Jerry Paul

1/10/03

Law of Marketing

Lynda J. Oswald

Louis and Myrtle Moskowitz Research
Professor of Business and Law

University of Michigan

WEST

™

THOMSON LEARNING

Australia · Canada · Mexico · Singapore · Spain · United Kingdom · United States

The Law of Marketing, by Lynda J. Oswald

Vice President/Publisher: Jack W. Calhoun
Senior Acquisitions Editor: Rob Dewey
Developmental Editor: Bob Sandman
Marketing Manager: Nicole Moore
Media Technology Editor: Vicky True
Media Developmental Editor: Peggy Buskey
Media Production Editor: John Barans
Production Editor: Daniel C. Plofchan
Design Projection Manager: Michelle Kunkler
Cover Design: Jennifer Lambert, Jen2 Design, Cincinnati
Internal Design: Ellen Pettengell Design, Chicago
Manufacturing Coordinators: Charlene Taylor, Sandee Milewski
Printer: Transcontinental Printing, Inc.
        Peterborough, ON
Production House: Shepherd, Inc.

For more information contact West Legal Studies in Business, South-Western College Publishing, 5101
Madison Road, Cincinnati, Ohio, 45227 or find us on the Internet at http://www.westbuslaw.com

For permission to use material from this text or product, contact us by
• **telephone: 1-800-730-2214**
• **fax: 1-800-730-2215**
• **web: http://www.thomsonrights.com**

Library of Congress Cataloging-in-Publication Data
Oswald, Lynda J.
    Law of marketing / by Lynda J. Oswald.
        p. cm
    Includes index.
    ISBN 0-324-00902-X (alk.paper)
    1. Marketing—Law and legislation—United States. 2. Trade regulation—United States.
    3. Business law—United States. I. Title.

KF1609.085 2002
343.73'084—dc21   2001031437

*To my husband, Brad, and our children,
Rhiannon, Nathaniel, and Kiernan.*

Brief Table of Contents

Table of Contents

Chapter 8   Legal Issues Relating to Promotion and Consumer Protection: Consumer Protection Law 266

Table of Cases

Preface

You wish to educate your students to become knowledgeable consumers of legal services. Your students desire to become successful managers, capable of planning to avoid legal problems and of making more informed decisions when confronted with legal issues regarding the marketing of goods and services. This textbook is designed for both you and your students.

Experienced marketing managers know that the law affects marketing activities in a multitude of ways. In the course of carrying out marketing duties, a manager may deal with such diverse issues as intellectual property, antitrust, franchise agreements, health and safety regulations, and products liability. Business students benefit immeasurably from a course that focuses on the many areas in which law and marketing intersect. *The Law of Marketing* is the book that will help you achieve your educational goals in a marketing law course.

Business students cannot assume that a single book or course on marketing law will make them an expert in the legal issues that might arise in their careers; nor can they assume that a single lawyer will be able to fully address all the legal concerns that they might encounter. However, by developing an understanding of the complexity and relevance of the various types of law that impact the marketing function, the informed student can meet these challenges head on and be better prepared to meet his or her career challenges.

Through a unique design that intertwines marketing principles, legal cases, and current business examples, *The Law of Marketing* focuses specifically and in detail on those legal principles of particular relevance to marketing activities. It addresses the pivotal topics necessary for understanding the impact that law has upon marketing activities and how law affects current marketing trends. The book also highlights the personal liability issues that your students, as future managers, might face.

Subject Matter and Organization of the Book

This textbook is designed to take the student through all aspects of marketing function. It covers the initial issues related to product development such as protection of intellectual property assets, legal issues relating to distribution and promotion of the product or service, and ultimately legal issues pertaining to the sale of the product or service, including attendant issues such as products liability and warranties.

This book is designed for both those students who have had a legal environment prerequisite and for those who are new to the study of business law. Thus, each individual chapter can stand alone. Students already possessing an understanding of the legal environment or who have previously taken courses addressing specialized legal topics will benefit from being able to jump almost immediately into the various marketing law topics covered in Chapters Two through Ten. For students who are new to the study of business law, Chapter One provides a very brief overview of the legal environment of marketing law, without belaboring any topics.

The book covers the following marketing law topics:

Product Development

Chapter Two: Legal Issues Relating to Product Development: Protection of Intellectual Property Assets Through Patent and Copyright Law

This chapter examines two of the four areas of law that protect intellectual property assets: patent law and copyright law.

Chapter Three: Legal Issues Relating to Product Development: Protection of Intellectual Property Assets Through Trade Secret Law, Contractual Agreements, and Business Strategies

This chapter addresses the third area of intellectual property law—trade secrets—as well as the law relating to the protection of unsolicited ideas, and business strategies for protecting and maximizing the value of intellectual property assets, including the use of contractual agreements.

Product Distribution

Chapter Four: Legal Issues Relating to Distribution of Products: Antitrust Law

This chapter addresses the major federal antitrust statutes, horizontal and vertical restraints of trade, monopolization, price discrimination, and the international implications of antitrust laws.

Chapter Five: Legal Issues Relating to Distribution Channels: The Franchisor-Franchisee Relationship

This chapter provides an overview of typical franchise agreements, the types of legal issues that commonly arise in franchise relationships, and state and federal regulation of franchises.

Product Promotion

Chapter Six: Legal Issues Relating to Promotion: Trademark Law

This chapter covers trademark law, including issues pertaining to international protection of marks and to the use of marks on the Internet.

Chapter Seven: Legal Issues Relating to Promotion: Commercial Speech and Regulation of Advertising

This chapter focuses on First Amendment restrictions on advertising and other forms of commercial speech, common law actions for deceptive or false advertising, and statutory causes of action for deceptive or false advertising arising under the Lanham Act and the Federal Trade Commission Act.

Chapter Eight: Legal Issues Relating to Promotion and Consumer Protection: Consumer Protection Law

This chapter addresses the regulation of direct marketing activities, labeling and packaging regulation, health and safety regulation, and consumer credit protection statutes.

Product Sale

Chapter Nine: Legal Issues Relating to the Sale of Services and Goods: Contracts and Sales of Goods Law

This chapter focuses on the fundamental common-law contract principles, the basic provisions of UCC law pertaining to the sale of goods, and the Convention on the International Sale of Goods.

Chapter Ten: Legal Issues Relating to the Sale of Goods: Warranties and Products Liability

This chapter examines the law pertaining to warranties on sales of goods and to products liability.

Features

The chapters consist of textual discussion of the relevant issues and rules of law, with cases and problems for discussion. Coverage of both international and Internet legal issues are integrated into each chapter.

Several tools are used to convey the ideas of each chapter. Each chapter contains two types of cases: "Focus Cases" and "Discussion Cases." The "Focus Cases" are short summaries of cases that illustrate a particular legal point discussed in the text. These cases are mostly paraphrased. When the original language of the court is used, it is indicated through quotation marks or through block quotes.

At end of each chapter there are three to six "Discussion Cases." These cases have been excerpted for length, but the language appearing on the page is entirely that of the court. Ellipses (. . .) have been used to indicate where a portion of a sentence has been omitted. Three asterisks (* * *) are used to indicate where a complete sentence or more has been omitted from a paragraph, and four asterisks (* * * *) to indicate where a complete paragraph or more has been omitted.

The Discussion Cases are somewhat longer than the cases found in most legal environment texts. Depending upon how the course is structured and how the text is used, instructors may assign all or just some of the cases, picking and choosing those that are most relevant to their own teaching objectives.

Why the long cases? Over my 13 years of teaching, I have noticed a trend toward cases being more and more heavily edited, often with the facts, issue, legal rule, and analysis being specifically labeled for the students. I am a firm believer in developing student's ability to "brief" cases, which enables the student to acquire the skill of analyzing a court's reasoning process and to hone her own reasoning skills. There is a real value in a student seeing the factual background of a case and the court's reasoning process and to working through the language used by the court. The longer cases provided within this textbook allow the students to engage in this process.

Most of the Focus Cases and the Discussion Cases are recent cases (usually decided within the last five years) and have been selected based upon their relevance to the function of marketing, their appeal to business students, and their effectiveness in highlighting key legal ideas. Several of them address Internet business activities.

At the end of each chapter are several Discussion Questions. Most of these problems are based on real cases (again, usually decided within the last five years) and give the students an opportunity to apply the concepts discussed in the chapter to real-life scenarios.

Scattered throughout the text are numerous Web addresses to Web sites of particular relevance to the topics being discussed throughout the book. These sites can be visited for additional background on topics of particular interest to the reader.

The U.S. Constitution and excerpts from several selected statutes, including the UCC, the Lanham Act, the Copyright Act, the Patent Act, and the Uniform Trade Secrets Act, are contained within the appendices and provide a quick and easy reference tool for the student. Finally, a glossary of major terms is provided. Key terms are also defined throughout the text and are usually indicated in italics.

Supplements

The text has a site on the World Wide Web devoted to the teaching and learning resources for the text: http://oswald.westbuslaw.com

In addition, the following supplemental resources are available:

- *Instructor's Manual with Test Bank* (ISBN: 0-324-04356-2) Prepared by the author, the *Instructor's Manual with its accompanying Test Bank* contains teaching tips, suggestions for background reading, and exam questions.
- *The New York Times Guide to Legal Studies in Business* (ISBN 0-324-04160-8), by Marianne Jennings and Jamie Murphy, is more than just a printed collection of articles. This guide gives you access, via password, to an on-line collection of the most current and relevant *New York Times* articles that are posted continually as news breaks. Also included are articles from *CyberTimes*, the on-line technology section of the *New York Times* on the Web.
- **InfoTrac College Edition** is an online library that contains hundreds of scholarly and popular periodicals, including *American Business Law Journal*, *Journal of International Business Studies*, *Environmental Law*, and *Ethics*. This can be included free with any West textbook. Contact your local Thomson Learning/West Legal Studies Sales Representative to set up a package for your course.
- **Videos** are available to qualified adopters using this text. You may access the entire library of West videos, a vast selection covering most business law issues on our Web site: http://www.westbuslawcom/video_library.html.

For more information about any of these ancillaries, contact your Thomson Learning/West Sales Representative for more details, or visit the Oswald *The Law of Marketing* Web site at http://oswald.westbuslaw.com.

Acknowledgments

No author could produce a book of this length without assistance from many people. I would be remiss if I did not thank several colleagues for their thoughtful reviews on specific chapters of the book, including:

Professor Norman Hawker, Western Michigan University
Professor Francine LaFontaine, University of Michigan
Professor Anne Lawton, University of Northern Ohio Law School
Professor Valerie Suslow, University of Michigan
Professor Frances Zollers, Syracuse University

Professor Elizabeth Cameron of Alma College provided invaluable assistance and input on Chapters Eight and Nine of the text in particular. Anthony Roehl (J.D., '02 University of Michigan) provided exceptional research assistance. I would also like to thank Rob Dewey, Nicole Moore, Bob Sandman, and Dan Plofchan of South-Western Publishing—without them, this book would not have been possible.

Lynda J. Oswald

CHAPTER 1

Overview of the Legal Environment of Marketing Activities

Introduction

This chapter is intended to provide you with a brief overview of the legal environment in which marketing activities occur. As is shown throughout the remainder of the book, many types of law impact marketing activities. Some of this law is statutory, while some arises under court opinions, the U.S. Constitution, or the rules and regulations of administrative agencies. Some of the law is found at the federal level, some at the state or even local level. Some types of law impose duties upon marketers in an effort to promote free competition, protect consumers, or foster fair business relationships. Other types of law grant rights to marketers, such as providing legal protection for patents, copyrights, and trademarks.

This chapter provides you with a framework within which you can start to analyze the various legal issues discussed in the following chapters. The topics touched upon briefly here appear in specific contexts throughout the book. In many respects, then, this chapter is a preview of coming attractions and is intended to help orient you as you begin your study of the law of marketing.

In light of this goal, this chapter begins by providing several classifications of the law so that you can understand the larger picture of the various types of law that exist within the American legal system. It then discusses the primary and secondary sources of the law and describes the American legal system, including the structure of the state and federal court systems. Finally, the chapter concludes with a short discussion of jurisdiction issues.

Classifications of the Law

The law has two main purposes: (1) it provides guidelines for decision making, and (2) it creates and enforces legal rights and duties. When we start to classify the law, we can see these two objectives come into play. Classifications also provide snapshots of the organization of the legal system and provide a sense of the wide variety of interests and activities that the law affects.

Law can be classified in many different ways. The first classification provided here is based upon the type of law involved (see Exhibit 1.1). The broad category of "law" can be divided into two basic areas: criminal law and civil law. *Criminal law* deals with a violation of the public order, i.e., it involves a wrong against the whole community. The purpose of a criminal prosecution is to punish the wrongdoer and to deter the wrongdoer and others from committing similar acts in the future. *Civil law*, on the other hand, deals with private relations between individuals or between individuals and the government and establishes the rights and responsibilities arising out of those relationships. The object of a civil lawsuit is to obtain relief for the injured party, most commonly in the form of monetary damages. Most of the law discussed in this book is civil law.

Each of these two basic categories can be further divided into procedural and substantive law. *Substantive law* actually defines, creates, and governs legal rights and duties. *Procedural law*, by contrast, defines the method by which people can enforce the rights given to them by the substantive law. For example, procedural law tells us the steps that must be taken to move a lawsuit through the legal system from its initial filing to its final judgment.

Substantive law can be further classified into public and private law. *Public law* deals with the relationship between the government as a sovereign and the individual and is typically enacted or created by a governmental body. Criminal law, for

EXHIBIT 1.1

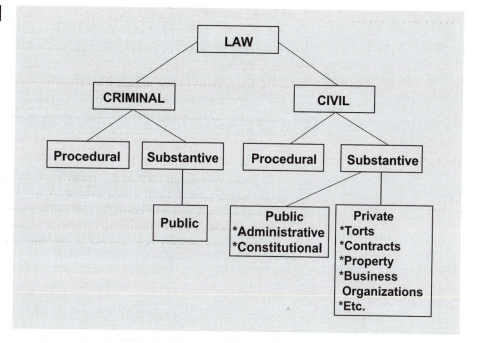

example, is public law, as is constitutional and administrative law. *Private law* deals with the rights and duties that arise as the result of a relationship between individuals, including legal entities such as corporations. *Private law* encompasses a wide variety of topics, including tort law, contract law, property law, and the law of business organizations.

The law can also be classified based upon political jurisdictions. In the United States, there are essentially three levels of political and legal jurisdictions: (1) federal, (2) state, and (3) local. All three jurisdictions can affect marketing activities, although our discussions focus primarily on federal and state regulation of these activities.

The *federal government* is the national government and is comprised of the legislative, executive, and judicial branches. Each of these has the ability to create law. Within its sphere, the federal government is superior to the state and local governments. Under the U. S. Constitution, however, the federal government is a government of limited powers. The federal government has no power to act in areas not granted to it under the Constitution. In the specific areas in which the federal government is authorized to act, such as patents and copyrights, the federal government is superior to the state and local governments.

The *state governments* also have legislative, executive, and judicial branches. The states retain all of the governmental power not explicitly granted to the federal government under the U.S. Constitution. This means that the states retain authority to regulate in a number of areas that implicate marketing activities, including trade secrets, contracts, warranties, and products liability. Some areas of the law—such as trademark law, which is discussed in Chapter 6—are regulated by both the federal and state governments.

Each state has the power to create its own state law. Thus, state laws can vary substantially from state to state. Marketers engaged in interstate or national marketing efforts need to be aware of the ramifications of differences in state laws. In some areas, such as sales of goods, the states have undertaken measures to foster uniformity among state laws, thus easing the burden on interstate businesses. These efforts are discussed at various points throughout the book.

Local governments, such as cities, towns, villages, and counties, can also regulate business activities, including marketing activities. The powers of local governments are delegated to them by their state legislatures and may be limited or modified by the states. To the extent that they are authorized to act, local governments can create local laws such as municipal ordinances and regulations. Although local regulations can impact certain types of marketing activities, such as issues relating to consumer protection, local regulation is of considerably less significance than federal or state regulation in the marketing law arena.

Finally, law can be classified based upon the branch of government that created it. At both the state and federal levels, each of the three branches can create law. The legislative branch enacts statutes; the judicial branch creates common law through its opinions; and the executive branch creates administrative rules and regulations through its power over administrative agencies. Numerous examples of all three types of law are found throughout this book.

Sources of the Law

The "law" can be found in many places. We look to *primary sources* when we want to find out what the legal rules "really are." We look to *secondary sources* when we want assistance in finding and interpreting the "law." There are numerous references to both primary and secondary sources throughout the book, both in the chapter discussions and in the judicial opinions.

PRIMARY SOURCES OF THE LAW

As already noted, there are two parallel legal systems in the United States: the federal system and the state systems. (And, in fact, there are 50 separate state systems, plus a system for the District of Columbia, making a total of 52 legal systems in the United States.)

Primary Sources of Federal Law

At the federal level, there are a number of primary sources of law: the U.S. Constitution, treaties, federal statutes, federal court opinions, and administrative rules and regulations.

The *U.S. Constitution* is said to be the "supreme law of the land." It establishes the three branches of the federal government—legislative, judicial, and executive—and addresses the powers and limitations of each of those branches. It restricts the power of the federal government and guarantees the rights and liberties of the people.

No law—whether created by the legislative, judicial, or executive branch or by the federal or a state government—is permitted to conflict with the U.S. Constitution. In addition, under the Constitution, federal statutes and treaties are superior to state constitutions and statutes. The U.S. Supreme Court, by virtue of its power of *judicial review,* has the authority to determine the constitutionality of all laws, federal or state.

A *treaty* is an agreement between or among nations. Under the U.S. Constitution, the President, with the advice and consent of the Senate, has sole authority to enter into treaties. A valid treaty has the legal force of a federal statute. If a treaty and a federal statute conflict, the last to have been adopted prevails.

In addition, as noted earlier, each of the three federal governmental branches can create law. First, Congress can enact *statutes*. We look at a number of such statutes in later chapters, including the Patent Act, the Copyright Act, the Sherman and Clayton Antitrust Acts, the Federal Trade Commission (FTC) Act, and the Lanham Act. Second, the courts can create *common law* through their judicial opinions. We examine many federal court opinions throughout the book. Third, administrative agencies are part of the executive branch and have the power to enact *administrative agency rules and regulations*. Later chapters examine the regulatory activities of several federal administrative agencies, such as the FTC and the Consumer Product Safety Commission.

Primary Sources of State Law

To a large extent, the primary sources of state law parallel those found at the federal level. The major exception is that treaties are found only at the federal and never the state level. Similarly, local government regulation is found only at the state and never the federal level.

Each state has its own *constitution*. Although often patterned upon the language of the federal Constitution, state constitutions are often more detailed than the federal Constitution. State constitutions cannot deprive individuals of federal constitutional rights, but they can give individuals additional rights beyond those found in the U.S. Constitution.

Each of the three branches of the state governments can create law, just as with the three branches of the federal government. The state legislatures can enact state *statutes*. Trade secrets and the right of publicity, for example, are governed by statute in many states, as are sales of goods. The executive branches of the state governments can enact state *administrative agency rules and regulations*. For example, state administrative agencies have undertaken several measures to protect consumers from unscrupulous marketing practices. Finally, the state courts can create *common law* through their opinions. Contract and tort law, for example, are still largely matters of state common law, which means that judicial opinions are an important primary source of state law.

SECONDARY SOURCES OF THE LAW

Numerous secondary sources of the law exist. Among the most influential of these are the *Restatements of the Law* compiled by the American Law Institute (ALI).[1] The ALI was formed in 1923 and consists of a group of distinguished lawyers, judges, and professors who compile authoritative statements of the common law in particular areas, including contracts, torts, and unfair competition. While the Restatements are not law themselves, the courts frequently look to and adopt the Restatements' positions on various points. Once adopted by a court, the Restatement language becomes a part of the common law of that jurisdiction. We see numerous references to various Restatements in later chapters.

As noted earlier, each state creates its own legal rules. The growth of interstate businesses was hampered by the fact that the laws could differ substantially from state to state, making planning and compliance difficult for businesses operating across state lines. In an effort to reduce some of the variation in state laws, the National Conference of Commissioners (NCC) on Uniform State Laws was created in 1892 to prepare uniform state legislation for presentation to and possible

---

[1] For general information on the ALI, see http://www.ali.org

adoption by the state legislatures.[2] Until adopted by a state legislature, these model laws have no binding legal effect and so are considered secondary sources of the law. Once adopted by a state legislature, of course, the model statute becomes a state statute and hence a primary source of law. The most widely adopted of the uniform laws is the *Uniform Commercial Code*, which was jointly created by the NCC and the ALI and which provides uniform rules regarding commercial transactions. The UCC has been adopted by all of the 50 states (although Louisiana has adopted only part of it) and the District of Columbia. The UCC is discussed in Chapter 9 and Chapter 10 in the context of sales of goods and warranties. The NCC still exists and is still active in drafting model uniform laws.

The courts may refer to legal encyclopedias, legal dictionaries, treatises, law review articles, and other secondary sources when trying to identify and interpret the legal rules contained within the primary sources of the law. Numerous examples of such secondary sources appear in the cases presented throughout this book.

The American Legal System

COMMON LAW AND EQUITY

The American legal system is a *common law*, or *Anglo-American*, legal system. This type of legal system is also found in other English-speaking countries, such as England, Canada (with the exception of Quebec), and Australia. In a common law system, much of the law is created by the judiciary and is found within court opinions. By contrast, much of the world, including Western Europe, Quebec, Scotland, Latin America, and parts of Africa and Asia, has a *civil law system*, in which the bulk of the law is found within legislative codes.

The American legal system is also an *adversary system*, which means that the parties, not the court, initiate and conduct litigation and gather evidence. The parties present their dispute to a neutral fact finder, the court. The theory behind the adversary system is that the two interested parties are most likely to vigorously litigate a case. Civil law systems, by contrast, often depend upon an *inquisitorial system*, in which the judiciary assists in initiating litigation, investigating facts, and presenting the evidence.

Because of the way that the common law developed in England historically, the primary form of legal relief available is monetary damages. Because money is not necessarily an appropriate form of relief in all cases, an additional system of judicial relief evolved that was known as *equity*. A court of chancery, sitting in equity, could award nonmonetary relief in instances where the monetary remedy available at law was inadequate. Among the primary forms of equitable relief found today are *injunctions*, which are court orders requiring a party to undertake an act or refrain from an act, and *specific performance*, which is an order to a party to fulfill its contractual obligations.

Today, virtually all jurisdictions in the United States have merged their courts of equity and law so that a single court can administer both forms of justice. Nonetheless, important distinctions remain. While a jury may be available in cases at law, only judges decide equity cases. In addition, equitable relief is available only at the discretion of the judge. In order to obtain equitable relief, the party seeking such relief must typically show that he or she has "clean hands," i.e., that he or she acted fairly and honorably toward the other party. There are numerous examples

---

[2] For general information on the NCC, see http://www.nccusl.org

of courts acting in equity throughout this book. Preliminary injunctions, for example, are a commonly requested form of relief in disputes involving marketers.

Within the American legal system, the operative doctrine is *stare decisis*, also known as the *doctrine of precedent*. Stare decisis is a Latin term that means "to stand by the decisions." Essentially, this doctrine tells us that each court is bound by its own "precedents," i.e., that each court must decide subsequent cases in the same way that it or a superior court decided earlier cases with similar facts. A court can overrule its own precedents, however, if it determines that a precedent was wrongly decided or that social or technological advances have rendered the precedent obsolete.

A court is not bound by *every* case that was decided earlier. As noted earlier, there are 52 court systems within the United States—the federal system, 50 state systems, and a system for the District of Columbia. In general, decisions of one court are binding only on that court and on *lower* courts within the same system. Thus, a Michigan trial court is bound by a decision of the Michigan Supreme Court but not by a decision of the Texas Supreme Court, which is outside its system. Similarly, the Michigan Supreme Court is not bound by a decision of the Michigan trial court, which is a lower court within its system. A decision of the U.S. Supreme Court on a *federal question* (i.e., a question involving the U.S. Constitution, a federal statute, or a treaty) is binding on all state and federal courts. Within the federal system, however, a decision of a specific circuit court of appeals is binding on that court and on all district (lower) courts within that circuit, but not on other circuit courts or upon the district courts outside its circuit.

COURT STRUCTURE

The doctrine of precedent means that it is important to understand how the court systems are arranged. All courts fulfill one of two basic types of judicial functions. First, some courts exercise *trial* functions and are said to have *original jurisdiction*. Cases originate in these courts, and the judges or juries (in appropriate cases) in these courts determine the facts of the case and take the first stab at applying the law to those facts.

In the American legal system, the person who starts a civil lawsuit is known as the *plaintiff*. The person who is being sued is known as the *defendant*. The plaintiff has the burden of proof, which means that the plaintiff must show, usually by a *preponderance of evidence*, that it should prevail. The most common remedies for a civil action are monetary damages and/or an injunction.

In a criminal case, the government, in its role as *prosecutor*, prosecutes an individual, known as the *defendant*, for a wrong that the individual allegedly committed against the whole community. The government bears the burden of proving that the defendant is guilty *beyond a reasonable doubt*. The punishment for crimes usually consists of imprisonment and/or fines.

The second type of court is said to have *appellate jurisdiction*. Appellate courts generally review only the lower court's theory of the law, not the trial court's findings of fact. Appellate courts do not conduct trials, hear evidence or testimony, or determine facts. Rather, appellate courts must accept the facts as determined by the trial court unless the trial court's decision is "clearly erroneous," which is a very difficult standard to meet. An appellate court reviews the factual *record* created by the trial court (e.g., the trial transcript and physical evidence introduced at trial). The appellate court's job is to resolve questions of law, i.e., to determine whether the trial was conducted in a procedurally proper manner and whether the appropriate law was applied correctly to the facts as determined by the trial court.

At the appellate level, the person who lost below and who is bringing the appeal is known as the *appellant* or the *petitioner.* The person who won below and who is defending the appeal is known as the *appellee* or the *respondent.* If the appellate court finds no prejudicial error in the lower court's determination, it will *affirm* the decision. If the court finds a prejudicial error, it will either *reverse* or *modify* the decision. If necessary, the appellate court can also *remand* the case back to the lower court for further proceeding.

We first examine the typical state court structure; then we examine the federal court structure.

State Court Structure

As already noted, each state has its own court system. There is great variety in state court systems. The most common state court structure is a four-tier judicial system, though some states use a three-tier system (see Exhibit 1.2). The first, or lowest, tier consists of *trial courts of limited jurisdiction.* These courts have jurisdiction over specific subject matters, such as minor criminal offenses and civil cases up to a fixed sum (e.g., $10,000). *Small claims courts* are found at this level. These are courts that hear civil cases involving relatively small sums of money. In most small claims courts, neither side is represented by an attorney, there is no jury, and the legal procedures are relaxed.

The second tier consists of *trial courts of general jurisdiction.* These courts conduct the trials on all cases not heard by the first tier courts, such as major crimes and civil cases involving larger sums of money. Juries are available in these courts in appropriate types of cases.

The third tier consists of *intermediate appellate courts.* Generally, the losing party in a case before the trial court is entitled to appeal to the intermediate appellate court provided that it can point to an alleged error of law (e.g., that the judge allowed evidence in that should have been excluded, that the jury instructions were incorrect, or that the wrong legal rule was applied). This is known as an *appeal of*

EXHIBIT 1.2

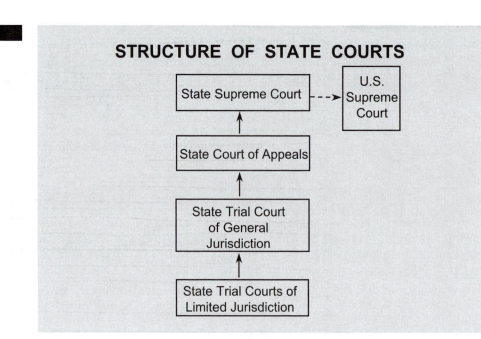

STRUCTURE OF STATE COURTS

State Supreme Court ---> U.S. Supreme Court

State Court of Appeals

State Trial Court of General Jurisdiction

State Trial Courts of Limited Jurisdiction

right because if the losing party can point to an alleged error of law, the appellate court must hear the appeal. Generally, a panel of three judges hears appeals at this level and a party must persuade two of the three in order to prevail.

Finally, the fourth tier consists of the *appellate court of last resort*, generally known as the supreme court in most (but not all) states. Usually, there are five to nine judges found on this court (they are generally referred to as justices) and all of them hear and decide each case. In most instances, the appealing party must ask the court's permission to appeal; there is usually no appeal of right at this level as there is with the intermediate appellate court. A party must generally persuade a majority of the justices in order to prevail. The decision of this court is usually final. A very few types of cases can be appealed from this court to the U.S. Supreme Court, but those cases must involve a federal question as discussed below. For the most part, cases that reach this level stop here.

Federal Court Structure

The federal court structure parallels the state court system in many ways. The main distinction between the two is that federal courts are courts of limited jurisdiction. They can only hear cases in areas granted to them under the U.S. Constitution. All other cases must go to state court (see Exhibit 1.3).

The first tier in the federal court system consists of the *trial courts*. These courts include *specialty tribunals*, such as the Patent and Trademark Office (PTO), which we discuss in Chapter 2 and Chapter 6. These tribunals have very limited jurisdiction over specific subject matter. The trial courts also include the *U.S. District Courts*. The district courts hear all cases not heard by the specialty tribunals, including general civil and criminal courts. Generally, one judge hears the case and juries are available in appropriate cases.

The second tier consists of the *U.S. Courts of Appeals*. These are reviewing courts with appellate jurisdiction, like the intermediate appellate courts in the

EXHIBIT 1.3

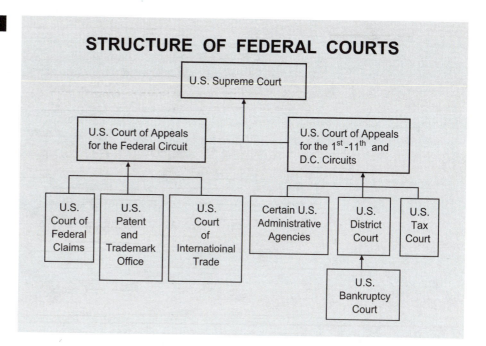

STRUCTURE OF FEDERAL COURTS

states. Parties who can point to an alleged error of law have an appeal of right to these courts. Typically, a panel of three judges hears each case (and a party must convince two of the three in order to prevail) although in some instance all of the judges of the circuit may sit *en banc* to hear a case.

There are 12 judicial circuits (the first through eleventh circuits, plus the D.C. Circuit). They hear appeals from the district courts as well as decisions of certain administrative agencies, the Tax Court, and the Bankruptcy Court. Certain appeals, including those from the Court of Federal Claims, the PTO, the United States Court of International Trade, and patent cases decided by a U.S. District Court, are heard by the Court of Appeals for the Federal Circuit (CAFC) (see Exhibit 1.4).

The final tier consists of the *U.S. Supreme Court*. Nine Justices sit on the Supreme Court, and typically all of them hear each case. The U.S. Supreme Court typically reviews federal appellate questions, although the Court does have original jurisdiction in a very few specific types of cases. In addition, a state court case can end up before the Supreme Court if it raises a federal question (i.e., if it contains an issue involving a federal statute, a treaty, or the federal Constitution).

For all practical purposes, there is no appeal of right to the U.S. Supreme Court. Rather, a party wishing to have its case heard by the Supreme Court must file a petition for a *writ of certiorari*. The Court may either grant the writ and agree to hear the case or, more likely, deny the writ, which means that the lower court's decision stands. The Court typically hears only a very small percentage of the cases

EXHIBIT 1.4

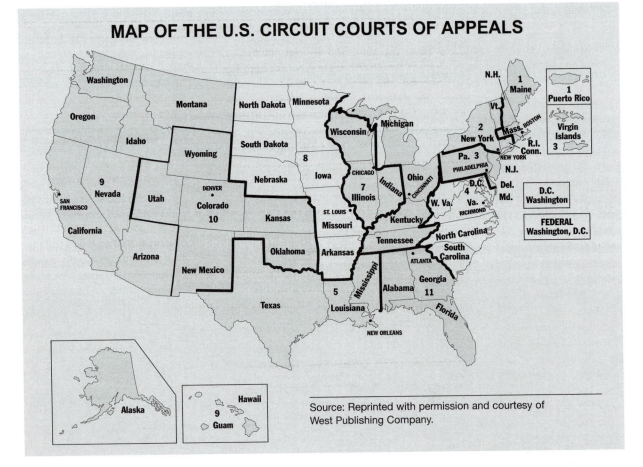

MAP OF THE U.S. CIRCUIT COURTS OF APPEALS

Source: Reprinted with permission and courtesy of West Publishing Company.

presented to it each year. Usually, the Court selects cases that involve a federal question of significant importance or a conflict among the U.S. Circuit Courts of Appeal.

Jurisdiction

Jurisdiction refers to the power or right of a court to hear or decide a case. The court must have two types of jurisdiction in order to have the power to resolve a case: (1) subject matter jurisdiction and (2) jurisdiction over the parties.

SUBJECT MATTER JURISDICTION

Subject matter jurisdiction refers to the power of a court to resolve a lawsuit involving a particular type of issue. The federal courts have limited subject matter jurisdiction, as set forth in Article III, Section 2, of the U.S. Constitution. That means that the federal courts can only hear cases where Congress or the Constitution has granted them the power to do so. The state courts have exclusive jurisdiction over all remaining cases.

The federal courts have exclusive jurisdiction over those areas where Congress has explicitly or implicitly so provided. These areas include certain admiralty issues, antitrust, bankruptcy, copyright and patent, federal criminal prosecutions, and suits against the United States.

The federal and state courts have *concurrent jurisdiction* in two instances. Concurrent jurisdiction means that either the state or the federal courts can hear the case. First, the state and federal courts have concurrent jurisdiction over *federal questions* in which the federal courts have not been given exclusive jurisdiction.

Second, the state and federal courts have concurrent jurisdiction in *diversity* cases. By definition, diversity cases involve state law issues that nonetheless are heard in federal court. Diversity jurisdiction arises where there is (1) "diversity of citizenship" between the two parties (e.g., when all of the plaintiffs are residents of a state or states different from the state or states of residence of all of the defendants or when the lawsuit is between citizens of the United States and citizens of a foreign country), and (2) the amount in controversy is more than $75,000. A party's place of residence is the state in which it resides or is domiciled. A corporation, however, is a resident of both the state in which it is incorporated and the state in which it has its principal place of business.

If a federal court hears a diversity case, it must apply state substantive law. (*Conflict of laws rules* determine which state's law applies.) The federal court generally applies federal procedural law, however.

In a concurrent jurisdiction case, the plaintiff has the option of bringing the case in either state or federal court. If the plaintiff files in state court, however, the defendant may usually have the case *removed* to federal court.

JURISDICTION OVER THE PARTIES

In addition to subject matter jurisdiction, a court must also have jurisdiction over the parties to the lawsuit, that is, the court must have the power to bind the parties involved in the dispute. This jurisdictional requirement can be satisfied in one of several ways.

First, the court has jurisdiction over a person who voluntarily comes before it and subjects himself to the court's jurisdiction. In a contract, for example, one party may agree that in the event of a lawsuit, the courts of the state of residence of the other party will have jurisdiction over the dispute.

Second, the court can exercise *in personam* jurisdiction, or *personal jurisdiction*, either over parties located within the state or over parties located outside the state to whom a "long-arm statute" applies. A *long-arm statute* is a state statute that allows a state court to exercise jurisdiction over nonresident defendants who have sufficient contacts (known as *minimum contacts*) with the state such that the exercise of jurisdiction does not offend "traditional notions of fair play and substantial justice."[3] Long-arm statutes typically apply to defendants who (1) have committed a tort within the state and the tort is the subject matter of the lawsuit, (2) own property within the state and the property is the subject matter of the lawsuit, (3) have entered into a contract within the state and the contract is the subject matter of the lawsuit, or (4) have transacted business within the state and the lawsuit involves that transaction.

Finally, the court can exercise *in rem jurisdiction*, which refers to the power of a state court to hear cases involving property situated within the state.

JURISDICTION ON THE INTERNET

The Internet raises special types of jurisdiction issues. Does a marketer located in Maine, for example, subject itself to the jurisdiction of the Hawaii courts simply because it has a website that is accessible to Hawaii residents? Or, must the marketer undertake more direct activities in Hawaii before it becomes subject to such jurisdiction?

The law is not yet settled regarding jurisdiction on the Internet. Courts generally have held that merely having a website that is accessible by residents in another state is insufficient to subject a defendant to the jurisdiction of that other state. Rather, courts generally look to see whether a defendant website owner has "purposefully availed" itself of the privilege of doing business in that state. Often, the courts have found this requirement is satisfied where a resident of the state has accessed the contents of the site or purchased goods or services offered on it. A recent court decision summarized the law thus:

> The likelihood that personal jurisdiction can be constitutionally exercised is directly proportionate to the nature and quality of commercial activity that an entity conducts over the Internet. . . . At one end of the spectrum are situations where a defendant clearly does business over the Internet. If the defendant enters into contracts with residents of a foreign jurisdiction that involve the knowing and repeated transmission of computer files over the Internet, personal jurisdiction is proper. At the opposite end are situations where a defendant has simply posted information on an Internet Web site which is accessible to users in foreign jurisdictions. A passive Web site that does little more than make information available to those who are interested in it is not grounds for the exercise [of] personal jurisdiction. The middle ground is occupied by interactive Web sites where a user can exchange information with the host computer. In these cases, the exercise of jurisdiction is determined by

---

[3] International Shoe Co. v. Washington 326 U.S. 310, 316 (1945).

examining the level of interactivity and commercial nature of the exchange of information that occurs on the Web site.[4]

Several state courts have held that successful solicitation of local residents is also sufficient to establish personal jurisdiction over the website owner. Websites that are purely local in nature, however, generally do not support exercise of jurisdiction, especially where the website contains conspicuous disclaimers to that effect.

[4] Molnlycke Health Care A.B. v. Dumex Medical Surgical Products, Inc., 64 F. Sup. 2d 448, 451 (E.D. Pa. 1999) (quoting Zippo Mfg Co. v. Zippo Dot Com, Inc., 952 F. Supp. 1119, 1124 [(W.D. Pa. 1997)).]

CHAPTER 2

Legal Issues Relating to Product Development

Protection of Intellectual Property Assets through Patent and Copyright Law

When a firm or an individual develops a new product or service, one of the very first legal issues that arises is protection of that new asset from competitors. If the firm waits until later in the product development or marketing process to consider this issue, it may find that it has lost the right to protect the asset. Thus, those creating a new product or service need to budget for and obtain legal advice on this issue very early in the development process. This chapter discusses ways in which patent and copyright law protect intellectual property assets and the steps that firms must take to obtain those protections.

Overview

Although businesspeople often think of intellectual property issues arising primarily in the context of high-technology ventures, *all* firms need to be concerned with intellectual property protection. Intellectual property law can be used to protect assets as sophisticated as computer software or as simple as soft drink formulas or customer databases.

CATEGORIES OF INTELLECTUAL PROPERTY LAW

Intellectual property assets consist of property rights in intangible products of investment, creative intellect, or labor. "Intellectual property law" is a broad legal term that is used to refer to a number of separate, but related, legal doctrines that relate to these assets. We examine the four basic categories of intellectual property law: (1) patent law, (2) copyright law, (3) trade secret law, and (4) trademark law. These doctrines provide overlapping protection. It is possible, for example, to protect different aspects of a single product through a combination of some or all of these four categories (see Exhibit 2.1). The decision as to which type or types of protection to pursue is a matter of both business and legal strategy and so requires the active participation of both management and its legal counsel.

Patent, copyright, and trade secret law comprise one major branch of intellectual property law. Each of these three mechanisms may be used to prevent others

EXHIBIT 2.1

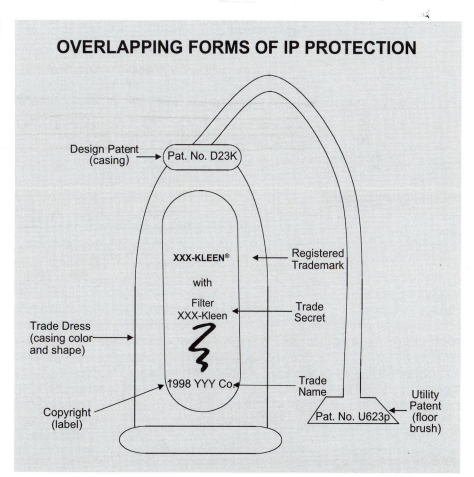

OVERLAPPING FORMS OF IP PROTECTION

Design Patent (casing) → Pat. No. D23K

XXX-KLEEN® ← Registered Trademark

with

Filter XXX-Kleen ← Trade Secret

Trade Dress (casing color and shape) →

1998 YYY Co. ← Trade Name

Copyright (label)

Pat. No. U623p — Utility Patent (floor brush)

from making or selling protected products or services. The second main branch of intellectual property law, which includes trademark and unfair competition law, allows firms to take action to prevent others from providing false and misleading information to consumers (see Exhibit 2.2).

This chapter addresses patent and copyright law. Trade secret law is addressed in Chapter 3, as is the law relating to covenants not to compete, nondisclosure agreements, and other contractual agreements and business strategies used to protect intellectual property assets. Trademark law and unfair competition law are discussed in Chapter 6, Chapter 7, and Chapter 8 which address legal issues related to the promotion of products and services.

Managerial interest in intellectual property issues has increased dramatically in recent years as a result of a stunning increase in the value of intellectual property over the past two decades. A number of "pure knowledge" companies, such as Microsoft, now derive much of their value from intellectual property rather than from tangible assets.

The federal government is also devoting much more attention to the international aspects of intellectual property law in recent years. The government wants to protect U.S. intellectual property rights overseas as much as possible. It also wants to harmonize intellectual property laws between the United States and other countries as much as possible to reduce transaction costs for global businesses and to provide a level playing field for American companies competing in foreign countries.

As a result of these initiatives, U.S. intellectual property law is currently changing very rapidly. Although every manager should have an understanding of the basic parameters of intellectual property law, firms should seek the expert advice of legal counsel before undertaking activities in this area.

UNDERLYING POLICY CONSIDERATIONS

Intellectual property law hinges on a fundamental policy conflict. The ultimate goal of intellectual property law is to provide a diverse, competitive marketplace. Thus, on the one hand, intellectual property law tries to promote creativity in an effort to encourage the provision of a wide variety of goods and services to the market. By giving inventors, writers, or artists property rights in their intangible creations, the

EXHIBIT 2.2

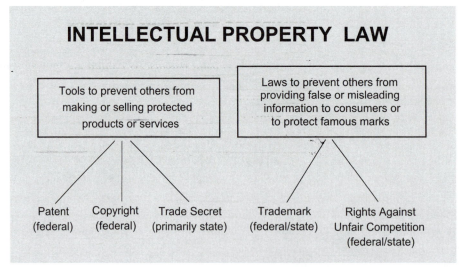

law gives them an opportunity to recoup their investment in the creative process and to earn a profit. On the other hand, the law wants to provide the freest possible public access to new products and services. Intellectual property law represents compromises between the goal of encouraging creativity and that of promoting public access. The net result is that intellectual property law is constantly changing as legislators attempt to strike a balance between these two competing goals.

Patent Law

A *patent* is a grant of an exclusive monopoly for a limited time period from the federal government to an inventor. The theory behind patent law is that the opportunity to obtain such an exclusive monopoly encourages investment in research and development. To receive a patent, the inventor must reveal to the public information about the invention. In return, the inventor may exclude others from making, using, selling, or offering to sell in the United States the patented invention or from making, using, selling, or offering to sell a substantial portion of components that, if combined, would infringe the patent. In addition, federal law prohibits the importation to the United States of products made from any process covered by a U.S. patent.

Patents are issued exclusively by the federal government. Article I, Section 8 of the U.S. Constitution provides:

> The Congress shall have power . . . To promote the Progress of Science and useful Arts, by securing for limited Times to Authors and Inventors the exclusive Right to their respective Writings and Discoveries.

States therefore may not issue patents.

Patents are issued under the auspices of the federal Patent and Trademark Office (PTO), in accordance with the provisions of the federal Patent Act.[1] In addition, Congress created the U.S. Court of Appeals for the Federal Circuit (CAFC) in 1982. The CAFC is a specialized appellate court with limited jurisdiction over certain types of legal issues, including patent law. All patent appeals are now heard by this court, which has developed expertise in this area of the law, rather than by the 12 regular circuit courts. As a result, patent law is now much more uniform and patents are more likely to be upheld than they were in the past.

STANDARDS FOR PATENT ISSUANCE

There are three kinds of patents in the United States: (1) utility patents, (2) design patents, and (3) plant patents. As Exhibit 2.3 indicates, utility patents are by far the most common. When people use the term "patent," they usually are referring to a utility patent.

Utility patents protect the function of articles or processes. *Design* patents protect the ornamental features of articles. *Plant* patents may be issued for asexually reproducible plants that are novel, nonobvious, and distinct. Because plant patents are such a narrow niche, our discussion focuses primarily on utility patents and secondarily on design patents.

An inventor can only have one patent per invention. If the item involved incorporates two or more inventions, however, the inventor can receive separate utility

[1]35 U.S.C. §§ 1 *et seq.*

EXHIBIT 2.3

1999 PATENT STATISTICS

Patent Documents Granted

(Calendar Year)

Utility Patents	153,493
Design Patents	14,732
Plant Patents	421
Reissue Patents	448
TOTAL -1999	169,094

Source: PTO, 2000

patents for each invention. In Exhibit 2.1, for example, separate utility patents could be obtained for the floor brush and the motor. In addition, an inventor can obtain both design and utility patents on a single item. Suppose a company invents a new kind of no-spill cup for children that is unusually effective at preventing spills and leaks and that has a unique and attractive shape. The company could obtain a utility patent on the no-spill lid and a design patent on the shape of the cup.

Utility Patents

Utility patents cover *useful* inventions that fall into one of five categories: processes (such as a gene-splicing procedure), machines, articles of manufacture (such as a tire or a chair),[2] a composition of matter (such as a new chemical compound), or improvements upon existing ideas that fall into any one of these categories. Utility patents protect only processes or tangible products. Patents may not be used to protect expressions of ideas (that is the function of copyright law); nor may patent law be used to obtain a monopoly on laws of nature, naturally occurring substances, mathematical formulas, or abstract ideas, for such a monopoly would stifle scientific inquiry and advancement.

The distinction between man-made and naturally occurring organisms has important implications for the biotechnology industry in particular. In *Diamond v. Chakrabarty*,[3] decided in 1980, the Supreme Court determined that while naturally occurring microorganisms cannot be patented, man-made microorganisms may be.

See Discussion Case 2.1.

---

[2] "Articles of manufacture" are generally simple objects without moving parts, as opposed to "machines," which generally have moving parts or electronic circuits.
[3] 447 U.S. 303 (1980).

The PTO has since interpreted *Chakrabarty* as authorizing patents on higher forms of genetically engineered mammals, such as mice and rabbits. The United States tends to be more liberal on this issue than most countries. Man-made organisms patentable in the United States may well not receive patent protection elsewhere in the world.

The categories of patentable subject matter can shift over time as courts respond to changing technology and circumstances. The most significant recent such change involves the patentability of *business methods* (i.e., patents that pertain to a method of doing or conducting business). In a 1998 decision, *State Street Bank & Trust Co. v. Signature Financial Group, Inc.*,[4] the CAFC held that software designed solely to make financial calculations is patentable.

See Discussion Case 2.2.

Prior to this decision, most finance, insurance, and banking companies had assumed that the best way to protect financial and other business software was through trade secret and copyright law.

Since *State Street Bank*, business method patent applications have grown dramatically, though they are still only a small fraction of the total number of patent applications filed each year. In fiscal year 1999, the PTO received 2,600 business method patent applications and issued 600 patents, a 100 percent increase over the 1998 figures.

The issuance of business method patents has been very controversial, as many commentators feel that the PTO is issuing patents for obvious inventions. In particular, many argue that the PTO is issuing patents for ways of doing business on the Internet that are common in the non-Internet business world. They fear that the growth in business method patents will hamper the development of the Internet as a commercial medium.

The *State Street Bank* decision has created problems as well as opportunities for businesses. Many businesses who had treated their business methods as trade secrets and had not attempted to patent them suddenly found themselves facing patent infringement claims from inventors who filed for business method patents long after the method had already been in use by others. Congress responded to this unexpected effect in the American Inventors Protection Act of 1999,[5] which created the "first investor defense." This defense allows a business that invented and used commercially a method of doing business at least one year before the date another person filed a business method patent application on it to continue using the method without infringing on any patent that might be granted.[6]

A utility patent gives its owner a monopoly of limited duration in an invention in return for full public disclosure of the invention's details (so that the public may learn from it). Patents currently have a term of 20 years from the date the application was filed. This term can be extended if the PTO fails to grant a patent within three years after filing because of administrative delay. Patent terms cannot otherwise be extended or renewed, however; and, once the term has expired, all members of the public (including competitors) are free to make or use the invention as they wish.

An inventor will not receive a patent merely because he has invented something. Rather, the inventor must show that the invention is worthy of a patent. The

---

[4] 149 F.3d 1368 (Fed. Cir. 1998).

[5] This act was signed by President Clinton on November 29, 1999, as part of the Omnibus Reform and Appropriations Act (Pub. L. No. 106-113).

[6] 35 U.S.C. § 273.

Patent Act requires that in order for a utility patent to issue, the invention must be (1) novel, (2) nonobvious, and (3) useful.

Novelty is covered in Section 102 of the Patent Act. Although Section 102 has numerous provisions covering a variety of types of circumstances, two are particularly important. Section 102(a) provides that a patent must be denied

> if the invention was known or used by others in this country, or patented or described in a printed publication in this or a foreign country, before the invention thereof by the applicant for a patent . . . .

The focus in Section 102(a) is on the actions of persons other than the applicant prior to the date that the applicant made the invention. Prior to that date, did other persons cause the invention to be known or used in the United States? Did they cause it to be patented or make it the subject of a printed publication anywhere else in the world? The policy behind Section 102(a) is to prevent a second inventor from obtaining a patent if a previous inventor has already placed the invention in the public domain before the second inventor made his invention.

Section 102(b) provides that a patent must be denied

> if the invention was patented or described in a printed publication in this or a foreign country or in public use or on sale in this country, more than one year prior to the date of application for patent in the United States . . . .

Section 102(b) focuses on the actions of the applicant and others more than one year before the application was filed. Essentially, once one of the listed events has occurred, the inventor has one year in which to file an application for patent, or the inventor loses the right to do so. There are several policy reasons behind this provision. First, it ensures that inventions in the public domain for one year remain there. Second, it allows the inventor one year in which to test market reaction before going to the considerable expense of filing for a patent. Third, it prevents the inventor from marketing the product for several years before applying for a patent in an effort to extend the effective patent time.

The *nonobviousness* standard asks whether the invention would have been obvious to someone skilled in the particular field as of the date of invention. If so, the invention is not patentable.

The *usefulness* standard requires that there be a current, significant, beneficial use for the invention. This is not a particularly high bar, and most inventions have no problem in meeting this requirement.

Design Patents

Design patents protect the *ornamental* features of an article of manufacture. As you can imagine, design patents are of great importance to many manufacturers, particularly manufacturers of consumer goods. Many goods—such as athletic shoes, coffeemakers, or chairs—may be virtually indistinguishable from each other except for their design, which then becomes critical to the marketing function.

To receive a design patent, the inventor must show that her design is (1) novel, (2) nonobvious, and (3) ornamental. With a few exceptions, the *novelty* requirement applies to design patents just as it does to utility patents. The test for *nonobviousness* of design patents is whether a professional designer of ordinary skill, viewing the overall appearance of the design as compared to prior designs, would consider the new design obvious. The *ornamentality* standard requires that the design be primarily ornamental and not dictated by functional considerations. If there are a variety of ways in which the article could be designed and still perform

Facts: The plaintiff, Robert Lee, sued the defendant, Dayton-Hudson Corp., claiming that the defendant had infringed his design patent for a massage device with an elongated handle with two opposing balls at one end. The plaintiff claimed that the defendant's device had different surface ornamentation but the same basic configuration as his invention.

The trial court found that the defendant had not infringed on the plaintiff's designs because "there [was] not a substantial identity of appearance between [the two devices] so as to deceive the ordinary observer." The plaintiff appealed.

Decision: The appellate court affirmed the decision of the trial court stating: "[B]y obtaining a design patent, not a utility patent, Mr. Lee limited his patent protection to the ornamental design of the article . . . . Design patents do not and cannot include claims to the structural or functional aspects of the article."

Thus, the court explained, "If the patented design is primarily functional rather than ornamental, the [design] patent is invalid. . . . [A] design patent is not a substitute for a utility patent. A device that copies the utilitarian or functional features of a patented design is not an infringement unless the ornamental aspects are also copied, such that the overall 'resemblance is such as to deceive.'" *Lee v. Dayton-Hudson Corp.*, 838 F.2d 1186 (Fed. Cir. 1988)

---

its function, the design is most likely ornamental and not functional. If the design affects the invention's function or performance, however, it must be protected, if at all, through a utility patent, not a design patent. Design patents are valid for a term of 14 years from the date of patent issuance—a much shorter term than that granted to utility patents (see Focus Case 2.1).

OWNERSHIP OF PATENTS

Under U.S. law, the *first to invent* is the only person who can file for and obtain a patent. In virtually every other country of the world, however, the *first to file* is entitled to the patent.

Very often, employees create inventions while at work. This situation raises two issues: (1) Who owns the invention—the inventor or the employer? and (2) Who may file for the patent—the inventor or the employer?

If the employee creates the invention in the context of fulfilling his specific job duties (i.e., the employee was "hired to invent"), the invention belongs to the employer and the employee is obligated to assign all rights to the invention to the employer. It is best, from the employer's perspective, to have a specific employment agreement in place providing that the employee will make such an assignment. In the absence of an explicit agreement, the common law will reach the same result.

If the employee does not create the invention as part of his official job duties but nonetheless invents something closely related to his duties or uses company resources in doing so, the employee will "own" the invention, but the employer will have "*shop rights*" to use the invention. Shop rights are an irrevocable, nontransferable, royalty-free license to use the invention. The theory behind shop rights is that the employer, whose resources contributed toward the invention, should have the right to use the invention in its business, although the employee retains the right to exploit the invention for all other purposes.

Employers generally are not satisfied with obtaining shop rights, however. Rather, they want to own the invention. Thus, employers often use "invention assignment agreements," in which the employee agrees in advance to assign all rights in an invention to the employer. (Invention assignment agreements are discussed in more detail in Chapter 3.)

Ownership of the *invention* does not resolve the question of who can apply for the *patent*, however. Recall that under U.S. law, only the *inventor* (i.e., the person who conceived of the invention) is entitled to apply for a patent. Thus, even if the employer has an invention assignment agreement transferring ownership of the invention to it, the inventor must still file for the patent; ownership of the patent can then be assigned to the employer by the inventor. Thus, the invention assignment agreement should contain a provision obligating the employee/inventor to cooperate in the application for the patent.

PATENT APPLICATION PROCEDURES

Applications for patents are made to the PTO in Washington, D.C. The PTO will examine the application and, if all of the statutory standards have been met, will issue a patent.

Inventors may represent themselves before the PTO. As a practical matter, however, because of the complexity and technicality of the documents required, it is usually advisable to seek the services of a patent agent or patent attorney who is skilled in drafting an application that is broad enough to protect the invention yet narrow enough to pass the scrutiny of the PTO examiner. Both patent lawyers and patent agents are individuals licensed to practice in patent cases before the PTO. The major distinction between the two is that patent agents cannot represent clients outside the PTO (for example, in litigation resulting from patent infringement), while patent lawyers, of course, can. Both patent lawyers and patent agents must have a bachelor's degree in a technical field, such as engineering or physics, and both must pass a PTO exam that tests knowledge of patent laws and rules and the ability to write a patent claim.

The process of obtaining a patent from the PTO is known as a *prosecution*. The application must describe the invention in detail and include a diagram or illustration. The application must set forth the *claims*—statements that describe the invention in a very formal and stylized manner and that articulate the basis for the monopoly that is to be granted to the inventor. Typically, a number of negotiations take place between the patent examiner and the patent lawyer or agent, which often result in the patent application being rewritten to result in a narrower monopoly being granted to the inventor. On average, it takes eighteen months to two years to obtain a patent, although the process can take much longer for complex or disputed patents.

Before filing an application, the applicant should conduct a *prior art search*. "Prior art" refers to any printed publication, prior patent or other document, or prior invention that references or makes use of the invention that is the subject of the patent application. The PTO may find that such prior art renders the applicant's invention obvious or nonnovel, making the issuance of a patent improper. A careful search for prior art helps the applicant to avoid the expense of filing an application that the PTO is unlikely to grant and helps the applicant to prepare responses in advance to issues likely to be raised by the PTO examiner. The applicant must disclose to the PTO all of the prior art of which it is aware. There are a number of professional firms that specialize in searching for prior art; there are a number of on-line databases available as well. Because the consequences of an improper prior art search can be both expensive and time-consuming, it is wise to seek professional assistance in this area. The PTO examiner also conducts a search for prior art in the course of evaluating the application.

The filing fee for a patent is relatively modest—typically, $710.[7] Of course, the filing fee is only one small part of the entire process. If the inventor hires a patent agent or patent lawyer to represent the inventor in the preparation of the patent application and in the negotiations with the PTO examiner, the inventor is likely to spend several thousand dollars to obtain his patent.

Historically, U.S. patent applications were kept secret and were not released to the public. That practice differed significantly from practices in the rest of the world, in which patent applications are typically published, or "laid open" to the public, within a specified time period (usually 18 months after filing). The American Inventors Protection Act of 1999, however, changed the U.S. practice of holding patent applications secret. Effective November 29, 2000, all U.S. utility patent applications that are also foreign-filed and published abroad will be published 18 months from their first effective filing date. The PTO will still hold utility patent applications that are filed solely in the United States and not abroad secret if the applicant so requests. If the patent application is made public, the inventor will gain several new advantages, including enhanced damages for infringement. The inventor will lose the opportunity to treat the invention as a trade secret in the event that the PTO does not issue the patent, however. (This topic is discussed further in Chapter 3.) Therefore, the inventor should discuss the implications of publishing the application versus holding it secret with legal counsel before proceeding with the application.

If a patent is issued, the patent is summarized and published in the *Official Gazette*, which is an official U.S. government publication.[8] At this point, the patent becomes a public document and anyone can examine it to determine the details of the invention. The theory is that, in return for receiving the limited monopoly granted by the patent, the patentee must make the invention available to the public so that others can make technological improvements upon it. At the end of the patent period, the invention is available to the public as a whole and anyone can make or use it without incurring liability.

The Patent Act requires that patent applicants fully disclose their inventions to the public as part of the "price" of obtaining a patent. The patent applicant is required to describe how to make and use the invention with sufficient clarity, precision, and detail to enable a person skilled in the relevant art to make and use it without undue experimentation. Failure to do so will result in either denial of the patent or, if the patent has already issued, invalidation of the patent.

If the patent examiner determines that the invention is not patentable, the applicant may take an administrative appeal to the PTO Board of Appeals. If the Board provides no relief, the applicant may appeal on the administrative record directly to the CAFC or may file suit against the Commissioner of Patents and Trademarks in the U.S. District Court, where a *de novo* review of patentability will be made. Appeals go to the CAFC (see Exhibit 2.4).

It is important to realize that issuance of the patent does not guarantee that the patentee has a valid patent. The PTO's issuance of a patent provides a *presumption* of validity, but this presumption can be overcome. For example, if the patentee attempts to enforce the patent in an infringement action, the alleged infringer can raise patent invalidity as a defense. A party can also challenge the validity of a patent through a *declaratory judgment action* before it has been charged with infringement by the patentee.

---

[7] For a complete and current PTO fee schedule, see the PTO's webpage at http://www.uspto.gov/
[8] The *Official Gazette* is available on-line on the PTO's webpage at http://www.uspto.gov/

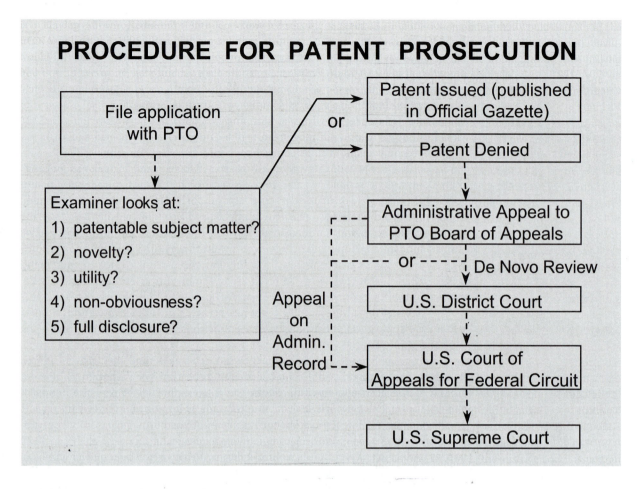

PROCEDURE FOR PATENT PROSECUTION

File application with PTO

or

Patent Issued (published in Official Gazette)

Patent Denied

Examiner looks at:
1) patentable subject matter?
2) novelty?
3) utility?
4) non-obviousness?
5) full disclosure?

Appeal on Admin. Record

Administrative Appeal to PTO Board of Appeals

or

De Novo Review

U.S. District Court

U.S. Court of Appeals for Federal Circuit

U.S. Supreme Court

EXHIBIT 2.4

The standards for obtaining a valid patent are stiff. The PTO denies many applications for patents, and, of the ones granted, a significant percentage are later invalidated by a court. A patentee cannot be complacent just because a patent has issued.

RIGHTS GRANTED BY A PATENT

A patent grants the patentee an exclusive monopoly (for a limited time period) to prevent others from making, using, selling, offering to sell, or importing the invention, even if those others independently create the invention. In most instances, the patentee may "work" the invention (i.e., put it into commercial use), license others to work the invention, or simply hold the patent and refuse to make the invention (or allow others to make it) during the patent period. Firms may use this latter tactic as a strategic measure to prevent competitors from entering specific markets.

Patentees do not automatically have a right to "work" their inventions in every instance, however. A patent does not grant the inventor the right to make, use, or sell the invention; rather, it grants the patentee the right to exclude others from doing so. Suppose that Inventor A holds a patent on a new type of widget that will revolutionize the widget-using industries. To make the widget, however, Inventor A must use a specific manufacturing process that has already been patented by Inventor B.

Inventor A therefore cannot manufacture her widgets without infringing upon Inventor B's patent. Inventor B's patent is known as a *blocking patent*, and it will have the effect of preventing Inventor A from commercializing her widget invention. Inventor A will have the right to prevent others from making her patented widget, but will be unable to make the widget herself unless she is able to negotiate a license with Inventor B for the use of the patented manufacturing method.

INFRINGEMENT

There are two dimensions of patent infringement issues that are relevant to marketers. First, a marketer may find that its patent has been infringed by another and may want to pursue legal remedies to protect the patent. Second, a marketer may find itself defending against an infringement action brought by a competitor. The marketer may have unintentionally infringed upon another's patent. Alternatively, a marketer may deliberately infringe a patent, believing that if its actions are challenged in court, the patent will be declared invalid.

Types of Infringement

The Patent Act provides that a person can be held liable for infringement if she (1) directly infringes a patent; (2) induces another to infringe a patent; (3) contributorially infringes a patent; (4) manufactures or sells certain components of a patented invention to be assembled abroad; or (5) imports, sells, offers to sell, or uses a product made abroad through a process protected by a U.S. patent.

The last provision prevents a business from avoiding a patentee's U.S. process patent by using the process abroad to manufacture products, then importing the products into the United States to sell or use. The use of the *process* abroad is not infringement, because U.S. patent laws do not have extraterritorial reach; but the subsequent importation, offer for sale, or use of the *products* in the United States is infringement. Theoretically, retailers and noncommercial users are subject to liability under this provision. However, the Patent Act provides that retailers and noncommercial users are held liable only if there is no adequate remedy against the primary manufacturers, importers, distributors, or wholesalers on the theory that the most culpable parties should be held liable first.

Direct infringement is most common. It occurs when the defendant makes, uses, sells, or imports the patented invention in the United States during the patent term. For example, in *Snuba International, Inc. v. Dolphin World, Inc.,*[9] Snuba International held a patent on a diving system. Snuba's invention consisted in part of a lightweight raft that carried compressed air tanks and that was attached to the diver by a harness and towline. Dolphin World sold a competing product called the "Free Diver," which used a "pod" and harness mechanism. Although Dolphin World attempted to argue that a "pod" was not a "raft" and that its system therefore did not infringe, the CAFC disagreed and found that Dolphin World had directly infringed Snuba's patent.

Inducement to infringe occurs when the defendant actively, intentionally, and knowingly solicits or assists a third party in directly infringing a patent. Direct infringement by a third party is a prerequisite to finding inducement to infringe. In *Snuba International*, for example, the CAFC found that the use of the Free Diver system by Dolphin World's customers constituted direct infringement and that Dolphin

---

[9] 2000 U.S. App. LEXIS 16946 (CAFC, July 11, 2000).

World had induced this infringement by disseminating sales information and promotional materials that encouraged consumers to purchase its Free Diver system.

Contributory infringement occurs when the defendant sells, offers to sell, or imports a material component of the patented invention that has no substantial use aside from use in the patented invention, provided that: (1) the defendant knows that the component he sold was specially made or adapted for use in the patented invention, has no other substantial use, and is likely to be used to infringe the patent; and (2) his actions contribute to another's direct infringement. Direct infringement is a prerequisite to finding contributory infringement. In *Snuba International*, the CAFC found that Dolphin World had notice of the Snuba patent and admitted that its Free Diver pod had no noninfringing use. Because the use of the Free Diver system by Dolphin World's customers was direct infringement, Dolphin World was liable for contributory infringement (in addition to inducement to infringement and its own direct infringement).

Finally, managers should be aware that the courts have held corporate officers—but not nonmanagement employees—personally liable for the infringing activities of their corporations in certain instances. While a corporate officer is not automatically held personally liable merely because of her status as an officer of the corporation, an officer may be held personally liable in instances in which she personally took part in the commission of the infringing act or specifically directed other officers, agents, or employees of the corporation to infringe the patent of another.[10] Often, officers can avoid this personal liability by showing that they obtained the advice of legal counsel and relied in good faith on that advice in structuring their behavior. Failure to obtain such advice or to heed it may well result in personal liability.

Defenses to Infringement Claims

A defendant charged with patent infringement can raise four basic defenses. First, the defendant can raise *patent invalidity*. If the defendant can show by clear and convincing evidence that the invention was not novel, nonobvious, and useful (for a utility patent) or not novel, nonobvious, and ornamental (for a design patent), the court will find the patent invalid and the defendant will not be liable for infringement.

Second, the defendant can raise *patent misuse* by the patentee. The patentee has misused his patent if he uses it to obtain more market power than Congress intended the patent to convey. Generally, this involves some sort of antitrust violation. Where patent misuse is shown, the patentee is denied enforcement of the patent until the misuse ceases; the defendant is not liable for infringement. Antitrust issues are discussed in more detail in Chapter 4.

Third, the defendant is relieved of liability for infringement if the defendant can show *inequitable conduct* on the part of the patentee. For example, if the patentee intentionally made a misrepresentation or withheld material information about the patentability of the invention during patent prosecution, the patent is unenforceable.

Finally, the defendant can raise the *experimental use defense*. This is a very narrow defense that permits a person to make or use a patented invention if that person's purpose is only to satisfy her scientific curiosity or to engage in an intellectual exercise. The experimental use defense does not apply if the defendant has any commercial motivation.

---

[10] *See, e.g.*, Orthokinetics, Inc. v. Safety Travel Chairs, Inc., 806 F.2d 1565 (Fed. Cir. 1986).

REMEDIES FOR PATENT INFRINGEMENT

Two basic forms of remedies are available for patent infringement: injunctions and monetary damages. In addition, patentees may recover attorney fees and treble damages under certain circumstances.

Injunctions

An *injunction* is a court order to a party requiring that party to either do something or to refrain from doing something. When infringement is found, the court usually awards the patentee both monetary damages and a *permanent injunction* against further infringement.

The patentee often seeks a *preliminary injunction* as well, which is much harder to obtain. This is a court order issued during the lawsuit that prevents the defendant from continuing its alleged infringing activities until the lawsuit is resolved. Courts traditionally have been reluctant to grant preliminary injunctions because they fear that if the defendant is ultimately found not to be infringing the plaintiff's patent, the defendant's market position might have been impaired or lost altogether. However, the CAFC has become much more liberal in recent years in granting preliminary injunctions. Generally, to receive a preliminary injunction, the patentee must show that (1) the patentee has a reasonable likelihood of success on the merits; (2) irreparable harm to the patentee will occur if the injunction is not granted; (3) the balance of hardships tips in the patentee's favor; and (4) the impact of the injunction is in the public interest (see Focus Case 2.2 on page 28).

Monetary Damages

The Patent Act requires the court to award monetary damages to a prevailing patentee in an amount "adequate to compensate for the infringement." The preferred measure of damages is the patentee's *lost profits* attributable to the infringement. To recover under this measure of damages, the patentee must demonstrate a reasonable probability that, but for the defendant's infringement, the patentee would have made the sales that the defendant made. Thus, the patentee generally must show (1) sufficient demand for the patented invention, and (2) an absence of noninfringing substitutes.

For example, suppose that *Inventor A* has a patent for a telephone answering machine. Several of *Inventor A*'s competitors sell comparable, noninfringing answering machines. *Inventor B* infringes *Inventor A*'s patent. *Inventor A* must show that, absent *Inventor B*'s infringement, *Inventor B*'s customers would have bought from *Inventor A*, not *Inventor A*'s competitors.

Obviously, many patentees find it difficult to meet this standard and obtain lost profits. In such instances, the patentee may still recover damages in the form of a *reasonable royalty*. This is the amount that a prospective licensee seeking a license to make, use, sell, or import the patented invention would be willing to pay and a reasonable patentee would be willing to accept in an arm's-length transaction at the time of the infringement.

The Patent Act requires the patentee to give *notice* to the public of its patent. Notice is given by putting the word "patented" or the abbreviation "Pat.," along with the patent number, on the items being marketed. If the patentee fails to provide notice, the patentee may still obtain injunctive relief against infringers. However, the patentee will receive monetary damages only if the defendant had specific notice that the defendant was being charged with infringement. In addition, damages will be limited to the infringement that occurred after the defendant received the notice. Thus, patentees should be careful to place the required notice on their goods.

Facts: In October 1999, Amazon.com filed a complaint in federal district court alleging that Barnesandnoble.com had infringed its '411 Patent. The '411 Patent describes a method and system for placing a purchase order via a communication network. It allows a purchaser to complete a purchase order for an item using the Internet through a single action (such as a single click of a computer mouse button).

Amazon.com alleged that Barnesandnoble.com's "Express Lane" ordering feature infringed its '411 Patent. Amazon.com filed a motion for a preliminary injunction with the trial court.

Decision: The district court granted Amazon.com's motion. In evaluating the motion for preliminary injunction, the court examined the standard four-factor test for such motions:

(1) Likelihood of Success on the Merits: Barnesandnoble.com argued that the motion should be denied because the '411 Patent was invalid because the invention (1) was obvious and (2) had been anticipated by prior art. Barnesandnoble.com also argued that Express Lane did not infringe any claims in the '411 Patent.

Because patents are presumed valid, Barnesandnoble.com bore the burden of demonstrating that the '411 Patent was invalid. Barnesandnoble.com failed to bear this burden. First, after reviewing the prior art references put forth by Barnesandnoble.com, the court concluded that there were key differences between each of the prior art references and the method and system described in the '411 Patent.

Second, the court found that the one-click shopping system was nonobvious. Expert testimony described Amazon.com's one-click system as "innovative," and industry analysts and the popular press had described it in similar terms. Although the method and system described in the '411 Patent were simple, that simplicity did not mean that the invention was obvious. The court stated: "The commercial success of the invention, the failure of others to solve the problem addressed by the patented invention, and the fact that the [invention] has become the industry standard is [sic] compelling objective evidence of the nonobviousness of the claimed invention."

The court concluded that the '411 Patent was most likely valid and that the strong similarities between Amazon.com's one-click system and Barnesandnoble.com's Express Lane suggested that Barnesandnoble.com had infringed the '411 Patent. Thus, Amazon.com had demonstrated a reasonable likelihood that it would succeed on the merits at trial.

(2) Irreparable Harm: Having established a reasonable likelihood of success on the merits, Amazon.com was entitled to a presumption of irreparable harm. Barnesandnoble.com was unable to rebut this presumption. Moreover, Amazon.com presented "ample evidence that the harm it asks the Court to prevent —losing the opportunity to distinguish itself and build customer loyalty at a critical time [the holiday shopping period]— cannot be reduced to a simple formula. There is no easy way to determine the value of the relationships and loyalties that millions of customers establish with Internet retailers over the next several months."

(3) Balance of Hardships: The court found that Barnesandnoble.com could easily modify Express Lane to avoid infringement of the '411 Patent by simply requiring customers to take an additional action to confirm orders. Amazon.com, on the other hand, would lose the primary value of its one-click option in the absence of a preliminary injunction.

(4) Public Interest: Finally, the court found that a preliminary injunction was in the public interest, stating:

> The public is served by innovation on the Internet and in electronic commerce, particularly now while it is still developing rapidly. Competition to provide unique, effective and enjoyable consumer experiences will lead to innovation and diversity in on-line commerce. On the other hand, innovation will be discouraged if competitors are permitted a free ride on each other's patented inventions. Protection of intellectual property rights in innovations will foster greater competition and innovation.

> * * * Encouraging Amazon.com to continue to innovate—and forcing competitors to come up with their own new ideas—unquestionably best serves the public interest.

Thus, the court issued a preliminary injunction against Barnesandnoble.com and required Amazon.com to pay a bond in the amount of $10,000,000. *Amazon.com, Inc. v. Barnesandnoble.com, Inc.*, 73 F. Supp. 2d 1228 (W.D. Wash. 1999)

The American Inventors Protection Act of 1999 granted a new damage remedy to inventors. While damages for infringement traditionally have been measured from the date of patent issuance, an inventor may now collect "reasonable royalties" for infringement that occurred during the period after publication of the application but before issuance of the patent. To take advantage of this remedy, though, the patentee must bring the published application to the infringer's attention.

Attorneys Fees and Treble Damages

Generally, under U.S. law, each side must bear its own legal costs in litigating a case. Thus, even a winning party is ordinarily required to pay for its own attorneys fees. Some statutes, such as the Patent Act, alter this rule by allowing the winning party to recover its legal fees from the losing party. The Patent Act authorizes the court to award *attorneys fees* to the prevailing party in exceptional cases, such as those in which: (1) the patentee has won and there was willful or deliberate infringement by the defendant, or (2) the defendant has won and there was bad faith conduct by the patentee in obtaining the patent or in suing for infringement.

A few statutes also provide for increasing the damage award in certain circumstances. Under the Patent Act, the court may award up to *treble damages* to the patentee if the defendant willfully infringed or acted in bad faith.

FILING FOR FOREIGN PATENTS

No single patent protects an invention in every country around the world. Rather, the inventor must file for a patent in each country in which the inventor wants to protect her intellectual property asset. Because of the expense and effort involved in filing for patent protection, the inventor generally must choose the countries in which patent protection makes the most commercial sense. To a large extent, this is determined by the inventor's assessment of potential markets and potential competitors and depends upon the inventor's plans for future marketing of the product.

The United States adheres to the Convention for the Protection of Industrial Property, more commonly known as the *Paris Convention*.[11] This is a multilateral treaty to which over 160 countries, including most industrialized countries, belong. The key provision of the Paris Convention is that it requires each country to grant "national treatment" to foreign patent applicants. This means that foreign applicants must be treated the same as domestic applicants and cannot be discriminated against. However, the Paris Convention provides little in the way of substantive rights to inventors, and no enforcement mechanisms apply if a member state does not comply with its obligations.

Inventors thus must look to the specific laws of the countries in which they seek patent protection. In general, all countries grant patents to new inventions and give the patentee some sort of limited monopoly in the invention. The length of the patent term varies from country to country, although 20 years is becoming the norm, at least in industrialized countries. Patentable subject matter also varies from country to country. As noted earlier, the United States tends to be more liberal than most countries. An inventor cannot assume that, just because a patent issues in the United States, the same invention is patentable elsewhere. The process of obtaining a patent varies from country to country as well. It is always important that an inventor have, in addition to whatever U.S. legal counsel the inventor may hire, a

---

[11] The Convention can be found at http://www.wipo.org/

local legal representative who is familiar with the language, laws, customs, and procedure of the country in which the inventor wants to seek a patent.

Generally, U.S. patent law is unlike that found in the rest of the world. First, the United States has a first-to-invent system, not a first-to-file system as exists in virtually every other country around the world. (The United States is currently considering legislation that would implement a first-to-file system, however.) Second, applications in the United States that are not also filed abroad may be held secret unless and until a patent issues. As we see in Chapter 3, if the PTO denies a patent application that is held secret, the inventor still has the option of treating the invention as a trade secret. In most countries, however, all patent applications are made public, either immediately or within 18 months after filing, making trade secret protection impossible if a patent is not issued. Third, in many countries, the inventor is required to "work" the invention within a certain time period. Some countries also impose "compulsory licensing," in which the inventor is required to license other parties within the country to produce the item at reasonable royalty rates. The United States does not require either "working" or compulsory licensing of inventions.

An inventor wishing to obtain patents in foreign countries can follow one of two paths. First, the inventor can file directly in each country in which the inventor wants patent protection. This process can be expensive, as the inventor must pay filing fees, translation costs, and prosecution costs in each country in which the inventor applies. However, the inventor can target specific countries. Depending upon the nature of the invention, such targeting may be the best business strategy.

Second, the inventor can seek patent protection indirectly through a *convention filing*. The two most widely known conventions are the *European Patent Convention* and the *Patent Cooperation Treaty*. The European Patent Convention permits an inventor to file a single patent application with the European Patent Office. If the patent is granted, patent rights arise in all member countries designated by the inventor in her application.[12]

As of October 2000, the Patent Cooperation Treaty had 108 member countries, including the United States.[13] Under this treaty, the inventor can file an international application with one of several specified receiving offices (which include the PTO and the European Patent Office). A patent examination is conducted and the results sent to all member countries designated by the inventor. At that point, the inventor has to hire translators and local attorneys to complete the patent application in each country and has to pay local filing fees.

Using a convention filing tends to be cheaper up-front than directly filing in foreign countries, although the registration fees at the end can be very high. Filings can generally be done in English, however, which makes the examination process quicker and cheaper.

Copyright Law

Copyright law gives the owner of a creative work of authorship the right to keep others from using the work without the owner's permission. The purpose of copyright

---

[12] As of October 2000, the members of the European Patent Convention were: Austria, Belgium, Cyprus, Denmark, Finland, France, Germany, Greece, Ireland, Italy, Liechtenstein, Luxembourg, Monaco, the Netherlands, Portugal, Spain, Sweden, Switzerland, and the United Kingdom. *See* http://www.european-patent-office.org

[13] A list can be found at http://www.wipo.org/eng/ratific/m-pct.htm

law is similar to that of patent law: to encourage creativity. Specifically, copyright law seeks to encourage creation of works of art, literature, music, and other "works of authorship."

We find the same type of fundamental policy tension in copyright law as in patent law. On the one hand, the law wants to encourage creativity by giving creators exclusive rights in their works through copyright protection. On the other hand, the law wants to foster a competitive marketplace by giving the public the freest possible access to works of authorship and the ideas they express.

Copyright law balances these two interests by limiting the author's property rights to the author's particular method of expressing an idea or information. The author can only copyright the *expression* of an idea and not the idea itself, facts, or information.

This is a key distinction between copyright and patent. Patent law gives the inventor an exclusive monopoly in an invention. In return for that monopoly, patent law imposes very strict substantive standards in the form of rigorous application procedures and standards. Copyright law, on the other hand, gives the author a monopoly in one way of expressing an idea—and even that monopoly is limited, because copyright law does not prohibit independently created works, as does patent law. As a result, the requirements for obtaining a copyright are much less stringent than those for obtaining a patent.

SOURCES OF COPYRIGHT LAW

Like patent law, the foundation of copyright law is the U.S. Constitution. The first copyright statute was passed in 1790 and underwent several major revisions. The current statute was adopted in 1976 but has been amended numerous times since then. Many of the most recent amendments resulted from the United States joining the *Berne Convention*[14] in 1988 and as result of the *Trade-Related Aspects of Intellectual Property Rights* (*TRIPs*)[15] agreement of the Uruguay Round of the General Agreement on Tariffs and Trade (GATT), which was completed in December 1993. The Berne Convention is an 1886 international treaty that standardizes basic copyright protection among its 100-plus member countries.

Prior to the Copyright Act of 1976, the United States had a dual system of copyright. Unpublished works were protected under state common-law copyright. Once the works were published, state protection ceased and federal copyright law applied, provided that proper copyright notice was affixed to the works.

In the 1976 Copyright Act, Congress provided that federal copyright protection attaches automatically as soon as a work is fixed in tangible form. Thus, federal law now covers unpublished as well as published works. Today, very little, if any, state copyright law survives.

Generally, copyrighted works today are covered by one of three laws, depending upon when the work was copyrighted and the issues involved: (1) the Copyright Act of 1909; (2) the Copyright Act of 1976, as originally enacted; or (3) the Copyright Act of 1976, as amended. Our discussion focuses on the latter category as it is applicable to the most recently copyrighted works.

The U.S. Copyright Office[16] registers copyrights, issues certificates of registration, keeps records of assignments and licenses, and regulates deposit of copyrighted material. It does not engage in the extensive, comprehensive review

---

[14] *See* http://www.wipo.org

[15] *See* http://www.wto.org

[16] The webpage of the Copyright Office can be found at http://www.loc.gov/copyright/

that the PTO undertakes in a patent application, however. Rather, the Copyright Office looks merely to see if the submitted work falls within a copyrightable subject matter area and whether the formal registration requirements have been met. As we will see below, works do not need to be registered in order to be protected by copyright. Rather, copyright arises automatically once the work is created and fixed in a tangible form. Registration merely provides additional rights to the copyright owner.

SUBJECT MATTER OF COPYRIGHTS

The Copyright Act provides for a long list of works that may be copyrighted, including literary works (which include computer programs, flowcharts, and advertising items such as catalogues, product labels, and directories); musical works; dramatic works; pantomimes and choreographic works; pictorial, graphic, and sculptural works; motion pictures and other audiovisual works; sound recordings; and architectural works. This is not an exclusive list, and the courts can extend copyright protection to new forms of work if the legislative history of the Copyright Act suggests that Congress would have intended to cover those works had it known of them at the time it passed the Act. Thus, the Copyright Act adjusts quite well to advances and changes in technology.

Section 102 of the Copyright Act defines copyrightable subject matter. It states that copyright exists

> in original works of authorship fixed in any tangible medium of expression, now known or later developed, from which they can be perceived, reproduced, or otherwise communicated, either directly or with the aid of a machine or device.

Thus Section 102 contains two important requirements: the work must be (1) "original" and (2) "fixed" in a tangible medium.

Originality

Originality simply means that the author must have created the work herself (as opposed to merely copying from someone else). Copyright law, unlike patent law, does not protect against independent creation. If a second person independently creates an identical form of work, the second person is entitled to a copyright as well as the first (provided there truly is no copying going on).

Originality also requires that the work contain some minimal amount of creativity, although the work does not have to be unique, novel, or of high quality. Thus, even product descriptions or labeling directions can qualify for copyright protection. There must be *some* level of creativity involved, however. For example, a person could not copyright the word "the" because there is no creativity on the part of the purported author. Moreover, granting such a copyright would remove an important word from common usage and make it difficult, if not impossible, for others to engage in normal expression.

According to a rule issued by the Copyright Office, words and short phrases (such as names, titles, and slogans), listings of ingredients or contents, and familiar symbols or designs are not copyrightable. Some of these things may be protected by trademark law, however, as discussed in Chapter 6.

The U.S. Supreme Court addressed the originality requirement in a 1991 case, *Feist Publications, Inc. v. Rural Telephone Service Co.*[17]

---

[17] 499 U.S. 340 (1991).

See Discussion Case 2.3.

The Court's decision that a phone company's compilation of names, addresses, and telephone numbers in its white pages was not entitled to copyright protection caused a great deal of consternation in the business world. Databases are a multibillion dollar industry in the United States. *Feist* is viewed as leaving the industry with little, if any, protection for these valuable assets. Data itself may not be protected by copyright. Rather, only the selection and arrangement of data may be so protected and only then if that selection and arrangement contain sufficient creativity.

In each of the past several legislative sessions, Congress has considered legislation that would close the gap on the protection of databases caused by *Feist* but no legislation has been enacted. The European Union, by contrast, passed a Database Directive in 1996 that provides for a 15-year protection period for databases created "through substantial investment."[18] This protection is available only on a reciprocal basis. Unless the United States enacts database legislation that provides protection equivalent to that of the Directive, U.S. database owners will not receive this heightened protection in the European Union.

Fixation

The *fixation* requirement prevents works that are not put into a tangible form—such as oral statements or unrecorded, unwritten musical improvisations—from receiving copyright protection. For example, if you go to Preservation Hall in New Orleans and hear jazz improvisation, those works are neither copyrighted nor copyrightable unless and until they are written down or recorded. The Copyright Act permits works to be fixed in a wide variety of tangible media, including paper, floppy disks, fabrics, records, tapes, and compact discs.

RIGHTS PROVIDED BY COPYRIGHT

The Copyright Act sets forth several exclusive *economic rights* that are granted to the copyright owner. Section 106 provides that the author, or the person to whom the author has transferred the copyright, has the exclusive right to do or authorize the following:

1. reproduce the copyrighted work;[19]
2. prepare derivative works based upon the copyrighted work;
3. distribute copies or phonorecords of the copyrighted work to the public;
4. publicly perform certain types of copyrighted works;
5. publicly display certain types of copyrighted works; and,
6. in the case of sound recordings, perform the copyrighted work publicly by means of a digital audio transmission.

In addition to these economic rights, Congress amended the Copyright Act in 1990 to provide for protection of *moral rights.* Many nations, especially civil law

---

[18]The Directive can be found at http://europa.eu.int/eur-lex/en/lif/dat/1996/en_39660009.html
[19]This right is subject to certain exceptions. For example, the lawful owner of a copy of a copyrighted computer program may make a backup copy. In addition, public libraries and archives are permitted to copy in many instances that would constitute infringement if done by a private party.

nations, view a work of authorship as an extension of the author's personality. These nations grant the author (1) *the right of attribution* (i.e., the right to prevent others from claiming authorship in the work, the right to be known as the author, and the right to avoid having others' works falsely attributed to an individual); and (2) *the right of integrity* (i.e., the right to prevent others from distorting, mutilating, or misrepresenting the author's work).

The United States traditionally did not recognize the moral rights of attribution and integrity. The Berne Convention requires member countries to provide protection for such rights, however, so the United States amended the Copyright Act so that it would be in compliance with its treaty obligations. Section 106A of the Copyright Act now provides that, in the case of works of visual art (which are narrowly defined as works of fine art but not objects of utility or mass production), the artist (not the copyright owner, who may be a different individual or entity) has the moral rights of attribution and integrity. Specifically, the artist has the right to

1. claim authorship in the work;
2. prevent the use of her name as the author of any work she did not create;
3. prevent the use of her name as the author of the work if the work has been distorted, mutilated, or otherwise modified such that the work would be prejudicial to her honor or reputation;
4. prevent any additional distortion, mutilation, or other modification of her work that would be prejudicial to her honor or reputation; and
5. prevent any intentional or grossly negligent destruction of her work, if the work is of recognized stature.

OWNERSHIP OF THE COPYRIGHT

Initially, the copyright is owned by the author of the work. If there are two or more authors, they are considered joint owners of a single copyright in the work. Unless the authors have agreed otherwise, each has an equal ownership share.

The author can transfer some or all of the economic rights in the copyright to others. Transfers of exclusive rights must be made in writing and signed by the author. Transfers of nonexclusive rights may be made through oral agreements. (As a practical matter, however, oral agreements are seldom a wise business practice.)

The exception to the rule that the author is the owner of the copyright involves two categories of works known as *works for hire*. First, when a work is prepared by an employee within the scope of his employment, the employer owns the copyright. Second, when a work is created by an independent contractor, the copyright belongs to the hiring party, provided that: (1) the parties expressly agree in a written, signed agreement that the work will be considered a work for hire, and (2) the work fits within one of nine broad categories listed in Section 101 of the Copyright Act. It can often be difficult to determine whether an individual is an employee or an independent contractor. The Supreme Court addressed this issue in *Community for Creative Non-Violence v. Reid*,[20] in which it set forth the types of factors a court should consider in making this critical determination.

See Discussion Case 2.4.

---

[20] 490 U.S. 730 (1989).

As a practical matter, a firm should always require anyone who creates copyrighted works for it (whether an employee or an independent contractor) to sign an agreement assigning any intellectual property rights that individual might have in the works to the firm. This topic is discussed in further detail in Chapter 3.

COPYRIGHT PROCEDURES

Copyright Creation

As previously noted, copyright arises automatically once an original work is expressed in a tangible form. This distinguishes copyrights from patents, which involve a lengthy and detailed application process.

Although an author need not do anything to obtain a copyright, there are certain steps that the author can take to strengthen the copyright protection he receives under the law. In particular, the author should provide a *copyright notice* on the work and should *register* the work with the Copyright Office.

Copyright Notice

Before 1989, the United States, unlike most of the rest of the world, had very strict requirements regarding the use of copyright notices. If the author failed to place the correct notice on his work, he lost his copyright protection.

Once the United States joined the Berne Convention, however, it was required to redraft its copyright laws in order to meet its treaty obligations. For works published after 1989, U.S. copyright arises automatically and attaches to the work without any formal action being required on the part of the author. Thus, the author is not required to register the work or place a copyright notice upon it in order to obtain copyright protection. Nonetheless, it is a good idea for authors to include a copyright notice on their works, as the notice tells the public who owns the copyright in a particular work. In addition, some foreign countries do not protect works that do not contain a copyright notice.

To encourage authors to include notices on their works, the Copyright Act provides a special remedy: where a proper copyright notice has been affixed to a work, a defendant may be barred from claiming an innocent infringement defense to mitigate actual or statutory damages. This defense is discussed in more detail below.

The form of copyright notice required is very simple. For example, an author named Jane Smith who created an original work in 2001 would place either of the following notations on her work:

"Copyright, 2001, Jane Smith" *or*
"© 2001 Jane Smith."

The notice should be placed on the first page or on a visible part of the work or copy. Although in the past it was customary to add the words "all rights reserved" as well in order to obtain complete protection around the world under a specific international copyright treaty, current international agreements have made the phrase unnecessary.

Deposit and Registration

Under the Copyright Act, the copyright owner of a published or unpublished work may register the work with the Copyright Office at any time. The purpose of this provision is to create a comprehensive record of U.S. copyright claims. The registration procedure is very simple:

1. the copyright owner fills out a very short application form;
2. the copyright owner mails the form and a filing fee ($30) to the Copyright Office; and
3. the copyright owner deposits one copy of an unpublished work or two copies of a published work with the Copyright Office.

Copyright application forms and a current fee schedule may be obtained from the Copyright Office's webpage (see Exhibit 2.5 for a sample registration form).

The Copyright Office reviews the application only for obvious errors or lack of copyrightable subject matter and then issues a certificate of registration. The process is relatively simple and can be accomplished by most individuals without the assistance of a lawyer.

Prior to adopting the Berne Convention, the United States required all copyright owners to register their works before suing for infringement. However, the Berne Convention prohibits member states from imposing formalities such as registration as a prerequisite to copyright protection. As a result, U.S. law now provides that only authors of works whose country of origin is the United States must register before they can bring suit for infringement. A work's country of origin is the United States if: (1) the work was first published in the United States; (2) the work was simultaneously published in the United States and another country; or (3) if unpublished, the work was created entirely by U.S. authors. Authors of works whose country of origin is another Berne Convention member state need not preregister.

Note that registration need not occur prior to the infringement but, rather, only prior to filing of the lawsuit. If the copyright owner waits to register until after infringement has occurred, however, she may be barred from receiving certain remedies. This is discussed more below. As a practical matter, then, a copyright owner who wants to ensure that she will have access to the greatest range of potential remedies in the event of an infringement should register her work promptly.

Copyright Duration

Prior to the 1976 Copyright Act, federal copyright protection began when the work was published, assuming proper notice had been affixed. Under the 1976 Copyright Act, copyright protection begins when the work is created and fixed in a tangible medium. Publication or registration is not necessary.

Moreover, Congress has recently extended copyright terms significantly through the Sonny Bono Copyright Term Extension Act.[21] This Act extends all existing copyrights by 20 years, thus harmonizing U.S. law with European Union law. Copyright duration for pre-1978 copyrighted works is extended to 95 years. For works created after January 1, 1978, copyrights now generally last for the life of the author plus 70 years. If there are joint authors, the copyright is measured by the life of the last to die plus 70 years. If the work is published anonymously or under a pseudonym or is a work for hire, copyright protection lasts for 95 years after first publication or 120 years after creation, whichever expires first. Moral rights in visual works created after June 1, 1991, last for the life of the author or, in the case of joint authors, for the life of the last to die (see Exhibit 2.6 on page 39).

---

[21]Pub. L. No. 105-298.

FORM TX
For a Nondramatic Literary Work
UNITED STATES COPYRIGHT OFFICE

REGISTRATION NUMBER

TX	TXU

EFFECTIVE DATE OF REGISTRATION

Month	Day	Year

DO NOT WRITE ABOVE THIS LINE. IF YOU NEED MORE SPACE, USE A SEPARATE CONTINUATION SHEET.

1

TITLE OF THIS WORK ▼

PREVIOUS OR ALTERNATIVE TITLES ▼

PUBLICATION AS A CONTRIBUTION If this work was published as a contribution to a periodical, serial, or collection, give information about the collective work in which the contribution appeared.   **Title of Collective Work ▼**

If published in a periodical or serial give: **Volume ▼**   **Number ▼**   **Issue Date ▼**   **On Pages ▼**

2
a

NAME OF AUTHOR ▼

DATES OF BIRTH AND DEATH
Year Born ▼   Year Died ▼

Was this contribution to the work a "work made for hire"?
☐ Yes
☐ No

AUTHOR'S NATIONALITY OR DOMICILE
Name of Country
OR { Citizen of ▶_____
Domiciled in▶_____

WAS THIS AUTHOR'S CONTRIBUTION TO THE WORK
Anonymous?   ☐ Yes ☐ No
Pseudonymous?   ☐ Yes ☐ No

If the answer to either of these questions is "Yes," see detailed instructions.

NATURE OF AUTHORSHIP Briefly describe nature of material created by this author in which copyright is claimed. ▼

NOTE

Under the law, the "author" of a "work made for hire" is generally the employer, not the employee (see instructions). For any part of this work that was "made for hire" check "Yes" in the space provided, give the employer (or other person for whom the work was prepared) as "Author" of that part, and leave the space for dates of birth and death blank.

b

NAME OF AUTHOR ▼

DATES OF BIRTH AND DEATH
Year Born ▼   Year Died ▼

Was this contribution to the work a "work made for hire"?
☐ Yes
☐ No

AUTHOR'S NATIONALITY OR DOMICILE
Name of Country
OR { Citizen of ▶_____
Domiciled in▶_____

WAS THIS AUTHOR'S CONTRIBUTION TO THE WORK
Anonymous?   ☐ Yes ☐ No
Pseudonymous?   ☐ Yes ☐ No

If the answer to either of these questions is "Yes," see detailed instructions.

NATURE OF AUTHORSHIP Briefly describe nature of material created by this author in which copyright is claimed. ▼

c

NAME OF AUTHOR ▼

DATES OF BIRTH AND DEATH
Year Born ▼   Year Died ▼

Was this contribution to the work a "work made for hire"?
☐ Yes
☐ No

AUTHOR'S NATIONALITY OR DOMICILE
Name of Country
OR { Citizen of ▶_____
Domiciled in▶_____

WAS THIS AUTHOR'S CONTRIBUTION TO THE WORK
Anonymous?   ☐ Yes ☐ No
Pseudonymous?   ☐ Yes ☐ No

If the answer to either of these questions is "Yes," see detailed instructions.

NATURE OF AUTHORSHIP Briefly describe nature of material created by this author in which copyright is claimed. ▼

3
a
YEAR IN WHICH CREATION OF THIS WORK WAS COMPLETED
This information must be given in all cases.
◀ Year

b
DATE AND NATION OF FIRST PUBLICATION OF THIS PARTICULAR WORK
Complete this information ONLY if this work has been published.
Month ▶ _____ Day ▶ _____ Year ▶ _____
◀ Nation

4

COPYRIGHT CLAIMANT(S) Name and address must be given even if the claimant is the same as the author given in space 2. ▼

See instructions before completing this space.

TRANSFER If the claimant(s) named here in space 4 is (are) different from the author(s) named in space 2, give a brief statement of how the claimant(s) obtained ownership of the copyright. ▼

DO NOT WRITE HERE OFFICE USE ONLY

APPLICATION RECEIVED

ONE DEPOSIT RECEIVED

TWO DEPOSITS RECEIVED

FUNDS RECEIVED

MORE ON BACK ▶ • Complete all applicable spaces (numbers 5-9) on the reverse side of this page.
• See detailed instructions.   • Sign the form at line 8.

DO NOT WRITE HERE
Page 1 of _____ pages

EXHIBIT 2.5

EXAMINED BY

CHECKED BY

CORRESPONDENCE
☐ Yes

FORM TX

FOR
COPYRIGHT
OFFICE
USE
ONLY

DO NOT WRITE ABOVE THIS LINE. IF YOU NEED MORE SPACE, USE A SEPARATE CONTINUATION SHEET.

PREVIOUS REGISTRATION Has registration for this work, or for an earlier version of this work, already been made in the Copyright Office?

☐ **Yes** ☐ **No** If your answer is "Yes," why is another registration being sought? (Check appropriate box.) ▼

a. ☐ This is the first published edition of a work previously registered in unpublished form.

b. ☐ This is the first application submitted by this author as copyright claimant.

c. ☐ This is a changed version of the work, as shown by space 6 on this application.

If your answer is "Yes," give: **Previous Registration Number** ▶   **Year of Registration** ▶

5

DERIVATIVE WORK OR COMPILATION

Preexisting Material Identify any preexisting work or works that this work is based on or incorporates. ▼

a

6

Material Added to This Work Give a brief, general statement of the material that has been added to this work and in which copyright is claimed. ▼

b

See instructions
before completing
this space.

DEPOSIT ACCOUNT If the registration fee is to be charged to a Deposit Account established in the Copyright Office, give name and number of Account.

Name ▼   **Account Number** ▼

a

7

CORRESPONDENCE Give name and address to which correspondence about this application should be sent. Name/Address/Apt/City/State/ZIP ▼

b

Area code and daytime telephone number ▶   Fax number ▶

Email ▶

CERTIFICATION* I, the undersigned, hereby certify that I am the

Check only one ▶ {
☐ author
☐ other copyright claimant
☐ owner of exclusive right(s)
☐ authorized agent of _____

of the work identified in this application and that the statements made
by me in this application are correct to the best of my knowledge.

Name of author or other copyright claimant, or owner of exclusive right(s) ▲

8

Typed or printed name and date ▼ If this application gives a date of publication in space 3, do not sign and submit it before that date.

Date ▶

Handwritten signature (X) ▼

X _

**Certificate
will be
mailed in
window
envelope
to this
address:**

Name ▼

Number/Street/Apt ▼

City/State/ZIP ▼

YOU MUST:
• Complete all necessary spaces
• Sign your application in space 8

**SEND ALL 3 ELEMENTS
IN THE SAME PACKAGE:**
1. Application form
2. Nonrefundable filing fee in check or money order
payable to *Register of Copyrights*
3. Deposit material

MAIL TO:
Library of Congress
Copyright Office
101 Independence Avenue, S.E.
Washington, D.C. 20559-6000

As of
July 1,
1999,
the
filing
fee for
Form TX
is $30.

9

*17 U.S.C. § 506(e): Any person who knowingly makes a false representation of a material fact in the application for copyright registration provided for by section 409, or in any written statement filed in connection
with the application, shall be fined not more than $2,500.

June 1999—200,000   ♻ PRINTED ON RECYCLED PAPER   ☆U.S. GOVERNMENT PRINTING OFFICE: 1999-454-879/49
WEB REV: June 1999

EXHIBIT 2.5

EXHIBIT 2.6

COPYRIGHT DURATION

Pre- 1/1/78 Works	Post- 1/1/78 Works	Moral Rights in Visual Works Created After 6/1/91
95 years	Life of Author + 70 years Work for Hire: 95 years after first publication or 120 years after creation, whichever expires first	Life of Author

COPYRIGHT INFRINGEMENT

Direct Infringement

An individual becomes liable for *direct infringement* if the individual violates any of the exclusive rights of the copyright owner or illegally imports copies of a copyrighted work into the United States. The most common form of violation is an infringement of the copyright owner's exclusive right to reproduce a work.

To prove copyright infringement, the plaintiff generally must show that the defendant's work was (1) copied from the plaintiff's work, and (2) "substantially similar" to the plaintiff's copyrighted work. The alleged infringer can then attempt to demonstrate one of the defenses discussed later in the chapter.

Copying is usually shown in one of two ways. First, the plaintiff may have direct evidence of the defendant's copying. This is relatively rare, as it requires an eyewitness or documentary evidence showing that the defendant copied or an admission of copying by the defendant. Second, the plaintiff may produce circumstantial evidence that the defendant had access to the copyrighted work and that the defendant's work is similar to the plaintiff's work. This is known as the *access plus similarity* test (see Focus Case 2.3 on page 40 for an example of the *access plus similarity* test).

Vicarious and Contributory Infringement

With one narrow exception,[22] the Copyright Act does not specifically provide for liability for infringement based on acts committed by another. Nonetheless, the courts have determined that a defendant may be liable for vicarious or contributory infringement.

Vicarious liability attaches in cases in which the defendant (1) had the right and ability to supervise the infringing acts of another, and (2) had an obvious and direct financial interest in the exploitation of the copyrighted materials. For example, owners of nightclubs have been held vicariously liable for unauthorized public performances by bands that they had hired, even though they did not direct the bands to engage in infringing behavior.[23]

Contributory infringement occurs in which the defendant (1) knew or had reason to know of someone else's directly infringing activity and (2) actively participated by inducing, materially contributing to, or furthering that other person's directly

---

[22] This exception involves semiconductor mask works. *See* 17 U.S.C. § 905(3).

[23] *See, e.g.,* ITSI T.V. Prods., Inc. v. California Auth. of Racing Fairs, 785 F. Supp. 854 (E.D. Cal. 1992); Cass County Music Co. v. Vineyard Country Golf Corp., 605 F. Supp. 1536 (D. Mass. 1985).

Facts: Salvino Figurine Manufacturing, Inc., entered into a license agreement with the Major League Baseball Players Association to produce stuffed animal toys, known as Bamm Bears, bearing the names of individual players. Ty, Inc., who produces Beanie Babies stuffed toys, sued for copyright infringement, claiming that Salvino's bears were substantially similar to its Beanie Babies bears. Ty requested a temporary restraining order.

Decision: To obtain a temporary restraining order, the party requesting it must show (1) some likelihood of success on the merits, (2) that there is no adequate remedy at law, and (3) that it will suffer irreparable harm if the temporary restraining order is not issued.

To satisfy the first element—a likelihood of success on the merits—Ty must establish copyright infringement. This requires a showing of "(1) ownership of a valid copyright and (2) copying of constituent elements of the work that are original."

The first element was easily satisfied. Ty had registered its copyrights, which was "prima facie evidence of the validity of the copyright."

To demonstrate the second element, copying, the plaintiff must show that (1) the defendant had access to the copyrighted work and (2) the allegedly infringing work is substantially similar to the copyrighted work. The parties did not dispute that Salvino had access to Ty's bears.

The basic axiom of copyright is that only the expression of an idea is protected, not the idea itself. Thus, "substantial similarity' is determined by a two-part test: (1) whether the defendant copied from the plaintiff's work, and (2) whether the copying constitutes an improper appropriation."

The trial court found that Salvino had clearly engaged in "some copying here" as the two sets of bears were "the same size, ha[d] the same general shape, and ha[d] approximately the same degree of stuffing." Nonetheless, the court found that there was no substantial similarity between the bears:

The bear's face is the main expressive element. The facial features on the two bears are different. The Ty bear's nose is flat and somewhat "pug," while the Salvino bear's nose is much larger, more like a snout. Moreover, the protruding snout makes the Salvino bear's head larger than the Ty bear's. In addition, the Ty bear's eyes are set close together, while the Salvino bear's eyes are separated by the base of the snout and are farther apart, giving the bear a substantially different appearance.

The identifying tag sewn into the left back of the Salvino bear also differentiates the bears. Furthermore, the Salvino bears have embroidered on the front a number and in some cases a date and place; on the back of each is an embroidered name and number of a major league baseball player. Most of Ty's bears also bear an embroidered imprint, but it is solely on the front of the bear and consists of a small shamrock, a heart, a peace symbol or national flag.

An ordinary, reasonable person would not overlook the differences in the two products. Hence, there is no substantial similarity here.

Because the court found that there was no substantial similarity between the bears, it concluded that Ty had not shown a likelihood of success on the merits and thus was not entitled to a temporary restraining order. *Ty, Inc. v. Salvino Manufacturing, Inc.,* 1998 U.S. Dist. LEXIS 16977 (N.D. Ill. 1998)

infringing acts. As with patent law, however, contributory infringement does not attach in situations in which the products or materials supplied are capable of "substantial noninfringing uses." The Supreme Court clarified this rule in a 1984 decision, *Sony Corp. of Am. v. Universal City Studios* (see Focus Case 2.4 on page 41).

Corporate officers should be aware that they can be held personally liable for the copyright infringement of their employees even if they had no knowledge of the infringing activities. For example, the courts have held corporate officers vicariously liable in situations in which: (1) the officer personally participated in the actual infringement; (2) the officer derived financial benefit from the infringing activities, either as a major shareholder in the corporation or through some other means such as receiving a percentage of the revenues from the activity giving rise to the infringement; (3) the officer used the corporation as an instrument to carry out a deliberate infringement of copyright; or (4) the officer was the dominant influence

Facts: Universal City Studios and Walt Disney Productions, which owned the copyrights on a number of television programs broadcast on the public airwaves, sued Sony Corp., the maker of Betamax, a brand of VCR. The plaintiffs alleged that individuals directly infringed upon their copyrights by using Betamaxes to copy some of plaintiffs' copyrighted works that had been aired on commercially sponsored television. Because it is impossible to find and sue those anonymous people, the plaintiffs sued Sony for contributory infringement for marketing a product that makes such direct infringement possible. The trial court ruled for Sony. The appellate court reversed and Sony appealed to the U.S. Supreme Court.

Decision: The Supreme Court noted that the Copyright Act does not specifically address liability for acts committed by others, but found that the Act's silence on this issue was not conclusive:

> The absence of such express language in the copyright statute does not preclude the imposition of lia-

bility for copyright infringements on certain parties who have not themselves engaged in the infringing activity. For vicarious liability is imposed in virtually all areas of the law, and the concept of contributory infringement is merely a subspecies of the broader problem of identifying the circumstances in which it is just to hold one individual accountable for the actions of another.

While the Court held that the Copyright Act does allow recovery for contributory infringement, it determined that contributory infringement of a copyright does not exist where the item in question has some substantial noninfringing use as well. Betamaxes can be used for home "time-shifting" (e.g., recording a broadcast program for private, noncommercial viewing at a later date or time), which the Court found to be a fair use. Because Betamaxes had a substantial noninfringing use, Sony's sale of them did not constitute contributory infringement (even though some purchasers of Betamaxes may have put them to illegal uses). *Sony Corp. of Am. v. Universal City Studios,* 464 U.S. 417 (1984)

---

in the corporation and determined the policies that resulted in the infringement.[24] A corporate officer who fails to adequately monitor the activities of employees may well find himself personally liable for copyright infringement.

DEFENSES TO COPYRIGHT INFRINGEMENT

A defendant charged with copyright infringement can raise a number of defenses, including that: (1) the later work was independently created, (2) the use of an earlier work was permitted by statute, or (3) the earlier work was not copyrightable (e.g., because it did not contain sufficient originality).

The most common defense, however, is the *fair use defense*. Because this is an equitable doctrine, it is purposely vague and must be applied on a case-by-case basis, depending upon the facts before the court. Essentially, the defense states that, although technically infringement did occur, it should be excused under the circumstances. Section 107 of the Copyright Act lists four factors that the court should consider in determining whether the fair use defense should apply:

1. *The purpose and character of the use.* Commercial use is least likely to be regarded as a fair use; nonprofit educational use is most likely to be classified as a fair use.
2. *The nature of the copyrighted work.* Unpublished works receive more copyright protection than published works on the theory that the copyright owner should have the right to determine the time and manner of the first publication of his work. In addition, factual works receive less copyright protection than fictional works.

---

[24] *See* Famous Music Corp. v. Bay State Harness Horse Racing & Breeding Assoc., Inc., 423 F. Supp. 341 (D. Mass. 1976), *aff'd*, 554 F.2d 1213 (1st Cir. 1977).

3. *The amount and substantiality of the portion used in relation to the copyrighted work as a whole.* This factor examines both the quantity and the importance of the work copied by the defendant.
4. *The effect of the use on the potential market for or value of the copyrighted work.* The Supreme Court has stated that this is the most important factor.

A court evaluating a fair use defense is to consider all of these factors and is not to treat any of them as conclusive. In addition, these factors are not exclusive and a court should consider whatever other factors are relevant under the circumstances before it.

See Discussion Case 2.5.

Parodies are a special category of fair use. Parody is considered an important form of social commentary within U.S. society. Because the authors of serious works are unlikely to authorize others to parody their work, the courts have recognized that the fair use doctrine is important in ensuring that parodies will be created.

In determining whether a parody was a fair use, the courts consider (1) whether the defendant's purpose was at least in part to parody the plaintiff's work, (2) the amount of the copyrighted material taken, and (3) the effect of the parody on the plaintiff's market (including the effect on the market for derivative works). The Supreme Court addressed these issues in a 1994 case, *Campbell v. Acuff-Rose Music, Inc* (see Focus Case 2.5 on page 43).

REMEDIES FOR COPYRIGHT INFRINGEMENT

Copyright law, like patent law, provides for two basic forms of remedies: (1) injunctions and (2) monetary damages. The Copyright Act also allows infringing materials to be impounded and destroyed under certain circumstances.

Injunctions

Preliminary and permanent injunctions are available against both copyright infringement and violation of moral rights.

Impoundment

Under Section 503 of the Copyright Act, the court may impound allegedly infringing materials prior to judgment and may destroy them if a final judgment is entered against the defendant.

Monetary Damages

Section 504 of the Copyright Act gives the copyright owner the choice of recovering either (1) actual damages and any additional profits of the infringer or (2) statutory damages.

The plaintiff can recover any actual damages she suffered as a result of the defendant's actions, plus any of the defendant's profits attributable to the infringement that are not taken into account in calculating actual damages. Actual damages are usually measured either by (1) the *lost sales* that the plaintiff suffered as a result of the defendant's infringement, or (2) the *reasonable royalty* that the plaintiff would have received had the defendant purchased a license to carry out its infringing activities.

Facts: 2 Live Crew, a popular rap music group, released a parody of Roy Orbison's rock ballad, "Oh, Pretty Woman." Acuff-Rose Music, Inc., which held the copyright to Orbison's song, sued for copyright infringement. 2 Live Crew defended on the grounds that its parodic use was a fair use under § 107 of the Copyright Act. The District Court granted summary judgment to 2 Live Crew based on fair use. The Court of Appeals reversed, holding that the defense of fair use was barred by the song's commercial character and by excessive borrowing from the original. 2 Live Crew appealed to the U.S. Supreme Court.

Decision: The Supreme Court reversed the decision of the Court of Appeals. The Court noted first that 2 Live Crew's song would clearly infringe Acuff-Rose's rights absent of finding of fair use through parody.

The Court examined the role of § 107's four-factor test in fair use cases:

> It is uncontested that 2 Live Crew's song would be an infringement of Acuff-Rose's rights in "Oh, Pretty Woman" but for a finding of fair use through parody. The task [of evaluating fair use] is not to be simplified with bright-line rules, for [Section 107] calls for case-by-case analysis. Nor may the four statutory factors be treated in isolation, one from another. All are to be explored, and the results weighed together, in light of the purposes of copyright.

The Court thus found that the appellate court had erred in treating the first factor, the purpose and character of the use, as determinative. Although 2 Live Crew's use was commercial, the commercial character of the use is but one factor to consider under § 107.

The Court then stated that the second factor, "the nature of the copyrighted work," is "not much help in this case, or ever likely to help much in separating the fair use sheep from the infringing goats in a parody case, since parodies almost invariably copy publicly known, expressive works."

The third factor, which "asks whether 'the amount and substantiality of the portion used in relation to the copyrighted work as a whole,' are reasonable in relation to the purpose of the copying," looks not only to the quantity of the material copied from the original but to its quality and importance as well. This factor requires careful application in a parody case. As the Court noted:

> Parody's humor, or in any event its comment, necessarily springs from recognizable allusion to its object through distorted imitation. Its art lies in the tension between a known original and its parodic twin. When parody takes aim at a particular original work, the parody must be able to "conjure up" at least enough of that original to make the object of its critical wit recognizable. What makes for this recognition is quotation of the original's most distinctive or memorable features, which the parodist can be sure the audience will know. Once enough has been taken to assure identification, how much more is reasonable will depend, say, on the extent to which the song's overriding purpose and character is to parody the original or, in contrast, the likelihood that the parody may serve as a market substitute for the original. But using some characteristic features cannot be avoided.

The fourth fair use factor examines "the effect of the use upon the potential market for or value of the copyrighted work." Under this factor, the court must consider not only harm to the market for the original work but also harm to the market for derivative works.

Parody can affect market demand in ways that do not violate the Copyright Act. The Court stated:

> [A]s to parody pure and simple, it is more likely that the new work will not affect the market for the original in a way cognizable·under this factor, that is, by acting as a substitute for it. This is so because the parody and the original usually serve different market functions.

> We do not, of course, suggest that a parody may not harm the market at all, but when a lethal parody, like a scathing theater review, kills demand for the original, it does not produce a harm cognizable under the Copyright Act. Because "parody might quite legitimately aim at garrotting the original, destroying it commercially as well as artistically," the role of the courts is to distinguish between "biting criticism [that merely] suppresses demand [and] copyright infringement[, which] usurps it."

Because 2 Live Crew's parody was also rap music, the lower court should have considered the impact of the parodic rap song on the market for a nonparodic rap version of "Oh, Pretty Woman." Thus, the Supreme Court remanded the case to the lower court for further proceedings. *Campbell v. Acuff-Rose Music, Inc.*, 510 U.S. 569 (1994)

In situations in which it is too difficult to prove actual damages, the plaintiff may elect instead to receive statutory damages, provided that the copyright owner registered the work within the proper time frame (i.e., before infringement occurred for unpublished works or within three months after first publication for published works). Statutory damages are set by the court and must be between $750 and $30,000. If the defendant willfully infringed, the court may increase the statutory damages up to $150,000. If the defendant can show that its infringement was innocent (i.e, that it did not know and had no reason to think that it was infringing), the court may reduce the statutory damages to not less than $200. However, the defendant may not use this defense if a proper copyright notice appeared on the copy of the work to which the defendant had access.

Attorneys Fees and Costs

Section 505 of the Copyright Act provides that the court, in its discretion, may award costs to either side if the opposing side acted in bad faith. In addition, prevailing parties may receive attorneys fees, although copyright owners who failed to register their works in a timely manner are barred from this relief.

Criminal Penalties

Section 506 of the Copyright Act also allows for criminal penalties for willful infringement (1) for commercial advantage or private financial gain and (2) "by the reproduction or distribution, including by electronic means, during any 180-day period, of 1 or more copies or phonorecords of 1 or more copyrighted works, which have a total retail value of more than $1,000." The Act provides for fines and imprisonment for up to 10 years, depending upon the nature of the offense (e.g., how many copies were made or whether it was a first offense), as well as forfeiture and destruction of the infringing works and all equipment used to produce them.

Section 506 also provides for criminal sanctions (of fines of up to $2,500) for fraudulent copyright notice, fraudulent removal of copyright notice, and false representations in applications for copyright registrations. Criminal sanctions are not provided for violations of moral rights, however.

COPYRIGHT LAW ON THE INTERNET

The advent of the Internet, with its ability to enable millions of people to instantaneously access, reproduce, and disseminate information, including copyrighted material, is having a significant impact on copyright law. While the Internet makes distribution of copyrighted works much easier and cheaper, it also makes it far more difficult for a copyright owner to protect its copyright and prevent piracy of its works. Commentators are currently debating whether copyright law will, or should, survive the Internet. Some argue for the free and unhindered flow of information; others maintain that individuals who engage in creative endeavors should continue to be rewarded for their efforts through the use of copyrights.

This debate is a complex and highly controversial one and is beyond the scope of this book. Several types of webpage-related activities, such as linking, framing, and the use of metatags, can have very real effects upon businesses and their marketing activities. These topics also implicate trademark law and so are addressed in Chapter 6.

Several new technologies are available to assist businesses in identifying and halting copyright and/or trademark infringement on the Internet. In particular, several providers now offer on-line business intelligence services that use specialized software to track trademark and copyright infringement, counterfeited goods, and bootlegged videos and music.

INTERNATIONAL COPYRIGHT LAW ISSUES

There is no "international copyright" that automatically protects a work around the world. Copyright protection within a specific country depends upon the laws of that country. The United Nations' World Intellectual Property Organization (WIPO) has been working to harmonize national copyright laws, and there is a substantial amount of international cooperation in this area. Nonetheless, some countries provide little or no copyright protection to foreign works and foreign piracy of copyrighted works can be hard to combat.

There are two principal international copyright conventions: (1) the Berne Union for the Protection of Literary and Artistic Property (*Berne Convention*), initiated in 1886,[25] and (2) the *Universal Copyright Convention of 1952* (UCC).[26] The United States was originally a member of the UCC and became a signatory of the Berne Convention in 1989. Even if a work is not protected under one of these two conventions, it may be protected by a bilateral agreement between the United States and the other country or under the other country's national laws.

International copyright issues are particularly relevant to copyrighted materials appearing on the Internet. While the Internet is global in reach, copyright law is inherently national. The Berne Convention provides some protection in this area, however, because it states that member countries must provide at least the same protection to citizens of other member countries as they do to their own. In addition, once copyright protection is obtained in one Berne Convention country, it is automatic in all other member countries as well. The Berne Convention has few substantive restrictions and weak enforcement provisions, however. Its only enforcement mechanisms are two nonmandatory provisions for the seizure of infringing materials.

Generally, an author should check to see what protection is available for foreign authors in each country in which the author wants copyright protection. The author should do this before the work is published anywhere because in some countries copyright protection depends upon the facts existing at the time of first publication, regardless of where that publication occurred.

International copyright piracy is a very real and very expensive problem for businesses. The International Intellectual Property Alliance (IIPA)[27] surveyed 67 countries and found that U.S. copyright industries[28] lost an estimated $9.9 billion to copyright piracy in 1999. The IIPA estimates that worldwide losses from copyright piracy total between 20 and 22 billion dollars annually. Sixty-three percent of the pirated copyright materials involved business applications and entertainment software.

Obviously, international intellectual property piracy is a major concern for companies and managers. Although there are practical steps a company can take to

---

[25] *See* http://www.wipo.org

[26] *See* http://www.unesco.org/culture/law/copyright/html-eng/page/htm

[27] *See* http://www.iipa.com The IIPA is a private-sector coalition formed in1984 and comprised of seven trade associations. It represents U.S. copyright-based industries—business software, films, videos, music, sound recordings, books and journals, and interactive entertainment software— in efforts to increase the international protection of copyrighted materials.

[28] The IIPA reviewed piracy of motion pictures, records and music, business applications, entertainment software, and books.

protect its intellectual property, companies are often limited to seeking remedies for such piracy in the country or countries where such activities are taking place. These countries may not have copyright protections equivalent to those of the United States. In addition, pursuing these remedies in distant lands may prove too time-consuming, difficult, and/or expensive for many companies. As a result, much international intellectual property piracy goes on unhindered.

If pirated goods that violate U.S. patents, copyrights, mask works, trade secrets, or trademarks are being imported, the injured party can file a complaint with the International Trade Commission (ITC) under Section 337 of the U.S. Tariff Act. If the ITC determines that the imported goods do violate U.S. intellectual property rights, it can direct the U.S. Customs Service to prevent importation of the infringing goods. Section 337 does not provide for monetary damages to injured intellectual property owners, however.

If the piracy is occurring completely overseas—for example, a foreign company is making bootlegged copies of copyrighted books or films and is selling them in foreign markets—the aggrieved copyright owner often finds it difficult to obtain a meaningful remedy. At the governmental level, the U.S. government can bring pressure to bear upon countries in which piracy is rampant. Thus, companies and industry groups can lobby the United States Trade Representative (USTR) for trade sanctions against countries that fail to take effective action against intellectual property piracy within their jurisdictions. Similarly, the U.S. government can (and has) opposed membership in the World Trade Organization (WTO) by countries who fail to adequately protect intellectual property.

At the firm level, intellectual property owners faced with international piracy can directly pursue certain types of measures abroad. For example, some foreign countries have censorship offices that may require a marketer to demonstrate title to a copyrighted work before the marketer can obtain a license to sell the product. Some countries also require duplication licenses for copyrighted works. For example, in China, the central government requires that all copies have a certification sticker.

DISCUSSION CASES

2.1 Patent Law—Patentable Subject Matter

Diamond v. Chakrabarty, 447 U.S. 303 (1980)

OPINION: MR. CHIEF JUSTICE BURGER We granted certiorari to determine whether a live, human-made micro- organism is patentable subject matter under 35 U.S.C. § 101.

I

In 1972, respondent Chakrabarty, a microbiologist, filed a patent application, assigned to the General Electric Co. The application asserted 36 claims related to Chakrabarty's invention of "a bacterium from the genus *Pseudomonas* . . . ." This human-made, genetically engineered bacterium is capable of breaking down multiple components of crude oil. Because of this property, which is possessed by no naturally occurring bacteria, Chakrabarty's invention is believed to have significant value for the treatment of oil spills.

Chakrabarty's patent claims were of three types: first, process claims for the method of producing the bacteria; second, claims for an inoculum comprised of a carrier material floating on water, such as straw, and the new bacteria; and third, claims to the bacteria themselves. The patent examiner allowed the claims falling into the first two categories, but rejected claims for the bacteria. His decision rested on two grounds: (1) that micro-organisms are "products of nature," and (2) that as living things they are not patentable subject matter under 35 U.S.C. § 101.

* * * *

[Chakrabarty appealed to the Patent Office Board of Appeals, which affirmed the patent examiner's rejection. Chakrabarty then appealed to the Court of Customs and Patent Appeals, which reversed. (Today, the appeal would go to the CAFC). The Commissioner of Patents and Trademarks appealed to the Supreme Court.]

II

The Constitution grants Congress broad power to legislate to "promote the Progress of Science and useful Arts, by securing for limited Times to Authors and Inventors the exclusive Right to their respective Writings and Discoveries." Art. I, § 8, cl. 8. The patent laws promote this progress by offering inventors exclusive rights for a limited period as an incentive for their inventiveness and research efforts. * * *

The question before us in this case is a narrow one of statutory interpretation requiring us to construe 35 U.S.C. § 101, which provides:

> Whoever invents or discovers any new and useful process, machine, manufacture, or composition of matter, or any new and useful improvement thereof, may obtain a patent therefor, subject to the conditions and requirements of this title.

Specifically, we must determine whether respondent's micro-organism constitutes a "manufacture" or "composition of matter" within the meaning of the statute.

III

In cases of statutory construction we begin, of course, with the language of the statute. And "unless otherwise defined, words will be interpreted as taking their ordinary, contemporary, common meaning." We have also cautioned that courts "should not read into the patent laws limitations and conditions which the legislature has not expressed." * * * In choosing such expansive terms as "manufacture" and "composition of matter," modified by the comprehensive "any," Congress plainly contemplated that the patent laws would be given wide scope.

The relevant legislative history also supports a broad construction. The Patent Act of 1793, authored by Thomas Jefferson, defined statutory subject matter as "any new and useful art, machine, manufacture, or composition of matter, or any new or useful improvement [thereof]." * * * Subsequent patent statutes in 1836, 1870, and 1874 employed this same broad language. In 1952, when the patent laws were recodified, Congress replaced the word "art" with "process," but otherwise left Jefferson's language intact. The Committee Reports accompanying the 1952 Act inform us that Congress intended statutory subject matter to "include anything under the sun that is made by man."

This is not to suggest that § 101 has no limits or that it embraces every discovery. The laws of nature, physical phenomena, and abstract ideas have been held not patentable. Thus, a new mineral discovered in the earth or a new plant found in the wild is not patentable subject matter. Likewise, Einstein could not patent his celebrated law that $E = mc^2$; nor could Newton have patented the law of gravity. Such discoveries are "manifestations of . . . nature, free to all men and reserved exclusively to none."

Judged in this light, respondent's micro-organism plainly qualifies as patentable subject matter. His claim is not to a hitherto unknown natural phenomenon, but to a non-naturally occurring manufacture or composition of matter—a product of human ingenuity "having a distinctive name, character [and] use." * * * [T]he patentee has produced a new bacterium with markedly different characteristics from any found in nature and one having the potential for significant utility. His discovery is not nature's handiwork, but his own; accordingly it is patentable subject matter under § 101.

IV

* * * *

B

The [petitioner argues] that micro-organisms cannot qualify as patentable subject matter until Congress expressly authorizes such protection. His position rests on the fact that genetic technology was unforeseen when Congress enacted § 101. From this it is argued that resolution of the patentability of inventions such as respondent's should be left to Congress. The legislative process, the petitioner argues, is best equipped to weigh the competing economic, social, and scientific considerations involved and to determine whether living organisms produced by genetic engineering should receive patent protection. * * *

It is, of course, correct that Congress, not the courts, must define the limits of patentability; but it is equally true that once Congress has spoken it is "the province and duty of the judicial department to say what the law is." Congress has performed its constitutional role in defining patentable subject matter in § 101; we perform ours in construing the language Congress has employed. In so doing, our obligation is to take statutes as we find them, guided, if ambiguity appears, by the legislative history and statutory purpose. Here, we perceive no ambiguity. The subject-matter provisions of the patent law have been cast in broad terms to fulfill the constitutional and statutory goal of promoting "the Progress of Science and the useful Arts" with all that means for the social and economic benefits envisioned by Jefferson. Broad general language is not necessarily ambiguous when congressional objectives require broad terms.

* * * *

To buttress his argument, the petitioner . . . points to grave risks that may be generated by research endeavors such as respondent's. The briefs present a gruesome parade of horribles. Scientists, among them Nobel laureates, are quoted suggesting that genetic research may pose a serious threat to the human race, or, at the very least, that the dangers are far too substantial to permit such research to proceed apace at this time. We are told that genetic research and related technological developments may spread pollution and disease, that it may result in a loss of genetic diversity, and that its practice may tend to depreciate the value of human life. * * *

It is argued that this Court should weigh these potential hazards in considering whether respondent's invention is patentable subject matter under § 101. We disagree. The grant or denial of patents on micro-organisms is not likely to put an end to genetic research or to its attendant risks. * * *

What is more important is that we are without competence to entertain these arguments—either to brush them aside as fantasies generated by fear of the unknown, or to act on them. The choice we are urged to make is a matter of high policy for resolution within the legislative process after the kind of investigation, examination, and study that legislative bodies can provide and courts cannot. That process involves the balancing of competing values and interests, which in our democratic system is the business of elected representatives. Whatever their validity, the contentions now pressed on us should be addressed to the political branches of the Government, the Congress and the Executive, and not to the courts.

* * * Our task, rather, is the narrow one of determining what Congress meant by the words it used in the statute; once that is done our powers are exhausted. Congress is free to amend § 101 so as to exclude from patent protection organisms produced by genetic engineering. Or it may choose to craft a statute specifically designed for such living things. But, until Congress takes such action, this Court must construe the language of § 101 as it is. The language of that section fairly embraces respondent's invention.

Accordingly, the judgment of the Court of Customs and Patent Appeals is affirmed.

Questions for Discussion for Case 2.1

1. What are the limits of patentable subject matter?

2. What are the relative roles of the courts and the legislature in making and interpreting law?

3. What steps does a court take when it engages in statutory interpretation? What sources does it look to in determining what a statute means?

2.2 Patent Law—Patentable Subject Matter

State Street Bank & Trust Co. v. Signature Financial Group, Inc., 149 F.3d 1368 (Fed. Cir. 1998)

Signature Financial Group, Inc. (Signature) appeals from the decision of the United States District Court . . . granting a motion for summary judgment in favor of State Street Bank & Trust Co. (State Street), finding . . . the '056 patent . . . invalid on the ground that the claimed subject matter is not encompassed by § 101 [of the Patent Act]. We reverse and remand because we conclude that the patent claims are directed to statutory subject matter.

BACKGROUND

Signature is the assignee of the '056 patent which is entitled "Data Processing System for Hub and Spoke Financial Services Configuration." * * * The '056 patent is generally directed to a data processing system (the system) for implementing an investment structure which was developed for use in Signature's business as an administrator and accounting agent for mutual funds. In essence, the system, identified by the proprietary name Hub and Spoke®, facilitates a structure whereby mutual funds (Spokes) pool their assets in an investment portfolio (Hub) organized as a partnership. This investment configuration provides the administrator of a mutual fund with the advantageous combination of economies of scale in administering investments coupled with the tax advantages of a partnership.

State Street and Signature are both in the business of acting as custodians and accounting agents for multi-tiered partnership fund financial services. State Street negotiated with Signature for a license to use its patented data processing system described and claimed in the '056 patent. When negotiations broke down, State Street brought a declaratory judgment action . . . , and then filed a motion for partial summary judgment of patent invalidity for failure to claim statutory subject matter under § 101. The motion was granted and this appeal followed.

DISCUSSION

* * * We hold that . . . plaintiff State Street was not entitled to the grant of summary judgment of invalidity of the '056 patent under § 101 as a matter of law, because the patent claims are directed to statutory subject matter.

* * * The patented invention relates generally to a system that allows an administrator to monitor and record the financial information flow and make all calculations necessary for maintaining a partner fund financial services configuration. * * * The system determines the percentage share that each Spoke maintains in the Hub, while taking into consideration daily changes both in the value of the Hub's investment securities and in the concomitant amount of each Spoke's assets.

In determining daily changes, the system also allows for the allocation among the Spokes of the Hub's daily income, expenses, and net realized and unrealized gain or loss, calculating each day's total investments based on the concept of a book capital account. This enables the determination of a true asset value of each Spoke and accurate calculation of allocation ratios between or among the Spokes. The system additionally tracks all the relevant data determined on a daily basis for the Hub and each Spoke, so that aggregate year end income, expenses, and capital gain or loss can be determined for accounting and for tax purposes for the Hub and, as a result, for each publicly traded Spoke.

It is essential that these calculations are quickly and accurately performed. In large part this is required because each Spoke sells shares to the public and the price of those shares is substantially based on the Spoke's percentage interest in the portfolio. In some instances, a mutual fund administrator is required to calculate the value of the shares to the nearest penny within as little as an hour and a half after the market closes. Given the complexity of the calculations, a computer or equivalent device is a virtual necessity to perform the task.

* * * *

* * * Section 101 [of the Patent Act] reads:

Whoever invents or discovers any new and useful process, machine, manufacture, or composition of matter, or any new and useful improvement thereof, may obtain a patent therefor, subject to the conditions and requirements of this title.

The plain and unambiguous meaning of § 101 is that any invention falling within one of the four stated categories of statutory subject matter may be patented, provided it meets the other requirements for patentability set forth in [the Patent Act].

The repetitive use of the expansive term "any" in § 101 shows Congress's intent not to place any restrictions on the subject matter for which a patent may be obtained beyond those specifically recited in § 101. Indeed, the Supreme Court has acknowledged that Congress intended § 101 to extend to "anything under the sun that is made by man." *Diamond v. Chakrabarty*, 447 U.S. 303, 309 (1980). Thus, it is improper to read limitations into § 101 on the subject matter that may be patented where the legislative history indicates that Congress clearly did not intend such limitations.

The "Mathematical Algorithm" Exception

The Supreme Court has identified three categories of subject matter that are unpatentable, namely "laws of nature, natural phenomena, and abstract ideas." Of particular relevance to this case, the Court has held that mathematical algorithms are not patentable subject matter to the extent that they are merely abstract ideas. In [*Diamond v. Diehr*, 450 U.S. 175 (1981)], the Court explained that certain types of mathematical subject matter, standing alone, represent nothing more than abstract ideas until reduced to some type of practical application, i.e., "a useful, concrete and tangible result."

Unpatentable mathematical algorithms are identifiable by showing they are merely abstract ideas constituting disembodied concepts or truths that are not "useful." From a practical standpoint, this means that to be patentable an algorithm must be applied in a "useful" way . * * *

* * * *

Today, we hold that the transformation of data, representing discrete dollar amounts, by a machine through a series of mathematical calculations into a final share price, constitutes a practical application of a mathematical algorithm, formula, or calculation, because it produces "a useful, concrete and tangible result"—a final share price momentarily fixed for recording and reporting purposes and even accepted and relied upon by regulatory authorities and in subsequent trades.

* * * *

The Business Method Exception

As an alternative ground for invalidating the '056 patent under § 101, the court relied on the judicially-created, so-called "business method" exception to statutory subject matter. We take this opportunity to lay this ill-conceived exception to rest. Since its inception, the "business method" exception has merely represented the application of some general, but no longer applicable legal principle . . . . Since the 1952 Patent Act, business methods have been, and should have been, subject to the same legal requirements for patentability as applied to any other process or method.

* * * *

CONCLUSION

The appealed decision is reversed and the case is remanded to the district court for further proceedings consistent with this opinion.

Questions for Discussion Case 2.2

1. What did the court hold regarding the patentability of algorithms?

2. What did the court hold regarding the patentability of business methods?

3. Signature Financial had not sued State Street Bank for infringement of its '056 patent. Why, then, was State Street Bank in court litigating the validity of this patent?

2.3 Copyright—Originality, Fair Use, Infringement
Feist Publications, Inc. v. Rural Telephone Service Co., 499 U.S. 340 (1991)

OPINION: O'CONNOR, J. This case requires us to clarify the extent of copyright protection available to telephone directory white pages.

I

Rural Telephone Service Company, Inc., is a certified public utility that provides telephone service to several communities in northwest Kansas. * * * [A]s a condition of its monopoly franchise, Rural publishes a typical telephone directory, consisting of white pages and yellow pages. The white pages list in alphabetical order the names of Rural's subscribers, together with their towns and telephone numbers. The yellow pages list Rural's business subscribers alphabetically by category and feature classified advertisements of various sizes. Rural distributes its directory free of charge to its subscribers, but earns revenue by selling yellow pages advertisements.

Feist Publications, Inc., is a publishing company that specializes in area-wide telephone directories. Unlike a typical directory, which covers only a particular calling area, Feist's area-wide directories cover a much larger geographical range, reducing the need to call directory assistance or consult multiple directories. The Feist directory that is the subject of this litigation covers 11 different telephone service areas in 15 counties and contains 46,878 white pages list-

ings—compared to Rural's approximately 7,700 listings. Like Rural's directory, Feist's is distributed free of charge and includes both white pages and yellow pages. Feist and Rural compete vigorously for yellow pages advertising.

As the sole provider of telephone service in its service area, Rural obtains subscriber information quite easily. Persons desiring telephone service must apply to Rural and provide their names and addresses; Rural then assigns them a telephone number. Feist is not a telephone company, let alone one with monopoly status, and therefore lacks independent access to any subscriber information. To obtain white pages listings for its area-wide directory, Feist approached each of the 11 telephone companies operating in northwest Kansas and offered to pay for the right to use its white pages listings.

Of the 11 telephone companies, only Rural refused to license its listings to Feist. Rural's refusal created a problem for Feist, as omitting these listings would have left a gaping hole in its area-wide directory, rendering it less attractive to potential yellow pages advertisers. * * *

Unable to license Rural's white pages listings, Feist used them without Rural's consent. Feist began by removing several thousand listings that fell outside the geographic range of its area-wide directory, then hired personnel to investigate the 4,935 that remained. These employees verified the data reported by Rural and sought to obtain additional information. As a result, a typical Feist listing includes the individual's street address; most of Rural's listings do not. Notwithstanding these additions, however, 1,309 of the 46,878 listings in Feist's 1983 directory were identical to listings in Rural's 1982–1983 white pages. Four of these were fictitious listings that Rural had inserted into its directory to detect copying.

Rural sued for copyright infringement . . . taking the position that Feist, in compiling its own directory, could not use the information contained in Rural's white pages. Rural asserted that Feist's employees were obliged to travel door-to-door or conduct a telephone survey to discover the same information for themselves. Feist responded that such efforts were economically impractical and, in any event, unnecessary because the information copied was beyond the scope of copyright protection. The District Court granted summary judgment to Rural . . . . [T]he Court of Appeals for the Tenth Circuit affirmed . . . . We granted certiorari to determine whether the copyright in Rural's directory protects the names, towns, and telephone numbers copied by Feist.

II

A

This case concerns the interaction of two well-established propositions. The first is that facts are not copyrightable; the other, that compilations of facts generally are. * * *

There is an undeniable tension between these two propositions. Many compilations consist of nothing but raw data—*i.e.*, wholly factual information not accompanied by any original written expression. On what basis may one claim a copyright in such a work? Common sense tells us that 100 uncopyrightable facts do not magically change their status when gathered together in one place. Yet copyright law seems to contemplate that compilations that consist exclusively of facts are potentially within its scope.

The key to resolving the tension lies in understanding why facts are not copyrightable. The *sine qua non* of copyright is originality. To qualify for copyright protection, a work must be original to the author. Original, as the term is used in copyright, means only that the work was independently created by the author (as opposed to copied from other works), and that it possesses at least some minimal degree of creativity. To be sure, the requisite level of creativity is extremely low; even a slight amount will suffice. * * * Originality does not signify novelty; a work may be original even though it closely resembles other works so long as the similarity is fortuitous, not the result of copying. To illustrate, assume that two poets, each ignorant of the other, compose identical poems. Neither work is novel, yet both are original and, hence, copyrightable.

* * * *

* * * Census data therefore do not trigger copyright because these data are not "original" in the constitutional sense. The same is true of all facts—scientific, historical, biographical, and news of the day. * * *

Factual compilations, on the other hand, may possess the requisite originality. The compilation author typically chooses which facts to include, in what order to place them, and how to arrange the collected data so that they may be used effectively by readers. These choices as to selection and arrangement, so long as they are made independently by the compiler and entail a minimal degree of creativity, are sufficiently original that Congress may protect such compilations through the copyright laws. Thus, even a directory that contains absolutely no protectible written expression, only facts, meets the constitutional minimum for copyright protection if it features an original selection or arrangement.

This protection is subject to an important limitation. The mere fact that a work is copyrighted does not mean that every element of the work may be protected. Originality remains the *sine qua non* of copyright; accordingly, copyright protection may extend only to those components of a work that are original to the author. * * * Thus, if the selection and arrangement are original, these elements of the work are eligible for copyright protection. No matter how original the format, however, the facts themselves do not become original through association.

* * * *

This, then, resolves the doctrinal tension: Copyright treats facts and factual compilations in a wholly consistent manner. Facts, whether alone or as part of a compilation, are not original and therefore may not be copyrighted. A factual compilation is eligible for copyright if it features an original selection or arrangement of facts, but the copyright is limited to the particular selection or arrangement. In no event may copyright extend to the facts themselves.

* * * *

III

There is no doubt that Feist took from the white pages of Rural's directory a substantial amount of factual information. At a minimum, Feist copied the names, towns, and telephone numbers of 1,309 of Rural's subscribers. Not all copying, however, is copyright infringement. To establish infringement, two elements must be proven: (1) ownership of a valid copyright, and (2) copying of constituent elements of the work that are original. The first element is not at issue here; Feist appears to concede that Rural's directory, considered as a whole, is subject to a valid copyright because it contains some foreword text, as well as original material in its yellow pages advertisements.

The question is whether Rural has proved the second element. In other words, did Feist, by taking 1,309 names, towns, and telephone numbers from Rural's white pages, copy anything that was "original" to Rural? Certainly, the raw data does not satisfy the originality requirement. Rural may have been the first to discover and report the names, towns, and telephone numbers of its subscribers, but this data does not "owe its origin" to Rural. Rather, these bits of information are uncopyrightable facts; they existed before Rural reported them and would have continued to exist if Rural had never published a telephone directory. * * *

* * * *

The question that remains is whether Rural selected, coordinated, or arranged these uncopyrightable facts in an original way. As mentioned, originality is not a stringent standard; it does not require that facts be presented in an innovative or surprising way. It is equally true, however, that the selection and arrangement of facts cannot be so mechanical or routine as to require no creativity whatsoever. The standard of originality is low, but it does exist. * * *

The selection, coordination, and arrangement of Rural's white pages do not satisfy the minimum constitutional standards for copyright protection. * * *

* * * *

* * * The white pages do nothing more than list Rural's subscribers in alphabetical order. This arrangement may, technically speaking, owe its origin to Rural; no one disputes that Rural undertook the task of alphabetizing the names itself. But there is nothing remotely creative about arranging names alphabetically in a white pages directory. It is an age-old practice, firmly rooted in tradition and so commonplace that it has come to be expected as a matter of course. * * *

* * * *

Because Rural's white pages lack the requisite originality, Feist's use of the listings cannot constitute infringement. This decision should not be construed as demeaning Rural's efforts in compiling its directory, but rather as making clear that copyright rewards originality, not effort. * * *

The judgment of the Court of Appeals is reversed.

Questions for Discussion for Case 2.3

1. What does "originality" mean in the copyright area? How does it differ from "novelty" in the patent area?

2. What elements must be shown to establish copyright infringement? Which element or elements were at issue here?

3. Why were Rural's white pages not copyrightable?

2.4 Copyright—Work for Hire

Community for Creative Non-Violence v. Reid, **490 U.S. 730 (1989)**

OPINION: MARSHALL, J. In this case, an artist and the organization that hired him to produce a sculpture contest the ownership of the copyright in that work. To resolve this dispute, we must construe the "work made for hire" provisions of the Copyright Act of 1976 and in particular, the provision in § 101, which defines as a "work made for hire" a "work prepared by an employee within the scope of his or her employment."

I

Petitioners are the Community for Creative Non-Violence (CCNV), a nonprofit unincorporated association dedicated to eliminating homelessness in America, and Mitch Snyder, a member and trustee of CCNV. In the fall of 1985, CCNV decided to participate in the annual Christmastime Pageant of Peace in Washington, D.C., by sponsoring a display to dramatize the plight of the homeless. As the District Court recounted:

> Snyder and fellow CCNV members conceived the idea for the nature of the display: a sculpture of a modern Nativity scene in which, in lieu of the traditional Holy Family, the two adult figures and the infant would appear as contemporary homeless people huddled on a streetside steam grate. The family was to be black (most of the homeless in Washington being black); the figures were to be life-sized, and the steam grate would be positioned atop a platform "pedestal," or base, within which special-effects equipment would be enclosed to emit simulated "steam" through the grid to swirl about the

figures. They also settled upon a title for the work—"Third World America"—and a legend for the pedestal: "and still there is no room at the inn."

Snyder made inquiries to locate an artist to produce the sculpture. He was referred to respondent James Earl Reid . . . . In the course of two telephone calls, Reid agreed to sculpt the three human figures. CCNV agreed to make the steam grate and pedestal for the statue. * * * Reid . . . suggested, and Snyder agreed, that the sculpture would be made of a material known as "Design Cast 62," a synthetic substance that could meet CCNV's monetary and time constraints, could be tinted to resemble bronze, and could withstand the elements. The parties agreed that the project would cost no more than $15,000, not including Reid's services, which he offered to donate. The parties did not sign a written agreement. Neither party mentioned copyright.

After Reid received an advance of $3,000, he made several sketches of figures in various poses. At Snyder's request, Reid sent CCNV a sketch of a proposed sculpture showing the family in a crechelike setting: the mother seated, cradling a baby in her lap; the father standing behind her, bending over her shoulder to touch the baby's foot. Reid testified that Snyder asked for the sketch to use in raising funds for the sculpture. Snyder testified that it was also for his approval. Reid sought a black family to serve as a model for the sculpture. Upon Snyder's suggestion, Reid visited a family living at CCNV's Washington shelter but decided that only their newly born child was a suitable model. While Reid was in Washington, Snyder took him to see homeless people living on the streets. Snyder pointed out that they tended to recline on steam grates, rather than sit or stand, in order to warm their bodies. From that time on, Reid's sketches contained only reclining figures.

Throughout November and the first two weeks of December 1985, Reid worked exclusively on the statue, assisted at various times by a dozen different people who were paid with funds provided in installments by CCNV. On a number of occasions, CCNV members visited Reid to check on his progress and to coordinate CCNV's construction of the base. CCNV rejected Reid's proposal to use suitcases or shopping bags to hold the family's personal belongings, insisting instead on a shopping cart. Reid and CCNV members did not discuss copyright ownership on any of these visits.

On December 24, 1985, . . . Reid delivered the completed statue to Washington. There it was joined to the steam grate and pedestal prepared by CCNV and placed on display near the site of the pageant. Snyder paid Reid the final installment of the $15,000. The statue remained on display for a month. In late January 1986, CCNV members returned it to Reid's studio in Baltimore for minor repairs. Several weeks later, Snyder began making plans to take the statue on a tour of several cities to raise money for the homeless. Reid objected, contending that the Design Cast 62 material was not strong enough to withstand the ambitious itinerary. He urged CCNV to cast the statue in bronze at a cost of $35,000, or to create a master mold at a cost of $5,000. Snyder declined to spend more of CCNV's money on the project.

In March 1986, Snyder asked Reid to return the sculpture. Reid refused. He then filed a certificate of copyright registration for "Third World America" in his name and announced plans to take the sculpture on a more modest tour than the one CCNV had proposed. Snyder, acting in his capacity as CCNV's trustee, immediately filed a competing certificate of copyright registration.

Snyder and CCNV then commenced this action . . . , seeking return of the sculpture and a determination of copyright ownership. The District Court granted a preliminary injunction, ordering the sculpture's return. After a 2-day bench trial, the District Court declared that "Third World America" was a "work made for hire" under § 101 of the Copyright Act and that Snyder, as trustee for CCNV, was the exclusive owner of the copyright in the sculpture. The court reasoned that Reid had been an "employee" of CCNV within the meaning of § 101(1) because CCNV was the motivating force in the statue's production. Snyder and other CCNV members, the court explained, "conceived the idea of a contemporary Nativity scene to contrast with the national celebration of the season," and "directed enough of [Reid's] effort to assure that, in the end, he had produced what they, not he, wanted."

The Court of Appeals . . . reversed and remanded, holding that Reid owned the copyright because "Third World America" was not a work for hire. * * *

We granted certiorari to resolve a conflict among the Courts of Appeals over the proper construction of the "work made for hire" provisions of the Act. We now affirm.

II

A

The Copyright Act of 1976 provides that copyright ownership "vests initially in the author or authors of the work." As a general rule, the author is the party who actually creates the work, that is, the person who translates an idea into a fixed, tangible expression entitled to copyright protection. The Act carves out an important exception, however, for "works made for hire." If the work is for hire, "the employer or other person for whom the work was prepared is considered the author" and owns the copyright, unless there is a written agreement to the contrary. * * *

Section 101 of the 1976 Act provides that a work is "for hire" under two sets of circumstances:

(1) a work prepared by an employee within the scope of his or her employment; or

(2) a work specially ordered or commissioned for use as a contribution to a collective work, as a part of a motion picture or other audiovisual work, as a translation, as a supplementary work, as a compilation, as an instructional text, as a test, as answer material for a test, or as an atlas, if the parties expressly agree in a written instrument signed by them that the work shall be considered a work made for hire.

Petitioners do not claim that the statue satisfies the terms of § 101(2). Quite clearly, it does not. Sculpture does not fit within any of the nine categories of "specially ordered or commissioned" works enumerated in that subsection, and no written agreement between the parties establishes "Third World America" as a work for hire.

The dispositive inquiry in this case therefore is whether "Third World America" is "a work prepared by an employee within the scope of his or her employment" under § 101(1). * * *

* * * *

* * * To determine whether a work is for hire under the Act, a court first should ascertain, using principles of general common law of agency, whether the work was prepared by an employee or an independent contractor. After making this determination, the court can apply the appropriate subsection of § 101.

B

* * * In determining whether a hired party is an employee under the general common law of agency, we consider the hiring party's right to control the manner and means by which the product is accomplished. Among the other factors relevant to this inquiry are the skill required; the source of the instrumentalities and tools; the location of the work; the duration of the relationship between the parties; whether the hiring party has the right to assign additional projects to the hired party; the extent of the hired party's discretion over when and how long to work; the method of payment; the hired party's role in hiring and paying assistants; whether the work is part of the regular busi-

ness of the hiring party; whether the hiring party is in business; the provision of employee benefits; and the tax treatment of the hired party. No one of these factors is determinative.

Examining the circumstances of this case in light of these factors, we agree with the Court of Appeals that Reid was not an employee of CCNV but an independent contractor. True, CCNV members directed enough of Reid's work to ensure that he produced a sculpture that met their specifications. But the extent of control the hiring party exercises over the details of the product is not dispositive. Indeed, all the other circumstances weigh heavily against finding an employment relationship. Reid is a sculptor, a skilled occupation. Reid supplied his own tools. He worked in his own studio in Baltimore, making daily supervision of his activities from Washington practicably impossible. Reid was retained for less than two months, a relatively short period of time. During and after this time, CCNV had no right to assign additional projects to Reid. Apart from the deadline for completing the sculpture, Reid had absolute freedom to decide when and how long to work. CCNV paid Reid $15,000, a sum dependent on "completion of a specific job, a method by which independent contractors are often compensated." Reid had total discretion in hiring and paying assistants. "Creating sculptures was hardly 'regular business' for CCNV." Indeed, CCNV is not a business at all. Finally, CCNV did not pay payroll or Social Security taxes, provide any employee benefits, or contribute to unemployment insurance or workers' compensation funds.

* * * Thus, CCNV is not the author of "Third World America" by virtue of the work for hire provisions of the Act. * * * However, . . . CCNV nevertheless may be a joint author of the sculpture if, on remand, the District Court determines that CCNV and Reid prepared the work "with the intention that their contributions be merged into inseparable or interdependent parts of a unitary whole." In that case, CCNV and Reid would be co-owners of the copyright in the work.

For the aforestated reasons, we affirm the judgment of the Court of Appeals . . . .

Questions for Discussion for Case 2.4

1. Was Reid an independent contractor or an employee? What "test" did the Court apply in deciding this issue?

2. What is the legal effect of classifying Reid as a independent contractor or an employee for purposes of the Copyright Act?

3. What issue did the Court remand to the trial court for further determination?

2.5. Copyright—Infringement, Fair Use

Micro Star v. Formgen Inc., 154 F.3d 1107 (9th Cir. 1998)

Duke Nukem routinely vanquishes Octabrain and the Protozoid Slimer. But what about the dreaded Micro Star?

I

[FormGen] made, distributed and own[s] the rights to Duke Nukem 3D (D/N-3D), an immensely popular (and very cool) computer game. D/N-3D is played from the first-person perspective; the player assumes the personality and point of view of the title character, who is seen on the screen only as a pair of hands and an occasional boot, much as one might see oneself in real life without the aid of a mirror. Players explore a futuristic city infested with evil aliens and other hazards. The goal is to zap them before they zap you, while searching for the hidden passage to the next level. The basic game comes with twenty-nine levels, each with a different combination of scenery, aliens, and other challenges. The game also includes a "Build Editor," a utility that enables players to create their own levels. With FormGen's encouragement, players frequently post levels they have created on the Internet where others can download them. Micro Star, a computer software distributor, did just that: It downloaded 300 user-created levels and stamped them onto a CD, which it then sold commercially as Nuke It (N/I). N/I is packaged in a box decorated with numerous "screen shots," pictures of what the new levels look like when played.

Micro Star filed suit in district court, seeking a declaratory judgment that N/I did not infringe on any of Form-Gen's copyrights. FormGen counterclaimed, seeking a preliminary injunction barring further production and distribution of N/I. Relying on *Lewis Galoob Toys, Inc. v. Nintendo of Am., Inc.*, 964 F.2d 965 (9th Cir. 1992), the district court held that N/I was not a derivative work and therefore did not infringe FormGen's copyright. The district court did, however, grant a preliminary injunction as to the screen shots, finding that N/I's packaging violated FormGen's copyright by reproducing pictures of D/N-3D characters without a license. The court rejected Micro Star's fair use claims. Both sides appeal their losses.

* * * *

III

To succeed on the merits of its claim that N/I infringes FormGen's copyright, FormGen must show (1) ownership of the copyright to D/N-3D, and (2) copying of protected expression by Micro Star. FormGen's copyright registration

creates a presumption of ownership . . . . We therefore focus on the latter issue.

FormGen alleges that its copyright is infringed by Micro Star's unauthorized commercial exploitation of user-created game levels. In order to understand FormGen's claims, one must first understand the way D/N-3D works. The game consists of three separate components: the game engine, the source art library and the MAP files. The game engine is the heart of the computer program; in some sense, it *is* the program. It tells the computer when to read data, save and load games, play sounds and project images onto the screen. In order to create the audiovisual display for a particular level, the game engine invokes the MAP file that corresponds to that level. Each MAP file contains a series of instructions that tell the game engine (and, through it, the computer) what to put where. For instance, the MAP file might say scuba gear goes at the bottom of the screen. The game engine then goes to the source art library, finds the image of the scuba gear, and puts it in just the right place on the screen. The MAP file describes the level in painstaking detail, but it does not actually contain any of the copyrighted art itself; everything that appears on the screen actually comes from the art library. * * * When the player selects one of the N/I levels, the game engine references the N/I MAP files, but still uses the D/N-3D art library to generate the images that make up that level.

FormGen points out that a copyright holder enjoys the exclusive right to prepare derivative works based on D/N-3D. According to FormGen, the audiovisual displays generated when D/N-3D is run in conjunction with the N/I CD MAP files are derivative works that infringe this exclusivity. Is FormGen right? The answer is not obvious.

The Copyright Act defines a derivative work as

> a work based upon one or more preexisting works, such as a translation, musical arrangement, dramatization, fictionalization, motion picture version, sound recording, art reproduction, abridgment, condensation, or any other form in which a work may be recast, transformed, or adapted. A work consisting of editorial revisions, annotations, elaborations, or other modifications which, as a whole, represent an original work of authorship, is a "derivative work."

The statutory language is hopelessly overbroad, however, for "[e]very book in literature, science and art, borrows and must necessarily borrow, and use much which was well known and used before." To narrow the statute to a manageable level, we have developed certain criteria a work must satisfy in order to qualify as a derivative work. One of these is that a derivative work must exist in a "concrete or permanent form," and must substantially incorporate protected material from the preexisting work. Micro Star argues that N/I is not a derivative work because the audiovisual displays generated when D/N-3D is run with N/I's MAP files are not incorporated in any concrete or permanent form, and the MAP files do not copy any of D/N-3D's protected expression. It is mistaken on both counts.

* * * Obviously, N/I's MAP files themselves exist in a concrete or permanent form; they are burned onto a CD-ROM. But what about the audiovisual displays generated when D/N-3D runs the N/I MAP files—i.e., the actual game level as displayed on the screen? Micro Star argues that, because the audiovisual displays in *Galoob* didn't meet the "concrete or permanent form" requirement, neither do N/I's.

In *Galoob*, we considered audiovisual displays created using a device called the Game Genie, which was sold for use with the Nintendo Entertainment System. The Game Genie allowed players to alter individual features of a game, such as a character's strength or speed, by selectively "blocking the value for a single data byte sent by the game cartridge to the [Nintendo console] and replacing it with a new value." Players chose which data value to replace by entering a code; over a billion different codes were possible. The Game Genie was dumb; it functioned only as a window into the computer program, allowing players to temporarily modify individual aspects of the game.

Nintendo sued, claiming that when the Game Genie modified the game system's audiovisual display, it created an infringing derivative work. We rejected this claim because "[a] derivative work must incorporate a protected work in some concrete or permanent form." The audiovisual displays generated by combining the Nintendo System with the Game Genie were not incorporated in any permanent form; when the game was over, they were gone. Of course, they could be reconstructed, but only if the next player chose to reenter the same codes.

* * * [W]hereas the audiovisual displays created by Game Genie were never recorded in any permanent form, the audiovisual displays generated by D/N-3D from the N/I MAP files are in the MAP files themselves. * * *

* * * Because the audiovisual displays assume a concrete or permanent form in the MAP files, *Galoob* stands as no bar to finding that they are derivative works.

* * * *

Micro Star further argues that the MAP files are not derivative works because they do not, in fact, incorporate any of D/N-3D's protected expression. In particular, Micro Star makes much of the fact that the N/I MAP files reference the source art library, but do not actually contain any art files

themselves. Therefore, it claims, nothing of D/N-3D's is reproduced in the MAP files. In making this argument, Micro Star misconstrues the protected work. The work that Micro Star infringes is the D/N-3D story itself—a beefy commando type named Duke who wanders around post-Apocalypse Los Angeles, shooting Pig Cops with a gun, lobbing hand grenades, searching for medkits and steroids, using a jetpack to leap over obstacles, blowing up gas tanks, avoiding radioactive slime. A copyright owner holds the right to create sequels, and the stories told in the N/I MAP files are surely sequels, telling new (though somewhat repetitive) tales of Duke's fabulous adventures. A book about Duke Nukem would infringe for the same reason, even if it contained no pictures.

Micro Star nonetheless claims that its use of D/N-3D's protected expression falls within the doctrine of fair use, which permits unauthorized use of copyrighted works "for purposes such as criticism, comment, news reporting, teaching (including multiple copies for classroom use), scholarship, or research." 17 U.S.C. § 107. Section 107 instructs courts "determining whether the use made of a work in any particular case is a fair use" to consider four factors: (1) the purpose and character of the use, including whether it is commercial in nature; (2) the nature of the copyrighted work; (3) the amount and substantiality of the copied material in relation to the copyrighted work as a whole; and (4) the effect of the use on the potential market for the copyrighted work.

* * * *

Our examination of the section 107 factors yields straightforward results. Micro Star's use of FormGen's protected expression was made purely for financial gain. While that does not end our inquiry, "every commercial use of copyrighted material is presumptively an unfair exploitation of the monopoly privilege that belongs to the owner of the copyright." The Supreme Court has explained that the second factor, the nature of the copyrighted work, is particularly significant because "some works are closer to the core of intended copyright protection than others, with the consequence that fair use is more difficult to establish when the former works are copied." The fair use defense will be much less likely to succeed when it is applied to fiction or fantasy creations, as opposed to factual works such as telephone listings. Duke Nukem's world is made up of aliens, radioactive slime, and freezer weapons—clearly fantasies, even by Los Angeles standards. N/I MAP files "expressly use the [D/N-3D] story's unique setting, characters, [and] plot," both the quantity and importance of the material Micro Star used are substantial. Finally, by selling N/I, Micro Star "impinged on [FormGen's] ability to market new versions of the [D/N-3D] story." Only FormGen has the right to enter that market;

whether it chooses to do so is entirely its business. "[N/I] neither falls into any of the categories enumerated in section 107 nor meets the four criteria set forth in section 107." It is not protected by fair use.

* * * *

IV

Because FormGen will likely succeed at trial in proving that Micro Star has infringed its copyright, we reverse the dis-

trict court's order denying a preliminary injunction and remand for entry of such an injunction. Of course, we affirm the grant of the preliminary injunction barring Micro Star from selling N/I in boxes covered with screen shots of the game.

Affirmed in part, reversed in part, and remanded. * * *

Questions for Discussion for Case 2.5

1. Why did Micro Star, who was the alleged infringer, file this lawsuit?

2. What characteristics must a work have in order to be a "derivative" work?

3. What benefits did FormGen gain from having previously registered its copyright?

4. What must a party show in order to establish copyright infringement? Did FormGen succeed in demonstrating these elements?

5. What factors does a court examine in evaluating a fair use defense? Has Micro Star engaged in fair use?

6. Does this opinion resolve the underlying dispute between these two parties?

DISCUSSION QUESTIONS

1. Which of the following would receive patent or copyright law protection?
  a. A method of manufacturing cereal that enables the product to remain fresh longer after the box has been opened.
  b. Nike's slogan: "Just do it."
  c. A new theory involving market segmentation strategies.
  d. Common seaweed when manipulated in particular ways that render it an effective drug for several types of illnesses.
  e. A new, nonfunctional shape for a flashlight.
  f. A new, functional shape for a flashlight.

2. Seiko Epson Corp. sued Nu-Kote International, alleging that Nu-Kote had infringed on its design patent for ink cartridges for printers. The district court held that Seiko Epson's design patent was invalid because (1) the cartridge is not visible after its installation and during use and thus its design was "not a matter of concern to consumers" and (2) the design is not aesthetically pleasing. Is the district court's reasoning

correct? What are the requirements for a valid design patent? *Seiko Epson Corp. v. Nu-Kote International*, 190 F.3d 1360 (Fed. Cir. 1999)

3. Rotec Industries is the assignee of the '291 patent for a crane conveyor belt system used to carry concrete over long distances for construction projects such as river dams. The defendants, a group of corporations including Mitsubishi Corp., signed an agreement with the Chinese government to provide a crane conveyor belt system for its Three Gorges Dam project. Rotec alleged that the defendants were offering to sell a conveyor system that infringed upon its '291 patent.

Rotec sued for patent infringement. The evidence at trial showed: (1) the agreement among the defendants called for all of the conveyor components to be made in Japan and China; (2) no components were made in the United States; (3) the bid proposal, including the description of the product and the proposed price, was finalized in Hong Kong and presented in China; (4) all negotiations with the Chinese government prior to signing the agreement took place in China; and (5) the agreement was signed in China. How should the court rule on Rotec's claim and why? *Rotec Industries v. Mitsubishi Corp.*, 215 F.3d 1246 (Fed. Cir. 2000)

4. Chung filed for a design patent for a cigarette packet that allowed the cigarettes to be pulled out of the packet lengthwise rather than by their ends. In explaining the reason for his design, Chung stated: "I was motivated . . . to design a new cigarette package . . . when I . . . happened to see . . . workers pull out cigarettes from the packages holding their filter-tip top with dirty fingers during work to smoke them. Some even used their teeth to pull them out so as not to contaminate the filter-tip end with dirty fingers, and some others tore open the bottom part of the package to take out cigarettes from the bottom."

Does Chung's invention satisfy the requirements for a design patent? Why or why not? *In re Uie S. Chung*, 2000 U.S. App. LEXIS 24916 (Fed. Cir. Oct. 4, 2000)

5. Sun Hill Industries, Inc., holds a design patent on a lawn bag with vertical strips and Halloween-style "happy" and "scary" jack-o-lantern faces on opposing sides. The design patent does not mention color or size or material. Sun Hill markets a version of the patent design as the GIANT STUFF-A-PUMPKIN. The GIANT STUFF-A-PUMPKIN is a large, orange, plastic lawn bag. When stuffed with leaves or other debris and tied at the top, the bag resembles a huge Halloween pumpkin. The prior art included the Noteworthy bag, a yellow plastic Halloween trick-or-treat bag sold by Noteworthy Industries. This bag has vertical stripes and opposing identical happy jack-o-lantern faces.

Easter Unlimited, Inc., designed a line of orange plastic Halloween lawn bags of various sizes, consulting with its attorneys during the design process in an attempt to avoid liability for infringement. Its bags have a jack-o-lantern face on only one side, no stripes, and a different bottom closure than that claimed in Sun Hill's patent.

Sun Hill sued Easter Unlimited for patent infringement. What test should the court use to determine whether infringement has occurred? What result should the court reach? Would your answer change if Sun Hill had included the color and material of the bag in its patent? *Sun Hill Industries, Inc. v. Easter Unlimited, Inc.*, 48 F.3d 1193 (Fed. Cir. 1995)

6. OddzOn Products, Inc., is a toy and sporting goods company that holds a design patent on and sells the popular "Vortex" tossing ball, a foam football-shaped ball with a tail and fin structure. Just Toys, Inc., another toy and sporting goods company, sells a competing line of "Ultra Pass" balls.

OddzOn sued Just Toys for design patent infringement. Just Toys denied infringement and asserted that the patent was invalid due to obviousness. For "inspiration," the inventor of the OddzOn design reviewed two prior confidential ball designs. If an inventor relies on prior art in making his invention, he is not entitled to a patent. Should confidential designs that are not publicly available qualify as prior art? *OddzOn Products, Inc. v. Just Toys, Inc.*, 122 F.3d 1396 (Fed. Cir. 1997)

7. Jeffrey Mendler, a professional photographer, signed a licensing agreement with Winterland Production, Ltd., a manufacturer of screen-printed apparel, that allowed Winterland to use several photographs that Mendler had taken of the America's Cup yacht race as "guides, models, and examples, for illustrations to be used on screenprinted T-shirts or other sportswear." Several years later, Mendler discovered that Winterland had put out a line of T-shirts that displayed a digitally altered version of the image from one of Mendler's photographs. Winterland had scanned Mendler's photograph and had flipped the image horizontally, had reconstructed the missing tip of a sail that had been cut off in the original photograph, and had altered the colors of the sky somewhat.

Mendler complained that the licensing agreement did not authorize such a use and that Winterland had infringed upon his copyright. Winterland argued that the changes that it had made had altered the image on the T-shirt from a photograph to an illustration based on a photograph. The parties agree that the license does not authorize Winterland to use photographic reproductions of Mendler's work but only to use the photographs as a "guide, model, or example" to achieve an end result that was an "illustration" and not a photographic reproduction. What must a plaintiff show to establish copyright infringement? Has infringement occurred here? *Mendler v. Winterland Production, Ltd.*, 207 F.3d 1119 (9th Cir. 2000)

8. Fashion Victim, Inc., sells a T-shirt called Skeleton Woopee with a fanciful design depicting skeletons engaging in sexual activity in seven different positions. Skeleton Woopee is Fashion's best-selling product.

Fashion sold 55,000 shirts since the shirts' introduction in 1990. In 1992, Sunrise Turquoise, Inc., featured a shirt in its catalogue that was very similar to the Skeleton Woopee T-shirt. Fashion Victim sued Sunrise for copyright infringement. At trial, the evidence indicated that Sunrise had heard of the idea of a T-shirt depicting skeletons in sexual positions from a potential customer but had not seen or directly copied the Skeleton Woopee shirt. Should Sunrise be held liable for copyright infringement? Why or why not? *Fashion Victim, Ltd. v. Sunrise Turquoise, Inc.*, 785 F. Supp. 1302 (N.D. Ill. 1992)

9. When Universal City Studios, Inc., and Amblin' Entertainment, Inc., were producing the movie *How to Make an American Quilt*, they contracted with Barbara Brown, a well-known professional quilter. Brown agreed to design patterns for 15 quilt blocks for $50 per block. One of these designs was known as the Wedding Block. Under the contract, Brown was to retain the copyright to the designs, but Universal was authorized to use the design to create two copies of a prop quilt (known as the "The Life Before" quilt) for the movie.

In designing a second quilt for the movie, Universal's technical consultant, Patricia McCormick, created a block design known as the Marriage Block. Both McCormick's Marriage Block and Brown's Wedding Block depict a scene with a black bird flying over a man and a woman holding hands. In the Marriage Block, however, the crow points downward, while the crow in the Wedding Block points upward. In addition, the Marriage Block includes a figure of the sun, but the Wedding Block does not. McCormick later wrote a book in which she stated: "I made [the Marriage Block] by using the pattern Barbara Brown had designed for . . . The Life Before quilt. . . . The block in this quilt is a duplication of the . . . block in The Life Before quilt."

Brown sued for copyright infringement. Does McCormick's Marriage Block design infringe on Brown's Wedding Block design? Why or why not? *Brown v. McCormick*, 87 F. Supp. 2d 467 (D. Md. 2000)

10. Cory Van Rijn, Inc., (CVR) copyrighted various humanized raisin characters that it had developed. The California Raisin Advisory Board then developed Claymatic raisin characters for use in an advertising campaign. While both sets of characters had raisin bodies, the Board's characters had detailed eyes with eyebrows and upper and lower lids; detailed mouths with upper and lower lips; detailed noses with nostrils; long and wire-like arms and legs; four-fingered, gloved hands; high-top basketball sneakers; and blue, red, and yellow sunglasses. CVR's raisin characters had exaggerated, cartoon-like eyes; lipless mouths or no mouths at all; short and pudgy arms; no legs; three-fingered, gloveless hands; various types of shoes (none of which were high-top sneakers); and black, mirrored sunglasses. CVR conceded that the characters were not identical but argued that the characters were similar enough that an ordinary reasonable person would perceive the two groups as being "cousins in an extended raisin family."

CVR sued the Board for copyright infringement. How should the court rule on CVR's claim and why? *Cory Van Rijn, Inc. v. California Raisin Advisory Board*, 697 F. Supp. 1136 (E.D. Cal. 1987)

11. Iowa Pedigree (IP) wanted to develop software for use in its business of assisting dog breeders and brokers in complying with American Kennel Club licensing and registration requirements. In May 1989, IP asked Gary Harter to develop this program for it. For the next six years, Harter worked on a variety of projects for IP. He developed several computer programs, maintained IP's computers, and serviced the software of IP's clients.

Throughout Harter's employment with IP, IP reported his pay to the IRS on form 1099 as payment to an independent contractor. Harter reported the pay as self-employed income. IP did not withhold for income or social security taxes. Harter received payment on an irregular basis, sometimes being paid as often as three times within one month and sometimes going as long as seven months without payment. Harter did not punch a time clock or submit the hours worked to IP except in the form of an invoice. IP directed the hours and days that he would work. Harter did some work at home but primarily worked at IP's offices, using its equipment.

Harter also continued to consult for other companies during his employment with IP. In 1992, Harter hired an assistant to work on a particular project and paid the assistant himself. Harter received no medical, retirement, or vacation benefits from IP. Harter traveled extensively with the owner of IP throughout the six-month period to service clients. Harter attended several trade shows for IP as well, in which he wore an IP "uniform" and worked at the IP booth answering

CHAPTER 3

Legal Issues Relating to Product Development

Protection of Intellectual Property Assets Through Trade Secret Law, Contractual Agreements, and Business Strategies

In this chapter, we consider the third category of intellectual property law protection, trade secret law, as well as the law relating to protection of unsolicited ideas. The chapter also discusses strategies that businesses can follow to best protect their intellectual property assets, including the use of contractual agreements such as covenants not to compete and nondisclosure agreements (NDAs).

Trade Secret Law

Trade secret protection is a critical issue for businesses in two respects. First, businesses need to know what to do to protect their trade secrets from being misappropriated. An estimated annual $63 billion in trade secret misappropriation went on in the mid-1990s.[1] Misappropriation most commonly involves illegal disclosures by former employees or raids by competitors and, somewhat less frequently, misappropriation by foreign enterprises. Misappropriation is a particular risk in high-tech industries in which employee mobility and turnover are high. Second, businesses need to understand the consequences of deliberately or inadvertently misappropriating another's trade secrets. What civil and/or criminal penalties might apply?

DEFINITION OF "TRADE SECRET"

While patent and copyright law arise under federal law, trade secret law[2] is primarily state law, although, as we will see, the federal Economic Espionage Act addresses theft of trade secret information in certain circumstances.

Originally, trade secret law was developed through the common law. A few states, including Missouri, New Jersey, New York, Pennsylvania, Tennessee, Texas, and Wyoming, continue to protect trade secrets under the common law. These states generally follow the definition of a *trade secret* found in the Restatement of Torts § 757, comment b:

> A trade secret may consist of any formula, pattern, device or compilation of information which is used in one's business, and which gives him an opportunity to obtain an advantage over competitors who do not know or use it.

Forty-one states and the District of Columbia have codified the common law of trade secrets by adopting some version of the Uniform Trade Secrets Act (USTA). The USTA defines a *trade secret* as:

> information, including a formula, pattern, compilation, program, device, method, technique, or process, that:
> (i) derives independent economic value, actual or potential, from not being generally known to, and not being readily ascertainable by proper means by, other persons who can obtain economic value from its disclosure or use, and
> (ii) is the subject of efforts that are reasonable under the circumstances to maintain its secrecy.[3]

The definitions of trade secret under the USTA and the Restatement are quite similar.[4] In general, trade secrets include business and commercial information that (1) has commercial value, (2) is not in the public domain, and (3) is subject to

---

[1] *See* S. Rep. No. 359, 104th Cong., 2d Sess. 79 (Aug. 27, 1996) (citing survey by the American Society for Industrial Security International).

[2] For general information on trade secret law, see "The Trade Secrets Home Page" at http://www.execpc.com/~mhallign

[3] The USTA can be viewed at the Web site of the National Conference of Commissioners on Uniform State Laws at http://www.nccusl.org

[4] The most recent attempt to organize the law of trade secrets occurred in the Restatement (Third) of Competition § 39 (1995), which provided a similar definition of trade secret: "A trade secret is any information that can be used in the operation of a business or other enterprise and that is sufficiently valuable and secret to afford an actual or potential economic advantage over others."

Focus Case 3.1

Facts: Mark Brown, Deborah Christopher, and David Graben (the "defendants") were employees of Allied Supply Company, Inc., an industrial supply company. All three held managerial positions; Brown and Christopher were also corporate officers. On January 19, 1988, the three individuals resigned and formed their own industrial supply company.

Allied filed suit against them, alleging that the defendants had misappropriated customer and vendor lists before they left Allied, that those lists were trade secrets, and that, by misappropriating the lists, the defendants had violated both the common law and the Alabama Trade Secrets Act.

The trial court granted summary judgment to the defendants, finding that Allied had failed to make reasonable efforts to maintain the secrecy of the lists. The defendants appealed.

Decision: The appellate court affirmed, noting that "at least 10 Allied employees had free access to the lists. In addition, the lists were not marked 'confidential'; the lists were taken home by employees; multiple copies of each list existed; and the information on the lists was contained in the receptionist's Rolodex file." Thus, the lists were not trade secrets and the defendants could not be liable for misappropriating them. *Allied Supply Company, Inc. v. Brown*, 585 So. 2d 33 (Ala. 1991).

reasonable steps to maintain secrecy. Trade secrets include any information that can be of value to a company and its competitors, such as formulas, processes, computer programs, customer and supplier lists, strategic business data, financial projections, research results, marketing strategies, customer needs and profiles, business or product plans, and negative know-how (i.e., knowledge of what does or does not work), provided the information meets the requirements for secrecy. Thus, trade secret law protects assets that are not patentable as well as those that are.

The requirement that trade secrets have "commercial value" does not mean that the business must currently have competitors who might value the information. Rather, it means only that there must be actual or potential value from the information being held secret; potential rather than actual competition is sufficient.

In addition, trade secret information need not be kept absolutely secret, just "reasonably" secret. What is "reasonable" will vary with the circumstances; but, generally, companies should limit the information to those employees who have a need to know and should take precautions to ensure confidentiality. Obviously, the firm must share trade secret information with necessary employees and even with outsiders, such as consultants, in certain circumstances. To maintain the trade secret status of the information, however, the company must ensure that only a few, authorized outsiders know of the information and that those persons make an effort to keep it secret (see Focus Case 3.1).

Public or readily available or ascertainable information is not entitled to trade secret protection. For example, trade secret information that can be quickly and easily reverse-engineered is entitled to little or no protection. (*Reverse-engineering* refers to the process of starting with a product and working backward to identify the process that led to its development or manufacture.) However, publicly known information that is compiled or combined in a way that provides a competitive advantage that is not generally known in the industry may be protected as a trade secret.

See Discussion Case 3.1.

Trade secret protection lasts only as long as the secret is maintained. Once the trade secret information enters the public domain, whether through careless security measures by the trade secret owner or through misappropriation or independent creation by another, the trade secret is lost.

PATENT PROTECTION VERSUS TRADE SECRET PROTECTION

In many instances, an invention may qualify for either patent or trade secret protection. In these cases, the inventor must choose which form of protection to pursue, as these are mutually exclusive options. A single invention cannot be protected through both patent and trade secret. For example, if the inventor makes secret commercial use of the invention for more than one year, the inventor loses the right to seek patent protection under the Patent Act and must protect the invention, if at all, as a trade secret. Conversely, once a patent is issued or after the patent application is laid open, the information becomes public and trade secret protection is no longer possible.

United States law provides inventors with more flexibility in choosing between patent and trade secret protection than virtually any other country in the world, although that flexibility has been considerably reduced in light of the 1999 amendments to the Patent Act (discussed in Chapter 2). If the inventor does not file for foreign patents and his application for a U.S. patent is denied, the inventor can request that the application not be released to the public. The inventor can then treat the invention as a trade secret.

Most other countries do not offer inventors even this limited choice. Rather, they treat patent applications as public information and typically lay open the application within 18 months of its filing. Filing for a patent application in these countries thus automatically takes the information into the public domain and makes trade secret protection unavailable even if the patent ultimately does not issue. Similarly, if a U.S. inventor files for foreign patents, its U.S. patent application is also automatically laid open and its opportunity to seek trade secret protection lost. U.S. inventors should keep this limitation in mind in evaluating whether to pursue foreign patents on their inventions.

In deciding which form of protection—patent or trade secret—to pursue, the inventor must consider several factors:

- *Duration of protection.* Patents are limited to a term of 20 years, while trade secret protection lasts as long as the information remains secret. Theoretically, a trade secret can last forever, though, in practical terms, the life of a trade secret varies greatly depending upon the type of invention and the industry involved. The formula for Coca-Cola, which is a trade secret, is over one hundred years old; a trade secret in the rapidly changing computer industry, on the other hand, may last only a year or two.
- *Scope of protection.* Patent protection is stronger than trade secret protection because it prevents even someone who independently invented the invention from making, using, selling, offering to sell, or importing the invention during the patent period. Trade secret protection, on the other hand, only prohibits persons from using or disclosing the information if they learned of it improperly. It does nothing to prevent persons who acquired the information independently or through legitimate means, such as reverse-engineering, from using the information.

- *Cost.* While it can be expensive and time-consuming to acquire a patent, trade secrets arise automatically under the law. There is no application procedure and no formalities that must be followed. It can be expensive to maintain a trade secret, however, as discussed below.

OWNERSHIP OF TRADE SECRETS CREATED BY EMPLOYEES

Ownership issues arise when the trade secret involved is not a preexisting one revealed to the employee in the scope of her employment but, rather, is a trade secret created by the employee. If the parties had the foresight to sign an express agreement assigning ownership of such trade secrets to one party or the other, that agreement controls. In the absence of such an agreement, the question becomes whether the trade secret is the property of the employer or the employee.

Generally, the trade secret belongs to the employer if (1) the employee was hired specially to do research of the type that led to the trade secret, and (2) the employer has put substantial time and resources at the disposal of the employee to develop the trade secret. For example, a research scientist who develops a new substance while in his research lab at work has created a trade secret that belongs to the employer. In such instances, the employee is under a duty not to use or disclose the trade secret, even in the absence of an express employment contract so stating. If these two conditions are not met, however, the trade secret belongs to the employee. For example, if Employer, a manufacturer of treadmills, hires Employee as a salesperson assigned to its wholesale clients and Employee, in her garage and on or her own time, invents an improved treadmill, the trade secret belongs to Employee.

If the employee was not hired to do research and development but nonetheless created a trade secret related to the employer's business during working hours or using the employer's equipment or materials, the employee owns the trade secret. The employer, however, has *shop rights* in the trade secret. Shop rights are an irrevocable, nontransferable, royalty-free right or license to use the trade secret in the employer's business.

Generally, employers are not satisfied with obtaining shop rights in such trade secrets and want to own the trade secret outright. An *invention assignment agreement* (discussed below) is critical in such instances.

MISAPPROPRIATION OF A TRADE SECRET

Generally, *misappropriation* of a trade secret can occur in one of two ways: (1) an employee or other person with a duty of confidentiality toward the trade secret owner may wrongfully disclose or use the information, or (2) a competitor may wrongfully obtain the information.

Violation of a Duty of Confidentiality

If the defendant has a *duty of confidentiality* toward the trade secret owner, the defendant's disclosure or use of the trade secret is misappropriation. The duty of confidentiality most commonly arises as a result of a special relationship between the parties, such as an employer-employee, partner, or attorney-client relationship. This duty arises automatically under the law and does not depend upon the existence of any type of contract. An employee, for example, has a legal duty not to use or disclose his employer's trade secrets without permission if the employee learned of those secrets within the scope of his employment even if the employee has not signed an employment agreement or other contract expressly addressing this topic. This duty of confidentiality binds the employee even after he leaves the employer's employ. Thus, an employee cannot take the employer's trade secrets to a new job.

Although not legally required, from the employer's perspective it is always better to have an express, written *nondisclosure agreement* (NDA). The NDA usually requires the employee to expressly agree not to use or disclose any trade secrets belonging to the employer and often requires the employee to assign in advance to the employer all trade secrets he might create. (This topic is discussed further below.) The courts generally enforce such agreements provided that they are not unconscionable.

Another type of express agreement that is often used is a *covenant not to compete*, also known as a noncompete agreement. These agreements generally require the employee not to compete or to work for a competitor for a specified time period in a specified geographic region after leaving the employer's employ. The advantage, from the employer's perspective, of using such an agreement is that the agreement can cover confidential proprietary information that might not rise to the level of a trade secret. The disadvantage is that the courts dislike noncompete agreements as a matter of public policy and carefully scrutinize them to make certain that they do not infringe upon an employee's ability to make a living. Noncompete agreements are invalid in a few states, such as California. (Noncompete agreements are discussed in more detail below.)

A number of courts have adopted the *inevitable disclosure rule*, which permits an employer to obtain an injunction prohibiting an employee from working for a direct competitor, even in the absence of a noncompete agreement, when it would be difficult for the employee to perform his new job without disclosing or relying upon the former employer's trade secrets. This rule recognizes that people cannot easily segregate general information or knowledge from the trade secrets and confidential information of former employers.

The courts hesitate to issue injunctions under the inevitable disclosure rule, however, because of their concern that individuals not be deprived of their livelihoods. The Pennsylvania Supreme Court described the policy conflicts that nondisclosure rules generally raise, noting that trade secret law

> brings to the fore a problem of accommodating competing policies in our law: the right of a businessman to be protected against unfair competition stemming from the usurpation of his trade secrets and the right of an individual to the unhampered pursuit of the occupations and livelihoods for which he is best suited. . . . Society as a whole greatly benefits from technological improvements. Without some means of post-employment protection to assure that valuable developments or improvements are exclusively those of the employer, the businessman could not afford to subsidize research or improve current methods. * * *
>
> On the other hand, any form of post-employment restraint reduces the economic mobility of employees and limits their personal freedom to pursue a preferred course of livelihood. The employee's bargaining position is weakened because he is potentially shackled by the acquisition of alleged trade secrets; and thus, paradoxically, he is restrained, because of his increased expertise, from advancing further in the industry in which he is most productive.[5]

---

[5] Wexler v. Greenberg, 160 A.2d 430, 434–35 (Pa. 1960).

See Discussion Case 3.2.

   To avoid liability for misappropriation of a competitor's trade secrets, a company should take care when recruiting new employees. In some instances, it may be best not to recruit particular individuals. The recruit should be informed at the beginning of the interview process that the interviewing company does not want information about or access to any competitor's trade secrets. If the recruit is hired, she should be informed again (in writing) of this policy. The recruit should not bring confidential documents or materials to the new job and should not be placed into jobs in which she might be tempted to use such information, even inadvertently, including jobs that involve reverse-engineering or independent creation of products similar to those of the previous employer. If the recruit has entered into a noncompete agreement or NDA with the former employer, the new employer should review it carefully to ensure that the new employment does not violate any of the valid provisions of the agreements. The new employer should document in writing all efforts undertaken to avoid trade secret misappropriation in the event that the previous employer alleges misappropriation at some point in the future (see Exhibit 3.1).

Unlawful Acquisition of a Competitor's Trade Secret Information

Certain types of behavior are regarded as unlawful means of obtaining trade secret information. *Illegal conduct*, such as theft, trespass, fraud, misrepresentation, wiretapping, and bribery, is not permitted. Acquisition of a competitor's trade secrets through *industrial espionage*, such as electronic surveillance or spying, is also not permitted. Moreover, a competitor who purchases trade secret information, knowing that it was improperly obtained, is liable for misappropriation just as though the competitor had engaged in the misappropriation directly (see Focus Case 3.2 on page 67).

EXHIBIT 3.1

TRADE SECRET MISAPPROPRIATION

Does the information qualify as a trade secret?

   ¥ commercially valuable
   ¥ not in public domain <u>and</u>
   ¥ subject to reasonable security measures

If no,
no misappropriation

If yes, did the D acquire,
use, or disclose the
information improperly?

If no, no
misappropriation

If yes,
misappropriation

Focus Case 3.2

Facts: When E.I. du Pont de Nemours and Company was building a new plant to accommodate a new process for producing methanol, workers noticed an airplane taking aerial photographs of the site. The photographers had been hired by an unidentified third party. Du Pont claimed that its new methanol process was a trade secret developed after expensive and time-consuming research. It claimed that it had taken special precautions to safeguard the process and that the process gave it a competitive advantage over other producers.

Du Pont sued the photographers for misappropriation of trade secrets. Du Pont feared that a competitor could reverse-engineer the process from the photographs. It sought damages for disclosure of the trade secret and temporary and permanent injunctions prohibiting further disclosure.

The trial court, applying Texas law in this diversity case, ordered the photographers to release the name of their client. The photographers appealed this order.

Decision: The appellate court affirmed the order of the trial court. The appellate court found that the photographers' actions fell below generally accepted standards of commercial morality. While du Pont could legitimately be expected to place a fence around the site or a roof over the plant once it was completed, du Pont was not required to construct a temporary roof over the site to shield the construction process (particularly because the roof would have blocked access to the site). The court concluded: "We should not require a person or corporation to take unreasonable precautions to prevent another from doing that which he ought not to do in the first place." *E. I. du Pont de Nemours & Co. v. Christopher,* 431 F.2d 1012 (5th Cir. 1970).

Lawful Acquisition of a Competitor's Trade Secret Information

There are a number of legitimate means by which a competitor can gain access to trade secret information. If the owner (or its employee) puts the information into the public domain, e.g., by publishing it in brochures or other materials, or by talking about it in public places, competitors may legally use that information. In addition, competitors are permitted to reverse-engineer trade secret information through inspection of a product or examination of published literature. Competitors may also independently create the information without incurring liability for misappropriation.

It is also legal for a company to obtain public information about its competitor's trade secrets through *competitive intelligence* activities. These activities include the gathering of either primary data (i.e., information gathered from direct sources such as telephone or in-person interviews) or secondary data (i.e., information gathered from indirect sources, such as consultants, published documents, or patents). For example, competitive intelligence information can be obtained through Internet searches, examination of trash, attendance at trade shows, interviews with securities analysts and suppliers, examinations of UCC filings, visits to competitors' facilities, or discussions with competitors' customers.

While competitive intelligence is a long-established practice in Europe and Asia, it is still relatively new in the United States. It is a rapidly growing field, however. An estimated 10 percent of large corporations have in-house competitive intelligence units, and the Society for Competitive Intelligence Professionals (SCIP) has a membership of over 6,000.[6] While a firm can use competitive intelligence techniques proactively to enhance its own market position, the firm also

---

[6] Their webpage is located at http://www.scip.org

EXHIBIT 3.2

Lawful Acquisition of a Competitor's Trade Secrets	Unlawful Acquisition of a Competitor s Trade Secrets
¥ accessing information in public domain ¥ competitive intelligence ¥ reverse-engineering ¥ independent creation	¥ violation of duty of confidentiality ¥ duty implied by law as result of special relationship ¥ duty created by express contract ¥ illegal conduct ¥ industrial espionage ¥ knowingly obtaining information misappropriated by another

needs to be aware that it may be the target of such actions by its competitors as well. Although a firm cannot block all such activities by its competitors, simple steps such as shredding sensitive documents before placing them in the trash, monitoring factory visits from outsiders, and controlling access to sensitive data can minimize the risks (see Exhibit 3.2).

REMEDIES FOR TRADE SECRET MISAPPROPRIATION

Two general types of remedies are available for trade secret misappropriation: (1) injunctions and (2) monetary damages. In addition, the federal Economic Espionage Act provides for criminal penalties for certain types of trade secret misappropriation.

Injunctions

Generally, it is relatively easy to get an injunction for trade secret misappropriation. The more difficult question typically is how long the injunction should last. The majority of courts limit the injunction to the life of the trade secret. This can be measured up front by how long the court estimates the trade secret will endure. Alternatively, the court can issue an injunction of indefinite length that allows the defendant to petition the court to have the injunction lifted if and when the trade secret enters the public domain (e.g., through reverse-engineering or independent creation by others).

A minority of courts will issue a perpetual injunction on the theory that the defendant's breach of confidence or improper conduct warrants such punishment. This prevents the defendant from using the trade secret information even once it is generally known within the industry and is available to other competitors. It thus puts the defendant at a considerable disadvantage compared both to the plaintiff and to other competitors.

Monetary Damages

Depending upon the circumstances, the court may select from a variety of types of monetary damages:

1. the *lost profits* that the trade secret owner has incurred as a result of the defendant's misappropriation of the trade secret;
2. *unjust enrichment damages,* often measured as the amount of *profits* that the defendant made as a result of the misappropriation; or
3. a *reasonable royalty* for the defendant's use of the trade secret during the time at issue (measured by the amount that reasonable parties would have agreed to if they had willingly negotiated for a license to use the trade secret during an arm's-length transaction).

Double Damages and Attorneys Fees

Under the USTA, the court can award up to *double damages* for willful and malicious trade secret misappropriation. In addition, the court can award *attorneys fees* to the prevailing party in cases of willful and malicious misappropriation by the defendant or bad faith by the trade secret owner. As noted in Chapter 2, enhanced damages and awards of attorneys fees are rare in the U.S. legal system and are available only where specifically authorized by statute.

Criminal Prosecution

Both civil and criminal proceedings can be brought against an individual alleged to have engaged in misappropriation. As of 1996, only about one half of the states had statutes imposing criminal sanctions for theft of a trade secret. To address this gap in enforcement, Congress enacted the Economic Espionage Act,[7] which took effect January 1, 1997. This federal statute provides that individuals convicted of trade secret theft can be fined up to $250,000 and corporations up to $5 million. In both instances, the fines can be doubled if the defendant acted in concert with a foreign instrumentality. In addition to the fines, the court may impose jail terms of up to 10 years (15 years if the defendant acted in concert with a foreign instrumentality) and subject the defendant to forfeiture of property.

Congress's main purpose in enacting the Economic Espionage Act was to provide redress for illegal activities of foreign governments, although the Act applies to purely domestic trade secret misappropriation as well. The Department of Justice, which enforces the Act, has stated that it will exercise restraint in bringing federal charges under the Act, noting that civil remedies for trade secret misappropriation are generally available under state law. In determining whether federal criminal prosecution is also appropriate in any particular circumstance, the Department of Justice considers factors such as "(a) the scope of the criminal activity, including evidence of involvement by a foreign government, foreign agent or foreign instrumentality; (b) the degree of economic injury to the trade secret owner; (c) the type of trade secret misappropriated; (d) the effectiveness of available civil remedies; and (e) the potential deterrent value of the prosecution."[8]

As of October 2000, there were 23 reported criminal arrests under the Economic Espionage Act (and the FBI was investigating approximately 800 other cases). Most of these arrests have led to pleas of guilty by the defendants and have resulted in substantial prison sentences and/or fines.[9] In January 2000, for example, a federal district judge sentenced the former chief executive officer of Four Pillars Enterprise, Ltd., a Taiwanese adhesives company with annual sales of approximately $150 million, to a fine of $250,000, 6 months' home confinement, and 18 months' probation. The executive's daughter, a former company executive, was

---

[7] 18 U.S.C. §§ 1831–1839.
[8] UNITED STATES ATTORNEY'S MANUAL, SECTION 9-59.100 (available at http://www.usdoj.gov/).
[9] For a summary of these cases, see http://www.execpc.com/~mhallign/indict.html

sentenced to a fine of $5,000 and one year of probation. The company itself was fined $5 million. The defendants had been convicted of two counts of trade secret theft under the Act. The defendants had secretly paid a research scientist at Avery Dennison Corp., a leading pressure-sensitive adhesive manufacturer, to provide them with adhesive formulas and other confidential technical information over an eight-year period. Avery Dennison also brought a civil suit against Four Pillars and, in February 2000, was awarded $10 million for trade secret misappropriation, $10 million for RICO (Racketeer Influenced and Corrupt Organizations) violations, $10 million for conversion, and $30.16 million in punitive damages.[10] The RICO award was automatically trebled, making the total verdict $80.16 million.

Trade secret theft can also be prosecuted under other federal statutes, such as wire fraud. One of the more-publicized recent cases involved Jose Ignacio Lopez de Arriortua, who, in May 2000, was indicted by federal prosecutors on four counts of wire fraud and two counts of violating federal interstate transportation laws. Lopez is alleged to have copied extensive General Motors computer files on auto parts costs and future car models and to have provided those to his new employer, competitor Volkswagen AG. His actions led not only to the filing of federal criminal charges against him but also to a civil lawsuit between the two companies. General Motors sued Volkswagen, alleging that Lopez had misappropriated confidential documents. In 1996, Lopez was forced to resign from Volkswagen as part of an out-of-court settlement between the two companies. Volkswagen also agreed to pay General Motors $100 million and to purchase $1 billion in General Motors parts.[11]

PROTECTION OF TRADE SECRETS

Businesses must have reasonable security precautions in place in order to claim protection for their trade secrets. A proactive policy is best. The company should start by conducting a trade secret audit to gain an understanding of what trade secrets it owns and how well its current company policy protects those secrets. The audit should be repeated periodically to ensure that appropriate measures are taken to protect new trade secrets as well.

Employees are the largest source of leaks of trade secrets, so careful management of the employer-employee relationship is needed. All employees should be informed about the company's trade secret policies and the consequences of violating those policies. The company should develop written policies regarding trade secret protection and should communicate those policies clearly and emphatically to all employees who might have access to such secrets. Access to trade secrets should be limited to those employees who have a need to know specific information, and the employees should be explicitly instructed that the information is a trade secret. The company should clearly label confidential documents as such but should avoid labeling every piece of information "confidential." In addition to making it difficult for employees to distinguish between truly secret information and routine information, incorrect or excessive designation of information as confidential may weaken the company's ability to assert trade secret protection in the event of misappropriation or litigation.

---

[10] Margaret Cronin Fisk, *Accusations Stick in the Adhesive Industry*, National Law Journal, Feb.19, 2001 at c15. *See U.S. Court Imposes Maximum Fine After Taiwan Firm Is Convicted of Economic Espionage*, INTERNATIONAL ENFORCEMENT LAW REPORTER, Feb. 2000; http://www.execpc.com/~mhallign (summarizing cases).

[11] See Jeffrey McCracken, *Lopez Accused of Giving Secrets, Documents to VW*, Detroit Free Press, May 23, 2000, at p. 1A.

The company should destroy written information once it is no longer needed. The company should instruct employees to use passwords and security codes on sensitive computer files and to lock desks, filing cabinets, and offices when not in use. It should caution employees not to discuss confidential information in the presence of outsiders, over unsecure phone lines (particularly over cell phones), or in public. The company should also monitor and restrict access by plant visitors, including repair or service personnel.

The most important element of a proactive trade secret program, however, is the use of express contractual agreements, especially NDAs. This is a contractual promise by an employee not to make unauthorized use or disclosure of trade secrets. Senior managers and technical staff should also be required to sign noncompete agreements. NDAs and noncompete agreements are discussed in more detail below.

Finally, the company should conduct exit interviews to remind departing employees of their obligation to maintain the employer's trade secrets even after they have ceased working for the employer.

INTERNATIONAL ASPECTS OF TRADE SECRET PROTECTION

As with patent law, the ability of the United States to regulate trade secrets abroad is constrained by its territorial boundaries. When a U.S. court is unable to obtain jurisdiction over the parties or when the infringing goods are not imported into the United States, U.S. courts and government agencies are generally powerless to restrict a foreign party's exploitation of a competitor's trade secrets abroad, even if the exploitation would be illegal under U.S. law.

As a result, businesses need to be very careful when they license or transfer trade secrets abroad. Whenever a business establishes foreign operations, enters into ventures with foreign partners, or shares information or personnel with foreign sources, the business needs to carefully investigate the host country's trade secret laws, as those laws will likely govern in the event of a dispute or problem.

Laws regarding trade secret protection vary greatly around the world, but generally we are seeing a movement toward greater protection of trade secrets and greater harmonization of national laws. Japan, Korea, and Mexico enacted their first trade secret protection statutes in 1991; China followed in 1993.[12] In addition, the Trade-Related Aspects of Intellectual Property Rights (TRIPS) Agreement of the Uruguay Round of GATT requires member countries to protect against the acquisition, disclosure, or use of a party's trade secrets "in a manner contrary to honest commercial practices." This agreement should ultimately lead to stronger and more harmonized trade secret protection laws among member countries.

The Law of Unsolicited Ideas

Very often, individuals develop ideas for new products or services that they are unable or unwilling to pursue on their own. The inventor will offer the idea to an established company, hoping that the company will compensate the inventor in exchange for the right to commercialize the invention. Both inventors who approach companies and the companies who are approached need to be careful about the manner in which the relationship develops, lest they find themselves in an undesirable legal position.

[12] The trade secret law of several countries is summarized on "The Trade Secrets Home Page," http://www.execpc.com/~mhallign

Focus Case 3.3

 Facts: Mark Landsberg wrote a book on strategies for winning Scrabble, a popular board game. He contacted Selchow & Richter Co., the owner of the Scrabble trademark, for permission to use the mark. Selchow & Richter requested a copy of the manuscript and entered into lengthy negotiations with Landsberg regarding its possible publication. Eventually, the parties ceased negotiations and Selchow & Richter published its own Scrabble strategy book. Landsberg sued for copyright infringement and breach of contract. The trial court found for Landsberg on the breach of contract claim. Selchow & Richter appealed.

Decision: Although the appellate court ruled that the two books were not sufficiently similar to support a copyright infringement claim, it did find for Landsberg on the breach of contract claim. The court stated: "California law allows for recovery for the breach of an implied-in-fact contract when the recipient of a valuable idea accepts the information knowing that compensation is expected and subsequently uses the idea without paying for it. If disclosure occurs before it is known that compensation is a condition of its use, however, no contract will be implied."

The facts indicated that Landberg's initial disclosure of his manuscript was confidential. Moreover, the lengthy negotiations for the use of the manuscript by Selchow & Richter Co. indicated that Landsberg reasonably believed that the company would not use the manuscript without paying him for it. *Landsberg v. Scrabble Crossword Game Players, Inc.*, 802 F.2d 1193 (9th Cir. 1986).

FROM THE INVENTOR'S PERSPECTIVE

Before disclosing his invention to the company, the inventor must make certain that the company recognizes that either it must pay for the idea or, if it chooses not to purchase the invention, that it must keep the idea confidential. If the inventor simply reveals the details of his invention without first obtaining this understanding, the inventor could inadvertently lose his rights in the invention.

Thus, before revealing the invention, the inventor should contact the company to make certain that the company understands that the inventor is seeking to sell or license the invention. As a practical matter, the inventor should get the company to sign an agreement stating that the company will review the invention but will keep the invention confidential and will pay a reasonable purchase price or royalties if it pursues the idea. Often, such agreements state that the company is not obligated to pay if it was already familiar with the invention or if the invention was already publicly known. Even if the parties do not enter into an express contract, the courts may well "imply" the existence of a contract that protects the interests of the inventor provided the inventor has made his position clear prior to revealing his ideas (see Focus Case 3.3).

FROM THE COMPANY'S PERSPECTIVE

Companies who may be approached by inventors with unsolicited ideas face a different set of problems. Many companies are inundated by calls and letters from inventors regarding unsolicited ideas and inventions. The companies may well already be aware of similar inventions or may be working on similar inventions themselves. The companies are legitimately concerned that rejected inventors will conclude that a company who later comes out with a similar invention stole the unsolicited idea from the inventor and will sue.

Most companies have standard procedures for dealing with the submission of unsolicited ideas. Many simply do not consider unsolicited ideas under any circumstances and return the letter of inquiry to the sender without reviewing the ideas contained in it. For example, Hershey Foods' idea submission policy on its Web site states that it "does not accept or consider any creative ideas or suggestions relating to products or marketing plans unless it has specifically requested them." It also states that any communications or materials transmitted to the company will be treated as "non-confidential and non-proprietary" and states that "Hershey is free to use any ideas or concepts contained in any communication [sent] to [its] Web site for any purpose whatsoever, including but not limited to developing, manufacturing and marketing products using such information."[13]

Some companies review unsolicited ideas but generally require the inventor to first sign a written waiver (supplied by the company) that relieves the company of any liability for disclosing confidential information and that explicitly states that no relationship is formed between the parties as a result of the company's review of the inventor's materials. Many of these companies review the invention only if it is already covered by a patent. This policy ensures that the ownership rights in the invention are both clear and assignable in the event the company wishes to pursue the invention.

Business Strategies for Protecting Intellectual Property Assets

Companies can take a number of actions to protect their intellectual property assets. Specifically, in many (but not all) instances, firms may be able to use contractual agreements, such as covenants not to compete and NDAs, to protect these assets. More generally, companies should conduct periodic intellectual property audits to determine the nature and scope of their assets and to evaluate protection measures in place. In addition, several specialized software programs are now on the market to assist companies in managing their intellectual property assets.

CONTRACTUAL AGREEMENTS

There are several different types of contractual agreements that employers should consider using to protect their interests in intellectual property assets, including covenants not to compete, NDAs, and invention assignment agreements. Each of these agreements is governed by state law.

Covenants Not to Compete
Covenants not to compete are agreements in which the employee agrees not to compete with the employer in certain specified manners after leaving its employ. Noncompete covenants are also commonly used when a business is sold (to prevent the former owner from competing with the new owner) or when a partnership is dissolved (to prevent one partner from competing with another). Typically, these agreements restrict the ability of the former employee to work for competitors, conduct or solicit business from the former employer's customers, or use the former employer's confidential business information. Covenants not to compete are governed by the common law regarding restraints of trade (discussed further in Chapter 4).

As a matter of public policy, courts dislike noncompete covenants. The courts are concerned that such agreements may prevent an employee from making a

---

[13] *See* http://www.hersheys.com/legal/index.shtml

livelihood in his profession. In addition, the courts favor the free flow of labor and fear that widespread use of noncompete covenants could impede a competitive marketplace for labor. As a result, some states do not permit such agreements. Many other states place significant restrictions upon the use of such agreements, permitting them, for example, in the sale of a business but not in the employment context.

In general, covenants not to compete must meet several legal requirements. First, they must be ancillary (or subordinate) to another contractual agreement. In an employee-employer relationship, this generally means that the parties must have entered into a formal, written employment contract. In the absence of such an employment contract, many courts regard the covenant not to compete as an illegal restraint on trade.

Second, the covenant not to compete must be narrowly drawn so as to protect only the legitimate interests of the employer. Mere protection of the employer from competition is insufficient. Rather, the covenant must be designed to protect business assets such as trade secrets of the employer, a customer base, confidential business information, or business goodwill.

Third, the covenant not to compete must be restricted in terms of both (1) duration and (2) geographic scope. These determinations are highly fact-specific and are made on a case-by-case basis. Covenants with a duration of one year or less are generally considered valid; covenants of several years are generally considered overbroad. As a general rule, the covenant should not exceed the period of any employment contract given to the employee. Thus, if the employee has a two-year employment contract, the covenant not to compete should not extend more than two years after termination of that employment.

The advent of the Internet and the increasingly rapid pace at which technology is changing are having profound impacts on the way in which courts evaluate the reasonable duration of covenants not to compete. Even one-year noncompete agreements that historically would have been found valid in virtually every instance have been held invalid in the fast-paced high-technology world. Employers may need to revise their standard boilerplate noncompete agreements and tailor them to the specifics of the industry in which they operate (see Focus Case 3.4 on page 76).

Permissible geographic scope is determined by the scope of the company's activities. As a general rule, the geographic area covered by the covenant cannot exceed the area in which the employer currently does business. As commerce continues to become more national and international in scope, however, this rule is likely to erode. A recent court decision—*Intelus Corp. v. Barton*—addressed this issue (see Focus Case 3.5 on page 77).

The most common remedy granted for breach of a valid covenant not to compete is an *injunction* that requires the employee to adhere to the terms of the covenant and to cease any impermissible competition. *Monetary damages* are also available in some instances.

See Discussion Case 3.3.

Nondisclosure Agreements

A *nondisclosure agreement* (also known as a *proprietary information agreement*) is a contractual agreement that prohibits an employee from revealing or using trade secrets or proprietary information. Although the common law of unfair competition generally prohibits employees from using or disclosing trade secrets or other confidential information even in the absence of an explicit contractual agreement, it is still wise for employers to use an NDA.

Focus Case 3.4

Facts: Mark Schlack was employed by Earth-Web, Inc., as a vice president responsible for "content" on the company's Web sites. Earth-Web provides on-line products and services to business professionals in the information technology industry. Eleven months after he was hired, Schlack resigned to accept a position with ITworld.com, a subsidiary of International Data Group, Inc., which was scheduled to launch the following year and which was to provide information technology print-based data.

EarthWeb immediately filed suit to enjoin Schlack from beginning employment with ITworld.com, alleging potential loss of trade secrets and breach of his noncompete agreement. Schlack had signed an employment contract with EarthWeb that had contained a one-year noncompete agreement.

Decision: The trial court refused to enforce the noncompete agreement. It stated that "the one-year duration of EarthWeb's restrictive covenant is too long given the dynamic nature of this industry, its lack of geographical borders, and Schlack's former cutting-edge position with EarthWeb where his success depended on keeping abreast of daily changes in content on the Internet." The court found that enforcing such a provision would "work a significant hardship on Schlack." The court explained: "When measured against the IT industry in the Internet environment, a one-year hiatus from the workforce is several generations, if not an eternity." *EarthWeb, Inc. v. Schlack*, 71 F. Supp. 2d 299 (S.D. N.Y. 1999).

Use of such agreements not only strengthens the employer's legal position in the event of a breach by showing that the employer has taken reasonable measures to protect its trade secrets but also serves to emphasize to the employee the importance of trade secret protection. In addition, the NDA may protect confidential information that does not rise to the level of a trade secret and thus is not protected under common law. Courts do not like NDAs as a matter of public policy, however, and often impose significant limitations on them.

An NDA can be a stand-alone document or can be part of a larger employment contract. *Every* employee with potential access to trade secrets, including clerical and custodial staffs, should be required to sign an NDA. In addition, consultants, independent contractors, potential investors, and others with access to trade secrets should be required to sign a confidentiality agreement before any confidential information is released to them.

See Discussion Case 3.4.

Even states that do not allow covenants not to compete typically allow NDAs. Although a few states impose the same restrictions upon NDAs as they do upon noncompete agreements (i.e., restrictions on duration, geographic area, and scope), most states do not hold NDAs to the same level of scrutiny as they do noncompete agreements.

A properly drawn NDA does several things. First, the NDA provides clear notice to the employee of the confidential nature of the information at issue. Generally, the law does not impose a duty upon an employee to maintain the confidentiality of information when the employee has not been notified that the information is secret. Second, the NDA informs the employee as to her responsibilities regarding such information (particularly required efforts to maintain its confidentiality). Finally, an NDA should contain a promise (covenant) from the

---

Focus Case 3.5

Facts: Bernard Barton was hired as an account manager in 1993 by Intelus Corporation, which develops, sells, and supports software programs for the health care industry. At that time, he signed a noncompete agreement that barred him from calling on or soliciting any customer or account of Intelus to sell any competitive product or from engaging in any business that competed directly for Intelus's customer accounts for a period of six months after leaving Intelus's employ. In 1998, Barton resigned from Intelus and went to work for MedPlus, Inc., a direct competitor of Intelus's in the field of sales of electronic record systems to health care organizations. When Intelus filed suit to enforce the covenant not to compete, Barton argued that the covenant was not valid because it did not state any geographic restriction.

Decision: The trial court, applying Maryland law in this diversity case, rejected Barton's argument. It stated: "[C]ompetition unlimited by geography can be expected where the nature of the business concerns computer software and the ability to process information. . . . The court anticipates that restrictive covenants will grow in importance with the continued emergence of technology-driven and information-based industries. An employee who can use a computer and a modem to solicit and service customers anywhere in the world can easily jump from competitor to competitor, potentially taking with him a collection of clients."

The court found that Barton was not unduly harmed by enforcement of the covenant. The covenant prevented him from working only at the 10 firms that were direct competitors of Intelus during the 6-month period, while permitting him to work for the 100 companies that also sold computer software generally to the health care industry, but which were not direct competitors of Intelus. Moreover, the public interest favored the enforcement of such restrictions because they are important to the growth of businesses that are based primarily upon the provision of superior customer service. *Intelus Corp. v. Barton,* 7 F. Supp. 2d 635 (D. Md. 1998).

---

employee prohibiting the employee from disclosing or using such information after termination of employment (see Exhibit 3.3 on page 78).

Invention Assignment Agreements

An *invention assignment agreement* is one in which the employee agrees to assign to the employer any inventions that he or she may conceive of or create during her term of employment. The courts will enforce such agreements but will scrutinize them to make certain that they are fair. Thus, both the duration of the agreement and the scope of the rights granted must be reasonable under the circumstances.

The agreement should require the employee to disclose any preexisting inventions to which the employee claims ownership, as well as require the employee to disclose all inventions made during the course of employment as they occur. The agreement should also require the employee to cooperate in the pursuit of patents or copyrights on the inventions (see Exhibit 3.4 on pages 79–80).

INTELLECTUAL PROPERTY AUDITS

Every business should periodically conduct an *intellectual property audit*—a systematic review of the patent, copyright, trade secret, and trademark assets of the firm and an analysis of the company's procedures for protecting those assets. A thorough intellectual property audit not only discloses the nature and extent of the intellectual property assets owned by the company but also reveals gaps in existing company policy by uncovering information, ideas, or inventions that should be

EXHIBIT 3.3

PROPRIETARY INFORMATION AGREEMENT

This Agreement between XYZ, Inc. including its direct and indirect subsidiaries and affiliate (hereinafter "XYZ, Inc.") and _____ (herein after "Employee") shall govern the responsibilities of Employees with respect to proprietary information. Entering into this agreement is a condition of Employee's employment by XYZ, Inc. but the agreement does not purport to set forth the terms of said employment.

WITNESSETH:

WHEREAS, Employee is or desires to be employed by XYZ, Inc. or one of its direct or indirect subsidiaries or affiliates in a capacity in which Employee may receive or contribute to proprietary information which may or may not be patentable;

WHEREAS, XYZ, Inc. and its direct and indirect subsidiaries and affiliates develop and use valuable technical and non-technical proprietary information which XYZ, Inc. may wish to protect either by patents or by keeping material secret and proprietary;

NOW THEREFORE, in consideration of Employee's employment by XYZ, Inc. or the relevant direct or indirect subsidiary or affiliate, it is agreed as follows:

1. Employee shall not disclose or use for Employee or others at any time either during or subsequent to said only employment proprietary information of XYZ, Inc. of which Employee becomes informed during said employment, whether or not developed by Employee, without first obtaining the written consent of XYZ, Inc. over the signature of a company officer. Employee understands that the term "proprietary information" means any information not generally known or previously published by XYZ, Inc. which gives or is intended to give XYZ, Inc. an advantage over its competitors who do not have the information. Such proprietary information includes but is not limited to, secret information relating to marketing plans, products, formulas, processes, manufacturing techniques, personnel information, financial data, production information, software, and the like.

2. Misuse or unauthorized disclosure of proprietary information may result in legal and/or disciplinary action up to and including termination.

3. The obligations of Employee under this agreement shall continue beyond the termination of employment with respect to proprietary information received by Employee during the period of employment and shall be binding upon Employee's assigns, executors, administrators, and legal representatives.

4. This agreement supersedes and replaces any existing agreement, written or otherwise, entered into by Employee and XYZ, Inc. relating generally to the same subject matter. It is expressly understood, however, that nothing contained herein shall in any way alter the terms of any agreement between XYZ, Inc. and Employee, or any representative of Employee, with respect to collective bargaining agreements, termination, or any other aspects of employment which may be present and form part of an employment agreement between XYZ, Inc. and Employee.

Employee is to be employed at _____, a direct or indirect subsidiary of XYZ, Inc..

XYZ, Inc.   **Employee**

By_____   By_____

Date_____   Date_____

EXHIBIT 3.4

INVENTION AND WORK PRODUCT AGREEMENT

This agreement, between _____, including its direct and indirect subsidiaries and affiliates (hereafter "XYZ, Inc."), and _____ (hereinafter "Employee") shall govern the responsibilities of Employee with respect to inventions. Entering into this agreement is a condition of Employee's employment by XYZ, Inc. but the agreement does not purport to set forth the terms of said employment.

WHEREAS, Employee is or desires to be employed by XYZ, Inc. or one of its direct or indirect subsidiaries or affiliates in a capacity in which Employee may contribute to and/or make inventions which may or may not be patentable;

WHEREAS, XYZ, Inc. and its direct and indirect subsidiaries and affiliates develop and use valuable technical and non-technical proprietary information and inventions which XYZ, Inc. and/or its direct and indirect subsidiaries and affiliates may wish to prevent others from using either by patents or by keeping this material secret and proprietary;

NOW, THEREFORE, in consideration of Employee's employment or continued employment by XYZ, Inc. or the relevant direct or indirect subsidiary or affiliate, it is agreed as follows:

1. Employee agrees to make a prompt and complete disclosure of every invention (as hereafter defined) which Employee conceives of or reduces to practice, and any patent application which Employee files, during the term of Employee's employment and further agrees that every said invention and patent application is the property of XYZ, Inc. Employee understands that the term "invention" means any discoveries, developments, concepts, and ideas whether patentable or not, which relate to any present or prospective activities of XYZ, Inc. with which activities Employee is acquainted as a result or consequence of Employee's employment with XYZ, Inc. Such inventions would include, but not be limited to, processes, methods, products, software, apparatus, trade mark, trade names, advertising, and promotional material, as well as improvements therein and know-how related thereto. Employee further agrees that upon XYZ, Inc.'s request, but without expense to Employee, Employee will execute any so-called applications, assignments, and other instruments which XYZ, Inc. shall deem necessary or convenient for the protection of its said property in the United States and/or foreign countries and to render aid and assistance in any litigation or other proceeding pertaining to said property.

2. XYZ, Inc. agrees that any invention made by Employee in which XYZ, Inc. states in writing over the signature of its President & Vice President that it has no interest, may be freely exploited by Employee.

3. Employee agrees that all writings, illustrations, models, and other such materials produced by Employee or put into Employee's possession by XYZ, Inc. during the term of and relating to Employee's employment are at all times XYZ, Inc.'s property and Employee will deliver the same over to XYZ, Inc. upon request or upon termination of Employee's employment and shall be work made for hire under U.S. Copyright Laws. To the extent that such works are not works made for hire as defined by U.S. Copyright Law, Employee hereby assigns,

continued

protected by intellectual property laws but are not. The ultimate outcomes of the audit should be an inventory of the intellectual property assets held by the company and the creation of processes and procedures that will ensure that these assets are identified and protected in the future.

Because intellectual property assets implicate legal, technological, and business concerns, audits should be conducted by a team of persons from the marketing, research, manufacturing, information technology, and legal functions. The actual performance of the audit will vary according to the extent and nature of the company's intellectual property activities.

transfers, and grants to XYZ, Inc. any and all rights (including but not limited to copyrights) in and to all works provided hereunder. Any and all copyright ownership claims which Employee may raise as a result of work undertaken pursuant to this agreement are hereby assigned, transferred, and granted to XYZ, Inc.

4. This Agreement does not apply to an invention for which no equipment, supplies, facility, or trade secret information of employer was used and which was developed entirely on the Employee's own time, and (1) which does not relate (a) directly to the business of the employer or (b) to the employer's actual or demonstrably anticipated research or development, or (2) which does not result from any work performed by the Employee for the employer.

5. The obligations of Employee under this agreement shall continue beyond the termination of employment with respect to inventions conceived or made by Employee during the period of employment, and shall be binding upon Employee's assigns, executors, administrators, and other legal representatives.

6. This Agreement supersedes and replaces any existing agreement, written or otherwise, entered into by Employee and XYZ, Inc. relating generally to the same subject matter. It is expressly understood, however, that nothing contained herein shall in any way alter the terms of any agreement between XYZ, Inc. and Employee, or any representative of Employee, with respect to collective bargaining agreements, termination, or any other aspects of employment which may be present and form part of an employment agreement between XYZ, Inc. and Employee.

Employee is to be employed at (insert XYZ, Inc. company) a direct or indirect subsidiary of XYZ, Inc.

XYZ, Inc.   **Employee**

By_____   By_____

Date_____   Date_____

This document is reprinted with the permission of the American Corporate Counsel Association (ACCA) as it originally appeared in the ACCA's Intellectual Property InfoPAK[SM] Copyright 1997, the American Corporate Counsel Association, all rights reserved.

In general, the audit team should inventory all inventions made by the company and should determine whether appropriate patents are in place. In particular, the company should evaluate its business processes to determine whether it should pursue business method patents on any of those processes. The audit team should determine whether third parties are infringing upon patents belonging to the company or whether the company is, even inadvertently, infringing upon the patents of others.

The audit team should identify all confidential or proprietary information held by the company and should review and assess the company's trade secret efforts. If necessary, the company should implement additional measures to ensure that confidential information retains its secret status. In particular, the company should institute explicit E-mail and Internet-use policies regarding the distribution of sensitive or confidential information and should employ state-of-the-art computer security and encryption technology.

The audit team should inventory all copyrighted works owned by the company. The audit team should review all agreements entered into with third parties who have created "works for hire" to ensure that proper assignments of the copyright to the company have been made. The company should also review the actions of its employees, as the company may incur copyright infringement liability for employee activities such as the loading of unlicensed software onto the company's network or the unauthorized photocopying of materials. The company should clarify employee policies prohibiting such practices, if necessary.

The audit team should identify all trademarks being used by the company. It should evaluate unregistered marks to determine whether the company should register those marks. The audit team should determine whether third parties are infringing upon the company's trademarks or whether the company is infringing, even inadvertently, upon the marks of others.

Finally, the audit team should scrutinize employment agreements to make certain that the company is using and enforcing appropriate invention assignment agreements, noncompete covenants, and NDAs (see Exhibit 3.5).

EXHIBIT 3.5

SUMMARY OF U.S. INTELLECTUAL PROPERTY LAW

	Asset Protected	Source of Protection	How Asset Created	Length of Protection	Standards	What Constitutes Infringement
Patent – Utility	Machines, industrial processes, compositions of matter, and articles of manufacture	Patent Act (federal statute)	By US PTO upon application of inventor	Application filed after 6/8/95: 20 years from date of application Earlier applications: 17 years from date of issuance	Must be novel, nonobvious, and useful	Manufacture, use, offer for sale, or sale in U.S.; or use or sale in U.S. if invention made outside U.S by patented process
Patent – Design	Ornamental designs for manufactured articles	Patent Act (federal statute)	By US PTO upon application of inventor	14 years from date of issuance	Must be novel, nonobvious, and ornamental	Designs appear same to ordinary observer
Copyright	Expressions of ideas fixed in tangible form	Copyright Act (federal statute)	Automatically upon creation of a work of authorship	For Post-1978 works: Life of author plus 70 yrs.; works for hire: at least 95 yrs. after publication or 120 yrs. after creation	Must be original work of authorship fixed in tangible medium	Copying
Trade Secret	Business and commercial information	State statute or common law	Automatically upon investment of time and money, provided security measures are taken	As long as information remains confidential	Must be confidential and commercially valuable information	Misappropriation
Trademark	Identifying words, names, symbols, or devices	Lanham Act (federal statute); common law	1) Through adoption and use or 2) Through intent to use plus registration	As long as mark is used commercially	Must identify and distinguish goods or services	Confusion, mistake, or deception likely

3.1 Trade Secrets—Required Elements

Electro-Craft Corp. v. Controlled Motion, Inc., 332 N.W.2d 890 (Minn. 1983)

Respondent Electro-Craft Corporation ("ECC") sued appellants Controlled Motion, Inc. ("CMI") and CMI's president, John Mahoney (a former employee of ECC), for misappropriation of trade secrets. ECC claimed that CMI and Mahoney improperly copied the designs of ECC's electric motors. The district court found that misappropriation had occurred. . . . We reverse the order for judgment based on misappropriation.

THE PRODUCTS

* * * *

* * * John Mahoney is the president and founder of CMI. Mahoney was formerly national sales manager for ECC. While at ECC, Mahoney established ECC's customer relationships with Storage Technology Company and IBM, customers for the motors involved in this lawsuit.

ECC and CMI manufacture high performance D.C. motors, called "servo" motors . . . . These motors are useful for such high technology applications as computer disc drives and printers and industrial robots. In this action ECC claims misappropriation of trade secrets with respect to one moving coil motor and one brushless motor.

* * * *

According to Mr. Edward Kelen, president of ECC, ECC was one of only three significant producers of small moving coil motors in 1980. Also, although seven companies produced brushless servo motors, ECC had more than half of the private sector domestic market. * * * Moreover, Kelen testified that the total brushless motor market is growing rapidly; in five years (from 1980) it was projected to grow from two million dollars to fifty or sixty million dollars per year.

* * * *

About 1974, Robert Schept, Engineering Manager at ECC, designed the successful ECC 1600 moving coil motor. Schept studied various other motors on the market to try to determine the best combination of dimensions for the motor. Subsequently, Schept designed the 1125 moving coil motor for ECC. * * * Schept testified that it took four to five months to design prototypes for the 1125 and around a year to start actual production. * * * The model involved in this case is the 1125-03-003, designed for a specific computer system built by Storage Technology Co.

ECC's brushless motors are of more recent origin than that of ECC's moving coil motors. Nonetheless, a long

process of trial and error, using new developments in technology and costing approximately two million dollars, has been involved in the development of workable models. ECC initially sent prototypes to several customers. Finally ECC worked with IBM to develop a prototype motor for an IBM printer. This model was a very successful enterprise for ECC, since ECC became the only known source of motors for the IBM project. For around five years, ECC has also been working with Ford Motor Company on a new application for ECC brushless motors. * * * ECC has produced several prototypes for Ford and hopes to begin production in 1983.

THE EVENTS

In May of 1980, John Mahoney, while employed by ECC, began to explore the possibility of starting his own business. Mahoney already had many contacts in the business, including people at Storage Technology and at IBM—ECC customers for the ECC 1125-03-003 and brushless motors. Mahoney had also guided development of the IBM project and the Ford project. On June 12, 1980, Mahoney hired an attorney as counsel for the proposed new business, and counsel helped Mahoney prepare a prospectus which was circulated to prospective investors. Mahoney met with several prospective investors during June and July but apparently received no investments before August 1980.

The prospectus indicates that Mahoney proposed to compete with ECC in its IBM and Ford applications. Mahoney planned to complete prototypes for IBM in twelve weeks and obtain IBM approval in another week. Mahoney planned to try eventually to enter the market for the Ford systems. The prospectus projected revenues in the third month from sales of the prototype brushless motors but projected no research and development expenses for the first few months.

In June of 1980 Mahoney met with several of his fellow ECC employees about their joining the new business. On August 6, 1980, Mahoney resigned from ECC. Mahoney and ECC's president, Kelen, met briefly regarding trade secrets and Mahoney told Kelen not to worry. On September 16, 1980, four other ECC employees resigned in order to work for Mahoney's company, now called CMI. The four employees were:

(1) William Craighill, a mechanical engineer who worked with ECC on the design of the ECC 1125 and the brushless motor for IBM. * * *

(2) James West, previously Quality Assurance Manager at ECC for electric motors. West was acting plant manager at one ECC plant for six months.

(3) William Anderson, who had worked for ECC as a technician for about two years. * * *

(4) Lynn Klatt, Buyer's Assistant at ECC, who was familiar with ECC's vendors and with the parts used in ECC's motors.

All of these employees, as well as Mahoney, had signed confidentiality agreements[1] when hired by ECC. None of these agreements, however, included a non-competition clause. When these four employees left ECC, ECC's management conducted exit interviews. The employees were asked to sign acknowledgment forms which outlined the areas that ECC considered confidential; only Anderson signed the acknowledgment.

On September 17, 1980, Mahoney met with some IBM representatives about developing a CMI motor as an alternative to the ECC brushless motor. The IBM representatives said that IBM would not deal with such a new company and that Mahoney should try again in 6 months.

On September 18, Mahoney traveled to Colorado to meet representatives of Storage Technology Co. [who at the time used ECC and Honeywell motors]. * * * Mahoney delivered prototypes of a CMI motor, the CMI 440, to Storage Technology on December 15, 1980; the motor was finally approved on March 1, 1981.

The evidence is conflicting as to how CMI produced the 440. The CMI 440 is almost identical in dimensions and tolerances to the ECC 1125-03-003. William Craighill, the former ECC employee who developed the CMI 440, testified that he did not copy, nor even possess, an ECC 1125 motor when he designed the CMI 440. Craighill claimed that he used only a similar Honeywell motor, the Storage Technology specifications, and his own calculations to develop the CMI 440. On the other hand, circumstantial evidence pointed to the conclusion that CMI employees copied the ECC 1125. The similarity of the motors suggests copying, although the motors are not absolutely identical. Furthermore, the manufacturing processes, adhesives, and other

materials are nearly identical. Expert testimony differed as to how long it should have taken CMI to "reverse engineer" the motor by taking apart an ECC 1125, measuring the parts and testing the material, and putting the plans together. A CMI expert estimated that it should have taken two to three months to develop a prototype motor. An expert for ECC estimated that the process would take at least six months to a year. Kelen estimated it would take a year.

CMI has, by reverse engineering, also been able to market remanufactured ECC and Honeywell motors. In remanufacturing, CMI replaces the parts to a broken motor, rebuilds it and rewarrants it.

THE ACTION

On September 26, 1980, about six weeks after Mahoney's resignation, ECC sued CMI and Mahoney . . . claiming that CMI misappropriated ECC's trade secrets. * * *

A trial was held before Judge Arthur, [who] . . . found that CMI had misappropriated ECC's trade secrets and enjoined CMI from producing or selling any "brushless or low inertia electric motor or tachometer" with dimensions within 10% of the dimensions of ECC's 1125 motor or ECC's brushless motor produced for IBM. The injunction was to be in effect for 12 months after the expiration of the last stay of execution of the order. The court also awarded ECC $50.00 in exemplary damages (but no compensatory damages) for each offending motor sold.

* * * *

THE ISSUES

* * * We must affirm the final order if we can ascertain that (1) ECC has protectable trade secrets . . .; (2) that ECC's trade secrets, if they exist, have been misappropriated by CMI; and (3) that the relief granted in the final order was appropriate. * * *

A. *Trade Secret Status*

The Uniform Trade Secrets Act, Minn. Stat. §§ 325C.01–325C.08 allows the protection of certain types of information through an action for misappropriation. Misappropriation is defined as improper acquisition, disclosure, or use of a "trade secret." Without a proven trade secret there can be no action for misappropriation, even if defendants' actions were wrongful.

1. * * * *

2. In order to determine the existence of trade secrets, we must first determine what trade secrets are claimed by ECC and what trade secrets were found by the district court. * * *

---

[1] The agreements were part of the employment agreements, reading in part as follows:

FOURTH—Employee shall not directly or indirectly disclose or use at any time, either during or subsequent to the said employment, any secret or confidential information, knowledge, or data of Employer (whether or not obtained, acquired or developed by Employee) unless he shall first secure the written consent of Employer. Upon termination of his employment Employee shall turn over to Employer all notes, memoranda, notebooks, drawings or other documents made, compiled by or delivered to him concerning any product, apparatus or process manufactured, used or developed or investigated by Employer during the period of his employment; it being agreed that the same and all information contained therein are at all times the property of the Employer.

* * * *

With respect to the moving coil motors, ECC claims that the dimensions, tolerances, adhesives, and manufacturing processes of the ECC 1125-03-003 motor are trade secrets. The thrust of ECC's claim is that the specific combination of details and processes for the 1125 motor is a trade secret, and the evidence of the specific features of the 1125 motor sold to Storage Technology adequately identifies the information which ECC claims constitutes a trade secret. * * *

3. In determining whether ECC has proven the existence of a trade secret in the 1125 motor, we look to the common law and the Uniform Trade Secrets Act, Minn. Stat. §§325C.01–325C.08. * * *

* * * *

[Under] Minn. Stat. § 325C.01, subd. 5 (1982):

"Trade secret" means *information*, including a formula, pattern, compilation, program, device, method, technique, or process, that:

(i) derives *independent economic value*, actual or potential, *from not being generally known to, and not being readily ascertainable by proper means by, other persons* who can obtain economic value from its disclosure or use, *and*

(ii) is the subject of *efforts that are reasonable under the circumstances to maintain its secrecy.*

Applying the statutory test, we hold that . . . ECC has not met its burden of proving the existence of any trade secrets. Therefore, we must reverse the district court's order . . . . * * *

(a) *Not generally known, readily ascertainable.* The trial court found the information regarding the ECC 1125-03-003 to be secret. * * * First, the trial court found . . . that CMI could not *readily* (i.e. quickly) reverse engineer a motor with exactly the same dimensions, tolerances, and materials as the ECC 1125-03-003. * * * Reverse engineering time is certainly a factor in determining whether information is readily ascertainable. The complexity and detail of dimensional data also bears on its ascertainability.

Second, the district court found that the exact combination of features of the 1125-03-003 is unique, even though none of the processes or features are unique in the industry and the 1125-03-003 is not the only way to achieve the required performance. Novelty is not a requirement for trade secrets to the same extent as for patentability. On the other hand, some novelty is required; mere variations on widely used processes cannot be trade secrets. * * * In the present case the exact combination of features of the 1125-03-003 could be characterized as a unique solution to the needs of one customer in the industry.

* * * *

(b) *Independent economic value from secrecy.* This statutory element carries forward the common law requirement of competitive advantage. * * *

The statute requires that a trade secret "[derive] independent economic value . . . from not being generally known . . . and not being readily ascertainable . . . ." This does not mean, as CMI contends, that the owner of the trade secret must be the only one in the market. Several developers of the same information, for example, may have trade secret rights in that information. If an outsider would obtain a valuable share of the market by gaining certain information, then that information may be a trade secret if it is not known or readily ascertainable.

* * * That ECC expended time and money between 1966 and 1975 in the development of the 1125 motor and its predecessors does not support a finding of competitive advantage unless, under the present state of the art, a prospective competitor could not produce a comparable motor without a similar expenditure of time and money. The trial court found, however, that such time and money *would* be required of a prospective competitor today . . . . The ECC 1125, therefore, did provide ECC with economic value from its secrecy, as the statute requires—value that ECC would lose if any prospective competitor could enter the market (cutting into ECC's market share) without a substantial development expense.

(c) *Reasonable efforts to maintain secrecy.* It is this element upon which ECC's claim founders. The district court found that, even though ECC had no "meaningful security provisions," ECC showed an *intention* to keep its data and processes secret. This finding does not bear upon the statutory requirement that ECC use "efforts that are reasonable under the circumstances to maintain . . . secrecy." * * *

This element of trade secret law does not require maintenance of absolute secrecy; only partial or qualified secrecy has been required under the common law. * * * [However,] the employer cannot complain of the employee's use of information if the employer has never treated the information as secret.

It is this aspect of trade secret law which truly sets it apart from the other two means through which employers can protect information—patents, and employment contracts containing a non-competition clause. The latter two remedies depend on only a single act by the employer. Trade secret protection, on the other hand, depends upon a continuing course of conduct by the employer, a course of conduct which creates a confidential relationship. This relationship, in turn, creates a reciprocal duty in the employee to treat the information as confidential insofar as the employer has so treated it . . . .

[W]e hold that ECC did not meet its burden of proving that it used reasonable efforts to maintain secrecy as to the ECC 1125-03-003. We acknowledge that ECC took minimal precautions in screening its Handbook and publications for confidential information and by requiring some of its employees to sign a confidentiality agreement, but these were not enough.

First, ECC's physical security measures did not demonstrate any effort to maintain secrecy. By "security" we mean the protection of information from discovery by outsiders. Security was lax in this case. For example, the main plant had a few guarded entrances, but seven unlocked entrances existed without signs warning of limited access. Employees were at one time required to wear badges, but that system was abandoned by the time of the events giving rise to this case. * * * Discarded drawings and plans for motors were simply thrown away, not destroyed. Documents such as motor drawings were not kept in a central or locked location, although some design notebooks were kept locked.

The relaxed security by itself, however, does not preclude a finding of reasonable efforts by ECC to maintain secrecy. Other evidence did not indicate that industrial espionage is a major problem in the servo motor industry. Therefore, "security" measures may not have been needed, and the trial court could have found trade secrets if ECC had taken other reasonable measures to preserve secrecy.

However, ECC's "confidentiality" procedures were also fatally lax . . . . By "confidentiality" in this case we mean the procedures by which the employer signals to its employees and to others that certain information is secret and should not be disclosed. Confidentiality was important in this case, for testimony demonstrated that employees in the servo motor business frequently leave their employers in order to produce similar or identical devices for new employers. ECC has hired many employees from other corporations manufacturing similar products. If ECC wanted to prevent its employees from doing the same thing, it had an obligation to inform its employees that certain information was secret.

ECC's efforts were especially inadequate because of the nonintuitive nature of ECC's claimed secrets here. The dimensions, etc., of ECC's motors are not trade secrets in as obvious a way as a "secret formula" might be. ECC should have let its employees know in no uncertain terms that those features were secret.

Instead, ECC treated its information as if it were not secret. None of its technical documents were marked "Confidential", and drawings, dimensions and parts were sent to customers and vendors without special marking. Employee access to documents was not restricted. ECC never issued a policy statement outlining what it considered to be secret. Many informal tours were given to vendors and customers without warnings as to confidential information. Further, two plants each had an "open house" at which the public was invited to observe manufacturing processes.

* * * *

The exit interviews also did not constitute reasonable efforts to maintain secrecy. The exit interviews, a procedure initiated by ECC only after it became clear that the employees were about to work for Mahoney, occurred a mere ten days before the commencement of this litigation. These "interviews" were little more than attempts to intimidate or threaten employees, to prevent them from leaving ECC and engaging in legitimate competition using their skill and expertise. Such thinly-veiled threats certainly do not qualify as ongoing efforts to maintain the secrecy of specific information. The law of trade secrets does not condone, and this court certainly will not reward, ECC's conduct.

In summary, ECC has not met its burden of proof in establishing the existence of any trade secrets. The evidence does not show that ECC was ever consistent in treating the information here as secret.

B. *Misappropriation*

Since no trade secrets existed to be misappropriated, we technically need not reach the issue of whether misappropriation occurred. However, as we noted above, the concept of trade secret status and the concept of misappropriation should not be artificially separated. In the present case the concepts are so interrelated that we feel compelled to discuss the tort of misappropriation. Misappropriation involves the acquisition, disclosure, or use of a trade secret through improper means. "Improper means" are defined as

> [T]heft, bribery, misrepresentation, breach or inducement of breach of a duty to maintain secrecy, or espionage through electronic or other means.

Minn. Stat. § 325C.01, subd. 2. In the employer-employee context of the present case, ECC was required to show some duty on the part of the employee not to disclose the information. ECC claims that the employees' duty here arose from the employee agreements and from a confidential employer-employee relationship.

However, a common law duty of confidentiality arises out of the employer-employee relationship only as to information which the employer has treated as secret:

> [T]he employee is entitled to fair notice of the confidential nature of the relationship and what material is to be kept confidential.

Therefore, in the present case, ECC's failure to make reasonable efforts to maintain secrecy, discussed above, was fatal to its claim of a confidential relationship. The employees were never put on notice of any duty of confidentiality. The employee agreements do not help ECC's claim for the same reason—ECC never treated specific information as secret. Therefore, the agreements' vague language prohibiting the employee from taking "secrets" did not create a duty of confidentiality in the employee, and no misappropriation occurred.

Questions for Discussion for Case 3.1

1. Why did the court find that ECC did not have a protectable trade secret?

2. Why did the court find that CMI had not engaged in misappropriation?

3. What steps should ECC have taken in order to protect its alleged trade secrets?

We reverse the district court's final order of October 19, 1981.

* * * *

4. Although the court found CMI's actions to be legal, do you think that those actions were ethical? Why, or why not?

3.2 Trade Secrets—Inevitable Disclosure Rule
PepsiCo, Inc. v. Redmond, 54 F.3d 1262 (7th Cir. 1995)

Plaintiff PepsiCo, Inc., sought a preliminary injunction against defendants William Redmond and the Quaker Oats Company to prevent Redmond, a former PepsiCo employee, from divulging PepsiCo trade secrets and confidential information in his new job with Quaker and from assuming any duties with Quaker relating to beverage pricing, marketing, and distribution. The district court agreed with PepsiCo and granted the injunction. We now affirm that decision.

I.

The facts of this case lay against a backdrop of fierce beverage-industry competition between Quaker and Pepsico, especially in "sports drinks" and "new age drinks." Quaker's sports drink, "Gatorade," is the dominant brand in its market niche. PepsiCo introduced its Gatorade rival, "All Sport," in March and April of 1994, but sales of All Sport lag far behind those of Gatorade. Quaker also has the lead in the new-age-drink category. * * * PepsiCo's products have about half of Snapple's market share. [Quaker owns the Snapple brand.] Both companies see 1995 as an important year for their products: PepsiCo has developed extensive plans to increase its market presence, while Quaker is trying to solidify its lead by integrating Gatorade and Snapple distribution. Meanwhile, PepsiCo and Quaker each face strong competition from Coca Cola Co., which has its own sports drink, "PowerAde," and which introduced its own Snapple-rival, "Fruitopia," in 1994, as well as from independent beverage producers.

William Redmond, Jr., worked for PepsiCo in its PepsiCola North America division ("PCNA") from 1984 to 1994. Redmond became the General Manager of the Northern California Business Unit in June, 1993, and was promoted one year later to General Manager of the business unit covering all of California, a unit having annual revenues of more than 500 million dollars and representing twenty percent of PCNA's profit for all of the United States.

Redmond's relatively high-level position at PCNA gave him access to inside information and trade secrets. Redmond, like other PepsiCo management employees, had signed a confidentiality agreement with PepsiCo. That agreement stated in relevant part that he

> would not disclose at any time, to anyone other than officers or employees of [PepsiCo], or make use of, confidential information relating to the business of [PepsiCo] . . . obtained while in the employ of [PepsiCo], which shall not be generally known or available to the public or recognized as standard practices.

Donald Uzzi, who had left PepsiCo in the beginning of 1994 to become the head of Quaker's Gatorade division, began courting Redmond for Quaker in May, 1994. Redmond met in Chicago with Quaker officers in August, 1994, and on October 20, 1994, Quaker, through Uzzi, offered Redmond the position of Vice President—On Premise Sales for Gatorade. Redmond did not then accept the offer but continued to negotiate for more money. Throughout this time, Redmond kept his dealings with Quaker secret from his employers at PCNA.

On November 8, 1994, Uzzi extended Redmond a written offer for the position of Vice President—Field Operations for Gatorade and Redmond accepted. Later that same day, Redmond called William Bensyl, the Senior Vice President of Human Resources for PCNA, and told him that he had an offer from Quaker to become the Chief Operating Officer of the combined Gatorade and Snapple company but had not yet accepted it. Redmond also asked whether he should, in light of the offer, carry out his plans to make calls upon certain PCNA customers. Bensyl told Redmond to make the visits.

Redmond also misstated his situation to a number of his PCNA colleagues, including Craig Weatherup, PCNA's President and Chief Executive Officer, and Brenda Barnes, PCNA's Chief Operating Officer and Redmond's immediate superior. As with Bensyl, Redmond told them that he had been offered the position of Chief Operating Officer at Gatorade and that he was leaning "60/40" in favor of accepting the new position.

On November 10, 1994, Redmond met with Barnes and told her that he had decided to accept the Quaker offer and was resigning from PCNA. Barnes immediately took Redmond to Bensyl, who told Redmond that PepsiCo was considering legal action against him.

True to its word, PepsiCo filed this diversity suit on November 16, 1994, seeking a temporary restraining order to enjoin Redmond from assuming his duties at Quaker and to prevent him from disclosing trade secrets or confidential information to his new employer. * * *

From November 23, 1994, to December 1, 1994, the district court conducted a preliminary injunction hearing on the same matter. At the hearing, PepsiCo offered evidence of a number of trade secrets and confidential information it desired protected and to which Redmond was privy. First, it identified PCNA's "Strategic Plan," an annually revised document that contains PCNA's plans to compete, its financial goals, and its strategies for manufacturing, production, marketing, packaging, and distribution for the coming three years. Strategic Plans are developed by Weatherup and his staff with input from PCNA's general managers, including Redmond, and are considered highly confidential. The Strategic Plan derives much of its value from the fact that it is secret and competitors cannot anticipate PCNA's next moves. PCNA managers received the most recent Strategic Plan at a meeting in July 1994, a meeting Redmond attended. * * *

Second, PepsiCo pointed to PCNA's Annual Operating Plan ("AOP") as a trade secret. The AOP is a national plan for a given year and guides PCNA's financial goals, marketing plans, promotional event calendars, growth expectations, and operational changes in that year. The AOP, which is implemented by PCNA unit General Managers, including Redmond, contains specific information regarding all PCNA initiatives for the forthcoming year. The AOP bears a label that reads "Private and Confidential—Do Not Reproduce" and is considered highly confidential by PCNA managers.

In particular, the AOP contains important and sensitive information about "pricing architecture"—how PCNA prices its products in the marketplace. Pricing architecture covers both a national pricing approach and specific price points for given areas. Pricing architecture also encompasses PCNA's objectives for All Sport and its new age drinks with reference to trade channels, package sizes and other characteristics of both the products and the customers at which the products are aimed. Additionally, PCNA's pricing architecture outlines PCNA's customer development agreements. These agreements between PCNA and retailers provide for the retailer's participation in certain merchandising activities for PCNA products. As with other information contained in the AOP, pricing architecture is highly confidential and would be extremely valuable to a competitor. Knowing PCNA's pricing architecture would allow a competitor to anticipate PCNA's pricing moves and underbid PCNA strategically whenever and wherever the competitor so desired. PepsiCo introduced evidence that Redmond had detailed knowledge of PCNA's pricing architecture and that he was aware of and had been involved in preparing PCNA's customer development agreements with PCNA's California and California-based national customers. Indeed, PepsiCo showed that Redmond, as the General Manager for California, would have been responsible for implementing the pricing architecture guidelines for his business unit.

PepsiCo also showed that Redmond had intimate knowledge of PCNA "attack plans" for specific markets. Pursuant to these plans, PCNA dedicates extra funds to supporting its brands against other brands in selected markets. To use a hypothetical example, PCNA might budget an additional $500,000 to spend in Chicago at a particular time to help All Sport close its market gap with Gatorade. Testimony and documents demonstrated Redmond's awareness of these plans and his participation in drafting some of them.

Finally, PepsiCo offered evidence of PCNA trade secrets regarding innovations in its selling and delivery systems. Under this plan, PCNA is testing a new delivery system that could give PCNA an advantage over its competitors in negotiations with retailers over shelf space and merchandising. Redmond has knowledge of this secret because PCNA, which has invested over a million dollars in developing the system during the past two years, is testing the pilot program in California.

Having shown Redmond's intimate knowledge of PCNA's plans for 1995, PepsiCo argued that Redmond would inevitably disclose that information to Quaker in his new position, at which he would have substantial input as to Gatorade and Snapple pricing, costs, margins, distribution systems, products, packaging and marketing, and could give Quaker an unfair advantage in its upcoming skirmishes with PepsiCo. Redmond and Quaker countered that Redmond's primary initial duties at Quaker as Vice President—Field Operations would be to integrate Gatorade and Snapple distribution and then to manage that distribution as well as the promotion, marketing and sales of these products. Redmond asserted that the integration would be conducted according to a pre-existing plan and that his special knowledge of PCNA strategies would be irrelevant. This irrelevance would derive not only from the fact that Redmond would be implementing pre-existing plans but also from the fact that PCNA and Quaker distribute their products in entirely different ways: PCNA's distribution system is vertically integrated (i.e., PCNA owns the system) and delivers its product directly to retailers, while Quaker ships its product to wholesalers and customer warehouses and relies on independent distributors. The defendants also pointed out that Redmond had signed a confidentiality agreement with Quaker preventing him from disclosing "any confidential information belonging to others," as well as the Quaker Code of Ethics, which prohibits employees from engaging in "illegal or improper acts to acquire a competitor's trade secrets." Redmond additionally promised at the hearing that should he be faced with a situation at Quaker that might involve the use or disclosure of PCNA information, he would seek advice from Quaker's in-house counsel and would refrain from making the decision.

PepsiCo responded to the defendants' representations by pointing out that the evidence did not show that Redmond would simply be implementing a business plan already in place. On the contrary, as of November, 1994, the plan to integrate Gatorade and Snapple distribution consisted of a single distributorship agreement and a two-page "contract terms summary." Such a basic plan would not lend itself to widespread application among the over 300 independent Snapple distributors. Since the integration process would likely face resistance from Snapple distributors and Quaker had no scheme to deal with this probability, Redmond, as the person in charge of the integration, would likely have a great deal of influence on the process. PepsiCo further argued that Snapple's 1995 marketing and promotion plans had not necessarily been completed prior to Redmond's joining Quaker, that Uzzi disagreed with portions of the Snapple plans, and that the plans were open to reevaluation. Uzzi testified that the plan for integrating Gatorade and

Snapple distribution is something that would happen in the future. Redmond would therefore likely have input in remaking these plans, and if he did, he would inevitably be making decisions with PCNA's strategic plans and 1995 AOP in mind. Moreover, PepsiCo continued, diverging testimony made it difficult to know exactly what Redmond would be doing at Quaker. Redmond described his job as "managing the entire sales effort of Gatorade at the field level, possibly including strategic planning," and at least at one point considered his job to be equivalent to that of a Chief Operating Officer. Uzzi, on the other hand, characterized Redmond's position as "primarily and initially to restructure and integrate our—the distribution systems for Snapple and for Gatorade, as per our distribution plan" and then to "execute marketing, promotion, and sales plans in the marketplace." Uzzi also denied having given Redmond detailed information about any business plans, while Redmond described such a plan in depth in an affidavit and said that he received the information from Uzzi. Thus, PepsiCo asserted, Redmond would have a high position in the Gatorade hierarchy, and PCNA trade secrets and confidential information would necessarily influence his decisions. Even if Redmond could somehow refrain from relying on this information, as he promised he would, his actions in leaving PCNA, Uzzi's actions in hiring Redmond, and the varying testimony regarding Redmond's new responsibilities, made Redmond's assurances to PepsiCo less than comforting.

On December 15, 1994, the district court issued an order enjoining Redmond from assuming his position at Quaker through May, 1995, and permanently from using or disclosing any PCNA trade secrets or confidential information. * * * The court . . . found that Redmond's new job posed a clear threat of misappropriation of trade secrets and confidential information that could be enjoined under Illinois statutory and common law. The court also emphasized Redmond's lack of forthrightness both in his activities before accepting his job with Quaker and in his testimony as factors leading the court to believe the threat of misappropriation was real. This appeal followed.

II.

* * * *

A.

The Illinois Trade Secrets Act ("ITSA"), which governs the trade secret issues in this case, provides that a court may enjoin the "actual or threatened misappropriation" of a trade secret. A party seeking an injunction must therefore prove both the existence of a trade secret and the misappropriation. * * * [The parties agreed that trade secrets existed.]

The question of threatened or inevitable misappropriation in this case lies at the heart of a basic tension in trade secret law. Trade secret law serves to protect "standards of commercial morality" and "encourage[ ] invention and innovation" while maintaining "the public interest in having free and open competition in the manufacture and sale of unpatented goods." Yet that same law should not prevent workers from pursuing their livelihoods when they leave their current positions. * * *

This tension is particularly exacerbated when a plaintiff sues to prevent not the actual misappropriation of trade secrets but the mere threat that it will occur. * * *

* * * [A] plaintiff may prove a claim of trade secret misappropriation by demonstrating that defendant's new employment will inevitably lead him to rely on the plaintiff's trade secrets. * * * Questions remain, however, as to what constitutes inevitable misappropriation . . . .

PepsiCo presented substantial evidence at the preliminary injunction hearing that Redmond possessed extensive and intimate knowledge about PCNA's strategic goals for 1995 in sports drinks and new age drinks. The district court concluded on the basis of that presentation that unless Redmond possessed an uncanny ability to compartmentalize information, he would necessarily be making decisions about Gatorade and Snapple by relying on his knowledge of PCNA trade secrets. It is not the "general skills and knowledge acquired during his tenure with" PepsiCo that PepsiCo seeks to keep from falling into Quaker's hands, but rather "the particularized plans or processes developed by [PCNA] and disclosed to him while the employer-employee relationship existed, which are unknown to others in the industry and which give the employer an advantage over his competitors." * * *

Admittedly, PepsiCo has not brought a traditional trade secret case, in which a former employee has knowledge of a special manufacturing process or customer list and can give a competitor an unfair advantage by transferring the technology or customers to that competitor. PepsiCo has not contended that Quaker has stolen the All Sport formula or its list of distributors. Rather PepsiCo has asserted that Redmond cannot help but rely on PCNA trade secrets as he help plots Gatorade and Snapple's new course, and that these secrets will enable Quaker to achieve a substantial advantage by knowing exactly how PCNA will price, distribute, and market its sports drinks and new age drinks and being able to respond strategically. This type of trade secret problem may arise less often, but it nevertheless falls within the realm of trade secret protection under the present circumstances.

Quaker and Redmond assert that they have not and do not intend to use whatever confidential information Redmond has by virtue of his former employment. They point out that Redmond has already signed an agreement with Quaker not to disclose any trade secrets or confidential information gleaned from his earlier employment. They also note with regard to distribution systems that even if Quaker wanted to steal information about PCNA's distribution plans, they would be completely useless in attempting to integrate the Gatorade and Snapple beverage lines.

The defendants' arguments fall somewhat short of the mark. Again, the danger of misappropriation in the present case is not that Quaker threatens to use PCNA's secrets to create distribution systems or coopt PCNA's advertising and marketing ideas. Rather, PepsiCo believes that Quaker, unfairly armed with knowledge of PCNA's plans, will be able to anticipate its distribution, packaging, pricing, and marketing moves. Redmond and Quaker even concede that Redmond might be faced with a decision that could be influenced by certain confidential information that he obtained while at PepsiCo. In other words, PepsiCo finds itself in the position of a coach, one of whose players has left, playbook in hand, to join the opposing team before the big game. * * *

The district court also concluded from the evidence that Uzzi's actions in hiring Redmond and Redmond's actions in pursuing and accepting his new job demonstrated a lack of candor on their part and proof of their willingness to misuse PCNA trade secrets, findings Quaker and Redmond vigorously challenge. The court expressly found that

> Redmond's lack of forthrightness on some occasions, and out and out lies on others, in the period between the time he accepted the position with defendant Quaker and when he informed plaintiff that he had accepted that position leads the court to conclude that defendant Redmond could not be trusted to act with the necessary sensitivity and good faith under the circumstances in which the only practical verification that he was not using plaintiff's secrets would be defendant Redmond's word to that effect.

The facts of the case do not ineluctably dictate the district court's conclusion. Redmond's ambiguous behavior toward his PepsiCo superiors might have been nothing more than an attempt to gain leverage in employment negotiations. The discrepancy between Redmond's and Uzzi's comprehension of what Redmond's job would entail may well have been a simple misunderstanding. The court also pointed out that Quaker, through Uzzi, seemed to express an unnatural interest in hiring PCNA employees: all three of the people interviewed for the position Redmond ultimately accepted worked at PCNA. Uzzi may well have focused on recruiting PCNA employees because he knew they were good and not because of their confidential knowledge. Nonetheless, the district court, after listening to the witnesses, determined otherwise. That conclusion was not an abuse of discretion.

* * * *

Thus, when we couple the demonstrated inevitability that Redmond would rely on PCNA trade secrets in his new job at Quaker with the district court's reluctance to believe that Redmond would refrain from disclosing these secrets in his new position (or that Quaker would ensure Redmond did not disclose them), we conclude that the district court correctly decided that PepsiCo demonstrated a likelihood of success on its statutory claim of trade secret misappropriation.

* * * *

For the foregoing reasons, we affirm the district court's order enjoining Redmond from assuming his responsibilities at Quaker through May, 1995, and preventing him forever from disclosing PCNA trade secrets and confidential information.

AFFIRMED.

Questions for Discussion for Case 3.2

1. Why is this state law claim being heard in federal court?

2. Do you believe that Redmond's actions were ethical? Why, or why not?

3. Why does the court find that an injunction is proper here?

4. What could Redmond have done differently to have avoided this litigation?

3.3 Covenants Not to Compete

Ticor Title Insurance Co. v. Cohen, **1998 U.S. Dist. LEXIS 9700 (S.D. N.Y. 1998)**

Plaintiffs seek an injunction to prevent their former employee, the defendant, from working for a competitor for six months. * * * For the reasons that follow, a permanent injunction is granted.

FACTUAL BACKGROUND

The plaintiffs, Ticor Title Insurance Co. and Chicago Title Insurance Co. (hereinafter collectively "Ticor"), are affiliated companies that sell title insurance nationwide.

The defendant, Kenneth Cohen, began working for Ticor in 1981 as a sales account manager. By 1987, he was a senior vice president. In 1995, Ticor and Cohen entered into an employment contract. It provided that if Cohen quit prior to a certain date, he promised not to work in the title insurance business in the state of New York for six months. The contract promised Cohen a minimum annual pay of $600,000—a base salary of $200,000 plus commissions. He received more than $1.1 million in 1997 from Ticor. Cohen negotiated the contract with the advice of counsel, who was actively involved in the negotiations.

On April 20, 1998, TitleServ, a direct competitor of Ticor, offered to employ Cohen. Obviously anticipating that Ticor would attempt to enforce the covenant not to compete, TitleServe agreed to indemnify Cohen by paying him his salary during the six-month period even if he was enjoined from working. Cohen sent Ticor a letter on April 21, 1998, notifying it of his resignation effective May 21, 1998. He agreed to begin with TitleServ on May 27, 1998.

DISCUSSION

Courts in New York enforce covenants not to compete made between an employee and employer only if reasonable. They must be reasonable in time and geographic area, and they will be enforced only to the extent necessary to protect the employer's legitimate interests. There are two main reasons for such scrutiny. First, such covenants can restrict a person's ability to earn a livelihood. Second, they restrain competition in the market.

Thus, even once a court finds a covenant reasonable in time and area, it will still not enforce it unless it falls into one of two categories. The first is where enforcement of the covenant is needed to prevent the ex-employee from disclosing or using trade secrets or confidential customer information. The second is where an employee's services are special, unique, or extraordinary.

* * * Recently, . . . the Supreme Court in New York County enforced a covenant not to compete based upon the unique services category. *Maltby v. Harlow Meyer Savage, Inc.*, 166 Misc. 2d 481, 633 N.Y.S.2d 926 (Sup. Ct. 1995), *aff'd*, 223 A.D.2d 516, 637 N.Y.S.2d 110 (1996). The facts in *Maltby* are so similar to those here that the Court is compelled to follow *Maltby* in granting an injunction.

In *Maltby*, the departing employees were brokers each earning more than $100,000 per year plus "substantial bonuses." Each signed the employment contracts incorporating the noncompete clause after consulting with counsel. The agreements recited that each employee possessed unique skills. Each employee promised not to compete for six months after termination of employment in or near New York, Los Angeles, Toronto, London, or continental Europe. In exchange, the employer promised to continue to pay the employee her base salary during the "Restriction Period." The employees quit and began working for the employer's direct competitor.

The employees argued the restrictive covenant would interfere with their livelihood because during the six-month restrictive period they would lose the long-term relationships they had developed with clients. The employer argued that the employees developed these relationships during the course of their employment, largely at the employer's expense and encouragement through entertaining these clients.

The court found the covenant reasonable, noting that the trend in New York law has been to enforce such covenants when not unduly burdensome. At the threshold, the court found the geographic area and time restrictions to be reasonable. The court also found the covenant was justified because it fell within the "unique services" category. "Plaintiffs all have unique relationships with the customers with whom they have been dealing that have been developed while employed at HMS and, partially, at HMS expense." The court also found that a trader's absence from the market for six months "does not render him unemployable within the industry or substantially impair his ability to earn a living." * * *

The facts here are in most respects identical to those in *Maltby*. All of Cohen's clients came to him during his time at Ticor; about half he developed and about half he inherited from another, departing salesman. Cohen developed these new relationships, and maintained his old ones, at least in part by way of a substantial entertainment expense account provided by Ticor. In 1997, Cohen spent about $170,000 entertaining clients and in the first five months of 1998 he spent about $138,000.

Cohen's relationships with his clients were important, and made his services special, beyond that of an ordinary salesman, for several reasons. First, the cost and terms of title insurance in New York is fixed by law. Therefore, bases of competition other than price and terms, including personal relationships, loom larger than in some other industries. Second, the identity of the potential clients, New York law firms with real estate practices, is well known throughout the industry. Maintaining current clients and wooing new ones from an established group becomes important. Therefore, as in *Maltby*, Cohen's relationships with his clients are special enough to fall into this unique services category.

Also as in *Maltby*, Cohen here negotiated this contract with the help of a lawyer, and there is no dispute that he was aware of and agreed to the noncompete clause. The testimony also demonstrated that the very purpose of the covenant was to protect Ticor against exactly this sort of departure, one in which the employee takes with him both the clients he developed while at Ticor and their pending transactions. * * * Absent a contract, an employee may, of course, continue to do business with his clients after he has left his old job. Here, however, Cohen promised that he would not compete for six months, and when that covenant relates to unique services as they do here, it is enforceable.

Cohen argues that his absence from the business for six months would irreparably harm him because he would lose his relationships. However, the evidence overall does not support this contention. The transactions at issue typically last several months, but not usually years. Therefore, most of the transactions Cohen does not participate in during his hiatus will have been completed by his return in any case. In addition, it defies common sense that clients he had developed over numerous years would forget him in six months; Cohen provided no evidence to support the contention that lawyers at major real estate law firms are so fickle. On the other hand, without this six-month period Ticor would likely lose clients. * * *

Defendant, in an effort to distinguish *Maltby*, has placed great emphasis on a single difference. In *Maltby*, the employees were paid their base salary of at least $100,000 per year during the restriction period, whereas Mr. Cohen will receive nothing during his six month hiatus. One of the two main dangers of non-compete provisions is that they prevent a person from earning a livelihood. However, Mr. Cohen earned $1 million per year from Ticor, which should be enough to sustain Mr. Cohen until he can return to work. After all, part of that $1 million was in exchange for his promise not to compete for six months after termination.

* * * *

* * * There is nothing unfair in holding Mr. Cohen to be bound to the contract term that he accepted in return for highly lucrative employment. The non-compete provision served to protect legitimate business interests of Ticor. Ticor invested substantial sums to enable its sales staff to develop the type of relationships with clients that would generate substantial business. It would be unfair to allow a competitor to appropriate Ticor's investment by simply hiring away its employees. The restrictive covenant is narrowly drawn to protect Ticor's legitimate business interest. It gives Ticor no more than an even playing field in the title insurance business.

* * * *

CONCLUSION

For the foregoing reasons, the defendant, Kenneth Cohen, is enjoined from working in the Title Insurance business as defined in the Employment Contract within the state of New York and from appropriating Ticor's corporate opportunities to engage in the business of Title Insurance with its current or prospective customers for a period of six months, commencing June 10, 1998.

SO ORDERED.

Questions for Discussion for Case 3.3

1. Why does this court feel "compelled" to apply the reasoning of *Maltby?*

2. What factors led this court to conclude that the noncompete agreement was enforceable?

3. How does the court balance the interests of the employee and employer in deciding whether to issue an injunction?

3.4 Nondisclosure Agreements

Thomas & Betts Corp. v. Panduit Corp., 1999 U.S. Dist. LEXIS 6298 (E.D. April 8, 1999)

Plaintiffs Thomas & Betts Corporation and Thomas & Betts Holdings, Inc., brought this ten-count action against its former employee, Jeffrey Wimmer, and his current employer, Panduit Corporation. Plaintiffs claim, among other things, that Mr. Wimmer has breached the nondisclosure agreement he signed while a Thomas & Betts employee. * * *

BACKGROUND

Jeffrey Wimmer (Wimmer) began his employment with Thomas & Betts (T&B) on April 12, 1965. Fifteen years later, on May 6, 1980, while still employed by the company, he signed an agreement titled "Employment Priority Information & Invention Agreement" (the confidentiality and non-disclosure agreement). Twelve years later, on January 2, 1992, T&B merged with another electronics company, American Electric Co. Shortly thereafter, on February 6, 1992, Wimmer's employment was terminated. In June 1992, Wimmer accepted employment with Panduit, another company engaged in the selling of electrical component parts. In 1993 T&B brought this suit.

ANALYSIS

[P]laintiffs allege that Wimmer breached his agreement with T&B by taking two computers, several floppy disks, documents and records containing confidential information about the conduct of T&B's business, and by disclosing this information to Panduit and its employees. * * * Wimmer first argues that the non-disclosure agreement he signed while employed by T&B is nonenforceable because it is too broad and consequently unreasonable, unenforceable and void. The agreement provides in part:

* * * *

5. Since the work for which I am employed and upon which I shall be engaged will include Company knowledge and information of a private, confidential, or secret nature, I shall not, during the period of my employment by the Company or after termination of such employment without regard for the causes thereof, except as required by the Company, publish, disclose, or make use of, or authorize anyone else to publish, disclose, or otherwise make use of any such knowledge or information, of a confidential nature to and the secret property of the Company or other information which in any way relates to the business of the Company or the design, construction, manufacture or sale of the Company's products or services.

In Illinois, employers unquestionably have the right to protect confidential and secret information through the use of employee non-disclosure agreements. The enforceability of such covenants is "dependent on whether, given the particular facts of the case, the restraints imposed thereby are reasonably necessary for the protection of the employer's business from unfair or improper competition." * * *

We now turn to the question of how broad a restriction may be with respect to the content of the information protected. It is clear that a provision barring the employee from disclosing any information about the company to any person forever is overly broad. Similarly, any provision that would render an employee virtually unemployable in his field of expertise or another field, or restrict his ability to earn a living in that field throughout an entire geographic area, is too broad and will be considered void as against public policy. On the other hand, non-disclosure agreements that itemize the particular types of information covered are generally permitted. However, an agreement prohibiting the disclosure of any and all information about innumerable specific categories of information will not be enforced. By contrast, contracts that seek to protect only confidential information and trade secrets are more likely to find favorable treatment from the courts.

The non-disclosure agreement in this case falls somewhere between these two extremes. * * *

* * * [In the fifth paragraph of the agreement], Wimmer agrees to not disclose or use both "information of a private, confidential, or secret nature," and any "other information which in any way relates to the business of [T&B] or the design, construction, manufacture or sale of the company's products." The case is a close one, but we conclude that the portion restricting the disclosure of confidential material is sufficiently specific . . . . Although the contract does not specifically lay out the categories of confidential information precluded by disclosure, the documents produced by T&B indicate that the company had a specific procedure for designating material "confidential" and repeatedly reminded its employees that material so designated was not for release to anyone outside of the company. For example, in a memorandum dated October 31, 1991, that accompanied the Corporate Policies Manual, James Hay, then T&B's general counsel, defined three different confidentiality classifications used by the company. Documents with no restrictions could be widely circulated to other employees. Documents marked "T&B Confidential" or "Vitramon Confidential" could be used by the recipient for a designated task and distributed to other employees who also needed the document for a specific purpose, but could not be passed to anyone else. Documents marked "Personal and Confidential" were for the eyes of the recipient alone. Moreover, the defendants have not shown that Wimmer's inability to disclose T&B's confidential material would prevent him from working for Panduit or any other company. Thus, we find that any information so marked,[2] or any other information T&B can prove that it made a serious and demonstrable effort to keep secret and confidential, is subject to the non-disclosure provision which we find sufficiently specific to be valid and enforceable at law.

* * * *

The second portion of paragraph five, that prohibiting the release of any "other information which in any way relates to the business of [T&B] or the design, construction, manufacture, or sale of the company's products," gives us greater pause. * * * It gives Wimmer little guidance about what material is included, is not limited to confidential or secret material, and by its terms would include information that might otherwise be available to the public. Its unlimited language renders it overly broad and unenforceable. * * *

All is not lost for T&B, however. In Illinois, if a court determines that a non-disclosure agreement is overly broad, it may modify the contract so that it comports with the law or sever the unenforceable provisions. * * * If, . . . portions of the agreement can be redacted without affecting the agreement as a whole, and if the agreement was generally fair and does not appear designed to be oppressive, the court has the discretion to strike the offending part and retain the rest.

We think the latter is the case here. Removing the last clause of paragraph five does not affect the validity of the prohibition against the disclosure of confidential information contained in the preceding clause. Moreover, contrary to defendants' assertions, we do not see evidence that T&B acted in bad faith in executing the contract, or required Wimmer to undertake job responsibilities that would force him to violate his obligation to keep confidential information secret. Accordingly, we strike from the agreement the clause beginning with "or other information which" and ending at the end of paragraph five. The remainder of the agreement will be enforced pursuant to its terms.

* * * *

CONCLUSION

For the reasons stated above, defendants' motion for summary judgment is granted in part and denied in part.

---

[2] Obviously, any information marked "confidential" that T&B did not actually attempt to keep that way will not be covered by the non-disclosure agreement.

Questions for Discussion for Case 3.4

1. What part of this NDA is unenforceable, and why? How might the employer have rewritten this NDA to have avoided this problem of unenforceable language?

2. What effect does the unenforceable language have on the validity of the rest of this NDA?

DISCUSSION QUESTIONS

1. Stutz Motor Car of America, Inc., an automotive manufacturer, received a patent in 1986 for a "shock absorbing air bladder" for use in footwear. However, Stutz never manufactured a shoe with this innovation. In 1989, Reebok began producing the PUMP, a very successful line of athletic shoes with an air bladder different in design but similar in concept to Stutz's invention. Because Reebok's design was not sufficiently similar to Stutz's to constitute patent infringement, Stutz sued instead for trade secret misappropriation. Should Stutz prevail on its misappropriation claim? Why, or why not? *Stutz Motor Car of America, Inc. v. Reebok International, Ltd.*, 113 F.3d 1258 (Fed. Cir. 1997)

2. Palm Beach Blood Bank, a nonprofit organization, hired several employees who used to work for American Red Cross, another nonprofit organization. One of the employees took Red Cross's blood donor list to Palm Beach, and Palm Beach used the list to recruit donors. Many of the Red Cross donors advertised that they were Red Cross donors, and the Red Cross posted the donor list on a computer bulletin board. How should the court rule on Red Cross's claim of trade secret misappropriation? Are there any policy arguments against enjoining the use of the donor list by Palm Beach Blood Bank? *American Red Cross v. Palm Beach Blood Bank, Inc.*, 143 F.3d 1407 (11th Cir. 1998)

3. Christopher M. developed a secret recipe for fudge. His fudge is very popular, and he closely guarded his secret by keeping only one copy of his recipe and storing it at a location outside his factory. Additionally, he divided up the manufacturing process and allowed his employees to see only the part of the manufacturing process in which they were engaged. However, one employee, Hennon, gained Christopher M.'s confidence and through the course of his year-long employment was able to see most of the manufacturing process. Hennon also learned the ingredients of the fudge recipe because he had the sensitive task of typing the ingredients into a computer system. Hennon left Christopher M.'s factory, taking several confidential computer disks and documents. He then produced his own line of fudge with similar, if not identical, properties. Hennon had not signed a confidentiality agreement. Christopher M. sued for trade secret misappropriation. Should he win? Why, or why not? *Christopher M.'s Hand Poured Fudge, Inc. v. Hennon*, 699 A.2d 1272 (Penn. Super. Ct. 1997)

4. Northeast Coating Technologies, Inc. (NCT), is a start-up corporation in the business of "vacuum coating" metals. To lure potential investors, NCT created a prospectus that included its business plan, including its orders from suppliers. This prospectus was widely distributed and contained a disclaimer that the information in the prospectus was confidential. Several copies of the prospectus ended up in the hands of potential competitors of NCT. The competitors used the business plan in NCT's prospectus to plan strategies to prevent NCT from successfully competing with them. If NCT sues for misappropriation of the "trade secret" material in the prospectus, should it win? Why, or why not? *Northeast Coating Technologies, Inc. v. Vacuum Metallurgical Co., Ltd.*, 684 A.2d 1322 (Me. 1996)

5. I Can't Believe It's Yogurt (ICBIY), a frozen yogurt company, required potential franchise owners to attend "Yogurt University"—a training program designed to teach owners how to run an ICBIY store. In addition to teaching potential owners how to mix and freeze yogurt, Yogurt University also teaches potential owners how to structure the store. ICBIY claimed that particular floor tile patterns move customers through the store more efficiently. In addition, ICBIY used certain paint color schemes, logos, menu boards, windows, and common business marketing practices to distinguish an ICBIY store and improve business results. ICBIY considered these store designs and practices to be trade secrets. However, ICBIY did not require potential owners to sign a confidentiality agreement until the individual signed a franchise agreement. Gunn attended Yogurt University, became a franchisee, and set up his store. Irregular yogurt shipments from ICBIY and late payments of franchise royalties by Gunn created a rocky relationship between the parties, however. Eventually, ICBIY canceled Gunn's franchise. Gunn continued to use ICBIY's logo and trade secret information in his business. ICBIY sued Gunn for trade secret misappropriation. Should ICBIY win? Why, or why not? *I Can't Believe It's Yogurt v. Gunn*, 1997-2 Trade Cas. (CCH) 71879 (D. Colo. 1997)

6. Carolina Chemical Equipment Company (CCEC), a company involved in sales of chemical and cleaning supplies, required its employees to sign a covenant not to divulge trade secrets. The covenant provided in part:

> [Employee] agrees not to divulge any trade secrets of the Corporation. Trade secrets means any knowledge or information concerning any aspect of the business of the Corporation which could, if divulged to a direct or indirect competitor,

adversely affect the business of the Corporation, its prospects or competitive position. Seller shall not use for his own benefit any trade secret of the Corporation in any manner whatsoever.

Muckenfuss signed the agreement when he was hired. He also signed a covenant not to compete for one year after leaving the company. After several years of employment, Muckenfuss left CCEC. He did not work in the chemical industry for over one year, but eventually he went to work for one of CCEC's direct competitors, where he sold products to some of CCEC's customers that were essentially the same products that CCEC sells. CCEC sued Muckenfuss for trade secret misappropriation. Should CCEC win? Why, or why not? *Carolina Chemical Equipment Co. v. Muckenfuss*, 471 S.E.2d 721 (S.C. App. 1996)

7. Cybex, a division of Lumex, is the largest manufacturer of exercise and weight training equipment. Pursuant to its normal business practices, Cybex required its worldwide head of marketing, Greg Highsmith, to sign a noncompete agreement. The agreement provided that Highsmith was not to work for a competitor for six months after leaving Cybex. However, the agreement allowed Highsmith to work for a competitor whose business was "diversified," provided Highsmith worked on product lines that were not in direct competition with Cybex products. The agreement also provided for six months of compensation and employee benefits in the event that Highsmith left Cybex and the terms of the restrictive covenant prevented him from obtaining another job during the noncompete period.

Highsmith left Cybex and went to work for Life Fitness, a competitor, within a matter of days. Although Life Fitness sent several letters to Cybex, assuring Cybex that it had not and would not induce Highsmith to violate his duty of confidentiality, Cybex filed suit for a preliminary injunction prohibiting Highsmith from working for Cybex for a period of six months. Should the court grant the injunction? Why, or why not? *Lumex, Inc. v. Highsmith*, 919 F. Supp. 624 (E.D.N.Y. 1996)

8. Phillips manufactures "single-pole" tree stands—a device that allows hunters to sit perched in a tree to await deer or other game. A group of investors expressed interest in buying the venture, and purchase negotiations began. In the course of the process, Phillips sent the investors information about his company, including prospecti and videotapes. Phillips also gave the investors a tour of the plant and showed them firsthand the manufacturing process. Although Phillips

had never patented his tree stand, he knew that without knowledge of the manufacturing process, building the stand would be cost-prohibitive. During the course of the negotiations, the investors bought several samples of the stand. Although Phillips wanted to sell the company and tried to make several concessions in the purchase price, the investors were unable to obtain financing, and the deal fell through. Sometime later, a company founded by the investors began to manufacture nearly identical "single pole" tree stands. Phillips sued for trade secret misappropriation, but the investors claimed that they had lawfully reverse-engineered the tree stand. Which party should win and why? What type of remedy, if any, should the court award? *Phillips v. Frey*, 20 F.3d 623 (5th Cir. 1994)

9. In 1983, J & K Ventures, Inc., signed a 10-year franchise agreement with American Speedy Printing Centers with plans to establish a printing center in Tampa, Florida. In addition, J & K Ventures signed a nondisclosure agreement that also contained a covenant not to compete within a 10-mile radius of the franchise. J & K Ventures operated the Tampa printing center until July 1993, as agreed in the franchise agreement. Toward the end of the 10 years, however, the relationship between the two companies deteriorated, so J & K Ventures decided to allow the franchise agreement to expire without renewal. No other Speedy franchises operated within the 10-mile radius agreed to under the franchise agreement. Following the expiration of the agreement, J & K Ventures maintained a printing center at the same location and telephone number under the name Express Printing Center. Express Printing Center expanded its basis of operations and offered more expanded services under the new name.

Speedy brought suit for violation of the noncompetition covenants. J & K Ventures asserted that Florida Statute § 542.33(2)(b) makes the noncompete agreement void. Section 542.33(2)(b) states: "[Licensee] may agree with the licensor to refrain from carrying on or engaging in a similar business and from soliciting old customers within a reasonable limited time and area, so long as the licensor . . . continues to carry on a like business therein." How should the court rule on Speedy's claim, and why? *American Speedy Printing Ctrs. v. J & K Ventures*, 1997 U.S. Dist. LEXIS 13269 (E.D. Mich. July 15, 1997)

10. Communication Technical Systems, Inc. (CTS), began providing computer programming services for Gateway 2000, Inc. (Gateway), in July 1994. Rickey Densmore, a programmer for CTS, worked on the

Gateway account in Chicago for two weeks before transferring to Gateway's South Dakota production site. In September, Gateway entered into an agreement with CTS called the "Agreement Not to Recruit," in which Gateway promised not to hire, solicit, or recruit any CTS employee while CTS was working on the Gateway account, nor for a one-year period after CTS ceased working on the account.

In December, Densmore expressed his dissatisfaction with CTS to a Gateway employee, who suggested that Densmore talk to Gateway's legal counsel about possibly being hired by Gateway. Densmore talked to Gateway counsel, but they refused to discuss the possibility, citing the "Agreement Not to Recruit." On December 15, Gateway gave CTS proper 30-day notice of its intent to terminate CTS's services. On January 20, 1995, Densmore resigned from CTS to begin his own consulting firm, Corinium Consulting, Inc. Densmore contacted Gateway, stating that he was now free to program for Gateway and was free of any restrictions imposed by the "Agreement Not to Recruit." Three days later, Gateway hired Densmore's firm for a five-month programming job. Section 53-9-8 of the South Dakota statutes states: "Every contract restraining exercise of a lawful profession, trade, or business is void to that extent . . . ." Section 53-9-11 provides an important exception, however, that allows noncompete covenants. CTS brought this suit against Densmore for breach of the "Agreement Not to Recruit." How should the court rule on CTS's claim, and why? *Communication Tech. Sys. v. Densmore*, 583 N.W.2d 125 (S.D. 1998)

11. Donald Ray Dawson was an initial 49 percent investor and promoter in Temps Plus, Inc., a Blytheville, Arkansas, temporary-employment agency. In May 1996, Temps Plus bought all of Dawson's 49 percent interest in the corporation for $95,000. As part of the transaction, Dawson agreed "that for a period of five (5) years from the execution of this Agreement, he will not directly or indirectly, whether as an owner, partner, or employee, compete with Temps Plus, Inc., within a radius of seventy (70) miles from Blytheville, Arkansas." Dawson later did not recall reading that portion of the agreement.

Approximately one year later, Dawson, along with his brother, hired two employees away from Temps Plus in anticipation of creating the Dawson Employment Agency. Two weeks later, Dawson and his brother formed their own employment agency corporation, Steve Dawson Employment Services, Inc. (SDES), in Blytheville. In April, Temps Plus sued

SDES for breach of the noncompete agreement. How should the court rule, and why? *Dawson v. Temps Plus, Inc.*, 987 S.W.2d 722 (Ark. 1999)

12. In the mid-1980s, Deere & Co. became interested in installing a draft sensor device on its tractors, which would regulate the depth and mechanical forces on the plow. In June 1986, Deere entered an agreement with Revere Transducers to install the "Gozinta" strain gauge on Deere tractors to serve as draft sensor devices. Revere and Deere worked jointly on the project, taking four years to develop the product. Revere specially hired two men, engineer Francis Delfino and product manager Greg Eckart, in late summer 1986 to work on the "Gozinta" project. Both signed nondisclosure agreements, in which they agreed not to disclose any inventions or discoveries either during their employment or for a one-year period after their employment. No other formal agreements existed between Revere and the two men who, in all other respects, were at-will employees.

The "Gozinta" turned out to be a failure. Deere believed the defect resulted from Revere's decision to use poor-quality knurls without consulting Deere. Due to significant downsizing, Delfino and Eckart were told that they would be released in 1989, at about the same time Eckart was independently studying the viability of a sensor that could be welded to the plow instead of pressed—an idea previously rejected by Revere. Delfino and Eckart spoke with Deere about the possibility of starting a new company to supply Deere with the welded sensors, and Deere stressed that, if they proceeded, it was vital that they took no documents, models, or engineering drawings from Revere.

In March 1989, Delfino and Eckart started their own company—D & E Sensor Manufacturing, Inc. D & E formally proposed its idea for the new sensor—the "weldzinta"—to Deere and received a purchase order from Deere for $172,900. Revere sued Deere for tortious interference of contract. Deere argued that the suit should be dismissed on the grounds that the nondisclosure contract is not enforceable. Under Iowa law, restrictive covenants are evaluated under a three-pronged test: (1) is the restriction reasonably necessary for the protection of the employer's business?; (2) is the restriction unreasonably restrictive of the employee's rights?; and (3) is the restriction prejudicial to the public interest? Is the NDA enforceable? Why, or why not? *Revere Transducers v. Deere & Co.*, 595 N.W.2d 751 (Iowa 1999)

CHAPTER 4

Legal Issues Relating to Pricing and Distribution of Products and Services

Antitrust Law

"Antitrust laws . . . are the Magna Carta of free enterprise. They are as important to the preservation of economic freedom and our free-enterprise system as the Bill of Rights is to the protection of our fundamental personal freedoms."[1]

---

[1] United States v. Topco Assoc., Inc., 405 U.S. 596, 610 (1972).

Overview

The purpose of the federal antitrust laws is to control private economic power by promoting and encouraging competition. Competition is valued highly within our legal and economic system for a variety of reasons. Competition is believed to: (1) keep costs and prices lower and quality higher, (2) encourage product and service innovation and efficient allocation of resources, and (3) give consumers broader choices in the marketplace. In short, competition maximizes consumer welfare. In a truly competitive market, firms try to attract consumers by cutting prices and increasing the quality of the products or services they offer.

At the same time, however, antitrust law recognizes that efficiency concerns also come into play. While we want to foster competition, we do not want to inhibit innovation; nor do we want to restrict economies of scale or economies of scope. We also want to promote lower transaction costs and improved quality. Thus, antitrust law must balance a number of competing concerns.

Federal antitrust law is founded on four statutes: the Sherman Act, the Clayton Act, the Robinson-Patman Act, and the Federal Trade Commission (FTC) Act. Each of these federal statutes is designed to reach certain types of anticompetitive behavior. The language of these statutes is often extremely broad and general. As a result, much of antitrust law has been formed through the court opinions that interpret and apply these statutes. As you can imagine, the courts' analyses of the antitrust statutes are heavily influenced by economic concepts such as supply and demand curves, cost, revenue, and market structure.

Antitrust litigation is usually lengthy and complex and the outcomes highly fact-specific. While monopolization that results from unfair business practices is illegal, monopolization that results from business skill is not. Identical pricing that results from collusion among competitors is illegal, but identical pricing that results from intense marketplace competition is not. Cooperation among competitors that results in reduced competition that harms consumers is illegal, but cooperation that increases competition and benefits consumers (such as industry standardization for component parts) is not.

In addition, as the U.S. Supreme Court has emphasized, antitrust laws are designed for the "protection of competition, not competitors."[2] Harm to an individual firm by a competitor, even if motivated by pure malice, does not lead to an antitrust violation unless the competitive process itself is harmed (e.g., through an increase in market prices or decrease in market production).

It is important that management and marketing personnel alike understand the basics of antitrust law and the parameters of legal and illegal competitive behaviors. Managers are often surprised to discover that actions that they regard as sound competitive strategies not only are illegal but subject the firm to substantial fines and/or civil damages. In addition, the individual managers involved in antitrust violations may personally face similar fines and/or damages and may even be imprisoned in certain instances. Thus, knowledge of the antitrust laws is important not only to the firm but also to the manager personally.[3]

Companies should work closely with their corporate or outside legal counsel to develop a compliance program that informs officers, managers, salespersons, and other employees about their responsibilities under the antitrust laws. A well-designed

---

[2] Brown Shoe Co. v. United States, 370 U.S. 294, 320 (1962).
[3] For general information on antitrust law, including a list of links to other antitrust-related Web sites, see http://www.antitrustinstitute.org

compliance program outlines proper policies and procedures to minimize the likelihood of antitrust violations and provides for periodic monitoring of firm activities and individual actions to ensure that the firm is meeting its compliance goals.

Common Law Contracts in Restraint of Trade

Although antitrust law is primarily statutory today, it is important to realize that the common law also prohibits contracts in restraint of trade and monopolistic combinations, at least in some instances. Because the common law rules arise under state law, they can vary from state to state.

The Restatement (Second) of Contracts states that a contract is in "restraint of trade" if "its performance would limit competition in any business or restrict a promisor in the exercise of a gainful occupation."[4] Contracts in restraint of trade are not automatically illegal; rather, *unreasonable* contracts in restraint of trade are unenforceable on public policy grounds. A contract is considered unreasonable if: (1) the restraint is greater than that needed to protect the promisee's legitimate interest, or (2) the restraint poses an undue hardship on the promisor or excessive likely injury to the public.[5]

Generally, the types of enforceable restraints include covenants not to compete by the seller of a business, by a partner in a business, or by an employee. Covenants not to compete in the context of employment agreements are discussed in greater detail in Chapter 3.

The enforceability of a covenant not to compete that relates to the activities of a business depends upon the factual circumstances in which the covenant was used. "Naked" covenants (e.g., covenants that are not incidental to the sale of a business) are generally considered unreasonable. Thus, an agreement between *Company A* and *Company B* in which *A* pays *B* not to compete with *A*'s business would generally be unenforceable. Similarly, if *A* and *B* were already competitors, an agreement between *A* and *B* that *B* would cease competing with *A* would also be unenforceable. If *A* were to purchase *B*'s business, on the other hand, *A* and *B* could legally enter into a covenant prohibiting *B* from competing with *A*.

Covenants not to compete that are ancillary to the sale of a business are limited to a reasonable geographic location and to a reasonable time duration, often measured by the length of time that the buyer carries on the business. A reasonable geographic location is usually defined as the territory in which the business was previously conducted plus the area in which it may be conducted in the reasonably foreseeable future. Where the covenant is broader in geographic scope or time duration than is necessary and legal, many courts use the "blue pencil rule" to rewrite the covenant to limit it to whatever geographic or time restraint the court deems is appropriate under the circumstances. Other courts simply hold that the covenant is invalid and refuse to enforce it at all.

The usual remedy given for the violation of a valid covenant is *injunctive relief* that prevents the promisor from violating the covenant. *Monetary damages* may be available in certain instances, though this remedy often does not fully compensate the promisee for the injury it suffered as a result of the violation.

The federal antitrust statutes are by far the most important source of law regarding illegal restraints of trade and monopolistic combinations today. The remainder of this chapter focuses on these statutes.

[4] Restatement (Second) of Contracts § 186.
[5] *Id.* § 188.

The Federal Antitrust Statutes

The federal antitrust statutes arose out of dissatisfaction with the common law's treatment of contracts in restraint of trade. In particular, the common law was seen as providing inadequate protection to injured parties. While the common law protects the parties to the covenants at issue, it does not generally provide relief or remedies to the public or to third parties harmed by such restraints of trade. In addition, the common law is not uniform but, rather, varies from state to state, making it difficult for interstate businesses to monitor their behavior.

As the United States moved from an agrarian economy to an industrialized one in the late nineteenth century, there were increasing abuses within the economy by large industrial interests, such as railroads and manufacturers. Many of these large businesses engaged in predatory practices, driving out small competitors and then restricting output and increasing prices. In particular, there was great societal concern about "trusts" (i.e., combinations of companies that were able to control entire industries so as to increase monopoly power). The Standard Oil Trust created by John D. Rockefeller was one of the first such trusts, but trusts were created in other industries as well, such as the whiskey, sugar, and lead industries. Ultimately, Congress responded to these concerns by passing a series of antitrust acts. The major statutes are described here briefly, followed by a discussion of specific types of illegal anticompetitive behaviors.

THE SHERMAN ACT

The first federal legislation passed to address the economic abuses by large trusts was the Sherman Act of 1890.[6] This Act created a new, federal cause of action to reach two types of anticompetitive behavior: (1) restraints of trade and (2) illegal monopolization or attempts to monopolize. As the Supreme Court explained:

> The Sherman Act was designed to be a comprehensive charter of economic liberty aimed at preserving free trade and unfettered competition as the rule of trade. It rests on the premise that the unrestrained interaction of competitive forces will yield the best allocation of our economic resources, the lowest prices, the highest quality and the greatest material progress, while at the same time providing an environment conducive to the preservation of our democratic political and social institutions.[7]

Section 1 of the Sherman Act prohibits contracts, combinations, and conspiracies that restrain trade; Section 2 prohibits certain monopolies and attempts to monopolize. The language of these two provisions is surprisingly brief:

Section 1: Every contract, combination in the form of trust or otherwise, or conspiracy, in restraint of trade or commerce among the several States, or with foreign nations, is hereby declared to be illegal . . . .

Section 2: Every person who shall monopolize, or attempt to monopolize, or combine or conspire with any other person or persons, to monopolize any part of the trade or commerce among the several States, or with foreign nations, shall be deemed guilty of a felony . . . .

---

[6] 15 U.S.C. § 107 *et seq.*
[7] Northern Pacific Railway Co. v. United States, 356 U.S. 1, 4 (1958).

The courts have provided many layers of interpretation to this short and seemingly simple language. For example, Section 1 of the Sherman Act prohibits "every contract, combination . . . or conspiracy in restraint of trade." Taken literally, the language of Section 1 would make illegal virtually all business contracts, even those that benefit society and the economy. Every contract between a buyer and a seller, no matter how simple in content or short in duration, limits the market activity of those two parties in the subject matter of that contract and for the duration of the transaction. Thus, in 1911, the Supreme Court determined that only agreements that *unreasonably* restrain trade are unlawful.[8]

As discussed below, certain restraints of trade are deemed automatically unreasonable and so are illegal *per se*, while others are adjudged on a case-by-case basis under the "rule of reason." In addition, it is not necessarily illegal for a company to have or to try to obtain a monopoly position; rather, Section 2 only prohibits maintenance or acquisition of a monopoly position through unfair or abusive methods.

Note as well that Section 1 requires the actions of two or more persons acting together, as it is impossible for an individual to contract, combine, or conspire alone. Much antitrust litigation centers on whether concerted action has occurred. While the Supreme Court has ruled that an agreement between a parent corporation and its wholly owned subsidiary does not violate Section 1[9] (because the two entities are viewed as a single firm), it is unclear whether agreements between a parent and a less-than-wholly owned subsidiary may potentially violate Section 1.

Section 2 of the Sherman Act applies both to persons acting in concert and to those acting alone. In practice, Section 2 is generally applied to firms acting alone to illegally gain monopoly power, while combinations and conspiracies to monopolize are usually prosecuted under Section 1.

THE CLAYTON ACT

In 1914, Congress enacted the Clayton Act[10] in response to perceived shortcomings in the Sherman Act. Unlike the Sherman Act, which is essentially remedial in nature (in that it reaches actual anticompetitive behavior), the Clayton Act is preventative in nature, as it is directed toward trying to prevent anticompetitive behavior "in its incipiency" and before it harms the public.

The Clayton Act addresses behavior such as certain exclusionary practices, mergers, and interlocking directorates. In particular, Section 3 of the Clayton Act provides:

> **Section 3:** [I]t shall be unlawful for any person in commerce . . . to lease or make a sale or contract for the sale of goods for use, consumption, or resale within the United States . . . on the condition, agreement or understanding that the lessee or purchaser thereof shall not use or deal in the goods . . . of a competitor . . . of the lessor or seller, where the effect of such lease, sale . . . or such condition, agreement, or understanding may be to substantially lessen competition or tend to create a monopoly in any line of commerce.

Section 3 thus prohibits activities such as tie-in sales, exclusive dealing arrangements, and requirements contracts in which the effect of such arrangements "may be to substantially lessen competition or tend to create a monopoly." Note, however, that this section applies only to the sale of goods, not to the sale of services.

[8] *See* Standard Oil Co. of New Jersey v. United States, 221 U.S. 1 (1911).
[9] Copperwald Corp. v. Independence Tube Corp., 467 U.S. 752 (1984).
[10] 15 U.S.C. §§ 12–27; 44.

Among its other provisions, Section 4 of the Clayton Act allows private parties injured by violations of the Sherman or Clayton Act to sue for treble damages. This provision thus encourages private parties to bring actions to enforce these antitrust statutes. Section 7 prohibits mergers or acquisitions in which the effect "may be substantially to lessen competition, or tend to create a monopoly" in "any line of commerce in any section of the country." Section 8 prohibits certain interlocking directorates but has not been vigorously enforced. These latter two provisions are less important to the marketing function and so are not discussed further.

THE FEDERAL TRADE COMMISSION ACT

The Federal Trade Commission (FTC) Act[11] was also enacted in 1914. The FTC Act created the Federal Trade Commission (FTC), a consumer protection agency, and gave that agency broad powers to enforce certain antitrust acts.[12] Under a 1938 amendment to the FTC Act, the FTC has two mandates: (1) to protect the marketplace from unfair methods of competition and (2) to prevent unfair or deceptive practices that harm consumers. Specifically, Section 5(a)(1) of the FTC Act provides:

> **Section 5(a)(1):** Unfair methods of competition in or affecting competition and unfair or deceptive acts or practices in or affecting commerce, are hereby declared unlawful.

Section 5 authorizes the FTC to take preemptive action against potential violations of the Sherman or Clayton Acts—"to stop in their incipiency acts and practices which, when full blown, would violate" those statutes.[13] Section 5 also reaches unfair or deceptive conduct that is outside the provisions of the antitrust statutes.

Only the FTC may sue to enforce Section 5; private individuals have no cause of action under this statute. The FTC also has authority, concurrent with the Department of Justice (DOJ)[14] and private parties, to enforce the Clayton Act and the Robinson-Patman Act. In addition, while the FTC does not have express authority to enforce the Sherman Act, the courts have read Section 5 of the FTC Act broadly enough that violation of Section 1 or Section 2 of the Sherman Act generally is also a violation of Section 5; thus, the FTC may issue cease-and-desist orders against violations of the Sherman Act.

This chapter focuses on the provisions of the FTC Act directed toward anti-competitive behavior. The "unfair or deceptive acts or practices" provisions of the FTC Act and the consumer protection role of the FTC are discussed further in Chapter 7 and Chapter 8.

THE ROBINSON-PATMAN ACT

The Robinson-Patman Act of 1936[15] is actually an amendment of Section 2 of the Clayton Act. The Robinson-Patman Act was designed to address very specific types of pricing behaviors, particularly those behaviors that favored chain stores, which were in their infancy at the time of the statute's enactment, over traditional small

---

[11] 15 U.S.C. §§ 41–57a.
[12] The FTC's home page, which contains information about its antitrust enforcement activities, is found at http://www.ftc.gov
[13] FTC v. Motion Picture Advertising Service Co., 344 U.S. 392, 394 (1953).
[14] The Department of Justice's home page, which contains information about its antitrust enforcement activities, is found at http://www.usdoj.gov
[15] 15 U.S.C. § 13.

independent retailers. Thus, this federal statute makes it illegal to give, induce, or receive discriminatory prices or supplementary services, except under certain specified circumstances, where the effect of the discrimination would be to substantially lessen competition or tend to create a monopoly.

There are three main sections to the Robinson-Patman Act. Section 2 (there is no Section 1) addresses price discrimination. In particular, Section 2(a) provides:

> **Section 2(a) Price Discrimination.** [I]t shall be unlawful for any person engaged in commerce, in the course of such commerce, either directly or indirectly, to discriminate in price between different purchasers of commodities of like grade and quality, where either or any of the purchases involved in such discrimination are in commerce, where such commodities are sold for use, consumption, or resale, within the United States . . . and where the effect of such discrimination may be substantially to lessen competition or tend to create a monopoly in any line of commerce, or to injure, destroy, or prevent competition with any person who either grants or knowingly receives the benefit of such discrimination, or with customers of either of them . . . .

Section 3 establishes criminal liability for certain types of discriminatory pricing. (This provision is seldom enforced.) Section 4 exempts cooperative associations and nonprofit institutions from the Act.

Thus, Section 2 of the Robinson-Patman Act would prohibit a lumber supplier from offering a discount (including allowances for advertisements, counter displays, and samples) to a large home improvement chain unless a "proportional discount" is given to independent lumber supply stores as well. (What is "proportional" is a question of fact to be decided on a case-by-case basis.) Similarly, a firm cannot offer a *wholesaler's* or *broker's discount* to a customer who is not a true wholesaler, even if that customer is a large retail chain that purchases more than the average wholesaler. Cooperative advertising and other promotional assistance are permitted, provided such assistance is offered to all customers on proportionally equal terms.

THE ANTITRUST STATUTES GENERALLY

The antitrust statutes apply to most parties involved in business transactions, including corporations, partnerships, sole proprietorships, individuals, trade associations, professionals (such as doctors and lawyers), and certain activities of nonprofit organizations. Labor unions and agricultural organizations are essentially exempt from the provisions of the Sherman and Clayton Acts; and certain other industries, such as export trade associations, the insurance industry, stock exchanges, utilities, railroads, and shipping, may be exempt from specific provisions as well, at least in certain instances.

The antitrust laws are complex, and it can be difficult for a company to know whether a particular contemplated action is legal. Thus, both the DOJ and the FTC have a procedure by which a company can seek an advisory opinion on the legality of a proposed action before undertaking it. Each has also published guidelines on how the antitrust implications of specific actions or issues, such as the licensing of intellectual property, international operations, collaborations among competitors, and health care industry practices, are analyzed.[16]

While the federal antitrust statutes reach only activities that affect interstate or foreign commerce, this encompasses most U.S. business activities. The courts have

---

[16] These guidelines generally can be located on the Web sites of the FTC and the DOJ.

interpreted the interstate commerce requirement as requiring only that the business or activity, even if otherwise purely intrastate, have a substantial economic effect on interstate commerce. As the Supreme Court stated, "[i]f it is interstate commerce that feels the pinch, it does not matter how local the operation that applies the squeeze."[17]

THE RULE OF REASON VERSUS PER SE VIOLATIONS

Alleged antitrust practices are judged under one of two standards. Certain practices, such as price-fixing, are regarded as so inherently harmful to competition and consumers that they are deemed *per se* violations and are automatically illegal. In such instances, the plaintiff need only demonstrate that the prohibited practice occurred; the plaintiff need not show that the practice had an anticompetitive effect, nor may the defendant argue that the practice was in fact procompetitive. The Supreme Court described the illegal *per se* category as follows:

> [T]here are certain agreements or practices which because of their pernicious effect on competition and lack of any redeeming virtue are conclusively presumed to be unreasonable and therefore illegal without elaborate inquiry as to the precise harm they have caused or the business excuse for their use. This principle of *per se* unreasonableness not only makes the type of restraints which are proscribed by the Sherman Act more certain to the benefit of everyone concerned, but it also avoids the necessity for an incredibly complicated and prolonged economic investigation into the entire history of the industry involved, as well as related industries, in an effort to determine at large whether a particular restraint has been unreasonable—an inquiry so often wholly fruitless when undertaken.[18]

In recent years, in particular, the courts have been reluctant to label conduct as *per se* illegal and the number of activities that qualify as *per se* violations has declined. Instead, most alleged antitrust violations are examined under the *rule of reason* and are deemed illegal if the practice significantly restricts competition and has no overriding business justification. This flexible standard mandates a case-by-case determination that takes into consideration a number of factors, "including specific information about the relevant business, its condition before and after the restraint was imposed, and the restraint's history, nature, and effect."[19] In short, it requires the court to balance the anticompetitive effects of the restraint against its procompetitive effects. The sole focus under the rule of reason is the effects of the challenged action on competition; the social or political effects of the challenged action are irrelevant, no matter how beneficial they may be.

The Supreme Court has also enunciated a third—intermediate—standard, known as the "quick look" analysis. Under this analysis, certain types of activities are presumed to be anticompetitive unless the defendant shows that the activity has a procompetitive effect. If the defendant can make such a showing, the activity is judged under the rule of reason; if the defendant cannot, the conduct is illegal *per se*.

See Discussion Case 4.1.

---

[17] United States v. Women's Sportswear Manufacturers Assoc., 336 U.S. 460, 464 (1949).
[18] Northern Pacific Railway Co. v. United States, 356 U.S. 1, 5 (1958).
[19] State Oil Co. v. Khan, 522 U.S. 3, 10 (1997).

REMEDIES FOR ANTITRUST VIOLATIONS

The federal antitrust laws provide for civil or criminal actions against violators. (In some instances, both civil and criminal actions can be filed for the same conduct.) Depending upon the nature of the violation, remedies may include fines, imprisonment, money damages, injunctive relief, court-ordered restructuring of a firm, or some combination of these.

The federal antitrust laws are enforced through a variety of mechanisms. The Antitrust Division of the DOJ can bring criminal and civil enforcement actions. The Bureau of Competition of the FTC can bring civil enforcement actions (but not criminal actions). The state attorneys general can bring civil suits under the Clayton Act on behalf of injured consumers in their states. Finally, private parties can bring antitrust actions to redress injuries.

Both the government and private plaintiffs can sue for *equitable relief* for antitrust violations. Most antitrust violations result in equitable relief. The relief can take many forms, including a restraint on particular acts or conduct, compelled licensing of a patent or other intellectual property asset on a reasonable royalty basis, or the cancellation of contracts. *Preliminary injunctions* are also available to both the government and private parties against conduct that would irreparably injure the plaintiff, provided the plaintiff can show a likelihood of success on the merits and a public interest in the injunction.

Damages are also available in antitrust cases. In fact, in an effort to encourage private enforcement of the antitrust laws, Section 4 of the Clayton Act authorizes "any person . . . injured in his business or property by reason of anything in the antitrust laws" to recover treble damages, plus costs and attorneys fees.

The Clayton and the FTC Acts do not provide for *criminal sanctions*. Violations of Sections 1 and 2 of the Sherman Act, on the other hand, can be prosecuted as felonies. Individuals may be fined up to $350,000 and/or may be imprisoned for up to three years for each offense. Corporations may be fined up to $10 million for each offense.

These criminal sanctions bear real teeth. In May 2000, for example, two German pharmaceutical manufacturers (Merck KgaA and Degussa-Hals AG) and two U.S. pharmaceutical companies (Nepera, Inc., and Reilly Industries, Inc.) agreed to plead guilty and to pay criminal antitrust fines totaling $33 million for participating in two international conspiracies to suppress and eliminate competition in the vitamin industry. Two former executives of Nepara agreed to plead guilty, pay criminal fines totaling $150,000, and serve time in prison for their roles in the conspiracy.[20]

The annual amount of criminal fines obtained by the Antitrust Division has skyrocketed over the last decade (see Exhibit 4.1). In addition, the federal Amended Sentencing Guidelines, which became effective in 1991, make it substantially more likely than in the past that individuals convicted for antitrust violations will serve a prison sentence.[21]

As a practical matter, the DOJ generally seeks criminal sanctions under the Sherman Act only for *per se* violations of the statutes (discussed below) or for egregious predatory conduct. In recent years, the DOJ has particularly focused on the prosecution of international cartels that victimize American businesses and consumers. The DOJ may prosecute actions that constitute antitrust violations under other statutes as well, such as statutes that prohibit perjury, obstruction of justice,

[20] U.S. Department of Justice Press Release, May 5, 2000 (at http://www.usdoj.gov/atr).
[21] Trade Reg. Rep. (CCH) Para. 13,250, U.S. Sentencing Guidelines Part R. The guidelines are also available on-line at http://www.ussc.gov

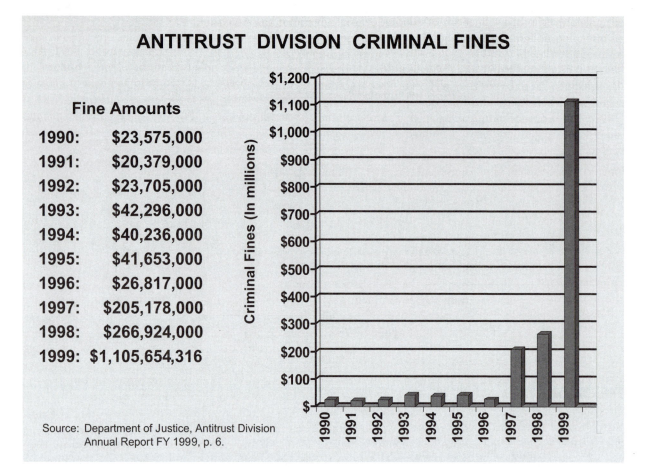

ANTITRUST DIVISION CRIMINAL FINES

Fine Amounts

1990:	$23,575,000
1991:	$20,379,000
1992:	$23,705,000
1993:	$42,296,000
1994:	$40,236,000
1995:	$41,653,000
1996:	$26,817,000
1997:	$205,178,000
1998:	$266,924,000
1999:	$1,105,654,316

Source: Department of Justice, Antitrust Division
Annual Report FY 1999, p. 6.

EXHIBIT 4.1

conspiracies to defraud the United States, and mail and wire fraud (see Focus Case 4.1 on page 107).

The federal Amended Sentencing Guidelines provide real incentives for companies to establish compliance programs. Under the Guidelines, if a company has an effective compliance program "to prevent and detect violations of law" but an antitrust violation nonetheless occurs, the fines assessed against the company may be substantially reduced. In addition, if a company's compliance program reveals the existence of an antitrust violation, the company and its management and employees who admit involvement may avoid criminal prosecution if they report the illegal activity to the DOJ at an early stage and if they meet certain other requirements.[22] A separate leniency program applies to individuals who report illegal antitrust activity to the DOJ in the absence of a company admission of culpability.[23]

The following discussion focuses on those antitrust actions most relevant to marketing practices: (1) horizontal restraints among competitors, (2) vertical

[22] U.S. Department of Justice, Antitrust Division, Corporate Leniency Program, Trade Reg. Rep. (CCH) Para. 13,113 (Aug. 10, 1993). This program can be found on-line at http://www.usdoj.gov
[23] U.S. Department of Justice, Antitrust Division, Leniency Policy for Individuals, Trade Reg. Rep. (CCH) Para. 13,114 (Aug. 10, 1994). This policy can be found on-line at http://www.usdoj.gov

---

Focus Case 4.1

Facts: Mark Albert Maloof was the southern regional sales manager for Bay Industries, Inc., a company that produces and sells metal building insulation. Bay opened a Houston office in 1993 and sharply reduced its prices in order to attract customers. Bay's competitors responded by reducing their prices as well.

In 1993, fiberglass manufacturers doing business in Texas announced a price increase and reduction in the supply of fiberglass insulation, one of the major components of metal building insulation. In response, Bay's general manager prepared a price sheet in November 1993 outlining a new pricing scheme for Bay's sales representatives.

On January 3, 1994, Maloof called Wally Rhodes, vice president of sales for Mizell Brothers Company, one of Bay's competitors. Rhodes testified that he and Maloof discussed the effect of the insulation supply reduction and that Maloof suggested adopting uniform pricing to ensure that neither company would quote or sell under the other's prices. Maloof then faxed Bay's price sheet to Rhodes. Telephone records documented daily phone calls and faxes between Maloof and Mizell over the following week. Rhodes testified that the purpose of the calls was to revise Mizell's price sheet to conform to Bay's pricing. Rhodes also testified that prior to a laminators'

trade association meeting on January 11, 1994, he and Maloof agreed to ask representatives of other insulation suppliers to join in the price-fixing scheme.

The fiberglass manufacturers imposed three price increases in 1994 and one in 1995. Government witnesses testified that after each increase, Maloof shared Bay's pricing sheet with representatives of Mizell and two other competitors. Rhodes and one other representative testified that they agreed upon a pricing scheme with Maloof before distributing new price sheets to their sales representatives.

In 1994, Bay sales representatives began to receive complaints from some customers that competing sales representatives consistently gave quotes identical to Bay's for 3-inch white vinyl insulation. Ultimately, Jan Smith, a Bay division manager under Maloof's supervision, reported Maloof's activities to the FBI.

Decision: At trial, Maloof was convicted of one count of conspiracy to restrain trade in violation of Section 1 of the Sherman Act and one count of conspiracy to commit wire fraud. He was sentenced to 30 months' imprisonment on each count, to run concurrently, and fined $30,847. The appellate court affirmed the convictions. *United States v. Maloof*, 205 F.3d 819 (5th Cir. 2000).

---

restraints between buyers and sellers, (3) maintenance or creation of a monopoly, and (4) price discrimination.

Horizontal Restraints Among Competitors

Trade restraints can be either horizontal or vertical. *Horizontal restraints* occur among competitors at the same level in the chain of distribution, such as among manufacturers or among wholesalers (see Exhibit 4.2). *Vertical restraints* occur among parties at different levels in the chain of distribution, such as between a manufacturer and a wholesaler.

To compete horizontally, firms must be at the *same level of distribution* and compete in the same *product* and *geographic* markets. For example, if *Firm A* and *Firm B* both sell potato chips in the southeast Michigan region, they compete horizontally. If *Firm A* sells in southeast Michigan and *Firm B* in the northern California region, however, they would be operating in different geographic markets and would not be competing horizontally. If both operate in southeast Michigan, but *Firm A* sells potato chips and *Firm B* sells processed cheese, they would be operating in different product markets and again would not compete horizontally.

EXHIBIT 4.2

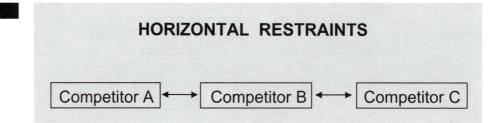

HORIZONTAL RESTRAINTS

| Competitor A | ←→ | Competitor B | ←→ | Competitor C |

These determinations are very fact-specific in most instances. If *Firm A* sells potato chips, for example, and *Firm B* sells pretzels, the court would need to determine whether the relevant product market should be defined as potato chips or whether it would include some broader definition of snack foods, such as salty, hand-held snacks. Not surprisingly, when an illegal horizontal restraint is alleged, the issue of the correct definition of the relevant market is usually hotly litigated.

Certain agreements among competitors may be legal because they have the effect of benefiting consumers (for example, by promoting standardization within an industry that allows interchangeability of products, such as component parts). Similarly, competitors can safely lobby together for legislative or regulatory change and can participate in trade association activities that do not stray into the realm of competitive decision making, such as pricing decisions or market allocations.

Other agreements among competitors may have the effect of reducing competition, however, and so are illegal. Certain horizontal restraints, such as price-fixing, are presumed to always be anticompetitive in effect and so are deemed illegal *per se*. Other horizontal restraints are viewed as being potentially procompetitive and so are evaluated under the rule of reason (see Exhibit 4.3).

Horizontal restraint cases raise difficult issues of proof. To succeed in an action under Section 1 of the Sherman Act, the plaintiff must show the existence of an agreement among the defendants. (Recall that Section 1 does not reach unilateral conduct but only agreements among two or more parties.) *Direct evidence*, such as written documentation of the agreement, minutes of a meeting in which agreement was reached, or testimony by a person with personal knowledge of the agreement, while most probative, can be difficult to obtain, if indeed it exists at all.

EXHIBIT 4.3

POTENTIAL ILLEGAL HORIZONTAL RESTRAINTS AMONG COMPETITORS

- price-fixing and bid-rigging

- group boycotts and concerted refusals to deal

- horizontal market allocations

- agreements to restrict advertising

- joint ventures

Because direct evidence of an antitrust violation generally is so difficult to obtain, many cases turn on *circumstantial evidence*. As the Supreme Court put it, "circumstantial evidence is the lifeblood of antitrust law."[24] Thus, agreements can be shown by inference—i.e., by a combination of circumstantial evidence, such as the existence of a meeting among the competitors before they implemented certain practices (even if the plaintiff has no evidence of the actual agenda of the meeting), records of telephone calls, or signaling behavior. *Signaling behavior* occurs when one company indirectly tells a competitor that it intends to raise prices by a specified amount. Competitors often disseminate information regarding things such as prices, costs, or inventories through mechanisms such as trade associations or the popular press. The courts usually (but not always) regard the exchange of price information as a violation of Section 1 of the Sherman Act. Most antitrust lawyers advise their clients not to share price information with competitors as a result. Courts generally are less concerned about the exchange of nonprice information, such as joint market surveys or joint advertising, unless such sharing lessens competition.

Circumstantial evidence of a Section 1 violation may be demonstrated through parallel behavior (known as *conscious parallelism*) by independent firms, such as persistent setting of prices at the same level or simultaneous changing of prices. Parallel behavior might just as easily result from intense competition, however, as from anticompetitive behavior, making it an ambiguous indicator of an antitrust violation. Where the parallel business behavior can be explained in terms of the independent business judgment of each defendant, no antitrust violation would occur. (Such acts may violate the prohibition in Section 5 of the FTC Act against "unfair methods of competition," however.) The courts thus usually require additional evidence of illegal behavior (known as *"plus factors"*), such as complex actions that would benefit each competitor only if all competitors acted in a prescribed manner (see Focus Case 4.2).

PRICE-FIXING

Horizontal price-fixing occurs when competitors agree on price or price-related issues (such as credit terms). According to the Supreme Court, "[u]nder the Sherman Act, a combination formed for the purpose and with the effect of raising, depressing, fixing, pegging, or stabilizing the price of a commodity in interstate or foreign commerce is illegal *per se.*"[25] The list of behaviors that are defined as "price-fixing" is extensive, including the setting of minimum prices, the setting of maximum prices, the setting of "list prices" (even where the list price is simply the starting point for customer negotiations, such as in automobile sales), production limits (even where no actual price is fixed), agreements regarding the availability of short-term credit, and agreements not to advertise prices. Regulated industries, such as railroads and public utilities, may fix prices or rates without violating the antitrust laws, however, provided they act within the limits established by their regulatory agencies.

See Discussion Case 4.2.

Although we most commonly think of price-fixing as occurring among sellers of goods or services, agreements among buyers to set the price that they will pay for goods or services or the quantities that they will purchase is also price-fixing.

---

[24] United States v. Falstaff Brewing Co., 410 U.S. 526, 532 n.13 (1973).
[25] United States v. Socony-Vacuum Oil Co., 310 U.S. 150, 223 (1940).

Focus Case 4.2

Facts: Plaintiffs, who were direct purchasers of baby food from the defendant manufacturers, including wholesalers and supermarket chains, sued the major manufacturers of baby food: Gerber Products Company, H. J. Heinz Co., and Beech-Nut (which was owned at first by Nestle Food Company and later by Ralston Purina Company). Collectively, the three defendants accounted for over 98 percent of all baby food products manufactured and sold in the United States. Gerber, in particular, accounted for 70 percent of the total U.S. market.

Gerber had positioned itself as the "premium" brand. Heinz had carved out a market niche as the "value" brand. Beech-Nut was originally positioned as a "value" brand but repositioned itself as a "premium" brand with a strong regional presence in the northeast United States.

The plaintiffs alleged that from 1975 to 1993, the defendants engaged in an unlawful conspiracy in violation of Section 1 of the Sherman Act "to fix, raise, and maintain wholesale prices and price levels of baby food in the United States." In particular, the plaintiffs alleged that the defendants exchanged information with each other regarding future price increases before they announced those increases to the public. The plaintiffs argued that the defendants had no legitimate business reason for informing each other before informing the public. The plaintiffs alleged that if Gerber, the dominant company in the industry and the price leader, decided to raise its prices, the other competitors had to follow the price increase immediately or the time gap between Gerber's increases and the other companies' increases would disturb their respective market shares. Giving advance notice solved this problem. The plaintiffs argued that advance notice did occur, showing that an agreement to conspire existed among the defendants.

Decision: The trial court granted summary judgment to the defendants, and the appellate court affirmed.

Although plaintiffs lacked direct evidence of price-fixing, the appellate court noted that they could support their claim with circumstantial evidence of conscious parallelism. "The theory of conscious parallelism is that uniform conduct of pricing by competitors permits a court to infer the existence of a conspiracy between those competitors. The theory is generally applied to highly concentrated markets where few sellers exist and where

they establish their prices, not by express agreement, but rather in a consciously parallel fashion. Thus, when two or more competitors in such a market act separately but in parallel fashion in their pricing decisions, this may provide probative evidence of an understanding by the competitors to fix prices."

The court explained:

In an oligopolistic market, meaning a market where there are few sellers, interdependent parallelism can be a necessary fact of life but be the result of independent pricing decisions.

In a market served by three large companies, each firm must know that if it reduces its price and increases its sales at the expense of its rivals, they will notice the sales loss, identify the cause, and probably respond. In short, each firm is aware of its impact upon the others. Though each may independently decide upon its own course of action, any rational decision must take into account the anticipated reaction of the other two firms. Whenever rational decision-making requires an estimate of the impact of any decision on the remaining firms and an estimate of their response, decisions are said to be "interdependent." Because of their mutual awareness, oligopolists' decisions may be interdependent although arrived at independently.

Because the evidence of conscious parallelism is circumstantial in nature, courts are concerned that they do not punish unilateral, independent conduct of competitors. They therefore require that evidence of a defendant's parallel pricing be supplemented with "plus factors." The simple term "plus factors" refers to "the additional facts or factors required to be proved as a prerequisite to finding that parallel action amounts to a conspiracy." They are necessary conditions for the conspiracy inference. They show that the allegedly wrongful conduct of the defense was conscious and not the result of independent business decisions of the competitors. The plus factors may include, and often do, evidence demonstrating that the defendants: (1) acted contrary to their economic interests, and (2) were motivated to enter into a price fixing conspiracy.

* * * *

Once the plaintiffs have presented evidence of the defendants' consciously parallel pricing and sup-
continued

plemented this evidence with plus factors, a rebuttable presumption of conspiracy arises.

The court found that the evidence was insufficient to prove conscious parallelism on the part of the defendants. Because Gerber controlled 70 percent of the baby food market and was the acknowledged industry leader, Gerber's pricing most likely did influence its competitors' pricing. However, the court stated, "Conscious parallelism . . . will not be inferred merely because the evidence tends to show that a defendant may have followed a competitor's price increase."

In the absence of "probative proof of concerted action" by the defendants, the appellate court affirmed the district court's grant of summary judgment to the defendants. *In re Baby Food Antitrust Ligitation*, 166 F.3d 112 (3d Cir. 1999).

The plaintiff bears the burden of proving price-fixing. This can be a difficult burden to meet. Price similarities or simultaneous changes in prices may result from normal economic conditions rather than from illegal firm behavior. If the price of raw timber increases as a result of changing conditions in the international timber markets, for example, the net effect may be a change in the wholesale price of lumber that causes competing lumber yards in a particular area to raise their retail prices by the same amount at the same time. In the absence of an agreement among the lumber yards to set the price, there would be no antitrust violation.

Price-fixing and its parallel behavior, *bid-rigging* (i.e., when two or more firms agree not to bid against each other to supply products or services to governmental units, or when they agree on the level of their individual bids), are considered by the DOJ to be the worst type of antitrust violation because such behavior invariably harms consumers by raising prices. The DOJ has made criminal prosecution of such behavior a top antitrust enforcement priority, and many corporate officers and managers have been imprisoned for such violations. The federal sentencing guidelines mandate a prison term for individuals convicted of price-fixing or bid-rigging; a 6 to 12 month minimum sentence for first-time offenders is typical.

GROUP BOYCOTTS AND CONCERTED REFUSALS TO DEAL

As the Supreme Court has stated, a firm has the "right to deal, or refuse to deal, with whomever it likes, as long as it does so independently."[26] Thus, a *unilateral* refusal to deal does not violate Section 1 of the Sherman Act, although it may violate Section 2 as an illegal monopolization or attempt to monopolize, as discussed beow.

Section 1 of the Sherman Act prohibits *group boycotts* or *concerted refusals to deal*. These are agreements among competitors not to deal with another person or business, to deal only on certain terms, or to coerce suppliers or customers not to deal with that person or business. Such an agreement violates the antitrust laws if it forces that party to pay higher prices, prevents a firm from entering a market, or disadvantages a competitor.

Although group boycotts or concerted refusals to deal historically were treated as *per se* violations, the law is unclear on this issue, and most such actions are analyzed under the rule of reason today.

[26] Monsanto Co. v. Spray-Rite Service Corp., 465 U.S. 752, 761 (1984).

HORIZONTAL MARKET ALLOCATIONS

Agreements among competitors to divide markets (defined by geographic territories, customer types, or product classes) are illegal *per se* as such agreements effectively give each firm a monopoly within its assigned territory.

See Discussion Case 4.2.

AGREEMENTS TO RESTRICT ADVERTISING

Agreements among competitors to restrict price advertising may be illegal if the restrictions deprive customers of valuable information. Similarly, restrictions on nonprice advertising may also be illegal if the restrictions have anticompetitive effects and no reasonable business justification.

JOINT VENTURES

A *joint venture* is a business association between two or more firms organized to carry out a specific business endeavor, such as joint research or a joint sales agency. If the purpose of the joint venture is to engage in behavior that is illegal *per se*, such as price-fixing or horizontal market allocation, the joint venture itself is illegal *per se*. Otherwise, the joint venture is evaluated under the rule of reason.

In 1984, Congress enacted the National Cooperative Research Act to alleviate concerns among businesses that joint research and development ventures might somehow violate the antitrust statutes. Joint ventures covered by the Act are evaluated under the rule of reason, are liable only for single (not treble) damages, and may qualify for "safe harbor" protection if they have less than a 20 percent market share. In 1993, the Act was extended to protect joint production ventures as well.

In April 2000, the FTC and the DOJ jointly issued *Antitrust Guidelines for Collaborations Among Competitors.*[27] These guidelines address the various types of horizontal agreements that competitors may form, such as joint ventures and strategic alliances, and provide an analysis that firms and their lawyers may apply in evaluating whether a proposed collaboration is likely to run afoul of the antitrust laws.

Vertical Restraints Against Competition

While relationships among competitors are described as being "horizontal," the relationships created between suppliers, manufacturers, wholesalers, retailers, and consumers of a product are described as "vertical" (see Exhibit 4.4). Certain agreements between such parties are illegal under Sections 1 and 2 of the Sherman Act and Section 3 of the Clayton Act. Some such agreements are illegal *per se*, while others are evaluated under the rule of reason (see Exhibit 4.5 on page 114).

RESALE PRICE MAINTENANCE AGREEMENTS

Manufacturers often want to establish the prices at which their distributors sell to customers. A manufacturer who has established a marketing program that positions its product as a high-prestige item will not want its distributors to dilute that product image by selling at a discount. The manufacturer would thus want to set a *minimum*

---

[27] The guidelines are available on the DOJ's Web site. *See* http://www.usdoj.gov.

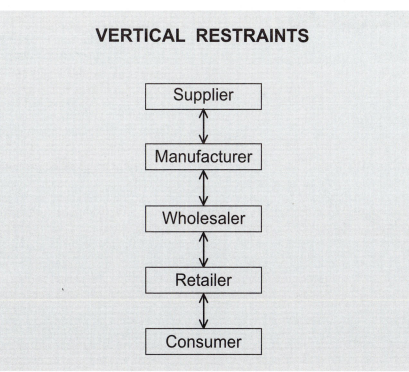

VERTICAL RESTRAINTS

price at which its distributors may sell. On the other hand, a manufacturer who is seeking high-volume sales, perhaps in an effort to establish economies of scale in production or to gain a prominent market share, will not want its distributors to reduce those sales by over-pricing. The manufacturer would thus want to set a *maximum* price at which its distributors may sell.

In either event, the manufacturer's and the distributors' interests may well diverge. The distributors' total profits, for example, may be higher if sales are lower but prices are higher than those sought by the manufacturer.

Until recently, it was thought that it was a *per se* violation of Section 1 of the Sherman Act for a seller to set either the minimum or the maximum price at which the buyer could resell the product. In 1997, however, in *State Oil Co. v. Khan*,[28] the Supreme Court ruled that vertical maximum resale price-fixing is not a *per se* unlawful restraint of trade but, rather, must be evaluated under the rule of reason because in some situations such agreements can benefit customers by preventing dealers from charging a noncompetitive price. Minimum resale price-fixing remains *per se* unlawful.

See Discussion Case 4.3.

Manufacturers are free to announce "suggested retail prices" as long as the prices are merely suggested and the action is unilateral. In *United States v. Colgate & Co.*,[29] the Supreme Court stated:

[28] 522 U.S. 3 (1997).
[29] 250 U.S. 300, 307 (1919).

EXHIBIT 4.5

POTENTIAL ILLEGAL VERTICAL RESTRAINTS AGAINST COMPETITION

- resale price maintenance agreements

- non-price agreements between manufacturer and dealer

- tying arrangements

In the absence of a purpose to create or maintain a monopoly the [Sherman] act does not restrict the long recognized right of a trader or manufacturer engaged in an entirely private business, freely to exercise his own independent discretion as to parties with whom he will deal; and, of course, he may announce in advance the circumstances under which he will refuse to sell.

In addition, the manufacturer may even announce that it will terminate its dealings with any retailer who fails to adhere to the suggested pricing. As long as the manufacturer adheres strictly to its policy, it will likely avoid any antitrust problems. A manufacturer who announces such a policy and then engages in a pattern of suspending and reinstating retailers who first fail to adhere but then agree to do so, however, or who engages in other mechanisms to obtain adherence to its retail prices may well find that it is liable for unlawful resale price maintenance.

An unlawful vertical price-fixing agreement can be either express, as evidenced by written or oral agreements, or inferred from the course of conduct between the parties, such as withholding dealer allowances or increasing wholesale prices to dealers who do not comply with suggested prices.

Most cases in this area are brought by private parties — usually dealers who claim that they were unlawfully terminated because they failed to adhere to the manufacturer's prices (see Focus Case 4.3).

NON-PRICE AGREEMENTS BETWEEN A MANUFACTURER AND A DEALER

Arrangements in which the manufacturer imposes limitations on how or where a dealer may sell a product (i.e., such things as location restrictions, service obligations, or customer or territorial limitations) are judged under the rule of reason and are generally upheld.

These types of agreements may reduce *intrabrand competition* between local dealers selling a particular manufacturer's products but may well enhance *interbrand* competition between dealers selling competing manufacturers' products. Generally, courts are more concerned with protecting interbrand rather than intrabrand competition. If there is no interbrand competition for the product, however (i.e., the manufacturer has no competitors), the courts may view intrabrand competition as more critical and may thus restrict the manufacturer's right to pick and choose among its prospective dealers or distributors.

Focus Case 4.3

 Facts: Spray-Rite Service Corp., an agricultural herbicide distributor, sued Monsanto Co., a chemical manufacturer, under Section 1 of the Sherman Act, alleging that Monsanto and some of its distributors had conspired to fix the resale prices of Monsanto's herbicides and that Monsanto had terminated Spray-Rite's distributorship in furtherance of this policy and had encouraged distributors to boycott Spray-Rite.

From 1957 to 1968, Spray-Rite had sold agricultural herbicides manufactured by Monsanto. Spray-Rite was a family-owned discount operation, which bought in large quantities and sold at a low margin. In 1968, Monsanto refused to renew Spray-Rite's one-year distributorship term. At the time, Spray-Rite was Monsanto's tenth largest distributor (out of approximately 100 distributors) and 16 percent of its sales were Monsanto products. Although Spray-Rite was subsequently able to purchase some Monsanto products from other distributors, it was unable to purchase as much of Monsanto's products as it wanted or as early in the growing season as it wanted.

Monsanto argued that it had terminated Spray-Rite's distributorship because of Spray-Rite's failure to hire trained salesmen and to promote sales to dealers adequately.

Decision: At trial, the jury found that Spray-Rite's termination was the result of a conspiracy between Monsanto and its distributors to set resale prices and awarded $3.5 million in damages, which the District Court trebled to $10.5 million. The U.S. Court of Appeals for the Seventh Circuit affirmed on the grounds that there was sufficient evidence to show that there was a conspiracy to set resale prices because proof of termination following competitor complaints is sufficient to support an inference of concerted action. The evidence at trial had shown numerous complaints from distributors to Monsanto about Spray-Rite's price-cutting practices.

The U.S. Supreme Court also affirmed but found that the Court of Appeals had applied an incorrect standard to the evidence in the case. The Supreme Court stated:

[T]he fact that a manufacturer and its distributors are in constant communication about prices and marketing strategy does not alone show that the distributors are not making independent pricing decisions. A manufacturer and its distributors have legitimate reasons to exchange information about the prices and the reception of their products in the market.

Inferring a price-fixing agreement from the existence of complaints from other distributors, or even from the fact that termination resulted in response to complaints, could deter or penalize legitimate conduct. Something more than mere complaints is necessary.

Thus, the Supreme Court held, to support a finding of an unlawful contract, combination, or conspiracy, "the antitrust plaintiff should present direct or circumstantial evidence that reasonably tends to prove that the manufacturer and others 'had a conscious commitment to a common scheme designed to achieve an unlawful objective.'"

The Supreme Court found that there was sufficient evidence for the jury to have concluded that Monsanto and its distributors had conspired to maintain resale prices and to terminate price cutters. The evidence included: (1) threats that Monsanto would not ship adequate supplies of Monsanto products to price-cutting distributors; (2) after Monsanto complained to a parent company about its subsidiary's price-cutting, the parent instructed the subsidiary to comply, and the subsidiary assured Monsanto that it would; and (3) a Monsanto distributor's newsletter, sent to its dealer-customers, which could reasonably have been interpreted as referring to agreements that distributors and dealers would maintain prices, that Monsanto's company-operated distributors would not undercut those prices, and that discounters would be terminated.

Moreover, there was circumstantial evidence showing that Spray-Rite's termination was made pursuant to a conspiracy between Monsanto and its competitors. Spray-Rite's president had testified that Monsanto made explicit threats to terminate Spray-Rite unless it raised its prices. In a post-termination meeting between Spray-Rite and Monsanto, Monsanto mentioned the many complaints it had received about Spray-Rite's prices as a factor in its termination decision. *Monsanto Co. v. Spray-Rite Service Corp.*, 465 U.S. 752 (1984).

Similarly, *exclusive dealing* agreements, in which a supplier prohibits its distributors from selling the products of competing suppliers, are evaluated under the rule of reason and are generally legal if the supplier can show that that there is a legitimate business reason for the arrangement, such as a franchisor's need to protect its mark and goodwill. If the effect is to restrict competition, however, courts will likely find the agreement illegal.

As a practical matter, the vast majority of nonprice vertical restraint cases are decided in favor of the defendant. It is very difficult for a plaintiff to show an illegal nonprice vertical restraint.

TYING ARRANGEMENTS

Tying arrangements or *tie-in sales* involve the sale of a desired product or service (the *tying product*) upon the condition that the buyer purchase a second product or service (the *tied product*) that the customer may not want or may be able to purchase elsewhere at lower cost. To get the desired product, the purchaser must accept the undesired product as well. For example, a PC manufacturer who requires a purchaser to buy an expensive printer in order to get access to a new and desirable computer would be tying the purchase of the computer (the tying product) to the purchase of the printer (the tied product).

Tying arrangements are governed by several of the antitrust acts. Section 3 of the Clayton Act prohibits tying arrangements involving goods but not those involving services, intangibles, or real property. Section 1 of the Sherman Act also applies to tying arrangements, including the services, intangibles, and real property instances not covered by the Clayton Act. Section 5 of the FTC Act covers tying arrangements that would be illegal under either the Clayton or the Sherman Acts. The analysis is the same under all of the acts.

A tying arrangement is illegal *per se* if

1. the tying and tied products or services are two separate products or services;
2. the seller possesses sufficient economic power in the tying market to be able to restrain appreciably competition in the tied market; and
3. the arrangement involves a "not insubstantial" amount of interstate commerce.

The concern is that a seller in such a position can force out existing producers of tied products and can block new entrants by forcing them to enter both the tied and tying markets in order to compete.

Tying arrangements that do not meet these three standards are evaluated under the rule of reason and may be legal, though the courts generally view such arrangements with disfavor because of their potential anticompetitive effects. The courts often uphold tying arrangements in the franchisor-franchisee context, however, because of business justifications supporting such arrangements. Franchising law is discussed further in Chapter 5.

Firms may attempt to use tying arrangements for a variety of reasons. If the firm has monopoly power in the tying product market, it may be able to use the tying arrangement to obtain monopoly power in the tied product market as well. Firms may also use this arrangement in an attempt to avoid price controls or to engage in price discrimination. Firms may engage in such behavior for legitimate reasons as well. For example, the firm may be attempting to take advantage of efficiencies or economies of scale. Similarly, the firm may attempt to protect its goodwill by refusing to provide replacement parts to nonauthorized service providers. The courts view such actions with a skeptical eye, however. As the Supreme Court stated, "The only situation . . . in which the protection of goodwill may necessitate the use of tying clauses is where specifications for a substitute would be so detailed that they could not practicably be supplied."[30]

Monopolization and Attempts to Monopolize

MONOPOLIZATION BY A SINGLE FIRM

Antitrust law is concerned that firms with *monopoly power* will exclude competitors from the market, reduce output, and thus raise prices for goods and services. In a truly competitive market, a firm has no power to control the prices at which it sells its products as those prices are dictated by market conditions beyond its control. In an imperfect market, firms with monopoly or oligopoly power can raise their prices without losing all of their customers. Their *market power* (i.e., their power to profitably reduce output and raise prices above marginal costs) is limited only by the availability of other products that customers would find suitable substitutes or by the lack of barriers to entry by other firms.

It is not illegal for a firm to have a monopoly position in a market if that power results from a superior product or service, business acumen, or historical accident. As the U.S. Court of Appeals for the Second Circuit once noted: "The successful competitor, having been urged to compete, must not be turned upon when he wins."[31] However, Section 2 of the Sherman Act makes it illegal for a firm to maintain or to attempt to create a monopoly through actions that unreasonably exclude firms from the market or that significantly impair their ability to compete. Such antitrust violations may involve a single firm acting unilaterally or a group of firms acting together to monopolize a market. Conspiracies to monopolize are usually prosecuted under Section 1 of the Sherman Act and are discussed below. Section 2 of the Sherman Act applies to *monopsony* power (i.e., monopoly buying power), as well as to monopoly power.

According to the U.S. Supreme Court, *monopolization* consists of two elements:

1. the possession of monopoly power in the relevant market; and
2. unfair attainment or maintenance of that power, as opposed to growth or development as a consequence of a superior product, business acumen, or historic accident.[32]

Monopoly Power in the Relevant Market

Firms that possess a large amount of market power in their relevant market are said to have "monopoly power." For purposes of the antitrust statutes, a firm does not have to have 100 percent of the market in order to have a monopoly position. Rather, a firm with a market share in excess of 70 percent is likely to be deemed to have monopoly power. A firm with a market share of less than 40 percent is unlikely to be found to have monopoly power. If the firm has between 40 percent and 70 percent market share, the court has to make a case-by-case determination as to whether the firm possesses monopoly power. Even where a firm has a high market

---

[30] Standard Oil Co. of California v. United States, 337 U.S. 293 (1949).
[31] United States v. Aluminum Co. of America, 148 F.2d 416, 430 (2d Cir. 1945).
[32] United States v. Grinnell Corp., 384 U.S. 563 (1966).

share, it is not deemed to have monopoly power if the barriers to entry are so slight that other competitors could easily enter the market.

In determining whether a company has monopoly power, the relevant market must be defined. To answer this, the court must determine (1) the relevant geographic market and (2) the relevant product market.

The defendant, of course, will try to define both of these markets broadly, which will reduce the defendant's relevant market share and make it less likely that the defendant will be found to have monopoly power. The plaintiff, on the other hand, will try to define each of these markets narrowly, which will increase the defendant's relevant market share and increase the likelihood that the court will find the defendant to be a monopolist. Thus, the definition of the relevant geographic and product markets tends to be litigated vigorously.

The relevant *geographic market* can be international, national, regional, or local, depending upon the type of product or service at issue. It is usually defined as the area in which the defendant and competing sellers sell the product at issue, considering factors such as transportation costs, delivery limitations, customer convenience and preferences, and the locations and facilities of other producers and distributors. According to the U.S. Court of Appeals for the 11th Circuit, "A geographic market is only relevant for monopoly purposes where these factors show that consumers within the geographic area cannot realistically turn to outside sellers should prices rise within the defined area."[33]

The relevant *product market* is determined primarily by customer preferences and the extent to which customers view products as being reasonably interchangeable. Obviously, this determination is subject to a large amount of interpretation and is the subject of much litigation. While two brands of potato chips are logically viewed as being in the same product market, are potato chips and tortilla chips? Potato chips and pretzels? Potato chips and other salty snack foods, such as peanuts? Potato chips and all snack foods, including cookies, candy, and ice cream?

See Discussion Case 4.4.

Most products or services fall into the *multiple brand product market* in which several products or services are viewed as interchangeable substitutes and thus compete. However, in a 1992 case, *Eastman Kodak Co. v. Image Technical Services, Inc.,*[34] the Supreme Court held that a single brand of a product or service could constitute a separate market under certain circumstances. Kodak controlled nearly all of the parts market and 80 percent to 95 percent of the service market on its equipment. The Supreme Court found that: "Because service and parts for Kodak equipment are not interchangeable with other manufacturers' service and parts, the relevant market from the Kodak equipment owner's perspective is composed only of those companies that service Kodak machines."

Unfair Attainment or Maintenance of Monopoly Power

The second required element of illegal monopolization is that the firm have engaged in some form of prohibited market behavior. As already noted, the possession of monopoly power itself is not illegal; rather, it is the possession of monopoly power through predatory or coercive behavior that is prohibited. Judge

---

[33] T. Harris Young & Associates, Inc. v. Marquette Electronics, Inc., 931 F.2d 816 (11th Cir. 1991).
[34] 504 U.S. 451 (1992).

Learned Hand, in a famous case known as *The Alcoa Case*,[35] stated that illegal monopoly power exists where the firm purposefully and intentionally acquired, maintained, or exercised that power, unless it is shown that the monopoly power was either: (1) attained by "superior skill, foresight, or industry" or (2) "thrust upon" the firm as a result of a thin market or economies of scale. This latter category encompasses "innocently acquired" or "natural" monopolies, such as those enjoyed by a small town newspaper where the market will support only one such paper,[36] by a professional football team in a city in which there are insufficient fans to support more than one such team,[37] or when large economies of scale exist, such as those enjoyed by oil pipeline distribution networks or electricity suppliers.

The types of acts that constitute predatory or coercive behavior include conduct that excludes or bars competitors from the marketplace (such as increasing production capacity to supply all demand before a competitor can enter the field[38]), predatory pricing, and certain refusals to deal.

Predatory pricing is usually defined as pricing below average variable cost. The concern is that a firm attempting to create a monopoly will set prices low to eliminate competition and then raise prices once it has driven all the other firms from the market. It can be difficult and expensive for a plaintiff to show that predatory pricing has occurred. According to the Supreme Court, for predatory pricing to occur under Section 2 of the Sherman Act: (1) the plaintiff must prove below-cost pricing by the defendant (measured by average variable cost) and (2) the defendant must have a dangerous probability of recouping the money that it lost on below-cost pricing.[39] If the defendant is not in a position to recoup its losses, consumer welfare (and competition) is actually enhanced because consumers face lower aggregate prices in the marketplace. Individual competitors may be harmed by such a strategy but, as stated earlier, the antitrust laws are designed to protect consumers and competition as a whole, not individual competitive firms.

Generally, as already discussed, firms may unilaterally *refuse to deal* with particular competitors or purchasers without violating the antitrust laws. There is an exception to this general rule, however, known as the *essential facilities doctrine*. If a firm has exclusive access to a facility that is "essential" to competition, the courts may require the firm to provide access to that facility to its competitors on a reasonable, nondiscriminatory basis. To prove monopolization of an "essential facility," the plaintiff generally must show: "(1) control of the essential facility by a monopolist; (2) a competitor's inability practically or reasonably to duplicate the essential facility; (3) the denial of the use of the facility to a competitor; and (4) the feasibility of providing the facility."[40] Because of the difficulties of meeting this standard of proof, this doctrine is seldom used.

See Discussion Case 4.4.

ATTEMPTED MONOPOLIZATION

Section 2 of the Sherman Act also prohibits "attempts to monopolize." *Attempted monopolization* generally requires a showing that: (1) the defendant has engaged in

---

[35] United States v. Aluminum Co. of America, 148 F.2d 416 (2d Cir. 1945).
[36] Union Leader Corp. v. Newspapers of New England, Inc., 284 F.2d 582 (1st Cir. 1960).
[37] American Football League v. National Football League, 323 F.2d 124 (4th Cir. 1963).
[38] United States v. Aluminum Co. of America, 148 F.2d 416 (2d Cir. 1945).
[39] Brooke Group, Ltd. v. Brown & Williamson Tobacco Corp., 509 U.S. 209 (1993).
[40] MCI Communications Corp. v. American Tel. & Tel. Co., 708 F.2d 1081, 1132–33 (7th Cir. 1983).

predatory or anticompetitive conduct (2) with a specific intent to monopolize and (3) that there is a dangerous probability of the defendant's success.

The required specific intent can be proved by direct evidence (such as internal memos outlining the firm's plans to illegally obtain a monopoly) or by inference from unfair conduct on the part of the defendant, such as inducing other firms to boycott the defendant's competitors or discriminatory pricing. The same types of predatory or anticompetitive behavior that are condemned in monopolization cases are condemned in attempt to monopolize cases.

See Discussion Cases 4.4, 4.5.

CONSPIRACY TO MONOPOLIZE

Section 2 of the Sherman Act states that it is illegal for any person "to conspire with any other person or persons to monopolize . . . ." Any such violation is also a violation of Section 1's prohibition against conspiracies in restraint of trade. Such actions are almost always prosecuted under Section 1's broader language.

Price Discrimination

The Robinson-Patman Act prohibits discrimination in the prices charged or supplementary services offered to competing purchasers where such discrimination harms competition unless there is a legitimate business justification for the difference. It is intended primarily to protect small, independent businesses from injury caused by discriminatory pricing. *Price discrimination* is defined as identical or similar products being sold at prices that have different ratios to the marginal costs of producing the products.

Price discrimination can enhance profits for the seller who charges a higher price to those customers willing to pay more for the product or service and lower prices to those unwilling to pay. Price discrimination can only exist in markets with a few sellers or with differentiated products or services. In competitive markets with homogenous products, firms do not have the ability to charge different prices to different buyers. Moreover, price discrimination is more common with services than with goods. If a buyer is able to resell the goods, for example, there is an opportunity for an arbitrageur to buy the good at the lower price and resell it at the higher price. Services, on the other hand, are more difficult to resell. However, the Robinson-Patman Act does not reach sales of services, only sales of goods.

As a practical matter, the DOJ and the FTC seldom take enforcement actions under the Robinson-Patman Act today. Private plaintiffs, on the other hand, (particularly resellers charged the higher price) bring frequent suits. Recently, for example, Intimate Bookshop, Inc., an independent book retailer, brought a price discrimination suit against Barnes & Noble, Inc., Borders Group, Inc., and Walden Acquisition Co., the industry leaders. Intimate Bookshop alleged that the defendants were violating the Robinson-Patman Act by coercing lower prices from publishers in the form of advertising allowances and promotional payments that exceeded the costs of the services, as well as coercing discounts in excess of those offered to independent book retailers.[41]

---

[41] *Independent Bookseller Throws Book at Industry Giants*, ANTITRUST LITIGATION REPORTER, Apr. 2000, at p. 16. The outcome of the case was still pending at the time of the publication of this book.

Private plaintiffs face a difficult burden of proof in Robinson-Patman Act suits. Even if the plaintiff wins at trial, it is likely to find its victory overturned by the appellate court.

Many states also have laws prohibiting price discrimination. Often, these laws are modeled on the Robinson-Patman Act, but they typically apply only to intrastate activities. Several state acts regulate price discrimination involving services as well as commodities.

ELEMENTS OF PRICE DISCRIMINATION

The requirements of the Robinson-Patman Act are set forth in Section 2(a) of the Clayton Act. This section makes it unlawful for any person (1) engaged in commerce (2) to discriminate in price between different purchasers (3) of commodities of like grade and quality (4) where the effect may be to substantially lessen competition in any line of commerce, or tend to create a monopoly, or (5) to injure, destroy, or prevent competition with any person who either grants or knowingly receives the benefits of such discrimination, or with the customers of either of them. Thus, even if all other elements of a Robinson-Patman Act case are satisfied, there is no violation if there is no reasonable likelihood of injurious effects on competition.

There are some key points to recognize from this statutory languge. First, both the seller who offers and the buyer who knowingly receives discriminatory prices or supplementary services are guilty of violating the Act. In addition, a buyer who knowingly induces an unlawful discriminatory price or supplementary service is in violation of the Act. Thus, a buyer cannot use its superior purchasing power to force sellers into granting discriminatory prices or supplementary services.

Second, the Robinson-Patman Act applies only to "commodities," which includes only tangible goods. Services and intangibles, such as brokerage services, newspaper advertising, cable television, cellular telephone services, mutual fund shares, patent licenses, leases, and real property, are excluded. Electricity, however, is considered a commodity for purposes of the Act.

Third, for a violation to occur, there must be at least two sales (leases, consignments, and license agreements do not count) to two different purchasers, at least one of which must be across a state line. The purchases must occur at fairly contemporaneous times, as determined by market conditions (see Focus Case 4.4 on page 122).

Fourth, the Robinson-Patman Act reaches indirect, as well as direct, price discrimination. Thus, discrimination that results from preferential credit terms, quantity discounts, or supplementary services, such as promotional assistance, is illegal. The Act also prohibits certain other types of discounts, rebates, and allowances and prohibits the selling of goods at unreasonably low prices for the purpose of destroying competition or eliminating a competitor.

Fifth, to be of "like grade or quality," the two products need not be identical but must be viewed by buyers as being interchangeable and substitutable.

Sixth, the Act permits recovery for three categories of price discrimination. *Primary-line price discrimination* occurs when a seller's price discrimination harms competition with its direct competitors and usually takes the form of predatory pricing. (Recall that predatory pricing may also violate the Sherman Act.) *Secondary-line price discrimination* occurs when a seller's price discrimination impacts competition among the seller's purchasers (i.e., there are purchasers who compete with each other, some of whom receive the favored price and some of whom do

Focus Case 4.4

Facts: An electric cogenerator brought several antitrust allegations against a utility that had refused to purchase energy from it. One of the allegations involved price discrimination. Specifically, the cogenerator alleged that the utility had offered to sell electricity to the cogenerator's customers at a lower price than that offered by the cogenerator, that the reduced price was not offered to all customers, and that such an action violates the Robinson-Patman Act.

Decision: In affirming the trial court's dismissal of the claim, the appellate court stated:

> The Robinson-Patman Act, which amended the Clayton Act, prohibits price discrimination "where the effect of such discrimination may be substantially to lessen competition or tend to create a monopoly." In order to state a claim under the Robinson-Patman Act, a plaintiff must allege facts to demonstrate that

(1) the defendant made at least two contemporary sales of the same commodity at different prices to different purchasers; and (2) the effect of such discrimination was to injure competition.

The appellate court found that the plaintiff had not satisfied the first element because it had alleged only that the defendant had "offered" to sell electricity at a rate lower than that charged by the plaintiff, rather than actually engaging in a sale. As the court noted, "[m]erely offering lower prices to a customer does not state a price discrimination claim."

Moreover, the plaintiff had not satisfied the second element either, as it had made no allegation of predatory conduct or other injury to competition, such as below-market prices. Merely approaching the plaintiff's customer does not constitute an antitrust violation. *Crossroads Cogeneration Corp. v. Orange & Rockland Utilities, Inc.*, 159 F.3d 129 (3d Cir. 1998).

---

not). *Tertiary-line price discrimination* occurs when a seller's price discrimination harms competition between customers of the favored and disfavored purchasers, even though the favored and disfavored purchasers do not compete directly against one another. This occurs when the recipient of a favored price passes that lower price along to purchasers in the next level of distribution. Purchasers from other secondary-line sellers are injured because they do not receive the lower price. These purchasers may sue and recover damages from the discriminating secondary-line seller.

Finally, the Robinson-Patman Act does not apply to sales to the federal, state, or local governments; nonprofit institutions; cooperative associations; or export sales.

Price discrimination in goods and services may also violate the Sherman Act if it constitutes a restraint of trade or an attempt to monopolize, or may violate Section 5 of the FTC Act if it is an unfair method of competition.

DEFENSES

There are three statutory *defenses* that sellers can raise in response to allegations of illegal price discrimination: (1) cost justification, (2) response to market conditions, and (3) meeting competition.

Section 2(a) of the Robinson-Patman Act states that "nothing herein contained shall prevent differentials which make only due allowance for differences in the cost of manufacture, sale, or delivery resulting from the differing methods or quantities in which such commodities are sold or delivered." If the defendant can prove a *valid cost justification* for the price discrimination, it has an absolute defense to allegations of violation of the Act. This requires the defendant to make a detailed showing of *actual* cost savings attributable to the quantity sold, such as showing that the lower price simply represents the passing on of cost savings achieved through producing and shipping in large quantities. As a practical matter, it is difficult for defendants to calculate and prove such actual cost savings; thus, this defense is rarely used.

Section 2(a) also allows price variations designed to meet fluid product or market conditions, such as the deterioration of perishable goods, obsolescence of seasonal goods, a distress sale under court order, or a legitimate going-out-of-business sale. This defense, which is seldom used, is known as the *market conditions* defense.

Section 2(b) provides that a seller can defend by showing that its lower price was "made in good faith to meet an equally low price of a competitor"—the so-called *"meeting competition in good faith defense."* To use this defense, the seller must show (1) that at the time the price concession was made, the facts before it "would lead a reasonable and prudent person to believe that the granting of a lower price would in fact meet the equally low price of a competitor"[42] and (2) that the price concession met but did not beat the competitive price for a similar product.

Antitrust and the Internet

The rapid growth of information technology and the Internet have raised new types of antitrust issues. Some commentators have argued that antitrust enforcement is less important in such an environment as new entrants can easily enter markets and supplant dominant market participants who try to assert market power or otherwise abuse their market position. The Antitrust Division of the DOJ, however, has taken the position that first-mover advantages associated with information technology systems raise special risks that dominant market participants will be able to capture markets and engage in anticompetitive behaviors. The Division feels that antitrust enforcement may well be even more important in such an environment.

Federal antitrust regulators have recently turned their attention to business-to-business (B2B) electronic marketplaces. These are software systems that allow buyers and sellers of similar goods to carry out procurement activities using common, industry-wide computer systems. B2B marketplaces raise some unique antitrust issues, particularly in the context of illegal combinations or collusion, while at the same time having the potential for substantial efficiencies, such as reducing transaction costs, generating volume-related scale economies, improving inventory management, and facilitating bidding processes. The FTC reportedly is currently investigating a site planned by Ford Motor Corp., General Motors Corp., and Daimler-Chrysler A-G. The site is designed to buy as much as $250 million per year in auto parts and supplies.[43]

The FTC held a workshop in June 2000 to bring together designers, owners, and operators of B2B electronic businesses, as well as buyers and sellers, to discuss how such markets can be structured to achieve efficiency while avoiding anticompetitive effects.[44] The panelists concluded that B2B activities are amenable to traditional antitrust analysis.

State Antitrust Enforcement

Although the discussion in this chapter has focused primarily on federal antitrust laws, states are also active in antitrust enforcement. Most states have antitrust

---

[42] FTC v. A. E. Staley Mfg. Co., 324 U.S. 746 (1945).

[43] Andrea Foster, *B2Bs Raise Antitrust Concerns*, THE NATIONAL LAW JOURNAL, May 8, 2000, at p. B1.

[44] *See* http://www.ftc.gov/bc/b2b/index.htm

statutes, which are often patterned after the federal statutes. These statutes are enforced through the offices of the state attorneys general and, in many states, by private plaintiffs as well. These statutes address intrastate anticompetitive behavior rather than the interstate behavior targeted by the federal statutes. Over 40 states provide for criminal enforcement of state antitrust laws, with 25 of those states making antitrust violations felonies. Like the federal statutes, state antitrust law generally provides for recovery of treble damages, costs, and reasonable attorneys fees.

The impact of state antitrust enforcement actions should not be underestimated. In October 1998, for example, the FTC issued a final order finding that Toys "R" Us had violated Section 1 of the Sherman Act by unlawfully using its dominant market power in order to form and enforce agreements between itself and toy manufacturers and among toy manufacturers to restrict the sale of toys to "wholesale" clubs, such as Sam's Club, Price-Costco, and BJ's Wholesale Club. The FTC enjoined Toys "R" Us from engaging in such conduct with respect to sales to any toy discounter and from engaging in other conduct, such as gathering and sharing of information, that had facilitated that unlawful activity.[45]

At the same time, 45 states had filed claims against Toys "R" Us and toy manufacturers. The states had claimed that, in an effort to limit the competitive threat posed by low-margin, high-volume warehouse clubs, Toys "R" Us had unlawfully used its market power to get toy manufacturers to agree to limit the sale of certain toys to discounters or to sell toys to those discounters only in "combination packs" that made it difficult for consumers to compare the retail prices charged by the discounters to those charged by Toys "R" Us. The defendants entered into a settlement with the states. Under the terms of the settlement, Toys "R" Us was to pay $40.5 million in cash and toys, Mattel was to pay $8,222,900 in cash and toys, and Little Tykes Co. was to pay $1,316,250 in cash and toys. Hasbro had previously agreed to pay $5.95 million in cash and toys.[46]

International Implications of Antitrust Laws

The United States enforces its antitrust laws abroad, both civilly and criminally, and, in fact, is far more aggressive than any other country in the world in extending the extraterritorial reach of such laws. Under U.S. Supreme Court doctrine, conduct that would violate U.S. law if it occurred in the United States is also a violation if it occurred abroad but affected imports into the U.S.[47] The DOJ's *Antitrust Guidelines for International Operations*[48] state two purposes behind the extraterritorial application of U.S. antitrust law: (1) to protect U.S. consumers from conduct that raises prices or limits choices and (2) "to protect American export and investment opportunities against privately imposed restrictions."

The DOJ has specifically targeted international price-fixing and market-allocation cartels in its enforcement efforts, stating that it will focus its enforcement efforts primarily on boycotts and cartels that injure American exports or affect American consumers.[49] Not only have the cartel fines collected by the

[45] In re Toys "R" Us, Inc., 1998 F.T.C. LEXIS 119 (Oct. 13, 1998), *aff'd*, Toys "R" Us v. FTC, 221 F.3d 928 (7th Cir. 2000).
[46] The Settlement was approved by the U.S. District Court. *See* In re Toys "R" Us Antitrust Litigation, 191 F.R.D. 347 (E.D. N.Y. 2000).
[47] United States v. Aluminum Co. of America, 148 F.2d 416 (2d Cir. 1945).
[48] *See* http://www.usdoj.gov/atr/public/guidelines/guidelin.htm

Antitrust Division risen dramatically in recent years, but top executives of cartels (including foreign nationals) have been sentenced to imprisonment and cartels have been subjected to civil treble damage liability.[50] Many foreign nations have followed the United States' lead and are also focusing their antitrust enforcement efforts more intensely on international cartels. The United States has entered into cooperation agreements with several nations, including Australia, Brazil, Canada, the European Union, Germany, Israel, and Japan. These agreements are designed to enhance the abilities of governmental authorities to investigate and prosecute international cartel activities.

As you can imagine, the extension of U.S. antitrust law to foreign firms has created some serious policy conflicts with foreign governments. Under the *sovereign immunity doctrine*, the United States does not apply its laws to foreign governments. Thus, if a foreign firm's activities are mandated (as opposed to merely tolerated) by its government, the U.S. antitrust laws do not apply to it.

Over 80 foreign nations also have antitrust litigation.[51] Most Southeast Asian and Latin American countries have or are drafting antitrust laws. The European Union's competition policy is found within Articles 85 and 86 of the Treaty of Rome and is similar to Sections 1 and 2 of the Sherman Act. Most foreign antitrust laws, like the U.S. laws, provide for extraterritorial jurisdiction if the defendant's conduct affects markets in those nations. Thus, a company cannot assume that just because it has no assets in a particular foreign nation that it is not subject to that nation's antitrust provisions.

---

[49] Department of Justice, Antitrust Division, 1999 Annual Report, at p. 5.

[50] *See* Stephen D. Brown & George G. Gordon, *International Cartel Enforcement: How to Avoid Becoming a Target*, The Metropolitan Corporate Counsel (May, 2000).

[51] Information on many of these laws can be found at the "The World's Biggest Competition, Antitrust and Regulatory Sites List" at http://www.clubi.ie/competition/compframesite/index.htm

---

DISCUSSION CASES

4.1 The Rule of Reason vs. *Per se* Violations

Continental Airlines, Inc. v. United Air Lines, Inc., 120 F. Supp. 2d 556 (E.D. Va. 2000)

This . . . action grows out of the collective decision of defendants United Air Lines ("United") and Dulles Airport Airline Management Council ("AMC") to employ carry-on baggage "templates" to restrict the size of carry-on bags allowed to pass through security checkpoints at Washington Dulles International Airport ("Dulles"). Plaintiffs, Continental Airlines, Inc., and its wholly owned subsidiary, Continental Express, Inc., filed a . . . complaint against defendants . . . for violation of the Sherman Act, 15 U.S.C. § 1 . . . . * * * For the reasons that follow, defendants' motion to dismiss must be denied.

I

Delays associated with checking luggage at airport ticket counters and with collecting luggage at destination airports are endemic and major irritants of air travel. Accordingly, many airline passengers—particularly business travelers—avoid checking luggage and prefer to travel with lightweight and mobile luggage that is easy to carry onto the aircraft. This consumer preference, plaintiffs allege, creates no safety issue provided the aircraft's overhead bins accommodate and secure such stowed luggage. In fact, no federal law or regulation mandates any specific or uniform limit on the size or number of allowable carry-on bags. Instead, the FAA allows each carrier to adopt a carry-on baggage policy that is tailored to its particular circumstances. Thus, limits on carry-on baggage are at the discretion of each airline and vary among air carriers.

Plaintiffs . . . claim that, in response to passenger preference for avoiding the need to check baggage, they have invested approximately $15 million in outfitting their aircraft with larger overhead bins to accommodate larger carry-on bags than can be carried in the overhead bins of their competitors' aircraft. Given this, plaintiffs have adopted a liberal "gate-checking" policy on commuter flights. Plaintiffs allege that airlines compete for passengers on a variety of fronts, including, *inter alia*, price, convenience of flight schedules, type of aircraft, seating comfort, frequent-flyer incentive programs, and carry-on baggage policies. Indeed, plaintiffs allege that their carry-on baggage policies are an important element of their aggressive nationwide competitive strategy of providing high-quality service to the flying public. * * *

* * * * The AMC is an association of domestic and international air carriers that provide passenger service to and from Dulles. Its membership includes, in addition to United and plaintiffs, Air Canada, Air Tran, All Nippon Airways, Atlantic Coast, British Airways, BWIA, Delta Airlines, Korean Air, Lufthansa, Sabena, Spanair, Swissair, TACA, and TWA, among other air carriers.

By virtue of its position as the largest carrier at Dulles, United operates the security checkpoints at Dulles, including the metal detectors through which passengers must pass and the x-ray equipment that screens all carry-on bags and personal belongings. Control of operations at these checkpoints is shared between United and the AMC. In April of this year, a majority of the members of the AMC, at the urging of United, agreed to install baggage "templates" at the front of x-ray screening units in order to restrict the size of bags that passengers may carry on to the aircraft. Passengers with bags that do not fit the template must return to the ticket counter and check the "oversized" bag.

Plaintiffs objected to the installation of these carry-on baggage templates out of concern that use of the templates to restrict the size of carry-on bags would erode the competitive advantage they enjoy owing to their policy of allowing travelers greater flexibility with respect to carry-on bags. According to plaintiffs, defendants' agreement is not grounded in any security concerns . . . . Plaintiffs also claim that defendants' agreement to restrict the size of carry-on bags was in reality an agreement to forestall competition among air carriers on the basis of baggage-handling policies and, consequently, to deprive plaintiffs of the fruits of their investment in adopting consumer-friendly carry-on baggage policies. This decision, plaintiffs argue, is a naked restriction on the ability of individual air carriers to engage in nonprice competition. * * * Plaintiffs further allege that because their customers have been unable to take advantage of plaintiffs' liberal carry-on baggage policies, they have lost any competitive advantage stemming from their carry-on baggage policy and the profits attributable to that policy. In addition, plaintiffs claim that defendants' agreement has reduced the

competitive pressure on other airlines to change their aircraft and policies to accommodate customer preferences for larger carry-on bags.

Plaintiffs' motion to dismiss . . . presents the following questions . . . :

1. Whether the complaint states a valid Sherman Act Section 1 claim under the rule of *per se* illegality.

* * * *

II

* * * *

A. Plaintiffs' Antitrust Claims

"Designed to be a comprehensive charter of economic liberty aimed at preserving free and unfettered competition as a rule of trade," the Sherman Act provides that "every contract, combination[,] . . . or conspiracy, in restraint of trade or commerce among the several States . . . is declared to be illegal." Yet, only those agreements or conspiracies that are "unreasonably restrictive of competitive conditions" are prohibited; Section 1 does not reach de minimis restraints of trade. Thus, a plaintiff asserting a claim for violation of Section 1 must plead: (1) an agreement or conspiracy among two or more separate entities that (2) unreasonably restrains trade and (3) affects interstate or foreign commerce. Defendants' dismissal motion focuses on the second element—namely, that the AMC's agreement to restrict the size of carry-on bags at Dulles was an unreasonable restraint of trade. * * * [Certain] categories of restraints . . . are deemed to be *per se* unreasonable restraints on competition. These agreements have such a "pernicious effect on competition and lack of any redeeming virtue" that they "are conclusively presumed to be unreasonable and therefore illegal without elaborate inquiry as to the precise harm they have caused or the business excuse for their use." Thus, a court confronted with a *per se* unreasonable restraint on competition need not study the market involved, the effects of such an agreement on competition, or the purpose for its adoption before concluding that the plaintiff has satisfied the second element of a Section 1 violation.

The proper analytical approach "where the economic impact of certain practices is not immediately obvious," however, is the "Rule of Reason," which requires a court to analyze a restraint's impact on competition in a relevant market. Under this mode of analysis, which is the presumptive standard for most categories of restraints, "the factfinder weighs all of the circumstances of a case in deciding whether a restrictive practice should be prohibited as imposing an unreasonable restraint on competition." In doing so, a court must "take into account a variety of factors, including specific information about the relevant business, its condition before and after the restraint was imposed, and the restraint's history, nature, and effect" in assessing the anticompetitive effect of an agreement. "The true test of legality" under the Rule of Reason "is whether the restraint imposed is such as merely regulates and perhaps thereby promotes competition or whether it is such as may suppress or even destroy competition."

* * * "[T]here is often no bright line separating *per se* from Rule of Reason analysis," for the dispositive question is whether an agreement impermissibly restrains competition. In this regard, the analysis is inevitably fact-intensive . . . ."

1. Per se Illegality

Agreements that are subject to a determination of *per se* unreasonableness are those which "facially appear to be one[s] that would always or almost always tend to restrict competition and decrease output," and which are not "designed to 'increase economic efficiency and render markets more, rather than less competitive.'" Thus, where an agreement has a "pernicious effect on competition and lack[s] . . . any redeeming virtue," *per se* treatment is appropriate. Examples of restraints held to be *per se* illegal under Section 1 include inter alia, price-fixing, group boycotts, tying arrangements, and market-allocation agreements among competitors. The common thread uniting these *per se* violations of Section 1 is that they are all "naked restraints on trade with no purpose except stifling of competition." This is precisely the complaint's characterization of the defendants' agreement to restrict the size of carry-on bags at Dulles. Specifically, the complaint alleges that defendants' agreement is a restraint designed to eliminate competition for airline passengers on the basis of carry-on baggage size. The complaint further alleges that the agreement is a restraint of trade that is neither related to, nor justified by, any legitimate safety or security concerns. Indeed, the complaint also reflects that the FAA allows individual carriers to adopt carry-on baggage policies specifically tailored to a carrier's equipment, operational policies, and competitive strategy. These allegations, which are assumed to be true at this stage, are plainly sufficient to allege a *per se* violation of Section 1.

* * * *

[I]t is certainly true, as defendants contend, that *per se* analysis is the exception rather than the rule, and that *per se* analysis traditionally has been applied only to limited categories of agreements, none of which precisely describes the agreement at issue here. Yet, . . . the question is not whether the specific restraint here at issue has been judicially labeled a *per se* violation in the past (it has not), but rather, whether it should now be so labeled. * * * *Per se* treatment is appropriate . . . to any agreement restricting competition that has no purpose other than the stifling of competition. * * * [B]ecause an agreement to eliminate competition on the size of carry-on baggage has not yet been subjected to judicial scrutiny, "considerable inquiry into market conditions [is required] before the evidence justifies the presumption of anticompetitive conduct"—i.e., *per se* treatment under Section 1. * * * At this stage in the proceedings, for the claim of *per se* illegality to survive threshold attack, it is sufficient that plaintiffs have alleged a restraint on trade in the form of a horizontal agreement among competitors not to compete—here, on the basis of carry-on luggage capacity—that is arguably analogous to horizontal agreements that have been held to be *per se* illegal.

* * * *

An appropriate order has been issued.

Questions for Discussion for Case 4.1

1. What are the significant differences between the rule of reason and the *per se* rule? Which rule would a plaintiff prefer to have apply? Which rule would a defendant prefer?

2. How does a court determine which rule applies in any given case?

3. Which rule is the court applying in this case, and why?

4.2 Horizontal Price-Fixing, Horizontal Market Allocation

Palmer v. BRG of Georgia, Inc., 498 U.S. 46 (1990)

OPINION: PER CURIAM. In preparation for the 1985 Georgia Bar Examination, petitioners contracted to take a bar review course offered by respondent BRG of Georgia, Inc. (BRG). [T]hey contend that the price of BRG's course was enhanced by reason of an unlawful agreement between BRG and respondent Harcourt Brace Jovanovich Legal and Professional Publications (HBJ), the Nation's largest provider of bar review materials and lecture services. The central issue is whether the 1980 agreement between respondents violated § 1 of the Sherman Act.

HBJ began offering a Georgia bar review course on a limited basis in 1976, and was in direct, and often intense, competition with BRG during the period from 1977 to 1979. * * * In early 1980, they entered into an agreement that gave BRG an exclusive license to market HBJ's material in Georgia and to use its trade name "Bar/Bri." The parties agreed that HBJ would not compete with BRG in Georgia and that BRG would not compete with HBJ outside of Georgia. Under the agreement, HBJ received $100 per student enrolled by BRG and 40% of all revenues over $350. Immediately after the 1980 agreement, the price of BRG's course was increased from $150 to over $400.

[T]he District Court held that the agreement was lawful. The United States Court of Appeals for the Eleventh Circuit, with one judge dissenting, agreed with the District Court that *per se* unlawful horizontal price fixing required an explicit agreement on prices to be charged or that one party have the right to be consulted about the other's prices. The Court of Appeals also agreed with the District Court that to prove a *per se* violation under a geographic market allocation theory, petitioners had to show that respondents had subdivided some relevant market in which they had previously competed. * * *

In *United States v. Socony-Vacuum Oil Co.*, 310 U.S. 150 (1940), we held that an agreement among competitors to engage in a program of buying surplus gasoline on the spot market in order to prevent prices from falling sharply was unlawful, even though there was no direct agreement on the actual prices to be maintained. We explained that "under the Sherman Act a combination formed for the purpose and with the effect of raising, depressing, fixing, pegging, or stabilizing the price of a commodity in interstate or foreign commerce is illegal *per se*."

The revenue-sharing formula in the 1980 agreement between BRG and HBJ, coupled with the price increase that took place immediately after the parties agreed to cease competing with each other in 1980, indicates that this agreement was "formed for the purpose and with the effect of raising" the price of the bar review course. It was, therefore, plainly incorrect for the District Court to enter summary judgment in respondents' favor. Moreover, it is equally clear that the District Court and the Court of Appeals erred when they assumed that an allocation of markets or submarkets by competitors is not unlawful unless the market in which the two previously competed is divided between them.

In *United States v. Topco Associates, Inc.*, 405 U.S. 596 (1972), we held that agreements between competitors to allocate territories to minimize competition are illegal:

> One of the classic examples of a *per se* violation of § 1 is an agreement between competitors at the same level of the market structure to allocate territories in order to minimize competition. . . . This Court has reiterated time and time again that "[h]orizontal territorial limitations . . . are naked restraints of trade with no purpose except stifling of competition." Such limitations are *per se* violations of the Sherman Act.

The defendants in *Topco* had never competed in the same market, but had simply agreed to allocate markets. Here, HBJ and BRG had previously competed in the Georgia market; under their allocation agreement, BRG received that market, while HBJ received the remainder of the United States. Each agreed not to compete in the other's territories. Such agreements are anticompetitive regardless of whether the parties split a market within which both do business or whether they merely reserve one market for one and another for the other. Thus, the 1980 agreement between HBJ and BRG was unlawful on its face.

The petition for a writ of certiorari is granted, the judgment of the Court of Appeals is reversed, and the case is remanded for further proceedings consistent with this opinion.

It is so ordered.

JUSTICE SOUTER took no part in the consideration or decision of this case.

Questions for Discussion for Case 4.2

1. What is the relevant market?

2. What do you think the purpose of the agreement between these two firms was? Do you think that the managers of these companies could have legitimately thought that their contract was not against the public interest?

3. Do you think that the result would have been the same if the companies had decided to form a joint venture in Georgia? What standard would the court use to review a joint venture?

4. Recall from the chapter discussion that a joint venture is illegal *per se* where its purpose is to engage in behavior that is illegal *per se*. Do you think that it is harder to prove that a joint venture has an illegal purpose or to prove the existence of a horizontal market allocation?

5. Does your answer to Question 4 suggest greater leeway for joint ventures? Can you think why courts might allow joint ventures greater freedom than two independent companies?

4.3 Rule of Reason, Vertical Maximum Resale Price Maintenance
State Oil Co. v. Khan, 522 U.S. 3 (1997)

OPINION: JUSTICE O'CONNOR delivered the opinion of the Court.

Under § 1 of the Sherman Act, "[e]very contract, combination . . . , or conspiracy, in restraint of trade" is illegal. In *Albrecht v. Herald Co.*, 390 U.S. 145 (1968), this Court held that vertical maximum price fixing is a *per se* violation of that statute. In this case, we are asked to reconsider that decision in light of subsequent decisions of this Court. We conclude that *Albrecht* should be overruled.

I

Respondents, Barkat U. Khan and his corporation, entered into an agreement with petitioner, State Oil Company, to lease and operate a gas station and convenience store owned by State Oil. The agreement provided that respondents would obtain the station's gasoline supply from State Oil at a price equal to a suggested retail price set by State Oil, less a margin of 3.25 cents per gallon. Under the agreement, respondents could charge any amount for gasoline sold to the station's customers, but if the price charged was higher than State Oil's suggested retail price, the excess was to be rebated to State Oil. Respondents could sell gasoline for less than State Oil's suggested retail price, but any such decrease would reduce their 3.25 cents-per-gallon margin.

* * * *

Respondents sued State Oil . . . , alleging in part that State Oil had engaged in price-fixing in violation of § 1 of the Sherman Act by preventing respondents from raising or lowering retail gas prices. According to the complaint, but for the agreement with State Oil, respondents could have charged different prices based on the grades of gasoline, . . . thereby achieving increased sales and profits. * * *

* * * [T]he District Court entered summary judgment for State Oil on respondents' Sherman Act claim.

The Court of Appeals for the Seventh Circuit reversed. * * *

We granted certiorari to consider . . . whether State Oil's conduct constitutes a *per se* violation of the Sherman Act . . . .

II

A

Although the Sherman Act, by its terms, prohibits every agreement "in restraint of trade," this Court has long recognized that Congress intended to outlaw only unreasonable restraints. As a consequence, most antitrust claims are analyzed under a "rule of reason," according to which the finder of fact must decide whether the questioned practice imposes an unreasonable restraint on competition, taking into account a variety of factors, including specific information about the relevant business, its condition before and after the restraint was imposed, and the restraint's history, nature, and effect.

Some types of restraints, however, have such predictable and pernicious anticompetitive effect, and such limited potential for procompetitive benefit, that they are deemed unlawful *per se*. *Per se* treatment is appropriate "[o]nce experience with a particular kind of restraint enables the Court to predict with confidence that the rule of reason will condemn it." * * *

A review of this Court's decisions leading up to and beyond *Albrecht* is relevant to our assessment of the continuing validity of the *per se* rule established in *Albrecht*. Beginning with *Dr. Miles Medical Co. v. John D. Park & Sons Co.*, 220 U.S. 373 (1911), the Court recognized the illegality of agreements under which manufacturers or suppliers set the minimum resale prices to be charged by their distributors. By 1940, the Court broadly declared all business combinations "formed for the purpose and with the effect of raising, depressing, fixing, pegging, or stabilizing the price of a commodity in interstate or foreign commerce" illegal *per se*. *United States v. Socony-Vacuum Oil Co.*, 310 U.S. 150 (1940). Accordingly, the Court condemned an agreement between two affiliated liquor distillers to limit the maximum price charged by retailers in *Kiefer-Stewart Co. v. Joseph E. Seagram & Sons, Inc.*, 340 U.S. 211 (1951), noting that agreements to fix maximum prices, "no less than those to fix minimum prices, cripple the freedom of traders and thereby restrain their ability to sell in accordance with their own judgment."

In subsequent cases, the Court's attention turned to arrangements through which suppliers imposed restrictions on dealers with respect to matters other than resale price. In *White Motor Co. v. United States*, 372 U.S. 253 (1963), the Court considered the validity of a manufacturer's assignment of exclusive territories to its distributors and dealers. The Court determined that too little was known about the competitive impact of such vertical limitations to warrant treating them as *per se* unlawful. Four years later, in *United States v. Arnold, Schwinn & Co.*, 388 U.S. 365 (1967), the Court reconsidered the status of exclusive dealer territories and held that, upon the transfer of title to goods to a distributor, a supplier's imposition of territorial restrictions on the distributor was "so obviously destructive of competition" as to constitute a *per se* violation of the Sherman Act.* * *

Albrecht, decided the following Term, involved a newspaper publisher who had granted exclusive territories to independent carriers subject to their adherence to a maximum price on resale of the newspapers to the public. Influenced by its decisions in *Socony-Vacuum*, *Kiefer-Stewart*, and *Schwinn*, the Court concluded that it was *per se* unlawful for the publisher to fix the maximum resale price of its newspapers. * * *

Albrecht was animated in part by the fear that vertical maximum price-fixing could allow suppliers to discriminate against certain dealers, restrict the services that dealers could afford to offer customers, or disguise minimum price fixing schemes. * * *

* * * *

Nine years later, in *Continental T. V., Inc. v. GTE Sylvania Inc.*, 433 U.S. 36 (1977), the Court overruled *Schwinn*, thereby rejecting application of a *per se* rule in the context of vertical nonprice restrictions. The Court acknowledged the

principle of *stare decisis*, but explained that the need for clarification in the law justified reconsideration of *Schwinn*:

> Since its announcement, *Schwinn* has been the subject of continuing controversy and confusion, both in the scholarly journals and in the federal courts. The great weight of scholarly opinion has been critical of the decision, and a number of the federal courts confronted with analogous vertical restrictions have sought to limit its reach. In our view, the experience of the past 10 years should be brought to bear on this subject of considerable commercial importance.

* * * *

* * * Subsequent decisions of the Court . . . have hinted that the analytical underpinnings of *Albrecht* were substantially weakened by *GTE Sylvania*. * * *

* * * *

B

Thus, our reconsideration of *Albrecht*'s continuing validity is informed by several of our decisions, as well as a considerable body of scholarship discussing the effects of vertical restraints. Our analysis is also guided by our general view that the primary purpose of the antitrust laws is to protect interbrand competition. "Low prices," we have explained, "benefit consumers regardless of how those prices are set, and so long as they are above predatory levels, they do not threaten competition." * * *

So informed, we find it difficult to maintain that vertically-imposed maximum prices could harm consumers or competition to the extent necessary to justify their *per se* invalidation. * * *

* * * *

After reconsidering *Albrecht*'s rationale and the substantial criticism the decision has received, . . . we conclude that there is insufficient economic justification for *per se* invalidation of vertical maximum price-fixing. * * *

* * * *

C

Despite what Chief Judge Posner aptly described as *Albrecht*'s "infirmities, [and] its increasingly wobbly, moth-eaten foundations," there remains the question whether *Albrecht* deserves continuing respect under the doctrine of *stare decisis*. The Court of Appeals was correct in applying that principle despite disagreement with *Albrecht*, for it is this Court's prerogative alone to overrule one of its precedents.

We approach the reconsideration of decisions of this Court with the utmost caution. *Stare decisis* reflects "a policy judgment that 'in most matters it is more important that the applicable rule of law be settled than that it be settled right.'" It "is the preferred course because it promotes the evenhanded, predictable, and consistent development of legal principles, fosters reliance on judicial decisions, and contributes to the actual and perceived integrity of the judicial process." This Court has expressed its reluctance to overrule decisions involving statutory interpretation, and has acknowledged that *stare decisis* concerns are at their acme in cases involving property and contract rights. Both of those concerns are arguably relevant in this case.

But "*[s]tare decisis* is not an inexorable command." In the area of antitrust law, there is a competing interest, well-represented in this Court's decisions, in recognizing and adapting to changed circumstances and the lessons of accumulated experience. Thus, the general presumption that legislative changes should be left to Congress has less force with respect to the Sherman Act in light of the accepted view that Congress "expected the courts to give shape to the statute's broad mandate by drawing on common-law tradition." * * * Accordingly, this Court has reconsidered its decisions construing the Sherman Act when the theoretical underpinnings of those decisions are called into serious question.

* * * *

* * * In overruling *Albrecht*, we of course do not hold that all vertical maximum price-fixing is *per se* lawful. Instead, vertical maximum price-fixing, like the majority of commercial arrangements subject to the antitrust laws, should be evaluated under the rule of reason. * * *

* * * We therefore vacate the judgment of the Court of Appeals and remand the case for further proceedings consistent with this opinion.

It is so ordered.

Questions for Discussion for Case 4.3

1. What is the doctrine of *stare decisis?* Under what circumstances will the Supreme Court reverse its own precedents?

2. How could vertical maximum price-fixing benefit consumers?

3. Why would a company want to set a maximum price for its goods?

4. Do you think it would be legal for a company to set a maximum price for its distributors but not for itself?

4.4 Monopolization, Attempted Monopolization, Essential Facilities

America Online, Inc. v. GreatDeals.Net, 49 F. Supp. 2d 851 (E.D. Va. 1999)

* * * The issue[*] presented [is] . . . whether Defendants' claim of monopolization and attempted monopolization in violation of antitrust laws constitutes a claim upon which relief can be granted . . . . For the reasons stated below, the Court grants Plaintiff's Motion to Dismiss . . . .

I. Background

Defendant Martindale Empowerment ("Martindale") is a Virginia corporation in the business of providing commercial electronic-mail ("e-mail") service to advertisers. Great-Deals.Net is an Internet domain name belonging to Martindale Empowerment and GreatDeals is a trade name belonging to Martindale Empowerment. Until September 1998, Martindale's business included sending commercial electronic advertising over the Internet in the form of e-mail to e-mail addresses throughout the United States.

Plaintiff America Online, Inc. ("AOL") is the largest commercial online service with more than sixteen million individual subscribers across the United States. From late 1996 to September 1998, Martindale transmitted commercial e-mail messages advertising goods and services to AOL subscribers among others. Martindale marketed computers and computer-related equipment. Martindale claims that it ceased transmitting messages to AOL subscribers because AOL created various mechanisms to block these transmissions and succeeded in blocking virtually all such transmissions. Martindale contends that AOL has established itself as the only entity that can advertise to AOL subscribers.

AOL brought a complaint seeking damages and an injunction to prohibit Defendants from continuing their practice of sending unsolicited bulk e-mail ("UBE") advertisements to AOL subscribers. * * * AOL alleged that Defendants used deceptive practices to mask the source and quantity of their transmissions and thereby avoid AOL's filtering technologies. AOL further alleged that Defendants continued such transmissions after specific notice from AOL that their use of AOL's computer network was unauthorized and that AOL was receiving thousands of complaints from its subscribers who received Defendants' UBE.

Defendants admit that they transmitted UBE containing their advertisements for computer equipment to AOL subscribers. * * * [D]efendants claimed that . . . AOL violated antitrust laws by engaging in monopolization and attempted monopolization . . . .

AOL has filed a motion to dismiss . . . .

* * * *

IV. Violations of Antitrust Laws
(Counts III & IV)

* * * *

A. Monopolization

* * * *

To prevail on a monopolization claim, a party must show: (1) possession of monopoly power in a relevant market [and] (2) willful acquisition or maintenance of that power in an exclusionary manner . . . . * * *

1. Relevant Market

AOL argues that Defendants have failed to allege a viable relevant market . . . . Defendants argue that the proper market for purposes of this case is e-mail advertising and that Internet subscribers who are accessed through the facilities which AOL controls constitute a distinct sub-market. * * * The Court holds that Defendants' monopolization claim should be dismissed for failure to plead a relevant market.

A relevant market has two dimensions: (1) the relevant product market, which identifies the products or services that compete with each other, and (2) the relevant geographic market, which identifies the geographic area within which competition takes place. The outer boundaries of a relevant market are determined by reasonable interchangeability of use. Reasonable interchangeability of use refers to consumers' practicable ability to switch from one product or service to another. Thus, the Court must consider whether there are any substitutes for Defendants' e-mail advertising to AOL subscribers.

In defining the relevant product or service market, the Court finds that there are reasonable substitutes for advertising through AOL. Thus, it must reject Defendants' proposed relevant market. First, the Court rejects Defendants' attempt to restrict the market to e-mail advertising. There are numerous substitutes for e-mail advertising, some of which are less expensive, including use of the World Wide Web, direct mail, billboards, television, newspapers, radio, and leaflets, to name a few. Even if the Court restricted the market to e-mail advertising, interchangeable substitutes include other paid e-mail subscription services such as Microsoft Network or Prodigy, or free e-mail services like Hotmail and Yahoo. The Court will not restrict the market to AOL subscribers because it is improper to define a market simply by identifying a group of consumers who have purchased a given product. Instead, the market consists of the array of "interchangeable" products that those consumers confronted when making their product selection. Here, AOL subscribers could have chosen another paid e-mail service or a free e-mail service. Thus, those entities are part of the relevant market. * * * In this case, there are other e-mail services that provide the same type of service as AOL. Defendants could have advertised through another e-mail service and still reached the Internet-accessing public.

With respect to the relevant geographic market in which competition takes place, the Court finds that the Internet cannot be defined with outer boundaries. It is not a place or location; it is infinite. The Internet is a "giant network which interconnects innumerable smaller groups of linked computer networks." The network "allows any of literally tens of millions of people with access to the Internet to exchange information." Defendants ignore the fact that they have multiple means of advertising their computer equipment to the Internet-accessing public. The geographic market may not be restricted to AOL subscribers not only because there are other persons with access to the Internet, but also because there are other means of advertising to those persons and to AOL subscribers.

* * * *

2. Exclusionary or Anti-Competitive Conduct

The second element of a monopolization claim requires that Defendants prove willful acquisition or maintenance of the monopoly power in an exclusionary manner. Whether conduct is exclusionary is not defined by the effect of such conduct on Defendants. The Court should consider the impact of such conduct on consumers and competitors. If Defendants show that AOL has harmed consumers and competition by making a short-term sacrifice in order to further its exclusive, anti-competitive objectives, then Defendants establish predation by AOL. Exploiting competitive advantage that is legitimately available, however, does not amount to predatory conduct, even for a firm with monopoly power. Thus, general intent to gain monopoly status is not sufficient absent some predatory conduct.

Here, Defendants make no showing of harm to consumers or to AOL's competition.[6] Furthermore, Defendants do not point to any exclusive, anti-competitive objectives other

---

[6] It is important to note that Defendants cannot claim harm as a competitor of AOL because Defendants do not compete in the same market as AOL. Defendants are advertisers and sellers of computer equipment whereas AOL sells information services.

than AOL's requirement that advertisers pay for the right to advertise on AOL's network to AOL's subscribers. Even if the Court views AOL as a monopoly power in the Internet access or information services market because AOL has 16 million subscribers, there is no proof of exclusionary conduct by AOL. Defendants' allegation that AOL discouraged other information service providers from permitting Martindale to advertise on their networks does not amount to anti-competitive conduct. Defendants fail to allege or demonstrate any impact of the purported anti-competitive conduct on consumers or competitors. Indeed, Defendants' claim seems to rest on the fact that AOL has been successful in the information services market. Where, as here, there is no predatory conduct and a successful entrepreneur competing in the infinite Internet market, there can be no claim of monopolization. Thus, Defendants cannot prevail on this aspect of the monopolization claim and dismissal is appropriate.

B. Attempted Monopolization

To establish attempted monopolization, a party must show: (1) specific intent to monopolize the market; (2) anti-competitive or predatory conduct designed to further that intent; and (3) a dangerous probability of success.

1. Specific Intent to Monopolize

Defendants claim intent may be inferred from the acts of the party allegedly attempting to monopolize. * * * The only evidence thus far is that AOL blocked Defendants' advertisements, refused to accept compensation from Defendants for the right to advertise to AOL subscribers on AOL's network,[7] and allegedly threatened to stop dealing with other entities who do business with Defendants.

Unlike monopolization, which requires intent only, attempted monopolization requires proof that the accused party had a "specific intent to destroy competition or build monopoly." A desire to increase market share or even to drive a competitor out of business through vigorous competition on the merits is not sufficient. The monopolizing party must have sought to create a monopoly by circumventing the competitive process. * * *

* * * *

* * * [D]efendants have failed to allege any conduct that would support an inference of specific intent. The only anti-competitive practice that Defendants allege is that AOL allegedly threatened other providers who dealt with Defendants with lack of access to AOL subscribers if they did not

---

[7] There is no evidence that AOL prohibited Defendants from participating in the normal application process for businesses that want to advertise on AOL's network. Defendants did not apply; instead, they advertised through UBE then offered to pay AOL after being caught.

stop dealing with Defendants. * * * AOL's vigorous attempts to protect its subscribers from UBE and to prevent Defendants from circumventing AOL's technical means to prevent the transmission of UBE to its subscribers do not show intent to monopolize.

2. Anti-Competitive or Predatory Conduct

As established in the discussion above on monopolization, Defendants have not alleged any anti-competitive conduct. Thus, there is nothing to show that AOL acted to further a specific intent to monopolize. * * *

3. Dangerous Probability of Success

To determine whether there is a dangerous probability of success in monopolizing the market, courts often consider the relevant market and a participant's ability to lessen or destroy competition in that market. The Court holds that in this case there cannot be a probability that AOL will monopolize the information services market because the Internet is infinite. Indeed, the Court is unable to measure AOL's market share because the market in which AOL participates is not defined. The Internet is not regulated and an entrant's ability to participate in the market and offer services like that offered by AOL is without boundary. Thus, even if the Court determined AOL's market share to be relatively high, there is no dangerous probability of successful monopolization where there are no substantial barriers to entry and there are other factors that make the exercise of monopoly power unlikely.

Because Defendants can establish none of the factors necessary to show attempted monopolization, dismissal of this claim is appropriate.

C. Denial of Essential Facilities

* * * To plead monopolization through the "essential facilities" doctrine, Defendants must allege (1) control of the essential facility by a monopolist; (2) a competitor's inability practically or reasonably to duplicate the essential facility; (3) the denial of the use of the facility to a competitor; and (4) the feasibility of providing the facility to competitors. "An 'essential facility' is one which is not merely helpful but vital to the claimant's competitive viability."

Here, Defendants allege that AOL controls an essential facility for access to all persons who obtain access to the Internet through AOL. Defendants contend that there is no other way to obtain access to such persons other than through nodes controlled by AOL. Defendants allege that AOL has used its control of Internet nodes to prevent Martindale from transmitting commercial electronic messages to AOL subscribers. At the same time, Defendants contend that AOL does transmit commercial electronic messages for non-AOL advertisers, and thus monopolizes the market for such commercial electronic messages to its subscribers.

* * * *

Elements two, three, and four require that the monopolist and the plaintiff are competitors. The essential facilities doctrine is inapplicable where the alleged monopolist and the plaintiff do not compete. In the present case, Martindale fails to allege or plead any facts from which the Court could infer that Defendants and AOL are competitors.

* * * *

The pleadings also have another defect as to element two. Martindale failed to plead that it could not reasonably duplicate or pursue a reasonable alternative to the essential facility. In fact, Martindale even concedes that in "rare" cases persons such as Martindale can obtain access to such persons other than through nodes controlled by AOL. As stated by another court, "Internet users are not a 'captive audience' to any single service provider, but can transfer from one service to another . . . ." Anyone can acquire the computer equipment necessary to provide Internet access services on a smaller scale with a relatively minor capital investment. As argued by AOL, Martindale could develop its own commercial online system or advertising web site and charge a competitive rate. Due to the other means by which Martindale could reach AOL subscribers, Martindale cannot properly plead element two of the essential facilities doctrine.

* * * *

VI. Conclusion

For the reasons stated above, Plaintiff's Motion to Dismiss Defendants' Counterclaims is granted. * * *

Questions for Discussion for Case 4.4

1. What are the required elements of a monopolization claim? Attempted monopolization?

2. How do we define the limits of a "relevant market" for antitrust purposes?

3. Do you think that the court was correct in stating that the relevant market was broader than just e-mail advertising? Are the substitutes that the court listed (the Web, direct mail, billboards, television, newspapers, radio, and leaflets) reasonably interchangeable with direct e-mail? What factors would you consider in determining whether other media are suitable substitutes for e-mail advertising?

4. Why does the court state that the defendant must show harm to consumers or to AOL's competition in order to support its monopolization claim?

5. Why does the court find that the essential facilities doctrine is inapplicable here? Do you think that the barriers to entry for a firm like GreatDeals.Net to form its own on-line service that would be competitive with AOL would be great or slight?

4.5 Attempted Monopolization
Taylor Publishing Co. v. Jostens, Inc., 36 F. Supp. 2d 360 (E.D. Tex. 1999)

Introduction

Plaintiff, Taylor Publishing Company, and Defendant, Jostens, Inc., are competitors in the manufacture and sale of scholastic yearbooks. The major competitors in the yearbook market are Plaintiff, Defendant, Herff-Jones, Lifetouch, and Walsworth. Defendant and Plaintiff hold the number one and number two market positions, respectively.

Plaintiff brought claims for damages against Defendant alleging that Defendant violated federal law by attempting to monopolize the national yearbook market in violation of Section 2 of the Sherman Antitrust Act . . . .

For purposes of Plaintiff's attempted monopolization claim, the parties agreed that the relevant geographic market was limited to sales within the United States, however, the parties disagreed as to the relevant product market. Plaintiff contended that the product market was limited to "yearbooks," those products prepared by students, with some teacher input, that incorporate individual student pictures as well as candid shots of various activities within the school. Plaintiff argued that "picture books," those products usually limited to individual student pictures and often prepared by teachers with little or no input from students, should not be included in the product market. On the other hand, Defendant claimed the relevant product market included both yearbooks and picture books.

The case was tried with a jury beginning on May 4, 1998. * * * Plaintiff claimed that Defendant planned to eliminate Plaintiff from the market and implemented such plan by the use of many predatory practices. * * *

* * * The jury returned with a verdict containing findings against Defendant . . . . * * *

Defendant files the current motion and renews its Motion for Judgment as a Matter of Law . . . . * * *

* * * *

LEGAL STANDARD FOR JUDGMENT AS A MATTER OF LAW

Judgment as a matter of law is proper if "there is no legally sufficient evidentiary basis for a reasonable jury to find for that party on that issue." * * *

DISCUSSION

* * * *

II. Defendant's Motion for Judgment as a Matter of Law

* * * *

A. Attempted Monopolization Under Section 2 of the Sherman Act

1. *The Applicable Law*

An attempted monopoly in violation of Section 2 of the Sherman Act consists of 3 elements: (1) that the defendant engaged in predatory or anticompetitive conduct, (2) that the defendant specifically intended to acquire monopoly power in the relevant market, and (3) a dangerous probability that an actual monopoly position will ultimately be achieved. * * *

2. *Court's Analysis*

In short, Defendant contends that Plaintiff's Section 2 claim fails as a matter of law because Plaintiff presented insufficient evidence of substantial predatory conduct which created a dangerous probability of monopolization. * * *

a. *Predatory or Anticompetitive Conduct*

The first element of an attempted monopolization claim requires Plaintiff to show that Defendant engaged in anticompetitive or predatory conduct designed to further an intent to monopolize. "Predatory or anticompetitive conduct is that which unfairly tends to be exclusionary or tends to destroy competition." "Exclusionary conduct is conduct that tends to exclude or restrict competition and is not supported by a valid business reason." "[I]n order to rise to a § 2 violation, however, the exclusionary conduct must appear reasonably capable of contributing *significantly* to creating or maintaining monopoly power."

At trial, Plaintiff claimed that Defendant engaged in the following anticompetitive activities: (1) sham pricing; (2) predatory pricing; (3) raiding Plaintiff's sales force; (4) acquiring Plaintiff's confidential information; (5) interfering with Plaintiff's term agreements with customers; and (6) predatory disparagement.

* * * The Court will address each area of conduct.

i. *Sham Pricing or Upgrading*

"Sham pricing" was the predominant type of conduct Plaintiff pointed to in support of its claim of predatory, anticompetitive conduct by Defendant. Plaintiff claimed that Defendant's sales representatives made false or sham price quotes in order to win yearbook accounts from Plaintiff without the intention of fulfilling the contracts at the quoted prices. Plaintiff contended that after Defendant entered into contracts with the converted customers, it then charged higher prices to the customer. Plaintiff offered . . . , a memorandum written by one of Defendant's personnel that described the process of upgrading as providing the lowest price to a customer in order to obtain the business and then reselling a new program to this customer after the customer has committed to having Defendant publish the yearbook. Additionally, Plaintiff identified other evidence of training programs on upgrading that were offered by Defendant to its sales representatives. Plaintiff claimed that over the 4-year period of 1995 to 1998, 840 of its former customers were victims of Defendant's sham pricing and that such conduct caused $9,602,000 in damages to Plaintiff.

While Plaintiff characterizes this conduct as "sham" or "false pricing," Defendant contends this conduct is known as "upgrading" in the industry and is the process of selling additional yearbook features to customers. The sale of additional features results in a final invoice price greater than the original contract price, however, Defendant argues this is not fraudulent or illegal, anticompetitive conduct. * * *

* * * Absent evidence that Defendant's original contracts misrepresented what the customer would be receiving for the stated price or that Defendant falsely quoted prices to the customer, the Court finds that Plaintiff failed to prove that Defendant's actions constituted predatory, anticompetitive conduct.

ii. Predatory Pricing

A claimant alleging predatory pricing in violation of Section 2 of the Sherman Act must establish two elements for recovery. First, a plaintiff must prove that a rival's low prices are below an appropriate measure of the rival's costs. The second element of a predatory pricing claim requires the plaintiff to demonstrate that the rival had a dangerous probability of recouping its investment in below-cost prices. "For recoupment to occur, below-cost pricing must be capable, as a threshold matter, of producing the intended effects on the firm's rivals, whether driving them from the market, or, . . . causing them to raise their prices to supracompetitive levels . . . ." * * *

* * * Plaintiff argued that as part of Defendant's attempt to monopolize the yearbook market, Defendant priced its yearbooks to customers at prices below its [average variable cost (AVC)], thus taking a loss on the yearbook. Plaintiff offered evidence that Defendant sold below its AVC to 66 customers over the 4-year period of 1995 to 1998 and that from this, Plaintiff's actual losses and future lost profits for a 10-year period amounted to $591,000.

* * * *

The Court finds that Plaintiff's evidence on predatory pricing fails to support a finding of anticompetitive conduct in violation of the Sherman Act. First, through its accounting expert . . . Plaintiff offered evidence that throughout the entire United States, Defendant sold below its AVC to 27 of Plaintiff's former customers in 1995, 26 in 1996, and 13 in 1997. Since Plaintiff annually serviced 7,000 schools on average, this evidence amounts to a customer loss of less than 1% of Plaintiff's annual sales. The Court finds that with an impact of less than 1%, Defendant's below-cost pricing was not capable, as a threshold matter, of driving its competitors from the market. * * *

iii. Predatory Hiring

In *Associated Radio Service Co. v. Page Airways, Inc.*, 624 F.2d 1342 (5th Cir. 1980), the Fifth Circuit recited the following principles from a treatise on antitrust law:

> Areeda and Turner are adamant in their view that the mere hiring away of employees from a rival is *per se* legal under the antitrust laws . . . . [However] no similar virtue would redeem efforts to induce such disloyal performance by a rival's employee as disclosure of trade secrets or other private information; [or] steering customers, researchers, or others away from his employer and to the monopolist. [S]uch practices would be grounds for Section 2 liability *if the actual effect was significant.*

* * * *

In the present case, Plaintiff offered evidence that Defendant hired the following three sales representatives from Plaintiff: Jeff Graffam, Jan Day DeFalco, and Dan DeFalco, who was regarded as a "lynchpin" that would bring $1.4 million in sales to Defendant. Since sales representatives are very important to a yearbook company, Plaintiff contended that Defendant's hiring of Plaintiff's sales representatives was an effective way to put Plaintiff out of business. Additionally, Plaintiff claimed Defendant induced these individuals to reveal confidential information concerning Plaintiff. Plaintiff asserted that it lost 49 customers during 1995 to 1998 due to Defendant's raiding of Plaintiff's sales force and that such loss resulted in actual lost profits and projected lost profits of $664,000 over a 10-year period.

* * * *

[T]he Court is unable to find sufficient evidence that Defendant either induced disclosure of confidential information by Graffam or the DeFalcos or that these sales representatives steered customers away from Plaintiff and to Defendant while the sales representatives were still employed by Plaintiff. Moreover, the Court finds the loss sustained by Plaintiff was insignificant. Evidence at trial showed that Plaintiff had over 200 sales representatives; therefore, the loss of 3 represented 1.5% of its sales force. Further, less than 1% of Plaintiff's customers, a figure representing 49 of Plaintiff's 7,000 total customers, transferred to Defendant. Additionally, the monetary loss of $664,000 over 10 years represented less than 1% of the approximate $70 million in sales that Plaintiff has in 1 year. The Court finds Defendant's hiring of the 3 representatives had a negligible impact upon Plaintiff's competitive position.

iv. Acquisition of Confidential Information or Trade Secrets

[T]he Court finds that Plaintiff offered some evidence that Defendant possessed confidential information of Plaintiff. However, the Court is of the opinion that the acquisition of such information by Defendant had an insubstantial effect on Plaintiff. Plaintiff claimed damages in the amount of $1,446,576 from Defendant's acquisition of confidential information. This amount constitutes only 2% of Plaintiff's total sales in one year. Such impact does not rise to the level of contributing significantly to creating or maintaining monopoly power; therefore, this conduct cannot support a finding of a Section 2 violation.

* * * *

vi. Predatory Disparagement

[I]solated incidents of disparagement do not constitute sufficient evidence to support an attempted monopolization claim.

Defendant contends that Plaintiff presented no evidence of disparagement at trial. At best, Defendant states the only testimony which might be considered such was testimony that one of Defendant's sales representatives told a teacher that Plaintiff was having problems with its plant in 1994.

While Plaintiff alleged disparagement by Defendant, . . . Plaintiff failed to support such allegation. Further, the Court is not aware of any damages suffered by Plaintiff as a result of disparagement. Therefore, the Court finds that as a matter of law, the jury could not have based a finding of predatory, anticompetitive conduct on alleged disparagement.

In summary, the Court finds that not one of the instances of improper conduct would lead to Section 2 liability. The analysis remains unchanged when the acts are viewed as a whole. The evidence showed that the aggregated conduct had an insubstantial effect on Plaintiff and does not support the jury's verdict that Defendant attempted to monopolize the yearbook market. Since the Court is of the opinion that Plaintiff failed to prove predatory conduct that unfairly tended to be exclusionary or tended to destroy competition, Plaintiff's attempted monopolization claim fails for lack of this element.

b. Dangerous Probability of Achieving Monopoly Power

Even though the Court believes Plaintiff's attempted monopolization claim fails for lack of sufficient anticompetitive conduct, the Court also finds that the claim fails for lack of a dangerous probability that Defendant would have achieved monopoly power. As part of Plaintiff's attempted monopolization claim, Plaintiff had to prove there was a dangerous probability that the attempted monopolization would succeed. Monopoly power is the power to control prices or exclude competition. In determining whether there is a dangerous probability of monopolization, courts have found it necessary to consider the relevant market and the defendant's ability to lessen or destroy competition in that market. Further, this element is assessed by evaluating the defendant's market share in the relevant market.

Plaintiff contends that Defendant devised and implemented a plan to put Plaintiff out of business. The most significant evidence presented by Plaintiff in support of its claim was the collection of statements by Jack Thornton, the indi-

vidual who ran Defendant's yearbook business during the relevant time period, pertaining to Thornton's dream of becoming the only national yearbook company in the industry. Additionally, Plaintiff offered minimal evidence of predatory conduct: (1) that Defendant hired 3 of Plaintiff's 200 sales representatives; (2) that Defendant sold below its AVC to a total of 66 customers over 4 years; and (3) that Defendant obtained some of Plaintiff's confidential information.

While the most significant pieces of evidence Plaintiff relied upon to establish a dangerous probability of monopolization were statements of intent to become the only national yearbook company by Defendant's personnel, this evidence did not establish that Defendant realistically possessed the power to create a monopoly. Instead, the undisputed evidence at trial indicated that throughout the period of alleged predation, Plaintiff was a large, profitable company whose sales remained constant during the relevant period of time—$100.4 million in 1994, $98.6 in 1995, $99 in 1996, $98.2 in 1997, and an estimated $102.2 in 1998. There was no evidence that any conduct by Defendant caused Plaintiff to exit any markets or product lines, lay off any employees, sell assets, or do anything to place its business in peril. The evidence at trial was insufficient to support a finding that the predatory acts on which Plaintiff relied resulted in a dangerous probability that an attempted monopoly would succeed. Rather, the evidence indicated Defendant did not control prices or exclude competition; therefore, no dangerous probability of Defendant monopolizing the market existed.

* * * *

CONCLUSION

For the foregoing reasons, the Court finds that judgment as a matter of law should be granted in Defendant's favor on all of Plaintiff's claims.

IT IS SO ORDERED.

Questions for Discussion for Case 4.5

1. What are the required elements of an attempted monopolization claim? Did the plaintiff succeed in showing either of these elements?

2. The jury found for the plaintiff in this case, yet the defendant ultimately won. Why?

3. Does it seem like Taylor Publishing had many small grievances and few major ones? Do you think that this had an impact on how the court viewed its claims?

DISCUSSION QUESTIONS

1. In 1968, Business Electronics Corp. (BEC) became the exclusive retailer in the Houston area of electronic calculators manufactured by Sharp Electronics Corp. In 1972, Sharp appointed Gilbert Hartwell as a second retailer in the Houston area. At the time, electronic calculators cost up to $1,000 and were sold primarily to business customers. Sharp published a list of suggested minimum retail prices, but its written dealership agreements with BEC and Hartwell did not require either of them to honor those prices or to charge any other specific prices. BEC's retail prices were often below Hartwell's retail prices, although Hartwell sometimes priced below Sharp's suggested retail prices as well. Hartwell complained to Sharp a number of times about BEC's prices. In June 1973, Hartwell delivered an ultimatum to Sharp that Hartwell would terminate his dealership unless Sharp ended its relationship with BEC within 30 days. Sharp terminated BEC's dealership the next month. BEC sued Sharp and Hartwell alleging that: (1) they had conspired to terminate BEC and (2) such a conspiracy was illegal *per se* under Section 1 of the Sherman Act. Should the *per se* standard apply here? Why, or why not? *Business Electronics Corp. v. Sharp Electronics Corp.*, 485 U.S. 717 (1988)

2. Russell Stover Candies, Inc., sells and ships its box chocolates and candies to more than 18,000 retailers throughout the country. Most of the retailers are department, drug, card, and gift stores. Russell Stover designates resale prices for all of its products and communicates those prices to retailers by price lists, invoices, order forms, and preticketing of all of its products. Russell Stover also announces to each prospective retailer the circumstances under which it will refuse to sell; i.e., whenever Russell Stover reasonably believes that a prospective retailer will resell Stover products at less than designated prices and whenever an existing retailer has actually sold Stover products at less than designated prices. Russell Stover does not request or accept express assurances from existing or prospective retailers regarding resale prices, however. Russell Stover has, in the past, refused to sell to prospective retailers or has terminated existing retailers based on these policies. As a result, 97.4 percent of Stover products are sold at or above the designated resale price.

The FTC determined that Russell Stover had violated Section 1 of the Sherman Act by illegally combining with the retail dealers to fix retail prices.

Russell Stover has appealed the FTC's decision to the Court of Appeals. How should the appellate court rule on this issue? *Russell Stover Candies, Inc. v. FTC*, 718 F.2d 256 (8th Cir. 1983)

3. Anti-Monopoly, Inc., developed and marketed a family board game called Anti-Monopoly. It possessed less than 1 percent of the market for family board games. Hasbro, Inc., the leading manufacturer of family board games, has more than 80 percent of the market. Toys "R" Us is the largest retailer of family board games, with about 35 percent to 40 percent of the retail market. K-Mart is the second largest such retailer, with about 15 percent of the retail market. Anti-Monopoly and Hasbro compete directly for space in retail stores such as these. Anti-Monopoly brought suit against Hasbro, alleging that Hasbro exercised control over Toys "R" Us and K-Mart by conditioning the sale of its family board games to such retailers on the retailers not purchasing family board games from Anti-Monopoly and other small competitors. Anti-Monopoly alleged that Hasbro's control of Toys "R" Us and K-Mart constituted monopolization of an essential facility in violation of Section 2 of the Sherman Act. How should the court rule on this claim? *Anti-Monopoly, Inc. Hasbro, Inc.*, 1995-2 Trade Cas. (CCH) P71,095 (S.D.N.Y. 1995)

4. Jimi Rose owned a business, first known as Hollywood Nights and then as Goodfellas, which he wanted to advertise in the *Morning Call*, a local newspaper. He alleged that space and layout restrictions were placed on his ads and that on several occasions, his ads were not run at all, while white competitors in similar businesses faced no such restrictions. He alleged that he was told by the *Morning Call* that his ads were prurient and inferior to those of his white competitors, yet the *Morning Call* accepted prurient and sexually suggestive ads from those competitors. He further alleged that the *Morning Call* refused to accept his ads for over a year and that the ban extended to the classified want ads, which prevented him from seeking new employees. Finally, Rose alleged that the ban on his advertising cost him valuable business, as hotel guests and convention participants did not know that his business existed. Rose contended that the *Morning Call's* behavior toward him was racially motivated.

Rose sued the *Morning Call*, alleging that the *Morning Call* enjoyed monopoly power over an essential facility, newspaper advertising, and that its use of that power to exclude Rose from advertising his business and from placing classified ads had an anticompetitive effect. Rose described the relevant geographic market as the Lehigh Valley in Pennsylvania and the relevant product market as advertising in the *Morning Call*. He alleged that the *Morning Call*'s actions diminished his ability to compete in the marketplace and caused "serious and permanent damage" to him and his business. Is the *Morning Call* an essential facility? Has Rose defined the relevant markets correctly? If you were the judge, how would you rule on this claim, and why? *Rose v. The Morning Call, Inc.*, 1997-1 Trade Cas. (CCH) P71,775 (E.D. Penn. 1997)

5. Cancall Communications, Inc., a distributor of prepaid wireless telephone services, acquired airtime on Omnipoint Corp.'s network that it then resold to its customers. In the prepaid wireless telecommunications industry, each consumer must use a telephone handset that is specifically programmed to access a specific network. The service providers supply Subscriber Identification Module Cards (SIM Cards) to each of their customers. The SIM cards contain specific information about each consumer and enable that consumer to access the network. Omnipoint refused to sell Cancall SIM cards alone, but instead required that Cancall's customers purchase new handsets, which were manufactured by three handset manufacturers (the Equipment Manufacturers) and supplied to Omnipoint for use with its network. While direct Omnipoint customers could purchase the handsets from Omnipoint for $49, Omnipoint charged Cancall $189 for the same handsets. The Equipment Manufacturers refused to sell the handsets directly to Cancall. Cancall has alleged that the Equipment Manufacturers have violated the Robinson-Patman Act. Have they? Why, or why not? *Cancall, PCS, LCC v. Omnipoint Corp.*, 2000 ITrade Co (ccm) p 72,855 (S.D.N.Y. 2000)

6. Digital Equipment Corp. (DEC) manufactures computer hardware. In April 1994, DEC introduced its Alpha line of mid-range servers. It offered a three-year warranty on the servers, even though the industry standard at the time was to offer a one-year warranty. DEC offered the longer warranty as part of its strategy to compete with its industry rivals, such as IBM, Sun Microsystems, and Hewlett-Packard.

SMS Systems Maintenance Services, Inc., an independent service organization (ISO) that operates nationally and specializes in servicing DEC equipment, accused DEC of violating Section 2 of the Sherman Act, alleging that longer warranties unfairly constrained consumers' ability to choose their preferred service providers and thus paved the way for a monopoly in the services aftermarket for DEC computers. There is a strong aftermarket for servicing computers, and many ISOs compete vigorously with manufacturers for this business. SMS argued that a purchaser with a warranty will not use an ISO because the purchaser will not want to pay twice for the same service. In framing its argument, SMS alleged that the relevant market was the aftermarket for repair services for DEC computers. Has SMS defined the relevant market correctly? How should the court rule on its claim? *SMS Systems Maintenance Services, Inc. v. Digital Equipment Corp.*, 188 F.3d 11 (1st Cir. 1999)

7. Full Draw Productions, an archery trade show promoter, held its first Bowhunting Trade Show (BTS) in 1990. At the time, it was the only merchandise mart devoted solely to archery equipment. Archery manufacturers and distributors purchased exhibition space, and dealers paid a fee to attend. The same year, Full Draw entered into a five-year agreement with AMMO, a trade association, in which Full Draw paid AMMO 10 percent of its BTS gross revenues in exchange for AMMO's endorsement of the show. In 1994, AMMO tried to increase this fee to 30 percent. AMMO also discussed buying the BTS from Full Draw and threatened to boycott the BTS unless Full Draw sold the show to AMMO on the terms offered by AMMO. AMMO and Full Draw did not reach an agreement.

In 1995, AMMO decided that it would present its own archery trade show, to be held one week after the 1997 BTS. Several archery manufacturers and distributors, a publishing company, and a representative for archery manufacturers (the defendants) had supported and participated in AMMO's actions against Full Draw to date. The defendants decided to boycott the BTS to eliminate it as a competitor to AMMO's new trade show. The defendants allegedly (1) advertised that they would attend only the AMMO trade show in 1997; (2) informed others at the 1996 BTS that they would attend only the AMMO show the following year; (3) persuaded others to boycott the BTS and attend only the AMMO show by repeatedly stating that key manufacturers and distributors would not attend the 1997 BTS and that the BTS would be a failure and probably not even occur; (4) created a "climate of fear of retribution and loss of business" for attending the BTS and retaliated against businesses that did attend the 1997 BTS; (5) agreed among themselves and caused other

AMMO members to agree not to attend the 1997 BTS; and (6) actually boycotted the 1997 BTS.

The 1997 BTS failed financially and was eliminated as a competitor to future AMMO shows, leaving AMMO as the only supplier in the market of archery trade shows in the United States.

Full Draw sued the defendants, claiming a violation of the Sherman Act. The district court dismissed Full Draw's antitrust claims, noting that Full Draw had alleged that the defendants' actions had driven it out of business, but had not alleged that those acts caused harm to consumers or competition;

> "and this is unsurprising where Defendants are many of the relevant consumers and their acts increased, albeit temporarily, competition. By definition, it would seem that where a majority of consumers believe that a monopoly producer is not performing adequately and decide to provide an alternative for themselves and other consumers, there can be no antitrust injury, particularly where, as here, there have been no allegations that harm was caused to any other consumers (e.g., the other exhibitors or the attendees of the shows) by reduced output or increased prices."

Full Draw has appealed. How should the appellate court rule? Is the trial court's analysis correct and persuasive? Why, or why not? *Draw Productions v. Easton Sports, Inc.,* 182 F.3d 745 (10th Cir. 1999)

8. Plaintiffs operate lodges and provide lodging referral services in the Big Bear Valley recreational area. For years, the two ski resorts in the area, Snow Summit, Inc., and Bear Mountain, Inc., offered bulk discounts on lift tickets to lodges and tourist businesses, including Plaintiffs. Plaintiffs would then offer "ski packages" of lodging and lift tickets at attractive prices to consumers.

Plaintiffs alleged as follows: In 1994, the president of Snow Summit helped form a local association to promote the Big Bear Valley. Plaintiffs were told that unless they joined the association (and paid up to 2.5 percent of their incomes as dues), neither Snow Summit nor Bear Mountain would sell them discount lift tickets nor honor any tickets purchased by them. Association members were also prohibited from selling, trading, or conveying discount lift tickets to Plaintiffs. The Association then adopted rules prohibiting members from belonging to other local referral services in which nonmembers participated and from referring business to nonmembers. Association members also agreed on uniform rates and charges for lodge accommodations, ski packages, and resort services and published advertising materials reflecting these rates. Plaintiffs alleged both price-fixing and group boycott violations on the part of the Association, Snow Summit and Bear Mountain, and certain other members of the Association.

The district court dismissed Plaintiffs' complaint, stating: "This is not an antitrust case, period." Plaintiffs have appealed. How should the appellate court rule, and why? *Big Bear Lodging Ass'n v. Snow Summit, Inc.,* 182 F.3d 1096 (9th Cir. 1999)

9. National Parcel Service is a "zone shipper," a shipping company that receives packages from mail order and retail catalog merchants and delivers them in bulk to U.S. Postal Service (USPS) bulk mail distribution centers. This enables National to charge lower prices than United Parcel Service (UPS), because UPS charges a premium for residential deliveries, and to offer faster service than USPS.

J. B. Hunt is an interstate trucking company. In mid-1994, a J. B. Hunt subsidiary entered the zone shipping market, targeting the customers of National and another zone shipper, CTC, with low prices. J. B. Hunt's initial strategy was to make "whatever price concessions you need to give or whatever, get us in the business quickly." J. B. Hunt's revenues grew quickly even though it lost money, while National lost business. National brought a suit, seeking damages for predatory pricing under Section 2 of the Sherman Act. Has J. B. Hunt engaged in predatory pricing? Why, or why not? *National Parcel Services v. J. B. Hunt Logistics, Inc.,* 150 F.3d 970 (8th Cir. 1998)

10. From 1992 to 1996, Generac Corp. served as a dealer of certain generators that it manufactured under license from Caterpillar, Inc. The license agreement gave Generac the right to develop and manufacture a line of generators that were marketed under Caterpillar's Olympian trademark and that were distributed by Caterpillar dealers in specified territories. Generac was assigned North, Central, and South America, as well as 17 countries in the Far East. Caterpillar agreed not to license anyone else to sell generator sets within Generac's territory under the Olympian trademark but could sell or license others to sell generators in the Generac territory under a different trademark. In the United States and Canada, Generac was permitted to sell Olympian products only to Caterpillar dealers who had been designated by Caterpillar as a Power Systems Distributor (PSD). Generac also promised not to appoint any new distribution outlets for its own branded sets in a Caterpillar dealer's territory as long as the dealer was adequately covering its sales territory for Olympian sets. The agreement was for an indefinite duration and could be terminated by either party upon 24 months' written notice or with cause upon 120 days' notice.

Through June 1996, Generac spent $10.5 million on sales, service, and warranties to promote and support the Olympian line and invested more than $660,000 in the engineering and development of the line. It constructed a new manufacturing facility at a cost of $5.24 million. It paid Caterpillar more than $5.6 million in fees and generated sales of Olympian products of more than $124.4 million. Ultimately, Olympian products represented about 58 percent of Generac's total industrial sales.

In May 1996, Caterpillar informed Generac that it was terminating the agreement effective June 30, 1998, so that it could form a new business relationship with Emerson Electric Company. Generac felt that it was the victim of a "classic free ride"—that it had invested millions to develop the market for the Olympian line, only to be deprived of the opportunity to reap the long-term benefits.

Generac sued for antitrust violations, claiming that the restrictions placed on it violated Section 1 of the Sherman Act as a *per se* unlawful horizontal market division. Is Generac right? Why, or why not? *Generac Corp. v. Caterpillar, Inc.*, 172 F.3d 971 (7th Cir. 1999)

CHAPTER 5

Legal Issues Relating to Distribution Channels

The Franchisor-Franchisee Relationship

Since World War II, franchising has become a growth industry, both in the United States and internationally. There are over 600,000 franchised locations in the United States, and a new franchise outlet opens, on average, every eight minutes of each business day. Many types of businesses use franchise systems, including automobile dealerships, gasoline stations, convenience stores, soft drink bottlers, travel agencies, restaurants, car rental agencies, pet stores, cleaning services, and day care centers.[1] Although no definitive recent statistics exist, analysts generally agree that 35 percent to 40 percent of retail sales occurs through franchised businesses.[2] This chapter addresses legal issues that are specific to the franchisor-franchisee relationship.

[1] The Web site of the International Franchise Association, a franchising advocacy group, is found at http://www.franchise.org Other information on franchising opportunities can be found at http://www.frannet.com and http://www.franchise1.com

[2] *See* Francine Lafontaine, *Myths and Strengths of Franchising*, FINANCIAL TIMES, Mastering Strategies Series, Nov. 22, 1999, *reprinted in* MASTERING STRATEGY: THE COMPLETE MBA COMPANION IN STRATEGY, FT Prentice Hall, London, 2000, pp. 140–45.

Overview

The term *franchise* refers to a contractual relationship where one party (the *franchisor*) licenses another party (the *franchisee*) to use the franchisor's trade name, trademarks, copyrights, and other property in the distribution and sale of goods or services in accordance with established practices and standards. "Franchise" is used to refer both to the contractual agreement between the franchisor and the franchisee and to the franchise outlet itself.

Both the franchisor and the franchisee can obtain significant benefits from a well-conducted franchise relationship. The franchisee receives the opportunity to start and own a business, even though the franchisee may have limited capital and/or experience. The franchisee also obtains access to the franchisor's goodwill, training, and supervision, as well as access to product supplies and marketing expertise generally available only to larger business concerns. The franchisor receives the influx of the franchisee's capital (which facilitates expansion), a larger asset base, enhanced goodwill generated by the franchisee's business efforts, and access to a known distribution network.

The franchise system poses risks for both parties as well, however. The franchisor must work to ensure consistent quality and operational standards throughout the franchise system, which can be both costly and difficult. The franchisee, on the other hand, must guard against abuses by the franchisor of its generally superior knowledge of the business and market power.

As discussed later in this chapter, the federal government, acting through the Federal Trade Commission (FTC), regulates only limited aspects of the franchise relationship—primarily issues relating to disclosure. Most regulation of the franchise relationship occurs at the state level.

Types of Franchises

There are two primary categories of franchises: *product and trade name franchises* and *business format franchises*. In a *product and trade name franchise*, the franchisor licenses a franchisee to sell its product, either exclusively or with other products. The franchisee often has the exclusive right to sell the product in a designated area or territory. These franchises essentially function as a distribution system for the franchisor's goods. Automobile dealerships and beer distributorships, for example, fall within this category.

In a *business format franchise*, the franchisee operates a business under the franchisor's trade name and is identified as a member of a select group of persons who deal in this particular good or service. The franchisor sells a "way of doing business" to the franchisee in exchange for royalties and fixed fees. Generally, the franchisee must follow a standardized or prescribed format as to methods of operation, including things such as use of trade or service marks, site selection, design of the facility, hours of business, and qualifications and training of employees. Fast-food restaurants, hotels, and rental services are generally set up as business format franchises.

Definition of a "Franchise"

It is often difficult to distinguish between a franchise and other forms of branded distribution. The label that the parties attach to their relationship does not necessarily control. In many states, "franchise" is defined statutorily. The Illinois Franchise Disclosure Act is typical:

> "Franchise" means a contract or agreement, either expressed or implied, whether oral or written, between two or more persons by which:
>
> (a) a franchisee is granted the right to engage in the business of offering, selling, or distributing goods or services, under a marketing plan or system prescribed or suggested in substantial part by a franchisor; and
>
> (b) the operation of the franchisee's business pursuant to such plan or system is substantially associated with the franchisor's trademark, service mark, trade name, logotype, advertising, or other commercial symbol designating the franchisor or its affiliate; and
>
> (c) the person granted the right to engage in such business is required to pay, directly or indirectly, a franchise fee of $500 or more.[3]

Most state statutes and the federal Franchise Disclosure Rule (discussed below) provide that, in order for a franchise relationship to exist, there must be a contract or agreement, either express or implied, oral or written, that meets three requirements:

1. *Use of mark.* The franchisee must receive a license to use the franchisor's trade or service mark, trade name, logotype, advertising, or other commercial symbol in connection with the sale or distribution of goods or services.

2. *Assistance to or control over franchisee's business.* The franchisor must somehow assist or control the franchisee's business, usually through the provision of a marketing plan or system prescribed in total or substantial part by the franchisor. Under the FTC Franchise Disclosure Rule, this assistance or control can take any of the following forms:

   - restrictions on business location or sales area;
   - furnishing management, marketing, or personnel advice;
   - restrictions on customers, location, or sales area;
   - formal sales, repair, or business training programs;
   - furnishing a detailed operations manual;
   - promotional campaigns requiring participation or financial contribution;
   - mandatory personnel policies and practices;
   - control over production techniques;
   - establishing accounting systems or requiring accounting practices;
   - location and site approval;
   - location design or appearance requirements; or
   - control over hours of operation.[4]

3. *Franchise fee.* Under most (though not all) state franchise statutes, a franchise relationship does not exist in the absence of a payment of a "franchise fee." This requirement is easily met, however, as most state statutes define a franchise fee as any payment above a minimal amount (usually $500) required for the right to enter into the franchise business (excluding purchases or leases of

---

[3] 815 Ill. Comp. Stat. 705/3 (West 2000).

[4] Disclosure Requirements and Prohibitions Concerning Franchising and Business Opportunity Ventures; Promulgation of Final Interpretative Guides, 44 Fed. Reg. 49,966, 49,967 (1979).

Focus Case 5.1

Facts: Jerome-Duncan, Inc. (JDI), a Ford dealership, entered into a five-year contract with Auto-by-Tel (ABT), which operated an Internet site through which it referred potential customers to car dealers. Under the contract, JDI was to be the exclusive dealer to which ABT would refer potential Ford customers in a four-county area. Either party could terminate the contract on 30-days' notice. After JDI refused ABT's request to renegotiate the contractual terms, ABT gave notice that it was terminating the contract. JDI sued, claiming that the contract was a "franchise agreement" under the Michigan Franchise Investment Law (MFIL) and therefore could not be terminated without good cause, despite the express termination provision.

Decision: The trial court noted that the policy behind the MFIL was to remedy perceived abuses by large franchisors against unsophisticated investor franchisees. JDI, which was the largest Ford dealership in the metro Detroit area and which had annual sales in excess of $130 million, was not the type of franchisee that the MFIL was intended to protect.

Moreover, the MFIL defines a "franchise agreement" as one in which: (1) the franchisee is subject to a marketing plan or system prescribed in substantial part by the franchisor; (2) the franchisee is allowed to use the mark, trade name, or other commercial symbol of the franchisor; and (3) the franchisee is required to pay a franchise fee.

The trial court found that neither of the first two requirements had been met. First, JDI attempted to classify ABT's Web site as a "virtual dealership" and argued that JDI thus operated an ABT "virtual dealership" franchise. JDI pointed to the specific guidelines given by ABT regarding customer contacts, the training provided by ABT to a JDI executive who was to serve as the "ABT representative," and the limited territory that it received from ABT. The trial court rejected this argument, find-

ing that because JDI was selling Ford products, not ABT goods or services, it was not operating under a "marketing plan prescribed by a franchisor."

Second, JDI was not engaged in distributing goods or services substantially associated with the mark of ABT. Although ABT required JDI to place the ABT logo on certain print advertisements, place an "authorized Auto-by-Tel dealer" sign in its showroom, use the ABT logo on business cards, and assign titles such as "Auto-by-Tel manager" to its employees, the court found that JDI's sales were still primarily associated with the Ford mark borne by the cars it sold. Thus, the second requirement of the MFIL was also not met.

The court listed several other factors that courts consider in determining whether a relationship is a "franchise": "(1) franchisor control over hours and days of operation; (2) placing of signs advertising the franchisor; (3) loans by franchisor of equipment; (4) franchisor auditing of franchisee's books; (5) franchisor inspection of franchisee's premises; (6) franchisor control over lighting at franchisee's place of business; (7) franchisor requiring the franchisee to wear uniforms; (8) franchisor control over the setting of prices; (9) franchisor licensing of sales quotas; (11) [sic] franchisor training of employees; and (12) offer by franchisor of financial support." The majority of these factors were not present in this case.

The trial court did note that JDI had paid a start-up fee of $3,500 and was required to pay a monthly fee of $500. These payments would likely constitute a "franchise fee" under the MFIL had the other two elements of a franchise been satisfied.

Because the contractual agreement between JDI and ABT did not meet the definition of a franchise agreement, the MFIL did not apply. Thus, the termination provisions of the agreement controlled and ABT had not violated any state law by terminating the relationship. The trial court awarded summary judgment to ABT. *Jerome-Duncan, Inc. v. Auto-by-Tel*, 989 F. Supp. 838 (E.D. Mich. 1997), *aff'd*, 176 F.3d 904 (6th Cir. 1999).

real property and purchases of goods at bona fide wholesale prices). It does not matter whether the parties have labeled the payment a "franchise fee" or not.

Thus, business arrangements such as licenses, joint ventures, strategic alliances, distribution agreements, dealer or sales agent agreements, and subcontractor agreements may potentially be regulated as franchises, even if the parties did not contemplate a franchise relationship (see Focus Case 5.1).

To avoid the inadvertent creation of a franchise, a supplier or manufacturer should be careful about licensing others to use its marks, should exercise restraint in providing assistance to or control over a distributor's business, and should not require any payment from its dealers above a bona fide wholesale price. A more extensive (but often impractical) strategy is for the supplier or manufacturer to use its own sales force and retail outlets and avoid the use of dealers altogether.

See Discussion Cases 5.1, 5.2.

Creation of a Franchise

Franchisors usually recruit franchisees by advertising their particular business. Interested parties then contact the franchisor, who sends out a "franchise kit." The kits tend to describe the franchise business in very positive terms, which can be misleading to unsophisticated potential franchisees. The federal and state disclosure rules discussed later in this chapter are intended to alleviate this problem.

Once the parties agree to the franchise relationship, they typically sign a detailed contractual agreement. The agreement is almost always drafted by the franchisor and, not surprisingly, often tends to favor that party substantially. These agreements are usually long (often 30 to 50 pages) and are often very complicated. Because of the disparity in bargaining power between the parties, in the event of litigation, the courts often scrutinize the agreements to make sure that the stronger party (the franchisor) has not taken unfair advantage of the weaker party (the franchisee).

Generally, the franchise agreement imposes a limited variety of obligations upon the franchisor. The franchisor typically gives the franchisee the right to use its trademark and/or standardized product or service in exchange for a franchise fee. The franchisor generally advertises the product or service in exchange for an advertising fee (often calculated as a percentage of gross sales). The franchisor also provides training programs and manuals and sets out detailed guidelines for the day-to-day operation of the business. Established franchisors often designate a particular location for the franchise outlet, design and arrange for standardized construction of the facility, and install fixtures and equipment.

The franchisee, on the other hand, is generally required to follow the procedures specified by the franchisor or risk termination. The franchise agreement usually mandates strict accounting procedures and authorizes the franchisor to inspect the books and records at any time. The franchisee is required to a pay a number of types of fees as well, such as

- an initial license fee (i.e., a lump-sum payment for receiving the franchise);
- a royalty fee (i.e., a payment for the use of the franchisor's trade name, property, and assistance, usually calculated as a percentage of gross sales and payable on a monthly basis);
- an assessment fee (which covers things such as advertising, promotional, and administrative costs and which is usually calculated as either a flat monthly or annual fee or as a percentage of gross sales);
- lease fees (i.e., payments for any equipment or land leased from the franchisor); and
- costs of supplies (i.e., payments for any supplies purchased from franchisor).

The franchise agreement also typically requires the franchisee to obtain liability insurance to protect both the franchisor and the franchisee against casualty losses and tort suits and requires the franchisee to comply with state law workers' compensation requirements.

The franchise agreement usually sets forth the duration of the franchise (typically 10 to 20 years) and usually provides for renewals of the term. Typically, the agreement contains a covenant not to compete, which prohibits the franchisee from competing with the franchisor for a stated period after termination of the franchise relationship. (Covenants not to compete are discussed in more detail in Chapter 3.)

Finally, the agreement usually requires the franchisor to give the franchisee a certain time period (e.g., 10 days) to cure any default under the agreement. The franchisor typically must then give notice of termination. In states that regulate termination and nonrenewal of franchises, the franchisor must generally wait a set time period after giving notice (often 90 days) before the termination is actually effective. Most states do not regulate termination and nonrenewal, however. In those states, the franchisee receives only those protections provided by the franchise agreement.

Regulation of the Franchise Relationship

On the one hand, franchise relationships can promote competitive markets, which, as we have noted before, the law favors. On the other hand, the disparity in the bargaining relationship between the franchisor and the franchisee can lead to abuses. Franchise law thus generally attempts to facilitate the franchise relationship while putting in place safeguards to prevent overreaching behavior by the franchisor (who typically is the dominant party in the relationship).

Prior to the 1970s, there was little regulation of franchise relationships at either the state or the federal levels. With the exception of disclosure requirements (discussed below), there are only two areas of significant federal regulation of the franchise relationship today. First, the federal Automobile Dealers' Franchise Act[5] prevents automobile company franchisors from terminating their dealers without just cause. (Many state legislatures have also passed statutes protecting automobile dealerships from the disproportionately greater power of car manufacturers.) Second, the federal Petroleum Marketing Practices Act[6] protects motor fuel distributors and dealers from arbitrary terminations.

Today, most regulation occurs at the state level, which means, of course, that regulation can vary from state to state. Franchisors are subject to the laws of each state in which they offer franchises and thus must plan their business activities carefully to avoid inadvertently incurring legal liability.

DISCLOSURE

Federal Disclosure Rules

Existing federal law primarily addresses *disclosure* issues. In 1979, the FTC issued its FTC Franchise Disclosure Rule,[7] which requires every regulated franchisor to prepare an extensive disclosure document for each potential franchise purchaser.

---

[5] 15 U.S.C. § 1221 *et seq.*
[6] 15 U.S.C. §§ 2801–2806, 2821–2824, 2841.
[7] 16 C.F.R. Part 436. The FTC's Web site, http://www.ftc.gov, contains various types of information on franchises, including a Guide to the FTC Franchise Rule.

The FTC Rule applies to business format franchises, product franchises, and vending machine and display rack business opportunity ventures.

Under the federal Rule, the franchisor's disclosure must include a number of types of information, including: (1) the history of the franchisor, (2) required fees and investment costs, (3) information about the franchisor, (4) financial statements of the franchisor, (5) the litigation and bankruptcy history of the franchisor, and (6) a copy of the franchisor's standard franchise agreement. The written disclosures must be provided to the potential franchisee at the earlier of the first "personal meeting" or at least ten business days before the prospective franchisee signs the franchise agreement or makes any payment. The Rule also mandates that certain cautionary statements be explicitly and conspicuously made in the document (see Exhibit 5.1).

The FTCs Rule does not require that the franchisor file its disclosure with the FTC, and no government agency reviews or approves the contents of the disclosure. Nonetheless, the Rule is a federal trade regulation with the full force and effect of federal law, so if the FTC discovers that the franchisor made an inaccurate disclosure, the FTC may seek injunctions, civil penalties (including fines of up to $10,000 for each violation), and consumer redress as remedies. These penalties can be severe. The courts have imposed civil penalties of up to $870,000 in a single case and have ordered consumer redress of up to $4.9 million. The Rule does not provide a cause of action to private parties (such as a potential franchisee misled by an incorrect disclosure), however. The FTC is currently considering making substantial changes to the Rule.

Many analysts argue that the FTC Disclosure Rule has no real teeth. A July 1993 audit by the General Accounting Office found that the FTC acted on fewer than 6 percent of the franchise complaints brought to its attention. Congress has reacted to this problem by periodically introducing (but not enacting) legislation that would provide greater protection to franchisees.

EXHIBIT 5.1

The FTC Franchise Disclosure Rule requires a disclosure document to carry certain notices printed in bold-face type of not less than 12-point size, such as:

**Information for Prospective Franchisees
Required by Federal Trade Commission**

***

To protect you, we've required your franchisor to give you this information. We haven't checked it, and don't know if it's correct. It should help you make up your mind. Study it carefully. While it includes some informtion about your contract, don't rely on it alone to understand your contract. Read all of your contract carefully. Buying a franchise is a complicated investment. Take your time to decide. If possible, show your contract and this information to an advisor, like a lawyer or an accountant. If you find anything important that's been left out, you should let us know about it. It may be against the law. There may also be laws on franchising in your state. Ask your state agencies about them.

FEDERAL TRADE COMMISSION, Washington, D.C.
and
CAUTION
These figures are only estimates of what we think you may earn. There is no assurance you'll do as well. If you rely upon our figures, you must accept the risk of not doing as well.

Source: 16 C.F.R. Part 436

State Disclosure Rules

Fifteen states have franchise investment laws that require franchisors to provide disclosures to potential purchasers as well.[8] Franchisors can file the Uniform Franchise Offering Circular (UFOC), which will satisfy the requirements of both the federal and state disclosure laws. Unlike the FTC Disclosure Rule, the state disclosure laws will permit private parties to sue for violations. Thus, the state statutes can provide a more direct remedy for aggrieved investors.

Thirteen of these states require registration as well as disclosure.[9] In effect, these states treat the sale of a franchise like the sale of a security. These states generally require the franchisor to file a registration document with state regulators and to obtain their approval before offering franchises to potential buyers. Some states also require franchisors to submit advertisements for franchises for review or approval prior to publication.

Finally, 24 states also have *business opportunity statutes*, which regulate the offer and sale of distribution arrangements directed at unsophisticated "consumer" dealers or distributors.[10] Unlike "franchises," "business opportunities" do not require the use of the seller's trademark. (This is the key distinction between the two categories in most states.)

The definition of a business opportunity is quite broad in most states, encompassing virtually any type of business activity that might be offered for sale. Under Texas law, for example, the existence of a marketing program and a payment exceeding $500 suffices. These statutes generally require registration and disclosure similar to those required by franchise laws. (The FTC Franchise Disclosure Rule applies to vending machine and display rack business opportunities but not to other types of business opportunities.) These state statutes also usually regulate the ongoing business relationship between the seller and the buyer. In addition to providing for a private cause of action for damages and rescission, the business opportunity statutes often give the buyer the right to rescind the agreement within one year of execution and to receive a refund in the event the seller violates the statute. In many instances, a single transaction may be subject to both the business opportunity statute and the state franchise laws.

Legal Issues Arising from the Franchise Relationship

Many types of legal issues can arise in the franchisor-franchisee relationship. These are generally state law issues.

EXISTENCE OF A FRANCHISE RELATIONSHIP

It is sometimes difficult to tell whether the relationship between the parties is truly a franchisor-franchisee relationship or whether it involves an employer-employee or principal-agent relationship. It is important from the franchisor's perspective that this relationship be clear, as franchisors are generally not liable for the torts or

---

[8] These states are California, Hawaii, Illinois, Indiana, Maryland, Michigan, Minnesota, New York, North Dakota, Oregon, Rhode Island, South Dakota, Virginia, Washington, and Wisconsin.

[9] These states are California, Hawaii, Illinois, Indiana, Maryland, Minnesota, New York, North Dakota, Rhode Island, South Dakota, Virginia, Washington, and Wisconsin.

[10] These states are California, Connecticut, Florida, Georgia, Illinois, Indiana, Iowa, Kentucky, Louisiana, Maine, Maryland, Michigan, Minnesota, Nebraska, New Hampshire, North Carolina, Ohio, Oklahoma, South Carolina, South Dakota, Texas, Utah, Virginia, and Washington.

Focus Case 5.2

Facts: West Sanitation Services, Inc., provides restroom sanitizing services to commercial customers. Glenroy Francis was hired in 1986 as a serviceperson for specified routes. In 1987, West began a franchise program. Francis signed a 23-page franchise agreement. As a franchisee, he performed the same functions that he had as an employee. In 1992, West terminated Francis's franchise for cause. Francis then applied for unemployment insurance benefits. Employees are entitled to such benefits, but franchisees are not.

Decision: The New York Unemployment Insurance Appeal Board determined that West "exercised a sufficient degree of direction and control over [Francis] . . . to establish an employment relationship." Among the factors cited by the Board were West's assignment of a territory and/or customers to Francis; retention of active client control, including billing; establishing weekly schedules for customer service; "paying" Francis; specification of products that could be used; provision of new customer accounts; inspection and evaluation of Francis's performance; requirement that Francis use West's logo; requirement that Francis submit reports; and restrictions on Francis's right to transfer his interest in the customer accounts.

Thus, the Board ruled that West was liable for unemployment insurance contributions for Francis and other similarly situated individuals. The Appellate Division of the New York Supreme Court upheld the Board upon appeal. *In re Francis*, 668 N.Y.S.2d 55 (N.Y. App. Div. 3d Dep't 1998).

---

contractual breaches of their franchisees, but employers or principals may be liable for the torts or breaches of their employees or agents.

It is also important from the franchisee's perspective that the franchisor-franchisee relationship be clear. In some instances, franchisees get certain rights under state law that employees, agents, or other parties do not. For example, many state laws prohibit termination of a franchise without good cause but permit termination of other types of dealers without cause if the underlying contract so permits. On the other hand, if the purported franchisee is found to be an employee, she may be protected by laws regarding unemployment insurance, wages, civil rights, and other employment-related regulation that would not apply to franchisees (see Focus Case 5.2).

VICARIOUS LIABILITY OF A FRANCHISOR

Although a franchise relationship ordinarily shields a franchisor from liability for the torts or contractual breaches of its franchisee, customers, patrons, or other injured parties may nonetheless succeed in holding the franchisor vicariously liable for the wrongful acts of its franchisees under certain circumstances. There are three theories under which a franchisor might potentially be held liable: (1) the franchisor was *negligent;* (2) the franchisee was an *actual agent* of the franchisor; or (3) the franchisee was an *apparent agent* of the franchisor. All three theories are based to some extent upon the franchisor's exertion of "control" over some aspect of the franchisee's activities. For example, if the franchisor exercises control over the terms and conditions of employment of the franchisee's employees, it may find itself liable for the franchisee's violations of labor or employment laws or for acts of the employees that violate antidiscrimination laws.

Negligence claims against a franchisor usually arise in the context of premises liability claims. To recover for negligence, the plaintiff must prove: (1) that the franchisor owed a duty of care to the plaintiff, (2) that the duty of care was breached, (3) that the breach caused the plaintiff's injury, and (4) that the plaintiff suffered actual injury.

Thus, if a person is assaulted in a franchise outlet, the franchisor typically is not liable for any resulting injuries because the franchisor does not generally owe a legal duty of care to persons who enter the franchisee's premises. (The franchisee, on the other hand, depending upon the circumstances, might incur liability for failing to provide a secure setting.) The franchisor might assume such a duty of care, however, by exercising control over things such as lighting, security, and general layout of the building. The issue raised in most such cases, then, is whether the franchisor indeed assumed such a duty of care. This is a highly fact-specific inquiry that the court must undertake on a case-by-case basis (see Focus Case 5.3 on page 152).

If the franchisor is too closely involved with the operation of the franchisee, the franchisee may be treated as being the *actual agent* of the franchisor. Under agency law, the principal (the franchisor) may be held liable for the wrongful acts of the agent (the franchisee). If individuals are led to believe that they are dealing with the franchisor directly, rather than with a franchisee operation or with an authorized agent of the franchisor, the franchisor can be held liable under an *apparent agency* theory.

See Discussion Case 5.3.

Franchisors should be careful about the degree of control that they exercise over their franchisees' activities lest they find themselves liable in unexpected situations. Franchisors should take care not to involve themselves in issues such as employment-related decisions or the day-to-day operations of their franchisees (see Focus Case 5.4 on page 153).

Franchisors generally are permitted to exercise control to the extent necessary to ensure that the franchisees conform to specified quality or operational standards. In many franchise industries, such as fast-food restaurants, this may well be a very extensive amount of control. The franchise agreement should specify, however, that the franchisor's control is based solely on the need to ensure compliance with stated quality standards and that any comments made by the franchisor regarding other issues are merely suggestions and not commands. Many franchise agreements also contain *indemnification clauses*, which provide that if a third party (including an employee) brings a claim against the franchisor, the franchisee will bear all costs related to the suit and any resulting liability. Franchisors may also require franchisees to carry insurance policies covering employment-related or premises liability claims. Finally, all franchise operations should be required to prominently display signs indicating local ownership. This simple measure can help the franchisor avoid an apparent agency relationship, although it may not completely insulate the franchisor from liability.

FRANCHISE ANTITRUST ISSUES

Tying Arrangements

A great deal of the antitrust tie-in litigation (discussed earlier in Chapter 4) over the past 20 years has dealt with franchise contracts, particularly fast-food franchises. Most franchise antitrust claims involve allegations of illegal *tying* by the franchisor. A tying arrangement occurs when a seller conditions the sale of a desired (*tying*) item on the purchase of a second (*tied*) item. The U.S. Supreme Court has established that a tie is unlawful *per se* if the seller possesses economic power in the market for the tying item and if the arrangement involves a "not

Focus Case 5.3

Facts: Wendy Hong Wu was an employee of a 24-hour donut store owned by Turnway Donuts, Inc., under a franchise agreement with Dunkin' Donuts, Inc. Early one morning, when Wu was working alone at the store, two teenagers entered the store, gained access to the employee area behind the counter, and brutally attacked and raped Wu. Wu filed suit against Dunkin' Donuts, arguing that the attack resulted in part from the vicarious negligence of Dunkin' Donuts. In particular, she argued that Dunkin' Donuts was vicariously liable for the franchisee's negligent provision of security.

Decision: According to the trial court, the issue presented was whether a franchisor's making of recommendations regarding security matters to its franchisees renders the franchisor legally responsible for ensuring the safety of its franchisees' employees.

The court identified the applicable legal rule as follows: "In deciding whether a franchisor may be held vicariously liable for acts of its franchisees, courts determine whether the franchisor controls the day-to-day operations of the franchisee, and more specifically, whether the franchisor exercises a considerable degree of control over the instrumentality at issue in a given case." The cases from this and other jurisdictions indicate that the franchisor must exercise very specific control over the franchisee and its operations before vicarious liability will attach. For example, a franchisor who retains the right to terminate the relationship for failure to meet standards or to reenter premises and inspect generally does not exercise sufficient control over the franchisee's security practices so as to give rise to a legal duty on the part of the franchisor.

The trial court concluded that "absent a showing of actual control over the security measures employed by the franchisee, franchisors have no legal duty in such cases." Wu pointed to three particular practices that she argued showed that Dunkin' Donuts retained actual control over security measures. She argued that Dunkin' Donuts (1) required that the franchisee remain open 24 hours a day, (2) controlled the purchase of security equipment and required a functioning alarm system, and (3) required a site plan that revealed to passersby that Wu was alone.

The court quickly dismissed the first argument, stating that while the requirement that the franchisee stay open 24 hours a day may have heightened the need for adequate security, Dunkin' Donuts did not mandate specific security measures or otherwise control or limit the franchisee's response to this increased risk. Thus, Dunkin' Donuts could not be held vicariously liable on these grounds.

Nor did the evidence support Wu's second argument. While Dunkin' Donuts made security equipment available for purchase and suggested that alarms and other burglary prevention techniques were important, Dunkin' Donuts did not mandate or otherwise exercise control over the purchase of security equipment. Indeed, the franchisee here had unilaterally hired a security consultant and had installed its own security system, including a plexiglass partition, alarm system, and video camera.

Finally, the evidence also did not support Wu's claim that Dunkin' Donuts had required a site plan that revealed to persons outside the store that Wu was working alone. While Dunkin' Donuts did provide a standard site plan to its franchisees, the franchise agreement did not require franchisees to conform to this standard plan and, in fact, the franchisee in this instance had made significant interior alterations to the store without seeking or receiving Dunkin' Donuts' prior approval.

The court concluded by noting a public policy concern raised by Wu's arguments: "The possibility . . . that the recommended security measures might have helped protect Wu highlights a public policy concern that the court also believes counsels against imposing liability on Dunkin' Donuts under the circumstances of this case. Dunkin' Donuts expressed a laudable desire to assist its franchisees in protecting their employees and customers. Imposing liability on the basis of such advice could discourage franchisors such as Dunkin' Donuts from taking steps to promote an awareness of security issues among franchisees."

Because "there [was] no evidence that Dunkin' Donuts actually mandated specific security equipment or otherwise controlled the steps taken by its franchisees in general, and [this franchisee] in particular, to protect employees," the court held that Dunkin' Donuts was not vicariously liable for Wu's injuries. The court granted summary judgment to Dunkin' Donuts. *Wu v. Dunkin' Donuts, Inc.*, 105 F. Supp.2d 83 (E.D. N.Y. 2000).

Focus Case 5.4

Facts: Plaintiffs Abby Fogt and Mary Carter worked at a Motel 6 franchise located in Troy, Ohio. The franchise was owed by BVP, Inc., and the motel was managed by Lisa Serafini. Plaintiffs alleged that they were sexually harassed, assaulted, and abused by Serafini during their employment. Plaintiffs informed Motel 6, the franchisor, of their allegations. Both testified at trial that they were told to "keep it quiet" and that Motel 6 would conduct an on-site investigation. The Director of Franchise Operations for Motel 6 admitted in a deposition that he had received a call from someone complaining of sexual harassment at the Troy Motel 6, that he had told the caller that he would speak to the franchise owner about the matter, that he did refer the complaint to the franchise owner, and that he did not follow up on the complaint.

Plaintiffs filed suit against the franchisor, Motel 6, alleging that: (1) an actual or apparent agency relationship existed between Motel 6 and BVP such that Motel 6 should be held liable for the actions of its franchisee, and (2) that Motel 6 had voluntarily assumed a duty of care to investigate sexual harassment complaints made by employees of its franchisees.

The trial court granted summary judgment to Motel 6. Plaintiffs appealed.

Decision: The appellate court rejected plaintiffs' argument that an actual agency relationship existed between Motel 6 and BVP, stating: "The key factor in determining the existence of an agency relationship is the right of control vested in the principal."

The court noted that the franchise agreement at issue here, at first glance, appeared to give Motel 6 the right to control employment decisions for its franchisees. The franchise agreement provided that Motel 6 had the authority to approve any manager with authority over the "day-to-day" operations of its franchisees and that Motel 6 could terminate the franchise of any franchisee who did not "comply promptly" with the standards contained in its confidential manuals. The manuals specifically stated that Motel 6 "will not tolerate discrimination or the appearance of discrimination of any kind" with regard to either employment practices or room availability. The manuals also stated that employees "may" be dismissed

for "offending, disrupting, or harassing guests or fellow employees" at the franchisee's discretion.

However, the franchise agreement also specifically stated that the franchisee is "solely responsible" for all employment decisions, including firing, hiring, training, wages, and discipline. BVP did not ask Motel 6 for assistance in making employment decisions and Motel 6 did not involve itself with such issues. The appellate court concluded that Motel 6 did not have the right to control employment decisions of the franchisee. The court thus rejected plaintiffs' claim that Motel 6 was liable under an actual agency theory.

Even when actual agency does not exist, "apparent agency may be conferred if the principal holds its agent out to the public as possessing sufficient authority to act on its behalf and the person dealing with the agent knew these facts and, acting in good faith, had reason to believe that the agent possessed the necessary authority." Here, however, plaintiffs had both testified that they knew that Motel 6 did not own the motel, that BVP was their employer, that Motel 6 was not involved with employee discipline, and that Serafini made the hiring and firing decisions at the Troy franchise. Thus, no apparent agency relationship existed here either.

The appellate court concluded, however, that the statements made by the Director of Franchise Operations for Motel 6 raised a genuine issue of material fact with regard to plaintiffs' claim that the Motel 6 voluntarily assumed the duty of investigating and rectifying the alleged harassment. The court also found that there was a genuine issue of fact as to whether Motel 6 exercised ordinary care in carrying out this duty (assuming such a duty existed). While a jury might find that Motel 6 did exercise ordinary care by referring the complaint to the franchisee, the jury might instead find that the Motel 6 was obligated to do something more.

The appellate court thus reversed the trial court's grant of summary judgment to Motel 6 and remanded the case for further proceedings on the issue of whether Motel 6, a franchisor, voluntarily assumed a duty to investigate sexual harassment complaints made by employees of its franchisee. The court affirmed the lower court's rulings on the agency arguments. *Hamlin v. Motel 6,* 2000 Ohio App. LEXIS 2439 (June 9, 2000).

insubstantial" amount of interstate commerce.[11] Some tying arrangements are legal, however, although courts generally view them with disfavor because of their potential anticompetitive effects.

Tie-in arrangements are common in the franchise setting. A franchisor invariably wants to impose quality control standards on its franchisees, so the standard franchise agreement contains quality control restrictions. Very often the agreement requires the franchisee to purchase supplies and products from the franchisor at set prices or from suppliers who can meet the exact specifications and standards of the franchisor. Usually, the franchisor designates "approved" suppliers from which the franchisees may purchase.

In most franchise tie-in litigation, the plaintiff is a franchisee (or class of franchisees) and the defendant is the franchisor. The complaint is usually that the franchisee was able to obtain a franchise only on the condition that it purchase some additional item or items from the franchisor or a franchisor-approved vendor as well. Thus, the tying item is the franchise itself and the tied item is essential food ingredients or the primary product sold by the franchisor or its approved vendor.

Originally, franchisees won many of these cases. In recent years, however, franchisors have tended to prevail. *Queen City Pizza, Inc. v. Domino's Pizza, Inc.*[12] is an important recent example of this trend.

See Discussion Case 5.4.

Under the rationale of the *Domino's Pizza* court, if a product that is substitutable for the tied product is available in the marketplace, it will be difficult for a franchisee to plead a relevant antitrust market in the tied product, even if the franchise agreement prohibits the franchisee from purchasing that product.

Other courts have rejected the *Domino's Pizza* approach, stating that the validity of a tying claim by a franchisee must be determined by the amount of information possessed by the franchisee at the time it signed the franchise agreement and by the cost barriers to franchisees' switching franchises, not by whether the tied product has substitutes in the marketplace.[13]

Vertical Price Restraints

Although many franchisors would like to be able to control the price at which their franchisees sell their products or services, vertical price restraints have long been illegal under the antitrust laws. It is illegal *per se* for franchisors to set *minimum* prices at which their franchisees may sell. Until recently, it was also illegal *per se* for franchisors to set the *maximum* price at which their franchisees could sell.

In November 1997, however, the U.S. Supreme Court decided *State Oil Co. v. Khan*,[14] in which the Court determined vertical maximum price-fixing was no longer illegal *per se* but, rather, must be judged by a rule of reason. The Court ruled that a supplier's imposition of maximum resale prices upon its distributors may have procompetitive effects and actually result in lower prices for consumers. In such an instance, the price-fixing ought not to be barred. The court must make a fact-specific inquiry into the specific challenged conduct, the industry and market involved, the purported justification for the conduct, and intended and actual

---

[11] Northern Pacific Railroad Co. v. United States, 356 U.S. 1, 6 (1958).

[12] 124 F.3d 430 (3d Cir. 1997).

[13] *See* Collins v. International Dairy Queen, 980 F. Supp. 1252 (M.D. Ga. 1997); Wilson v. Mobil Oil Corp., 940 F. Supp. 944 (E.D. La. 1996).

[14] 522 U.S. 3 (1997). This case is reproduced at Discussion Case 4.2.

effects of the conduct on interbrand competition. If the conduct is found to have anticompetitive effects, it is illegal.

Although it is still too soon to determine what effect *State Oil Co.* will have upon franchisor conduct, it will most likely result in increased attempts by franchisors to impose resale price ceilings on their franchisees. It may also facilitate advertising and promotional campaigns or special offers for specific products and services by enabling franchisors to promote specific prices. Franchisors should be aware, however, that even if a vertical maximum price-fixing scheme is allowed under the federal antitrust laws, it might still be illegal under state laws relating to consumer protection, unfair trade practices, or franchises. Thus, a franchisor considering a price ceiling should always seek legal counsel before implementing such a price scheme. Antitrust law is discussed in greater detail in Chapter 4. Consumer protection and unfair trade practice laws are discussed in Chapter 8.

CO-BRANDING

Co-branding involves the operation of two or more types of franchises or nonfranchised businesses under a single roof. Many fast-food franchises have entered into co-branding relationships, such as Taco Bell and KFC, and Burger King and TCBY. Co-branding allows franchisors to expand into nontraditional locations, opens up access to desirable sites, allows for cost savings and operating efficiencies, and promotes competitive positioning of the brands. Co-branding works best when it provides synergy between the offerings, such as offering a dessert (frozen yogurt) at a burger chain.

Co-branding results in a complex legal relationship. Suppose, for example, a donut chain and a Mexican fast-food chain decide to co-brand on the theory that the relationship will increase each party's sales in its weaker daily sales time slots. Typically, one party will be the "host franchisor," who already has in place an existing franchise system, has control over the physical sites on which the co-branded business will operate, and who will exercise some control over how the franchisees operate the "guest" brand. The host and guest franchisors will have to decide upon a structure, which can be as complex as a *subfranchise* (in which the guest franchisor grants a "master franchise" to the host franchisor, who then subfranchises the co-brand to its franchisees) or a *cofranchise* (in which the guest franchisor offers the co-brand directly to the host's franchisees with the consent of the host franchisor), or as simple as a *lease* or a *license*. Whatever the structure agreed upon, the parties will probably need to alter their standard franchise agreements to cover topics such as protection of trade secrets and proprietary information, noncompete covenants, royalty arrangements, and termination provisions.[15] Co-branding can also raise issues of "encroachment."

ENCROACHMENT

Encroachment has been defined as expansion by the franchisor beyond the point that the franchisor would have expanded had it owned all its own outlets.[16] It occurs when a franchisor sells a franchisee an outlet in a particular location, then sells

---

[15] *See generally* Kenneth R. Costello, *Baskin Donuts: Hidden Pitfalls in Co-Branding*, Franchising Business & Law Alert, vol. 3, no. 11, p. 1 (July 1997).

[16] "Warren S. Grimes, *When Do Franchisors Have Market Power? Antitrust Remedies for Franchisor Opportunism*, 65 Antitrust L.J. 105, 138 (1996).

another outlet in close vicinity to a different franchisee. The original franchisee is harmed because the new outlet draws customers and revenue from the original outlet. The franchisor, on the other hand, benefits because royalties from two stores, even though they may cannibalize each other, are greater than royalties from a single store.

Particularly as a result of the growth in co-branding, encroachment issues have been very prominent and prevalent in recent years. Generally, the contractual language of the franchise agreement determines whether impermissible encroachment has occurred. If, under the terms of the agreement, the franchisee received an exclusive territory, the franchisor is clearly prohibited from locating other units within that territory. (The franchisor may try to avoid such restrictions by offering a similar, but not identical, product, such as a different brand of hotel franchise, within the territory.) Similarly, if the franchise agreement explicitly states that the franchisor has an unrestricted right to locate additional units or that the franchisee does not have an exclusive territory, that language will control as well.

Many encroachment cases involve a middle ground, however, in which the franchise agreement grants a small, protected territory to the franchisee. The franchisor then locates a new unit outside that protected territory but close enough to have a negative impact on the revenues or profitability of the original franchisee. These cases generally implicate the *implied covenant of good faith*. Under the Restatement (second) of Contracts, "[e]very contract imposes upon each party a duty of good faith and fair dealing . . . ."[17] This implied covenant is overridden by express language, such as a contractual provision stating that the franchisor has complete discretion to establish new franchises at any location outside the protected territory even if the new units harm the existing franchisee. Where such explicit contractual provisions are missing, however, the courts have to determine whether the franchisor's actions violated its duty of good faith and fair dealing. In general, the franchisors have tended to win these disputes (see Focus Case 5.5 on page 157).

As a practical matter, franchisors should state their encroachment policies explicitly within their franchise agreements so as to avoid litigation with disappointed franchisees. Other mechanisms, such as granting franchisees the right of first refusal on new units, can be used to address these problems as well.

TERMINATION ISSUES

Generally, franchise agreements provide that the franchisor can terminate the franchise if certain events occur. Most provide for termination "for cause," which includes situations such as the franchisee failing to meet quality control standards or failing to pay required fees. Some state laws restrict the franchisor's ability to terminate or refuse to renew a franchise without cause. A minority of states require that the franchisor provide notice—often 90 or 180 days in advance—before terminating or refusing to renew a franchise.

The courts are concerned that terminations will leave a franchisee with little or nothing to show for what might have been a very large investment of time and money. Thus, the courts often try to protect the franchisee in termination cases. They do not, however, prevent a franchisor from terminating franchisees that fail to meet the obligations of their franchise agreements.

In addition, even in states that require "good cause" for termination, the courts recognize that the franchisor's own economic circumstances are relevant to the

---

[17]Restatement (second) of Contracts § 205.

Focus Case 5.5

Facts: Linquist & Craig, which owned several Holiday Inn franchises, sued Holiday Inns, its franchisor, after Holiday Inns opened three new hotels near its hotels in Venture and Costa Mesa, California. Linquist & Craig claimed that the Holiday Inns had expressly breached (1) its license agreements and (2) the implied covenant of good faith and fair dealing.

Decision: The court rejected both of the arguments raised by Linquist and Craig and granted summary judgment to Holiday Inns.

The license agreements for both of Linquist & Craig's hotels stated: "This License does not limit the right of Licensor or of its affiliates . . . to engage in or license any business activity at any other location." Linquist & Craig pointed to additional language in the agreement that prohibited "arbitrary and capricious" behavior by Holiday Inns. Linquist & Craig argued that the two provisions, read together, prohibited Holiday

Inns from licensing additional franchises in close proximity to its existing hotels.

The trial court rejected this argument, stating that the "arbitrary and capricious" language prohibited arbitrary and capricious "enforcement" of the agreement, such as in requiring compliance with standards or conducting inspections. Because licensing of additional franchises is not an "enforcement" action, the express language of the agreement permitting Holiday Inns to license "any business activity in any location" controlled.

The court also rejected Linquist & Craig's claim that Holiday Inns had violated the implied covenant of good faith and fair dealing. Because the license agreement expressly reserved to Holiday Inns the right to license additional franchisees in any location it wished, Holidays Inns could not be said to have violated any obligation of good faith or fair dealing to Linquist & Craig. *Linquist & Craig Hotels & Resorts, Inc. v. Holiday Inns Franchising, Inc.*, CCH Bus. Fran. Guide ¶ 11,514 (C.D. Cal. 1998).

determination of whether termination was justified. Thus, the courts generally do not second-guess the franchisor's decision to terminate when it is supported by evidence of losses, flat or declining profits or sales, or cancellation of an entire product line.

MULTILEVEL MARKETING

Multi-level marketing, also known as *network* or *matrix marketing*, involves sales of goods or services through distributors, where distributors are typically promised commissions both on their own sales and on sales their recruits have made. *Pyramid schemes*, which are a form of multilevel marketing that involves paying commissions to distributors only for recruiting new distributors, are illegal in most states. Pyramid schemes inevitably collapse once no new distributors can be recruited, causing most people involved (except those at the very top) to lose their money.

To avoid prohibitions against pyramid schemes, multilevel marketing plans should pay commissions only on sales and not for recruitment of new participants. If the multilevel marketing plan involves the sale of business opportunities or franchising, it must comply with the requirements of applicable disclosure laws.

Franchising and the Internet

Franchisors have been quick to take advantage of the opportunities that the Internet provides. In many respects, however, franchising law has not kept up with the technological advances of the Internet. The rules governing the use of the Internet in this setting are uncertain. In addition, many established franchisors had not anticipated the opportunities that the Internet would create and so had not planned properly in their franchise agreements to address the host of issues that this new communication medium raises.

Franchisors face several issues with regard to Internet activities, including: (1) what disclosure obligations apply to a franchisor's advertising of franchises on the Internet? (2) what control does a franchisor have over its franchisee's Internet activities? and (3) when do Internet activities rise to the level of "encroachment"?

"OFFERING" FRANCHISES ON THE INTERNET

Many franchisors maintain Internet sites that contain general information about their franchise system that could be construed as an "offer" of a franchise, thus triggering state disclosure and registration requirements. In addition, the franchise laws in several states require that all franchise advertisements proposed for use within the state be submitted to (and often approved by) state officials prior to use. Definitions of advertisements are broad enough to include Web site content. California, for example, defines an "advertisement" as "any written or printed communication or any communication by means of recorded telephone messages or spoken on radio, television, or similar communications media, published in connection with the offer or sale of a franchise."[18]

Thus, franchisors with Web sites must be concerned with two issues: (1) must they register in all of the states requiring franchise registration? and (2) must they submit the content of their Web sites to those states that require franchise advertisements to be approved by state authorities before use?

Currently, the marketing of franchises on-line is not directly regulated in most states; thus, it not yet clear how most state franchise laws apply to activities on the Internet. Web sites reach individuals in every state, and the owner of the site cannot control its dissemination. It initially would appear, therefore, that if a franchisor's Web site contains information that would cause the site to be a "franchise offer," the site must be registered in all states requiring registration.

States have taken action to lessen this burden on franchisors. In December 1997, Indiana became the first state to clarify its position on these issues. The Indiana Securities Administrator issued an order stating that an Internet offer of a franchise will be exempt from Indiana registration requirements if: (1) the offer indicates that franchises will not be sold to persons in Indiana; (2) an offer is not otherwise addressed to any person in Indiana; and (3) no sales of franchises are made in Indiana as a result of the Internet offer.[19] Thus, to avoid registration in Indiana, the franchisor must post a statement on its Web site stating that franchises are not available within the state and are not sold within the state. Similar rules apply in the other states that regulate franchise advertising.

As already noted, some states require submission or approval of advertisements for franchises. It is not yet clear whether franchisors must submit their Web site content for approval in states requiring submissions or approvals of advertisements, but it would appear that they should not. Most states exempt advertisements appearing in publications with at least two-thirds of their circulation outside the state from these regulations. Although the states have not yet provided their formal positions on this issue, Web sites would seem to fall squarely within this exemption.

---

[18] Cal. Corp. Code § 31003 (West 2000).
[19] Admin. Order 97-0378AO. The order can be found at http://www.state.in.us/sos/security/orpol. html#970378ao

FRANCHISOR CONTROL OVER FRANCHISE INTERNET ACTIVITIES

Cybersquatting—the use of an Internet domain name by a company or individual who does not hold the trademark or trade name in that name—is a common problem. Domain names such as "mcdonalds.com," "mtv.com," "panavision.com," and "coke.com" were all originally held by persons other than the registered trademark owners. Cybersquatting issues are discussed in more detail in Chapter 6.

The franchise relationship adds another dimension to the cybersquatting problem; a franchisee may register and use a domain name belonging to its franchisor. For example, California Closets Co., a franchisor of closet organization system stores, obtained a temporary restraining order preventing its franchisee from using the domain name "californiacloset.com."[20]

Many existing franchise agreements were drafted before the explosion in Internet activity and do not explicitly address Internet issues. Existing language in these documents addressing the franchisor's intellectual property rights in its marks and trade names may prove insufficient to protect the franchisor's interests. New franchise agreements should explicitly address these issues, of course, including topics such as the franchisee's right to establish an Internet site and restrictions upon its content (generally, prior approval of the franchisor of all content is required), permissible domain names, and required "links" between the franchisee's site and the franchisor's site.

INTERNET "ENCROACHMENT" ISSUES

In addition, the Internet poses a special type of encroachment issue for franchisees. While a franchisee might have been granted an exclusive territorial area under its franchise contract, an Internet "virtual store" operated by the franchisor can easily interfere with the franchisee's sales, placing the franchisor in direct competition with its franchisees. While properly drawn new franchise agreements should explicitly address this issue, older agreements that predate the growth of the Internet do not. Franchisees and franchisors thus often find themselves in litigation as they struggle to determine whether existing contract language should be applied to a situation neither party could have anticipated at the time of contracting.

In September 2000, for example, a three-arbitrator panel ruled that Drug Emporium, Inc., a franchisor, violated its franchise agreements with 16 franchisees when it went on-line with its DrugEmporium.com retailing business. Drug Emporium marketed its Web site as a "the full service online drug store" and offered deeply discounted promotional items to on-line purchasers. The panel found that the Drug Emporium had encroached on the territories of its franchisees in violation of its franchise agreements. As a remedy, the panel ordered that the Web site should direct purchasers to the franchisees' brick-and-mortar stores and that the Web site should not ship into franchisees' territories.

International Issues in Franchising

U.S. franchisors often wish to expand their operations abroad. Federal and state franchising laws generally do not govern such transactions; rather, the franchisor must adhere to the laws of the country or countries in which it wishes to offer franchises.

---

[20] California Closet Co. v. Space Organization Systems, Inc., CCH Bus. Franchise Guide ¶ 11,150 (E.D. Wis. 1997).

Three basic forms of franchising are found at the international level. The most common form is the use of a *master franchise agreement*. Under this arrangement, the franchisor enters into a master franchise agreement with a subfranchisor (usually a foreign national), which authorizes the subfranchisor to (1) develop and operate franchises and (2) grant subfranchises to others. *Direct franchising*, in which the franchisor contracts directly with franchisees in the host country, works best when the laws and customs of the host country are similar to that of the United States. Finally, the franchisor may enter into a *joint venture* with an overseas partner. There are, of course, many variations on these basic categories. The choice of method used depends upon cultural differences between the home and host countries; legal constraints imposed by the host country; and business factors, such as financial and personnel constraints, difficulty of managing relationships over long distances, and differences in commercial practices between the two countries involved.

Offering franchises in foreign countries raises a number of legal issues that are different from those found in domestic franchising relationships. Intellectual property issues become particularly critical in foreign franchising activities. The franchisor faces two separate tasks with regard to intellectual property issues in foreign franchising activities. First, it must determine whether existing marks, trade names, and logos will function in the new country, both in terms of being culturally and linguistically acceptable and in terms of whether the mark is sufficiently distinct from other marks already in use. Second, the franchisor must be concerned with protection of intellectual property assets. Will the host country's laws adequately protect marks, trade secrets, and copyrights? Should the franchisor apply for additional patents? (Intellectual property law issues are discussed in more detail in Chapter 2, Chapter 3, and Chapter 6.)

In addition, the franchisor must be concerned with the franchise laws, specifically, and business laws, generally, of the host country. Most countries do not regulate franchises, but the franchisor must determine whether disclosure and/or registration laws apply; what securities or antitrust restrictions might be imposed; whether foreign investments and technology transfers are regulated; what contract, commercial, taxation, and labor laws apply, whether import or export controls are in place; what packaging, labeling, or food and drug regulations apply; and what impact the immigration laws might have on staffing and personnel decisions.

DISCUSSION CASES

5.1 Existence of Franchise Relationship

To-Am Equipment Co., Inc. v. Mitsubishi Caterpillar Forklift America, Inc., **152 F.3d 658 (7th Cir. 1998)**

Legal terms often have specialized meanings that can surprise even a sophisticated party. The term "franchise," or its derivative "franchisee," is one of those words. The question in this case is whether the district court correctly ruled that certain payments that To-Am Equipment Company made to Mitsubishi Caterpillar Forklift America (MCFA), in connection with To-Am's distributorship for certain Mitsubishi products, could constitute franchise fees within the meaning of the Illinois Franchise Disclosure Act of 1987. That ruling in turn set the stage for a jury verdict in To-Am's favor

awarding it $1.525 million in damages for MCFA's termination of its distribution agreement. MCFA challenges the lower court's legal ruling on appeal. * * * We affirm.

I

The Mitsubishi keiretsu (the traditional Japanese form of conglomerate) is a well known manufacturer of heavy equipment, including forklift trucks. In June 1985, To-Am entered into a dealership agreement for these forklifts with [MCFA]. * * * To-Am had been doing business in south

Chicago since 1973, servicing, renting, and repairing fork-lifts. Over the years it also sold a number of different brands of forklifts . . . , though prior to its contract with MCFA it sold only used forklifts. Before allowing To-Am to become a Mitsubishi dealer MCFA required To-Am to relocate to a larger showroom. To-Am complied and moved to Frankfort, Illinois. During the years it served as a Mitsubishi dealer To-Am continued to handle used forklifts manufactured by Mit-subishi's competitors—in other words, the dealership did not require exclusivity on To-Am's part. On the other hand, the agreement conferred on To-Am an exclusive Area of Primary Responsibility (APR), consisting of four Illinois counties and one county in Indiana, in which MCFA did not have and agreed not to create a competing dealership.

Under the 1985 contract . . . , To-Am was required to participate in Mitsubishi's warranty program. This meant, among other things, that To-Am had to maintain trained personnel and provide prompt warranty and non-warranty service on all Mitsubishi products within its APR. To com-ply with these requirements, To-Am participated in all of MCFA's training programs, apparently for the most part at its own expense. Article III para. 14 of the agreement expressly required To-Am to "maintain an adequate supply of current [MCFA] sales and service publications." To-Am did so by keeping a master set of manuals in its parts depart-ment, a second set in its service department, and additional manuals in its mobile service vehicles. . . . MCFA provided one set of these manuals in 1985 when To-Am became a dis-tributor, but thereafter To-Am had to order additional man-uals for the other locations where it kept manuals, for updating, and when manuals wore out. MCFA invoiced To-Am for these additional manuals, and over the years To-Am paid over $1,600 for them. * * *

In February 1994, MCFA notified To-Am that it was terminating the dealership agreement effective April 2, 1994, in accordance with Article XI para. 1 of the agreement, which permitted either party to terminate upon 60 days' written notice "or as required by law." This step was a blow to To-Am's business . . . . The reason was simple: Mitsubishi fork-lifts were the only new vehicles that To-Am had been selling. Even though new truck sales are themselves relatively low profit generators for dealers, they can create substantial downstream business, ranging from trade-ins that could be resold as used equipment or carried as rental equipment, to service and parts sales. Testimony at trial indicated that, while dealer profit margins on new equipment sales might be as low as 3%, the margins on these downstream business opportuni-ties ranged from 30% to 50%. Thus, the loss of To-Am's line of new trucks had ripple effects on its business going far beyond the immediate lost sales.

To-Am therefore brought this suit against MCFA. * * * To-Am alleged violations of the Illinois Franchise Disclo-sure Act for the wrongful termination of its franchise with-out good cause. * * *

* * * Prior to trial MCFA conceded that To-Am met the requirement under the Franchise Disclosure Act that the franchisee's business be substantially associated with the fran-chisor's trademark. MCFA also conceded that the termina-tion was without good cause, as the Act uses the term. * * *

II

* * * *

A. Franchise Fees

The Franchise Disclosure Act defines a franchise fee as follows:

> [A]ny fee or charge that a franchisee is required to pay directly or indirectly for the right to enter into a business or sell, resell, or distribute goods, services or franchises under an agreement, including, but not limited to, any such payments for goods or services, provided that the Administrator may by rule define what constitutes an indirect franchise fee, and pro-vided further that the following shall not be considered the payment of a franchise fee [setting forth six exceptions, none of which MCFA argues apply here].

As this section specifically contemplates, the Illinois Attorney General, as the Administrator of the statute, has issued a number of pertinent implementing regulations. First, he has elaborated on the definition of the term "fran-chise fee":

> A franchise fee within the meaning of Section 3(14) of the Act may be present regardless of the designation given to or the form of the fee, whether payable in lump sum or installments, definite or indefinite in amount, or partly or wholly contingent on future sales, profits or purchases of the franchise business.

14 Ill. Admin. Code § 200.104. In addition, § 200.105 explains:

> (a) Any payment(s) in excess of $500 that is required to be paid by a franchisee to the franchisor or an affiliate of the franchisor constitutes a franchise fee unless specifically excluded by Sec-tion 3(14) of the Act.
> . . .
> (c) A payment made to a franchisor or affiliate for equipment, materials, real estate services, or other items shall not consti-tute a franchise fee if the purchase of the items is not required by the franchisor or the franchisee is permitted to purchase the items from sources other than the franchisor or its affiliates and the item is available from such other sources.

These definitions are obviously sweeping in their scope. The sum of $500, all that has to be paid over the entire life of a franchise, is less than small change for most businesses of any size. Furthermore, the regulations explicitly allow this small amount to be paid either in a lump sum or in installments, to be "definite or indefinite" in amount, and to be "partly or wholly contingent" on different, possibly quite unpredictable, variables. In short, the Illinois legislature and the designated Administrator, the Attorney General, could not have been more clear. They wanted to protect a wide class of dealers, distributors, and other "franchisees" from specified acts, such as terminations of their distributorships (franchises) for anything less than "good cause." * * *

MCFA begins with the factual assertion that To-Am was not required to pay it anything under the terms of the agreement, and certainly no form of franchise fee. It is true that the agreement has no article entitled "Periodic Franchise Payments," but the Illinois statute and administrative regulations we have just quoted make it clear that no such precision is required. Article III para. 14 says that the dealer was required to "maintain an adequate supply of current [MCFA] sales and service publications." The jury was enti-

tled to view this as an indirect fee or charge for the right to enter into the business of distributing MCFA lift trucks, which was payable over time, and which exceeded the statutory floor of $500 by a factor of more than three. Given MCFA's control of the supply of these manuals, it easily could have built a franchise fee into their price. * * *

* * * *

Like many manufacturers, MCFA simply did not appreciate how vigorously Illinois law protects "franchisees." This does not mean that terminations are impossible, but it does mean that they usually must be the subject of negotiation unless the manufacturer is able to show "good cause." MCFA has conceded that it cannot meet that standard . . . . While we understand MCFA's concern that dealerships in Illinois are too easily categorized as statutory franchisees, that is a concern appropriately raised to either the Illinois legislature or Illinois Attorney General, not to this court. We therefore AFFIRM the judgment of the district court.

Questions for Discussion for Case 5.1

1. How does the Illinois Franchise Disclosure Act define a "franchise"? What elements of that definition were at issue here?

2. Do you think that either To-Am or MCFA thought it was creating a franchise when the parties first entered into this relationship?

3. Do you think that the outcome of this case is fair? What public policy considerations might support this outcome?

4. Where should franchisors such as MCFA go to seek redress from this statute and its broad definition of franchises?

5.2 Existence of Franchise Relationship
Mary Kay, Inc. v. Isbell, 999 S.W.2d 669 (Ark. 1999)

This case requires our interpretation of the Arkansas Franchise Practices Act and whether the Act applies to the business relationship established between appellee Janet Isbell and appellant Mary Kay, Inc. This court's jurisdiction is also invoked because the case presents issues of first impression and of substantial public interest and issues involving the need for clarification and development of the law.

Isbell's relationship with Mary Kay commenced in 1980 when she signed an agreement to be a beauty consultant for Mary Kay. As a consultant, Isbell was denominated an independent contractor, and, as such, she agreed to promote and sell Mary Kay products to customers at home demonstration parties; she was prohibited by the agreement from selling or displaying those products in retail sales or service establish-

ments. Instead, a Mary Kay consultant's locations for selling products are her home or those of her potential customers.

After serving a short period as a beauty consultant and recruiting a sufficient number of her customers to be Mary Kay consultants, Isbell became entitled to be a unit sales director. Isbell signed her first sales director agreement on September 1, 1981, and a second one on July 1, 1991. As a director, Isbell continued to recruit beauty consultants and to help and motivate members of her unit in the sale of Mary Kay cosmetics. She also continued to serve as a beauty consultant. Isbell earned compensation in the form of a commission on sales she made directly to customers as a consultant; as sales director, she additionally received override commissions based on sales made by the consultants she recruited.

In 1994, Isbell leased storefront space in a Little Rock mall and used the space as a training center. It was about this time when Mary Kay began receiving complaints about Isbell's operation. By letter dated April 11, 1994, Mary Kay's legal coordinator, Sherry Gragg, referred Isbell to the parties' Sales Director Agreement and the company's Director's Guide which was made a part of that agreement. Gragg related that Isbell's office or training center was to be used only as a teaching center and to hold unit meetings. Gragg further instructed that Isbell's office or center should not give the appearance of a cosmetic studio, facial salon, or retail establishment, or be used to display or store Mary Kay products. Gragg reiterated that, under the parties' agreement, a sales director's office could not appear to be a Mary Kay store or be used to make direct sales to customers. Finally, Gragg admonished Isbell to discontinue all photo sessions of potential customers at such location and to remove any window sign advertising "glamour tips" or face makeover programs taking place at the center. Mary Kay also received complaints of Isbell's (1) overly aggressive recruiting, (2) listing of fictitious recruits as consultants, and (3) check kiting practices.

Eventually, in September of 1995, Mary Kay's vice president of sales development, Gary Jinks, notified Isbell by letter that, under the terms of their agreement, the company was terminating its beauty consultant and sales director agreements, and the termination was effective thirty days from the date of the letter. Isbell filed suit against Mary Kay . . . , alleging that she was a franchisee under Arkansas's Franchise Practices Act and that Mary Kay failed to comply with the provisions of the Act when terminating Isbell. Isbell asserted, among other things, that Mary Kay's letter of termination failed to comply with § 4-72-204 of the Act because the letter did not give her ninety days' notice or set forth the reasons for her termination. * * *

[The trial court ruled as a matter of law that Mary Kay's termination of Isbell had violated the Act and the jury returned a verdict in Isbell's favor in the amount of $110,583.33. Both sides appealed.]

* * * *

The threshold issue to be decided is whether the Arkansas Franchise Practices Act applies, because if it does, Isbell would be entitled to the designation of franchisee and permitted to invoke the protections and benefits of that Act. The other five issues raised by the respective parties come into play only if the Act is ruled applicable to this case. * * *

To determine whether the Arkansas Franchise Practices Act applies to this case depends upon our interpretation and construction of the pertinent provisions of the Act. In this view, we turn first to Ark. Code Ann. § 4-72-202 (1), which in relevant part defines "franchise" to mean the following:

[A] written or oral agreement for a definite or indefinite period, in which a person grants to another a license to use a trade name, trademark, service mark, or related characteristic within an exclusive or nonexclusive territory, or to sell or distribute goods or services within an exclusive or nonexclusive territory, at wholesale, retail, by lease agreement, or otherwise.

Clearly, Mary Kay entered into a written agreement with Isbell so that Isbell, as an independent contractor, could use Mary Kay's trademark and name to sell its products as provided by their agreement. * * *

While the Act's definition of franchise is helpful, that definition alone is not dispositive of the issue as to whether Isbell, under the parties' agreement, is or is not a franchisee. * * * Section 4-72-203 clearly provides the Act applies only to a franchise that contemplates or requires the franchise to establish or maintain a place of business in the state. Next, § 4-72-202 (6) defines "place of business" under the Act as meaning "a fixed geographical location at which the franchisee [1] displays for sale and sells the franchisor's goods or [2] offers for sale and sells the franchisor's services. * * * In sum, citing these two statutes, Mary Kay submits that no fixed geographical location for selling products or services was ever contemplated, much less required, by the parties' agreement, and this reason is sufficient alone to preclude Isbell's reliance on the Act. We agree.

We first should note that Isbell concedes that, as a sales director, her agreements with Mary Kay provided that she could not display for sale or sell Mary Kay products from an office, whether that office was located in her home or her training center. * * *

While conceding that the parties' agreements never contemplated that Isbell would or could sell the franchisor's *goods* from a fixed location, she argues no such prohibition prevented her from selling Mary Kay *services* from her home or training center. Specifically, Isbell suggests the facial makeovers and "Glamour Shots" photo sessions that were a part of Mary Kay's demonstration and training program constituted services that the parties contemplated could be sold by Isbell from her center. * * *

* * * [Mary Kay's] Director's Guide, which was made a part of the parties' agreements, very clearly provided that a sales director's office, albeit it her home or training center, could only be used to interview potential recruits and hold unit meetings and other training events. The Guide further provided that the office or center should not give the appearance of a cosmetic studio, facial salon or retail establishment, or give the appearance of being a "Mary Kay" store. * * * Thus, nowhere in the parties' Guide or agreements can it be fairly said that the parties ever contemplated that Isbell could use her office or center as a fixed location to display or sell Mary Kay products or services.

* * * *

Finally, Isbell argues that her home constituted a place of business under the Act because as a consultant she occasionally displayed and sold products there. This argument, however, is not supported by the parties' agreement, since it never contemplated a fixed location for the display and sale of products. As previously stated, a Mary Kay consultant's locations for selling products are her home or those of her potential customers. * * * It is thus clear that the requirement of a fixed location is not satisfied by occasional sales from either Isbell's home or the homes of her potential customers.

In sum, we conclude that the agreements between Janet Isbell and Mary Kay did not contemplate the establishment of a fixed place of business as that term is defined in Ark. Code Ann. § 4-72-202 (6). As such, the business relationship entered into by Isbell and Mary Kay was not a franchise within the protection of the Arkansas Franchise Practices Act, and the court below erred in so holding. We therefore reverse and dismiss.

Questions for Discussion for Case 5.2

1. Why has the Arkansas Supreme Court agreed to hear this case?

2. Why is it important from each party's perspective whether Isbell had a fixed place of business?

5.3 Vicarious Liability of Franchisor

Miller v. McDonald's Corp., 945 P.2d 1107 (Or. App. 1997)

Plaintiff seeks damages from defendant McDonald's Corporation for injuries that she suffered when she bit into a heart-shaped sapphire stone while eating a Big Mac sandwich that she had purchased at a McDonald's restaurant in Tigard. The trial court granted summary judgment to defendant on the ground that it did not own or operate the restaurant; rather, the owner and operator was a non-party, 3K Restaurants (3K), that held a franchise from defendant. Plaintiff appeals, and we reverse.

Most of the relevant facts are not in dispute. * * * 3K owned and operated the restaurant under a License Agreement (the Agreement) with defendant that required it to operate in a manner consistent with the "McDonald's System." The Agreement described that system as including proprietary rights in trade names, service marks and trademarks, as well as

> designs and color schemes for restaurant buildings, signs, equipment layouts, formulas and specifications for certain food products, methods of inventory and operation control, bookkeeping and accounting, and manuals covering business practices and policies.

The manuals contain "detailed information relating to operation of the Restaurant," including food formulas and specifications, methods of inventory control, bookkeeping procedures, business practices, and other management, advertising, and personnel policies. 3K, as the licensee, agreed to adopt and exclusively use the formulas, methods, and policies contained in the manuals, including any subsequent modifications, and to use only advertising and promotional materials that defendant either provided or approved in advance in writing.

The Agreement described the way in which 3K was to operate the restaurant in considerable detail. It expressly required 3K to operate in compliance with defendant's prescribed standards, policies, practices, and procedures, including serving only food and beverage products that defendant designated. 3K had to follow defendant's specifications and blueprints for the equipment and layout of the restaurant, including adopting subsequent reasonable changes that defendant made, and to maintain the restaurant building in compliance with defendant's standards. 3K could not make any changes in the basic design of the building without defendant's approval.

The Agreement required 3K to keep the restaurant open during the hours that defendant prescribed, including maintaining adequate supplies and employing adequate personnel to operate at maximum capacity and efficiency during those hours. 3K also had to keep the restaurant similar in appearance to all other McDonald's restaurants. 3K's employees had to wear McDonald's uniforms, to have a neat and clean appearance, and to provide competent and courteous service. 3K could use only containers and other packaging that bore McDonald's trademarks. The ingredients for the foods and beverages had to meet defendant's standards, and 3K had to use "only those methods of food handling and preparation that [defendant] may designate from time to time." * * * The manuals save further details that expanded on many of these requirements.

In order to ensure conformity with the standards described in the Agreement, defendant periodically sent field consultants to the restaurant to inspect its operations. 3K trained its employees in accordance with defendant's materials and recommendations and sent some of them to training programs that defendant administered. Failure to comply with the agreed standards could result in loss of the franchise.

Despite these detailed instructions, the Agreement provided that 3K was not an agent of defendant for any purpose. Rather, it was an independent contractor and was responsible for all obligations and liabilities, including claims based on injury, illness, or death, directly or indirectly resulting from the operation of the restaurant.

Plaintiff went to the restaurant under the assumption that defendant owned, controlled, and managed it. So far as she could tell, the restaurant's appearance was similar to that of other McDonald's restaurants that she had patronized. Nothing disclosed to her that any entity other than defendant was involved in its operation. The only signs that were visible and obvious to the public had the name "McDonald's," the employees wore uniforms with McDonald's insignia, and the menu was the same that plaintiff had seen in other McDonald's restaurants. The general appearance of the restaurant and the food products that it sold were similar to the restaurants and products that plaintiff had seen in national print and television advertising that defendant had run. To the best of plaintiff's knowledge, only McDonald's sells Big Mac hamburgers.

In short, plaintiff testified, she went to the Tigard McDonald's because she relied on defendant's reputation and because she wanted to obtain the same quality of service, standard of care in food preparation, and general attention to detail that she had previously enjoyed at other McDonald's restaurants.

Under these facts, 3K would be directly liable for any injuries that plaintiff suffered as a result of the restaurant's negligence. The issue . . . is whether there is evidence that would permit a jury to find defendant vicariously liable for those injuries because of its relationship with 3K. Plaintiff asserts two theories of vicarious liability, actual agency and apparent agency. We hold that there is sufficient evidence to raise a jury issue under both theories. * * *

The kind of actual agency relationship that would make defendant vicariously liable for 3K's negligence requires that defendant have the right to control the *method* by which 3K performed its obligations under the Agreement. * * *

* * * *

* * * The Delaware Supreme Court stated the [right to control] test as it applies to [a franchise relationship]:

If, in practical effect, the franchise agreement goes beyond the stage of setting standards, and allocates to the franchisor the right to exercise control over the daily operations of the franchise, an agency relationship exists.

* * * *

[W]e believe that a jury could find that defendant retained sufficient control over 3K's daily operations that an actual agency relationship existed. The Agreement did not simply set standards that 3K had to meet. Rather, it required 3K to use the precise methods that defendant established, both in the Agreement and in the detailed manuals that the Agreement incorporated. Those methods included the ways in which 3K was to handle and prepare food. Defendant enforced the use of those methods by regularly sending inspectors and by its retained power to cancel the Agreement. That evidence would support a finding that defendant had the right to control the way in which 3K performed at least food handling and preparation. In her complaint, plaintiff alleges that 3K's deficiencies in those functions resulted in the sapphire being in the Big Mac and thereby caused her injuries. Thus, * * * there is evidence that defendant had the right to control 3K in the precise part of its business that allegedly resulted in plaintiff's injuries. That is sufficient to raise an issue of actual agency.

Plaintiff next asserts that defendant is vicariously liable for 3K's alleged negligence because 3K was defendant's apparent agent.[4] The relevant standard is in *Restatement (Second) of Agency*, § 267, which we adopted in *Themins v. Emanuel Lutheran*, 637 P.2d 155 (Or. App. 1981):

One who represents that another is his servant or other agent and thereby causes a third person justifiably to rely upon the care or skill of such apparent agent is subject to liability to the third person for harm caused by the lack of care or skill of the one appearing to be a servant or other agent as if he were such.

We have not applied § 267 to a franchisor/franchisee situation, but courts in a number of other jurisdictions have done so in ways that we find instructive. In most cases the courts have found that there was a jury issue of apparent agency. The crucial issues are whether the putative principal held the third party out as an agent and whether the plaintiff relied on that holding out.

We look first at what may constitute a franchisor's holding a franchisee out as its agent. In the leading case of *Gizzi v. Texaco, Inc.*, 437 F.2d 308 (5th Cir. 1971), the plaintiff purchased a used Volkswagen van from a Texaco service station. He was injured when the brakes failed shortly thereafter. The franchisee had worked on the brakes before selling the

---

[4] Apparent agency is a distinct concept from apparent authority. Apparent agency creates an agency relationship that does not otherwise exist, while apparent authority expands the authority of an actual agent.

car. The station prominently displayed Texaco insignia, including the slogan "Trust your car to the man who wears the star." Texaco engaged in considerable national advertising to convey the impression that its dealers were skilled in automotive servicing. About 30 percent of Texaco dealers sold used cars. There was a Texaco regional office across the street from the station, and those working in that office knew that the franchisee was selling cars from the station. Based on this evidence, the court concluded, under New Jersey law, that the question of apparent agency was for the jury.

* * * *

In *Crinkley v. Holiday Inns, Inc.*, 844 F.2d 156 (4th Cir. 1988), the defendant required the use of the Holiday Inn trade name and trademarks, was the original builder of the hotel, and engaged in national advertising that promoted its system of hotels without distinguishing between those that it owned and those that it franchised. The only indication that the defendant did not own this particular Holiday Inn was a sign in the restaurant that stated that the franchisee operated it. Based on this evidence, the court concluded, under North Carolina law, that apparent agency was a question for the jury.

In each of these cases, the franchise agreement required the franchisee to act in ways that identified it with the franchisor. The franchisor imposed those requirements as part of maintaining an image of uniformity of operations and appearance for the franchisor's entire system. Its purpose was to attract the patronage of the public to that entire system. The centrally imposed uniformity is the fundamental basis for the courts' conclusion that there was an issue of fact whether the franchisors held the franchisees out as the franchisors' agents.

In this case, for similar reasons, there is an issue of fact about whether defendant held 3K out as its agent. Everything about the appearance and operation of the Tigard McDonald's identified it with defendant and with the common image for all McDonald's restaurants that defendant has worked to create through national advertising, common signs and uniforms, common menus, common appearance, and common standards. The possible existence of a sign identifying 3K as the operator does not alter the conclusion that there is an issue of apparent agency for the jury. There are issues of fact of whether that sign was sufficiently visible to the public, in light of plaintiff's apparent failure to see it, and of whether one sign by itself is sufficient to remove the impression that defendant created through all of the other indicia of its control that it, and 3K under the requirements that defendant imposed, presented to the public.

Defendant does not seriously dispute that a jury could find that it held 3K out as its agent. Rather, it argues that there is insufficient evidence that plaintiff justifiably relied on that holding out. It argues that it is not sufficient for her to prove that she went to the Tigard McDonald's because it was a McDonald's restaurant. Rather, she also had to prove that she went to it because she believed that *McDonald's Corporation* operated both it and the other McDonald's restaurants that she had previously patronized. * * *

Defendant's argument both demands a higher level of sophistication about the nature of franchising than the general public can be expected to have and ignores the effect of its own efforts to lead the public to believe that McDonald's restaurants are part of a uniform national system of restaurants with common products and common standards of quality. * * *

Plaintiff testified in her affidavit that her reliance on defendant for the quality of service and food at the Tigard McDonald's came in part from her experience at other McDonald's restaurants. * * * A jury could find that it was defendant's very insistence on uniformity of appearance and standards, designed to cause the public to think of every McDonald's, franchised or unfranchised, as part of the same system, that makes it difficult or impossible for plaintiff to tell whether her previous experiences were at restaurants that defendant owned or franchised.

* * * *

[P]laintiff testified that she relied on the general reputation of McDonald's in patronizing the Tigard restaurant and in her expectation of the quality of the food and service that she would receive. Especially in light of defendant's efforts to create a public perception of a common McDonald's system at all McDonald's restaurants, whoever operated them, a jury could find that plaintiff's reliance was objectively reasonable. The trial court erred in granting summary judgment on the apparent agency theory.

Reversed and remanded.

Questions for Discussion for Case 5.3

1. What is the difference between actual and apparent agency? What tests are used to evaluate whether each is present in a given case?

2. How visible and obvious do you think signs should be telling customers that a franchisee owns and operates a business? On your last trip to a fast-food restaurant, did you notice who owned the restaurant?

3. Is it fair to hold McDonald's Corporation liable when its franchisee cooks the food and is most likely in the best position to control whether foreign objects enter the food? What public policy considerations come into play when you make this determination?

4. What can a franchisor do to protect itself against liability arising out of the acts of its franchisee?

5. Procedurally, what will happen next in this case?

5.4 Franchise Antitrust Issues

Queen City Pizza, Inc. v. Domino's Pizza, Inc., 124 F.3d 430 (3d Cir. 1997)

* * * Eleven franchisees of Domino's Pizza stores and the International Franchise Advisory Council, Inc. filed suit against Domino's Pizza, Inc., alleging violations of federal antitrust laws . . . . The district court dismissed the antitrust claims for failure to state a claim for which relief can be granted, because the plaintiffs failed to allege a valid relevant market. * * * We will affirm.

I. Facts and Procedural History

A.

Domino's Pizza, Inc. is a fast-food service company that sells pizza through a national network of over 4,200 stores. Domino's Pizza owns and operates approximately 700 of these stores. Independent franchisees own and operate the remaining 3,500. Domino's Pizza, Inc. is the second largest pizza company in the United States, with revenues in excess of $1.8 billion per year.

A franchisee joins the Domino's system by executing a standard franchise agreement with Domino's Pizza, Inc. Under the franchise agreement, the franchisee receives the right to sell pizza under the "Domino's" name and format. In return, Domino's Pizza receives franchise fees and royalties.

The essence of a successful nationwide fast-food chain is product uniformity and consistency. Uniformity benefits franchisees because customers can purchase pizza from any Domino's store and be certain the pizza will taste exactly like the Domino's pizza with which they are familiar. This means that individual franchisees need not build up their own good will. Uniformity also benefits the franchisor. It ensures the brand name will continue to attract and hold customers, increasing franchise fees and royalties.

For these reasons, section 12.2 of the Domino's Pizza standard franchise agreement requires that all pizza ingredients, beverages, and packaging materials used by a Domino's franchisee conform to the standards set by Domino's Pizza, Inc. Section 12.2 also provides that Domino's Pizza, Inc. "may in our sole discretion require that ingredients, supplies

and materials used in the preparation, packaging, and delivery of pizza be purchased exclusively from us or from approved suppliers or distributors." Domino's Pizza reserves the right "to impose reasonable limitations on the number of approved suppliers or distributors of any product." To enforce these rights, Domino's Pizza, Inc. retains the power to inspect franchisee stores and to test materials and ingredients. Section 12.2 is subject to a reasonableness clause providing that Domino's Pizza, Inc. must "exercise reasonable judgment with respect to all determinations to be made by us under the terms of this Agreement."

Under the standard franchise agreement, Domino's Pizza, Inc. sells approximately 90% of the $500 million in ingredients and supplies used by Domino's franchisees. These sales, worth some $450 million per year, form a significant part of Domino's Pizza, Inc.'s profits. Franchisees purchase only 10% of their ingredients and supplies from outside sources. With the exception of fresh dough, Domino's Pizza, Inc. does not manufacture the products it sells to franchisees. Instead, it purchases these products from approved suppliers and then resells them to the franchisees at a markup.

B.

The plaintiffs in this case are eleven Domino's franchisees and the International Franchise Advisory Council, Inc. ("IFAC"), a Michigan corporation consisting of approximately 40% of the Domino's franchisees in the United States, formed to promote their common interests. The plaintiffs contend that Domino's Pizza, Inc. has a monopoly in "the $500 million aftermarket for sales of supplies to Domino's franchisees" and has used its monopoly power to unreasonably restrain trade, limit competition, and extract supra-competitive profits. Plaintiffs point to several actions by Domino's Pizza, Inc. to support their claims.

First, plaintiffs allege that Domino's Pizza, Inc. has restricted their ability to purchase competitively priced dough. Most franchisees purchase all of their fresh dough from Domino's Pizza, Inc. Plaintiffs here attempted to lower costs by making fresh pizza dough on site. They contend that in response, Domino's Pizza, Inc. increased processing fees and altered quality standards and inspection practices for store-produced dough, which eliminated all potential savings and financial incentives to make their own dough. Plaintiffs also allege Domino's Pizza, Inc. prohibited stores that produce dough from selling their dough to other franchisees, even though the dough-producing stores were willing to sell dough at a price 25% to 40% below Domino's Pizza, Inc.'s price.

Next, plaintiffs object to efforts by Domino's Pizza, Inc. to block IFAC's attempt to buy less expensive ingredients and supplies from other sources. In June 1994, IFAC entered into a purchasing agreement with FoodService Purchasing Cooperative, Inc. (FPC). Under the agreement, FPC was appointed the purchasing agent for IFAC-member Domino's franchisees. FPC was charged with developing a cooperative purchasing plan under which participating franchisees could obtain supplies and ingredients at reduced cost from suppliers other than Domino's Pizza, Inc. Plaintiffs contend that when Domino's Pizza, Inc. became aware of these efforts, it intentionally issued ingredient and supply specifications so vague that potential suppliers could not provide FPC with meaningful price quotations.

Plaintiffs also allege Domino's Pizza entered into exclusive dealing arrangements with several franchisees in order to deny FPC access to a pool of potential buyers sufficiently large to make the alternative purchasing scheme economically feasible. In addition, plaintiffs contend Domino's Pizza, Inc. commenced anti-competitive predatory pricing to shut FPC out of the market. For example, they maintain that Domino's Pizza, Inc. lowered prices on many ingredients and supplies to a level competitive with FPC's prices and then recouped lost profits by raising the price on fresh dough, which FPC could not supply. Further, plaintiffs contend Domino's Pizza, Inc. entered into exclusive dealing arrangements with the only approved suppliers of ready-made deep dish crusts and sauce. Under these agreements, the suppliers were obligated to deliver their entire output to Domino's Pizza, Inc. Plaintiffs allege the purpose of these agreements was to prevent FPC from purchasing these critical pizza components for resale to franchisees.

Finally, plaintiffs allege Domino's Pizza, Inc. refused to sell fresh dough to franchisees unless the franchisees purchased other ingredients and supplies from Domino's Pizza, Inc. As a result of these and other alleged practices, plaintiffs maintain that each franchisee store now pays between $3000 and $10,000 more per year for ingredients and supplies than it would in a competitive market. Plaintiffs allege these costs are passed on to consumers.

C.

* * * *

Domino's Pizza, Inc. moved to dismiss the antitrust claims for failure to state a claim, contending the plaintiffs failed to allege a "relevant market," a basic pleading requirement for claims under both § 1 and § 2 of the Sherman antitrust act.

[The district court agreed that the plaintiffs had failed to allege a relevant market, and the plaintiffs appealed.]

* * * *

III. Discussion

* * * *

A.

* * * *

Plaintiffs have the burden of defining the relevant market. * * *

B.

Plaintiffs allege Domino's Pizza, Inc. has willfully acquired and maintained a monopoly in the market for ingredients, supplies, materials and distribution services used in the operation of Domino's stores, in violation of § 2 of the Sherman Act. Section 2 sanctions those "who shall monopolize, or attempt to monopolize, or combine or conspire with any other person or persons, to monopolize any part of the trade or commerce among the several states, or with foreign nations." "The offense of monopoly under § 2 of the Sherman Act has two elements: (1) the possession of monopoly power in the relevant market and (2) the willful acquisition or maintenance of that power as distinguished from growth or development as a consequence of a superior product, business acumen, or historic accident."

The district court dismissed plaintiffs' § 2 monopoly claims for failure to plead a valid relevant market. Plaintiffs suggest the "ingredients, supplies, materials, and distribution services used by and in the operation of Domino's pizza stores" constitutes a relevant market for antitrust purposes. We disagree.

[T]he outer boundaries of a relevant market are determined by reasonable interchangeability of use. "Interchangeability implies that one product is roughly equivalent to another for the use to which it is put; while there may be some degree of preference for the one over the other, either would work effectively. A person needing transportation to work could accordingly buy a Ford or a Chevrolet automobile, or could elect to ride a horse or bicycle, assuming those options were feasible." When assessing reasonable interchangeability, "[f]actors to be considered include price, use, and qualities." Reasonable interchangeability is also indicated by "crosselasticity of demand between the product itself and substitutes for it." As we [have] explained, "products in a relevant market [are] characterized by a cross elasticity of demand, in other words, the rise in the price of a good within a relevant product market would tend to create a greater demand for other like goods in that market."

Here, the dough, tomato sauce, and paper cups that meet Domino's Pizza, Inc. standards and are used by Domino's stores are interchangeable with dough, sauce and cups available from other suppliers and used by other pizza companies. * * * Thus, the relevant market, which is defined to include all reasonably interchangeable products, cannot be restricted solely to those products currently approved by Domino's Pizza, Inc. for use by Domino's franchisees. For that reason, we must reject plaintiffs' proposed relevant market.

Of course, Domino's-approved pizza ingredients and supplies differ from other available ingredients and supplies in one crucial manner. Only Domino's-approved products may be used by Domino's franchisees without violating section 12.2 of Domino's standard franchise agreement. Plaintiffs suggest that this difference is sufficient by itself to create a relevant market in approved products. We disagree. The test for a relevant market is not commodities reasonably interchangeable by a particular plaintiff, but "commodities reasonably interchangeable by consumers for the same purposes." A court making a relevant market determination looks not to the contractual restraints assumed by a particular plaintiff when determining whether a product is interchangeable, but to the uses to which the product is put by consumers in general. Thus, the relevant inquiry here is not whether a Domino's franchisee may reasonably use both approved or non-approved products interchangeably without triggering liability for breach of contract, but whether pizza makers in general might use such products interchangeably. Clearly, they could. * * *

* * * *

Were we to accept plaintiffs' relevant market, virtually all franchise tying agreements requiring the franchisee to purchase inputs such as ingredients and supplies from the franchisor would violate antitrust law. Courts and legal commentators have long recognized that franchise tying contracts are an essential and important aspect of the franchise form of business organization because they reduce agency costs and prevent franchisees from free riding—offering products of sub-standard quality insufficient to maintain the

reputational value of the franchise product while benefiting from the quality control efforts of other actors in the franchise system. Franchising is a bedrock of the American economy. More than one third of all dollars spent in retailing transactions in the United States are paid to franchise outlets. We do not believe the antitrust laws were designed to erect a serious barrier to this form of business organization.

The purpose of the Sherman Act "is not to protect businesses from the working of the market; it is to protect the public from the failure of the market." * * * Plaintiffs need not have become Domino's franchisees. If the contractual restrictions in section 12.2 of the general franchise agreement were viewed as overly burdensome or risky at the time they were proposed, plaintiffs could have purchased a different form of restaurant, or made some alternative investment. They chose not to do so. [P]laintiffs here must purchase products from Domino's Pizza not because of Domino's market power over a unique product, but because they are bound by contract to do so. If Domino's Pizza, Inc. acted unreasonably when, under the franchise agreement, it restricted plaintiffs' ability to purchase supplies from other sources, plaintiffs' remedy, if any, is in contract, not under the antitrust laws.

For these reasons, we agree with the district court that plaintiffs have not pleaded a valid relevant market.

C.

Plaintiffs' claim for attempt to monopolize fails for the same reasons. To prevail on an attempted monopolization claim under § 2 of the Sherman Act, "a plaintiff must prove that the defendant (1) engaged in predatory or anticompetitive conduct with (2) specific intent to monopolize and with (3) a dangerous probability of achieving monopoly power." In order to determine whether there is a dangerous probability of monopolization, a court must inquire "into the relevant product and geographic market and the defendant's economic power in that market."

Plaintiffs' attempted monopoly claim is predicated on the identical proposed relevant market underlying its monopoly claim: a market in the ingredients, supplies, and materials used by Domino's pizza stores. Because the products within this proposed market are interchangeable with other products outside of the proposed market, the claim was properly dismissed.

D.

Plaintiffs allege exclusive dealing arrangements entered into by Domino's Pizza, Inc. have unreasonably restrained trade in violation of § 1 of the Sherman Act. Section 1 of the Sherman Act provides: "Every contract, combination in the form of trust or otherwise, or conspiracy, in restraint of trade or commerce among the several states, or with foreign nations, is declared to be illegal."

To establish a section 1 violation for unreasonable restraint of trade, a plaintiff must prove (1) concerted action by the defendants; (2) that produced anti-competitive effects within the relevant product and geographic markets; (3) that the concerted action was illegal; and (4) that the plaintiff was injured as a proximate result of the concerted action.

Plaintiffs allege defendant's actions caused anticompetitive effects within the market for ingredients and supplies used by Domino's pizza stores. Again, this claim fails because the products within the proposed market are interchangeable with products outside the proposed market.

E.

Plaintiffs allege Domino's Pizza, Inc. imposed an unlawful tying arrangement by requiring franchisees to buy ingredients and supplies from them as a condition of obtaining Domino's Pizza fresh dough, in violation of § 1 of the Sherman Act. "In a tying arrangement, the seller sells one item, known as the tying product, on the condition that the buyer also purchases another item, known as the tied product." "[T]he antitrust concern over tying arrangements is limited to those situations in which the seller can exploit its power in the market for the tying product to force buyers to purchase the tied product when they otherwise would not, thereby restraining competition in the tied product market." * * *

Here, plaintiffs allege Domino's Pizza, Inc. used its power in the purported market for Domino's-approved dough to force plaintiffs to buy unwanted ingredients and supplies from them. This claim fails because the proposed tying market—the market in Domino's-approved dough—is not a relevant market for antitrust purposes. Domino's dough is reasonably interchangeable with other brands of pizza dough, and does not therefore constitute a relevant market of its own. All that distinguishes this dough from other brands is that a Domino's franchisee must use it or face

a suit for breach of contract. As we have noted above, the particular contractual restraints assumed by a plaintiff are not sufficient by themselves to render interchangeable commodities non-interchangeable for purposes of relevant market definition. If Domino's had market power in the overall market for pizza dough and forced plaintiffs to purchase other unwanted ingredients to obtain dough, plaintiffs might possess a valid tying claim. But where the defendant's "power" to "force" plaintiffs to purchase the alleged tying product stems not from the market, but from plaintiffs' contractual agreement to purchase the tying product, no claim will lie. * * *

F.

Plaintiffs allege Domino's Pizza, Inc. imposed an unlawful tie-in arrangement by requiring franchisees to buy ingredients and supplies "as a condition of their continued enjoyment of rights and services under their Standard Franchise Agreement," in violation of § 1 of the Sherman Act. This claim is meritless. Though plaintiffs complain of an illegal tie-in arrangement, they have failed to point to any particular tying product or service over which Domino's Pizza, Inc. has market power. Domino's Pizza's control over plaintiffs' "continued enjoyment of rights and services under their Standard Franchise Agreement" is not a "market." Rather, it is a function of Domino's contractual powers under the franchise agreement to terminate the participation of franchisees in the franchise system if they violate the agreement.

* * * *

* * * Because this claim was not properly raised before the district court and is not properly before us, we decline to address it.

* * * *

IV.

For the foregoing reasons, we will affirm the judgment of the district court.

Questions for Discussion for Case 5.4

1. What is the test for an illegal monopoly under Section 2 of the Sherman Act? What is the test for an illegal attempt to monopolize under Section 2? What is the test for an unreasonable restraint of trade in violation of Section 1 of the Sherman Act?

2. How does a court determine what the relevant market is? How is the relevant market defined here?

3. Who ultimately pays the bill for the increase in the cost of pizza supplies? Should such a practical consideration matter in cases of this type?

DISCUSSION QUESTIONS

1. Several plaintiffs brought actions against Conoco, Inc., claiming that they had been discriminated against on the basis of their race when they attempted to make purchases at three gas stations in Texas operated under the Conoco brand. Conoco directly owned and operated one of the stations, and independent contractors licensed to use the Conoco trademark operated the other two stations. Evidence, including videotapes, indicated that the clerks had refused to serve the customers and had used racial epithets during some of the incidents. What factors should the court consider and what tests should it apply in determining whether Conoco should be held liable? *Arguello v. Conoco, Inc.*, 207 F.3d 803 (5th Cir. 2000)

2. Lockard worked as a waitress for a Pizza Hut franchise owned by A & M Food Services. The national Pizza Hut franchisor produces several training documents for employees, including a booklet on how to bring sexual harassment complaints to the manager or district representative. The Pizza Hut franchisees actually operated and controlled the restaurants' day-to-day business. Lockard claimed that the restaurant that she worked at maintained a hostile environment because the manager played songs on the jukebox with sexually explicit lyrics. Furthermore, the manager made her serve two specific customers who had a history of making sexual advances to her at the restaurant. She complained that she did not want to serve the customers, but the manager demanded that she do so. When she went back to their table, the customers grabbed and groped her as she tried to take their orders. Lockard quit and sued the franchisor and the franchisee. Should Lockard recover against the franchisor? The franchisee? *Lockard v. Pizza Hut, Inc.*, 162 F.3d 1062 (10th Cir. 1998)

3. University Motors, a West Virginia business, entered into a franchise agreement with General Motors Corp. (GMC). The agreement specified that University Motors would require approval from GMC if it wanted to sell another line of vehicles. University Motors began selling a Nissan line of vehicles without first obtaining GMC approval. GMC sought to terminate the franchise and hand-delivered a letter to University Motors stating that the franchise would end 90 days from receipt of the letter. GMC stated that the reason for the termination was the new vehicle line and various deficiencies in University Motor's sales. University Motors filed suit to prevent termination of the franchise, claiming that GMC had violated a West Virginia statute that required a franchisor to deliver a termination letter by certified mail and to give the franchisee 180 days to cure the problem. The statute also required that the franchisor have a good faith reason for terminating because of poor sales or service performance. Should GMC be permitted to terminate University Motors? Why, or why not? *University Motors, Ltd. v. General Motors Corp.*, 168 F.3d 484 (4th Cir. 1999)

4. Shell Oil Co. owned a gas station and property in Deerfield Beach, Florida. In 1995, Shell entered into a "Motor Fuel Station Lease" with A. Z. Services, Inc., which provided that A. Z. would lease the gas station and property for five years. The parties also entered into a "Dealer Agreement," which established a franchise agreement between the two parties. Under the Dealer Agreement, A. Z. had the right to operate the gas station under Shell's trademarks, brand name, service marks, and other Shell identifications in connection with the sale of motor fuel and other petroleum products. A year later, without notice to or consent by Shell, A. Z. removed all Shell trademarks and identification, stopped selling Shell products, and began selling the products of a Shell competitor, Skipper's Choice. Shell terminated the franchise agreement and filed suit seeking an injunction to prohibit A. Z. from selling Skipper's Choice products and to vacate the property. A. Z. defended by claiming that Shell had unlawfully tied the lease of the property to the sale of Shell fuel. How should the court rule on this antitrust claim? *Shell Oil Co. v. A. Z. Servs.*, 990 F. Supp. 1406 (S.D. Fla. 1997)

5. In 1995, Golf U.S.A. entered into a franchise agreement granting Express Golf the right to operate a retail store using Golf U.S.A.'s methods, name, designs, systems, and service marks. The franchise agreement also stated that "[a]ny and all disputes, claims and controversies arising out of or relating to this Agreement . . . shall be resolved by arbitration conducted in Oklahoma County, State of Oklahoma." Golf U.S.A. is an Oklahoma corporation. The golf retail store failed within nine months, and Charles Barker, the sole shareholder of Express Golf, brought this action against Golf U.S.A. for fraudulent misrepresentation. He alleged that Golf U.S.A. misrepresented the success of its retail operations, thereby leading him to sign the franchise agreement. Golf

U.S.A. moved to dismiss the case, arguing that the dispute should be decided by arbitration and not by the judiciary. Barker claimed that the arbitration clause was unconscionable and therefore unenforceable. No statute prohibits the inclusion of arbitration clauses in franchise agreements. Should Barker be permitted to litigate in court or should the arbitration clause of the franchise agreement control? *Barker v. Golf U.S.A., Inc.*, 154 F.3d 788 (8th Cir. 1998)

6. Weaver operated two Burger King restaurants under two separate franchise agreements. *Restaurant 1* was located in Great Falls, Montana, and Weaver leased the facility from Burger King. *Restaurant 2* was also located in Great Falls, but Weaver owned the facility. Both franchise agreements required Weaver to make monthly royalty payments and advertising contributions to Burger King Corp. and provided that Florida law would control in the event of a dispute. The agreement for *Restaurant 1* contained no provisions regarding geographic scope, but the agreement for *Restaurant 2* stipulated that "this franchise is for the specified location only and does not in any way grant or imply any area, market, or territorial rights proprietary to FRANCHISEE." Neither agreement contained any limitations on the locations of future Burger King restaurants.

In 1989, another Burger King franchise opened in Great Falls. Weaver was upset by the competition, felt that Burger King had breached its obligations under the franchise agreements, and stopped making rent, royalty, and advertising payments, though he continued to use Burger King's marks and system. Burger King sued for breach of contract. Weaver counterclaimed, arguing that Burger King had breached the implied covenant of good faith and fair dealing, which, under Florida law, is part of every contract. Florida law does not recognize actions for breach of an implied covenant of good faith and fair dealing when: (a) the party breaching the implied covenant has performed all of the express contractual provisions in good faith and (b) the implied duty that was breached would vary the express terms of the contract. Which party should prevail here, and why? *Burger King Corp. v. Weaver*, 169 F.3d 1310 (11th Cir. 1999)

7. In 1993, Airborne Freight Corp. (Airborne), a package delivery service, and East Wind Express, Inc. (East Wind), entered into a contract under which East Wind agreed to provide services to Airborne, such as pickup, transport, and delivery of shipments between Airborne's customers and facilities in northern Oregon. Customers would call Airborne and ask to have a package delivered to another area. Airborne would radio an East Wind driver, who would then pick up the customer's package. Airborne billed the customer and assumed all liability for the package from the time of arrival at its pickup to the package's final destination. Under the contract, Airborne paid East Wind based on the average number of packages carried per day, and East Wind was "not entitled to receive any portion of any charges made by Airborne to its shippers." The contract also stated that East Wind's use of Airborne's trademarks on its uniforms and trucks was an advertising service and was to be compensated according to advertising fees. Airborne specified the standards that applied to the use of its trademarks by East Wind.

Eventually, the relationship between the two companies disintegrated, and Airborne terminated the contract. East Wind brought this action against Airborne, asserting that at-will terminations violated the Washington Franchise Investment Protection Act. Airborne argued that East Wind was an independent contractor, who could be terminated at will, and not a franchisee. What are the requirements for a franchise relationship? Under these standards, is Airborne a franchisee or an independent contractor? *East Wind Express, Inc., v. Airborne Freight Corp.*, 974 P.2d 369 (Wash. Ct. App. 1999)

8. As of June 1995, Little Caesar Enterprises, Inc. (LCE), had 536 franchises nationwide operating 2,867 carryout-type restaurants. LCE also owned and operated 1,000 carryout restaurants and 500 restaurants located in K-Mart stores. Blue Line Distributing, Inc., purchased the necessary supplies for the restaurants, bundled them into single units, and sold them to the franchisees. In June 1989, LCE and Blue Line entered into a licensing agreement granting Blue Line the exclusive right to distribute products containing the Little Caesar logo. Franchise agreements used to give franchisees the right to use LCE-approved alternative suppliers, but the 1990 Franchise Agreement excluded logoed products from the list of products that could be obtained from alternative suppliers. Logoed products, such as paper products, condiments, and packaging, are necessary to the operation of a franchise.

Plaintiffs bought Little Caesar franchises between 1990 and 1995 and are operating under the 1990 Franchise Agreement. They argue that Blue Line charges supracompetitive prices for the logoed products and that the exclusive license granted to Blue Line precludes them from obtaining cheaper products from alternative suppliers. They have brought this class action, alleging that LCE has unlawfully tied Blue Line's products to the purchase of a Little Caesar franchise. LCE argues that plaintiffs knew about the Blue Line distributorship, agreed to the terms when signing the 1990 Agreement, and that LCE lacks sufficient market power to force a tying arrangement on plaintiffs. How should the court resolve this antitrust claim, and why? *Little Caesar Enterprises, Inc. v. Smith*, 34 F. Supp. 2d 459 (E.D. Mich. 1998)

9. Tosco Corporation is an independent refiner and marketer of petroleum products. In 1994, Tosco purchased from BP Exploration & Oil, Inc. ("BP"), all service stations owned by BP in northern California, along with a license to use the "BP" trademark in California. The license for the trademark expires on August 1, 2006, and Tosco pays BP royalties for the use of the marks. In accordance with the sale, BP terminated all franchises, and Tosco subsequently offered the terminated franchisees a new franchise agreement to sell petroleum products under the "BP" trademark. The new franchise agreements were scheduled to expire on April 15, 1998.

On March 31, 1997, Tosco purchased the 76 Products Company from Union Oil Company of California, which included approximately 900 service stations in California and the right to use the "Union 76" and "76" trademarks in perpetuity.

In 1997, Tosco decided that it would be most effective to sell products at the service stations under only one brand and chose to sell under the "Union 76" trademark because use of that mark required no royalty payments. In December 1997, Tosco offered all of its BP franchisees renewal of the franchise agreement on condition that they sell fuel under the "Union 76" mark.

Plaintiffs are service station dealers who refused to agree to the change in marks, preferring to retain the "BP" mark. Tosco notified plaintiffs that their franchises would not be renewed for failure to agree to a change in a provision of the franchise agreement. Plaintiffs brought this action, contending that under the Petroleum Marketing Practices Act (PMPA) Tosco could not condition renewal of a franchise agreement on the franchisee's consent to "rebrand" the product. The relevant portion of the PMPA states that such conditional agreements are lawful, as long as the "changes or additions are the result of determinations made by the franchisor in good faith and in the normal course of business" and not for the purpose of preventing renewal of the franchise.

What factors should the court consider in resolving this dispute? *Unified Dealer Group v. Tosco Corp.*, 16 F. Supp. 2d 1137 (N.D. Cal. 1998) aff'd, 216 F.3d 1085 (9th Cir. 2000)

10. Dana Hoffnagle was an employee at a McDonald's restaurant owned by a franchisee, Rapid-Mac, Inc. At 10:00 one evening, two men entered the restaurant, grabbed Hoffnagle, and took her out to the parking lot where they attempted to force her into their car. Tammy Geiger, a managerial employee, came to Hoffnagle's assistance and helped her escape from the men and return into the restaurant. Geiger noticed the two men driving their car around the parking lot, but did not lock the doors or telephone the police. Later, one of the men reentered the restaurant and again attempted to force Hoffnagle outside. Geiger intervened again, and the men left the restaurant premises. Geiger then telephoned the police department.

Hoffnagle filed for workers' compensation benefits from her employer, Rapid-Mac, which she received. She then filed suit against McDonald's Corp., which was Rapid-Mac's franchisor, arguing that McDonald's Corp. had the ability to control the operations of the franchisee and was liable for negligence for failing to exercise such control.

The contractual agreements between McDonald's and Rapid-Mac required the franchisee to adhere to the franchisor's standards and policies "for providing for the uniform operation of all McDonald's restaurants within the McDonald's system including, but not limited to, serving only designated food and beverage products, the use of only prescribed equipment and building layout and designs, strict adherence to designated food and beverage specifications and to prescribed standards of quality, service and cleanliness in [the] restaurant operation." The agreements also required Rapid-Mac to adopt and use business manuals prepared by McDonald's and for McDonald's to make training available at "Hamburger University" for the franchisee and its managerial employees. McDonald's had the right to inspect the restaurant at all reasonable times to ensure compliance with the standards and policies and had the right to terminate the franchisee if the standards and policies were not met.

Hoffnagle argued that these agreements gave McDonald's the right to control the restaurant and property upon which she was assaulted and that McDonald's was liable for negligence in failing to exercise that control, particularly in failing to provide adequate security or in failing to direct the franchisee to provide adequate security. Specifically, she argued that the franchisee's managerial employee, Geiger, was not appropriately trained because she failed to lock the doors or telephone the police after the first assault. Should McDonald's, as the franchisor, be liable for Hoffnagle's injuries? What factors would you consider in making this determination? *Hoffnagle v. McDonald's Corp.*, 522 N.W.2d 808 (Iowa 1994)

CHAPTER 6

Legal Issues Relating to Promotion

Trademark Law

This chapter discusses the fourth major category of intellectual property law: trademark law. (Patent and copyright law are discussed in Chapter 2 and trade secret law in Chapter 3.)

Trademarks are the words or symbols used by companies or individuals to distinguish or identify their goods or services, to indicate consistent source and quality, and to facilitate advertising and sales. Because trademarks are so effective in fulfilling these critical roles, they are extremely valuable to their owners. Businesses spend a great deal of time and money both creating and protecting their marks.

Companies need to consider trademarks at two important junctures. First, companies need to devote significant attention and resources to selection of the proper trademark during the development stage of their product or service. A carefully and wisely chosen mark can increase the likelihood that the product or service will prove marketable, generate valuable goodwill, and enhance the firm's bottom line. A poorly chosen mark can detract from the desirability or marketability of the product or service and even embroil the firm in expensive litigation.

Second, once the company has chosen the mark and has begun using it to promote the product or service, the firm must guard against unauthorized use of the mark by others. Failure to do so can result in the loss of a valuable intellectual property asset. Both of these issues are discussed in this chapter.

Overview

A *trademark* is a word, symbol, name, device, or combination thereof used by a manufacturer or merchant to identify and distinguish its goods from those manufactured or sold by others and to indicate the source of goods. Although we tend to think of trademarks as being words (such as *Rubbermaid* or *Rocsports*), many trademarks are actually symbols—the "Golden Arches" used by McDonald's, for example, or the "bitten apple" used by Apple computer products.

Trademarks serve four purposes:

1. they provide an identification symbol for a particular merchant's goods or services;
2. they indicate that the goods or services to which the trademark has been attached are from a single source;
3. they guarantee that all goods or services to which the trademark has been attached are of a consistent quality; and
4. they advertise the goods or services.

Essentially, the trademark tells the consumer what a product or service is called, where it comes from, and who is responsible for its creation. However, the trademark does not necessarily identify the manufacturer or provider of goods or services. *Yoplait* identifies a brand of yogurt, for example, but it does not necessarily indicate that the yogurt is manufactured by a company called Yoplait. The yogurt may be produced by a different company licensed to use the *Yoplait* mark.

Both consumers and businesses benefit from the use of trademarks. Consumers rely upon trademarks to identify the source of goods or services. The mark helps the consumer repeat purchases that were satisfactory and avoid repeating purchases that were not. Businesses use marks to help create and protect business goodwill. *Goodwill* refers to a business's image, good reputation, and expectation of repeat patronage and is a valuable asset in most industries.

While the primary function of trademarks themselves is to promote the interests of the mark owner, the primary focus of trademark *law* is to protect the consumer from deception, not to protect the value of the trademark to its owner. Protection of the trademark owner's rights is secondary.

Nonetheless, although trademark law is primarily concerned with consumer protection, confused or misled consumers may not sue for relief under trademark law. Rather, only the owners or users of marks have a cause of action. In addition, trademark law is self-policing. Trademark owners must sue to enforce their rights; no government agency will enforce those rights on their behalf.

ORIGINS OF TRADEMARK LAW

Patent and copyright law are federal law, while trade secret law is primarily state law. By contrast, trademark law arises under both state and federal law.

Trademark law originally started out as one of several related doctrines arising under the state law of unfair competition. (Unfair competition law is discussed in Chapter 7.) The federal Lanham Act,[1] which was enacted in 1946 and which addresses trademarks, codified and expanded these state common law notions. The most significant innovation under this act was the creation of a federal register (the *Principal Register*) for trademarks.

---

[1] 15 U.S.C. §§ 1051–1128.

The federal Lanham Act did not preempt state law. Thus, today trademark owners can sue for violation of their rights in their trademarks under:

1. the state common law of unfair competition;
2. state trademark statutes; and/or
3. the federal Lanham Act.

State and federal claims can be brought in the same suit. (This is an example of concurrent jurisdiction, discussed in Chapter 1).

TYPES OF MARKS

There are four different categories of marks, only one of which is actually properly referred to as a "trademark." For most purposes, the law regarding all four is the same, both under the Lanham Act and under state law. We tend to refer to all four categories as "marks" or—more commonly but imprecisely—as "trademarks."

A *trademark* is a word, name, symbol, device, or any combination thereof that is used to distinguish the goods of one person from goods manufactured or sold by others. Examples include Volvo automobiles, General Mills cereals, and Sony camcorders.

A *service mark* is much the same as a trademark but is used to identify services rather than goods. Examples include Red Lobster for restaurants and State Farm for insurance services.

A *certification mark* is used to certify that goods or services of others have certain characteristics, such as adhering to certain standards regarding quality or accuracy, regional origin, or method of manufacture. Well-known examples include Underwriters' Laboratories and the Good Housekeeping Seal of Approval. Because consumers tend to rely upon these certifications, the Lanham Act restricts their use in a number of ways. In particular, companies are not permitted to certify their own goods or services, and certifying entities must be objective and cannot discriminate in certifying the goods and services of others.

A *collective mark* can take one of two forms. A *collective membership mark* is used to indicate membership within an organization, such as a union or professional society. The mark "ILGWU" on clothing, for example, indicates that it was made by members of the International Ladies Garment Workers Union (as opposed to a nonunion shop). A *collective trademark* or *collective service mark* is adopted by a collective organization (such as a cooperative) for use by members in selling individual goods or services. The organization itself does not sell goods or services, although it may advertise or promote the goods or services sold under the mark by others. In many instances, the collective mark serves the same purpose as a certification mark.

Creating and Protecting a Mark

DISTINCTIVENESS OF THE MARK

A company faces a number of business considerations when it selects a mark. The mark should be easy to pronounce, easy to remember, and unique. It should convey a positive image about the product and company and should communicate product concepts and qualities. In this environment of global business activity, it should also work well around the world and should not invoke any negative connotations in other languages.

A company's primary legal consideration in choosing a mark should be its *distinctiveness* (see Exhibit 6.1). The more distinctive the mark is, the greater the legal protection that it receives.

Inherently distinctive marks receive the most protection. These include *fanciful marks*, which are marks that consist of made-up words or combinations of letters and numbers with no meaning other than their trademark meaning (such as Exxon, Clorox, or Kodak); and *arbitrary marks*, which are marks that have no real connection to the product or service being sold, such as Penguin books, Beefeater gin, or Blue Diamond nuts. Arbitrary and fanciful marks are considered inherently distinctive because a consumer would immediately connect them with their product or service, as there is no other meaning to attach to them.

Suggestive marks are also considered inherently distinctive. These are marks that do not immediately create an association with the product but indirectly describe the product or service that they identify. The consumer must expend some mental effort to associate them with a description of the product. Examples include Greyhound for a bus service, Intuit for software, and Chicken of the Sea for tuna.

Marks that are not inherently distinctive are protected only once they acquire a *secondary meaning*. This means that over time and with sufficient exposure consumers cease to recognize just the primary, descriptive meaning of the mark and, instead, develop a mental association between the mark and the source of the product. A mark owner can show the existence of a secondary meaning either through proof of long and extensive use of the mark, through long and extensive advertising, or through scientifically conducted consumer surveys.

Several types of marks fall within this category, including *descriptive marks*, *geographic terms*, and *personal names*. Examples include Sears department stores, Chapstick lip balm, Tender Vittles cat food, and McDonalds restaurants. The limitation on the use of personal names reflects the fact that people traditionally like to use

EXHIBIT 6.1

DISTINCTIVENESS OF MARKS

CLASSIFICATION OF MARK	PROTECTION
Inherently Distinctive • Fanciful Marks • Arbitrary Marks • Suggestive Marks	Protected immediately upon use
Not Inherently Distinctive • Descriptive Marks • Geographic Terms • Personal Names	Protected once secondary meaning arises
Nondistinctive • Generic Terms	None

their own surnames for their businesses. The law does not want to place too many barriers in their way in doing so. Once the first user has established a secondary meaning in the mark, however, later users may be barred from using the mark, even if it is indeed the user's own name.

Generic terms receive no trademark protection. Mark users are not permitted to monopolize a term to which all producers or providers need access. It does not matter that the term may acquire a secondary meaning over time. Thus, a producer could not use the mark "cider" to identify the product coming from a particular mill. Many terms that were once enforceable trademarks have become generic over time and are no longer protected by trademark law. For example, aspirin, escalator, yo yo, kerosene, mimeograph, and lineoleum all were once protected trademarks that have become genericized over time. Trademark owners must constantly police the use of their marks to prevent them from becoming generic terms (see Exhibit 6.2 on page 180).

WHAT MAY CONSTITUTE A MARK?

Marks may consist of words, drawings, abstract designs, slogans (e.g., "Just Do It"), distinctive packaging features, sounds (e.g., NBC's three-note chime, the roar of the MGM lion), smells (e.g., plumeria blossoms for sewing thread), or virtually anything else that can be used to identify the good or service involved. Most marks consist of words or numbers. These can be real or coined words, a combination of words and numbers, or numbers alone.

Drawings and other art forms may be used for marks. Realistic drawings of the product or service are generally considered descriptive and are protected only if they have obtained a secondary meaning. Nonrealistic drawings—such as the Mr. Peanut mark of a humanized peanut with a monocle, walking cane, and top hat—may be considered suggestive, arbitrary, or fanciful and so inherently distinctive.

Trade dress can also be registered and protected. Trade dress refers to things like a distinctive shape (the Coca-Cola bottle) or packaging (Kodak's yellow film box) or decor (Banana Republic clothing stores). Trade dress may be protected as a mark if it makes a separate commercial impression and if its impact on the consumer is primarily to identify or distinguish the product or service, not merely to serve as ornamentation.

Trade dress originally referred to the complete package or container in which a product was sold and that was typically discarded after purchase. Over the past two decades, however, the definition of trade dress has been expanded to include the appearance of the product itself. This expansion has lead to uncertainty in the legal rules that apply to protected trade dress. In the past few years, the U.S. Supreme Court has decided three cases that delineate the parameters of trade dress protection. The cases illustrate the iterative process that the courts go through as they try to develop common law principles that fit a variety of circumstances.

In *Two Pesos, Inc. v. Taco Cabana, Inc.*,[2] a 1992 decision, the Supreme Court determined that the trade dress of a restaurant could be protected without a showing of secondary meaning if it were inherently distinctive and not merely descriptive.

See Discussion Case 6.1.

---

[2] 505 U.S. 763 (1992).

EXHIBIT 6.2

In a 1995 decision, *Qualitex Co. v. Jacobson Products Co.*,[3] the Supreme Court held that *color* could be protected trade dress, provided it had obtained a secondary meaning (e.g., pink for NutraSweet packages).

See Discussion Case 6.2.

Most recently, in a 2000 decision, *Wal-Mart Stores, Inc. v. Samara Brothers, Inc.*,[4] the Supreme Court determined that trade dress that consists of the *appearance of the product* requires a showing of secondary meaning because appearance is usually not considered a means of identifying the source of a product.

See Discussion Case 6.3.

The Court reconciled these three cases by stating that the analysis of trade dress protection depends upon whether the asserted trade dress is considered a *package* or a *product design*—a distinction the Court acknowledged is not always easily made. Package trade dress (which apparently encompasses restaurant design of the type found in *Two Pesos*) does not require a showing of secondary meaning, but product design does.

Physical features of the product itself or its container may also be protected as a mark as long as those features are distinctive and nonfunctional. Functional features, however, must be protected, if at all, under utility patents. Companies may not use trademark law as a means of avoiding the restrictions of patent law or to obtain a monopoly on functional features (see Focus Case 6.1 on page 182).

A single design can be protected both by trademark and design patent laws, however, provided the design meets the statutory requirements for each. Black and Decker's Dustbuster vacuum cleaner, for example, was the subject of both trademark protection and a design patent.

Some types of things cannot be registered as marks. *Scandalous or immoral marks*, which are marks that offend the conscience or moral feeling or which are shocking to the sense of decency or propriety, receive no protection. For example, the Patent and Trademark Office (PTO) denied registration of a depiction of a defecating dog for shirts.[5]

Deceptive marks also receive no protection. These are marks that either falsely indicate that the good or service has a particular characteristic or is associated with a particular person or institution or which mislead consumers by incorrectly describing the good or service in a way that would be material to the average consumer.

TRADEMARK SEARCHES

Before a new mark is used, the proposed user should do a *trademark search* to ensure that the mark is not identical or substantially similar to a mark already in use. Trademark searches usually involve a review of the state and federal trademark registers and a review of telephone directories, magazines, and trade journals to see if the mark is in use. In addition, the PTO maintains an on-line database of every trademark that is pending or that has been issued.[6] Many private firms specialize in conducting trademark searches, and several private companies offer subscription

---

[3] 514 U.S. 159 (1995).
[4] 529 U.S. 205 (2000).
[5] The Greyhound Corp. v. Both Worlds, Inc., 6 U.S.P.Q.2d 1635 (T.T.A.B. 1988).
[6] *See* http://tess.uspto.gov

Focus Case 6.1

Facts: Leatherman Tool Group, Inc., was the first to market a multifunction pocket tool, which it sold under the name "Pocket Survival Tool" (PST). Cooper Industries, Inc., became aware of the PST and its market success. It admittedly copied the PST "almost exactly" and came out with a multipurpose tool, called the Toolzall, that differed in appearance from the PST in only three respects: (1) it was marked with a different name than the PST; (2) it had different fasteners than those used on the PST; and (3) it had a serrated blade, which the PST did not.

Leatherman filed suit and obtained a preliminary injunction prohibiting Cooper from marketing the Toolzall on the grounds that the overall appearance of the PST was protected trade dress. At trial, the jury found that Cooper had infringed on Leatherman's protected trade dress, and the court issued a permanent injunction prohibiting Cooper from marketing the original Toolzall. Cooper appealed.

Decision: On appeal, the Ninth Circuit found that Leatherman could not protect the "overall appearance"

of the PST as trade dress. The court stated: "[T]he physical details and design of a product may be protected under the trademark laws only if they are nonfunctional . . . ." Functional features, which the court defined as "features which constitute the actual benefit that the consumer wishes to purchase, as distinguished from an assurance that a particular entity made, sponsored, or endorsed a product," must be protected, if at all, through patent law.

The court found no evidence that the PST's appearance existed for any nonfunctional purpose. Its features were not ornamental or intended to identify its source but rather were designed in that manner because the product functioned better with such features.

The court concluded that the overall appearance of the PST was not protectable trade dress, "at least as against a competitor which clearly marks its own product with a distinct name and who uses distinct packaging." Thus, the court reversed the permanent injunction prohibiting Cooper from marketing its Toolzall. *Leatherman Tool Group, Inc. v. Cooper Industries, Inc.*, 199 F.3d 1009 (9th Cir. 1999).

---

access to on-line databases, such as Trademarkscan, that list international, federal, and/or state trademarks and/or domain names.[7]

If the proposed user has a particular domain name in mind to go along with the mark, it would be wise to search the Web sites of the domain name registration companies to determine if the domain name is available. If not, the proposed user may wish to select a different mark and corresponding domain name.

CREATION AND OWNERSHIP OF THE MARK

Creation of the Mark

To create a mark, the user must be the first to use it in trade and must continue to use it thereafter. This requires that the mark be physically attached to the goods, their labels or containers, and advertising and that the goods then be sold or distributed. For services, the mark must be used or displayed in the course of selling or advertising the services.

What happens if two persons use the same mark? For marks that are inherently distinctive, the first to use the mark (the "*senior user*") will have priority in the mark. The exception is where the second to use the mark (the "*junior user*") in good faith establishes a strong consumer identification with the mark in a separate geographic

---

[7] Trademarks, for example, may be searched through the Web site of Thomson & Thomson, http://thomson-thomson.com

area. The junior user will have priority in that (but no other) geographic area. If the senior user has federally registered the mark, however, the senior user will have nationwide rights to the mark in every area in which it is not already in use at the time the senior user began using it.

Registration of the Mark

A mark user is permitted (but not required) to place its mark on the federal trademark register (the Principal Register), provided (1) the mark is distinctive and (2) the mark is in use in commerce across state, territorial, or international lines. If the mark is used only on a local service business, such as a dance studio, it probably will not qualify for federal registration unless the user can show that the business has a significant number of interstate or international customers.

Placement on the Principal Register provides many legal advantages:

1. it provides constructive notice nationwide of the user's claim to the mark (thus preventing later users from claiming that they were using the mark in good faith);
2. it establishes evidence of the registrant's ownership of the mark;
3. it allows the owner to sue in federal (rather than state court) in the event of infringement or dilution;
4. it makes the registrant's right to the mark virtually (though not absolutely) incontestable after five years of continuous use;
5. it enables the registrant to seek assistance from the U.S. Customs Service in preventing importation into the United States of articles bearing an infringing mark; and
6. it can provide a basis for obtaining registration in foreign countries.

Application for Registration

The Lanham Act provides for two different types of registration on the Principal Register.[8] If the mark has already been used in trade, the user may file a "*use*" application with the PTO. One application can cover goods and services in several product and/or service categories. The applicant must select the classes to be included in the application and must pay a separate fee for each class so specified. Although the fees for obtaining a trademark are relatively modest (the filing fee is currently $325[9]), the fees can add up rapidly if the applicant files for several product and/or service categories. As a practical matter, however, the applicant should file as broad an application as possible so as to protect its mark from infringement by use in an unclaimed class.

The application is reviewed by an examiner. If the examiner approves the application, the mark is published in the *Official Gazette*. People who feel that they may be injured by the registration (for example, because the mark is confusingly similar to their own) may file an opposition challenging the registration. If the PTO decides that registration is appropriate, it issues a certificate of registration.

A registration is good for 10 years, although the mark owner must file an affidavit in the sixth year showing that the mark is still in use. The registration may be renewed for additional 10-year periods as long as the mark remains in commercial use. Realize that *registration* of the mark is separate from *ownership* of the mark. The mark owner owns the mark as long as the mark remains in commercial

---

[8] Application forms are available on the Web and can be filed electronically or can be downloaded, filled out, and mailed in. *See* http://www.uspto.gov
[9] For a complete fee schedule, *see* http://www.uspto.gov

use. While registration is a wise idea because of the many benefits it confers, it is not legally required.

If the PTO examiner rejects the registration application, the applicant may appeal to the Trademark Trial and Appeal Board. If the applicant loses before the Board, the applicant may appeal on the administrative record to the U.S. Court of Appeals for the Federal Circuit (CAFC) or *de novo* to the U.S. District Court (see Exhibit 6.3).

If the applicant has not yet used the mark in trade, but has a bona fide intent to do so in the near future, the applicant may file an "*intent to use*" application. The PTO makes an initial examination of the application and publishes it for opposition in the *Official Gazette*. The applicant then has six months to begin actual use of the mark. (This time period can be extended up to two and one-half years upon a showing of good cause.) When the applicant makes the first use of the mark in trade, the applicant must file a statement of use with the PTO. The PTO then conducts a second examination. If the mark is deemed acceptable, it is then placed on the Principal Register.

Cancellation of a Mark

During the first five years of registration, a person who believes herself to be injured by a registration may petition the PTO to cancel it. After five years, the mark can only be challenged on very limited grounds, such as the mark has become generic or has been abandoned or the mark was obtained through fraud. The mark *cannot* be challenged at this point on the grounds that it is not inherently distinctive and lacks secondary meaning, that it is confusingly similar to a more senior mark, or that it is functional. Recently, challenges by Native American activists resulted in the cancellation of six Washington Redskins marks on the grounds that

EXHIBIT 6.3

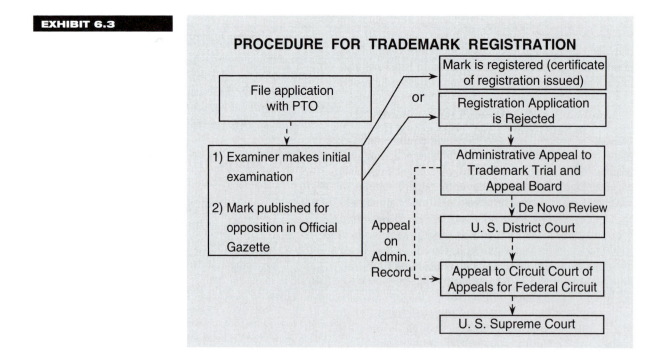

PROCEDURE FOR TRADEMARK REGISTRATION

the word *Redskins* is disparaging to Native Americans.[10] The cancellations do not prohibit the mark owner from continuing to use the marks but do prevent the owner from claiming any of the legal protections associated with registered marks.

Notice

Under the Lanham Act, registrants must provide notice of the registration by displaying the mark with the following words or symbol:

> "Registered in U.S. Patent and Trademark Office" *or*
> "Reg. U.S. Pat. & Tm. Off." *or*
> ®

What, then, does the familiar ™ or ˢᴹ symbol mean? It indicates that the user is using the word, phrase, symbol, or design as a trade or service mark but has not federally registered it. Such marks may still receive some protection under state or federal trademark law, but they do not receive the heightened protection given to federally registered marks.

If the registrant fails to provide proper notice of the registration, the registrant will only be able to recover profits and damages in the event of infringement if the registrant can prove that the defendant had *actual* notice of the registration. This can be very difficult to prove in many instances, so providing proper registration notice is an important preventative measure for mark owners to take.

Supplemental and State Registers

In addition to the Principal Register, the Lanham Act creates a *Supplemental Register*, which is used for marks that are not distinctive enough to be placed on the Principal Register. Most marks used to distinguish goods or services can be placed on the Supplemental Register, including descriptive and geographical terms and surnames. Generic marks may not be placed on the Supplemental Register, however, nor may immoral, deceptive, or scandalous marks.

Generally, the applicant should apply to the Principal Register first and apply to the Supplemental Register only if that application is denied. Although placement on the Supplemental Register confers few legal benefits, it often deters others from making use of an identical or substantially similar mark. In particular, marks that appear on the Supplemental Register may display the ® symbol or "Reg. U.S. Pat. Off." abbreviation, which is likely to discourage potential infringers. In addition, the PTO will not register a junior mark that is identical to a mark found on the Supplemental Register and used on closely related goods or services. Placement on the Supplemental Register for five years helps establish secondary meaning for the mark, which qualifies the mark for the Principal Register and all of the greater legal benefits that go along with such placement. Thus, marks can move from the Supplemental Register to the Principal Register as they gain distinctiveness over time.

In addition, every state has its own registration system. States do not provide for intent-to-use registration; thus, the mark must be in use before it can be registered with any state. State registration is particularly important to those mark users whose marks are not in interstate or international use and thus cannot be placed on the federal register.

---

[10] Harjo v. Pro Football, Inc., 50 U.S.P.Q.2d 1705 (T.T.A.B. 1999).

What are the benefits of state registration to a mark owner whose mark already appears on the Principal Register? State registration provides additional notice to junior users or potential infringers and, in a few states, provides some benefits in the event of successful litigation (e.g., recovery of attorneys fees or punitive damages). In addition, mark owners who register at both the state and federal levels have a choice of remedies and courts in which to sue. Thus, many mark owners opt to place their marks on both the federal and state registers.

U.S. CUSTOMS SERVICE ASSISTANCE

Under the U.S. Customs Act, a mark owner who has registered its mark on the Principal Register or a copyright owner who has registered its work with the Copyright Office may record that mark or copyright with the U.S. Customs Service, listing any authorized importers or sources of the goods. This record is placed on a national database that is available to all customs offices in every U.S. port of entry.

The customs inspectors are authorized to seize imported products that infringe on U.S. marks or copyrights. To get full benefit of these provisions, however, mark owners (or copyright owners) must monitor the importation of goods carefully themselves. Because of the sheer volume of imports entering the United States on a daily basis, the Customs Service responds most often to tips from owners rather than conducting its own independent investigations. Infringing products are destroyed at the importer's expense. If the counterfeit mark can be removed or obliterated without destroying the goods or if the mark owner agrees, the goods may be donated to a charitable organization. The mark owner can also waive its right to object to the infringing goods and allow the goods to be released to the importer.

If the Customs Service is not certain whether the goods involved infringe on U.S. marks or copyrights, it can detain the shipment. The U.S. mark or copyright owner has 30 days in which to file a Petition for Exclusion and a bond in an amount determined by the U.S. Customs Office. The U.S. Customs Headquarters then determines whether the goods are infringing. If so, the bond is returned to the mark or copyright owner and the goods are destroyed. If not, the goods are released for import and the importer receives the full amount of the bond to compensate it for its losses.

In FY 1998, the Customs Service seized more than 3,900 shipments with a value in excess of $76 million. The largest number of seized shipments originated in China.

Trademark Infringement and Dilution

Generally, mark owners are concerned with two types of potential injury. First, if the plaintiff and the defendant are direct competitors, the defendant's use of an identical or substantially similar mark may confuse consumers such that consumers purchase the defendant's goods or services when, in fact, they actually intended to buy the plaintiff's. This is *trademark infringement*. Second, even if the plaintiff and defendant are not in direct competition and even if customers are not confused by the use of identical or substantially similar marks, the defendant's use of the identical or similar mark may diminish the strength of the plaintiff's mark by tarnishing the reputation of the plaintiff's mark or by blurring the distinctiveness of the plaintiff's mark. This is *trademark dilution*.

INFRINGEMENT

Trademark infringement occurs when one party (the junior user) uses a trademark (the junior mark) that is identical or substantially similar to the existing mark (the senior mark) of another user (the senior user) on competing goods or services, such that prospective purchasers are likely to be confused, mistaken, or deceived as to the identity or source of the goods or services involved. Both the federal Lanham Act and the state law of every state provide a cause of action for trademark infringement. In order to establish trademark infringement, the plaintiff must show:

1. that the mark is valid (federally registered marks are presumed valid);
2. that the plaintiff is the senior user of the mark; and
3. that the junior user's use of the mark creates a *likelihood of confusion* in the minds of the purchasers of the product or service in question.

This last factor examines whether the defendant's use of its mark is likely to cause an appreciable number of consumers to be confused about the source, affiliation, or sponsorship of goods or services.

In determining whether a likelihood of confusion exists, the courts generally apply some variation of the so-called *Polaroid* factors.[11] These factors examine:

1. the strength of the plaintiff's mark;
2. the similarity between the two marks (e.g., appearance, sound, meaning);
3. the similarity of the products involved;
4. the likelihood that the plaintiff will enter the defendant's market (even if the plaintiff is not currently in the defendant's market, the court will consider how likely it is that the plaintiff may want to enter that market in the future);
5. the extent of actual consumer confusion;
6. the defendant's lack of good faith in adopting the mark;
7. the quality of the defendant's product; and
8. the sophistication of the buyers (the more sophisticated the consumers or the more expensive the goods or services, the less likely it is that consumers will be misled).

No factor is considered determinative, and the courts may weigh the factors differently depending upon the facts of the case before them.

Inherent within the notion of a likelihood of confusion is the requirement that the goods or services involved be similar. Trademark infringement is unlikely, for example, where the mark "Mayflower" is used both by a sailboat company and a moving company, because the typical consumer would not confuse the two companies and their products or services.[12]

A defendant can be held liable for *contributory infringement* if he intentionally suggests that another person infringe upon a mark and the other person actually does so. For example, suppose that the defendant manufactures goods that are identical to the plaintiff's goods and sells them to retailers, suggesting to the retailers that they sell these as the plaintiff's goods to customers who ask for the plaintiff's goods by name. If a retailer actually does so, the retailer is liable for trademark infringement and the defendant is liable for contributory infringement. A defen-

---

[11] These factors were articulated by the U.S. Court of Appeals for the Seventh Circuit in a 1963 case, Polaroid Corp. v. Polaraid, Inc., 319 F.2d 830 (7th Cir. 1963).

[12] *See* Aero Mayflower Transit Co. v. Snark Prods., Inc., 190 U.S.P.Q. 100, 106 (T.T.A.B. 1976).

Focus Case 6.2

Facts: Cherry Auction, Inc., operated a swap meet (also known as a flea market). Cherry Auction rented booth space to individual vendors and supplied parking, provided advertising, and reserved the right to exclude a vendor for any reason.

Cherry Auction was aware that vendors at its swap meet were selling counterfeit recordings that violated Fonovisa, Inc.'s trademarks and copyrights in those recordings. The County Sheriff's office had raided the swap meet in 1991 and seized more than 38,000 counterfeit recordings. In 1992, the Sheriff notified Cherry Auction by letter of ongoing counterfeit sales by individual vendors.

In 1993 Fonovisa sent an investigator to the swap meet who witnessed sales of counterfeit recordings. Fonovisa brought a copyright and trademark enforcement action against Cherry Auction. The trial court dismissed the suit, stating that, as a matter of law, Fonovisa could not hold a swap meet liable for sales by vendors who leased its premises. Fonovisa appealed.

Decision: The appellate court noted that the Sheriff's raid and subsequent letter clearly put Cherry Auction on notice of the illegal sales occurring at the swap meet. Further, "it would be difficult for the infringing activity to take place in the massive quantities alleged without the support services provided by" Cherry Auction, which included the provision of space, utilities, parking, advertising, plumbing, and customers. The court found that Cherry Auction "actively strives to provide the environment and the market for counterfeit recording sales to thrive."

The court thus found that Fonovisa had stated a cause of action for both contributory copyright infringement and contributory trademark infringement. It remanded the case to the trial court for further proceedings. *Fonovisa, Inc. v. Cherry Auction, Inc.*, 76 F.3d 259 (9th Cir. 1996).

dant can also be held liable for contributory infringement if the defendant sells the goods to a buyer knowing that the buyer will use the goods in direct infringement of the plaintiff's mark (see Focus Case 6.2).

Defenses to an Infringement Action

A defendant can raise *fair use* as a defense to an allegation of mark infringement. For example, if the plaintiff uses her surname as a mark for her product, the plaintiff is not permitted to assert a monopoly in that mark (unless the mark has acquired secondary meaning). The defendant is permitted to make "fair use" of the surname in selling his own goods. Fair use also encompasses comparative advertising, parodies involving the mark, journalistic uses of the mark, and use of the mark to describe compatability of aftermarket goods (see Focus Case 6.3 on page 189).

To determine whether a particular use is "fair," the courts consider (1) the manner in which the defendant used the mark, (2) whether the defendant is acting in good faith, and (3) whether the defendant's use is likely to confuse consumers. The last factor is the most important. While the courts may tolerate a small degree of consumer confusion if the other elements of fair use are present, if substantial confusion exists, there can be no fair use.

A defendant can also raise *abandonment* of a mark as a defense. Under the Lanham Act, abandonment occurs when the registrant discontinues its use throughout the United States and has no intent to resume the use within the reasonably foreseeable future. Nonuse of a mark for three consecutive years is evidence of abandonment. Abandonment also occurs when the registrant engages in acts that cause the mark to lose its significance, such as licensing others to use the mark without

Focus Case 6.3

Facts: Jordache Enterprises, Inc., manufactured and licensed the manufacture of a line of apparel, including designer blue jeans, under the mark *Jordache*. In 1984, Jordache sold 20 million pairs of Jordache jeans, with gross sales of $500 million and advertising expenses of $30 million. Hogg Wyld, Ltd. marketed large-sized designer blue jeans under the mark Lardashe. In 1984 (its first year of operation), Hogg Wyld sold approximately 1,300 pairs of jeans and did not advertise.

The Jordache mark consisted of the word "Jordache" in block letters superimposed over a drawing of a horse's head. The Lardashe mark consisted of the name "Lardashe" stitched in script lettering on the rear pocket of the jeans, an inverted-heart-shaped embroidered design on the pocket, and an embroidered applique of a pig's head and feet sewn onto the fabric so that the pig appeared to be peering out of the top of the pocket.

Jordache sued Hogg Wyld for trademark infringement.

Decision: Hogg Wyld argued that it had chosen the "Lardashe" name as a more polite variant of a childhood nickname used by one of its founders, and that it had not intended any similarity with the Jordache mark. The court did not believe Hogg Wyld's testimony on this issue, noting that other names considered and rejected by Hogg Wyld included "Calvin Swine," "Sow-soon," and "Horse's ashe."

However, the court also found that Hogg Wyld's "intent was to employ a name that, to some extent, parodied or played upon the established trademark Jordache." Parodies are permitted under trademark law where the junior mark is used only for humorous purposes and not to mislead or confuse the consumer. "That the defendant's joke mark calls the plaintiff's mark to mind is necessary for there to be a humorous parody at all . . . . But the requirement of trademark law is that a likely source of confusion of source, sponsorship or affiliation be proven, which is not the same things as a 'right' not to be made fun of."

Thus, the court found, because the Lardashe mark was an obvious parody of the Jordache mark, and because the two marks created "a very different concept, image, and 'feel'," it did not confuse consumers as to source, affiliation, or sponsorship, and so did not infringe. *Jordache Enterprises, Inc. v. Hogg Wyld, Ltd.*, 625 F. Supp. 48 (D. N.M. 1985), *aff'd*, 828 F.2d 1482 (10th Cir. 1987).

adequately supervising such use or failing to protest the unauthorized use of the mark by other parties.

Remedies for Infringement

There are two basic types of remedies for trademark infringement: (1) injunctions and (2) damages. Courts routinely grant *injunctions* in the trademark area. Both preliminary and permanent injunctions are available.

In addition, a prevailing plaintiff may recover *actual damages*. A plaintiff may suffer lost sales and injury to its reputation and goodwill as a result of the defendant's infringement. The plaintiff may recover these losses, but they can be difficult to prove and quantify. Therefore, the Lanham Act provides that courts can award up to *treble damages*, if necessary, to adequately compensate the plaintiff. As a practical matter, however, courts are reluctant to do so in the absence of willful behavior by the defendant.

The plaintiff may also recover the *profits* the defendant made from the infringing activity. In addition, the Lanham Act allows the court to award reasonable *attorneys fees* to the prevailing party in "exceptional" cases. Generally, this means that the infringement must have been malicious, fraudulent, deliberate, or willful.

Gray Markets/Parallel Importation

Gray markets (also called *parallel importation*) involve goods that are produced and sold for overseas markets but which are then imported (or reimported) into the United States. The result is a multibillion dollar a year industry that angers and frustrates U.S. manufacturers and diminishes their profits.

The gray market exists because U.S. manufacturers routinely sell consumer goods at deep discounts (often through distributors) in foreign markets. The discounts may reflect the fact that the foreign distributor, rather than the U.S. manufacturer, is incurring the foreign marketing and advertising costs or may simply reflect the U.S. manufacturer's business strategy in attempting to expand its foreign markets. The price difference may also be an unintended consequence of currency fluctuations. The price differential is often large enough that a distributor can then reimport the goods to the United States at a price that undercuts the domestic market.

The existence of gray markets raises a number of competing policy concerns. Gray marketeers argue that their activities are legal because the goods they sell are genuine and bear lawful trademarks. Thus, they contend, consumers are not confused as to the source or origin of their goods. Consumer advocates argue that the gray market is a good thing because it allows consumers to purchase goods at a lower cost, thus preventing price gouging by manufacturers. Manufacturers' groups, on the other hand, complain that gray marketeers are able to reap the benefits of the manufacturers' expensive marketing and advertising campaigns without incurring any of the accompanying costs. Companies that hold exclusive rights to distribute and sell products in the United States are also upset at facing unanticipated competition from importers and sellers of gray market goods.

Generally the importation and sale of gray market goods is not considered infringement of a U.S. mark if the imported goods are identical to the goods sold by the U.S. registrant (e.g., are of the same grade and quality, contain the same ingredients or components, and carry the same warranties and service commitments). Under the "material differences" test, however, if the imported goods are materially different in even one respect from goods produced for the domestic market, the importation and sale of the goods will infringe the U.S. mark. This test was originally articulated in *Original Appalachian Artworks, Inc. v. Granada Electronics, Inc.*[13] The defendant had imported gray market Cabbage Patch Kids dolls that had been intended for sale in Spain. Although the dolls bore the plaintiff's trademark, their "birth certificates" and "adoption papers" were in Spanish and could not be processed by the plaintiff's fulfillment houses in the United States. Thus, the buyers of the dolls could not participate in the "adoption process" that was critical to the dolls' commercial success. The Second Circuit found that this material difference created customer confusion over the source of the goods and diminished the plaintiff's goodwill. The dolls thus infringed on the plaintiff's U.S. trademark.

The material differences test recognizes that when the imported goods are identical to the U.S. goods and bear the same mark, customers will not be confused as to the source or origin of the goods.[14] However, where there is even one "material" difference (defined as a difference that consumers would likely consider in making their purchasing decision), customer confusion is likely and the U.S. trademark holder's goodwill is diminished. Because manufacturers often alter products

---

[13] 816 F.2d 68 (2d Cir. 1987).

[14] Courts have thus rejected trademark infringement claims where the gray market goods were identical to the domestic goods. *See* NEC Electronics v. CAL Circuit Abco, 810 F.2d 1506 (9th Cir. 1987); Weil Ceramics & Glass, Inc. v. Dash, 878 F.2d 659 (3d Cir. 1989).

to satisfy specific preferences in different national markets, such differences are likely to exist in many, though not all, instances.

In February 1999, the U.S. Customs Service issued its so-called *Lever* Rule.[15] This rule allows the U.S. trademark owner to restrict the importation of certain gray market goods that bear genuine trademarks if the goods are identical or substantially indistinguishable from those appearing on authorized goods so as to cause customer confusion. To restrict the importation of the gray market goods, however, the U.S. mark holder must submit an application to Customs that describes the physical and material differences between the gray market goods and the domestic goods.

If the importer of the goods can show that the imported goods are identical to the domestic goods, the Customs Service cannot detain the imported goods. In addition, the importer can exempt the goods from *Lever* Rule protection by attaching a tag or label that states: "This product is not a product authorized by the United States trademark owner for importation and is physically and materially different from the authorized product." The importer must place the label in close proximity to the trademark in its most prominent location on the article itself or its retail package.

In recent years, plaintiffs have also turned to copyright law for protection from gray marketeers. Many gray market items, such as books, videos, and CDs, are both copyrighted and trademarked. Even where the product itself is not copyrighted, its label, manual, or instructions may be. Analysts originally thought that copyright law would provide more protection to the U.S. registrants. In 1998, however, the U.S. Supreme Court issued a decision that casts doubt upon the amount of copyright protection available in this area (see Focus Case 6.4 on page 192).

In effect, the *L'Anza Research* Court indicated that gray market issues should be dealt with in the political and legislative arenas, not in the courts. So what can a manufacturer do to avoid the gray market problem? Unfortunately, options are limited. The manufacturer could simply not export its goods. That option is obviously unappealing to most businesses because it generally results in smaller markets and reduced profits. Companies can prohibit reimportation in their sales contracts (although such clauses can be hard to enforce). They can also label their products in the foreign language (thus making them harder to reimport and sell in the U.S. market) or can incorporate some other form of "material difference" in products manufactured for export.

Counterfeiting

Counterfeiting involves the intentional, knowing use of a false mark that is identical or substantially similar to a registered mark on goods or services of the same type.[16] It is considered to be a particularly egregious form of trademark infringement, and the courts are quick to sanction behavior they find inappropriate. For example, in a 1999 case, *Rolex Watch, U.S.A. v. Michel Co.,*[17] the Ninth Circuit ruled that a jeweler who had sold used Rolex watches that had been repaired or customized with non-Rolex parts without removing the original Rolex marks had engaged in counterfeiting.

---

[15] 19 C.F.R. § 133.23. The Rule implements the decision in Lever Bros. Co. v. United States, 981 F.2d 1330 (Fed. Cir. 1993).

[16] For general information on counterfeiting, see the Web site of the International Anti-Counterfeiting Coalition, at http://www.iacc.org

[17] 179 F.3d 704 (9th Cir. 1999).

Focus Case 6.4

Facts: L'Anza Research International, a U.S. manufacturer of hair products, limited its domestic sales to distributors who agreed to sell only to authorized retailers within limited geographic areas. L'Anza promoted its domestic sales with extensive advertising and special retailer training. L'Anza Research sold its shampoo to foreign distributors for 35 percent to 40 percent less than in the United States, but did not engage in comparable advertising or promotion.

L'Anza sold the shampoo at issue to a distributor in the United Kingdom, who sold it to a distributor in Malta, who sold it to Quality King Distributors, Inc. Quality King imported the shampoo for resale in the United States without L'Anza's permission and sold it at a discount to unauthorized retailers.

L'Anza held a copyright on the labels placed on the packaging. L'Anza did not argue that anyone had made unauthorized copies of the label, but rather argued that the domestic resales of the containers containing the labels violated its exclusive right to distribute copies of its labels. The Copyright Act makes unauthorized importation of copyrighted works illegal.

L'Anza sued Quality King for violation of its exclusive right to distribute its copyrighted materials. The trial court entered summary judgment for L'Anza. The Ninth Circuit affirmed. Quality King appealed to the Supreme Court.

Decision: The Supreme Court reversed. It found that under the "first sale" doctrine, the copyright owner's exclusive right to sell a work stops with the first sale of that work. The Court stated: "Once the copyright owner places a copyrighted item in the stream of commerce by selling it, he has exhausted his statutory right to control its distribution." Thus, once L'Anza sold the shampoo bottles to the first distributor, L'Anza lost the right to control further distribution of the labels. *Quality King Distributors, Inc. v. L'Anza Research Int'l, Inc.*, 523 U.S. 135 (1998).

Federal law provides special remedies for counterfeiting, including recovery of attorney fees, treble damages, and seizure of the offending goods. In addition, the Lanham Act provides for both civil and criminal penalties for counterfeiting, including statutory damages of up to $1 million per counterfeit mark, fines of up to $15 million, and prison terms of up to 20 years.

The line between traditional trademark infringement and counterfeiting is often blurry. If a manufacturer puts a false "Rolex" mark on a watch and markets it as a real "Rolex," the manufacturer has engaged in counterfeiting. If the manufacturer puts a "Polex" mark on the watch, the manufacturer has engaged in infringement (or possibly dilution).

DILUTION

Dilution occurs when a company uses a mark that is identical or substantially similar to a "famous" mark. The concern here is *not* that the consumer might be misled (that is an infringement notion) but that the value of the mark to the owner might be diminished because consumers will no longer associate the mark exclusively with the original user. Thus, unlike trademark infringement law, dilution law actually protects not the consumer but the value of the trademark to the mark owner.

Suppose, for example, that an authorized *Kodak* piano is sold in the marketplace. If consumers saw the piano and began thinking that Eastman Kodak Co. now sells musical instruments (or licenses another to do so under its mark), Eastman Kodak could sue for trademark infringement. If consumers recognized that Eastman Kodak was not in the piano business, but the presence of the *Kodak* piano led consumers to no longer exclusively associate the mark with Eastman Kodak and its photographic supplies (even though the consumers recognized the independent existence of the two separate entities using the mark), Eastman Kodak could sue for dilution.[18]

Until recently, dilution was only a state law action. Although over one-half of the states have dilution statutes, these state laws historically provided little relief to injured mark owners. Congress determined that a federal cause of action was necessary to provide protection to distinctive or well-known marks, which are generally used nationwide.

The Federal Trademark Dilution Act of 1995[19] created a federal cause of action for trademark dilution. We have seen a rapid increase in the number of dilution actions brought since this statute was passed. The federal Act did not preempt state law, so plaintiffs today may sue both under the Dilution Act and under any applicable state statute as well.

The Dilution Act defines dilution as

> The lessening of the capacity of a famous mark to identify and distinguish goods or services, regardless of the presence or absence of (1) competition between the owner of the famous mark and other parties; or (2) likelihood of confusion, mistake or deception.[20]

Under the Act, the plaintiff must demonstrate (1) that its mark is famous; (2) that the defendant adopted the junior mark after the plaintiff's senior mark had become famous; and (3) that the defendant's junior mark dilutes the plaintiff's senior mark by diminishing the capacity of the mark to identify and distinguish goods and services. Unlike trademark infringement, dilution law does not require that the goods or services be similar or competing; nor does it require the plaintiff to show that customers may be confused or deceived by the use of the junior mark.

To recover for dilution, the plaintiff must first show that its mark is "famous." The key purpose of dilution statutes, whether state or federal, is to protect a mark's "selling power." Weak or new marks have no such selling power to be protected and therefore cannot be diluted. Although there is no list of "famous marks" that one can turn to, the Act does set forth a list of eight factors that a court may consider in determining whether a particular mark is famous:

1. the degree of inherent or acquired distinctiveness of the mark;
2. the duration and extent of use of the mark in connection with the goods or services with which the mark is used;
3. the duration and extent of advertising and publicity of the mark;
4. the geographical extent of the trading area in which the mark is used;
5. the channels of trade for the goods or services with which the mark is used;
6. the degree of recognition for the mark in the trading areas and channels of trade used by the mark's owner and the person against whom the injunction is sought;
7. the nature and extent of use of the same or similar marks by third parties; and
8. whether the mark was registered under federal law.

See Discussion Case 6.4.

---

[18] See H.R. Rep. No. 104–374 at 3 (1995).
[19] 15 U.S.C. § 1125(c).
[20] 15 U.S.C. § 1127.

There are two forms of dilution actions: (1) tarnishment and (2) blurring. Although blurring is the more common type of dilution action brought, plaintiffs are generally more likely to win in tarnishment cases than they are in blurring cases.

Tarnishment

Tarnishment occurs when a junior user uses the senior user's mark or a similar mark in a manner that could hurt the reputation of the senior user's mark. Tarnishment typically involves the use of a famous mark on products of shoddy quality or the use of the mark in an unwholesome or unsavory context (usually involving sexual, obscene, or illegal activity). Examples of cases where the courts have issued preliminary injunctions prohibiting uses that tarnish a senior mark include the use of "Candyland" to identify a sexually explicit Internet site,[21] the use of "Buttwiser" on T-shirts,[22] and the use of "Adultsrus.com" for an Internet site on which sexual devices were sold.[23]

Blurring

Blurring occurs when a famous mark (or one very similar to it) is used in connection with the noncompeting goods or services of another, resulting in a "whittling away" of the senior mark's value over time as it is used in connection with the goods or services of another. Although consumers are not confused by the different uses of the mark, the concern is that over time they will cease to associate the mark exclusively with the mark owner's goods or services.

Blurring can be shown by one of two methods: (1) direct evidence or (2) circumstantial evidence. *Direct evidence* of blurring generally consists of some sort of survey of consumers that reveals that consumers have mistakenly associated the junior and senior marks. It is typically difficult to obtain direct evidence of blurring.

In most cases, *circumstantial evidence* is used to demonstrate blurring. Courts use a six-factor test set forth by Judge Sweet in his concurring opinion in *Mead Data Central, Inc. v. Toyota Motor Sales, U.S.A., Inc.*,[24] a 1989 decision of the U.S. Court of Appeals for the Second Circuit. Mead Data, the owner of the registered mark "Lexis," used for an on-line database of legal and news materials, sought to enjoin Toyota Motor Corp., a car manufacturer, from using a new mark, "Lexus," for automobiles, claiming that the junior mark violated the New York state dilution statute.

The Second Circuit overruled the trial court's determination that the junior mark "Lexus" diluted the senior mark "Lexis." The appellate court found that there was no blurring because: (1) the marks were not substantially similar; (2) the "Lexis" mark was recognized by only one percent of the general adult population (one-half of that one percent being attorneys or accountants) and that the mark was therefore not distinctive; and (3) no one would confuse a database with an automobile.

[21] Hasbro, Inc. v. Internet Entertainment Group, Ltd., 40 U.S.P.Q.2d 1479 (W.D. Wash. 1996). "CANDY LAND" is a registered mark for children's toys.
[22] Anheuser-Busch, Inc. v. Andy's Sportswear, Inc., 40 U.S.P.Q.2d 1542 (N.D. Cal. 1996).
[23] Toys "R" Us, Inc. v. Akkaoui, 40 U.S.P.Q.2d 1836 (N.D. Cal. 1996).
[24] 875 F.2d 1026 (2d Cir. 1989).

In his concurrence, Judge Sweet listed the following factors as relevant to evaluating the likelihood of dilution by blurring:

1. similarity of the marks;
2. similarity of the products covered by the marks;
3. sophistication of plaintiff's customers;
4. predatory intent of defendant;
5. renown of the senior mark; and
6. renown of the junior mark.

Each factor is to be considered, and all six are to be balanced in determining the likelihood of blurring.

Although it is rare for a concurring opinion to have such precedential effect, courts uniformly apply Judge Sweet's test in evaluating whether blurring has occurred in cases today, even in cases arising under the federal Act. Application of the test is very case-specific, and the outcomes are not always predictable. Thus, the junior mark "The Greatest Snow on Earth," used to promote the Utah ski travel industry, was found not to blur the senior mark, "The Greatest Show on Earth," used to promote a circus[25] because the court found that the marks were not substantially similar. The use of the junior mark "Don't Leave Home Without Me Pocket Address Book," on the other hand, was found to be so substantially similar to American Express's family of senior marks, "Don't Leave Home Without Us," "Don't Leave Home Without It," and "Don't Leave Home Without Them," as to result in blurring.[26]

See Discussion Case 6.4.

Defenses to Dilution Actions

Certain types of uses are permitted under the federal Dilution Act, including fair use of the mark in comparative advertising, noncommercial use of the mark, and all forms of news reporting and commentary.

Remedies Under the Dilution Act

The remedies provided by the act are extensive. A plaintiff whose famous mark has been diluted is entitled to a preliminary and/or permanent *injunction* against the junior user's commercial use of the mark. If the plaintiff can show that the offending party acted willfully, it may be entitled to additional remedies, including an *accounting of profits*, *actual damages* (including possible *treble damages*), *attorneys fees*, and an order requiring *destruction* of the offending items.

International Trademark Law Issues

When a company is considering expansion abroad, it is essential that the company consider its trademark strategy *before* it actually enters the foreign market. The company's ability to protect and use its chosen mark depends upon the laws of the countries in which it is operating. Thus, local legal counsel is almost always needed.

---

[25] Ringling Bros.–Barnum & Bailey Combined Shows, Inc. v. Utah Div. of Travel Dev., 955 F. Supp. 605 (E.D. Va. 1997), *aff'd*, 170 F.3d 449 (4th Cir. 1999).
[26] American Express Co. v. CFK, Inc., 947 F. Supp. 310 (E.D. Mich. 1996).

The company's first step should be to conduct a trademark search to see if the mark is available in other countries. If the mark is not available or not viable in the foreign market, the company needs to choose a different mark. In some countries, for example, letters and/or numbers may not be registered as marks.

Moreover, while in the United States the first to *use* the mark generally obtains the rights to it, in most other countries, the first to *register* receives the mark. As a result, many companies take the defensive maneuver of filing for marks even in countries where they have no immediate intention of operating, in order to stop trademark piracy. The applicant typically must use the mark within that country within a certain time period (usually three to five years) or lose the mark. As markets continue to globalize, however, countries are becoming more sympathetic to the owners of well-known marks. For example, K-Mart won the right to protect its mark from a pirate in Jamaica, even though K-Mart, which had registered its marks in Jamaica, was not actually doing business there. The court recognized that with the advent of international commercial technology and travel, greater protection of marks is required.[27]

Generally, the company must file for separate trademark protection in each country in which it wants to claim the mark. There are a few exceptions to the general rule that mark registrations must be filed on a country-by-country basis. For example, a single Benelux registration may be obtained for Belgium, the Netherlands, and Luxembourg. Beginning in 1996, the European Union has allowed a single application to be made to the Office of Harmonization of the Internal Market for a trademark that is good in all EU member countries. To qualify for a Community trademark, the trademark must be acceptable to all member countries. If the mark does not qualify for Community trademark status, the applicant can still file separate national registration applications in the various member countries.

Finally, the Protocol Relating to the Madrid Agreement Concerning the International Registration of Trademarks allows an applicant to file an international application automatically in any of the member countries upon registration of the mark in the home country. Each country has the right to refuse registration of the mark, however. As of January 2001, there were 49 parties to the Protocol, including all of the member countries of the EU.[28] The United States is not a party to the Madrid Agreement, which prevents U.S. companies from filing under this system (although their foreign affiliates in member countries can file).

Trademark registrations are potentially renewable forever in most countries. The initial term of the registration is generally 10 years in most countries, as it is in the United States. In most countries, the registration will be canceled if it is shown that the registrant has not used the mark commercially for a specified time period (usually three to five years).

Trademarks on the Internet

The advent of the Internet and E-commerce activities has greatly increased the number of trademark law issues that arise. The law has not yet evolved to adequately govern the use of trademarks in domain names and other Internet applications.

Domain names are the names given to groups of computers on the Internet. In the United States, domain names are managed by the Internet Corporation for

---

[27] Dyann L. Kostello, *When Goodwill Is Established, Rights May Follow*, THE NATIONAL LAW JOURNAL, May 18, 1998, p. C8.

[28] A list of member countries can be found at http://www.wipo.org

Assigned Names and Numbers (ICANN), a private, nonprofit organization created at the request of the government.[29] As of March 2001, ICANN had accredited 179 domain name registrars to register names in the generic top-level domains (gTLDs): ".com" (commercial), ".net" (network-related), and ".org" (nonprofit organizational). There are four additional gTLDS in the United States: .edu (educational), .gov (governmental), .int (international), and .mil (military). Country and territory names are designated by two-letter country-code top-level domains (ccTLDs), such as .uk or .gr. Domain names are usually registered on a first-come, first-served basis. The original registrar, Network Solutions, Inc., maintains and operates a shared, central registry used by all the registrars.

Because the number of domain names is rapidly expanding, there has been much talk lately of expanding the number of gTLDs available to include, for example, .name (for names), .biz (for business), or .aero (for the air-transport industry). It is expected that ICANN will begin introducing new gTLDs in 2001. Expanding the number of gTLDs will not really address the problems that businesses face in the domain name environment, however. Holders of strong marks, such as IBM or Apple, will want to claim their marks as domain names in every possible domain worldwide rather than allow someone else to use their mark in this manner.

Businesses often want to use their trademarks as domain names. Trademarks historically were limited in reach and operated only nationally. The law recognized that it would be inappropriate to allow one user to register or claim a mark in one country and then prevent everyone else in the world, even in a distant country and with a different product line, from using that same mark. Trademark law even today is territorially based, and rights obtained in one jurisdiction are good only in that particular jurisdiction. Use of a mark within the United States, for example, does not confer rights abroad; nor does use of a mark abroad confer rights in the United States. It is very possible, therefore, for separate firms or individuals to possess and use identical marks in different countries.

Domain names, on the other hand, are inherently global in reach and must be unique in order for the system to operate. Thus, only one user may possess any given domain name. Conflicts develop when multiple people want to use a particular name. The law has not yet developed adequately to fully resolve these conflicts. As a result, we see a number of legal issues involving trademarks and the Internet.

CYBERSQUATTING

Cybersquatting occurs when a user registers a well-known mark as a domain name and then attempts to sell the domain name back to the mark holder. For example, in 1998, Greg Smith, a resident of Greece, registered amazon.gr as an on-line bookstore with a Web site at http://www.amazon.gr that resembled the more well-known on-line bookstore site of http://www.amazon.com. Some mark holders sue (usually under theories of trademark infringement, trademark dilution, and/or unfair competition) to obtain the domain name from the cybersquatter; others pay the cybersquatter's price if they determine that paying would be cheaper than the costs of litigation. Generally, U.S. courts have proven more sympathetic to the mark holders than to the cybersquatters when these cases have made it to court, although the legal rules are not yet settled.

---

[29] For general information on ICANN, *see* http://www.icann.org

In addition, a new section of the Lanham Act, the *Anticybersquatting Consumer Protection Act*,[30] took effect on November 29, 1999. This federal statute is intended to combat the growing problem of trademark infringement and unfair competition on the Internet. The Act permits the owner of a registered or common law mark to sue anyone who, with a bad faith intent to profit, registers, traffics in, or uses a domain name that, among other provisions, (1) is identical or confusingly similar to a mark that is distinctive at the time when the domain name is registered or (2) is identical or confusingly similar to or dilutive of a mark that is famous at the time the domain name is registered.

The Act provides a long, nonexclusive list of factors that the court may consider in determining whether bad faith exists. These factors include: (1) intention to divert customers in a way that could harm the goodwill of a mark; (2) intention to sell the domain name for financial gain without having shown any intent to use the domain name in the bona fide offering of goods or services; and (3) registration of multiple marks that the registrant knows are identical or confusingly similar to a protected mark.

With certain exceptions, the Act also prohibits registration of a domain name that is identical or confusingly similar to another living person's name "with the specific intent to profit from such name by selling the domain name" to that person or a third party. This provision is directed primarily at protecting famous people, such as celebrities or athletes, who would have a specific interest in obtaining the domain names associated with their own names.

Generally, the remedies provided under the Act are the same as those provided for other Lanham Act violations: (1) return of the defendant's *profits*; (2) *actual damages*, which may be increased up to three times, in the court's discretion; and (3) *costs* of litigation. The Act also provides for *statutory damages* of $1,000 to $100,000 in the court's discretion, per domain name, in lieu of actual damages and profits. Finally, the Act allows for *injunctions* ordering cancellation or transfer of domain names that violate the Act. The only remedy available for registration of a domain name consisting of the name of a famous person is injunctive relief, however, as well as costs and attorneys fees, which may be awarded in the court's discretion. The first injunction under the Act was issued in January 2000 (see Focus Case 6.5).

Finally, the Act also allows *in rem* jurisdiction, which allows a mark owner to file an action against the domain name itself rather than against the cyberpirate. This allows the mark owner to sue even where the cyberpirate is unknown or personal jurisdiction over the cyberpirate cannot be established. The remedies for such an action are limited to an injunction ordering the forfeiture or cancellation of the domain name or the transfer of the domain name to the mark owner.

See Discussion Case 6.5.

As an alternative to federal litigation, ICANN adopted the Uniform Domain Name Dispute Resolution Policy (UDRP) on October 24, 1999. The policy sets forth an arbitration-type procedure for resolving some (though not all) domain name disputes. While the Anticybersquatting Consumer Protection Act makes bad faith registration alone actionable, the UDRP requires registration coupled with use of the domain name. ICANN anticipates that the dispute procedure, which is conducted primarily on-line, will take less than 45 days to complete and will cost approximately $1,000 in fees.

---

[30] 15 U.S.C. § 1125(d).

Focus Case 6.5

Facts: Perry Belcher of Tennessee registered the domain name "barginbid.com." Bargain Bid, an Internet start-up based in New York, had registered the name "bargainbid.com" for its on-line auction of computer goods. Bargain Bid claimed that Belcher was acting in bad faith in attempting to divert its customers away from its on-line business and moved for a preliminary injunction.

Decision: The trial court agreed with Bargain Bid and issued a preliminary injunction barring Belcher from: (1) using marks or domain names confusingly similar to plaintiff's domain names, including "barginbid.com"; (2) including any confusingly similar marks "in any position in connection with Internet Web sites that defen-dants have reason to believe would be read by an Internet search engine or other navigation aid and displayed to users of such search engine or aid as a title or source identifier, including the metatags thereof, or submitting a listing containing such marks to a search engine or navigation aid"; (3) offering for sale any marks confusingly similar to plaintiff's marks; (4) suggesting in any manner association between defendants' services and plaintiff's marks; (5) destroying or altering any documents concerning the offering of sale of marks confusingly similar to plaintiff's; and (6) using any names or email addresses obtained by defendants via the Web site "barginbid.com". *Bargain Bid LLC v. uBid, Inc.*, 2000 U.S. Dist. LEXIS 3021 (E.D. N.Y. Jan. 3, 2000).

Remedies under the UDRP are limited to requiring the cancellation or transfer of an infringing domain name. As of October 2000, ICANN had approved four dispute resolution providers. Complaints were accepted beginning December 1, 1999. As of March 2001, 3,184 proceedings had begun, involving 5,692 domain names, and a total of 2,298 decisions had been issued.

TYPOPIRACY

Typopiracy or *typosquatting* has also become a problem with Internet domain names. Here, Web sites try to take advantage of common typographical errors that users might make in typing in a Web address to direct users to a different Web site. The typopirate then sells advertising space on the site to businesses who want their banners seen by the accidental traffic generated. A number of large and legitimate Web businesses have placed banner ads on typopirates' sites.

In April 1999, a federal district court issued a preliminary injunction in what is believed to be the first typopiracy decision.[31] Paine Webber, Inc., maintained a Web site at http://www.painewebber.com. It filed suit for trademark infringement and dilution against Rafael Fortuny after it discovered that users who mistakenly omitted the "period" after "www" ended up at Fortuny's pornographic Web site. The company found the "typo" site after a customer complained about reaching the pornographic site while trying to access Paine Webber's webpage. A Paine Webber employee had incorrectly typed a "hot link" to Paine Webber's page, omitting the period after "www." The court ruled that Paine Webber was likely to succeed on the merits of its dilution claim because its mark is famous and would be tarnished by association with a pornographic site. The court also found an injunction was necessary to prevent irreparable harm to Paine Webber and ordered Network Solutions, Inc., the domain name registrar, to place the disputed name on hold pending the outcome of the litigation.

[31] Paine Webber, Inc. v. wwwpainewebber.com, 1999 U.S. Dist. Lexis 6552 (E.D. Va. April 9, 1999).

Focus Case 6.6

 Facts: Brookfield Communications, Inc., sells software called MovieBuff, which provides a searchable database of information such as movie credits, box office receipts, and release schedules. It also runs an Internet subscription database by the same name. Brookfield held a California trademark for the MovieBuff mark covering "computer software" in 1994 and applied for federal registration for the mark to designate both goods and services in 1994.

West Coast Entertainment Corp., a national video rental chain, federally registered a service mark for its retail stores in 1991—"The Movie Buff's Movie Store." In 1996, it registered the domain name "moviebuff.com" and used "moviebuff" as a metatag in its Web site.

In October 1998, Brookfield discovered that West Coast was launching a Web site at moviebuff.com that contained, among other things, a searchable entertainment database similar to Brookfield's. Brookfield filed suit in federal district court, claiming trademark infringement and unfair competition. The district court denied Brookfield's motion for a temporary restraining order preventing West Coast from using moviebuff.com.

Decision: On appeal, the Ninth Circuit determined that because Brookfield had marketed MovieBuff products before West Coast began using moviebuff.com in commerce, Brookfield was the senior user of the mark, and that West Coast's use of the mark would likely be confusing to consumers.

The Ninth Circuit based its decision on the metatags issue on what it termed "initial interest confu-sion." Although most Internet customers seeking Brookfield's MovieBuff software would not confuse West Coast's Web site with that of Brookfield, many would probably halt their search once they arrived at the West Coast site and saw its competing product. Thus, West Coast was improperly benefiting from the goodwill that Brookfield had generated from its "MovieBuff" mark.

The court analogized the situation to the use of billboards:

> Suppose West Coast's competitor (let's call it "Blockbuster") puts up a billboard on a highway reading—"West Coast Video: 2 miles ahead at Exit 7"—where West Coast is really located at Exit 8 but Blockbuster is located at Exit 7. Customers looking for West Coast's store will pull off at Exit 7 and drive around looking for it. Unable to locate it, but seeing the Blockbuster store right by the highway entrance, they may simply rent there . . . . Customers are not confused in the narrow sense; they are fully aware that they are purchasing from Blockbuster and they have no reason to believe that Blockbuster is related to, or in any way sponsored by, West Coast. Nonetheless, the fact that there is only initial customer confusion does not alter the fact that Blockbuster would be misappropriating West Coast's acquired goodwill.

The Ninth Circuit thus upheld Brookfield's motion for a preliminary injunction. *Brookfield Communications, Inc. v. West Coast Entertainment Corp.*, 174 F.3d 1036 (9th Cir. 1999).

METATAGS

Metatags are keywords that can be inserted into the source code of Web sites. Although Web users usually cannot see the metatags, search engines can read them. A search engine uses various algorithms to rank order webpages for hits on words or phrases, usually based on the domain name, text on the Web site, and metatags. Some search engines actually give more weight to metatags in search results than to visible text on the Web site. Often, an Internet business places the trademarks of competitors in the metatags of its site. Mark holders have begun challenging the use of metatags as trademark infringement, and the courts are proving receptive to their claims (see Focus Case 6.6).

As the *Brookfield* court emphasized, however, not all uses of metatags constitute trademark infringement. Competitors may use a competitor's metatag in *comparative advertising*. The *fair use defense* also applies to metatags. In a recent case, Terri

Welles, a former Playboy Playmate, set up a Web site on which she sold various products and services. She used "playboy" and "playmate" in the metatags for the site. Playboy Enterprises sought to enjoin her use of these metatags, claiming trademark infringement. The federal district court rejected Playboy's motion, finding that Welles had engaged in "fair use." The use of the words in her metatags accurately and fairly described her status as a former Playboy Playmate and were designed to give Internet users a better idea about the content of her webpage, not to trade off of Playboy's goodwill.[32] Welles did not use Playboy's bunny logo or stylized letters and had provided disclaimers on many of her pages.

PORTALS AND BANNER ADVERTISING

Trademark infringement issues can also arise through the use of *portals* or *banner advertising*. Businesses may register their Web sites through Internet *portals*, or directories. The business can often then select keywords that consumers may use to search the directory. If a business selects a competitor's trademark as a portal keyword, does it infringe upon the competitor's mark? Only a handful of cases have been brought in this area to date, so the answer is uncertain.[33]

Banner advertising is prominently displayed at the top of a screen when the user enters a keyword into the portal Web site. In addition to a list of search "hits," a large advertisement appears on the screen. Because most of the Internet sites that actually generate revenue do so through the sale of advertising space on the site, banner advertising is a very common practice.

Several lawsuits have been filed by companies as a result of advertisers using others' trademarks as keywords to trigger banner advertising for competitors' products or services. Estee Lauder, Inc., for example, sued Excite, Inc., because Excite allegedly sold the exclusive right to the Estee Lauder keyword "CLINIQUE" to The Fragrance Counter. When the keyword "CLINIQUE" is typed into Excite, a banner advertisement for The Fragrance Counter pops up. This prevents Estee Lauder from using its own trademark, Clinique, to trigger its own banner ads linked to its own Web site.[34]

LINKING ISSUES

Other Internet practices can also raise legal issues. *Hyperlinking* to a competitor's site without permission may also constitute trademark infringement, particularly where a logo, as opposed to a word mark, is used to designate the link. In *framing*, the linked site is retrieved as a "window" within the linking site. The linking site's URL is displayed on the user's browser, and the linking site may continue to display its own content, including paid advertising, as the frame or border of the linked site. Linking is thus analogous to picture-in-picture television. Because the URL does not change but continues to display the address of the linking rather than the linked site, framing can create false associations between the linking site

[32] Playboy Enterprises v. Welles, 7 F. Supp. 2d 1098 (S.D. Cal. 1998), *aff'd without opinion*, 162 F.3d 1169 (9th Cir. 1998).
[33] *See* Nettis Environment, Ltd. v. IWI, Inc., 46 F. Supp. 2d 722 (N.D. Ohio 1999); Playboy Enterprises v. Netscape Communications Corp., 55 F. Supp. 2d 1070 (S.D. Cal. 1999), *aff'd*, 202 F.3d 278 (9th Cir. 1999).
[34] Estee Lauder, Inc. v. The Fragrance Counter and Excite, Inc., (S.D.N.Y. complaint filed Mar. 5, 1999).

and its advertisers, on the one hand, and the linked site on the other. (It can also raise copyright infringement concerns.[35])

Deep linking occurs when the link takes the user to a page within the linked site, bypassing the linked site's home page and, very likely, its marks and paid advertising. Ticketmaster, for example, sued Microsoft, because Microsoft used a deep link to Ticketmaster's ticket-buying service. Ticketmaster alleged that this created a false impression of a business relationship between the two parties and enabled Microsoft customers to bypass Ticketmaster's advertisers, thus depriving it of revenue. The dispute was settled, with Microsoft agreeing to link directly to Ticketmaster's home page, rather than deep linking within its site.[36]

REMEDIES ISSUES

Finally, trademark infringement on the Internet raises difficult issues regarding remedies. Amazon Books, for example, has operated a feminist bookstore in Minneapolis since 1970. Amazon Books did not federally register its mark and thus does not have national rights to the Amazon name, but it clearly has obtained common law rights to use the name in its geographic market area. Amazon Books has challenged amazon.com's use of the Amazon name, claiming that the on-line bookstore is infringing on its mark.

Traditional law would recognize Amazon Books' senior use of the mark within its geographic market and would prohibit amazon.com from using the mark within that same geographic region but would allow amazon.com, as the junior user, to acquire rights everywhere else in the name. The Internet, however, does not recognize such geographic borders, which means that traditional remedies are not relevant. It is impossible, for example, to tell amazon.com that it can use the amazon name in every state except Minnesota, as there is no way to limit on-line users' access to the amazon.com Web site in that manner.

INTERNET STRATEGIES FOR BUSINESS

How should marketers manage these complex and often unresolved Internet trademark law issues? First, become aware of the Internet environment in which your trademark may be used. Look for typopiracy around your Web site. Run searches with your trademarks to determine whether your competitors may be using them in metatags, portals, or banner advertising. Second, evaluate your own activities for potential liability. Review your metatag, portal, and banner advertising practices to make certain that you are not infringing upon the trademark rights of your competitors and thus exposing your company to legal liability. Use of another's trademark for comparative advertising purposes is generally permissible, but other uses may not be. Avoid framing or deep linking, and use caution when linking to the sites of others. In many instances, it may be wise to enter into a specific linking agreement. Finally, post disclaimers for linked materials.

---

[35] *See* Futuredontics, Inc. v. Applied Anagramics, Inc., 1998 U.S. Dist. Lexis 2265 (C.D. Cal. Jan. 30, 1998).

[36] *Techweek; A Quick Look at the Latest Technology News; Lawsuits Challenge Net Advertising Policies,* The Atlanta Journal and Constitution, Feb. 21, 1999, p. O1H; Bob Tedeschi, *Ticketmaster and Microsoft Settle Suit on Internet Linking,* N.Y. Times, Feb. 15, 1999, at C6.

6.1 Trade Dress Protection—Distinctiveness of Marks, Secondary Meaning

Two Pesos, Inc. v. Taco Cabana, Inc., 505 U.S. 763 (1992)

OPINION: JUSTICE WHITE The issue in this case is whether the trade dress of a restaurant may be protected under § 43(a) of the Trademark Act of 1946 (Lanham Act), based on a finding of inherent distinctiveness, without proof that the trade dress has secondary meaning.

I

Respondent Taco Cabana, Inc., operates a chain of fast-food restaurants in Texas. * * * The first Taco Cabana restaurant was opened in San Antonio in September 1978, and five more restaurants had been opened in San Antonio by 1985. Taco Cabana describes its Mexican trade dress as:

> a festive eating atmosphere having interior dining and patio areas decorated with artifacts, bright colors, paintings and murals. The patio includes interior and exterior areas with the interior patio capable of being sealed off from the outside patio by overhead garage doors. The stepped exterior of the building is a festive and vivid color scheme using top border paint and neon stripes. Bright awnings and umbrellas continue the theme.

In December 1985, a Two Pesos, Inc., restaurant was opened in Houston. Two Pesos adopted a motif very similar to the foregoing description of Taco Cabana's trade dress. Two Pesos restaurants expanded rapidly in Houston and other markets, but did not enter San Antonio. In 1986, Taco Cabana entered the Houston and Austin markets and expanded into other Texas cities, including Dallas and El Paso where Two Pesos was also doing business.

In 1987, Taco Cabana sued Two Pesos . . . for trade dress infringement . . . . * * * [J]udgment was entered awarding damages to Taco Cabana. In the course of calculating damages, the trial court held that Two Pesos had intentionally and deliberately infringed Taco Cabana's trade dress.

The Court of Appeals [affirmed.] * * *

* * * We granted certiorari to resolve the conflict among the Courts of Appeals on the question whether trade dress that is inherently distinctive is protectible under § 43(a) without a showing that it has acquired secondary meaning. We find that it is, and we therefore affirm.

II

* * * *

Settle Suit on Internet Linking, N.Y. Times, Feb. 15,1999, at C6.

* * * In order to be registered, a mark must be capable of distinguishing the applicant's goods from those of others. Marks are often classified in categories of generally increasing distinctiveness; . . . they may be (1) generic; (2) descriptive; (3) suggestive; (4) arbitrary; or (5) fanciful. * * * The latter three categories of marks, because their intrinsic nature serves to identify a particular source of a product, are deemed inherently distinctive and are entitled to protection. In contrast, generic marks . . . are not registrable as trademarks.

Marks which are merely descriptive of a product are not inherently distinctive. When used to describe a product, they do not inherently identify a particular source, and hence cannot be protected. However, descriptive marks may acquire the distinctiveness which will allow them to be protected under the Act. Section 2 of the Lanham Act provides that a descriptive mark that otherwise could not be registered under the Act may be registered if it "has become distinctive of the applicant's goods in commerce." This acquired distinctiveness is generally called "secondary meaning."

The general rule regarding distinctiveness is clear: An identifying mark is distinctive and capable of being protected if it *either* (1) is inherently distinctive *or* (2) has acquired distinctiveness through secondary meaning. * * *

* * * *

Petitioner argues that the jury's finding that the trade dress has not acquired a secondary meaning shows conclusively that the trade dress is not inherently distinctive. * * *

* * * *

Engrafting onto § 43(a) a requirement of secondary meaning for inherently distinctive trade dress . . . would undermine the purposes of the Lanham Act. Protection of trade dress, no less than of trademarks, serves the Act's purpose to "secure to the owner of the mark the goodwill of his business and to protect the ability of consumers to distinguish among competing producers. National protection of trademarks is desirable, Congress concluded, because trademarks foster competition and the maintenance of quality by securing to the producer the benefits of good reputation." By making more difficult the identification of a producer with its product, a secondary meaning requirement for a nondescriptive trade dress would hinder improving or maintaining the producer's competitive position.

suggestions that . . . [t]he initial user of any shape or design would cut off competition from products of like design and shape are not persuasive. Only nonfunctional, distinctive trade dress is protected under § 43(a). [A] design is legally functional, and thus unprotectible, if it is one of a limited number of equally efficient options available to competitors and free competition would be unduly hindered by according the design trademark protection. * * *

On the other hand, adding a secondary meaning requirement could have anticompetitive effects, creating particular burdens on the startup of small companies. It would present special difficulties for a business, such as respondent, that seeks to start a new product in a limited area and then expand into new markets. Denying protection for inherently distinctive nonfunctional trade dress until after secondary meaning has been established would allow a competitor, which has not adopted a distinctive trade dress of its own, to appropriate the originator's dress in other markets and to deter the originator from expanding into and competing in these areas.

* * * *

III

We agree with the Court of Appeals that proof of secondary meaning is not required to prevail on a claim under § 43(a) of the Lanham Act where the trade dress at issue is inherently distinctive, and accordingly the judgment of that court is affirmed.

Questions for Discussion for Case 6.1

1. Why does the Supreme Court choose to hear this case?

2. What types of marks are inherently distinctive? What types of marks require secondary meaning? What types of marks get no protection?

3. Does the description of Taco Cabana's trade dress sound inherently distinctive? Why or why not?

4. What is the Court's concern about the effects on competition of requiring secondary meaning for inherently distinctive trade dress? Do you think the concern is a legitimate one?

6.2 Trademark Protection—Color as a Mark

Qualitex Co. v. Jacobson Products Co., 514 U.S. 159 (1995)

OPINION: JUSTICE BREYER The question in this case is whether the Trademark Act of 1946 (Lanham Act) permits the registration of a trademark that consists, purely and simply, of a color. We conclude that, sometimes, a color will meet ordinary legal trademark requirements. And, when it does so, no special legal rule prevents color alone from serving as a trademark.

I

The case before us grows out of petitioner Qualitex Company's use (since the 1950's) of a special shade of green-gold color on the pads that it makes and sells to dry cleaning firms for use on dry cleaning presses. In 1989, respondent Jacobson Products (a Qualitex rival) began to sell its own press pads to dry cleaning firms; and it colored those pads a similar green-gold. In 1991, Qualitex registered the special green-gold color on press pads with the Patent and Trademark Office as a trademark. Qualitex subsequently added a trademark infringement count to an unfair competition claim in a lawsuit it had already filed challenging Jacobson's use of the green-gold color.

Qualitex won the lawsuit in the District Court. But, the Court of Appeals for the Ninth Circuit set aside the judgment in Qualitex's favor on the trademark infringement claim because, in that Circuit's view, the Lanham Act does not permit Qualitex, or anyone else, to register "color alone" as a trademark.

The Courts of Appeals have differed as to whether or not the law recognizes the use of color alone as a trademark. Therefore, this Court granted certiorari. We now hold that there is no rule absolutely barring the use of color alone, and we reverse the judgment of the Ninth Circuit.

II

* * * Both the language of the [Lanham] Act and the basic underlying principles of trademark law would seem to include color within the universe of things that can qualify as a trademark. The language of the Lanham Act describes that universe in the broadest of terms. It says that trademarks "includ[e] any word, name, symbol, or device, or any combination thereof." Since human beings might use as a "symbol" or "device" almost anything at all that is capable of carrying meaning, this language, read literally, is not restrictive. The courts and the Patent and Trademark Office have authorized for use as a mark a particular shape (of a Coca-Cola bottle), a particular sound (of NBC's three chimes), and even a particular scent (of plumeria blossoms on sewing thread). If a shape, a sound, and a fragrance can act as symbols why, one might ask, can a color not do the same?

A color is also capable of satisfying the more important part of the statutory definition of a trademark, which requires that a person "us[e]" or "inten[d] to use" the mark

> to identify and distinguish his or her goods, including a unique product, from those manufactured or sold by others and to indicate the source of the goods, even if that source is unknown.

15 U.S.C. § 1127. True, a product's color is unlike "fanciful," "arbitrary," or "suggestive" words or designs, which almost *automatically* tell a customer that they refer to a brand. The imaginary word "Suntost," or the words "Suntost Marmalade," on a jar of orange jam immediately would signal a brand or a product "source"; the jam's orange color does not do so. But, over time, customers may come to treat a particular color on a product or its packaging (say, a color that in context seems unusual, such as pink on a firm's insulating material or red on the head of a large industrial bolt) as signifying a brand. And, if so, that color would have come to identify and distinguish the goods—i.e., "to indicate" their "source"—much in the way that descriptive words on a product (say, "Trim" on nail clippers or "Car-Freshner" on deodorizer) can come to indicate a product's origin. In this circumstance, trademark law says that the word (e.g., "Trim"), although not inherently distinctive, has developed "secondary meaning." ("[S]econdary meaning" is acquired when "in the minds of the public, the primary significance of a product feature . . . is to identify the source of the product rather than the product itself."). * * *

We cannot find in the basic objectives of trademark law any obvious theoretical objection to the use of color alone as a trademark, where that color has attained "secondary meaning" and therefore identifies and distinguishes a particular brand (and thus indicates its "source"). * * *

Neither can we find a principled objection to the use of color as a mark in the important "functionality" doctrine of trademark law. The functionality doctrine prevents trademark law, which seeks to promote competition by protecting a firm's reputation, from instead inhibiting legitimate competition by allowing a producer to control a useful product feature. It is the province of patent law, not trademark law, to encourage invention by granting inventors a monopoly over new product designs or functions for a limited time, after which competitors are free to use the innovation. If a product's functional features could be used as trademarks, however, a monopoly over such features could be obtained without regard to whether they qualify as patents and could be extended forever (because trademarks may be renewed in perpetuity). * * * This Court consequently has explained that, "[i]n general terms, a product feature is functional," and cannot serve as a trademark, "if it is essential to the use or purpose of the article or if it affects the cost or quality of the article," that is, if exclusive use of the feature would put competitors at a significant non-reputation-related disadvantage. Although sometimes color plays an important role (unrelated to source identification) in making a product more desirable, sometimes it does not. And, this latter fact—the fact that sometimes color is not essential to a product's use or purpose and does not affect cost or quality—indicates that the doctrine of "functionality" does not create an absolute bar to the use of color alone as a mark.

It would seem, then, that color alone, at least sometimes, can meet the basic legal requirements for use as a trademark. It can act as a symbol that distinguishes a firm's goods and identifies their source, without serving any other significant function. * * * [Qualitex's] green-gold color acts as a symbol. Having developed secondary meaning (for customers identified the green-gold color as Qualitex's), it identifies the press pads' source. And, the green-gold color serves no other function. * * * Accordingly, unless there is some special reason that convincingly militates against the use of color alone as a trademark, trademark law would protect Qualitex's use of the green-gold color on its press pads.

* * * *

IV

* * * For these reasons, the judgment of the Ninth Circuit is reversed.

Questions for Discussion for Case 6.2

1. Why does the Supreme Court choose to hear this case?

2. Can color be an inherently distinctive mark? When can color be protected as a mark?

3. Can color be a protected trademark if it enhances the performance of the product? Why or why not?

6.3 Trade Dress Protection—Unregistered Trade Dress

Wal-Mart Stores, Inc. v. Samara Brothers, Inc., 529 U.S. 205 (2000)

OPINION: JUSTICE SCALIA In this case, we decide under what circumstances a product's design is distinctive, and therefore protectible, in an action for infringement of unregistered trade dress under § 43(a) of the Trademark Act of 1946 (Lanham Act).

I

Respondent Samara Brothers, Inc., designs and manufactures children's clothing. Its primary product is a line of spring/summer one-piece seersucker outfits decorated with appliques of hearts, flowers, fruits, and the like. A number of chain stores, including JCPenney, sell this line of clothing under contract with Samara.

* * * In 1995, [Petitioner] Wal-Mart contracted with one of its suppliers, Judy-Philippine, Inc., to manufacture a line of children's outfits . . . . * * * Wal-Mart sent Judy-Philippine photographs of a number of garments from Samara's line, on which Judy-Philippine's garments were to be based; Judy-Philippine duly copied, with only minor modifications, 16 of Samara's garments, many of which contained copyrighted elements. In 1996, Wal-Mart briskly sold the so-called knockoffs, generating more than $1.15 million in gross profits.

In June 1996, a buyer for JCPenney called a representative at Samara to complain that she had seen Samara garments on sale at Wal-Mart for a lower price than JCPenney was allowed to charge under its contract with Samara. The Samara representative told the buyer that Samara did not supply its clothing to Wal-Mart. Their suspicions aroused, however, Samara officials launched an investigation, which disclosed that Wal-Mart and several other major retailers . . . were selling the knockoffs of Samara's outfits produced by Judy-Philippine.

After sending cease-and-desist letters, Samara brought this action in the United States District Court . . . against Wal-Mart, Judy-Philippine, Kmart, Caldor, Hills, and Goody's for copyright infringement under federal law, consumer fraud and unfair competition under New York law,

and—most relevant for our purposes—infringement of unregistered trade dress under § 43(a) of the Lanham Act. All of the defendants except Wal-Mart settled before trial.

After a weeklong trial, the jury found in favor of Samara on all of its claims. Wal-Mart then renewed a motion for judgment as a matter of law, claiming, *inter alia*, that there was insufficient evidence to support a conclusion that Samara's clothing designs could be legally protected as distinctive trade dress for purposes of § 43(a). The District Court denied the motion and awarded Samara damages, interest, costs, and fees totaling almost $1.6 million, together with injunctive relief. The Second Circuit affirmed the denial of the motion for judgment as a matter of law and we granted certiorari.

II

* * * In addition to protecting registered marks, the Lanham Act, in § 43(a), gives a producer a cause of action for the use by any person of "any word, term, name, symbol, or device, or any combination thereof . . . which . . . is likely to cause confusion . . . as to the origin, sponsorship, or approval of his or her goods . . . ." It is the latter provision that is at issue in this case.

* * * *

The text of § 43(a) provides little guidance as to the circumstances under which unregistered trade dress may be protected. It does require that a producer show that the allegedly infringing feature is not "functional," and is likely to cause confusion with the product for which protection is sought. Nothing in § 43(a) explicitly requires a producer to show that its trade dress is distinctive, but courts have universally imposed that requirement, since without distinctiveness the trade dress would not "cause confusion . . . as to the origin, sponsorship, or approval of [the] goods," as the section requires. * * *

In evaluating the distinctiveness of a mark . . ., courts have held that a mark can be distinctive in one of two ways. First, a mark is inherently distinctive if "[its] intrinsic nature serves to identify a particular source." In the context of word marks, courts have applied the now-classic test . . . , in which word marks that are "arbitrary" ("Camel" cigarettes), "fanciful" ("Kodak" film), or "suggestive" ("Tide" laundry detergent) are held to be inherently distinctive. Second, a mark has acquired distinctiveness, even if it is not inherently distinctive, if it has developed secondary meaning, which occurs when, "in the minds of the public, the primary significance of a [mark] is to identify the source of the product rather than the product itself."

* * * *

It seems to us that design, like color, is not inherently distinctive. The attribution of inherent distinctiveness to certain categories of word marks and product packaging derives from the fact that the very purpose of attaching a particular word to a product, or encasing it in a distinctive packaging, is most often to identify the source of the product. * * * Consumers are aware of the reality that, almost invariably, even the most unusual of product designs—such as a cocktail shaker shaped like a penguin—is intended not to identify the source, but to render the product itself more useful or more appealing.

* * * *

Respondent contends that our decision in *Two Pesos* forecloses a conclusion that product-design trade dress can never be inherently distinctive. In that case, we held that the trade dress of a chain of Mexican restaurants, which the plaintiff described as "a festive eating atmosphere having interior dining and patio areas decorated with artifacts, bright colors, paintings and murals," could be protected under § 43(a) without a showing of secondary meaning. *Two Pesos* unquestionably establishes the legal principle that trade dress can be inherently distinctive, but it does not establish that *product-design* trade dress can be. *Two Pesos* is inapposite to our holding here because the trade dress at issue, the decor of a restaurant, seems to us not to constitute product design. It was either product packaging—which . . . normally is taken by the consumer to indicate origin—or else some *tertium quid* that is akin to product packaging and has no bearing on the present case.

Respondent replies that this manner of distinguishing *Two Pesos* will force courts to draw difficult lines between product-design and product-packaging trade dress. There will indeed be some hard cases at the margin: a classic glass Coca-Cola bottle, for instance, may constitute packaging for those consumers who drink the Coke and then discard the bottle, but may constitute the product itself for those consumers who are bottle collectors, or part of the product itself for those consumers who buy Coke in the classic glass bottle, rather than a can, because they think it more stylish to drink from the former. * * * To the extent there are close cases, we believe that courts should err on the side of caution and classify ambiguous trade dress as product design, thereby requiring secondary meaning. * * *

We hold that, in an action for infringement of unregistered trade dress under § 43(a) of the Lanham Act, a product's design is distinctive, and therefore protectible, only upon a showing of secondary meaning. The judgment of the Second Circuit is reversed, and the case is remanded for further proceedings consistent with this opinion.

Questions for Discussion for Case 6.3

1. Is product-design trade dress inherently distinctive? Why or why not?

2. The Supreme Court says that this decision does not overrule *Two Pesos* because of the distinction between the décor of a restaurant and product design. Is the Court's analysis persuasive? How easy do you think it will be for businesses (and their lawyers) to apply this distinction?

3. Is the décor of a restaurant part of its product? Many people consider the atmosphere or ambience of a restaurant when determining which of several restaurants serving comparable food to patronize.

4. How would you protect the trade dress of your product shortly after initial marketing but before the design has become known widely enough to support a finding of secondary meaning?

6.4 Dilution—Fame of Mark, Blurring

Hershey Foods Corp. v. Mars, Inc., 998 F. Supp. 500 (M.D. Pa. 1998)

INTRODUCTION

The plaintiffs are Hershey Foods Corporation and Homestead, Inc. Hershey makes candy and sells it nationwide. Homestead is a related corporate entity that owns many of Hershey's trademarks and trade dress. (We will refer to Hershey and Homestead collectively as Hershey or the plaintiff.) This lawsuit was filed against Mars, Inc., another major candy maker, alleging violations of federal and state law governing competition. The suit stems from Mars' adoption of a trade dress for its peanut butter M&M's that Hershey asserts unlawfully resembles certain elements of its trade dress for its Reese's Peanut Butter Cups.

We are considering Hershey's motion for a preliminary injunction, seeking an order prohibiting Mars from using its current trade dress on the basis that it dilutes by blurring the Reese's trade dress. * * *

THE LAW OF DILUTION

A dilution claim protects a trademark holder's right in the mark's ability to act as a unique identifier of the mark's holder. This cause of action differs from [the federal trademark infringement law] by eliminating the need to show confusion; that is, the need to show that the defendant's mark causes consumers to confuse the defendant's goods with the plaintiff's. Instead, a dilution claim asserts that, while the defendant's mark does not confuse consumers as to the source of the goods, it leads consumers to believe that the plaintiff's mark now identifies two different sources of goods, thus diluting the mark's ability to identify the plaintiff's goods alone.

* * * *

Hershey's dilution-by-blurring claim is based on [the federal Dilution Act and the Pennsylvania anti-dilution statute]. The two laws are substantively similar.

* * * *

The federal statute requires that the mark be "famous" and provides that the court "may consider factors such as, but not limited to" the following in "determining whether a mark is distinctive and famous":

(A)   the degree of inherent or acquired distinctiveness of the mark;

(B)   the duration and extent of use of the mark in connection with the goods or services with which the mark is used;

(C)   the duration and extent of advertising and publicity of the mark;

(D)   the geographical extent of the trading area in which the mark is used;

(E)   the channels of trade for the goods or services with which the mark is used;

(F)   the degree of recognition of the mark in the trading areas and channels of trade used by the mark's owner and the person against whom the injunction is sought;

(G)   the nature and extent of use of the same or similar marks by third parties; and

(H)   whether the mark was registered under the Act of March 3, 1881, or the Act of February 20, 1905, or on the principal register.

15 U.S.C. § 1125(c)(1).

We read this language as giving the court flexibility in analyzing the enumerated factors so that their relative weight in any given case can be balanced.

In deciding whether the defendant's mark dilutes the plaintiff's by blurring, federal courts interpreting section 1125(c) have started from the framework first set forth in Judge Sweet's concurring opinion in *Mead Data Central, Inc. v. Toyota Motor Sales, U.S.A., Inc.*, 875 F.2d 1026 (2d Cir. 1989), which Judge Sweet used for interpreting the New York antidilution statute.

Judge Sweet used a six-factor test:

1)   similarity of the marks
2)   similarity of the products covered by the marks
3)   sophistication of consumers
4)   predatory intent
5)   renown of the senior mark
6)   renown of the junior mark

He believed there was a positive correlation between blurring and the similarity of the marks, the similarity of the products covered by the marks, the existence of predatory intent, and renown of the senior and junior marks, but that there was a negative correlation if the consumers were sophisticated.

Some commentators have disagreed on whether all of the factors are relevant to a dilution analysis. * * *

When these legal principles are put together, to prove dilution by blurring, the plaintiff must make the following showing: (1) that its mark is famous (as opposed to merely being a valid trademark); (2) that the defendant began using a mark in commerce after the plaintiff's mark became famous; and (3) that the "defendant's use causes dilution by lessening the capacity of the plaintiff's mark to identify and distinguish goods or services." In turn, dilution depends on at least how some of the factors set forth in *Mead Data Central* apply here.

FINDINGS OF FACT

THE PARTIES

1. Hershey Foods Corporation is a corporation organized under the laws of Delaware with its principal place of business in Hershey, Pennsylvania.
2. Homestead, Inc. is a corporation organized under the laws of Delaware with its principal place of business in Newark, Delaware.
3. Homestead manages and owns many of the trademarks and trade dresses that Hershey uses in connection with its confectionery products.
4. Mars, Incorporated is a corporation organized under the laws of Delaware with its principal place of business in McLean, Virginia.
5. The M&M/Mars Division of Mars, Incorporated is an operating division of Mars.
6. Hershey manufactures confectionery products, including chocolate and peanut butter candy. Hershey markets peanut butter cups under the trade name "Reese's" and sugar-shelled peanut butter candy under the trade name "Reese's Pieces."
7. Mars also manufactures and sells candy throughout the United States and in foreign countries. Mars sells varieties of its sugar-shelled chocolate candy under its trademark M&M's, two lower-case "m"s connected by an ampersand.
8. Hershey and Mars have long been the top two candy manufacturers in the United States. Hershey ranks number one and Mars number two in U.S. market share among marketers of confectionery products. Hershey gained the number one rank from Mars in 1988.
9. Reese's peanut butter cup candy and Reese's Pieces candy and the Mars peanut butter M&M's candy compete directly with each other.

THE PARTIES' PRODUCTS AND TRADE DRESS

A. *The Reese's Peanut Butter Cup and Reese's Pieces Products and Trade Dress*

10. Hershey's Reese's peanut butter cup candy has been Hershey's best-selling brand for decades. This is a chocolate peanut butter candy in a shallow cup shape with milk chocolate on the outside and peanut butter on the inside.
11. Hershey also markets Reese's Pieces candies, which is peanut butter encased in a candy shell.
12. Reese's peanut butter cup is sold in a package with a particular shade of background orange, the Reese's logo (its trade name in a slanted handwritten style in bright yellow with brown "keylining;" i.e., the yellow letters outlined in brown) and a brown rectangular bar with a sawtoothed top (imitating in two dimensions the top edge of a peanut butter cup) directly underneath the logo. The bar contains the message in bright yellow letters "PEANUT BUTTER CUPS." This is the "complete Reese's trade dress."
13. In this case, Hershey claims rights in the portion of that dress which consists of a particular shade of background orange as the principal element in combination with the brown and yellow elements, in a particular arrangement and juxtaposition used to create a distinctive overall impression. This is the "abbreviated Reese's trade dress."
14. The Reese's Pieces trade dress is similar in that it consists of the same shade of background orange, the Reese's logo (its trade name in a slanted handwritten style in bright yellow with brown keylining). However, it differs by having a so-called lozenge (a cartouche-shaped element) beneath the logo. The lozenge is brown with white keylining and has the words "peanut butter" in white letters.

B. *The Mars' M&M's Products and Trade Dress*

15. Mars has been selling its M&M's plain chocolate candies, bite-size individual chocolate candies with a sugar shell, in a package having a solid brown background with its distinctive M&M's logo in white lettering since 1949.
16. Mars began selling its M&M's peanut chocolate candies, a product with a peanut at the center, in the same style package, using a yellow background with the M&M's trademark (or logo) in its distinctive brown lettering style in 1964.
17. Mars began selling its M&M's almond chocolate candies, a product with an almond at the center, in the same style package using a tan background with the brown M&M's logo in 1987.
18. Mars began selling its M&M's chocolate candies in a mint chocolate variety in the early 1990's. The packaging for the M&M's mint chocolate candies uses a green background color with the M&M's logo.
19. Mars owns Federal trademark registrations for its M&M's variety packages Nos. 1,266,509, 1,272,035, and 2,005,935.
20. All of Mars' M&M's varieties packaging have included a display of cascading individual M&M's candy pieces (the "lentils") since at least as early as 1994. These candy pieces are "cultural icons" and highly recognizable by the public. They serve to identify the M&M's brand candies to consumers.
21. The design elements of the M&M's packages for these varieties, including the distinctive lettering style, the presence of the individual candy pieces or "lentils," and the lozenge indicating the variety situated below the M&M's trademark, are consistent throughout the range of these M&M's branded products.
22. The different varieties of M&M's brand of chocolate candies are together the largest selling brand of candy in the United States. In the last four years, Mars has sold approximately 4 billion dollars worth of M&M's brand candies in packaging bearing a display of the "cultural icon" images of the individual M&M's candies bearing the letter "m".

THE M&M'S PEANUT BUTTER VARIETY

A. *Background and Concept for the Peanut Butter M&M's Product*

1. Peanut Butter M&M's: 1988–1993

23. In November 1988, senior management of Mars approved a proposal to commence test marketing of a peanut butter

M&M's variety. The proposal stated: "The product [the proposed new M&M's variety] marries the benefits of two best selling brands-"M&M's" Chocolate Candies and Reese's Peanut Butter Cups-to grow M&M/Mars share of the chocolate candy market."

24. A test package for the Peanut Butter M&M's product employed a red background color and a yellow M&M logo, keylined in brown. The lozenge underneath the logo had a yellow background containing brown letters stating "Peanut Butter."

25. In 1990, Mars began to introduce Peanut Butter M&M's in phases. The initial package for the Peanut Butter M&M's product employed a red background color and a yellow M&M brand name, keylined in brown. Contrary to the test package, the lozenge had brown background containing yellow letters stating "Peanut Butter." Plaintiffs have referred to this package as "Trade Dress 1."

26. After some initial success, by 1993 the product was "a disappointment." Sales of Peanut Butter M&M's fell from a peak of $78 million in 1991 to $40 million in 1992 to $34 million in 1993.

2. 1993-1994 "Relaunch"

27. Notwithstanding disappointing sales, Mars had confidence that peanut butter M&M's could succeed and, in 1993, Mars developed a plan to "relaunch" Peanut Butter M&M's.

28. The relaunch plan was to reformulate the product and market it in a revised trade dress that would begin entering retail markets in 1994. The background color of the trade dress was changed from red to "a more orange red." The revised package also included a yellow "violator" (words in yellow on the left side of the package) that stated: NEW RECIPE/GREAT NEW TASTE! MORE PIECES! Plaintiffs have referred to this package as "Trade Dress 2."

B. *Hershey's Objections to Trade Dress 2*

29. Hershey became aware of Trade Dress 2 in the spring of 1995.

30. Hershey objected to Trade Dress 2 because it employed a color combination "dangerously close" to that used on the REESE'S Trade Dress.

31. In an April 27, 1995 letter, Hershey's counsel, Mr. Snyder, wrote to Mars' in-house counsel, expressing Hershey's concerns. Mr. Snyder specifically asked that Mars discontinue the use of the yellow violator.

32. In correspondence in June of 1995, Mars indicated its plans to remove the yellow violator, but reserved the right to use yellow violators in the future. Hershey similarly reserved the right to challenge such use by Mars in the future.

33. Subsequently, Mars removed the yellow violator. Plaintiffs have referred to the altered package, after removal of the violator, as "Trade Dress 3."

C. *Mars' PTO Application and the Parties' Negotiations Regarding Same*

34. On October 3, 1995, the Patent and Trademark Office ("PTO") published a notice that Mars had filed an appli-cation to register its Trade Dress 3, but describing the colors broadly as "orange" (for the background color) and brown (for the M&M mark).

35. Hershey was concerned that, because Mars did not limit the shade of colors referred to in its PTO application, the application would, if granted, allow Mars to use in the future a shade of orange similar to that used on the Reese's trade dress. Hershey communicated these concerns to Mars and demanded that Mars withdraw its PTO application or revise it to limit the shade of orange claimed by Mars. In response, counsel to Mars asserted that the shade of orange used in Mars' Trade Dress 3 was "distinctly different" from that used in the Reese's trade dress. The parties subsequently commenced negotiations of a possible settlement agreement relating to the shades of orange which each would be able to use to "avoid unnecessary litigation."

36. Pending these negotiations, Mars agreed to extend the time within which Hershey could file objections to Mars' PTO Application.

37. The negotiations continued until April 1997, but were unsuccessful. Hershey promptly thereafter filed an objection at the PTO to Mars' PTO Application.

38. Hershey initiated a resumption of the negotiations in early June 1997.

39. During the parties' negotiations, Mars was on full notice that Hershey objected to Mars' claim that Mars could adopt a color scheme similar to that used on the Reese's trade dress.

D. *1996: Mars' New Marketing Strategies*

40. After the relaunch of Peanut Butter M&M's in 1994, the product's performance continued to be disappointing. Sales for 1994 were down and sales for 1995 remained flat despite the "relaunch."

41. Peanut Butter M&M's continued to be a disappointing product for Mars and its survival was in doubt. Mars was in need of a strategy to stabilize sales of Peanut Butter M&M's to prevent further declines which might terminate its viability as a product.

42. In August 1996, a new brand manager was appointed for the Peanut Butter M&M's variety. She was assigned the task of advertising, promotion and packaging for the variety.

43. The brand manager targeted Reese's Pieces as one area where M&M's peanut butter candies could grow.

E. *New Package Design Project*

44. In October 1996, the brand manager prepared a "Packaging Design Brief," a formal document that identifies the objectives of the package redesign project. This document was signed by the brand manager and her superior.

45. Under a section entitled "Legal Constraints," it was written that "Background color of the 'M&M's' Peanut Butter pack cannot get any closer to the shade of orange on Reese's Pieces packs."

46. Mars sent the Packaging Design Brief to its packaging design firm.

47. The brand manager was familiar with the Reese's package and was aware at the time she wrote the Packaging Design brief that something had gone on between Hershey and Mars regarding the color orange.

48. The legal constraint on the Package Design Brief was subsequently removed. Under the section entitled "Review Packaging Brief," the brand manager wrote "Note amendments-removal of legal constraint on color of Peanut Butter package." The packaging design firm was made aware of the removal.

49. Mars adopted the shade of background orange for its current trade dress for M&M's Peanut Butter candy to copy the orange background of the Reese's trade dress.

50. Mars began making commercial use in commerce of the new Peanut Butter M&M's package, the trade dress at issue in this case, in late June 1997.

51. The new package was distributed on a rolling basis, gradually replacing the prior package.

52. Plaintiffs learned of the trade dress at issue around October 25, 1997, and filed this suit on November 10, 1997.

THE CURRENT M&M'S PEANUT BUTTER TRADE DRESS AND ITS CONTRAST WITH THE ABBREVIATED REESE'S TRADE DRESS

53. The current M&M's peanut butter trade dress (although Mars may vary it from time to time) uses the same orange background as used by Hershey in its Reese's trade dress, a brown M&M's logo slightly off center to the left of the package, cascading M&M's candies on the right of the package and a tannish yellow lozenge keylined in brown containing the words "Peanut Butter" in brown.

54. The current M&M's peanut butter trade dress does not use certain design elements that Hershey uses on its complete Reese's trade dress. It does not use: yellow letters, the Reese's name, slanted lettering for the M&M's trademark, cursive script lettering, brown keylining around the M&M's logo, a brown peanut butter cup design and it does not use a brown bar of any kind with yellow letters. The M&M's package uses a tannish yellow flavor lozenge and Reese's package does not.

DURATION AND EXTENT OF USE OF THE REESE'S TRADE DRESS

55. With the exception of the sawtoothed bar representing a peanut butter cup, the Reese's trade dress has been used for more than half a century, since 1947 or earlier, in connection with Reese's peanut butter cup candy.

56. This form of the Reese's trade dress was first used by the H.B. Reese Candy Company, which initially sold Reese's Peanut Butter Cups, and Hershey has continued this use since it acquired the H.B. Reese Candy Company in the 1960s. The sawtoothed bar first appeared in about 1974.

57. Hershey uses the Reese's trade dress with modifications on numerous products in addition to Reese's peanut butter cups. These include: Reese's Pieces candy; Reese's Crunchy Cookie Cups candy; Reese's Nutrageous candy; Reese's Peanut Butter Chips; Reese's Shell Ice Cream Topping; Reese's Sprinkles and Reese's Peanut Butter. The same orange color pervades all of the Reese's confectionery products.

58. Hershey sells hundreds of millions of dollars of products under the Reese's trade dress annually. Estimated factory sales to trade customers of Reese's peanut butter cups alone in 1997 totaled over $450 million; Hershey's estimated factory sales of all products bearing the Reese's trade dress during the same period totaled over $600 million.

59. Hershey's estimated retail sales of its products bearing the Reese's trade dress in 1997 totaled over $800 million.

60. Since 1990, Hershey's estimated factory sales of goods bearing the Reese's trade dress have exceeded $4 billion. Since 1990, Hershey's estimated retail sales of goods bearing the Reese's trade dress have exceeded $5.2 billion.

61. The Reese's peanut butter cup is currently the number one selling candy product in grocery stores. Reese's peanut butter cups have been among the top handful of all confectionery products in the United States for a number of years. In each year from 1990 to 1997, estimated retail sales of Reese's peanut butter cups alone totaled $400 million or more.

62. In addition to the many products bearing the Reese's trade dress that Hershey sells, other companies use a form of that trade dress under license from Hershey in marketing their own products. These include: Reese's Peanut Butter Puffs cereal, which is sold by General Mills; Reese's Peanut Butter Cups Ice Cream, which is sold by Friendly's; and Breyer's Good Humor ice cream that also contains pieces of Reese's Peanut Butter Cups.

DURATION AND EXTENT OF ADVERTISING AND PUBLICITY FOR THE REESE'S TRADE DRESS

63. Advertisements featuring some form of the Reese's trade dress have been printed and disseminated for decades, since at least as early as 1954.

64. As early as the 1960s, Hershey circulated print advertising alerting consumers to "Look for Reese's Peanut Butter Cups wherever candy is sold, in the familiar orange wrapper" and to "Look for the bright orange pack."

65. In addition, Hershey's television advertisements close with a shot of the candy package displaying the Reese's trade dress. Hershey's current television advertising campaign, which runs on all of the national networks and many independent stations, actually opens with a large screen in the shade of orange used in the Reese's trade dress, with elements of yellow and brown, and closes with a package shot and the orange background again.

66. The Reese's trade dress also features prominently in magazine advertising for Reese's peanut butter cups candy. For example, certain of Hershey's ads are set against a field of the bright orange color used in the Reese's trade dress, with yellow and brown elements.

67. Other advertising and promotional materials for the Reese's products also feature the Reese's trade dress. These include billboard advertisements displaying a massive field of orange and point of sale materials, such as cardboard cards placed on shelves at retail establishments.

68. Hershey devotes millions of dollars to advertising for the Reese's products each year. For example, during the period from 1985 to 1997, Hershey spent at least

$5 million on advertising per year for Reese's peanut butter cups alone. Hershey spent approximately $23 million in advertising for Reese's products in 1997, and has an advertising budget for the same amount in 1998. Since 1990 alone, Hershey has spent more than $121 million in advertising on Reese's products.

CHANNELS OF TRADE IN WHICH THE REESE'S TRADE DRESS IS USED

69.   The Reese's peanut butter cups product bearing the complete Reese's trade dress is sold nationwide.
70.   The complete Reese's trade dress in some modified form appears on products marketed in broad classes of trade to consumers of all ages. Reese's products are sold in grocery stores, drug stores, mass merchandise stores, vending machines, concession stands, theaters, and by fund raisers. The greatest volume of Reese's peanut butter cups is sold in grocery stores.

WHETHER THE REESE'S TRADE DRESS IS REGISTERED

71.   Plaintiffs have obtained a trademark registration with the U.S. Patent and Trademark Office for a mark that includes the complete Reese's trade dress as well as the word "REESE'S." (Registration No. 1,574,070).

PLAINTIFF'S SURVEY EVIDENCE

DR. JACOBY'S SURVEY

72.   Jacob Jacoby, Ph.D. designed, conducted and testified with respect to the plaintiff's survey evidence.
73.   The survey used respondents nationwide and attempted to determine (i) whether the abbreviated Reese's trade dress had achieved secondary meaning; (ii) whether the abbreviated Reese's trade dress is famous; and (iii) whether the current M&M's peanut butter trade dress is diluting the abbreviated Reese's trade dress.
74.   Dr. Jacoby surveyed consumers of (i) candy containing chocolate, peanuts, almonds or peanut butter in a sugar-coated shell; (ii) chocolate and peanut butter candies; or (iii) other kinds of peanut butter candies. Dr. Jacoby surveyed two distinct groups of such candy consumers.
75.   To conduct the survey, Dr. Jacoby created two stimuli, a representation of the abbreviated Reese's trade dress and a representation of the M&M's peanut butter trade dress at issue. The stimuli depicted their respective colors, as well as the proportion, arrangement and juxtaposition of those colors. The trade name "Reese's" was deleted and the sawtoothed top of the peanut butter cup shape which appears below the word mark was modified to a rectangular shape. The "M&M's" logo and the design mark consisting of "lentils" or "cascading M&M's" were deleted from the M&M's peanut butter stimulus. The lozenge beneath the "M&M's" logo was retained in the representation of the M&M's peanut butter package.

76.   One group was shown the Reese's stimulus and the other the M&M's stimulus.
77.   Both groups were also shown representations of six other brands; specifically, Snickers, Butterfingers, Nestle Crunch, Skor, Goldenberg's Peanut Chews and Milka. Milka is sold only in Europe. As a control, the two groups were also shown a representation of an "inverted Snickers" package, a package with all the design elements of a Snickers but with different colors than the actual Snickers package.
78.   In all of the representations, including the two test representations and all seven comparison representations, the designation "BRAND X" (in uppercase, slightly slanted block letters) was used in place of the word marks or brand names in the colors of the real words, and repeating letters "ABC" were used to replace other textual elements.
79.   The Reese's stimulus preserved the symmetrical pattern of the actual Reese's package; the "Brand X" logo was centered, where it would be on the real package. The logo was the same size, its type style was slanted, and the number of letters in Brand X equaled the number of letters in "Reese's."
80.   The Mars stimulus did not have certain identifying characteristics present on the real M&M's peanut butter package. It substituted a slanted Brand X logo for the upright two-letter M&M's logo. It did not have the cascading M&M's candy pieces, which normally appear on the right side of the package. In the absence of the M&M's, the Brand X logo was not asymmetrical but symmetrical, centered on the stimulus rather than slightly off to the left.
81.   Certain identifying characteristics were left on the comparison brands. The Milka stimulus retained all graphic illustrations and design elements of the actual package, including an illustration of a cow in the exact same form and location as on the commercial package. The Goldenberg's Peanut Chews representation retained a blue star in the same shape and location along with the words "bite size" inside the star. The Skor stimulus did not retain the picture of the candy bar that appears on the left hand side of the commercial package. However, the Brand X logo on that stimulus remained asymmetrical; it was not centered so that it would fill the space that would have been occupied by that picture.
82.   The objective of the survey with respect to one group of respondents was to determine whether the Reese's trade dress had achieved secondary meaning and fame. The objective of the survey with respect to the second group of respondents was to test the impact of the M&M's peanut butter color scheme contained on the current trade dress (the trade dress at issue).
83.   In the case of both groups of respondents, an interviewer first asked a series of questions in a "screener" to confirm that the individuals qualified as consumers of the relevant products and met other standard criteria for participation in such surveys. The interviewers then explained the procedure and asked a series of questions with respect to each of the representations of packages which were presented in random order. They were asked, "If you think you know, what brand of candy comes in this package?" After asking this question with respect to each of the representations, the interviewer questioned each respondent again

with respect to each of the representations of packages to determine the reason for the answers to the first question. Specifically, the interviewer asked, "What, in particular makes you think it is (brand previously named)?"

84. The survey was conducted in 19 geographically dispersed markets spread across the four U.S. Census Regions.

85. The survey results with respect to the representation of the Reese's trade dress were as follows: 94% of the respondents identified the Reese's stimulus as Reese's and only Reese's, and slightly less than 88% of those respondents indicated color as the reason for the Reese's identification; two respondents misidentified products other than the M&M's product as the Reese's trade dress and indicated color as the basis for the misidentification.

86. With respect to the M&M's stimulus, the results were as follows: 7% correctly identified the representation of the M&M's peanut butter package as M&M's, 51% misidentified it as Reese's and slightly less than 49% indicated color as the reason for the misidentification.

87. Eighty-eight % correctly identified the Butterfinger representation, 81% correctly identified the Snickers representation, 15% correctly identified the Skor representation, 6% correctly identified the Goldenberg's peanut chews representation and 0% correctly identified the Milka representation.

88. With respect to the representations used with both groups for comparison purposes: there were only two respondents who identified any of the comparison representations as Reese's based on color.

89. On the basis of the survey results, Dr. Jacoby formed the opinion (i) that the Reese's trade dress has achieved a high degree of secondary meaning; (ii) that the high degree of secondary meaning establishes that the Reese's trade dress is indeed famous; and (iii) that the M&M's peanut butter color scheme is dilutive of the Reese's trade dress.

90. The stimuli were shuffled before being presented to each respondent. Therefore, one or both of the Milka and Goldenberg's stimulus was shown to at least 2/3's of the respondents in the M&M's group before the M&M's stimulus. The presence of design elements on these stimuli would suggest to respondents that corresponding design elements on other stimuli would be retained if they existed. Thus, when exposed to the M&M's stimulus they might incorrectly understand that that package had no design elements.

91. The Skor stimuli would also have been shown to at least 1/2 of the respondents prior to the M&M's stimulus, thus improperly suggesting that the Mars stimulus was an accurate portrayal of a centered brand name rather than the asymmetric logo that M&M's really used.

92. Dr. Jacoby's study provides no evidence that the ability of the real Reese's package to serve as a unique identifier of the Reese's goods has been weakened or lessened because the public now associates that real package with M&M's.

DR. ROSS' PILOT SURVEY

93. In rebuttal of the defendant's critique of the Jacoby survey, plaintiff introduced a pilot survey or pretest conducted by Ivan Ross, Ph.D. which counsel for plaintiff commissioned in advance of this litigation, once again, to address (i) whether the Reese's trade dress had achieved secondary meaning; (ii) whether the Reese's trade dress is famous; and (iii) whether the M&M's trade dress at issue is diluting the Reese's trade dress, and other issues.

94. Dr. Ross surveyed consumers of "candy." His survey was not limited to consumers of peanut or peanut butter candy or candy sold in a candy shell.

95. Dr. Ross surveyed three separate groups of candy consumers with about 30 persons to a group. Each group viewed a single representation of a candy package, either (i) the Reese's trade dress; (ii) the color scheme of the M&M's trade dress at issue; or (iii) a previous version of the M&M's peanut butter color scheme with a reddish background which was used when the product was first introduced in 1988 until about 1994.

96. Dr. Ross also employed representations of the packages which removed all source identifying indicia other than color and the arrangement, proportion and juxtaposition of colors. In doing so, Dr. Ross substituted a series of four "X"s, i.e., "XXXX," appearing in standard type style (without any slant or other stylization) for the brand names to represent the colors utilized in the actual brand names.

97. In his screening questions, Dr. Ross used the word "candy" only, not "peanut" or "peanut butter," to identify appropriate respondents. He thus interviewed respondents who had eaten any type of candy, not just peanut butter candy.

98. Dr. Ross' survey results with respect to the Reese's trade dress representation indicated that 91% of the respondents identified that representation with Reese's products (either alone or together with other products) and 81% of the respondents identified the representation with Reese's products exclusively. Dr. Ross' results with respect to the representation of the M&M's trade dress at issue indicated a 6% correct identification of the package and a 53% misidentification of the package as Reese's.

99. On the basis of the survey results, Dr. Ross concluded: (i) that the Reese's trade dress has achieved a high degree of secondary meaning; (ii) that the high degree of secondary meaning establishes that the Reese's trade dress is famous; and (iii) that the color scheme of the M&M's trade dress at issue is dilutive of the Reese's trade dress.

100. Dr. Ross' survey is an insufficient basis on which to enjoin Mars' use of the current trade dress.

OTHER TRADE DRESS ASPECTS OF THIS CASE

101. Even were it true that the colors orange or yellow or brown were functional, the combination of those colors in the particular manner represented by the Reese's trade dress that creates the unique overall appearance achieved by that combination is not functional.

102. The color orange does not function to communicate peanut butter flavor.

103. The actual color of peanut butter is a shade of brown or tan, not orange.

104. The color orange appears on the packages of various food products on the market that contain no peanut butter flavor.
105. The packaging of some peanut butter candies and peanut butter products does not have the color orange.
106. There are at least several examples of trade dress similar to the abbreviated Reese's trade dress in the food industry alone.

NONSURVEY EVIDENCE BEARING ON DILUTION

107. The parties' marks are not similar. Looking at only the colors and their juxtaposition on the dress, the plaintiff uses a bright yellow for its trade name, keylined in brown, with a brown rectangular bar underneath with yellow lettering in the bar. The defendant uses a solid brown for its logo, not yellow with brown keylining, and the logo extends over a different area of the package. Its lozenge reverses the colors of the Reese's rectangular bar and uses a tannish yellow.
108. The consumers are not sophisticated. The parties' products are inexpensive, and targeted to children between the ages of 8 and 17 years of age.
109. The Reese's trade dress is highly renowned by the relevant consuming public.
110. The M&M's logo is also highly renown but was not the subject of this motion.
111. Mars developed the trade dress at issue to mimic the background orange on the Reese's trade dress.

CONCLUSIONS OF LAW

1. The abbreviated Reese's trade dress is not famous or distinctive under the federal or Pennsylvania dilution laws.
2. The M&M's peanut butter color scheme does not dilute the abbreviated Reese's trade dress.
3. Hershey has not demonstrated a likelihood of success on the merits, an essential factor to obtain preliminary injunctive relief.

DISCUSSION

* * * *

STANDARD FOR GRANTING A PRELIMINARY INJUNCTION

Hershey seeks a preliminary injunction, so it must satisfy the following standard:

> A preliminary injunction is appropriate when a party demonstrates the following: (1) that he is likely to suffer irreparable injury in the absence of injunctive relief; [and] (2) that he is likely to prevail on the merits. In addition, the district court may consider the injunction's effect on the adverse party and other interested parties, as well as the general public interest.

* * * We will address the likelihood of success on the merits by examining the strength of the plaintiff's dilution claim.

THE REESE'S TRADE DRESS AND ARGUMENTS AGAINST PROTECTABILITY

The parties dispute what should be included in the Reese's trade dress. We must therefore specify the exact nature of the dress, or the portions of it, that the plaintiff can protect before analyzing the dilution claim.

As the defendant points out, in most cases, the Reese's Peanut Butter Cup trade dress would consist of its overall appearance, including all the elements of the dress. * * *

Thus, the trade dress could be described as a particular shade of background orange, the Reese's logo (its trade name in a slanted handwritten style in bright yellow with brown "keylining;" i.e., the yellow letters outlined in brown) and a brown bar with a sawtoothed top (imitating in two dimensions the top edge of a peanut butter cup) directly underneath the logo with the bar containing the message in bright yellow letters "2 peanut butter cups." This is the complete Reese's trade dress.

However, the plaintiff asserts that certain portions of this trade dress, the abbreviated trade dress, have achieved distinction in their own right and are therefore entitled to trade dress protection. They maintain that this trade dress "consists of a unique shade of orange as the principal element in combination with and in juxtaposition to the colors yellow and brown, in an arrangement creating a distinctive overall appearance." Contrary to the defendant's contention, Hershey asserts it is not protecting the mere use of these colors on the package but the "particular *arrangement* . . . including the relative proportions of each color, the placement of each color on the package and the juxtaposition of each color in contact with the others."

This description of the trade dress omits the trade name, the slanted handwritten style of the trade name, the sawtoothed top of the brown bar, and the words inside the bar. The defendant asserts that the plaintiff cannot abbreviate the trade dress in this fashion, that Hershey must include all the elements of the dress for the purpose of its dilution claim.

We disagree with the defendant. * * *

[T]rade dress must be treated like a trademark for the purposes of the Lanham Act. * * * A certain combination of colors is protectable. * * * As the Seventh Circuit stated, a trademark:

> need not be the name of the brand; it need not even be a word; it can be a slogan, a symbol, a combination of words and symbols, an ornamental feature, a distinctive shape, or something else intended to remind the consumer of the brand.

In the instant case, the plaintiff asserts that "something else" besides its complete trade dress has come to signify its brand to the consuming public. We cannot say as a matter of law that it should be precluded from trying to protect this particular combination of elements as a mark.

Mars has also argued that the trade dress is not protectable because the colors are functional in that they distinguish the product and they stimulate appetite.

Functional elements are not protectable. However, the overall combination of features may be nonfunctional and thus protectable. The plaintiff seeks to protect not just the colors orange, brown and yellow, but peculiar shades of these colors in the combination found on its trade dress. We therefore reject the defendant's argument.

THE DILUTION CLAIM

A. *Fame*

As noted above, [the federal Dilution Act] lists certain factors we must consider on the fame element of a blurring claim.

1. Factor A, the degree of inherent or acquired distinctiveness of the mark, and Factor F, the degree of recognition of the mark in the trading areas and channels of trade used by the marks' owner and the person against whom the injunction is sought.

The plaintiff has combined these factors for analysis and we will follow its lead. To support its trade dress's claim of distinctiveness and recognition by candy consumers, the plaintiff relies on the nationwide survey it commissioned from Professor Jacob Jacoby of New York University. Using a stimulus that deleted the Reese's trade name and certain other aspects of its trade dress, so that the portions of its trade dress at issue in this case could be tested, Professor Jacoby found that 94% of those surveyed recognized it. Based on these results, Dr. Jacoby testified that in his opinion the abbreviated Reese's trade dress has achieved a high degree of secondary meaning and that it is famous.

In opposition, the defendant attacks the stimulus used to test the trade dress. Mars contends that the stimulus, in addition to the colors as they appear on the Reese's peanut butter cup package, used other elements of the trade dress. These purportedly included using "Brand X," which had the same number of letters as in Reese's, slanting Brand X at the same angle as Reese's and using almost the same script style for Brand X as Reese's, putting the Brand X in the same location as it appears on a real Reese's package, and reproducing the sawtoothed bar as a rectangular form of the same size and color. Mars contends that these additional elements meant that the stimulus did not test at all for the claimed

trade dress and gave the survey respondents additional clues for the source of the dress.

Second, Mars relies on the results for the stimulus used to represent the M&M's peanut butter trade dress. Since this stimulus left off certain specific elements of that trade dress, the cascading M&M's on the right side of the package and the geometric shape of the M&M's logo itself, the defendants contend that it is a truer test of the abbreviated Reese's trade dress, not the M&M's dress. Only 49% of the respondents surveyed for the Mars stimulus identified it as Reese's. Mars contends that this is not a sufficient percentage for fame or distinctiveness, as opined by Dr. Jacoby.

We disagree with both of the defendant's arguments. Its first argument erroneously asserts that the Reese's stimulus incorporates other elements of the trade dress. A review of the stimulus reveals the defendant's error. The slant is simply not important and using "Brand X" is proper because it roughly equals the space taken up by the trade name. Otherwise, the stimulus does not use the same script style nor does it have the sawtoothed illustration of a brown peanut butter cup.

The second argument erroneously assumes that Hershey is testing merely for the combination of colors. It is not; the colors must correspond to their placement on the trade dress. The M&M's stimulus does not have the same correspondence and cannot be used to defeat the results of testing the more accurate stimulus.

Hence, we conclude that the Hershey's trade dress has satisfied Factor A and F for assessing fame. The dress has acquired distinctiveness and it is recognized by purchasers of both Hershey and Mars products.

2. Factor B: the duration and extent of use of the mark in connection with the goods or services with which the mark is used.

The defendant does not attempt to contest this factor, and it is easily satisfied. [A] portion of the Reese's trade dress, the background orange and the brown keylined yellow, has been in use for half a century. Hershey's factory sales of goods bearing the Reese's trade dress or a modified version of it were approximately $628 million in 1997 and have exceeded $4 billion since 1990, and estimated retail sales since 1990 are more than $5.2 billion. The Reese's peanut butter cups, on which the trade dress is principally used, has been among the top handful of confectionery products in the United States in recent years, and for many years has been the number one or two selling confectionery item in this country.

3. Factor C: the duration and extent of advertising and publicity of the mark.

To satisfy this factor, plaintiff points out that it has spent more than $120 million nationwide advertising its Reese's products since 1990 alone. Hershey argues that, since these advertisements stress the trade dress, frequently including reproductions of the package for the Reese's peanut butter cups, its advertising expenditures support a finding that its mark is famous.

In opposition, the defendant contends that mere advertising expenditures alone, without an advertising strategy calling attention to the trade dress, is insufficient.

We do not believe that the advertisements must call attention to the dress but do believe that this factor is not especially strong here. It is true that the recent print advertisements feature the dress, but they strongly emphasis the background orange, not the overall color scheme since the orange is used as the background of the advertisements. Additionally, the earlier print ads specifically call attention to the orange package. In these circumstances, the plaintiff's advertisements satisfy factor C, but weakly.

4. Factor D: the geographical extent of the trading area in which the mark is used.

This factor favors the plaintiff. The defendant does not contest that the mark appears on Hershey's products nationwide.

5. Factor E: the channels of trade for the goods or services with which the mark is used.

This factor favors the plaintiff. The mark appears on Hershey's products wherever candy is sold.

6. Factor G: the nature and extent of use of the same or similar marks by third parties.

The defendant argues that this factor does not favor the plaintiff because numerous third-party food companies use marks that are similar to the Reese's abbreviated trade dress by employing a similar combination of the colors orange, brown, and yellow.

[Hershey argues that] it is not sufficient for the defendant merely to point out third-party uses of certain elements of the contested trade dress. Hershey contends that Mars must also establish that such third-party use confuses consumers as to source. * * *

We reject the plaintiff's argument. * * * [B]ecause we deal here with [dilution] and the statutory criteria for determining fame, we need only follow the statute, and if it simply requires us to determine the nature and extent of the use of the same or similar marks by third parties, we need not go further and determine confusion. * * *

* * * *

7. Factor H: whether the mark was registered under the Act of March 3, 1881, or the Act of February 20, 1905, or on the principal register.

The Reese's abbreviated trade dress is not federally registered. Federal registration is not a requirement to protect a mark, but a failure to register counts against a finding of fame. A person would be expected to register a famous mark.

WEIGHING THE FACTORS

Factors A, B, D, E and F favor the plaintiff. Factor C does so, but weakly. Factors G and H favor the defendant.

As noted above, however, we do not consider the fame analysis to be a mere arithmetical exercise. We would expect most businesses hoping to succeed under the federal dilution act to be able to satisfy factors A, B, C, D, E and F. Many companies doing business nationwide should be able to.

The important factors for us are G and H. The trade dress Hershey seeks to protect here, a particular combination of orange, brown and yellow, is similar to enough third-party marks in the food industry that we hesitate to preliminarily enjoin Mars' use of the color scheme on its M&M's peanut butter dress. Despite the evidence from the consumer survey, since plaintiff is not relying on its trade name, logo, and sawtoothed bar, the dress does not seem worthy of protection as famous.

Factor H is also significant because Hershey has registered its complete trade dress and has attempted to register its background orange but has never attempted to register the trade dress at issue here.

We conclude that the abbreviated Reese's trade dress at issue in this case has not been shown to be famous and Hershey has failed to establish the first element of its dilution claim.

B. *Assuming that Fame Had Been Established, Whether Mars' Use Causes Dilution.*

We will assume for the purpose of further analysis that plaintiff established the fame of its trade dress. We proceed to examine whether it has satisfied the remaining elements of a dilution claim. The plaintiff relies on . . . the *Mead Data Central* six-factor test.

* * * *

2. **The Mead Data Central Six-Factor Test.**

To reiterate, the *Mead Data Central* six-factor test is as follows:

1) similarity of the marks
2) similarity of the products covered by the marks
3) sophistication of consumers
4) predatory intent

5) renown of the senior mark
6) renown of the junior mark

As noted above, some commentators have questioned the relevance of all of these factors to a dilution claim. In our view, only the second factor is irrelevant. While the quintessential example of dilution is the use of famous mark on a product not made by the trademark holder, dilution can apply to competitors, as the federal and state statutes make clear, so whether the products are similar or not adds nothing to the analysis. We turn then to the remaining factors.

Under the first criterion, the marks need not be identical, but they should be substantially similar, and "the more similar the marks, the higher the likelihood of dilution." *Mead Data Central*, 875 F.2d at 1035.

[T]he defendant argues that the marks are not substantially similar because the real trade dress of the Reese's Peanut Butter Cup and the Mars' peanut butter M&M's must be compared, not just the elements that the plaintiff claims make up a distinctive trade dress on their own. * * *

[T]he defendant argues that:

Here the parties' *real* packages are distinctly different, the impressions conveyed by the combination of the respective logos, the quite different names or marks, the different graphics, including the cultural icons of the M&M's® candy pieces and/or M&M's® Characters preclude a finding of similarity.

Consistent with its approach of avoiding the logos and concentrating only on the colors and their relative positions on the trade dress, the plaintiff asserts that the marks are very similar:

sophisticated testing found the principal color of both packages to be virtually the same color [orange]. Both parties' trade dresses also employ brown, which is in direct contact with the orange background. Moreover, the Reese's trade name is written in yellow letters key-lined in brown; the "lozenge" on the Mars' package is similarly yellow and is similarly key-lined in brown. Indeed, both packages include the contrasting colors of yellow and brown in an oblong shape centered beneath the brand name. On both packages, the orange background extends to the edges of the rectangular face of the package, with no border or other outlining.

Examining the complete trade dress is an important part of the analysis of an infringement claim . . . because consumer confusion as to the source of the product is an essential element of that claim. Thus, if trade names and logos identify the source, and do so prominently enough, there can be no confusion.

Assuming that we were correct in deciding that a trade dress claim can be based on something less than the complete trade dress, it is more difficult to discern what purpose examining the trade names and logos would have in a dilution case. Confusion is not an element of a dilution cause of action. In

the dilution context, the consumer understands there are two different sources; the focus is instead on the consumer's connection of the same mark with the different sources.

Nonetheless, we need not resolve this issue. Even if we look only at the aspects of both trade dresses the plaintiff identifies, we conclude they are not substantially similar. Looking at only the colors and their juxtaposition on the dress, the plaintiff uses a bright yellow for its trade name, keylined in brown, with a brown rectangular bar underneath with yellow lettering in the bar. The defendant uses a solid brown for its logo, not yellow with brown keylining, and the logo extends over a different area of the package. Its lozenge reverses the colors of the Reese's rectangular bar and uses a tannish yellow. The overall look is different.

The only element the trade dresses have in common is the background orange, but the plaintiff is not claiming protection for orange alone on its preliminary injunction motion.

The next criterion is sophistication of the consumers. This factor works differently in a dilution claim than an infringement claim. Because confusion is an element of an infringement claim, the less sophisticated the consumers, the more likely there is infringement. However, the reverse is true in a dilution claim because the more sophisticated the consumers the more likely they will recognize that the mark has become associated with separate sources.

In the instant case the plaintiff argues that its primary customers are in the age group from eight- to 17-years-old, that they are unsophisticated, and that this factor favors Hershey.

However, based on our approach to the sophistication issue, this factor favors the defendant rather than the plaintiff. An unsophisticated consumer would confuse the products, and would not realize that the same mark was being blurred by use on what they knew were two different sources.

The next factor is predatory intent. In the infringement context, the Third Circuit has decided the defendant's intent to copy the plaintiff's trade dress is a weak indicator of infringement. Even this weak indicator does not favor the plaintiff. In the instant case, the defendant did not intend to copy the abbreviated trade dress, just the background orange.

The next factor is renown of the senior mark and it favors the plaintiff. We accept for the purposes of this motion that Dr. Jacoby's survey has established the renown of the plaintiff's mark, defined by the plaintiff as its trade dress in the colors of the Reese's package in a certain juxtaposition, and that this factor favors plaintiff. "The greater the fame of the mark, the greater the likelihood that consumers would make mental associations between the famous mark and similar junior marks."

The final factor is the renown of the junior mark. This factor is relevant to a blurring claim because when both the junior and senior marks are well known, it is easier for the junior mark, as an already recognized source, to adopt certain elements of the senior mark, and thus cause consumers to identify the mark with two different sources. * * * "Presumably, the potential for dilution is greater where the gap in renown is smaller." Here, the plaintiff argues that:

> both the REESE'S Trade Dress and the M&M's logo are famous. Indeed, because of the fame of the M&M's brand name, the color scheme which for decades has been associated uniquely with Reese's will quickly be associated with M&M's as well. Consumers will therefore no longer be able immediately to recognize Reese's products by the color scheme alone. This is the essence of dilution.

The problem with the plaintiff's analysis is that it relies on the M&M's word mark and logo to establish the renown of the M&M's peanut butter trade dress. This is improper in a case where the plaintiff is claiming that something less than that name and logo is blurring its abbreviated trade dress in its colors and their juxtaposition.

We conclude that the plaintiff has failed to satisfy our modified *Mead Data Central* test for blurring.

CONCLUSION

Since the plaintiff has failed to establish a likelihood of success on the merits, an essential element for granting a preliminary injunction, we will deny the motion seeking preliminary injunctive relief.

Questions for Discussion for Case 6.4

1. Was the abbreviated Reese's trade dress famous? What might Hershey have done to have strengthened its legal position?

2. In evaluating the fame of the mark, does the court give too much weight to the final two factors? Mars prevailed on almost all of the other factors.

3. How likely is it that consumers would be confused about these two products if the packaging colors were the same but the products had different logos?

4. Which of the *Mead Data* factors supported a finding of blurring? Which supported a finding of no blurring?

6.5 Anticybersquatting Consumer Protection Act of 1999
Sporty's Farm L.L.C. v. Sportsman's Market, Inc., 202 F.3d 489 (2d. Cir. 2000)

This case originally involved the application of the Federal Trademark Dilution Act ("FTDA") to the Internet. While the case was pending on appeal, however, the Anticybersquatting Consumer Protection Act ("ACPA") was passed and signed into law. That new law applies to this case.

* * * *

BACKGROUND

I

* * * The Internet (or "World Wide Web") is a network of computers that allows a user to gain access to information stored on any other computer on the network. Information on the Internet is lodged on files called web pages, which can include printed matter, sound, pictures, and links to other web pages. An Internet user can move from one page to another with just the click of a mouse.

Web pages are designated by an address called a domain name. A domain name consists of two parts: a top level domain and a secondary level domain. The top level domain is the domain name's suffix. * * * The secondary level domain is the remainder of the address, and can consist of combinations of letters, numbers, and some typographical symbols. To take a simple example, in the domain name "cnn.com," cnn ("Cable News Network") represents the secondary level domain and .com represents the top level domain. Each domain name is unique.

* * * *

For consumers to buy things or gather information on the Internet, they need an easy way to find particular companies or brand names. * * * As a result, companies strongly prefer that their domain name be comprised of the company or brand trademark and the suffix.com.

Until recently, domain names with the .com top level domain could only be obtained from Network Solutions, Inc. ("NSI"). Now other registrars may also assign them. But all these registrars grant such names primarily on a first-come, first-served basis upon payment of a small registration fee. They do not generally inquire into whether a given domain name request matches a trademark held by someone other than the person requesting the name.

Due to the lack of any regulatory control over domain name registration, an Internet phenomenon known as "cybersquatting" has become increasingly common in recent years. Cybersquatting involves the registration as domain names of well-known trademarks by non-trademark holders who then try to sell the names back to the trademark owners. * * *

II

Sportsman's is a mail order catalog company that is quite well-known among pilots and aviation enthusiasts for selling products tailored to their needs. In recent years, Sportsman's has expanded its catalog business well beyond the aviation market into that for tools and home accessories. The company annually distributes approximately 18 million catalogs nationwide, and has yearly revenues of about $50 million. Aviation sales account for about 60% of Sportsman's revenue, while non-aviation sales comprise the remaining 40%.

In the 1960s, Sportsman's began using the logo "*sporty*" to identify its catalogs and products. In 1985, Sportsman's registered the trademark *sporty's* with the United States Patent and Trademark Office. Since then, Sportsman's has complied with all statutory requirements to preserve its interest in the *sporty's* mark. *Sporty's* appears on the cover of all Sportsman's catalogs; Sportsman's international toll free number is 1-800-4sportys; and one of Sportsman's domestic toll free phone numbers is 1-800-Sportys. Sportsman's spends about $10 million per year advertising its *sporty's* logo.

Omega is a mail order catalog company that sells mainly scientific process measurement and control instruments. In late 1994 or early 1995, the owners of Omega, Arthur and Betty Hollander, decided to enter the aviation catalog business and, for that purpose, formed a wholly-owned subsidiary called Pilot's Depot, LLC ("Pilot's Depot"). Shortly thereafter, Omega registered the domain name sportys.com with NSI. Arthur Hollander was a pilot who received Sportsman's catalogs and thus was aware of the *sporty's* trademark.

In January 1996, nine months after registering sportys.com, Omega formed another wholly-owned subsidiary called Sporty's Farm and sold it the rights to sportys.com for $16,200. Sporty's Farm grows and sells Christmas trees, and soon began advertising its Christmas trees on a sportys.com web page. When asked how the name Sporty's Farm was selected for Omega's Christmas tree subsidiary, Ralph S. Michael, the CEO of Omega and manager of Sporty's Farm, explained . . . that

in his own mind and among his family, he always thought of and referred to the Pennsylvania land where Sporty's Farm now operates as *Spotty's farm*. The origin of the name . . . derived from a childhood memory he had of his uncle's farm in upstate New York. As a youngster, Michael owned a dog named Spotty. Because the dog strayed, his uncle took him to his upstate farm. Michael thereafter referred to the farm as Spotty's farm. The name Sporty's Farm was . . . a subsequent derivation.

There is, however, no evidence in the record that Hollander was considering starting a Christmas tree business when he registered sportys.com or that Hollander was ever acquainted with Michael's dog Spotty.

In March 1996, Sportsman's discovered that Omega had registered sportys.com as a domain name. Thereafter, and before Sportsman's could take any action, Sporty's Farm brought this declaratory action seeking the right to continue its use of sportys.com. Sportsman's counterclaimed and also sued Omega . . . for . . . (1) trademark infringement, (2) trademark dilution pursuant to the FTDA, and (3) unfair competition under state law. Both sides sought injunctive relief to force the other to relinquish its claims to sportys.com. While this litigation was ongoing, Sportsman's used "sportys catalogs.com" as its primary domain name.

* * * *

The district court * * * issued an injunction forcing Sporty's Farm to relinquish all rights to sportys.com. And Sportsman's subsequently acquired the domain name. Both Sporty's Farm and Sportsman's appeal. Specifically, Sporty's Farm appeals the judgment insofar as the district court granted an injunction in favor of Sportsman's for the use of the domain name. * * *

III

As we noted above, while this appeal was pending, Congress passed the ACPA. That law was passed "to protect consumers and American businesses, to promote the growth of online commerce, and to provide clarity in the law for trademark owners by prohibiting the bad-faith and abusive registration of distinctive marks as Internet domain names with the intent to profit from the goodwill associated with such marks—a practice commonly referred to as 'cybersquatting'." In particular, Congress viewed the legal remedies available for victims of cybersquatting before the passage of the ACPA as "expensive and uncertain." * * * In short, the ACPA was passed to remedy the perceived shortcomings of applying the FTDA in cybersquatting cases such as this one.

The new act accordingly amends the Trademark Act of 1946, creating a specific federal remedy for cybersquatting. New 15 U.S.C. § 1125(d)(1)(A) reads:

A person shall be liable in a civil action by the owner of a mark, including a personal name which is protected as a mark under this section, if, without regard to the goods or services of the parties, that person—

(i)   has a bad faith intent to profit from that mark, including a personal name which is protected as a mark under this section; and

(ii) registers, traffics in, or uses a domain name that—

(I)   in the case of a mark that is distinctive at the time of registration of the domain name, is identical or confusingly similar to that mark;

(II) in the case of a famous mark that is famous at the time of registration of the domain name, is identical or confusingly similar to or dilutive of that mark; . . .

The Act further provides that "a court may order the forfeiture or cancellation of the domain name or the transfer of the domain name to the owner of the mark," if the domain name was "registered before, on, or after the date of the enactment of this Act." It also provides that damages can be awarded for violations of the Act, but that they are not "available with respect to the registration, trafficking, or use of a domain name that occurs before the date of the enactment of this Act."

DISCUSSION

* * * *

B. "Distinctive" or "Famous"

Under the new Act, we must first determine whether sporty's is a distinctive or famous mark and thus entitled to the ACPA's protection. The district court concluded that sporty's is both distinctive and famous. We agree that sporty's is a "distinctive" mark. As a result, . . . we need not, and hence do not, decide whether sporty's is also a "famous" mark.[10]

* * * *

Distinctiveness refers to inherent qualities of a mark and is a completely different concept from fame. A mark may be distinctive before it has been used—when its fame is nonexistent. By the same token, even a famous mark may be so ordinary, or descriptive as to be notable for its lack of distinctiveness. We have no doubt that sporty's, as used in con-

nection with Sportsman's catalogue of merchandise and advertising, is inherently distinctive. * * *

C. "Identical and Confusingly Similar"

The next question is whether domain name sportys.com is "identical or confusingly similar to" the sporty's mark. * * * [A]postrophes cannot be used in domain names. As a result, the secondary domain name in this case (sportys) is indistinguishable from the Sportsman's trademark (sporty's). We therefore conclude that, although the domain name sportys.com is not precisely identical to the sporty's mark, it is certainly "confusingly similar" to the protected mark under § 1125(d)(1)(A)(ii)(I).

D. "Bad Faith Intent to Profit"

* * * The statute lists nine factors to assist courts in determining when a defendant has acted with a bad faith intent to profit from the use of a mark.[12] * * * The factors are . . . expressly described as indicia that "may" be considered along with other facts.

---

[12] These factors are:

(I)   the trademark or other intellectual property rights of the person, if any, in the domain name;

(II) the extent to which the domain name consists of the legal name of the person or a name that is otherwise commonly used to identify that person;

(III) the person's prior use, if any, of the domain name in connection with the bona fide offering of any goods or services;

(IV) the person's bona fide noncommercial or fair use of the mark in a site accessible under the domain name;

(V)   the person's intent to divert consumers from the mark owner's online location to a site accessible under the domain name that could harm the goodwill represented by the mark, either for commercial gain or with the intent to tarnish or disparage the mark, by creating a likelihood of confusion as to the source, sponsorship, affiliation, or endorsement of the site;

(VI) the person's offer to transfer, sell, or otherwise assign the domain name to the mark owner or any third party for financial gain without having used, or having an intent to use, the domain name in the bona fide offering of any goods or services, or the person's prior conduct indicating a pattern of such conduct;

(VII) the person's provision of material and misleading false contact information when applying for the registration of the domain name, the person's intentional failure to maintain accurate contact information, or the person's prior conduct indicating a pattern of such conduct;

(VIII) the person's registration or acquisition of multiple domain names which the person knows are identical or confusingly similar to marks of others that are distinctive at the time of registration of such domain names, or dilutive of famous marks of others that are famous at the time of registration of such domain names, without regard to the goods or services of the parties; and

(IX) the extent to which the mark incorporated in the person's domain name registration is or is not distinctive and famous within the meaning of subsection (c)(1) of section 43.

15 U.S.C. § 1125(d)(1)(B)(i).

---

[10] In most respects, sporty's meets the rigorous criteria laid out in § 1125(c)(1), requiring both fame and distinctiveness for protection under the FTDA. The mark (1) is sufficiently distinctive (as we discuss in the text), (2) has been used by Sportsman's for an extended period of time, (3) has had millions of dollars in advertising spent on it, (4) is used nationwide, and (5) is traded in a wide variety of retail channels. Moreover, the record does not indicate that anyone else besides Sportsman's uses sporty's, and the mark is, of course, registered with federal authorities.

We hold that there is more than enough evidence in the record below of "bad faith intent to profit" on the part of Sporty's Farm (as that term is defined in the statute) . . . . First, it is clear that neither Sporty's Farm nor Omega had any intellectual property rights in sportys.com at the time Omega registered the domain name. Sporty's Farm was not formed until nine months after the domain name was registered, and it did not begin operations or obtain the domain name from Omega until after this lawsuit was filed. Second, the domain name does not consist of the legal name of the party that registered it, Omega. Moreover, although the domain name does include part of the name of Sporty's Farm, that entity did not exist at the time the domain name was registered.

The third factor, the prior use of the domain name in connection with the bona fide offering of any goods or services, also cuts against Sporty's Farm since it did not use the site until after this litigation began, undermining its claim that the offering of Christmas trees on the site was in good faith. Further weighing in favor of a conclusion that Sporty's Farm had the requisite statutory bad faith intent, as a matter of law, are the following: (1) Sporty's Farm does not claim that its use of the domain name was "noncommercial" or a "fair use of the mark," (2) Omega sold the mark to Sporty's Farm under suspicious circumstances and, (3) as we discussed above, the sporty's mark is undoubtedly distinctive.

The most important grounds for our holding that Sporty's Farm acted with a bad faith intent, however, are the unique circumstances of this case, which do not fit neatly into the specific factors enumerated by Congress but may nevertheless be considered under the statute. We know from the record and from the district court's findings that Omega planned to enter into direct competition with Sportsman's in the pilot and aviation consumer market. As recipients of Sportsman's catalogs, Omega's owners, the Hollanders, were fully aware that sporty's was a very strong mark for consumers of those products. It cannot be doubted, as the court found below, that Omega registered sportys.com for the primary purpose of keeping Sportsman's from using that domain name. Several months later, and after this lawsuit was filed, Omega created another company in an unrelated business that received the name Sporty's Farm so that it could (1) use the sportys.com domain name in some commercial fashion, (2) keep the name away from Sportsman's, and (3) protect itself in the event that Sportsman's brought an infringement claim alleging that a "likelihood of confusion" had been created by Omega's version of cybersquatting. Finally, the explanation given for Sporty's Farm's desire to use the domain name, based on the existence of the dog Spotty, is more amusing than credible. * * *

E. Remedy

Based on the foregoing, we hold that . . . Sporty's Farm violated Sportsman's statutory rights by its use of the sportys.com domain name. * * * The Act permits a court to "order the forfeiture or cancellation of the domain name or the transfer of the domain name to the owner of the mark," for any "domain name[] registered before, on, or after the date of the enactment of [the] Act." That is precisely what the district court did here . . ., when it directed a) Omega and Sporty's Farm to release their interest in sportys.com and to transfer the name to Sportsman's, and b) permanently enjoined those entities from taking any action to prevent and/or hinder Sportsman's from obtaining the domain name. * * * We therefore affirm the district court's grant of injunctive relief.

* * * *

CONCLUSION

The judgment of the district court is AFFIRMED in all particulars.

Questions for Discussion for Case 6.5

1. How does a "distinctive" mark differ from a "famous" one?

2. How similar do you think a domain name has to be to a trademark for the ACPA to apply?

3. How should the courts read the ACPA's "confusing similar" standard? Do you think that the ACPA covers domain name misspellings, which, when looked at plainly, are not confusingly similar?

4. Does the ACPA afford any protection to a person who was the first to register a famous domain name? Is this fair? Why should companies automatically have the rights to domain names when they do not have automatic rights to other forms of identification, such as toll-free telephone numbers?

5. What facts lead the court to conclude that Sporty's Farm had acted in bad faith? Do you agree with this characterization of its behavior?

DISCUSSION QUESTIONS

1. Steinway & Sons, the makers of high-quality pianos, sued a company that produced clip-on beverage can handles under the mark "STEIN-WAY." Under what theory would Steinway & Sons sue? Should Steinway & Sons prevail? *Steinway & Sons v. Robert Demars & Friends*, 210 U.S.P.Q. 954 (C.D. Cal. 1981)

2. Identify each of the following marks as arbitrary or fanciful, suggestive, descriptive, or generic:
   a. "Hard Rock Cafe" for a restaurant/bar
   b. "Raisin Bran" for breakfast cereal
   c. "Coppertone" for sun lotion
   d. "Nyquil" for cold medicine
   e. "Pioneer" for sugar
   f. "Brim" for coffee
   g. "Lite Cola" for a reduced-calorie soft drink

3. In the late 1980s, L'Oreal wanted to introduce a "hair cosmetic" product that gave hair a blue, green, or other vivid color tint. L'Oreal wanted to market the product under the name "Zazu" and began to investigate the availability of this trademark. L'Oreal found out that the mark was in use by a clothing manufacturer and a hair salon, Zazu Hair Design (ZHD). L'Oreal contacted both companies to inquire about their intended use of the mark. L'Oreal paid $125,000 to the clothing manufacturer, which was producing clothing with the mark, for the right to use the mark for its hair cosmetic. However, when L'Oreal asked ZHD if it were producing products with the mark, ZHD informed L'Oreal that it had not yet produced products but was "working on it."

Satisfied that the ZHD state trade name did not prevent its use of the mark, L'Oreal applied for federal registration of the Zazu mark on June 12, 1986, and began advertising and shipping large quantities of product in August 1986. However, in the meantime, ZHD began to develop a line of hair care products under the Zazu name in 1985. During November 1985 and February 1986, ZHD sold two bottles of its new formula to friends and one carton of bottles to another hair salon. These sales were informal, and the product was sold in plain bottles with a ZHD business card taped to the product. ZHD was confident of its line's success and placed a large manufacturing order in late 1985. Additionally, ZHD began selling small quantities of hand-filled and -labeled bottles of the products from its salon in September 1986. ZHD sued to enjoin L'Oreal from using the trademark Zazu and

for damages. What result? *Zazu Designs v. L'Oreal, S.A.*, 979 F.2d 499 (7th Cir. 1992)

4. Jim Henson's popular characters, the Muppets, starred in the movie *Muppet Treasure Island*, in which Henson's production company introduced a new character—a wild boar named Spa'am. Hormel Foods, which manufactures Spam luncheon meat, took offense at its mark being associated with this character. Hormel sued Henson's production company to enjoin the use of the mark. Should the court prohibit the production company from using the mark? Why, or why not? *Hormel Foods Corp. v. Jim Henson Prods., Inc.*, 73 F.3d 497 (2d Cir. 1996)

5. In 1991, Shark Products began the manufacture and sale of a hair care product under the name "Miracle Gro." Stern's, which has been producing the Miracle-Gro line of plant foods since 1951 and had federally registered the mark, objected to Shark's use of the mark. In prelitigation negotiations, Shark assured Stern's that it would modify its packaging of the Miracle Gro hair products. Although Shark did modify the packing of its hair care products, it did not remove the words "Miracle Gro" from the product. Stern's sued for trademark infringement and dilution. Which *Polaroid* and *Mead Data* factors would the court consider most relevant? What result? *Stern's Miracle-Gro Prods. v. Shark Prods., Inc.*, 823 F. Supp. 1077 (S.D.N.Y. 1993)

6. Tour 18 is a golf course that replicates distinctive holes from some of the world's most famous golf courses. The course offers replicas from 16 different golf courses including Pinehurst, Pebble Beach, and Sea Pines' Harbour Town course. Tour 18's promotional material, tee markers, course signs, and dining room menus all make reference to the more well-known courses. For example, Tour 18 refers to the replica of Harbour Town's famous 18th hole as the "Lighthouse Hole," which is also what golfers call Harbour Town's hole. In addition, Tour 18's dining room offers "Pebble Beach" French toast and "Pinehurst" tuna salad. Tour 18 does use a disclaimer that notes that none of the replicas are sponsored or endorsed by the more famous golf courses. Nevertheless, Pebble Beach, along with several other courses, objects to the copying of its hole designs and the use of its registered service marks. It sues for trademark and trade dress infringement as well as trademark dilution. What result? *Pebble Beach Co. v. Tour 18 I, Ltd.*, 155 F.3d 526 (5th Cir. 1998)

7. When the New Kids on the Block were a popular musical group, several newspapers and magazines ran polls in which fans were asked to vote for their favorite member of the group. The ads for the polls contained copy such as "Who is the most popular New Kid?" Fans called 900 numbers to vote, and the companies running the polls charged a fee per vote. The New Kids on the Block took exception to the use of their name in such a moneymaking enterprise and sued for trademark infringement. What result? *New Kids on the Block v. News America Pub., Inc.*, 971 F.2d 309 (9th Cir. 1992)

8. Harley-Davidson motorcycles are often called "hogs." Indeed, some dictionaries even define "hog" as a motorcycle, especially a large one. While Harley-Davidson had mixed feelings about its products being referred to as a "hog," with the unsavory Hell's Angels image that the term conjures, it also recognized the marketing potential of the term. As a result, Harley-Davidson finally registered the term "hog" as trademark for its motorcycles in 1990.

Ronald Grottanelli, like many motorcycle enthusiasts, had used the term "hog" when referring to Harley-Davidson motorcycles for many years. In fact, he had been operating a motorcycle repair shop since 1969 under the name "The Hog Farm." In addition, Grottanelli offered products such as Hog Wash, an engine degreaser, and a "Hog Trivia" board game. Harley-Davidson sued for trademark infringement and dilution. What result? *Harley-Davidson, Inc. v. Grottanelli*, 164 F.3d 806 (2d Cir. 1999)

9. Mana Products and Columbia Cosmetics both sell cosmetic products to beauty salons and other retailers. The retailers then label the products with their own names and resell them to the public. One of Mana's products is an unusually shaped black makeup compact; Columbia sells an identical item. Mana claims that the shape and black color of its compact case are protectable trade dress, and it sues Columbia for infringement. Can the color of a compact case be a protectable trade dress? What are the possible consequences if it is? *Mana Prods., Inc. v. Columbia Cosmetics Mfg., Inc.*, 65 F.3d 1063 (2d Cir. 1995)

10. Disc Golf Association (DGA) manufactures equipment for the game of "disc golf." Disc golf is played like normal golf, but with flying discs like Frisbees. The object of the game is to throw the disc into the "hole" in as few attempts as possible. DGA manufactures disc golf "holes," which consist of a target of suspended loose chains that are designed to deflect a thrown disc into a basket below. DGA's patent on this device expired in 1994. Champion Discs, a competitor, subsequently began to make similar disc golf targets. DGA sued for trademark and trade dress infringement. What result? *Disc Golf Assoc., Inc. v. Champion Discs, Inc.* 158 F.3d 1002 (9th Cir. 1998)

CHAPTER 7

Legal Issues Relating to Promotion

Commercial Speech and the Regulation of Advertising

Marketers who wish to advertise their goods or services—and few marketers do not—find themselves faced with an extensive and often bewildering array of state and federal laws regulating their activities. Most of the regulation is designed to protect consumers from false or deceptive advertising, but it does so in widely divergent ways. Some of the laws arise under state common law, some under state or federal statutory law, and some under federal or state agency regulation. Some give the injured consumer the right to sue and recover redress; some give aggrieved competitors the right to sue; and others permit only the government to sue, with redress sometimes going to the government and sometimes to the consumer.

All such laws are constrained by the First Amendment to the U.S. Constitution, however, which protects free speech, including commercial speech. Thus, regulations affecting advertising practices reflect a tension between protecting the advertiser's right to free speech, on the one hand, and the consumer's right to not be misled or deceived, on the other. This chapter first discusses commercial free speech, then examines various forms of state and federal regulation of advertising practices.

Commercial Free Speech

Commercial speech is expression that is related to the economic interests of the speaker and his audience. It is protected under the First Amendment to the U.S. Constitution, which provides in relevant part: "Congress shall make no law . . . abridging the freedom of speech . . . ." The most common form of commercial speech, not surprisingly, is advertising. As Justice Stevens stated in a recent commercial speech case:

> Advertising has been a part of our culture throughout our history. Even in colonial days, the public relied on "commercial speech" for vital information about the market. Early newspapers displayed advertisements for goods and services on their front pages, and town criers called out prices in public squares. Indeed, commercial messages played such a central role in public life prior to the Founding that Benjamin Franklin authored his early defense of a free press in support of his decision to print, of all things, an advertisement for voyages to Barbados.[1]

All speech is not protected under the First Amendment, however; nor does all protected speech receive the same degree of protection. Some speech, such as obscenity, receives no protection at all. At the other end of the spectrum, political speech, which is considered essential to the functioning of a democracy, receives the greatest degree of First Amendment protection from government intrusion.

Until the 1970s, the Supreme Court had ruled that commercial speech was not entitled to protection under the First Amendment. The Court then recognized that such speech is important for the functioning of a free market. In 1976, in *Virginia State Board of Pharmacy v. Virginia Citizens Consumer Council, Inc.,*[2] the Supreme Court reversed its former stance. The Court explained: "[P]eople will perceive their own best interests if only they are well enough informed, and the best means to that end is to open the channels of communication to them rather than close them."[3]

Today, commercial speech is afforded an intermediate level of First Amendment protection. The Supreme Court has determined that commercial speech is entitled to "'a limited measure of protection commensurate with its subordinate position in the scale of First Amendment values,' and is subject to 'modes of regulation that might be impermissible in the realm of noncommercial expression.'"[4] Commercial free speech claims are evaluated under a four-part analysis articulated by the Supreme Court in *Central Hudson Gas & Electric Corp. v. Public Service Commission of New York*[5] in 1980. The *Central Hudson* test asks:

1. Is the speech protected by the First Amendment (i.e., does it concern lawful activity and is it not misleading)?
2. Is the asserted governmental interest in the regulation substantial?
3. Does the regulation directly advance the governmental interest asserted to a material degree?
4. Is the regulation no more extensive than necessary to serve that interest?

In subsequent cases, the Supreme Court has refined the *Central Hudson* test, establishing, for example, that to satisfy the third factor, the government bears the

---

[1] 44 Liquormart, Inc. v. Rhode Island, 517 U.S. 484, 495 (1996).
[2] 425 U.S. 748 (1976). This case involved the constitutionality of a Virginia statute that defined the advertising of prescription drug prices by licensed pharmacists as a form of unprofessional conduct.
[3] 425 U.S. at 770.
[4] Board of Trustees of State University of New York v. Fox, 492 U.S. 469, 477 (1989) (citations omitted).
[5] 447 U.S. 557 (1980).

burden of showing that its regulation will advance its governmental interest "to a material degree."[6] In addition, the Court has clarified that under the fourth factor, the government is not required to employ the least restrictive regulation possible to accomplish its goal, but that it must show a "reasonable 'fit' between the legislature's ends and the means chosen to accomplish those ends."[7]

The Supreme Court's current commercial speech doctrine is not completely settled. A few years ago, the Supreme Court seemed to be stepping back from First Amendment protection of commercial speech. The Supreme Court's 1996 decision in *44 Liquormart, Inc. v. Rhode Island*,[8] however, revived the commercial speech doctrine. The *44 Liquormart* Court reversed a decision of the First Circuit, which had upheld a Rhode Island statute banning the advertising of retail liquor prices. The statute was challenged by in-state and out-of-state liquor vendors who wanted to advertise their prices in Rhode Island. The statute was defended by the State of Rhode Island and by local Rhode Island liquor stores who wished to maintain their prices. They argued that advertising liquor prices would lead to price wars and the lowering of prices, which would then lead to more sales and excessive drinking.

The Supreme Court held that the ban on price advertising was a violation of commercial free speech because it did not directly advance the state's interest in the promotion of temperance and because it was more extensive than necessary to serve that interest. (In short, the state statute failed the third and fourth prongs of the *Central Hudson* test.) Although the Court was unanimous in agreeing that the statute was unconstitutional, the Court could not agree on the reasoning supporting that decision. Ultimately, the Justices issued four separate opinions. Despite the Justices' inability to agree on the proper rationale for striking down the regulation at issue, *44 Liquormart* seems to indicate that the Court will examine the third prong of the *Central Hudson* test carefully and will likely strike down any absolute prohibition on commercial speech that is not closely tailored to protect consumers from false or deceptive information.

See Discussion Cases 7.1, 7.3, 7.4.

Because misleading speech is not protected by the First Amendment, the government may regulate and prohibit advertising that is false, deceptive, or misleading. The government may also prohibit the advertising of illegal activities and may impose time, manner, or place restrictions on advertising. As the following discussion indicates, both the federal and state governments are very active in the regulation of advertising.

Common Law Causes of Action

Theoretically, a consumer who has been injured by false or deceptive advertising could rely upon common law contract or tort causes of action for relief. Realistically, the common law causes of action are less efficacious and thus less used than the statutory and regulatory causes of action. For example, a consumer who has been misled by false advertising could sue for *breach of contract*. The consumer might encounter difficulty in proving the existence of a contract, however, for, as discussed

---

[6] *See* Edenfield v. Fane, 507 U.S. 761, 771 (1993).
[7] *See* Board of Trustees of State University of New York v. Fox, 492 U.S. 469, 480 (1989).
[8] 517 U.S. 484 (1996).

in Chapter 9, the courts generally view advertisements merely as invitations to negotiate, not as offers to enter into a contract on the terms stated in the advertisement.

Similarly, a consumer could sue for the tort of *fraudulent misrepresentation* (also known as *deceit* or *fraud*). To prove fraud, the plaintiff must show that the defendant intentionally misled the plaintiff by making a material misrepresentation upon which the plaintiff relied and that the plaintiff suffered injury as a result of that misrepresentation. The plaintiff must demonstrate that the defendant knew the misrepresentation was false, which can create difficult questions of proof. Furthermore, the misrepresentation must involve a statement of fact, not opinion, which can be a murky distinction in the advertising area.

In addition, the laws of *unfair competition* evolved to prevent false, deceptive, and unauthorized business practices, particularly in the areas of sales and advertising. Unfair competition law is an evolving and expanding field that encompasses a number of different theories used to control improper conduct in the marketplace. The most common of causes of action in this area are (1) the right of publicity, (2) palming off (or passing off), (3) false advertising, and (4) disparagement. All of these causes of action originally started out as state common law torts. Today, the last three (but not the right of publicity) now have federal causes of action arising under the Lanham Act. Although a plaintiff is likely to state a claim under both state and federal law for these actions, federal law is generally regarded as the more important source of protection and relief in most instances.

The right of publicity is discussed next. The remaining three causes of action are discussed below in the context of the federal Lanham Act.

RIGHT OF PUBLICITY

The *right of publicity* "signifies the right of an individual, especially a public figure or celebrity, to control the commercial value and exploitation of his name and picture or likeness and to prevent others from unfairly appropriating this value for commercial benefit."[9] "Commercial," in this context, is generally defined narrowly as being undertaken in the course of advertising or of promoting or selling a product or service, not simply of being part of a business venture or profit-motivated endeavor. Thus, the right of publicity generally does not prohibit the use of an individual's name, picture, or likeness "in news reporting, commentary, entertainment, works of fiction or nonfiction, or in advertising that is incidental to such uses."[10]

The right of publicity is somewhat akin to copyright law, but it differs from copyright law in a very key respect. To be copyrighted, works must exist in a tangible form; the right of publicity, on the other hand, protects the identity and/or persona of an individual and thus protects "intangible" as well as tangible forms of expression, such as a voice or live performance. Where copyright law and the right of publicity overlap, federal copyright law preempts state publicity right law. (Copyright law is discussed in Chapter 2.)

The right of publicity arises under state law and is relatively new, having been first articulated about 50 years ago.[11] About one-half of the states recognize the right of publicity as either a common law or statutory right.[12] In a few states, it arises under both common and statutory law.

---

[9] Presley's Estate v. Russen, 513 F. Supp. 1339 (D.N.J. 1981).
[10] Restatement (Third) of Unfair Competition § 47.
[11] *See* Haelan Labs., Inc. v. Topps Chewing Gum, Inc., 202 F.2d 866 (2d Cir. 1953).
[12] J. T. McCarthy, The Rights of Publicity and Privacy § 6.6 (2000).

How might a plaintiff's identity be appropriated? First, an unauthorized use of a name, likeness, or nickname is clearly not permitted. "Crazylegs Hirsh," for example, a famous football player and team manager, recovered against a cosmetics company that used the name "Crazylegs" to market and promote a shaving cream for women's legs.[13] Similarly, Muhammad Ali recovered against *Playgirl* when the magazine published a drawing of a nude, black man sitting on a stool in a corner of a boxing ring with hands taped and arms outstretched on the ropes, captioned "Mystery Man," but also labeled "The Greatest."[14]

Second, the unauthorized use of phrases associated with the plaintiff is prohibited. Johnny Carson, for example, recovered against a defendant who rented out "Here's Johnny!" portable toilets and advertised itself as "The World's Foremost Comodian."[15]

Third, the unauthorized use of impersonators is prohibited. Bette Midler recovered against Ford Motor Co., who had hired a singer to imitate Midler's famous rendition of "Do You Want to Dance" after Midler had refused to perform in the commercial herself.[16] Tom Waits won a similar suit against Frito-Lay, Inc., and its ad agency for imitating Waits in a radio ad for Salsa Doritos.[17]

In about one-half of the states recognizing this legal right, the right of publicity ceases at death. In the remaining states, the right is considered an economic interest that passes to the heirs at the individual's death. In the states in which it does survive death, it lasts for either the same time as copyright protection extends (typically, the life of the author plus 70 years) or for a specific time period set by the state. The typical remedies for violation of the right of publicity include *preliminary* and/or *permanent injunctions, monetary damages*, and, in extreme cases, *punitive damages*.

Statutory and Regulatory Causes of Action

STATE STATUTES

Aggrieved consumers may sue under state statutory law for injury resulting from deceptive advertising. For example, if the advertising can be construed as creating an express warranty, an injured consumer may sue for breach of express warranty under the Uniform Commercial Code (UCC). (Warranty issues are discussed in Chapter 10.) In addition, approximately 16 states have private attorney general laws that permit consumers to bring suits for deceptive trade practices. In 1995, for example, a class action suit was brought under California law against Kenner Corporation. Kenner had claimed that its Easy Bake Oven allowed children to bake treats in under 10 minutes. The plaintiffs claimed that the toy ovens actually took 29 to 34 minutes to bake the treats. The case was ultimately settled under a confidentiality agreement.[18]

Generally, however, the state statutes are seldom used. Instead, most false or deceptive advertising cases arise under the federal Lanham Act or under regulation

---

[13] Hirsch v. S. C. Johnson & Son, Inc., 280 N.W.2d 129 (Wis. 1979).
[14] Ali v. Playgirl, Inc., 447 F. Supp. 723 (S.D.N.Y. 1978).
[15] Carson v. Here's Johnny Portable Toilets, Inc., 810 F.2d 104 (6th Cir. 1987).
[16] Midler v. Ford Motor Co., 849 F.2d 460 (9th Cir. 1988).
[17] Waits v. Frito-Lay, Inc., 978 F.2d 1093 (9th Cir. 1992).
[18] *See* Jeff Barge, *Advertising Legal Wars Heating Up: Lawsuits Filed Over Pitches for Long-lasting Antacid, Quick-Baking Toy Ovens*, 82 A.B.A. J. 32 (Apr. 1996).

arising under the Federal Trade Commission (FTC) Act. The rest of this chapter focuses primarily on these federal causes of action.

THE LANHAM ACT

In addition to providing for the registration and protection of trademarks (discussed in Chapter 6), the federal Lanham Act[19] forbids false designations of origin and false or misleading descriptions or representations of fact.

The Lanham Act provides a cause of action to competitors (but not consumers) who are injured by false advertising. The purpose of the Lanham Act is to ensure truthfulness in advertising and to prohibit misrepresentations of quality regarding either the advertiser's products or the products of its competitor. Thus, the Act prohibits the use of any false "description or representation" in connection with any goods or services. Many of the causes of action provided by the Lanham Act are also actionable under state law, so often a plaintiff may sue under either or both.

Passing Off

Passing off, also known as *palming off*, occurs when the defendant makes some sort of false representation that misleads consumers into thinking that the defendant's goods or services originate from, are sponsored by, or are affiliated with the plaintiff. Essentially, it is an attempt by the defendant to fool customers into thinking that the defendant's own goods or services are those of a competitor. *Reverse passing off* occurs when the defendant sells the plaintiff's product or service as the defendant's own (see Focus Case 7.1 on page 230).

Passing off can take a number of different forms. The defendant may make a direct false representation, such as telling customers that goods come from the plaintiff when they do not. Passing off can also involve an indirect false representation, such as the defendant showing the customer "samples" that are actually the plaintiff's goods and not its own. Passing off often involves the use of a trademark, trade name, or trade dress that is identical or confusingly similar to a mark, name, or trade dress of a competitor. A single act of the defendant can often be challenged both as passing off and as trademark infringement (discussed in Chapter 6).

Passing off is actionable under both common law and the federal Lanham Act. Remedies available under the common law for passing off include *injunctions* against further passing off and *damages* (measured by plaintiff's loss and/or defendant's profits). *Punitive damages* may also be available in egregious cases. Remedies for passing off under the Lanham Act are the same as the remedies for trademark infringement (discussed in Chapter 6): *preliminary* and/or *permanent injunctions* and *damages*, as well as the possible recovery of *treble damages* and *attorneys fees*.

False Advertising

State and federal laws provide several causes of action for *false advertising*. A plaintiff may sue under state common law for false advertising when a competitor misrepresents the nature or characteristics of her own goods to consumers by making untrue, unsupported, or deceptive claims. The plaintiff must be able to demonstrate, however, that the defendant's false advertising resulted in an actual loss of customers for the plaintiff, which is a difficult burden of proof to meet. If the plaintiff and the defendant are the only competitors in the market, the plaintiff may be able to meet this burden. If there are several competitors, however, the plaintiff

[19] 15 U.S.C. §§ 1051–1129.

Focus Case 7.1

Facts: By-Rite Distributing, Inc., operated and sold self-service soft drink dispensing systems under the name "Carb-A-Drink." By-Rite used the system in some of its own convenience stores and marketed the system to others. The Carb-A-Drink system consisted of a large unit of fountain dispensing equipment, equipped with 10–20 heads dispensing up to 40 flavors of soft drinks. The fountain heads bore the trademarks of the products being dispensed. A customer would obtain an empty two-liter bottle bearing the trademark "CARB-A-DRINK" and would fill the bottle at the dispensing station. The customer was encouraged to return to the store and refill the bottle or other package of his own at the fountain. Thus, customers could and did fill empty bottles containing the trademarks of one soft drink manufacturer with products manufactured by another company. By-Rite also marketed a 6-pack carrying case so that customers could fill and take home a number of bottles at one time. The bottles (and their contents) could remain in the customers' possession for three or more weeks and were often consumed by individuals other than those who purchased the products.

Several major soft drink producers, including The Coca-Cola Company, PepsiCo, Inc., Sunkist Soft Drinks, Inc., and Seven-Up USA, Inc., filed for a preliminary injunction, contending that By-Rite's activities constituted reverse passing off in violation of the Lanham Act.

Decision: The federal trial court agreed, stating: "Although purchasers at a Carb-A-Drink fountain will believe that they are buying the . . . defendants' products because they can see the trademarks on the fountain heads, other users who later drink these beverages at home, at picnics or elsewhere, will see only the CARB-A-DRINK trademark on the bottle, and they may be led to believe that it is a CARB-A-DRINK product. To the extent that they are satisfied with the product, only CARB-A-DRINK will benefit."

The court thus issued a preliminary injunction preventing By-Rite from selling in bottles soft drinks mixed from the defendants' fountain syrups. By-Rite was permitted to sell the products in cups, however. *By-Rite Distributing, Inc. v. The Coca-Cola Co.,* 577 F. Supp. 530 (D. Utah 1983).

---

may well find it impossible to prove that in the absence of the defendant's false advertising customers would have bought from the plaintiff (as opposed to one of the other competitors).

To counter this difficult burden of proof, many states now have statutes prohibiting false advertising. The statutes vary considerably from state to state. Some allow state agencies to sue; some allow consumers to sue; and others allow competitors to sue. The 12 or so states that have adopted the Uniform Deceptive Trade Practices Act (UDTPA) allow any person "likely to be damaged" by the false advertising to sue for injunctive relief.

The federal Lanham Act provides a cause of action for false advertising that is considerably broader than the common law action for false advertising. Section 43(a) of the Act provides:

> Any person who, on or in connection with any goods or services, or any container for goods, uses in commerce any . . . false or misleading description of fact, or false or misleading representation of fact, which . . . in commercial advertising or promotion, misrepresents the nature, characteristics, qualities, or geographic origin of his or her or another person's goods, services, or commercial activities, shall be liable to a civil action by any person who believes that he or she is likely to be damaged by such act.[20]

---

[20] 15 U.S.C. § 1125(a).

Focus Case 7.2

 Facts: Sandoz Pharmaceuticals Corp. brought suit, alleging that representations by Richardson-Vicks, Inc. ("Vicks"), regarding its product, Vicks Pediatric Formula 44, constituted false and deceptive advertising under Section 43(a) of the Lanham Act. Specifically, Sandoz challenged: (1) Vicks's assertion that Pediatric 44 starts to work the instant that it is swallowed, and (2) Vicks's advertising claims that Pediatric 44 is superior to its competitors. Sandoz requested that the court issue a preliminary injunction against Vicks's advertising claims.

Decision: Because Sandoz had not met its burden of showing that the claims were either literally false or misleading to the public, the appellate court affirmed the trial court's denial of Sandoz's request for a preliminary injunction against Vicks. The court noted that "Vicks's advertising claims with regard to Pediatric 44 are based on the effect of certain locally-acting, inert sugary liquids known as 'demulcents,' which operate directly on cough receptors in the recipient's throat and respiratory passages." Vicks had test results that supported, "if only marginally," these claims. The court further noted, however, that "the [Food and Drug Administration (FDA)] has never approved any 'demulcents' as effective for the relief of coughs, and whether Vicks's level of testing could meet the high standards for drug approval set by the FDA is far from certain."

The court went on to point out, however, that in a Lanham Act case, the plaintiff bears the burden of proving that the defendant's claims are false; the defendant need not prove that they are true.

The key distinction between the FTC and Lanham Act plaintiff turns on the burdens of proof and the deference accorded these respective litigants. The FTC, as a plaintiff, can rely on its own determination of deceptiveness. In contrast, a Lanham Act plaintiff must prove deceptiveness in court. * * *

Accordingly, consumer testimony regarding actual deception is not necessary when the FTC claims that an advertisement has the capacity to deceive or mislead the public. * * * A Lanham Act plaintiff, on the other hand, is not entitled to the luxury of deference to its judgment. Consequently, where the advertisements are not literally false, plaintiff bears the burden of proving actual deception by a preponderance of the evidence. Hence, it cannot obtain relief by arguing how consumers could react; it must show how consumers actually do react.

Sandoz failed to show that the claims made by Vicks were literally false. Sandoz also failed to provide consumer surveys indicating whether the claims made were misleading to the public. The court stated: "The law does not presume that consumers assume that all [over-the-counter] drug advertising claims are substantiated. Accordingly, a plaintiff must produce consumer surveys or some surrogate therefor to prove whether consumers expect an advertising claim to be . . . greater than that which the defendant has performed." *Sandoz Pharmaceuticals Corp. v. Richardson-Vicks, Inc.,* 902 F.2d 222 (3d Cir. 1990).

To receive *injunctive relief* under Section 43(a), the plaintiff must show: (1) the defendant made a false or misleading statement of fact in advertising about its own product; (2) the statement actually deceived or had the capacity to deceive a substantial segment of the audience; (3) the deception was material (i.e., it was likely to influence consumers' purchasing decisions); (4) the defendant caused its goods to enter interstate commerce; and (5) the plaintiff was or is likely to be injured as a result. Note that to receive an injunction the plaintiff need not show actual injury— the potential for injury is sufficient (see Focus Case 7.2).

To receive *monetary damages*, the plaintiff must prove that the advertisement was false, that consumers actually relied upon the false advertisement, and that the plaintiff's business incurred economic injury.

Under the Lanham Act, the defendant's statements need not be literally false. Rather, to establish a false advertising claim under the Lanham Act, the plaintiff

Focus Case 7.3

Facts: Clorox Co. ran 15- and 30-second television advertisements showing a water-filled Slide-Loc food storage bag manufactured by its competitor, S.C. Johnson & Sons, Inc., turned upside-down. The advertisements showed water leaking out of the bag at a rapid rate, with air bubbles forming in the bag. As stated by the trial court, "the overall impression, that is, the overall depiction in the commercial itself is of a rapid and substantial leakage and flow of water out of the Slide-Loc bag. This is rendered even more graphic because there is a goldfish depicted in the bag which is shown to be in jeopardy because the water is running out at such a rate."

S.C. Johnson & Co. filed suit, claiming that the advertisement was literally false and requesting an injunction prohibiting further airing of the advertisements.

Decision: The court found that when the Slide-Loc bags and Clorox's own Glad bags were subjected to the same quality control tests, two-thirds of both types of the bags showed some leakage. However, the "great majority" of the leaks were small and very slow and occurred only when the bags were held upside-down. Because normal consumers do not use the bags to hold water, particularly upside-down, and because the commercial greatly exaggerated the leakage of Slide-Loc bags, the court found that aspect of the advertisements to be literally false. It enjoined Clorox Co. from running the advertisements.

Three months later, the parties were back before the same court. Clorox Co. had revised its advertisement and was airing a new 15-second commercial as well as running a print ad in a popular women's magazine. The new commercial, like the original one, displayed a bag filled with water, containing a goldfish, and held upside-down. It did not, however, display a rate of leakage as fast as that shown in the original ad. The print ad had a single image of a Slide-Loc bag with a large drop of water about to fall away and the goldfish in danger of suffocating.

The court again found that both advertisements were literally false because they did not indicate that leakage occurs in only a certain percentage of such bags rather than all of them, and because nothing indicated the degree of risk of such leakage.

Thus, the court issued an injunction against both the new commercial and the print advertisement. *S.C. Johnson & Son v. Clorox Co., 2000 U.S. Dist. LEXIS 3621 (S.D.N.Y. Jan. 7, 2000); S.C. Johnson & Son v. Clorox Co., 2000 U.S. Dist. LEXIS 4977 (S.D. N.Y. April 6, 2000).*

---

must show either (1) that the advertisement is literally false as a factual matter, or (2) although literally true, the advertisement actually deceives or confuses consumers. Thus, representations that are literally true but because of innuendo, omission, or ambiguity may be deemed "implicitly false" subject the defendant to liability. Where representations are implicitly, rather than literally, false, the plaintiff is required to demonstrate that consumers were in fact misled by the representations. This is usually accomplished through consumer surveys or market studies (see Focus Case 7.3).

See Discussion Cases 7.2, 7.3.

Commercial Disparagement

Commercial disparagement, also known as *product disparagement*, is closely related to false advertising. It arises when the defendant makes false or deceptive representations about the quality of *plaintiff's* goods or services (as opposed to false or deceptive representations about the quality of defendant's own goods or services, which would be false advertising).

Commercial disparagement, like false advertising, can arise under state common law. The requirements vary from state to state, but, generally, the plaintiff is required to show (1) a false representation and (2) a specific economic loss (also known as "special damages"). General statements of comparison ("Product X is better than Product Y") or "puffing" (i.e., obviously exaggerated claims about a product or service or vague generalizations, such as "Product X is the best") do not constitute commercial disparagement. The special damages element requires the plaintiff to show that it suffered actual, specific harm as a result of the defendant's disparagement, such as lost business and revenue. Some jurisdictions also add a third element by requiring the plaintiff to show that the defendant intended to harm the plaintiff or at least acted with a reckless disregard for the effect of the disparagement on the plaintiff.

The UDTPA allows injunctive relief against false or misleading statements of fact that disparage the goods, services, or business of another, if the plaintiff shows that it is "likely to be damaged" by the statements.

Section 43(a) of the federal Lanham Act prohibits disparaging statements about a plaintiff's goods or services as well as false statements about the defendant's own goods or services. It is similar to the common law's cause of action for commercial disparagement. Section 43(a) does not require a showing of intent to harm, however, nor does it require proof of specific economic loss to support injunctive relief (though proof of actual economic harm is required for recovery of monetary damages).

THE FEDERAL TRADE COMMISSION ACT

The Federal Trade Commission (FTC) is responsible for enforcement of the FTC Act,[21] which is designed to promote competition and to protect the public from unfair and deceptive acts and practices in the marketing of goods and services. The FTC was created by Congress in 1914 to bolster the country's then weak antitrust laws. (The antitrust role of the FTC is discussed in Chapter 4.)

Section 5 of the FTC Act provides that one of the FTC's tasks is to prevent "unfair or deceptive acts or practices [and] unfair methods of competition"; this is where the FTC's ability to regulate advertising is found. Today, the FTC has primary responsibility for regulating deceptive advertising in the United States. Although the discussion in this chapter focuses primarily on advertising issues, it is important to note that the FTC's jurisdiction extends to all kinds of deceptive or unfair acts, including marketing and promotional activities and sales practices in general, not just to advertising violations. These issues are discussed further in Chapter 8.

The FTC is an independent federal administrative agency. As such, it is not subject to political control as are executive branch agencies. The FTC is headed by five commissioners who are appointed by the President and confirmed by the Senate for staggered seven-year terms. The President also appoints one of the commissioners chair of the FTC.

Much of the FTC's regulation of deceptive or unfair acts or practices focuses on deceptive advertising, including deceptive price and quality claims, false testimonials, and the use of mock-ups. The FTC has issued a number of guides and policy statements that clarify these rules for industry and the public,[22] such as a guide on the use of endorsements and testimonials and a rule on retail food-store advertising and marketing practices. The FTC also promulgates policy statements on topics such as comparative advertising claims and substantiation for product claims. These guides and policy statements do not have the force of law, but they are very useful tools in helping businesses to understand what activities or practices are legal or illegal (see Exhibit 7.1 on page 234).

---

[21] 15 U.S.C. §§ 41–58.
[22] These are available on-line at http://www.ftc.gov

FTC POLICY STATEMENTS AND GUIDES

□ **Advertising**
Dot Com Disclosures: Information About Online Advertising
Advertising and Marketing on the Internet: The Rules of the Road
Frequently Asked Advertising Questions: A Guide for Small Business

□ **Advertising Substantiation**
FTC Policy Statement Regarding Advertising Substantiation

□ **Bait Advertising**
FTC Guides Against Bait Advertising

□ **Deception**
FTC Policy Statement on Deception

□ **Deceptive Pricing**
FTC Guides Against Deceptive Pricing

□ **Use of the Word "Free"**
FTC Guide Concerning the Use of the Word Free

□ **Endorsements and Testimonials**
FTC Guide Concerning the Use of Endorsements and Testimonials

□ **Unfairness**
FTC Policy Statement on Unfairness

□ **Dietary Supplements**
Dietary Supplements: An Advertising Guide for Industry
FTC Staff Comment on Draft Report of the Commission on Dietary Supplement Labels
FTC Staff Comment on FDA Proposed Rule on Statements Made for Dietary Supplements

□ **Eye-Care Surgery**
FDA/FTC Joint Letter on PRK
FTC Staff Guides on Refractive Eye Surgery

□ **Food Advertising**
Enforcement Policy Statement on Food Advertising

□ **Jewelry**
Guides for the Jewelry, Precious Metals, and Pewter Industries

□ **Furniture**
Guides for the Household Furniture Industry

□ **Vocational and Distance Education Schools**
Guides for Private Vocational and Distance Education Schools

Although the FTC's authority to regulate extends only to advertising that promotes goods and services involved in interstate commerce, the courts define interstate commerce so broadly that the majority of goods or services fall within this category. Truly local advertising is regulated, if at all, at the state level. Most states do have laws, known as "Little FTC Acts," that regulate state advertising activities.

The FTC has jurisdiction over most ads for most products and services. Certain other government agencies can investigate advertising by certain specialized industries, such as airlines, banks, insurance companies, telephone and cable companies, and companies that sell securities and commodities. Additional special laws apply to ads for certain products or services, such as consumer leases, credit, 900 telephone numbers, and products sold through mail order or telephone sales. These issues are discussed further in Chapter 8.

The FTC Act does not give consumers or competitors the right to sue; rather, only the FTC may bring suit under the Act. FTC action can originate from an FTC-initiated investigation of business behavior or from an informal complaint made by a competitor or consumer. The FTC generally does not release the name of the complainant unless required to do so by law.

Because the FTC lacks the resources to respond to all complaints made, it investigates those that most directly implicate its mission of protecting consumers and fostering free competition. In particular, in making its enforcement decisions, the FTC tends to focus on national (as opposed to local) advertising, advertising that represents a pattern of deception (as opposed to an isolated dispute between a consumer and business or between two competitors), and cases that could affect consumer health or safety or result in widespread economic injury. The FTC's mandate is to act when it appears both that a company's advertising is deceptive *and* that FTC action is in the public interest. Thus, the FTC does not become involved in purely private disputes. While FTC investigations of an advertiser are confidential, FTC formal actions against an advertiser (such as filing a lawsuit or reaching settlement with the advertiser) are made public.

After investigating, the FTC staff submits a recommendation to the commission recommending that the case be closed, that the commission settle the case, or that the FTC issue a formal complaint against the respondent. If the case is settled, the parties enter into a *consent order* in which the FTC agrees not to pursue the case further in return for the business agreeing to refrain from engaging in specified acts. The business does not necessarily admit to having engaged in any illegal activities, however. Violation of a consent order is a civil infraction punishable by fines of up to $11,000 per day.

If a formal complaint is issued (and the FTC and the business do not agree on a settlement), the case is heard by an administrative law judge (ALJ) in an administrative hearing. The ALJ listens to evidence and arguments made by legal counsel for both the business and the FTC and issues an initial decision.

The decision of the ALJ becomes the decision of the full commission after 30 days unless the commission determines on its own to review it, or unless either party appeals to the commission. When the full commission reviews an ALJ decision, it may affirm the decision, modify it, or reverse it. If the commission affirms or modifies the decision, it issues an order against the business. Once the order is issued, the business has 60 days to appeal to the U.S. Court of Appeals. From there, either party may file for a writ of certiorari from the Supreme Court.

The penalties available under the FTC Act vary with the nature of the violation. The FTC or the courts can issue a *cease-and-desist order*, which requires the advertiser to stop running the deceptive or unfair ad or to stop engaging in the deceptive or unfair practice, to obtain substantiation for claims made in future ads, to report periodically to the FTC about that substantiation, and to pay a fine of $11,000 per day per ad if the advertiser violates the law in the future.

Violations can also result in *civil penalties* that can range up to millions of dollars depending upon the nature of the violation. In some cases, advertisers have been required to provide *consumer redress* in the form of full or partial refunds to all consumers who bought the product.

The FTC can also require an advertiser to engage in *corrective advertising*. This usually takes the form of requiring the advertiser to air a new ad to correct the misinformation contained in the original ad, to notify purchasers about deceptive claims in ads, or to provide other information to consumers. The FTC has required corrective advertising in a number of consent orders[23] but has ordered this remedy only twice in litigated cases. (Competitors do routinely seek, and often receive, corrective advertising in a number of other contexts, including under Section 43(a) of the Lanham Act,[24] however.)

In the 1970s, the FTC challenged Warner-Lambert Company's 40-year advertising campaign touting Listerine mouthwash as a cure for colds. The commission ordered the company to undertake $10 million of corrective advertising (its average annual advertising budget at the time), stating that corrective advertising is appropriate when: (1) the advertisement is deceptive; (2) the advertisement played a substantial role in creating or reinforcing in the public's mind a false and material belief; and (3) the belief survives even once the deceptive advertisement ceases.[25]

Many advertisers and their attorneys awaited the 1998 decision of the ALJ in *In re Novartis Corp.*[26] with great interest, as many analysts predicted that the ALJ would order corrective advertising. The outcome of the ALJ decision and the subsequent legal events surprised many.

Ciba-Geigy Corporation purchased the Doan's analgesic pain reliever brand in 1987. Ciba's consumer perception research indicated that its target market—back pain sufferers likely to use over-the-counter pain relievers—rated Doan's below its competitors in relieving back pain. From 1988 to 1996, first Ciba and then Novartis Corporation, its successor, engaged in a $55 million ad campaign that stressed that Doan's had a special efficacy in relieving back pain. Ciba/Novartis had no substantiation for claiming the product was superior to other over-the-counter analgesics in relieving back pain.

After the FTC took action, the advertising agency entered into a consent order with the FTC regarding its role in the ad campaign, agreeing to have scientific evidence to support claims regarding the efficacy, safety, benefits, or performance of any over-the-counter analgesic it advertised. The charges against Novartis were heard in an administrative hearing before an ALJ, who found the company liable for deceptive advertising. However, the ALJ declined to order corrective advertising, finding that the third element of the *Warner-Lambert* test (i.e., that the belief survives even once the deceptive advertising ceases) had not been met. In reaching this determination, the ALJ relied upon Novartis's evidence showing low 24- and 72-hour recall regarding the superiority claim and the fact that the ad campaign had been much shorter than the multi-decade Listerine campaign.

On appeal, the FTC ordered the company to carry the statement "Although Doan's is an effective pain reliever, there is no evidence that Doan's is more effective than other pain relievers for back pain" on all packaging and advertising materials for one year, excluding radio and television ads of less than 15 seconds, until it had expended on corrective advertising an amount equal to the average spent annually during the eight years of the advertising campaign.[27]

[23] *See, e.g.*, Eggland's Best, Inc., Docket No. C-3520 (Aug. 15, 1994); Unocal Corp., 117 F.T.C. 500 (1994); AHC Pharmaceuticals, Inc., 95 F.T.C. 528 (1980).

[24] *See* Alpo PetFoods, Inc. v. Ralston Purina Co., 720 F. Supp. 194 (D.D.C. 1989), *aff'd in pertinent part and vacated in part*, 913 F.2d 958 (D.C. Cir. 1990); John Wright, Inc. v. Casper Corp., 419 F. Supp. 292 (E.D. Pa. 1976), *aff'd in pertinent part sub nom.*, Donsco, Inc. v. Casper Corp., 587 F.2d 602 (3d Cir. 1978); Ames Publishing Co. v. Walker-Davis Publications, Inc., 372 F. Supp. 1 (E.D. Pa. 1974).

[25] Warner-Lambert Co. v. F.T.C., 86 F.T.C. 1398, 1499–1500 (1975), *aff'd*, 562 F.2d 749 (D.C. Cir. 1977).

[26] In re Novartis Corp., 1998 F.T.C. LEXIS 24 (Mar. 9, 1998).

[27] In re Novartis Corp., 1999 F.T.C. LEXIS 63 (May 27, 1999).

Novartis Corp. then appealed to the U.S. Court of Appeals, arguing that the advertisements were not "deceptive' because the claim made was not material. Novartis also argued that there was no evidence that consumers had actually relied upon the claims and that the FTC's action infringed on its First Amendment right to commercial speech. The Court of Appeals rejected all of Novartis's claims and upheld the FTC's findings.[28]

Finally, in extreme instances, the FTC has actually *banned* individuals from future participation within an industry or has required individuals to post a *bond* before continuing business.

GENERAL PRINCIPLES OF FTC REGULATION OF BUSINESS ACTS AND PRACTICES

Generally, the law requires that advertising be (1) truthful and not misleading, (2) substantiated (i.e., backed up by evidence), and (3) fair. In particular, the FTC can regulate business acts or practices that are either (1) unfair or (2) deceptive. A marketing practice can be unfair without being deceptive, and vice versa. Thus, separate rules apply to each of these areas.

Unfairness

The FTC Act does not list unfair trade practices, as Congress was aware that such a list would necessarily be incomplete and would quickly become outdated. Instead, the commission was given the task of identifying unfair trade practices, with the understanding that criteria for defining these would evolve and develop gradually.

The FTC's *Policy Statement on Unfairness*[29] explains the factors that the FTC now looks at in evaluating whether a business action is unfair. According to the *Policy Statement*, an advertisement or business practice is unfair: (1) if it causes or is likely to cause substantial consumer injury; (2) that a consumer could not reasonably avoid; and (3) the injury is not outweighed by any countervailing benefits to consumers or competition.

"Substantial injury" generally refers to monetary harm or unwarranted health and safety risks. Trivial, speculative, or merely emotional harms generally do not suffice to render an advertisement unfair. The *Policy Statement* specifically notes that certain practices may cause some consumer injury but that the injury may be offset by benefits to consumers. For example, an advertiser's failure to present technical data on the product may hamper a consumer's ability to choose but may also result in a reduced price. Such trade-offs are permissible provided that the net effect upon consumers is not injurious. Moreover, the FTC generally regards consumers as having free choice and expects that the marketplace will correct many unfair practices (i.e., consumers will simply refuse to buy from companies engaging in unfair practices). However, the FTC also recognizes that certain selling practices, such as withholding critical price or performance data, overt coercion, or undue influence over susceptible classes of purchasers (such as children or the terminally ill), may prevent the market from operating fairly and so may require agency intervention.

Deception

Advertising is more likely to run afoul of the ban against deceptive practices than it is the rules addressing unfair business practices. Deceptive practices involve acts

---

[28] Novartis Corp. v. FTC, 223 F.3d 783 (D.C. Cir. 2000).
[29] http://www.ftc.gov/bcp/policystmt/ad-unfair.htm

such as false oral or written representations, misleading price claims, sales of dangerous or systematically defective products or services without adequate disclosures, bait-and-switch tactics, and failure to meet warranty obligations.

Under the FTC's *Policy Statement on Deception*,[30] an advertisement or other type of business practice is *deceptive* (1) if it contains a representation, omission, or practice that (2) is likely to mislead consumers acting reasonably under the circumstances and (3) is "material" (i.e., is important to a consumer's decision to buy or use the product, such as representations about a product's performance, price, features, or effectiveness). Although this standard does not refer explicitly to an injury, the *Policy Statement* provides:

> Injury to consumers can take many forms. Injury exists if consumers would have chosen differently but for the deception. If different choices are likely, the claim is material, and injury is likely as well. Thus, injury and materiality are different names for the same concept.

The FTC can show that an advertisement is deceptive either by (1) proving its falsity or (2) showing that its proponent lacked a reasonable basis for asserting its truth. An advertiser can be liable even if it did not intend or did not know that its advertisement was deceptive.

To determine whether an advertisement is deceptive, the FTC begins by evaluating the ad from the perspective of the "reasonable consumer." As the FTC noted in an early case:

> An advertiser cannot be charged with liability in respect of every conceivable misconception, however outlandish, to which his representations might be subject among the foolish or feeble-minded. Some people, because of ignorance or incomprehension, may be misled by even a scrupulously honest claim. Perhaps a few misguided souls believe, for example, that all "Danish pastry" is made in Denmark. Is it "therefore" an actionable deception to advertise "Danish pastry" when it is made in this country? Of course not. A representation does not become "false and deceptive" merely because it will be unreasonably misunderstood by an insignificant and unrepresentative segment of the class of persons to whom the representation is addressed.[31]

If the representation or sales practice is targeted toward a specific audience, such as the children, the elderly, or doctors, the FTC considers the effect of the representation or practice upon a reasonable member of that group. Note, however, that the standard is whether the practice is *likely* to mislead consumers; actual deception is not required. However, the FTC does not pursue advertising claims based upon subjective claims (e.g., taste, feel, appearance, or smell) or upon cases involving puffing.

The FTC evaluates the entire ad—words, phrases, and pictures—to determine what message it conveys to consumers. The FTC also examines whether the ad omits information in such a way as to deceive or mislead the consumer. The makers of Campbell soup, for example, advertised that "most" Campbell soups were low in fat and cholesterol (a truthful statement) and were thus useful in fighting heart disease. However, the advertisements failed to point out that the soups were high in sodium and that high-sodium diets may increase the risk of heart disease. The FTC ruled that the company's failure to disclose the sodium content of the soups was deceptive. Campbell Soup Co. entered into a consent agreement in which it agreed to disclose the sodium content of any soup containing more than

---

[30] http://www.ftc.gov/bcp/policystmt/ad-decept.htm
[31] In re Heinz W. Kirchner, 63 F.T.C. 1282, 1290 (1963).

500 milligrams of sodium per eight-ounce serving in any ad that directly or by implication mentioned heart disease in connection with the soup. Campbell also agreed not to make any direct or implied representation regarding soup and the reduction of the risk of heart disease unless it possessed, at the time of the representation, "competent and reliable scientific or medical evidence" to that effect.[32]

The FTC evaluates both "express" and "implied" claims, and the advertisers must have proof to substantiate both types of claims made in an ad. An *express* claim is a statement literally made within the ad. An *implied* claim is made indirectly or through inference. Thus, a claim that "XYZ Sunscreen prevents skin cancer" is an express claim that the sunscreen does indeed prevent skin cancer. A claim that "XYZ Sunscreen blocks the harmful sun rays that cause skin cancer" is an implied claim. A reasonable consumer could conclude from the latter statement that XYZ Sunscreen prevents skin cancer.

The advertiser must disclose whatever qualifying information is necessary to ensure that the express or implied claims are not misleading to the consumer. All such disclosures must be clear, conspicuous, and in the same language as that used principally in the advertisement. A *disclosure* or *disclaimer* does not rectify a false or deceptive claim.

The FTC considers certain types of representations presumptively "material," including express claims, implied claims intentionally made by the seller, and claims or omissions involving health, safety, or other areas with which a reasonable consumer would be concerned, such as the efficacy or cost of the product or service, durability, performance, quality, or warranties. Thus, in scrutinizing advertising, the FTC pays the most attention to ads that make claims about health or safety (e.g., "XYZ Antibacterial Soap kills germs") and ads that make claims that consumers would have difficulty evaluating for themselves (e.g., "XYZ Laundry Detergent is safe for septic systems"). The FTC is less concerned with ads that make subjective claims or claims that consumers can easily judge for themselves (e.g., "Everybody loves XYZ cereal").

The FTC also scrutinizes carefully advertising that is aimed at children, because children are less-sophisticated consumers and are often more susceptible to deception. Advertising aimed at children is evaluated from a child's, not an adult's, perspective. The FTC works with the Children's Advertising Review Unit (CARU) of the Council of Better Business Bureaus (CBBB)[33] on children's advertising issues. CARU, created in 1974, is a private, self-regulatory group that promotes truthful, accurate, and socially responsible advertising that is sensitive to the needs of children. CARU monitors advertisements directed to children under the age of 12 in broadcast and cable television, radio, children's magazines, comic books, and on-line services.

The FTC Act also requires *substantiation* of advertising. A firm's failure to possess and rely upon a reasonable basis for objective claims made in advertisements is itself an unfair or deceptive trade practice. The advertiser bears the burden of demonstrating an ad is true. (Contrast this to the Lanham Act where the consumer or competitor bears the burden of demonstrating that the ad is false.) The FTC regards advertising substantiation as very important and has issued a *Policy Statement Regarding Advertising Substantiation*.[34] The advertiser and its ad agency must have evidence to support any claims made *before* the advertisement is run. The amount of

---

[32] In re Campbell Soup Co., 1991 F.T.C. LEXIS 303 (Apr. 17, 1991).
[33] The CBBB's website is http://www.bbb.org
[34] http://www.ftc.gov/bcp/guides/ad3subst.htm

LANHAM ACT v. FTC ACT

	Purpose	Who Can Be A Plaintiff	Who Bears Burden of Proof	Primary Remedies

Lanham Act	• Forbids false designation of origin and false or misleading descriptions or representations of fact
	• Includes:
	  • passing off
	  • false advertising
	  • commercial disparagement
		Competitors	Plaintiff must prove that ads are <u>literally</u> false <u>or</u> that there is an actual deception	• Injunctive Relief
				• Monetary Damages
				• Costs and Attorneys Fees in Exceptional Cases

FTC Act	• Prevents trade practices and acts that are:
	  • unfair *or*
	  • deceptive
	• Includes:
	  • deceptive pricing
	  • deceptive endorsements and testimonials
	  • deceptive mock-ups
	  • deceptive comparative advertising
		FTC	FTC must show ad has <u>capacity</u> to deceive or mislead the public	• Cease-and-desist Order
				• Civil Penalties
				• Consumer Redress
				• Corrective Advertising

EXHIBIT 7.2

evidence required depends upon the claim or claims made, but, at a minimum, the advertiser must have the level of evidence that it says that it has. Thus, if a toothpaste ad states that "three out of four dentists recommend" a particular brand, the advertiser must have competent and reliable *scientific* evidence to support that claim.

See Discussion Case 7.4.

Advertising agencies, Web site designers, and catalogue marketers, as well as advertisers themselves, may be held liable for deceptive ads. In considering whether a third party, such as an ad agency, should be held liable, the FTC looks at that party's participation in the preparation of the deceptive ad and whether it knew or should have known that the ad included false or deceptive claims. Ad agencies and Web site designers have a legal duty to independently verify the information used to substantiate claims and may not rely upon the advertiser's representation or assurance regarding claim substantiation.

SPECIFIC ADVERTISING PRACTICES

The FTC has issued guidances on several types of advertising practices to assist advertisers in determining what is or is not permissible.

Deceptive Pricing

The FTC has issued a *Guides Against Deceptive Pricing.*[35] The FTC defines *deceptive pricing* as any practice that tends to mislead or deceive consumers about the price that they are paying for goods or services. Deceptive pricing includes, for example, statements regarding the former or regular price of the merchandise that are false or two-for-one deals or offers of free merchandise coupled with a purchase where the advertiser has simply inflated the regular price of the merchandise bought to cover the costs of the supposedly "free" goods.

The *Deceptive Pricing Guides* provide some very specific rules regarding pricing strategies. For example, retail price comparisons ("Brand Y Printers, Price Elsewhere $329, Our Price $299") are permissible provided that a number of the principal retail outlets in the area regularly sell Brand Y Printers for $329. Where only a few outlets sell the printer for that price, however, and the majority sell the printer for less, the advertisement would contain deceptive pricing information. Similarly, it is permissible to advertise a discount from the manufacturer's list or suggested retail price only if a substantial number of sales are made in the area at the list or suggested retail prices. If most goods are sold in the area at a lower price, the consumer would be likely to be misled by the advertisement promising a reduction.

Bait-and-switch advertising is also regulated by the FTC. According to the FTC *Guides Against Bait Advertising,*[36] bait-and-switch advertising occurs when the seller (1) refuses to show, demonstrate, or sell the advertised item; (2) disparages the advertised product; (3) fails to have reasonable quantities of it on hand (unless the advertisement indicates the quantities are limited); (4) fails to take orders to deliver the item within a reasonable time; (5) shows a product that is defective or impractical for the use implied or stated in the advertisement; or (6) discourages salespersons from selling the item. In effect, the company has advertised a product but has no intention of actually selling the consumer that item. Rather, the company intends to sell the consumer a different product, usually at a higher price. The product advertised at the lower price serves as the "bait"; once the consumer is in the store, he or she is encouraged to "switch" to the higher-priced product. The FTC considers bait-and-switch advertising to be deceptive.

Endorsements and Testimonials

The FTC has issued a document entitled *FTC Guide Concerning Use of Endorsements and Testimonials in Advertising.*[37] Advertisers commonly use actors, sports stars, and other prominent public figures to endorse or provide testimonials about their products. Such *endorsements* or *testimonials* are considered deceptive if the person involved does not in fact use or prefer the product. The advertiser can only use the endorsement as long as the endorser continues to use and prefer the product.

To give an "expert" opinion regarding a product or service, the endorser must indeed be sufficiently qualified to be regarded as an expert in the field. In addition,

[35] http://www.ftc.gov/bcp/guides/decptprc.htm
[36] http://www.ftc.gov/bcp/guides/baitads-gd.htm
[37] http://www.ftc.gov/bcp/guides/endorse.htm

the expert must evaluate, examine, or test the product in the same manner that other experts in the field would normally use to substantiate the claims made in the advertisement.

If the advertisement contains an endorsement by what is represented to be an individual or group of "actual" consumers, actual consumers must be used or the advertisement must clearly and conspicuously disclose that the individuals depicted are actors, not actual consumers. In addition, the endorsement must reflect the *typical* experience of consumers who use the product, not the ideosyncratic experiences of one or a few consumers. The advertiser must disclose any payments made to the consumer for making the endorsement and generally must disclose any relationship between any endorser and the advertiser (such as an employee or family relationship) that might affect the weight or credibility of the endorsement.

Mock-ups

It is deceptive to show an advertisement that purports to be an actual product demonstration but is in fact a *mock-up* or *simulation*. Any use of a mock-up should be revealed, unless the mock-up or prop is necessary because of the difficulty of showing the actual product in the advertisements. This is why advertisers can use props, such as substituting mashed potatoes for ice cream (which would otherwise quickly melt under photographic lights), provided that the prop is not being used as actual proof of a product claim (such as the rich texture of the ice cream).

Volvo Corporation learned the dangers of not revealing mock-ups the hard way. It showed a television ad that depicted an oversized "monster" pickup truck driving over a row of cars. All of the cars except the Volvo were crushed. Volvo did not disclose that the Volvo automobile used in the ad had been structurally strengthened with steel and wood, while the other cars had been structurally weakened. Volvo and its advertising agency each paid a $150,000 fine to the FTC, though neither admitted to any wrongdoing. The consent order also prohibited further misrepresentations of the strength, structural integrity, or crashworthiness of any vehicle or of the safety of any occupant in a collision.[38]

The FTC also scrutinizes *product demonstrations* to make certain that they are truthful and not misleading. Advertisers should make certain that their product demonstrations accurately depict the product's qualities and capabilities and do not exaggerate or misrepresent the product or a competing product in any manner. In particular, advertisers should be certain that photographic techniques do not misrepresent or distort the product's characteristics or qualities in any way. Campbell Soup Co., for example, was held liable when its advertisement depicted bowls of soup filled with chunky ingredients. Marbles had actually been placed at the bottoms of the bowls in order to raise the ingredients to the surface.[39]

Comparative Advertising

The FTC has issued a *Statement of Policy Regarding Comparative Advertising*.[40] The FTC encourages the naming of or reference to competitors in advertising, even where the references are negative, provided that the statements are clear, truthful, and nondeceptive. Truthful and nondeceptive comparative advertising provides important information to consumers and can assist them in making informed, rational purchase choices. It can also lead to product innovation and improvement

---

[38] *F.T.C. Accords on Volvo Ads*, THE NEW YORK TIMES, Aug. 22, 1991, at D19.
[39] In re Campbell Soup Co., 77 F.T.C. 664 (1970). *See also* In re Mattel, Inc., 79 F.T.C. 667 (1971), *modified*, 104 F.T.C. 555 (1984) (toy car's speed exaggerated).
[40] http://www.ftc.gov/bcp/policystmt/ad-compare.htm

and to lower prices in the marketplace. For these reasons, the FTC generally opposes industry codes or standards that restrain comparative advertising or that require higher standards of substantiation for such advertising.

Sweepstakes and Contests

Sweepstakes-type promotions that require the participants to make a purchase are illegal. Each state also regulates sweepstakes and contests. It is imperative, therefore, that promoters examine the laws of each state in which they intend to advertise such activities.

State attorneys general have been particularly vigilant about sweepstakes abuses. For example, 39 states and the District of Columbia have reached multimillion dollar settlements with American Family Publishers (AFP) recently. The states had alleged that AFP, in an effort to sell magazine subscriptions, had conducted misleading sweepstakes campaigns that had tricked many people into believing that they had won $11 million. The states also alleged that dozens of elderly people had traveled to Tampa, Florida (the return address listed on the entry), to collect a prize that they had not in fact won.

As part of the settlements, AFP agreed to stop telling people that they were "winners" or "finalists" unless in fact they actually were. In addition, future language stating that the individual "may already be a winner" must include in type not less than half that size the disclaimer "if you have the winning ticket." Several of the settlements also created funds for consumer redress. AFP admitted to no wrongdoing in the settlements, however.[41]

The National Advertising Division

The National Advertising Division (NAD)[42] of the CBBB offers a private court that both consumers and companies can use to resolve disputes. The advantages of using this private court rather than normal litigation are that the process can be kept private (whereas litigation is necessarily public); it often is much cheaper (approximately $50,000 for a NAD proceeding versus $150,000 or more for litigation[43]); and disputes can be resolved quickly (often within 60 days).

The NAD was created by the advertising community in 1971 as part of its effort to foster voluntary self-regulation, minimize government regulation, and increase public confidence in the credibility of advertising. It responds to complaints about national advertising brought by a variety of parties, including individual consumers, advertisers, the Better Business Bureau, and trade associations. The NAD also monitors national broadcast and cable television and print advertising and initiates its own complaints. Approximately 20 percent of its cases originate from consumers and Better Business Bureaus, 50 percent from competing advertisers, and 30 percent from NAD's monitoring program.[44]

The NAD provides attorneys who review and evaluate claims substantiation and who investigate complaints about truth and accuracy in national advertising.

---

[41] *See American Family Publishers, Spokesmen Settle Sweepstakes Lawsuit*, THE ENTERTAINMENT LITIGATION REPORTER (July 31, 1999); Lisa Renze-Rhodes, *Attorney General Declares State a Winner*, THE INDIANA LAWYER (June 9, 1999), at p. 12; *NY Reaches $800,000 Settlement with American Family Publishers*, GAMING INDUSTRY LITIGATION REPORTER (Sept. 1998), p. 10.

[42] NAD's website can be found at http://www.bbb.org/advertising/advertiserAssist.asp

[43] Jeff Barge, *Advertising Legal Wars Heating Up*, 82 A.B.A. J. 32 (April, 1996).

[44] *See* http://www.bbb.org/advertising/advertiserAssist.asp#ques

The NAD recommends that the advertiser voluntarily modify and discontinue false or inaccurate claims, but it does not impose penalties. NAD decisions are published 10 times a year in the *NAD Case Reports* under two headings: "Advertising Substantiated" and "Advertising Modified or Discontinued." Unresolved controversies are referred to the National Advertising Review Board (NARB), a peer review group composed of 80 advertising professionals and public interest members. The dispute is heard by a five-person panel of NARB members at a roundtable review. The panel either overturns or upholds NAD's decision. If the advertiser fails to comply with a NAD or NARB panel decision, the NAD may refer the file to the appropriate government agency and release information regarding the referral to the public and the press.

Although NAD has functioned successfully for over 25 years, businesses appear to be shifting away from this private dispute resolution mechanism and back to litigation. First, attorneys note that NAD cannot award monetary damages, while monetary relief in false advertising litigation is skyrocketing. Second, preliminary injunctive relief can often be acquired from a court well within the 60-day NAD process period, suggesting that the NAD process is not necessarily faster than litigation. Finally, many plaintiffs, particularly competitors, want the publicity that comes from filing a suit, rather than the anonymity of NAD proceedings, where cases are not made public until the dispute is resolved.[45]

Advertising on the Internet

Advertising on the Internet raises a number of special legal issues. Some of these, such as metatags, deep linking, and banner advertisements, are discussed in Chapter 6 in the context of trademark law. The discussion in this chapter focuses on the FTC's on-line advertising guidelines and on privacy issues. Unsolicited commercial E-mail, or spam, is addressed in Chapter 8.

ON-LINE ADVERTISING

The FTC has issued two documents addressing on-line advertising activities—*Dot Com Disclosures: Information About Online Advertising*[46] and *Advertising and Marketing on the Internet: Rules of the Road.*[47] Generally, on-line advertising is subject to the same rules that apply to advertising in other media. The FTC takes its role in regulating Internet advertising seriously and since 1994 has brought over 100 enforcement actions to stop advertising abuses on-line.

The same *disclosure* requirements that apply to traditional advertising media apply to on-line advertising. To ensure that disclosures are clear and conspicuous in on-line ads, however, advertisers should consider

- the *placement* of the disclosure in the ad,
- the *proximity* of the disclosure to the relevant claim,

---

[45] *See* Wendy R. Leibowitz, *Advertisers Now Litigating Rivals' Fishy Claims*, NATIONAL LAW JOURNAL, p. A1 (June 23, 1997).
[46] This guide can be found at http://www.ftc.gov/bcp/conline/pubs/buspubs/dotcom/index.html
[47] This guide can be found at http://www.ftc.gov/bcp/conline/pubs/buspubs/ruleroad.htm

- the *prominence* of the disclosure,
- whether other parts of the ad *distract attention* from the disclosure,
- whether the ad is so long the disclosure should be *repeated*,
- whether audio disclosures are presented in *adequate volume and cadence*,
- whether visual disclosures appear for sufficient *duration*, and
- whether the language of the disclosure is *understandable* to the intended audience.

The on-line version of the *Dot Com Disclosures* document contains hyperlinks to mock ads illustrating these factors.

PRIVACY ISSUES

The growth in electronic commerce has lead to many concerns about *privacy* issues. On-line marketers can gather large amounts of information about actual or possible customers through the Web and the Internet. Web site owners can use "cookies"[48] to store user information for future retrieval on the individual hard drives of users visiting their sites. Internet service providers (ISPs) can track a user's navigation through the Web by capturing "click stream data" (i.e., electronic records of the user's activities).

While marketers may find this data very useful in determining consumer preferences or analyzing pricing schemes, surveys have indicated that many people do not participate in on-line activities because of concerns about lack of privacy.[49] Their fears appear well-founded. A 1997 public workshop on consumer information privacy conducted by the FTC revealed that 85 percent of Web sites gather personal information, with 14 percent providing notice of intended use and only 2 percent providing explicit comprehensive privacy policies.[50]

Currently, there is no federal law directly governing consumer privacy issues in the United States, although there is a patchwork of federal and state statutes and case law that provide protections in specific circumstances.

In the first FTC action involving Internet privacy actions, the FTC filed an action against Geocities.com for engaging in deceptive practices in violation of the FTC Act. The FTC alleged that Geocities had failed to follow its own privacy policies. In particular, the FTC alleged that Geocities (1) falsely represented that the information that it gathered would be used only for specifically requested advertisements but then sold the information for general advertising purposes; (2) falsely represented that certain information would not be disclosed without the customer's permission; and (3) falsely represented that it collected and maintained personal information from children when in fact the information was collected and maintained by other parties on Geocities' Web site.

The FTC and Geocities settled the case. Geocities agreed to post "a clear and prominent" privacy notice on its Web site informing consumers what information

---

[48] A "cookie" is "a small data text file that is transferred from a Web server computer and sent back to the server computer whenever an HTML file request is made." MICHAEL D. SCOTT, INTERNET TECHNOLOGY LAW DESK REFERENCE 111 (1999).

[49] *See* BUSINESS WEEK, Mar. 16, 1998, at 98 (recent poll showed majority of respondents cited privacy as primary reason they avoided the Internet).

[50] Lawrence J. Magid, *PC Focus: Efforts Aim to Protect Kids' Online Privacy*, L.A. TIMES, July 26, 1999, at C3.

is being collected and for what purposes, to whom it will be disclosed, and how consumers can access and remove the information. Geocities also agreed to obtain parental consent before collecting information from children under the age of 13.[51]

In addition to the FTC Act, other federal statutes address specific privacy issues. The *Electronic Communications Privacy Act,*[52] for example, restricts the monitoring of information flowing through the Internet and protects E-mail from use or disclosure by anyone other than the intended recipient.

Concerns about the on-line privacy of children led Congress to adopt the *Children's Online Privacy Protection Act of 1998* (COPPA).[53] COPPA regulates the operators of Web sites directed to children under the age of 13. It limits the use of personal information gathered on-line from such children and requires "verifiable parental consent" before such personal information can be collected.[54] The FTC enforces the provisions of COPPA.

The FTC promotes industry self-regulation in the privacy arena. Several trade associations have established privacy principles and guidelines for their members to follow in doing business on the Internet, including The Online Privacy Alliance,[55] The Direct Marketing Association,[56] and TRUSTe.[57] In addition, businesses can obtain "privacy seals" from various organizations, such as BBBOnLine, a subsidiary of the CBBB. These seals give customers assurance that a Web site is abiding by its posted privacy protection policy.

Generally, all businesses that collect data on-line should post a prominent privacy policy on their Web site addressing issues such as the identity of the data gatherer, the purposes of the data, how long and in what manner the data will be kept, and how individuals may access their data or correct inaccuracies in it.

The European Union and countries in the Pacific Rim (including Hong Kong and New Zealand) have been much more proactive than the United States in protecting personal information on the Internet. The *European Union Personal Data Directive,*[58] for example, became effective in October 1998. The Directive places limitations on the type of data that can be collected, the manner in which it can be collected, and the manner in which it may be used. It also grants certain rights, including access, to the provider of the information. The Directive also provides that the data can be transferred to another country only if the other country provides an "adequate level of protection" to the data. The United States, which does not currently meet this standard, is negotiating with the European Union to establish acceptable protections.

[51] A copy of the Agreement Containing the Consent Order can be found at http://www.ftc.gov/os/1998/9808/geo-ord.htm The FTC also settled a second Internet false advertising case involving children's privacy policies with Liberty Financial Companies, which operates the Young Investor website. The FTC alleged that the company falsely represented that information collected was anonymous. A description of the case and links to the consent order can be found at http://www.ftc.gov/opa/1999/9905/younginvestor.htm
[52] 18 U.S.C. § 2701.
[53] 15 U.S.C. §§ 6501–6506.
[54] The FTC's final rules pursuant to COPPA took effect on April 21, 2000. *See* 64 Fed. Reg. 59888 (1999) (codified at 16 C.F.R. pt. 312).
[55] http://www.privacyalliance.org
[56] http://www.the-dma.org
[57] http://www.truste.org
[58] Council Directive 95/46, 1995 O.J. (L 281) 31.

International Advertising Law

Regulation of advertising, whether on-line or conventional, varies greatly from country to country. Comparative advertising, for example, is prohibited in Germany, and several Scandinavian countries prohibit advertising directed at children. It is essential that marketers consult with attorneys of the country or countries in which they plan to advertise before beginning any advertising efforts overseas.[59] Internet advertisers, in particular, need to be sensitive to the different regulatory regimes to which their sites may be subject. Information on international advertising law can be found on-line. The FTC, for example, has posted materials from a June 1999 public workshop it held entitled "U.S. Perspectives on Consumer Protection in the Global Marketplace."[60] The European Commission's Consumer Protection Web site also contains valuable information on EC advertising law.[61]

[59] Contacts for foreign advertising counsel can be found at http://www.gala-marketlaw.com
[60] http://www.ftc.gov/bcp/icpw/index.htm
[61] http://www.europa.eu.int/comm/dg24/policy/index-en.html

DISCUSSION CASES

7.1 Commercial Speech

Rubin v. Coors Brewing Co., 514 U.S. 476 (1995)

OPINION: JUSTICE THOMAS Section 5(e)(2) of the Federal Alcohol Administration Act prohibits beer labels from displaying alcohol content. We granted certiorari in this case to review the Tenth Circuit's holding that the labeling ban violates the First Amendment because it fails to advance a governmental interest in a direct and material way. Because § 5(e)(2) is inconsistent with the protections granted to commercial speech by the First Amendment, we affirm.

I

Respondent brews beer. In 1987, respondent applied to the Bureau of Alcohol, Tobacco and Firearms (BATF), an agency of the Department of the Treasury, for approval of proposed labels and advertisements that disclosed the alcohol content of its beer. BATF rejected the application on the ground that the Federal Alcohol Administration Act (FAAA or Act) prohibited disclosure of the alcohol content of beer on labels or in advertising. Respondent then filed suit in the District Court for the District of Colorado seeking a declaratory judgment that the relevant provisions of the Act violated the First Amendment; respondent also sought injunctive relief barring enforcement of these provisions. The Government took the position that the ban was necessary to suppress the threat of "strength wars" among brewers, who, without the regulation, would seek to compete in the marketplace based on the potency of their beer.

The District Court granted the relief sought, but a panel of the Court of Appeals for the Tenth Circuit reversed and remanded. Applying the framework set out in *Central Hudson Gas & Elec. Corp. v. Public Serv. Comm'n of N. Y.*, 447 U.S. 557 (1980), the Court of Appeals found that the Government's interest in suppressing alcoholic "strength wars" was "substantial." * * * The court remanded for further proceedings to ascertain whether a "reasonable fit" existed between the ban and the goal of avoiding strength wars.

After further factfinding, the District Court upheld the ban on the disclosure of alcohol content in advertising but invalidated the ban as it applied to labels. * * * On the case's second appeal, the Court of Appeals affirmed the District Court. After reviewing the record, the Court of Appeals concluded that the Government had failed to demonstrate that the prohibition in any way prevented strength wars. The court found that there was no evidence of any relationship between the publication of factual information regarding alcohol content and competition on the basis of such content.

We granted certiorari to review the Tenth Circuit's decision that § 205(e)(2) violates the First Amendment. We conclude that the ban infringes respondent's freedom of speech, and we therefore affirm.

II

A

* * * The [FAAA] establishes national rules governing the distribution, production, and importation of alcohol and established a Federal Alcohol Administration to implement these rules. Section 5(e)(2) of the Act prohibits any producer, importer, wholesaler, or bottler of alcoholic beverages from selling, shipping, or delivering in interstate or foreign commerce any malt beverages, distilled spirits, or wines in bottles

> unless such products are bottled, packaged, and labeled in conformity with such regulations, to be prescribed by the Secretary of the Treasury, with respect to packaging, marking, branding, and labeling and size and fill of container . . . as will provide the consumer with adequate information as to the identity and quality of the products, the alcoholic content thereof (*except that statements of, or statements likely to be considered as statements of, alcoholic content of malt beverages are prohibited unless required by State law and except that, in case of wines, statements of alcoholic content shall be required only for wines containing more than 14 per centum of alcohol by volume,) the net contents of the package, and the manufacturer or bottler or importer of the product.*

27 U.S.C. § 205(e)(2) (emphasis added). The Act defines "malt beverage[s]" in such a way as to include all beers and ales.

Implementing regulations promulgated by BATF . . . prohibit the disclosure of alcohol content on beer labels. In addition to prohibiting numerical indications of alcohol content, the labeling regulations proscribe descriptive terms that suggest high content, such as "strong," "full strength," "extra strength," "high test," "high proof," "pre-war strength," and "full oldtime alcoholic strength." The prohibitions do not preclude labels from identifying a beer as "low alcohol," "reduced alcohol," "non-alcoholic," or "alcohol-free." By statute and by regulation, the labeling ban must give way if state law requires disclosure of alcohol content.

B

Both parties agree that the information on beer labels constitutes commercial speech. Though we once took the position that the First Amendment does not protect commercial speech, we repudiated that position in *Virginia Bd. of Pharmacy v. Virginia Citizens Consumer Council, Inc.*, 425 U.S. 748 (1976). There we noted that the free flow of commercial information is "indispensable to the proper allocation of resources in a free enterprise system" because it informs the numerous private decisions that drive the system. Indeed, we observed that a "particular consumer's interest in the free flow of commercial information . . . may be as keen, if not keener by far, than his interest in the day's most urgent political debate."

Still, *Virginia Board of Pharmacy* suggested that certain types of restrictions might be tolerated in the commercial speech area because of the nature of such speech. In later decisions we gradually articulated a test based on " 'the "commonsense" distinction between speech proposing a commercial transaction, which occurs in an area traditionally subject to government regulation, and other varieties of speech.' " *Central Hudson* identified several factors that courts should consider in determining whether a regulation of commercial speech survives First Amendment scrutiny:

> For commercial speech to come within [the First Amendment], it at least must concern lawful activity and not be misleading. Next, we ask whether the asserted governmental interest is substantial. If both inquiries yield positive answers, we must determine whether the regulation directly advances the governmental interest asserted, and whether it is not more extensive than is necessary to serve that interest.

We now apply *Central Hudson's* test to § 205(e)(2).

III

Both the lower courts and the parties agree that respondent seeks to disclose only truthful, verifiable, and nonmisleading factual information about alcohol content on its beer labels. Thus, our analysis focuses on the substantiality of the interest behind § 205(e)(2) and on whether the labeling ban bears an acceptable fit with the Government's goal. A careful consideration of these factors indicates that § 205(e)(2) violates the First Amendment's protection of commercial speech.

A

* * *[T]he Government contends that § 205(e)(2) advances Congress' goal of curbing "strength wars" by beer brewers who might seek to compete for customers on the basis of alcohol content. * * *

* * * *

Rather than suppressing the free flow of factual information in the wine and spirits markets, the Government seeks to control competition on the basis of strength by monitoring distillers' promotions and marketing. * * * [T]he Government here has a significant interest in protecting the health, safety, and welfare of its citizens by preventing brewers from competing on the basis of alcohol strength, which could lead to greater alcoholism and its attendant social costs. * * * Both panels of The Court of Appeals that heard this case concluded that the goal of suppressing strength wars constituted a substantial interest, and we cannot say that their conclusion is erroneous.

* * * *

B

The remaining *Central Hudson* factors require that a valid restriction on commercial speech directly advance the governmental interest and be no more extensive than necessary to serve that interest. * * * The Tenth Circuit found that § 205(e)(2) failed to advance the interest in suppressing strength wars sufficiently to justify the ban. We agree.

Just two Terms ago, in *Edenfield v. Fane*, 507 U.S. 761 (1993), we had occasion to explain the *Central Hudson* factor concerning whether the regulation of commercial speech "directly advances the governmental interest asserted." In *Edenfield*, we decided that the Government carries the burden of showing that the challenged regulation advances the Government's interest "in a direct and material way." That burden "is not satisfied by mere speculation or conjecture; rather, a governmental body seeking to sustain a restriction on commercial speech must demonstrate that the harms it recites are real and that its restriction will in fact alleviate them to a material degree." * * *

The Government attempts to meet its burden by pointing to current developments in the consumer market. It claims that beer producers are already competing and advertising on the basis of alcohol strength in the "malt liquor" segment of the beer market. The Government attempts to show that this competition threatens to spread to the rest of the market by directing our attention to respondent's motives in bringing this litigation. Respondent allegedly suffers from consumer misperceptions that its beers contain less alcohol than other brands. According to the Government, once respondent gains relief from § 205(e)(2), it will use its labels to overcome this handicap.

Under the Government's theory, § 205(e)(2) suppresses the threat of such competition by preventing consumers from choosing beers on the basis of alcohol content. It is assuredly a matter of "common sense" that a restriction on the advertising of a product characteristic will decrease the extent to which consumers select a product on the basis of that trait. * * *

We conclude that § 205(e)(2) cannot directly and materially advance its asserted interest because of the overall irrationality of the Government's regulatory scheme. While the laws governing labeling prohibit the disclosure of alcohol content unless required by state law, federal regulations apply a contrary policy to beer advertising. Like § 205(e)(2), these restrictions prohibit statements of alcohol content in advertising, but, unlike § 205(e)(2), they apply only in States that affirmatively prohibit such advertisements. As only 18 States at best prohibit disclosure of content in advertisements, brewers remain free to disclose alcohol content in advertisements, but not on labels, in much of the country.

The failure to prohibit the disclosure of alcohol content in advertising, which would seem to constitute a more influential weapon in any strength war than labels, makes no rational sense if the Government's true aim is to suppress strength wars.

Other provisions of the FAAA and its regulations similarly undermine § 205(e)(2)'s efforts to prevent strength wars. While § 205(e)(2) bans the disclosure of alcohol content on beer labels, it allows the exact opposite in the case of wines and spirits. Thus, distilled spirits may contain statements of alcohol content, and such disclosures are required for wines with more than 14 percent alcohol. If combating strength wars were the goal, we would assume that Congress would regulate disclosure of alcohol content for the strongest beverages as well as for the weakest ones. Further, the Government permits brewers to signal high alcohol content through use of the term "malt liquor." Although the Secretary has proscribed the use of various colorful terms suggesting high alcohol levels, manufacturers still can distinguish a class of stronger malt beverages by identifying them as malt liquors. One would think that if the Government sought to suppress strength wars by prohibiting numerical disclosures of alcohol content, it also would preclude brewers from indicating higher alcohol beverages by using descriptive terms.

* * * *

Even if § 205(e)(2) did meet the *Edenfield* standard, it would still not survive First Amendment scrutiny because the Government's regulation of speech is not sufficiently tailored to its goal. The Government argues that a sufficient "fit" exists here because the labeling ban applies to only one product characteristic and because the ban does not prohibit all disclosures of alcohol content—it applies only to those involving labeling and advertising. In response, respondent suggests several alternatives, such as directly limiting the alcohol content of beers, prohibiting marketing efforts emphasizing high alcohol strength (which is apparently the policy in some other western nations), or limiting the labeling ban only to malt liquors, which is the segment of the market that allegedly is threatened with a strength war. We agree that the availability of these options, all of which could advance the Government's asserted interest in a manner less intrusive to respondent's First Amendment rights, indicates that § 205(e)(2) is more extensive than necessary.

IV

In sum, although the Government may have a substantial interest in suppressing strength wars in the beer market, the FAAA's countervailing provisions prevent § 205(e)(2) from furthering that purpose in a direct and material fashion.

The FAAA's defects are further highlighted by the availability of alternatives that would prove less intrusive to the First Amendment's protections for commercial speech. Because we find that § 205(e)(2) fails the *Central Hudson* test, we affirm the decision of the court below.

Questions for Discussion for Case 7.1

1. Which prongs of the *Central Hudson* test were at issue in this case?

2. Why do you think that Coors wanted to put the alcohol content on its beer labels? The Court noted that Coors was concerned with the public's opinion that its beer had a low alcohol content. Does this turn alcohol content into a marketing point? Would this run counter to the government's significant interest in avoiding a "strength war"?

3. What other ways could the government have advanced its interest in preventing strength wars?

4. Does § 205(e)(2) fail on its own merits or because it was part of an inconsistent scheme of government regulation?

7.2 Lanham Act—False Advertising
Coca-Cola Co. v. Tropicana Products, Inc., 690 F.2d 312 (2d Cir. 1982)

A proverb current even in the days of ancient Rome was "seeing is believing." Today, a great deal of what people see flashes before them on their TV sets. This case involves a 30-second television commercial with simultaneous audio and video components. We have no doubt that the byword of Rome is as valid now as it was then. And, if seeing something on TV has a tendency to persuade a viewer to believe, how much greater is the impact on a viewer's credulity when he both sees and hears a message at the same time?

In mid-February of 1982 defendant Tropicana Products, Inc. (Tropicana) began airing a new television commercial for its Premium Pack orange juice. The commercial shows the renowned American Olympic athlete Bruce Jenner squeezing an orange while saying "It's pure, pasteurized juice as it comes from the orange," and then shows Jenner pouring the fresh-squeezed juice into a Tropicana carton while the audio states "It's the only leading brand not made with concentrate and water."

Soon after the advertisement began running, plaintiff Coca-Cola Company (Coke, Coca-Cola), maker of Minute Maid orange juice, brought suit . . . against Tropicana for false advertising in violation of section 43(a) of the Lanham Act. The statute provides that anyone who uses a false description or representation in connection with goods placed in commerce "shall be liable to a civil action by [anyone] . . . who believes that he is or is likely to be damaged by the use of . . . such false description or representation." Coke claimed the commercial is false because it incorrectly represents that Premium Pack contains unprocessed, fresh-squeezed juice when in fact the juice is pasteurized (heated to about 200 degrees Fahrenheit) and sometimes frozen prior to packaging. The court below denied plaintiff's motion for a preliminary injunction to enjoin further broadcast of the advertisement pending the outcome of this litigation. In our view preliminary injunctive relief is appropriate.

I

Scope of Review

A party seeking issuance of a preliminary injunction in this Circuit must always show that it is likely to suffer possible irreparable harm if the requested relief is not granted. In addition, it must demonstrate either (1) a likelihood of success on the merits of its case or (2) sufficiently serious questions going to the merits to make them a fair ground for litigation and a balance of hardships tipping decidedly in its favor.

* * * *

II

Irreparable Injury

Perhaps the most difficult element to demonstrate when seeking an injunction against false advertising is the likelihood that one will suffer irreparable harm if the injunction does not issue. It is virtually impossible to prove that so much of one's sales will be lost or that one's goodwill will be damaged as a direct result of a competitor's advertisement. Too many market variables enter into the advertising-sales equation. Because of these impediments, a Lanham Act plaintiff who can prove actual lost sales may obtain an injunction even if most of his sales decline is attributable to factors other than a competitor's false advertising. In fact, he need not even point to an actual loss or diversion of sales.

The Lanham Act plaintiff must, however, offer something more than a mere subjective belief that he is likely to be injured as a result of the false advertising; he must submit proof which provides a reasonable basis for that belief. The likelihood of injury and causation will not be presumed, but must be demonstrated in some manner.

Two recent decisions of this Court have examined the type of proof necessary to satisfy this requirement. Relying on the fact that the products involved were in head-to-head competition, the Court in both cases directed the issuance of a preliminary injunction under the Lanham Act. *Vidal Sassoon, Inc. v. Bristol-Meyers Co.*, 661 F.2d 272, 277 (2d Cir. 1981); *Johnson & Johnson v. Carter-Wallace, Inc.*, 631 F.2d 186, 189–91 (2d Cir. 1980).[2] In both decisions the Court reasoned that sales of the plaintiffs' products would probably be harmed if the competing products' advertising tended to mislead consumers in the manner alleged.[3] Market studies were used as evidence that some consumers were in fact misled by the advertising in issue. Thus, the market studies supplied the causative link between the advertising and the plaintiffs' potential lost sales, and thereby indicated a likelihood of injury.

Applying the same reasoning to the instant case, if consumers are misled by Tropicana's commercial, Coca-Cola probably would suffer irreparable injury. Tropicana and Coca-Cola are the leading national competitors for the chilled (ready-to-serve) orange juice market. If Tropicana's advertisement misleads consumers into believing that Premium Pack is a more desirable product because it contains only fresh-squeezed, unprocessed juice, then it is likely that Coke will lose a portion of the chilled juice market and thus suffer irreparable injury.

Evidence in the record supports the conclusion that consumers are likely to be misled in this manner. A consumer reaction survey conducted by ASI Market Research, Inc., and a Burke test, measuring recall of the commercial after it was aired on television, were admitted into evidence . . . . * * * Our examination of the Burke test results leads to the same conclusion [as that reached by the trial court], i.e., that a not insubstantial number of consumers were clearly misled by the defendant's ad. Together these tests provide sufficient evidence of a risk of irreparable harm because they demonstrate that a significant number of consumers would be likely to be misled. The trial court should have considered these studies on the issue of irreparable injury. If it had, we think that it would surely have concluded . . . that the commercial will mislead consumers and, as a consequence, shift their purchases from plaintiff's product to defendant's. Coke, therefore, demonstrated that it is likely to suffer irreparable injury.

III

Likelihood of Success on the Merits

Once the initial requisite showing of irreparable harm has been made, the party seeking a preliminary injunction must satisfy either of the two alternatives regarding the merits of his case. We find that Coca-Cola satisfies the more stringent first alternative because it is likely to succeed on the merits of its false advertising action.

Coke is entitled to relief under the Lanham Act if Tropicana has used a false description or representation in its Jenner commercial. When a merchandising statement or representation is literally or explicitly false, the court may grant relief without reference to the advertisement's impact on the buying public. When the challenged advertisement is implicitly rather than explicitly false, its tendency to violate the Lanham Act by misleading, confusing or deceiving should be tested by public reaction.

In viewing defendant's 30-second commercial at oral argument, we concluded that the trial court's finding that this ad was not facially false is an error of fact. * * * The visual component of the ad makes an explicit representation that Premium Pack is produced by squeezing oranges and pouring the freshly-squeezed juice directly into the carton. This is not a true representation of how the product is prepared. Premium Pack juice is heated and sometimes frozen prior to packaging. Additionally, the simultaneous audio component of the ad states that Premium Pack is "pasteurized juice as it comes from the orange." This statement is blatantly false—pasteurized juice does not come from

---

[2] In *Vidal Sassoon* it was assumed that two different shampoos competed for the same market, but in *Johnson & Johnson* the element of competition had to be proven because the two products, baby oil and a depilatory containing baby oil, were not obviously competing for the same consumer dollars.

[3] In *Vidal Sassoon* consumers were allegedly misled to believe that Body on Tap shampoo was an all-around superior product. In *Johnson & Johnson* consumers were allegedly misled into thinking that using NAIR depilatory with baby oil would obviate the need for using baby oil alone to moisturize the skin after shaving.

oranges. Pasteurization entails heating the juice to approximately 200 degrees Fahrenheit to kill certain natural enzymes and microorganisms which cause spoilage. Moreover, even if the addition of the word "pasteurized" somehow made sense and effectively qualified the visual image, Tropicana's commercial nevertheless represented that the juice is only squeezed, heated and packaged when in fact it may actually also be frozen.

Hence, Coke is likely to succeed in arguing that Tropicana's ad is false and that it is entitled to relief under the Lanham Act. The purpose of the Act is to insure truthfulness in advertising and to eliminate misrepresentations with reference to the inherent quality or characteristic of another's product. The claim that Tropicana's Premium Pack contains only fresh-squeezed, unprocessed juice is clearly a misrepresentation as to that product's inherent quality or characteristic. Since the plaintiff has satisfied the first preliminary injunction alternative, we need not decide whether the balance of hardships tips in its favor.

Because Tropicana has made a false representation in its advertising and Coke is likely to suffer irreparable harm as a result, we reverse the district court's denial of plaintiff's application and remand this case for issuance of a preliminary injunction preventing broadcast of the squeezing-pouring sequence in the Jenner commercial.

Questions for Discussion for Case 7.2

1. The court places great emphasis on advertising studies submitted into evidence to show that consumers were misled by the advertising. How high do you think that the standard ought to be in reviewing advertising studies?

2. Was Tropicana's main claim about being the only leading brand not made with concentrate or water true? What do you think was Coca-Cola's real concern with the commercial?

3. How could you design the advertisement to have the same message but not conflict with the court's decision?

7.3 Commercial Speech, Lanham Act—False Advertising
Castrol, Inc. v. Pennzoil Co., 1993 U.S. App. LEXIS 1778 (3d Cir. Feb. 4, 1993)

The primary issue raised by this appeal is whether one of this nation's major oil companies engaged in deceptive advertising in violation of the Lanham Act. The parties to this appeal further call upon this court to interpret the degree to which commercial speech is protected by the First Amendment to the United States Constitution.

Commercial advertising plays a dynamic role in the complex financial and industrial activities of our society, leading Norman Douglas to go so far as to observe that "you can tell the ideals of a nation by its advertisements." Because honesty and fair play are prominent arrows in America's quiver of commercial and personal ideals, Congress enacted Section 43(a) of the Lanham Act "to stop the kind of unfair competition that consists of lying about goods or services". Although "comparative advertising, when truthful and nondeceptive, is a source of important information to consumers and assists them in making rational purchase decision", the consumer called upon to discern the true from the false requires a fair statement of what is true and false.

The plaintiff-appellee in this case, Castrol Inc., (Castrol), a major motor oil manufacturer and distributor of its products, sued . . . , alleging that Pennzoil Company and Pennzoil Products Company (Pennzoil) advertised its motor oil in violation of Section 43(a) of the Lanham Act when it claimed that its product "outperforms any leading motor oil against viscosity breakdown." Additionally, Castrol challenged Pennzoil's related secondary claim that Pennzoil's motor oil provides "longer engine life and better engine protection." After a bench trial on the merits, the district court held that Pennzoil's advertisements contained claims of superiority which were "literally false".

Consequently, the court permanently enjoined Pennzoil from "broadcasting, publishing, or disseminating, in any form or in any medium" the challenged advertisements, or any "revised or reformulated versions" thereof. This injunction was superseded by a more narrowly tailored Amended Order and Final Judgment, which would prohibit only "revised or reformulated false or deceptive versions of the commercials." * * * Pennzoil immediately appealed on the grounds that its advertisements did not contain false claims and that the permanent injunction issued by the district court infringed on its right to free speech as protected by the First Amendment. We affirm.

I. FACTS

* * * Castrol's suit stems from a Pennzoil advertising campaign of its motor oil consisting of print and television commercials. These commercials feature either various members of national race car glitterati, or Arnold Palmer, a professional golf luminary of national repute, asserting that Pennzoil motor oil outperforms any leading motor oil against viscosity breakdown. The court found that the advertisements also implied that Pennzoil's products offered better protection against engine failure than any other leading motor oil.

Motor oils minimize metal-to-metal contact in an engine by providing an optimum protective film between moving parts. The measure of a motor oil's resistance to film is described as "viscosity." * * * Because it is critical to motor oil performance, viscosity is the basis on which motor oils are classified and marketed, by a grading system known as "SAE J300".

According to SAE J300, the viscosity of unused motor oils is measured by an industry-recognized laboratory test developed by the American Society for Testing and Materials (ASTM). * * * The court found that the Committee of Common Market Automobile Constructors (CCMC) has established "the most demanding viscosity breakdown standards." * * * CCMC motor oil specifications contain two viscosity breakdown requirements: (1) the Shear Stability or Stay-in-Grade test, and (2) the High Temperature/High Shear (HTHS) test.

* * * The Stay-in-Grade standard is a "pass/fail" standard, and it does not rank motor oils within each grade. * * * Both parties to the litigation have stipulated that Pennzoil does not outperform Castrol against the Stay-in-Grade viscosity breakdown standard.

The HTHS test is a more rigorous test . . . . * * * By this standard's measure, Pennzoil did not outperform Castrol in any way; rather, it was Castrol's motor oils which proved superior.

Pennzoil, however, does not rely on the aforementioned tests to lend credence to its claims of superiority with respect to viscosity breakdown and protection from engine wear. Rather, Pennzoil claimed superiority on the basis of research it conducted utilizing the ASTM D-3945 Test, promulgated by the American Society of Testing and Materials.

* * * These tests showed that Pennzoil motor oil suffered less viscosity loss percentage than Castrol motor oil. Rather, Pennzoil contends that percent viscosity loss is one method of measuring viscosity breakdown, and therefore asserts that this test substantiates its advertising superiority claims.

The district court, however, found that the ASTM-3945 Test was not a true measure of viscosity breakdown; it therefore relied upon the Stay-in-Grade and the HTHS tests. These tests, along with others conducted by Castrol, led the trial court to find that Pennzoil's claims of superiority for viscosity breakdown and engine protection were literally false. Pennzoil challenges these findings, and argues also that the district court's injunction infringes upon Pennzoil's right to freedom of speech.

II. THE VISCOSITY BREAKDOWN CLAIM

First, Pennzoil asserts that, absent any evidence of consumer confusion in this case, Castrol failed to meet its burden of proving literal falsity by the standard set forth in [*Sandoz Pharmaceuticals Corp. v. Richardson-Vicks, Inc.*, 902 F.2d 222 (3d Cir. 1990).] * * *

[T]here are two different theories of recovery for false advertising under Section 43(a) of the Lanham Act: "(1) an advertisement may be false on its face; or (2) the advertisement may be literally true, but given the merchandising context, it nevertheless is likely to mislead and confuse consumers."

> When a merchandising statement or representation is literally or explicitly false, the court may grant relief without reference to the advertisement's impact on the buying public. When the challenged advertisement is implicitly rather than explicitly false, its tendency to violate the Lanham Act by misleading, confusing or deceiving should be tested by public reaction.

Therefore, because the district court properly found that claims in this case were literally false, it did not err in ignoring Pennzoil's superfluous evidence relating to the absence of consumer confusion. * * *

Second, Pennzoil argues that Castrol failed to sustain its burden of proving literal falsity because Castrol never offered affirmative proof to refute Pennzoil's claims, but merely cast doubt upon Pennzoil's research. * * *

Yet Pennzoil's contention is meritless, as the trial record is replete with Castrol's affirmative evidence proving the literal falsity of Pennzoil's claims. For example, between October 25, 1991 and February 26, 1992, the Castrol Technical Center conducted the CCMC, the International Lubricant Standardization and Approval Committee (ILSAC) and Chrysler Stay-in-Grade Tests. Both Pennzoil and Castrol met the Stay-in-Grade requirements, thus refuting

Pennzoil's contention that it outperforms Castrol with respect to viscosity breakdown.

Between January 1, 1992, and March 25, 1992, the Castrol Technical Center conducted HTHS Tests, and all Castrol motor oils met the HTHS standard established by the CCMC, as well as all the other HTHS specifications. Pennzoil's 5W-30 and 10W-30 motor oils, however, failed to meet this standard, although other Pennzoil motor oils passed this test. Therefore, this test also did not substantiate Pennzoil's claims of *superiority*; on the contrary, it demonstrated Pennzoil motor oil's *inferiority* in some respects to Castrol motor oil. Thus, according to the only two industry accepted tests for measuring viscosity breakdown, Pennzoil's claims of superiority were literally false.

Castrol also presented expert testimony and field tests which affirmatively demonstrated that Pennzoil motor oil does not outperform Castrol motor oil with respect to viscosity breakdown. For example, the Southwest Research Institute conducted an automobile fleet test at Castrol's request. Researchers placed Pennzoil motor oil inside a group of three automobiles, each of a different model, and then placed Castrol motor oil inside three cars identical to the first set. The researchers then drove these automobiles through various tests, and compared the viscosity breakdown of the two motor oils. According to this test, Castrol motor oil outperformed Pennzoil's product with respect to viscosity breakdown, therefore discrediting Pennzoil's claims.

* * * *

In this case, Pennzoil made a claim of superiority, and when tested, it proved false. Hence, . . . the district court correctly found literal falsity. Therefore, Castrol sustained its burden of proof . . . .

* * * *

III. THE ENGINE WEAR CLAIM

First, Pennzoil asserts that its claims regarding superior engine protection constitutes common marketplace "puffery," and thus do not violate the Lanham Act. Puffery is an exaggeration or overstatement expressed in broad, vague, and commendatory language.

> Such sales talk, or puffing, as it is commonly called, is considered to be offered and understood as an expression of the seller's opinion only, which is to be discounted as such by the buyer. . . . The "puffing" rule amounts to a seller's privilege to lie his head off, so long as he says nothing specific.

Prosser & Keeton, *Handbook on the Law of Torts* § 109, at 756–57 (5th ed. 1984). Puffery is distinguishable from misdescriptions or false representations of specific characteristics of a product. As such, it is not actionable.

The predicate for Pennzoil's position—that its motor oil offered better protection against engine wear amounted to mere puffery—is that they were only general claims of superiority.

Pennzoil's claim of engine protection by contrast involves more than a mere generality. Here, the claim is both specific and measurable by comparative research. * * *

Pennzoil's failure to specifically mention its competitors in the sentence promoting engine protection also does not render the statement puffery. First, the district court found that the statement compared Pennzoil to its major competitors by necessary implication. Pennzoil stated it is superior to the other brands in protecting against viscosity breakdown, noting that viscosity breakdown leads to engine problems. It left the consumer with the obvious conclusion that Pennzoil is superior to the other leading brands in protection against engine problems. * * * Therefore, Pennzoil did, by implication, compare its effectiveness against engine wear to that of its competitors . . . .

Moreover, there need not be a direct comparison to a competitor for a statement to be actionable under the Lanham Act. Under Pennzoil's logic, as Castrol points out, the Ford Motor Company could claim that its Pinto model offers the best rear end protection as long as no competitor is specifically named. Such a result is impractical and illogical.

Second, Pennzoil asserts that the district court erred in holding that the claims relating to better engine protection were literally false by necessary implication. However, in assessing whether an advertisement is literally false, a court must analyze the message conveyed in full context.

* * * Pennzoil's advertisements claim that viscosity breakdown leads to engine failure. Pennzoil then claims, albeit falsely, that it outperforms *any leading motor oil* against viscosity breakdown. The implication is that Pennzoil outperforms the other leading brands with respect to protecting against engine failure, because it outperforms them in protecting against viscosity breakdown, the cause of engine failure. * * *

* * * *

Moreover, Castrol presented copious affirmative evidence to prove that Pennzoil's claim to superior protection from engine failure is false. * * *

Also, Pennzoil's Vice President of Product Support, Donald M. Johnson, candidly conceded that car owners who utilize Castrol motor oil do not run an enhanced risk of engine failure. In addition, Pennzoil's director of research, James Newsom, testified that under normal operating conditions, consumers would not experience engine wear whether they chose Castrol or Pennzoil. Furthermore, under the industry established test for engine wear protection, both Castrol and Pennzoil met the highest performance requirements of the American Petroleum Institute.

Therefore, there was ample evidence adduced at trial to prove that Pennzoil's claims of superior protection against engine wear were literally false, and the district court's finding was not clearly erroneous.

IV. THE FIRST AMENDMENT CONCERNS

Pennzoil also expansively contends that "[i]t is beyond dispute that the district court's order constitutes a plain restraint on Pennzoil's constitutional right to commercial free speech." Pennzoil urges that if its motor oil improves in the future and thereby provides better protection from viscosity breakdown than does Castrol motor oil, Pennzoil would nonetheless be restrained from advertising this truism.

The Supreme Court has held that commercial speech is within the ambit of First Amendment protection. Paragraph (c) of the permanent injunction granted by the district court prohibits Pennzoil from:

(c) broadcasting, publishing or disseminating, in any form or medium, any commercial or advertisement that claims, directly or by clear implication that:
   (i) Pennzoil motor oil outperforms any leading motor oil against viscosity breakdown;
   (ii) Pennzoil motor oil gives the most protection against viscosity breakdown of any leading motor oil;
   (iii) Pennzoil motor oil provides better protection against engine failure than any leading motor oil;
   (iv) Pennzoil motor oil provides better protection against engine wear than any leading motor oil; or
   (v) Pennzoil motor oil provides longer engine life or greater engine durability than any other leading motor oil.

In essence, the district court has enjoined Pennzoil only from broadcasting, publishing, or disseminating the very statements which the court found to be literally false. Pennzoil argues that this is a prior restraint, in contravention of the First Amendment of the United States Constitu-

tion. At this moment, however, these claims are false, and it is well settled that false commercial speech is not protected by the First Amendment and may be banned entirely. * * * The injunction is also not overbroad because it only reaches the specific claims that the district court found to be literally false. If, in the future, Pennzoil should improve its motor oil to surpass Castrol for viscosity breakdown, Pennzoil can at that time apply for a modification of the present injunction.

We therefore hold that commercial speech that is false when uttered does not enjoy the protection of the First Amendment. The district court thus committed no error in enjoining it.

V. CONCLUSION

In summary, the trial court, in a carefully written and exhaustive opinion, found Pennzoil's superiority claims to be literally false. These findings were based on Castrol's copious affirmative evidence, which included expert testimony, laboratory testing and field testing. The evidence proved that Pennzoil motor oil does not suffer less viscosity breakdown than Castrol; on the contrary, in that respect, Castrol motor oil is superior. Therefore, ample evidence adduced at trial supported the district court's findings of fact.

Pennzoil's claim that the district court unconstitutionally restrained commercial free speech is without merit. The only way to insure that Pennzoil will not duplicate its literally false claims in the context of a different advertisement is to enjoin the specific claims. The district court's retention of jurisdiction in the event its order needs modification facilitates adequate recourse if Pennzoil's claims of superiority should in the future become meritorious.

Accordingly, the judgment of the district court will be affirmed. * * *

Questions for Discussion for Case 7.3

1. What is the difference between puffery concerning a product and misrepresentation?

2. Could Pennzoil have maintained its claims if it had disclosed the empirical basis for the claims?

3. If Pennzoil had developed its own tests for measuring viscosity breakdown and found that its product was superior (in contradiction to the other more established tests), do you think Pennzoil could advertise that claim?

4. Practically speaking, why would a competitor want to argue that an advertisement is literally false rather than implicitly false?

5. If you think a competitor has issued a false or misleading advertisement, what types of information do you need to gather to get the court to award an injunction?

6. Could the FTC have brought an action against Pennzoil? If so, on what basis?

7.4 Commercial Speech, FTC Act—Deceptive Advertising
Kraft, Inc. v. FTC, 970 F.2d 311 (7th Cir. 1992)

Kraft, Inc. ("Kraft") asks us to review an order of the Federal Trade Commission ("FTC" or "Commission") finding that it violated §§ 5 and 12 of the Federal Trade Commission Act ("Act"). The FTC determined that Kraft, in an advertising campaign, had misrepresented information regarding the amount of calcium contained in Kraft Singles American Pasteurized Process Cheese Food ("Singles") relative to the calcium content in five ounces of milk and in imitation cheese slices. The FTC ordered Kraft to cease and desist from making these misrepresentations and Kraft filed this petition for review. We enforce the Commission's order.

I.

Three categories of cheese compete in the individually wrapped process slice market: process cheese food slices, imitation slices, and substitute slices. Process cheese food slices, also known as "dairy slices," must contain at least 51% natural cheese by federal regulation. Imitation cheese slices, by contrast, contain little or no natural cheese and consist primarily of water, vegetable oil, flavoring agents, and fortifying agents. * * * Substitute slices fit somewhere in between; they fall short of the natural cheese content of process cheese food slices yet are nutritionally superior to imitation slices. Consistent with FTC usage, we refer to both imitation and substitute slices as "imitation" slices.

Kraft Singles are process cheese food slices. In the early 1980s, Kraft began losing market share to an increasing number of imitation slices that were advertised as both less expensive and equally nutritious as dairy slices like Singles. Kraft responded with a series of advertisements, collectively known as the "Five Ounces of Milk" campaign, designed to inform consumers that Kraft Singles cost more than imitation slices because they are made from five ounces of milk rather than less expensive ingredients. The ads also focused on the calcium content of Kraft Singles in an effort to capitalize on growing consumer interest in adequate calcium consumption.

The FTC filed a complaint against Kraft charging that this advertising campaign materially misrepresented the calcium content and relative calcium benefit of Kraft Singles. The FTC Act makes it unlawful to engage in unfair or deceptive commercial practices, or to induce consumers to purchase certain products through advertising that is misleading in a material respect. Thus, an advertisement is deceptive under the Act if it is likely to mislead consumers, acting reasonably under the circumstances, in a material respect. * * * In implementing this standard, the Commission examines the overall net impression of an ad and engages in a three-part inquiry: (1) what claims are conveyed in the ad; (2) are those claims false or misleading; and (3) are those claims material to prospective consumers.

Two facts are critical to understanding the allegations against Kraft. First, although Kraft does use five ounces of milk in making each Kraft Single, roughly 30% of the calcium contained in the milk is lost during processing. Second, the vast majority of imitation slices sold in the United States contain 15% of the U.S. Recommended Daily Allowance (RDA) of calcium per ounce, roughly the same amount contained in Kraft Singles. Specifically then, the FTC complaint alleged that the challenged advertisements made two implied claims, neither of which was true: (1) that a slice of Kraft Singles contains the same amount of calcium as five ounces of milk (the "milk equivalency" claim); and (2) that Kraft Singles contain more calcium than do most imitation cheese slices (the "imitation superiority" claim).

The two sets of ads at issue in this case, referred to as the "Skimp" ads and the "Class Picture" ads, ran nationally in print and broadcast media between 1985 and 1987. The Skimp ads were designed to communicate the nutritional benefit of Kraft Singles by referring expressly to their milk and calcium content. The broadcast version of this ad on which the FTC focused contained the following audio copy:

Lady (voice over): I admit it. I thought of skimping. Could you look into those big blue eyes and skimp on her? So I buy Kraft Singles. Imitation slices use hardly any milk. But Kraft has five ounces per slice. Five ounces. So her little bones get calcium they need to grow. No, she doesn't know what that big Kraft means. Good thing I do.

Singers: Kraft Singles. More milk makes 'em . . . more milk makes 'em good.

Lady (voice over): Skimp on her? No way.

The visual image corresponding to this copy shows, among other things, milk pouring into a glass until it reaches a mark on the glass denoted "five ounces." The commercial also shows milk pouring into a glass which bears the phrase "5 oz. milk slice" and which gradually becomes part of the label on a package of Singles. In January 1986, Kraft revised this ad, changing "Kraft *has* five ounces per slice" to "Kraft is *made from* five ounces per slice," and in March 1987, Kraft added the disclosure, "one ¼ ounce slice has 70% of the calcium of five ounces of milk" as a subscript in the television commercial and as a footnote in the print ads.

The Class Picture ads also emphasized the milk and calcium content of Kraft Singles but, unlike the Skimp ads, did not make an express comparison to imitation slices. The version of this ad examined by the FTC depicts a group of school children having their class picture taken, and contains the following audio copy:

> *Announcer (voice over):* Can you see what's missing in this picture?
>
> Well, a government study says that half the school kids in America don't get all the calcium recommended for growing kids. That's why Kraft Singles are important. Kraft is made from five ounces of milk per slice. So they're concentrated with calcium. Calcium the government recommends for strong bones and healthy teeth!
>
> *Photographer:* Say Cheese!
>
> *Kids:* Cheese!
>
> *Announcer (voice over):* Say Kraft Singles. 'Cause kids love Kraft Singles, right down to their bones.

The Class Picture ads also included the subscript disclaimer mentioned above.

After a lengthy trial, the Administrative Law Judge (ALJ) concluded that both the Skimp and Class Picture ads made the milk equivalency claim. * * * Further, the ALJ concluded that both sets of ads falsely conveyed the imitation superiority claim . . . . According to the ALJ, both claims were material because they implicated important health concerns. He therefore ordered Kraft to cease and desist from making these claims about any of its individually wrapped slices of process cheese food, imitation cheese, or substitute cheese.

The FTC affirmed the ALJ's decision, with some modifications. As to the Skimp ads, the Commission found that four elements conveyed the milk equivalency claim: (1) the use of the word "has" in the phrase "Kraft has five ounces per slice"; (2) repetition of the precise amount of milk in a Kraft Single (five ounces); (3) the use of the word "so" to link the reference to milk with the reference to calcium; and (4) the visual image of milk being poured into a glass up to a five-ounce mark, and the superimposition of that image onto a package of Singles. It also found two additional elements that conveyed the imitation superiority claim: (1) the express reference to imitation slices combined with the use of comparative language ("hardly any," "but"); and (2) the image of a glass containing very little milk during the reference to imitation slices, followed by the image of a glass being filled to the five-ounce mark during the reference to Kraft Singles. The Commission based all of these findings on its own impression of the advertisements and found it unnecessary to resort to extrinsic evidence; it did note, however, that the available extrinsic evidence was consistent with its determinations.

The Commission then examined the Class Picture ads—once again, without resorting to extrinsic evidence— and found that they contained copy substantially similar to the copy in the Skimp ads that conveyed the impression of milk equivalency. It rejected, however, the ALJ's finding that the Class Picture ads made an imitation superiority claim, determining that the ads neither expressly compared Singles to imitation slices, nor contained any visual images to prompt such a comparison, and that available extrinsic evidence did not support the ALJ's finding.

The FTC next found that the claims were material to consumers. It concluded that the milk equivalency claim is a health-related claim that reasonable consumers would find important and that Kraft believed that the claim induced consumers to purchase Singles. The FTC presumed that the imitation superiority claim was material because it found that Kraft intended to make that claim. It also found that the materiality of that claim was demonstrated by evidence that the challenged ads led to increased sales despite a substantially higher price for Singles than for imitation slices.

Finally, the FTC modified the ALJ's cease and desist order by extending its coverage from "individually wrapped slices of cheese, imitation cheese, and substitute cheese" to "any product that is a cheese, related cheese product, imitation cheese, or substitute cheese." The Commission found that the serious, deliberate nature of the violation, combined with the transferability of the violations to other cheese products, justified a broader order. Kraft filed this petition to set-aside the Commission's order or, alternatively, to modify its scope.

* * * *

III.

Kraft['s] . . . principal claim is that the FTC erred as a matter of law in not requiring extrinsic evidence of consumer deception. Without such evidence, Kraft claims (1) that the FTC had no objective basis for determining if its ads actually contained the implied claims alleged, and (2) that the FTC's order chills constitutionally protected commercial speech. Alternatively, Kraft contends that substantial evidence does not support the FTC's finding that the Class Picture ads contain the milk equivalency claim. Finally, Kraft maintains that even if it did make the alleged milk equivalency and imitation superiority claims, substantial evidence does not support the FTC's finding that these claims were material to consumers. We address each contention in turn.

A.

1.

In determining what claims are conveyed by a challenged advertisement, the Commission relies on two sources of information: its own viewing of the ad and extrinsic evidence. Its practice is to view the ad first and, if it is unable on its own to determine with confidence what claims are conveyed in a challenged ad, to turn to extrinsic evidence. The most convincing extrinsic evidence is a survey "of what consumers thought upon reading the advertisement in question," but the Commission also relies on other forms of extrinsic evidence including consumer testimony, expert opinion, and copy tests of ads.

Kraft has no quarrel with this approach when it comes to determining whether an ad conveys *express* claims, but contends that the FTC should be required, as a matter of law, to rely on extrinsic evidence rather than its own subjective analysis in all cases involving allegedly *implied* claims.[4] The basis for this argument is that implied claims, by definition, are not self-evident from the face of an ad. This, combined with the fact that consumer perceptions are shaped by a host of external variables—including their social and educational backgrounds, the environment in which they view the ad, and prior experiences with the product advertised—makes review of implied claims by a five-member commission inherently unreliable. The Commissioners, Kraft argues, are simply incapable of determining what implicit messages consumers are likely to perceive in an ad. Making matters worse, Kraft asserts that the Commissioners are predisposed to find implied claims because the claims have been identified in the complaint, rendering it virtually impossible for them to reflect the perceptions of unbiased consumers.

Kraft buttresses its argument by pointing to the use of extrinsic evidence in an analogous context: cases brought under § 43(a) of the Lanham Act. Courts hearing deceptive advertising claims under that Act, which provides a private right of action for deceptive advertising, generally require extrinsic proof that an advertisement conveys an implied claim. Were this a Lanham Act case, a reviewing court in all likelihood would have relied on extrinsic evidence of consumer perceptions. While this disparity is sometimes justified on grounds of advertising "expertise"—the FTC presumably possesses more of it than courts—Kraft maintains this justification is an illusory one in that the FTC has no special expertise in discerning consumer perceptions. Indeed, proof of the FTC's inexpertise abounds: false advertising cases make up a small part of the Commission's work-

load, most commissioners have little prior experience in advertising, and the average tenure of commissioners is very brief. That evidence aside, no amount of expertise in Kraft's view can replace the myriad of external variables affecting consumer perceptions. Here, the Commission found implied claims based solely on its own intuitive reading of the ads (although it did reinforce that conclusion by examining the proffered extrinsic evidence). Had the Commission fully and properly relied on available extrinsic evidence, Kraft argues it would have conclusively found that consumers do not perceive the milk equivalency and imitation superiority claims in the ads.

While Kraft's arguments may have some force as a matter of policy, they are unavailing as a matter of law. Courts, including the Supreme Court, have uniformly rejected imposing such a requirement on the FTC, and we decline to do so as well. We hold that the Commission may rely on its own reasoned analysis to determine what claims, including implied ones, are conveyed in a challenged advertisement, so long as those claims are reasonably clear from the face of the advertisement.

* * * *

2.

The crux of Kraft's first amendment argument is that the FTC's current subjective approach chills some truthful commercial speech. * * * Society has a strong interest "in the free flow of commercial information" critical to a free market economy, and it is this interest the first amendment vindicates in protecting commercial speech. However, "[f]alse, deceptive, or misleading advertising" does not serve that interest and thus this category of commercial speech "remains subject to restraint."

Kraft contends that by relying on its own subjective judgment that an ad, while literally true, implies a false message, the FTC chills nonmisleading, protected speech because advertisers are unable to predict whether the FTC will find a particular ad misleading. Advertisers can run sophisticated pre-dissemination consumer surveys and find no implied claims present, only to have the Commission determine in its own subjective view that consumers would perceive an implied claim. Indeed, Kraft maintains that is precisely what happened here. Even more troubling, Kraft maintains that the ads most vulnerable to this chilling effect are factual, comparative ads, like the Five Ounces of Milk campaign, of greatest benefit to consumers. The net result of the Commission's subjective approach will be an influx of soft "feel good" ads designed to avoid unpredictable FTC decisions. The way to avoid this chilling effect, according to Kraft, is to require the Commission to rely on objective indicia of consumer perceptions in finding implied claims.

---

[4] Express claims directly represent the fact at issue while implied claims do so in an oblique or indirect way. To illustrate, consider the following. Suppose a certain automobile gets poor gas mileage, say, 10 miles per gallon. One advertisement boasts that it gets 30 miles per gallon while another identifies the car as the "Miser," depicts it rolling through the countryside past one gas station after another, and proclaims that the car is inexpensive to operate. Both ads make deceptive claims: the first does so expressly, the second does so impliedly.

Kraft's first amendment challenge is doomed by the Supreme Court's holding in *Zauderer v. Office of Disciplinary Counsel*, 471 U.S. 626 (1985) . . .* * * *

[Z]*auderer* teaches that consumer surveys are not compelled by the first amendment when the alleged deception although implied, is conspicuous. In both *Zauderer* and here, an omitted piece of information—the definition of a key contractual term in *Zauderer*; the effect of processing on nutrient content here—led to potential consumer deception, and in both cases the ads were literally true, yet impliedly misleading. Kraft's implied claims were reasonably clear from the face of the ads and not unpredictable to Kraft. * * * Because we conclude that the Commission was not required to rely on extrinsic evidence, we need not examine the extrinsic evidence proffered by Kraft that it says contravenes the Commission's findings. We note, however, that the Commission did thoroughly examine this evidence, albeit after the fact, and found that it did not refute the implied claim findings and that some of the evidence was based on unsound consumer testing methodologies.

Our holding does not diminish the force of Kraft's argument as a policy matter, and, indeed, the extensive body of commentary on the subject makes a compelling argument that reliance on extrinsic evidence should be the rule rather than the exception. Along those lines, the Commission would be well-advised to adopt a consistent position on consumer survey methodology—advertisers and the FTC, it appears, go round and round on this issue—so that any uncertainty is reduced to an absolute minimum.

B.

Alternatively, Kraft argues that substantial evidence does not support the FTC's finding that the Class Picture ads convey a milk equivalency claim. * * *

We find substantial evidence in the record to support the FTC's finding. Although Kraft downplays the nexus in the ads between milk and calcium, the ads emphasize visually and verbally that five ounces of milk go into a slice of Kraft Singles; this image is linked to calcium content, strongly implying that the consumer gets the calcium found in five ounces of milk. * * *

Kraft asserts that the literal truth of the Class Picture ads—they *are* made from five ounces of milk and they *do* have a high concentration of calcium—makes it illogical to render a finding of consumer deception. The difficulty with this argument is that even literally true statements can have misleading implications. Here, the average consumer is not likely to know that much of the calcium in five ounces of milk (30%) is lost in processing, which leaves consumers with a misleading impression about calcium content. The

critical fact is not that reasonable consumers might believe that a ¼ ounce slice of cheese actually contains five ounces of *milk*, but that reasonable consumers might believe that a ¼ ounce slice actually contains the *calcium* in five ounces of milk.

C.

Kraft next asserts that the milk equivalency and imitation superiority claims, even if made, are not material to consumers. A claim is considered material if it "involves information that is important to consumers and, hence, likely to affect their choice of, or conduct regarding a product." The Commission is entitled to apply, within reason, a presumption of materiality, and it does so with three types of claims: (1) express claims; (2) implied claims where there is evidence that the seller intended to make the claim; and (3) claims that significantly involve health, safety, or other areas with which reasonable consumers would be concerned. Absent one of these situations, the Commission examines the record and makes a finding of materiality or immateriality.

Here, the ALJ concluded that both claims were presumptively material because calcium is a significant health concern to consumers. The Commission upheld this conclusion, although it applied a presumption of materiality only to the imitation superiority claim. Kraft asserts the Commission's determination is not supported by substantial evidence. We disagree.

In determining that the milk equivalency claim was material to consumers, the FTC cited Kraft surveys showing that 71% of respondents rated calcium content an extremely or very important factor in their decision to buy Kraft Singles, and that 52% of female, and 40% of all respondents, reported significant personal concerns about adequate calcium consumption. The FTC further noted that the ads were targeted to female homemakers with children and that the 60 milligram difference between the calcium contained in five ounces of milk and that contained in a Kraft Single would make up for most of the RDA calcium deficiency shown in girls aged 9–11. Finally, the FTC found evidence in the record that Kraft designed the ads with the intent to capitalize on consumer calcium deficiency concerns.

Significantly, the FTC found further evidence of materiality in Kraft's conduct: despite repeated warnings, Kraft persisted in running the challenged ads. Before the ads even ran, ABC television raised a red flag when it asked Kraft to substantiate the milk and calcium claims in the ads. Kraft's ad agency also warned Kraft in a legal memorandum to substantiate the claims before running the ads. Moreover, in October 1985, a consumer group warned Kraft that it believed the Skimp ads were potentially deceptive. Nonetheless, a high-level Kraft executive recommended that the ad copy remain unaltered because the "Singles business is growing for the first time in four years due in large part to the copy." Finally, the FTC and the California Attorney General's Office independently notified the company in early 1986 that investigations had been initiated to determine whether the ads conveyed the milk equivalency claims. Notwithstanding these warnings, Kraft continued to run the ads and even rejected proposed alternatives that would have allayed concerns over their deceptive nature. From this, the FTC inferred—we believe, reasonably—that Kraft thought the challenged milk equivalency claim induced consumers to purchase Singles and hence that the claim was material to consumers.

With regard to the imitation superiority claim, the Commission applied a presumption of materiality after finding evidence that Kraft intended the challenged ads to convey this message. * * * It found this presumption buttressed by the fact that the challenged ad copy led to increased sales of Singles, even though they cost 40 percent more than imitation slices. Finally, the FTC determined that Kraft's consumer surveys were insufficient to rebut this inference and in particular criticized Kraft's survey methodology because it offered limited response options to consumers.

* * * *

IV.

The Commission's cease and desist order prohibits Kraft from running the Skimp and Class Picture ads, as well as from advertising any calcium or nutritional claims not supported by reliable scientific evidence. This order extends not only to the product contained in the deceptive advertisements (Kraft Singles), but to all Kraft cheeses and cheese-related products, which include Cracker Barrel, Velveeta, and Philadelphia Brand Cream Cheese. Kraft contends this order is too broad and must be set-aside or modified because it (1) bans constitutionally protected commercial speech, and (2) is not rationally related to Kraft's violation of the Act.

A.

First amendment infirmities arise, according to Kraft, from the sweep of the order: by banning commercial speech that is only *potentially* misleading, the order chills some non-deceptive advertising deserving of constitutional protection. * * *

* * * *

Kraft asserts that its advertisements are only potentially misleading . . . because the milk equivalency and imitation superiority claims are true and verifiable, there is no evidence that these claims actually misled consumers, and the advertising medium is not inherently conducive to deception. Alternative remedial measures were readily available to the Commission, such as modifications to the ads or prominent disclosures, and thus, Kraft contends, the order is broader than reasonably necessary to prevent deception. * * *

We reject Kraft's argument. To begin with, the Commission determined that the ads were *actually* misleading, not *potentially* misleading, thus justifying a total ban on the challenged ads. Moreover, even if we were to assume the order bans some potentially misleading speech, it is only constitutionally defective if it is no "broader than reasonably necessary to prevent the [deception]." We conclude that it is sufficiently narrow to pass constitutional muster. . . . [T]he restriction at issue here is an administrative cease and desist order directed toward one company's cheese ads and predicated on a specific finding of past deceptive practices.

To reiterate, the FTC's order does two things: it prohibits the Skimp ads and the Class Picture ads (as *currently* designed) and it requires Kraft to base future nutrient and calcium claims on reliable scientific evidence. Kraft mischaracterizes the decision as a categorical ban on commercial speech when in fact it identifies with particularity two nutrient claims that the Commission found actually misleading and prohibits only those claims. It further places on Kraft the (minor) burden of supporting future nutrient claims with reliable data. This leaves Kraft free to use any advertisement it chooses, including the Skimp and Class Picture ads, so long as it either eliminates the elements specifically identified by the FTC as contributing to consumer deception or corrects this inaccurate impression by adding prominent, unambiguous disclosures. We note one additional consideration further alleviating first amendment concerns; Kraft, like any party to an FTC order, may seek an advisory opinion from the Commission as to whether any future advertisements comply with its order, and this procedure has been specifically cited by courts as one method of reducing advertiser uncertainty.

For these reasons, we hold that the specific prohibitions imposed on Kraft in the FTC's cease and desist order are not broader than reasonably necessary to prevent deception and hence not violative of the first amendment. * * * The *subject* of Kraft's ads (i.e., the milk and calcium content of Singles) is obviously a perfectly legitimate subject of commercial advertising. It is only the *manner* of presentation that needs rectification. Kraft is free to continue advertising the milk and calcium content in its cheese products, and it can avoid future violations by correcting the misleading elements identified in the FTC's decision. Kraft could, for example, redesign the Skimp and Class Picture ads so that calcium content is accurately presented (i.e., "each Kraft Single contains the calcium equivalent of 3.5 ounces of milk") or it could add prominent, unambiguous disclosures about calcium loss in processing, either of which would put it in full compliance with the order.

B.

Alternatively, Kraft argues that the scope of the order is not "reasonably related" to Kraft's violation of the Act because it extends to products that were not the subject of the challenged advertisements. The FTC has discretion to issue multi-product orders, so-called "fencing-in" orders, that extend beyond violations of the Act to prevent violators from engaging in similar deceptive practices in the future. Such an order must be sufficiently clear that it is comprehensible to the violator, and must be "reasonably related" to a violation of the Act. Kraft does not challenge the order's clarity or precision but only its reasonableness.

In determining whether a broad fencing-in order bears a "reasonable relationship" to a violation of the Act, the Commission considers (1) the deliberateness and seriousness of the violation, (2) the degree of transferability of the violation to other products, and (3) any history of prior violations. Here, the ALJ found that Kraft had not engaged in a long-term pattern of deceptive advertising, and that this was an isolated incident in response to significant competitive pressures on Kraft; hence, the ALJ opted for a narrow order. The FTC disagreed; it concluded that Kraft's violations were serious, deliberate, and easily transferable to other Kraft products, thus warranting a broad fencing-in order.

We find substantial evidence to support the scope of the order. The Commission based its finding of seriousness on the size ($15 million annually) and duration (two and one-half years) of the ad campaign and on the difficulty most consumers would face in judging the truth or falsity of the implied calcium claims. Although Kraft disputes the Commission's $15 million figure, arguing it covers many non-deceptive or unchallenged advertisements, that does not obviate the fact that this was an expensive, nationwide campaign with highly effective results. Moreover, the FTC properly found that it is unreasonable to expect most consumers to perform the calculations necessary to compare the calcium content of Kraft Singles with five ounces of milk given the fact that the nutrient information on milk cartons is not based on a five-ounce serving.

As noted previously, the Commission also found that Kraft's conduct was deliberate because it persisted in running the challenged ad copy despite repeated warnings from outside sources that the copy might be implicitly misleading. Kraft challenges this finding, arguing it responded to these warnings by acting in good faith to modify the ads, and further that it commissioned a post-dissemination survey to determine whether the complaints had any merit. This survey found that only an insignificant percentage of respondents detected the alleged claims. We reject these contentions. The deceptive claims were apparent from the face of the ad, but even if they somehow eluded Kraft, the Commission reasonably concluded that the steady stream of warnings should have put Kraft on notice that its surveys were somehow inadequate or defective. Kraft made three modifications to the ads, but two of them were implemented at the very end of the campaign, more than two years after it had begun. This dilatory response provided a sufficient basis for the Commission's conclusion.

The Commission further found that the violations were readily transferable to other Kraft cheese products given the general similarity between Singles and other Kraft cheeses.
* * *

Finally, the FTC concluded that these factors outweighed Kraft's lack of prior violations. Kraft maintains that the Commission simply brushed aside its clean record even though prior violations are highly probative of propensity to commit future violations. This contention is also without merit because it is the circumstances of the violation as a whole, and not merely the presence or absence of any one of factor, that justifies a broad order. Hence, the FTC reasonably concluded that the seriousness, deliberateness, and transferability of the violations took precedence over the absence of any prior Kraft violations.

V.

For the foregoing reasons, Kraft's petition to set-aside the order is DENIED and the Commission's order is ENFORCED.

Questions for Discussion for Case 7.4

1. How is extrinsic evidence used in deceptive advertising cases brought under the FTC Act? In deceptive advertising cases brought under the Lanham Act?

2. The packages containing cheese products have printed nutritional information that consumers can compare to other brands. Why does this not alleviate the FTC's concerns about consumers being misled by the advertisements?

3. What was untrue about Kraft's revised advertisements? Why didn't a disclaimer on the bottom of the advertisement correct any deficiencies?

4. What factors do you think prompt the FTC to act on allegedly deceptive advertising? How might a manager limit each factor's influence?

DISCUSSION QUESTIONS

1. Since the late 1960s, Hot Wax, Inc., has produced and marketed car waxes to carwashes through the country. Its formula for car wax incorporates carnauba waxes at a considerable cost. Turtle Wax, Inc., entered the carwash supply industry in the mid-1970s, but it uses neither carnauba nor beeswax in its car waxes. Instead, it uses mineral seal oils or wax emulsions that are considerably cheaper than traditional wax ingredients. As a result, Turtle Wax has become a leader in the car wax industry. Hot Wax filed suit against Turtle Wax, alleging that Turtle Wax engaged in false advertising in violation of § 43(a) of the Lanham Act by promoting its products as "wax" when the products did not actually contain wax. Turtle Wax responded that Hot Wax's definition of "wax" was overly formalistic and introduced consumer surveys that indicated that consumers got exactly what they expected from a wax when they purchased Turtle Wax products—polish, shine, and protection. Hot Wax filed for summary judgment. Should the court grant summary judgment to Hot Wax? Why, or why not? *Hot Wax, Inc. v. Turtle Wax, Inc.*, 27 F. Supp. 2d 1043 (N.D. Ill. 1998), *aff'd*, 191 F.3d 813 (7th Cir. 1998)

2. In 1996, Miramax Films Corp. released a movie in the United States called "Scream," which had been directed by Wes Craven, an internationally renowned director of horror movies. In 1997, Columbia Pictures released "I Know What You Did Last Summer" in the United States. Shortly before the release, Miramax discovered that Columbia was marketing "Summer" as "From the Creator of Scream." The only link between "Scream" and "Summer" is the screenwriter Kevin Williamson. Williamson wrote an original screenplay for "Scream" and adapted a novel by another author for the screenplay of "Summer." In the advertisements, Williamson's name appeared in the small-print "credit block" of "Summer," but he was never named or otherwise identified as the "creator" to whom the advertisements refer.

Miramax filed suit against Columbia, alleging that Columbia was trying to profit from the popularity of "Scream" by inducing potential viewers of horror movies to see "Summer" in the false belief that it originated from the same source as "Scream." Miramax seeks a preliminary injunction against further use of the advertising. Should the court grant the relief requested to Miramax? Why, or why not? *Miramax Films Corp. v. Columbia Pictures Entertainment, Inc.*, 996 F. Supp. 294 (S.D.N.Y. 1998)

3. Abbott Laboratories makes and sells Ensure, a nutritional supplement beverage (NSB). Ensure has consistently held the greatest market share of all NSBs on the market. Gerber Products Co. reformulated a former product, Resource, into an NSB in 1997 and launched an advertising campaign. The campaign asserted, among other things, that "America Prefers Resource Over Ensure" and "National Preference Winner Resource Beats Ensure." Abbot asserts that Gerber's claim is false because the tests that Gerber relied upon to support its claim were conducted as taste tests and not as tests indicating overall preference. Resource and Ensure are both used for medicinal or medical reasons and are substantially similar in nutritional value. Abbot filed suit under § 43(a) of the Lanham Act, alleging that Gerber's advertising claims were literally false. Are they? Why, or why not? *Abbott Laboratories v. Gerber Products Co.*, 979 F. Supp. 569 (W.D. Mich. 1997)

4. Two Rivers, Wisconsin, enacted an extensive ordinance regulating the placement and nature of outdoor advertising. The preamble of the ordinance recognized "the need to protect the safety and welfare of the public; the need for well-maintained and attractive sign displays within the community; and the need for adequate business identification, advertising, and communication." Lavey is the President of the Lakeland Group, an advertising and public relations business. Lavey and the Lakeland Group have owned billboards for the last 15 years and have rented them to the public for the display of commercial and non-commercial messages. Two Rivers has frequently cited Lavey and the Lakeland Group for placing off-premises signs in areas where the ordinance does not permit such signs. Lavey brought this action seeking a declaration that the ordinance violates his First Amendment rights. How should the court analyze this issue? What result should it reach? *Lavey v. City of Two Rivers*, 171 F.3d 1110 (7th Cir. 1999)

5. The California Dental Association (CDA) is a voluntary nonprofit association of local dental societies to which about three-fourths of the dentists belong. The CDA lobbies and litigates in its members's interests and conducts marketing and public relations campaigns for their benefit. The dentists who belong to the CDA through the local associations agree to abide by a Code of Ethics (Code) that prohibits false and misleading advertising. The local associations enforce the Code by denying membership to new dentists who refuse to withdraw or revise objectionable advertisements and by subjecting current members who violate the Code to censure, suspension, or expulsion from the CDA.

The FTC brought a complaint against the CDA, alleging that it applied its guidelines so as to restrict truthful, nondeceptive advertising, and so violated § 5 of the FTC Act. In particular, the FTC alleged that the CDA had unreasonably restricted price advertising, particularly about discounted fees, and advertising relating to the quality of dental services. Has the CDA violated the FTC Act? Why, or why not? *California Dental Association v. FTC*, 526 U.S. 756 (1999)

6. Sabal is the manufacturer and seller of a line of over-the-counter topical hair loss products known as the "hair farming system." She claims that these products work by cleaning out congested pores and allowing hair to escape that would otherwise be trapped beneath the scalp. In 1993, Sabal entered into an exclusive marketing agreement with Mega Systems, Inc., to advertise her hair farming products on a nationally broadcast radio infomercial. During the infomercial, she stated that her products "can deep clean underneath the surface of the scalp, and clean out all the debris that prevents the hair or blocks the hair from reaching the surface." She also stated: "I have a right to this theory, whether the medical community believes me or not, although they soon will because I'll be written up in most of the major medical journals around the world. . . . It's guaranteed to work on every human being. . . . And everyone should have their hair back in six months to a year, permanently, painlessly, and never have to purchase anything again." In addition to the infomercial, Sabal published similar claims on an Internet Web site and in a book she published.

In 1996, the FTC charged her with deceptive advertising and fraudulent misrepresentation. How should the court rule on the FTC's motion for a preliminary injunction? *FTC v. Sabal*, 32 F. Supp. 2d 1004 (N.D. Ill. 1998)

7. Novell, Inc., produces its NetWare networking software in two forms: original and upgrade. The upgrade version is substantially identical to the original in function; the primary difference is its lower price as the upgrade is only available to owners of previous versions of the software. Network Trade Center, Inc. (NTC), purchased older versions of the NetWare software in bulk at discounted prices, and ordered the cheaper upgrade of the newer software from author-

ized Novell distributors. (At no time was NTC an authorized distributor of Novell software.) NTC then advertised the "upgrade" as "New Retail" or as a "Special Novell Promotional Package" while showing pictures of the "original" NetWare box, and sold it to end users. Many end users expressed confusion to both NTC and Novell about the extent of the license they obtained: some thought that they had received the "original" retail version, and others thought that they could register the upgrade with Novell. Some became so frustrated that they returned their copies to NTC. Once Novell discovered NTC's practice, Novell ordered NTC to stop, but NTC continued to advertise the product. Novell has filed suit, alleging, among other claims, that NTC is in violation of the Lanham Act's prohibition against false advertising. Has NTC engaged in false advertising? Why, or why not? *Novell, Inc. v. Network Trade Ctr.*, 25 F. Supp. 2d 1218 (D. Utah 1997)

8. Tommy Larsen, a Danish citizen, produces aesthetically pleasing functional objects, such as furniture. In 1992, Larsen designed a compact disc holder called the "CD 25," which holds 25 CDs. At first, Larsen distributed his product only in Europe, but he soon began exporting the CD 25 to the United States. Soon thereafter, Larsen looked for a U.S. distributor for his product and entered into a limited distributorship with Terk Technologies Corp. (Terk). Terk placed an order for 11,232 units at $1 per piece. Although the distribution agreement was not exclusive, Larsen treated it as though it were, allowing all orders in the United States to be fulfilled by Terk.

Despite the success of the CD 25 in high-end retail stores, Terk did not place other orders with Larsen, stating that demand did not warrant more units. In fact, however, Terk had placed an order with Allen Machine Products for 11,000 counterfeit units of the CD 25. Terk marketed these Allen-made CD 25s as the "TOMMY LARSEN" and "CD 25." The counterfeit holders also had markings indicating that the design was Danish and the product was produced in Denmark. The counterfeits were actually produced in New York.

Larsen, suspicious about the lack of orders from Terk, examined several of the distributed products and discovered the counterfeiting. He sued Terk, arguing that Terk had engaged in passing-off in violation of the Lanham Act. Has Terk violated the Lanham Act? Why, or why not? *Larsen v. Terk Techs. Corp.*, 151 F.3d 140 (4th Cir. 1998)

9. Synygy, Inc., produces Information Production and Distribution Systems, a software program that enables the user to integrate data from different sources. This software was targeted at companies in the pharmaceutical industry. Scott-Levin, Inc., compiles data for pharmaceutical companies that is used in computer programs such as those produced by Synygy. While working on a project for Bristol Meyers Squibb, Inc., Scott-Levin had disagreements with Synygy after Synygy changed file specifications without telling Scott-Levin and then blamed Scott-Levin for the conversion problems that ensued. In conversations with agents of Zeneca Pharmaceutical, Inc., a common customer of the two software companies, two Scott-Levin representatives discussed the problems they had working with Synygy in the past. Soon thereafter, Zeneca discontinued its relationship with Synygy. Zeneca claims that the discussions with the Scott-Levin representatives had no influence on that decision. In addition, during a client conference in 1997, Scott-Levin presented a slide show that contained the following slide: "simulate—to assume the outward qualities or appearance of, often with the intent to deceive." Simulate, Inc., was Synygy's name at the time of the client conference. Synygy sued Scott-Levin for commercial disparagement. Should Synygy prevail? Why, or why not? *Synygy, Inc. v. Scott-Levin, Inc.*, 51 F. Supp. 2d 570 (E.D. Pa. 1999)

10. Telebrands Corp. produces infomercials for television and distributes the products advertised on the commercials in retail stores. In 1996, Telebrands became the exclusive licensee of the "SAFETY CAN," a can opener that cuts cans from the side and not from the top, thereby eliminating the sharp, jagged edge. On the packaging of the SAFETY CAN was the statement "AS SEEN ON TV" in bright red lettering. As a result of the $3 million advertising campaign, Telebrands received over 300,000 direct response orders from consumers and over 1.9 million retail orders. In Summer 1997, Wilton Industries, Inc., also began selling a hand-held can opener that produces no sharp edges, known as the Betty Crocker "Safe Touch™." The packaging on the "Safe Touch™" also contained the "AS SEEN ON TV" logo. According to Wilton, *they* planned on showing an infomercial on national television, but *they* never did. The only television advertising that occurred for the "Safe Touch™" was small infomercials on cable preview channels in Chicago during June 1997. Telebrands alleged that the logo "AS SEEN ON TV" constitutes false advertising

in violation of the Lanham Act. Telebrands asked the court to issue a preliminary injunction enjoining Wilton from using the logo. Should the court issue the preliminary injunction? Why, or why not? *Telebrands Corp. v. Wilton Indus.*, 983 F. Supp. 471 (S.D.N.Y. 1997)

11. Clorox Co. produces the top-selling brand of roach bait insecticide called Combat. United Industries is a smaller, relatively new entrant in the roach bait industry that sells the Maxattrax brand of roach insecticide. To promote the Maxattrax product, United produced and distributed a 15-second television commercial entitled "Side by Side." The commercial opened with two boxes sitting on kitchen countertops—one was Maxattrax and the other was the generic "Roach Bait" but was vaguely similar to packaging used in the Combat brand. A voice-over asked, "Can you guess which bait kills roaches in 24 hours?" The camera then panned to show two differing views of the kitchen. On the Maxattrax side, the kitchen was neat and orderly; on the generic brand's side, the room was dirty and disheveled, ostensibly as a result of the roach infestation. The words, "Based on lab tests" appeared on the bottom of the screen, and another voice-over stated: "To kill roaches in 24 hours, it's hot-shot Maxattrax. Maxattrax, it's the no-wait roach bait."

Clorox asserted that this advertising campaign is not literally true and violates the Lanham Act's prohibition against false advertising because scientific tests conclude that Maxattrax (as well as all other roach bait products) can only exterminate those roaches that come into direct contact with the product during the 24-hour period. Clorox produced no evidence of consumer deception and therefore does not challenge the ad as being implicitly false or misleading. Clorox seeks a preliminary injunction enjoining United from using the ad in the future. Should the court issue the preliminary injunction? Why, or why not? *United Indus. Corp. v. Clorox Co.*, 140 F.3d 1175 (8th Cir. 1998)

12. General Motors Corp. aired a commercial in which a voice was heard asking who held the record for being selected most frequently as most valuable player of the National Athletic Association's basketball tournament. On the screen appeared the words "Lew Alcindor," former basketball star Kareem Abdul-Jabbar's name before his conversion to Islam. The ad went on to list the most valuable features of the Olds 88 as a "Definite First Round Pick." The current name, voice, signature, photograph, or likeness of

Kareem Abdul-Jabbar did not appear in the ad. The trial court granted summary judgment to General Motors on Abdul-Jabbar's right-of-publicity claim. Was the trial court's decision correct? Why, or why not? *Abdul-Jabbar v. General Motors Corp.*, 85 F.3d 407 (9th Cir. 1996)

13. Dillard Department Stores ran a newspaper advertisement for a shirt known as a "henley." The ad featured a photograph of a man wearing a henley shirt with the words "This is Don" in large print beside the picture and an arrow pointing toward the man's head from the words. Underneath the words was the statement, "This is Don's henley," with a second arrow pointing toward the shirt. The ad also contained the name of the retailer, general information about the sale price of the shirts, the name of the shirts' manufacturer, the available sizes, and the following: "Sometimes Don tucks it in; other times he wears it loose—it looks great either way. Don loves his henley; you will too."

Don Henley is a popular rock and roll musician. He founded The Eagles in the 1970s and in the 1980s and 1990s pursued a successful solo career. He has sued Dillard for violating his right of publicity. How should the court rule on his claim? Why? *Henley v. Dillard Dept. Stores*, 46 F. Supp. 2d 587 (N.D. Tex. 1999)

CHAPTER 8

Legal Issues Relating to Promotion and Consumer Protection

Consumer Protection Law

In this chapter, we consider some of the major sources of consumer protection law. A *consumer* is any individual who purchases goods or services for personal or household consumption.

Overview

Consumer protection laws are found at the federal, state, and local levels of government. State laws are usually governed through the state attorney general's office or through an office of consumer affairs. State laws can be very comprehensive and may well offer more protection than federal legislation in specific instances. However, we focus our discussion on federal legislation, which itself is very varied and is found in many different statutes and regulations.

Many of the topics that we discuss in Chapter 7, such as false or deceptive advertising or business practices and bait-and-switch tactics, could be viewed as consumer protection legislation. The Federal Trade Commission's (FTC's) *Policy Statement on Unfairness*, for example, which is discussed in the context of unfair advertisements in Chapter 7, applies equally to unfair business practices that adversely affect consumers, as the following case illustrates (see Focus Case 8.1 on page 268).

In this chapter, we focus specifically on legislation addressing direct marketing, labeling and packaging regulation, health and safety regulation, and statutes relating to consumer credit transactions, such as the Truth-in-Lending Act and the Consumer Credit Protection Act.

Direct Marketing Activities

Direct marketing refers to marketing efforts designed to persuade consumers to make a purchase from their home, office, or other nonretail setting. Examples include direct mail, catalogues, telemarketing, and electronic retailing (including solicitations made via e-mail). Because operating costs are lower, direct marketing can be less expensive for retailers than selling through a retail outlet. Direct marketing can also be much more convenient for consumers.[1]

These types of marketing techniques can also result in several types of abuses. Direct marketing thus tends to be fairly heavily regulated at the federal, state, and even local levels. The following discussion focuses on some of the more common forms of direct marketing regulation. Companies engaged in direct marketing should consult an attorney, however, to be certain that their proposed activities do not run afoul of any specialized laws, including any state or local laws that might apply.

TELEMARKETING

Telemarketing refers to the selling of goods or services by telephone or fax machine. It can consist of either sales calls (usually unsolicited) by the marketer or by orders placed by consumers, often through toll-free 800 numbers.

Telemarketing is regulated at both the federal and state levels. Not surprisingly, regulation of telemarketing has focused primarily on unsolicited sales calls, as opposed to customer-initiated sales orders.

Most states have statutes regulating telephone solicitation. State regulation may, in fact, impose more stringent requirements upon telemarketers than does federal regulation, such as requiring that the consumer give permission in writing before a telemarketing call may proceed or requiring telemarketers to create a "no-call list" of consumers who do not want to be contacted.

---

[1] Information about direct marketing activities is available at the Web site of The Direct Marketing Association, Inc., http://www.the-dma.org.

Focus Case 8.1

Facts: Between 1966 and 1975, Orkin Exterminating Company sold "lifetime" guarantees for extermination services. The contracts provided that the customer could renew his or her "lifetime" guarantee by paying an annual renewal fee in an amount specified in the contracts. The contracts did not provide for any increase in this fee.

By 1980, Orkin had determined that increasing costs and inflation rendered the contracts disadvantageous to Orkin. Orkin thus informed the customers that their annual renewal fees were going to be increased by 40%. Although many customers complained, they did not have any viable alternatives as switching to other competitors would have been no cheaper than paying Orkin's increased rates.

The FTC issued an administrative complaint that Orkin had committed an unfair act or practice in violation of Section 5 of the FTC Act. The ALJ agreed and issued an order requiring Orkin to roll back all fees in pre-1975 contracts to the levels specified in the contracts. Orkin appealed to the Commission, which affirmed the ALJ's decision. Orkin then appealed to the U.S. Court of Appeals.

Decision: The U. S. Court of Appeals noted that the FTC's *Policy Statement on Unfairness* provides:

> [T]o justify a finding of unfairness the injury must satisfy three tests. It must be substantial; it must not be outweighed by any countervailing benefits to consumers or competition that the practice pro-

duces; and it must be an injury that consumers themselves could not reasonably have avoided.

The court then reviewed the Commission's findings. The Commission had found that the first prong of the standard, requiring a finding of substantial injury to consumers, had been met. The Commission had stated: "The harm resulting from Orkin's conduct consists of increased costs for services previously bargained for and includes the intangible loss of the certainty of the fixed price term in the contract." In fact, Orkin's increase in annual fees generated more than $7 million in additional renewal fees.

In examining the second prong, the Commission had determined that the increase in annual fees did not result in any benefits to consumers, as it was not accompanied by an increase in the level or quality of the service provided.

Finally, with regard to the third prong, the Commission had found that the consumers could not have reasonably avoided the injury. The contracts had not given the consumers any indication that Orkin might raise the annual fees; thus "[a]nticipatory avoidance through consumer choice was impossible." Nor could consumers have avoided their injuries by switching their business to one of Orkin's competitors.

The Court of Appeals found no error in the Commission's findings and affirmed the Commission's cease-and-desist order. *Orkin Exterminating Co. v. FTC*, 849 F.2d 1354 (11th Cir. 1988).

At the federal level, the *Telephone Consumer Protection Act* (TCPA),[2] which was passed in 1991, regulates telemarketing activities. This Act prohibits telephone solicitation using an automatic telephone dialing system or a prerecorded voice. The TCPA also regulates direct marketing via fax transmissions. Fax advertising is enticing to marketers because it is often cheaper than direct mail advertising and receives a greater response from recipients. On the other hand, unlike "junk" mail, which can be easily thrown out, unsolicited fax advertisements impose costs upon the recipients in terms of paper, toner, and tied-up telephone lines. The TCPA thus makes it illegal to transmit fax ads without first obtaining the permission of the recipient.

The TCPA is enforced by the Federal Communications Commission (FCC). The TCPA also provides consumers with a private cause of action. Consumers sue in state court for violation of the TCPA and can recover either actual monetary damages resulting from a violation of the Act or $500 for each violation, whichever

[2] 47 U.S.C. § 227.

is greater. The court may treble the damage award if it determines that the defendant willfully or knowingly violated the TCPA.

Although marketers have brought several suits challenging the TCPA on First Amendment commercial free speech grounds, the courts have upheld the Act. Commercial free speech is discussed in more detail in Chapter 7.

See Discussion Cases 8.1, 8.2.

The FTC also has a role to play in regulating telemarketers. Under the *Telemarketing and Consumer Fraud and Abuse Prevention Act of 1994*,[3] the FTC has authority to establish rules regarding telemarketing and to bring actions against fraudulent telemarketers. The FTC's *Telemarketing Sales Rule of 1995*[4] covers most types of interstate telemarketing calls to consumers, including calls to pitch goods, services, sweepstakes, and prize promotion and investment opportunities. It also applies to calls that consumers make in response to postcards or other materials that they receive in the mail (except catalogues), unless the materials contain the information that is required to be disclosed under the Rule. If a solicitation occurs via an e-mail inviting the sender to place an order via a telephone call, that call and any subsequent sale must comply with the Telemarketing Sales Rule requirements. The Rule does not apply to transactions that occur entirely on-line, however.

The Rule also does not apply to entities that are specifically exempted from FTC jurisdiction, including (1) banks and other financial institutions; (2) long-distance telephone companies, airlines, and other common carriers; (3) nonprofit organizations; and (4) insurance companies that are otherwise regulated by state law. In addition, the Rule does not apply to certain types of calls, including (1) 900-number calls; (2) calls placed by consumers in response to a catalogue; (3) calls related to the sale of a franchise or certain business opportunities; (4) unsolicited calls from consumers; (5) calls that are part of a transaction involving a face-to-face sales presentation; (6) business-to-business calls that do not involve retail sales of nondurable office and cleaning supplies; and (7) most calls made in response to general media or direct mail advertising.

The Rule requires telemarketers, before they make their sales pitch, to inform the recipient that the call is a sales call and to identify the seller's name and the product or services being sold. The telemarketer must inform the recipient of the total cost and quantity of the product being sold; any material restrictions, limitations, or conditions on using or obtaining the goods; and whether the sale is final or nonrefundable. It is illegal for the telemarketer to misrepresent any information about the product, including cost, quantity, and other aspects or attributes of the product. Telemarketers are also prohibited from calling before 8 A.M. or after 9 P.M. and from calling customers who have previously indicated they do not want to be called (see Focus Case 8.2 on page 270).

Violations of the Telemarketing Sales Rule can result in civil penalties of up to $10,000 per violation, injunctions, and potential redress to injured consumers. The Rule is enforceable by the FTC and also by the state attorneys general, who can obtain nationwide injunctions against fraudulent telemarketers. Prior to the Rule, a state attorney general might have succeeded in closing down a fraudulent telemarketer within his own state but had no ability to prevent the telemarketer from relocating to a different state. The Rule has made it much more difficult for fraudulent telemarketers to simply relocate their operations. Private persons may also

---

[3] 15 U.S.C. §§ 6101–6108, available on-line at http://www.ftc.gov/bcp/rulemaking/tsr/index.html
[4] 16 C.F.R. §§ 310.1–310.8, available on-line at http://www.ftc.gov/bcp/rulemaking/tsr/index.html

Focus Case 8.2

Facts: David T. Umholtz and Wendy J. Foster are the owners, officers, and directors of Arlington Press, Inc., a corporation doing business under the name of "Consumer Data Service." Arlington operated a telemarketing business throughout the United States that advertised and marketed to consumers "how to" guides and lists concerning auctions of government-seized cars, home foreclosure sales, and at-home and government employment. Since its inception, Arlington has disseminated over 500 million flyers through direct mailings sent to consumers by coupon companies and placed advertisements in newspapers. The Arlington ads made claims such as "SEIZED CARS FROM $200" (with an accompanying picture of a late-model car) and "GOVERNMENT FORECLOSED HOMES for pennies on $1." Some of the guidebooks contained obvious information, such as "Never overbid" or "Remember to buy low!", but the bulk of the information in the books was instruction on how various auctions are conducted, definitions of auction terminology, information on how to obtain lists of auctions, etc.

The Arlington telemarketers were provided with scripts to follow when consumers called. The scripts contained responses that the telemarketers were to provide if they encountered sales resistance. For example, the "Auction Objection Responses" script suggested that the telemarketer state: "Oh, they just sold a '95 F150 pickup with 7,300 miles on it for only $2,700." The responses implied that it is possible to purchase good quality vehicles for a fraction of their fair market value. Similar scripts existed for the home foreclosure and employment guides.

In addition, the telemarketers told the callers that they could get a refund at any time. When customers actually sought a refund, however, they were told they could not get a refund until they had "worked with" the program for 90 days. Once the 90 days had passed, they would be told that they had to meet additional conditions and obtain the consent of a consumer research assistant before they would receive a refund.

The FTC brought an action against Arlington, Umholtz, and Foster, alleging that the defendants violated (1) the FTC Act's prohibition against unfair or deceptive acts and (2) the Telemarketing Sales Rule. The FTC sought a preliminary injunction extending the temporary restraining order that the court had entered the previous month.

Decision: The court found that Arlington had engaged in several practices that were likely to mislead and deceive consumers, such as misrepresenting that good quality, late-model cars were available for extremely small sums of money and misrepresenting that refunds were easily available. Thus, the court concluded that the FTC was likely to prevail on its claim that Arlington had violated the FTC Act.

The court also found that the FTC was likely to prevail on its claim that Arlington had violated the Telemarketing Sales Rule. The telemarketers had failed to disclose in a clear and conspicuous manner the total costs of goods and services and had not accurately disclosed the refund policy.

The court thus issued a preliminary injunction against the defendants in order to protect consumers. *FTC v. Arlington Press, Inc.,* 1999-1 Trade Cs. (CCH) P72,415 (C.D. Cal. Jan. 21, 1999).

bring suit in federal court to enforce the Rule if they have suffered $50,000 or more in actual damages.

The FTC's *Mail or Telephone Order Merchandise Rule*[5] applies to the sale of merchandise that is ordered by mail, telephone, fax, or computer "regardless of the method used to solicit the order."[6] Under the Rule, the marketer must have a reasonable basis for stating or implying that it can ship within a certain time when it advertises mail or telephone order merchandise. If the marketer does not make a specific statement regarding shipping, it must have a reasonable basis for believing

[5] 16 C.F.R. Part 435. The FTC's *Business Guide to the FTC's Mail or Telephone Order Merchandise Rule* is available at http://www.ftc.gov/bcp/conline/pubs/buspubs/mailordr/index.htm
[6] 16 C.F.R. § 435.2(a).

that it can ship within 30 days of the order. If the marketer later discovers that it cannot ship within the specified time period, it must obtain the customer's consent for the delayed shipment or refund all money paid. On-line merchants may send delay notices via e-mail.

ELECTRONIC RETAILING AND ADVERTISING

Electronic retailing includes activities such as shop-at-home television networks and on-line retailing. Obviously, there has been tremendous growth in Internet-based retailing in recent years, as on-line retailers expand their operations and as consumers become more familiar and comfortable with this alternative method of purchasing goods and services. Industry analysts predict that on-line consumer spending will increase from $7.8 billion in 1998 to approximately $108 billion by 2003—an almost 1,400 percent increase.[7]

While the Internet has opened up myriad new opportunities for retailing activities, it has also offered many possibilities for abusive retailing practices. Unsolicited commercial e-mail, also know as *junk e-mail* or *spam*, has proliferated in recent years. Many Internet users are outraged at the use of spam, but it remains a common direct marketing tool. Congress is contemplating regulation of such activities but has not yet acted. The FTC closely monitors the issue as well, although its concern focuses on how spam might be used to distribute false or misleading information about products or services.

The states have moved more quickly on this issue, and several states, including California, Nevada, and Washington,[8] have recently enacted regulation to control commercial e-mail. The challenge for businesses that participate in unsolicited commercial e-mail will be in ensuring that they comply with all of the various state statutes that might apply to their activities.

The California law, for example, prohibits any commercial e-mail message that "promotes, directly or indirectly, the sale or distribution of goods or services" and that is sent to a party with whom the sender does not have an "existing business or personal relationship" or from whom the sender does not have "express consent."[9] The e-mail must contain "ADV:" (for advertisement) in the subject line. If the advertisement contains sexual content, it must state "ADV:ADLT" in the subject line. This requirement is intended to enable users to employ filters to discard automatically any messages that contain these words in the subject line. The law provides for criminal penalties of a fine of $1,000 and/or six months' imprisonment for each violation of the statute. Individuals may also seek civil remedies in the form of injunctions. The law does not allow for damages or attorneys fees, however, which reduces the likelihood of civil enforcement of the statute.

The California statute also provides that any Internet service provider (ISP) or business that runs an e-mail delivery computer or that provides E-mail accounts through equipment located in California may adopt policies barring transmission of unsolicited commercial e-mail. The law provides for substantial civil penalties against senders who violate such policies. In addition, the law makes it a criminal offense to send an e-mail with a return address stolen from another person or

---

[7] Robert D. Hoff, *Is That E-Commerce Roadkill I See?*, BUSINESS WEEK, Sept. 27, 1999.
[8] *See* California (1998 A.B. 1676, A.B. 1629); Nevada, Nev. Rev. Stat. Ann. § 41.730 (1997); Virginia (1999 H.B. 1668, 1714, S.B. 881); and Washington (H.B. 2752, to be codified at Wash. Rev. Code Title 19).
[9] California Business and Professions Code §§ 17538.4 and 17538.45.

business—a tactic that some dishonest e-mail marketers have used when sending mass commercial messages.

HOME SOLICITATIONS

Home solicitation or *door-to-door sales* are regulated extensively at the state and federal levels. These are sales that are made at the buyer's home or in a place other than the seller's usual place of business. These types of sales are less likely to result in repeat transactions, so sellers have less incentive to seek to develop the goodwill of the customer and may engage in abusive or aggressive behavior.

For example, a woman and her parents brought suit for consumer fraud against Whirlpool Financial National Bank and Gulf Coast Electronics, charging them with "preying on the elderly and the illiterate" in the sale of satellite dishes. The purchase price of each dish was $1,100. With financing charges and a four-year loan term, the dishes cost $1,800, while the dishes were alleged to be available at stores for $199. In May 1999, a jury awarded the plaintiffs $975,000 in compensatory damages and $580 million in punitive damages. In August 1999, the trial court reduced the punitive damages award to $300 million. The trial judge acknowledged that the jury's verdict was "shocking and unexpected" but stated that it was "consistent with a finding that Whirlpool engaged in a 'malicious predatory sales practice,' designed to target and take advantage of the poor, under-educated, elderly, and African-American citizens of Alabama."[10] The case, along with 50 similar lawsuits, ultimately settled for a confidential amount.[11]

The FTC's *Cooling-off Rule*[12] requires sellers to give consumers three days to cancel and receive a full refund on any purchase of $25 or more made at the consumer's home or at certain locations other than the seller's normal place of business, such as hotel or motel rooms, convention centers, and fairgrounds. The seller must provide the buyer with (1) a summary of the right to cancel; (2) two copies of a cancellation form; and (3) a contract or receipt, which must be in the same language that was used in the sales transaction.

See Discussion Case 8.3.

Most states also have cooling-off laws that allow the buyers of goods sold door-to-door to cancel the contract within a specified time period (usually 48 to 72 hours).

UNSOLICITED MERCHANDISE, MERCHANDISE ON APPROVAL, AND NEGATIVE OPTION PLANS

Legally, only two types of unsolicited merchandise may be sent through the mail: (1) free samples, which must be clearly and conspicuously marked; and (2) merchandise mailed by a charitable organization that is seeking contributions. In both instances, the recipient may treat the merchandise as a gift.

Under the Postal Reorganization Act of 1970,[13] the mailing of any other type of unsolicited merchandise is considered an unfair trade practice and is illegal. The

---

[10] Margaret Cronin Fisk, *$300 Million in Punitives Upheld*, THE NATIONAL LAW JOURNAL, Sept. 13, 1999, at p. B7; *Alabama Court Reduces $581 Million Verdict Against Whirlpool Financial National Bank*, CONSUMER FINANCIAL SERVICES LAW REPORT, Sept. 20, 1999.

[11] *See Door-to-Door Sales Item Cost Nearly 800% More*, THE NATIONAL LAW JOURNAL, Feb. 28, 2000, at p. C19.

[12] *See* http://www.ftc.gov/bcp/conline/pubs/buying/cooling.htm

[13] 39 U.S.C. § 3009

recipient of such merchandise is entitled to retain, use, discard, or otherwise dispose of the merchandise and is not obligated to either pay for it or return it.[14] The recipient may also mark unopened packages "Return to Sender," and the Postal Service will return the packages with no additional postage charge to the recipient. In addition, a merchant who ships unordered merchandise knowing that it is unlawful to do so can be subject to civil penalties of up to $10,000 per violation.

However, marketers may engage in *"sales on approval"* transactions under certain circumstances. Under the FTC Act, the marketer must obtain the customer's express agreement to send merchandise on approval. Under this sales mechanism, the customer may return merchandise, usually after a "no obligation" or "free trial" period and does not have to pay for the merchandise until it is received and approved. Suppose, for example, that the marketer is selling a 30-volume set of encyclopedias with the understanding that a volume will be sent on approval to the customer each month. The marketer must explain the program in detail when soliciting the order and must obtain the customer's express agreement that a failure to return the cancellation document will be treated by both parties as a request to send the volume.

In addition, many music, book, and video club companies operate as *negative option plans*. Essentially, these marketers sell subscription plans to consumers who have agreed in advance to become subscribers. Under the FTC's *Negative Option Rule*, the marketer must provide certain information in the promotional materials, including how many selections the customer must buy, how and when the customer can cancel the membership, how and when to return the "negative option" form to cancel shipment of a selection, and how often a customer can expect to receive announcements and forms. Customers enrolled in the plan are then obligated to either return the negative option form within 10 days after receiving it or pay for the merchandise after receiving it.

900 NUMBERS

Providers of pay-per-call services (900 numbers) must comply with the FTC's *900-Number Rule*.[15] The provider must disclose the name of the 900-number company and the cost of the call in the introductory message of the call and must give the caller the opportunity to hang up without charge. Additional advertising disclosures must be made for services that promote sweepstakes or games of chance, provide information about a federal program but are not sponsored by a federal agency, or target children under the age of 18 years. Pay-per-call services and advertisements for them may not be targeted at children under the age of 12 years unless the advertisement is for a "bona fide educational service" as defined in the Rule.

WARRANTIES AND GUARANTEES

Under the FTC's *Rule on Pre-Sale Availability of Written Warranty Terms*,[16] sellers must make all written warranties on consumer products costing more than $15, whether extended by the manufacturer or by the seller, available to consumers before they purchase the product. If the marketer solicits orders for warranted

---

[14] *See* http://www.usps.gov/websites/depart/inspect/merch.htm (Postal Inspector Web site).

[15] *See* http://www.ftc.gov/bcp/conline/pubs/buspubs/900/intro.htm

[16] 16 C.F.R. Part 702.

consumer products through the mail or by telephone, it must either include the warranty in the catalogue or advertisement or include a statement informing customers how they may obtain a copy. Door-to-door sales companies must offer the consumer a copy of the written warranty before the transaction is completed. On-line merchants may use a clearly labeled hyperlink to lead to the full text of the warranty, but that text itself should be capable of being downloaded or printed so that the consumer can retain a copy. Warranties are discussed in more detail in Chapter 10.

Under the FTC Act, it is an unfair or deceptive practice for a marketer to fail to honor "satisfaction" and "money-back" guarantees fully and promptly. This requires return of the purchase price, shipping, handling, and other fees. Any limitations on the guarantee, such as requiring the customer to supply proof of purchase, requiring the return of the unused portion of the product, or time restrictions on the offer, must be stated clearly and conspicuously.

Labeling and Packaging Regulation

Labeling and packaging issues are regulated heavily at both the state and federal levels. Generally, these laws are designed to ensure that accurate information is provided about the product and that adequate warnings are given regarding the dangers of use or misuse.

Among the major federal labeling statutes are: the *Fair Packaging and Labeling Act of 1966*,[17] which requires that labels on consumer goods identify the product, the net quantity of the contents, the manufacturer, and the packager or distributor; the *Flammable Fabrics Act of 1953*,[18] which sets safety standards for flammable fabrics and materials in clothing; the *Federal Cigarette Labeling and Advertising Act*,[19] which requires specific warnings on cigarette packaging and most related advertising and which bans advertising on television and radio; the *Smokeless Tobacco Health Education Act of 1986*,[20] which requires specific health warnings on chewing tobacco packaging and most related advertising and which bans advertising on television and radio; and the *Wool Products Labeling Act of 1939*,[21] which requires that most wool and textile products be labeled as to fiber content, country of origin, and identity of manufacturer or other business responsible for marketing or handling the item. Special labeling requirements also apply to food and drug products, as discussed below.

There are numerous other federal and state labeling requirements. A marketer should always check to see if any specific labeling regulations apply to the particular products it is producing or selling. Two particular issues arise in the labeling context: (1) the use of the "Made in the U.S.A." label and (2) "green" marketing claims.

"MADE IN THE U.S.A." LABELING

United States content must be disclosed on automobiles and on textile, wool, and fur products. Most other products marketed in the United States are not required to disclose their amount of U.S. content. Many marketers choose to use the "Made in the U.S.A." label, however, as a way of distinguishing or marketing their goods.

---

[17] 15 U.S.C. §§ 1451–1461.
[18] 15 U.S.C. § 1191.
[19] 15 U.S.C. §§ 1331–1341.
[20] 15 U.S.C. §§ 4401–4408.
[21] 15 U.S.C. § 68.

Focus Case 8.3

Facts: USDrives Corporation is a subsidiary of a Taiwanese manufacturer and is headquartered in California. Until April 1998, USDrives manufactured and sold CD-ROM drives that were assembled in the U.S. In May 1998, USDrives moved its assembly operations to Asia.

The FTC alleged that the packages in which the CD-ROMs were marketed made both express and implied claims that the CD-ROMs were "made in the U.S.A." when, in fact, they were actually assembled in the U.S. of primarily imported parts. One package contained the statement "Made in the USA" in red and blue, with a depiction of an American eagle and the name "USDrives" in red, white, and blue. Another package depicted the American flag in red, white, and blue, surrounded by the statement "Well made in the U.S.A.," with depictions of the Statue of Liberty and of an American eagle and the name "USDrives" in red, white, and blue.

The FTC alleged that, prior to May 1998, the CD-ROMs were actually assembled in the U.S. of primarily imported parts and so did not qualify for the "Made in the U.S.A." designation. Once assembly moved to China in May 1998, USDrives added an inconspicuous statement "Made in China" to the bottom and side panels of the packages. The FTC alleged that this disclaimer did not offset the misleading impression that the rest of the packaging made regarding the country of origin.

Decision: The parties entered into a consent order on April 6, 1999, in which USDrives did not admit wrongdoing but nonetheless agreed, among other things:

1) not to misrepresent in its manufacturing, labeling, advertising, promotion, offering for sale, sale, or distribution, directly or by implication, the extent to which its CD-ROMs are made in the U.S.;

2) to maintain and make available to the FTC upon request for 5 years all packaging, labeling, advertisements, and promotional materials regarding representations as to whether the CD-ROMs were made in the U.S.; and

3) to provide a copy of the consent order to all current and future principals, officers, directors, managers, employees, agents, and representatives who might have responsibilities relating to the packaging, labeling, advertising, or promotion of the materials, and to obtain from them a signed and dated acknowledgment of receipt.

The order is to terminate 20 years from the date of issuance or 20 years from the most recent date that the FTC or the U.S. files suit alleging a violation of the order, whichever comes later. *In re USDrives Corp.*, 1999 F.T.C. LEXIS 8 (Jan. 19, 1999) (complaint); 1999 F.T.C. LEXIS 78 (Apr. 6, 1999) (decision and order).

The FTC, under its power to prevent deception and unfairness in the marketplace, requires that products advertised as "Made in the U.S.A." be "all or virtually all" made in the United States.[22] This means that all significant parts, processing, and labeling that go into the product must be of U.S. origin, with no or negligible foreign content. Products that contain a nonnegligible amount of foreign content should use a qualified "Made in the U.S.A." claim, such as "70% U.S. content" or "Made in U.S.A. of U.S. and imported parts."

The requirement applies to any U.S. origin claims that appear on products, labeling, advertising, or other promotional materials, including on-line marketing efforts. The requirement also applies to both express claims of U.S. origin and implied claims that might arise through the use of U.S. symbols (such as an American flag or eagle) or geographic references (see Focus Case 8.3).

The FTC enforces the "Made in the U.S.A." standard. The U.S. Customs Service has responsibility for enforcing requirements that imported goods be marked with their country of origin (e.g., "Made in China").

---

[22] *See* http://www.ftc.gov/os/statutes/usajump.htm

Many other countries have their own country-of-origin labeling requirements. Marketers must thus be aware of the rules applicable in the countries to which they intend to export their goods.

"GREEN" MARKETING

It has become very common for marketers to claim that their products are "environmentally safe," "recyclable," "degradable," or "ozone friendly." Because many consumers place great weight on environmental claims and because these claims are often open to interpretation and abuse, the FTC, with the cooperation of the Environmental Protection Agency (EPA), has developed *Guides for the Use of Environmental Marketing Claims*[23] for advertisers to ensure that green marketing claims do not mislead consumers. The original Guides were issued in 1992 and were most recently revised in 1998. In May 2000, the FTC issued a document entitled *Complying with the Environmental Marketing Guides* to assist businesses.[24] Generally, marketers may not exaggerate the environmental benefits of their products or packaging. Claims regarding environmental benefits must be specific and substantiated.

The Guides apply to environmental claims, whether explicit or implicit, made in labeling, advertising, promotional materials, and all other forms of marketing, including marketing through the Internet or e-mail. The Guides are not enforceable regulations and do not have the force and effect of law. However, failure to comply with the Guides may result in FTC investigation, which can lead to corrective action under Section 5 of the FTC Act if the FTC determines that the marketer's behavior leads to unfair or deceptive acts and practices.

If a product or package is labeled "recycled," for example, unless the product is 100 percent recycled, it must state how much of that product or package is recycled. This helps ensure that consumers are not misled into buying a product that contains only minimally recycled content. Similarly, if a product is labeled "nontoxic," "essentially nontoxic," or "practically nontoxic," the manufacturer must have reason to believe that the product does not pose any significant risk to people or the environment.

INTERNATIONAL LABELING CONSIDERATIONS

Marketers who sell their products overseas need to be concerned with the labeling laws of each of the countries in which they market their products. Most importantly, marketers need to be certain that ingredient, promotional, and instructional information on labels is translated accurately and into the appropriate language or languages. Some countries, such as Belgium and Finland, require labeling to be bilingual. Failure to adhere to local requirements can have severe consequences. Several years ago, for example, an Italian judge banned the distribution of bottled Coca-Cola in Italy because the ingredients were listed on the bottle caps rather than on the bottles.[25]

International marketers should be aware that laws vary substantially from country to country. Venezuela, for example, requires prices to be printed on the label while Chile prohibits this practice. Thus, the marketer must be certain to seek competent local counsel when making decisions about labeling in foreign countries.

[23] 16 C.F.R. Part 260. The Guides can also be found at http://www.ftc.gov/bcp/grnrule/guides 980427.htm
[24] *See* http://www.ftc.gov/bcp/conline/pubs/buspubs/greenguides.htm
[25] *See* Information Bank Abstracts, WALL STREET JOURNAL, Nov. 18, 1977, at p. 35, col. 2.

Eco-labeling also raises numerous international issues. Eco-labeling is the practice of including information on the labels of goods regarding the environmental quality of the production process. The first environmental label was issued in Germany in 1978. Canada initiated a similar program in 1988 and Japan in 1989. The European Union adopted a Community Regulation authorizing its Member Countries to issue eco-labels in 1992. Agenda 21 of the Rio Earth Summit in 1992 urged governments to expand "environmental labeling . . . to assist consumers to make informed choices." In addition, some developing countries, such as India, the Republic of Korea, and Singapore, have adopted eco-labeling programs.

Some forms of eco-labeling are voluntary and are undertaken by companies because of their appeal to consumers. The "dolphin-safe" label on canned tuna in the United States, for example, indicates that the company uses dolphin-safe methods of harvesting tuna—an issue of great interest and importance to many consumers.

While voluntary eco-labeling is seen as posing few, if any, serious trade implications, mandatory eco-labeling is a very controversial subject in the international arena, where it is often viewed as an illegal trade barrier. Many products can be produced with a variety of production processes, which may vary greatly from country to country. Eco-labeling, however, assumes that there is a global standard for production. Many developing countries argue that mandatory eco-labeling can be used as a trade barrier to keep such nations from participating in the global marketplace.

Countries that engage in mandatory eco-labeling need to be concerned about running afoul of the General Agreement on Tariffs and Trade (GATT). In 1992, for example, a GATT panel held that mandatory provisions of U.S. legislation regarding dolphin-safe tuna harvesting techniques were intended not only to protect dolphins but also to protect the U.S. fishing industry. The Panel found that the U.S. legislation was in violation of GATT Article III because it discriminated against imported products in favor of domestic products. The GATT Panel held that the primary goal of any environmental measures that affect trade must be to protect the environment rather than the domestic market. The Panel explained that if individual countries were allowed to impose their national environmental standards on other states:

> each contracting party could unilaterally determine the life or health protection policies from which other contracting parties could not deviate without jeopardizing their rights under the General Agreement. The General Agreement would then no longer constitute a multilateral framework for trade among all contracting parties but would provide legal security only in respect of trade between a limited number of contracting parties with identical internal regulations.[26]

Thus, the Panel concluded, "a contracting party may not restrict imports of a product merely because it originates in a country with environmental policies different from its own."[27]

Efforts to create international standards for eco-labeling have been hampered by the fact that there is no obvious forum for setting such standards. The World Trade Organization, for example, is primarily a trade forum and lacks expertise in environmental issues. Governmental agencies and nongovernmental organizations (NGOs) that do have environmental expertise, on the other hand, often lack a trade focus.

[26] GATT Panel Report on United States—Restrictions on Imports of Tuna, Feb. 18, 1992, GATT B.I.S.D. (39th Supp.), at 199, para. 5.27 (1993).
[27] *Id.* at 204, para. 6.2.

Health and Safety Regulation

In addition to labeling requirements, specific laws govern consumer health and safety issues. The two major federal statutes in this area are the federal *Food, Drug and Cosmetic Act* (FDCA), administered by the Food and Drug Administration (FDA), and the *Consumer Product Safety Act* (CPSA), administered by the Consumer Product Safety Commission (CPSC). As the following discussion illustrates, however, a number of additional federal statutes address health and safety issues as well.

FOOD, DRUG, AND COSMETIC LAWS

While the FTC regulates the *advertising* of food products, the FDA regulates the *safety* and *labeling* of such products. The federal FDCA,[28] enacted in 1938, governs the testing, manufacture, distribution, and sale of food, drugs, cosmetics, and medicinal products and devices. Under the FDCA, certain food additives, drugs, and medicinal devices may not be sold to the public unless they first obtain FDA approval.

The FDCA is administered by the FDA.[29] The FDA is a large federal agency with extensive powers. It is located within the Public Health Service, which itself is a part of the Department of Health and Human Services. The FDA regulates over $1 trillion worth of products, or 25 cents of every dollar spent annually by American consumers. To accomplish this massive task, the FDA has over 9,000 employees, including 2,100 scientists and 1,100 inspectors and investigators who cover 95,000 FDA-regulated businesses.

If the inspectors or investigators discover a violation of the FDCA, the FDA can encourage the firm to voluntarily correct the problem or to recall the product from the marketplace. However, the FDA has no authority to order recalls on its own initiative. In the absence of voluntary cooperation, the FDA can seek legal sanctions. The FDA has broad powers to obtain search warrants and conduct inspections. It can also seek court orders for the seizure and destruction of products, injunctions, and criminal penalties (including imprisonment) against willful violators.

About 3,000 products a year are either voluntarily recalled or seized under court order. In addition, about 30,000 import shipments are detained at the port of entry each year because the goods appear to be unacceptable.

Food

The FDCA establishes food standards, specifies safe levels of various food additives, and establishes classifications of food and food advertising. The Act prohibits the shipment, distribution, or sale of adulterated food, which is food that consists in whole or in part of any "filthy, putrid, or decomposed substance" or is otherwise "unfit for food." The Act does not require that food be pure or that it be completely free of any foreign substances. In a 1972 case, for example, a U.S. District Court concluded that a dairy corporation and its manager could not be held criminally liable for selling butter containing on average three miniscule particles of insect fragments per pound. The court concluded that "this contamination is a trifle, not a matter of concern to the law."[31] In fact, the FDA itself has set standards for the number of contaminants, or "defects," that are allowed in certain foods.[32]

---

[28] 21 U.S.C. § 301 *et seq.*
[29] The FDA's home page is found at http://www.fda.gov
[30] United States v. Capital City Foods, 345 F. Supp. 277, 279 (D. N.D. 1972).
[31] *See* 21 C.F.R § 110.110.

On the other hand, substantial contamination of food can lead to civil and/or criminal liability for both the corporation and the corporate manager in charge. Thus, managers need to be aware of the potential for individual liability, as well as corporate liability, under the FDCA.

See Discussion Case 8.4.

The FDCA also prohibits false and misleading labeling of food products. Most foods are required to carry nutrition labels as well, listing items such as total calories, calories from fat, total fat, saturated fat, cholesterol, sodium, total carbohydrates, dietary fiber, sugars, and certain vitamins.

States, too, may impose labeling requirements on food products in some instances. However, the ability of either the state or federal governments to impose such requirements is constrained by the First Amendment commercial speech doctrines discussed in Chapter 7, as the following case illustrates (see Focus Case 8.4 on page 280).

The federal regulatory regime addressing food products is expansive, and many agencies other than the FDA are involved in maintaining the safety and wholesomeness of the nation's food supply. For example, the Department of Agriculture inspects and grades meat and poultry that is to be consumed by humans, as well as administering the Agricultural Marketing Act of 1946,[32] the Poultry Inspection Act of 1957,[33] the Wholesome Meat Act of 1967,[34] and the Egg Products Inspection Act of 1970.[35] The Centers for Disease Control and Prevention oversee issues relating to food-borne disease outbreaks. The EPA oversees drinking water standards and regulates toxic substances and wastes to prevent their entry into the food chain, as well as regulating the use of pesticides. The Department of Commerce inspects and certifies fishing vessels, seafood processing plants, and retail facilities for federal sanitation standards. The Department of the Treasury, Bureau of Alcohol, Tobacco and Firearms regulates alcoholic beverages (with the exception of wine containing less than 7 percent alcohol). The U.S. Customs Service works with the various federal agencies to ensure that food products entering or exiting the United States meet U.S. laws and regulations.

Dietary Supplements

The line between food, drugs, and dietary supplements is blurring in the minds of many consumers, who are increasingly seeking health benefits from the foods they ingest. The regulatory line between these substances is blurring as well.

Traditionally, dietary supplements that made labeling claims for health or nutrition benefits were considered drugs by the FDA and were subject to rigorous preapproval, manufacturing, and labeling controls. Manufacturers who wished to avoid these expensive and time-consuming procedures could only inform the consumer of the product's contents but could not make any statements regarding possible or purported health benefits associated with the product.

Then Congress, believing that foods and dietary supplements do not raise the same risk as drugs and should not be held to the same substantiation standards, enacted two statutes. The *Nutrition Labeling and Education Act of 1990* (NLEA), which regulates both food products and dietary supplements, permits manufacturers to

---

[32] 7 U.S.C. § 1621.
[33] 21 U.S.C. § 451.
[34] 21 U.S.C. § 601.
[35] 21 U.S.C. § 1031.

Focus Case 8.4

Facts: In 1993, the FDA approved the use of recombinant Bovine Somatotropin (rBST), a synthetic growth hormone that increases milk production by cows. Because the FDA had found, "after exhaustive tests," that dairy products derived from herds treated with rBST were indistinguishable from products derived from untreated herds and that rBST posed no human safety or health concerns, the FDA declined to require labeling of products derived from cows treated with rBST.

In 1994, the state of Vermont enacted a statute requiring that milk or milk products derived from treated herds be labeled as such. The state imposed its requirement "to help consumers make informed shopping decisions."

International Dairy Foods Association, Milk Industry Foundation, International Ice Cream Association, National Cheese Institute, Grocery Manufacturers of America, Inc., and National Food Processors Association (collectively, the "plaintiffs") filed suit, arguing that the statute violated their First Amendment commercial free speech rights by compelling them to speak against their will. They requested a preliminary injunction. The trial court denied the injunction and the plaintiffs appealed.

Decision: The U.S. Court of Appeals determined that a preliminary injunction should issue because the plaintiffs had shown: (1) irreparable harm and (2) a likelihood of success on the merits. Although First Amendment claims usually center on the purposeful *suppression* of speech, the First Amendment also encompasses the right *not* to speak. The court concluded that compelling the plaintiffs to label their products, albeit truthfully, caused them irreparable harm.

The appellate court also found that the plaintiffs had shown a likelihood of success on the merits. The court applied the Supreme Court's *Central Hudson* test for determining whether a restriction on commercial speech is constitutional: (1) whether the expression concerns lawful activity and is not misleading; (2) whether the government's interest is substantial; (3) whether the disputed regulation directly serves that asserted interest; and (4) whether the regulation is no more extensive than necessary.

The appellate court found that the Vermont regulation failed the second prong of the test. The trial court had found that Vermont "does not claim that health or safety concerns prompted the passage of the Vermont Labeling Law," but instead defended the statute on the grounds of "strong consumer interest and the public's 'right to know' . . . ." The appellate court found these interests "insufficient to justify compromising protected constitutional rights." The court concluded that it was "aware of no case in which consumer interest alone was sufficient to justify requiring a product's manufacturers to publish the functional equivalent of a warning about a production method that has no discernable impact on a final product." Consumers interested in such information should, in the court's view, "exercise the power of their purses by buying products from manufacturers who voluntarily reveal it."

The appellate court thus remanded the case to the trial court for entry of a preliminary injunction enjoining enforcement of the statute.

International Dairy Foods Association v. Amestoy, 92 F.3d 67 (2d Cir. 1996).

make certain health-related claims about their products without triggering the much greater regulatory provisions applicable to drugs.

The *Dietary Supplement Health and Education Act of 1994* (DSHEA) permits manufacturers even more leeway in labeling dietary supplements. The DSHEA allows a manufacturer to make certain statements, such as claims about the role of a nutrient or dietary ingredient with respect to the structure or function of the human body and statements of general well-being arising from consumption of a nutrient or other dietary ingredient, without first seeking permission of the FDA, provided that the manufacturer has substantiation for the statements. As a result of the DSHEA, most of the nutritional and safety labeling requirements that apply to food and drugs do not apply to the marketing of dietary supplements. Rather, under the DSHEA, the manufacturer must have substantiation indicating that the claims are truthful and not misleading and must place the following disclaimer prominently on the label: "This statement has not been evaluated by the Food and Drug Administration. This product is not intended to diagnose, treat, cure, or prevent any disease." The manufacturer must also notify the FDA within 30 days of first marketing the product.

Drugs and Medical Devices

The FDCA sets up an elaborate procedure under which drugs must be proven to be both safe *and* effective before they may be marketed to the public. Thus, the FDA has authority to regulate the testing, manufacture, distribution, and sale of drugs. The FDA does not conduct research on the efficacy or safety of new drugs but, rather, evaluates the results of studies done by the manufacturers. This evaluation process may take several years, although expedited processes are available for drugs that address incurable diseases, such as AIDS. It can be very expensive and time-consuming for a manufacturer to perform the necessary testing to show that a drug is safe and effective.

Under the FDCA, all prescription and nonprescription drugs must be labeled with proper directions for use and with warnings about potential side effects. The manufacture, sale, or distribution of adulterated or misbranded drugs is prohibited.

Under the 1976 *Medical Device Amendment* to the FDCA,[36] the FDA regulates medical devices, such as pacemakers; kidney dialysis machines; defibrillators; and other diagnostic, therapeutic, and health devices. Medical devices that are life-supporting, life-sustaining, or implanted must receive agency approval before they can be marketed. The mislabeling of medical devices is prohibited, and the FDA can remove ineffective devices from the marketplace. Even after a drug or medical device is approved for marketing, the FDA continues to collect and analyze reports on such products to monitor the products for any unexpected adverse reactions.

In November 1997, President Clinton signed the *Food and Drug Administration Modernization Act of 1997*[37] (FDAMA), the most comprehensive reform of the regulation of these products in over 30 years. One of the FDAMA's most significant changes was the elimination of the existing prohibition on manufacturers disseminating information about unapproved uses of approved drugs, biologics,[38] and medical devices. When a drug or device manufacturer wants to market a new product, the manufacturer is required to submit the product, along with proposed labeling, to the FDA. The manufacturer is not required to submit labeling that indicates all possible uses of the drug or device. Rather, once the FDA has approved a label stating one intended use, the manufacturer may market the product.

It is common for physicians to make "off-label" uses of drugs or devices, i.e., uses that are not described on the approved label; in fact, it may be medical malpractice for a physician not to engage in certain off-label use practices. For example, over 80 percent of all AIDS patients are treated with at least one off-label drug[39] and approximately 65 percent of all anticancer drug use is off-label.[40] The new Act allows manufacturers to disseminate off-label drug use information under

[36] 21 U.S.C. § 360(c) *et seq.*
[37] Pub. L. No. 105-115, 111 Stat. 2296 (codified as amended in scattered sections of 21 U.S.C.).
[38] *Biologics* include blood and blood products, vaccines, allergenics, and biological therapeutics.
[39] Carol Brosgart, et al., *Off-Label Use in Human Immunodeficiency Virus Disease*, 12 J. Acquired Immune Deficiency Syndromes & Human Retrovirology 56, 57–58 (1996).
[40] General Accounting Office, Report to the Chairman, Comm. on Labor and Human Resources, U.S. Senate, Off-Label Drugs: Reimbursement Policies Constrain Physicians in Their Choice of Cancer Therapies 11, 13–14 (1991).

prescribed conditions to health care practitioners, pharmacy benefit managers, health insurance issuers, group health plans, and federal and state government agencies. Manufacturers may not disseminate such information directly to patients.

The new law illustrates the balancing that marketing managers must make when faced with new regulatory requirements. On the one hand, the FDAMA allows manufacturers to market their drugs for more purposes, thus potentially increasing sales and profits. On the other hand, the manufacturer must follow very strict requirements in marketing drugs for off-label uses or run the risk of incurring criminal or civil sanctions. In addition, the firm is likely to face increased products liability risks once it markets a drug for a use not approved by the FDA. Products liability issues are discussed in Chapter 10.

Cosmetics

Substances and preparations for cleansing, altering the appearance of, and promoting the attractiveness of a person are subject to FDA regulation. Ordinary household soap is exempted from such regulation.

The FDA may only regulate cosmetics *after* the products are released to the market. It has no authority to review or approve cosmetic products or ingredients prior to sale to the public. However, if a cosmetic product has drug properties (i.e., it cures, treats, mitigates, or prevents disease or affects the structure or function of the human body), it must be approved by the FDA as a drug.

The FDA also has no authority to require companies to do safety testing on their cosmetic products. If a product's safety has not been substantiated, however, it must bear a label stating: "WARNING: The safety of this product has not been determined." The FDA also has no power to order recalls of a cosmetic product; rather, to remove a product from the marketplace, the FDA must prove in court that the product is unsafe, improperly labeled, or otherwise in violation of law.

CONSUMER PRODUCT SAFETY LAW

The Consumer Product Safety Commission (CPSC)[41] is an independent federal agency, created in 1972 and charged with the task of protecting "the public against unreasonable risks of injuries and deaths associated with consumer products." The CPSC consists of five commissioners, each appointed by the President, with the advice and consent of the Senate, for a seven-year term. Specifically, the CPSC (1) conducts research on the safety of individual products, (2) maintains a clearinghouse on the risks associated with various consumer products, and (3) adopts rules and regulations to interpret and enforce the CPSA.

The CPSC regulates 15,000 types of consumer products used in the home or schools or for recreation, such as toys, clothing, appliances, furniture, and playground or sports equipment. It does not regulate products such as on-road motor vehicles, boats, aircraft, food, drugs, cosmetics, pesticides, alcohol, firearms, tobacco, or medical devices. The CPSC regulates every company, no matter how small, that manufactures, imports, distributes, or sells any type of consumer product covered by any law that the agency administers.

The primary act that the CPSC administers is the *Consumer Product Safety Act* (CPSA).[42] Under the CPSA, the CPSC is authorized to set mandatory safety

---

[41] The CPSC's home page is found at http://www.cpsc.gov General consumer information can be found at http://www.consumer.gov
[42] 15 U.S.C. §§ 2051–2084.

standards for consumer products and to ban the manufacture and sale of any product deemed by the Commission to pose an "unreasonable risk" to consumers. For example, the CPSC has set safety standards for bicycles and cigarette lighters and has banned the sale of lead-based paint. The CPSC also works with industry to develop voluntary industry standards.

The CPSC can require manufacturers of products it determines are "imminently hazardous" (i.e., products whose use can cause an unreasonable risk of death or serious injury or illness) to recall, repair, or replace the products or to take other corrective action.[43] The CPSC can seek injunctions, court orders to seize hazardous consumer products, and civil and/or criminal penalties. In addition, private parties can seek injunctions to prevent violations of the CPSA or of CPSC rules and regulations.

The CPSA imposes certain *reporting requirements* on businesses. First, any manufacturer, importer, distributor, or retailer of consumer products must notify the CPSA immediately if it concludes that one of its products (1) has a defect that creates a substantial risk of injury to the public, (2) creates an unreasonable risk of serious injury or death, or (3) violates a consumer product safety standard or ban of the product.[44]

Second, a manufacturer must report to the CPSC when any of its products has been involved in three or more lawsuits in a two-year period, if such lawsuits allege death or grievous bodily injury and result in a settlement or court judgment in favor of the plaintiff. Third, a manufacturer, distributor, retailer, or importer of marbles, small balls, latex balloons, or toys or games containing such items must report to the CPSC any incidents of children choking on those items.

The CPSC also enforces several other consumer product safety laws, including the *Federal Hazardous Substances Act*,[45] which regulates household substances and children's products that might be toxic, flammable, or corrosive; the *Flammable Fabrics Act*,[46] which applies to clothing, mattresses, carpets, and similar products; the *Poison Prevention Packaging Act*,[47] which requires child-resistant packaging for certain drugs and other hazardous household substances; and the *Refrigerator Safety Act*,[48] which requires household refrigerator doors to be easily opened from the inside to minimize the possibility of children becoming trapped.

Consumer Credit Protection

The federal government has enacted several pieces of legislation designed to protect consumers from abuses by creditors. The primary statute in this area is the *Truth-in-Lending Act*[49] (TILA), which was passed in 1968 as part of the Consumer Credit Protection Act.[50] A number of additional acts have been added as amendments to TILA in the last 30 years. TILA and some of its more important amendments are discussed below.

---

[43] A list of recalled products can be found at http://www.cpsc.gov/cpscpub/prerel/prerel.html
[44] 15 U.S.C. § 2064.
[45] 15 U.S.C. §§ 1261–1277.
[46] 15 U.S.C. § 1191.
[47] 15 U.S.C. §§ 1471–1476.
[48] 15 U.S.C. § 1211.
[49] 15 U.S.C. §§ 1601–1693.
[50] 15 U.S.C. § 1601 *et seq.*

THE TRUTH-IN-LENDING ACT

TILA is administered by the Federal Reserve Board. The goal of TILA is to assure that creditors and advertisers engage in meaningful disclosure of consumer credit and lease terms so that consumers can shop around for the best financing arrangements. TILA's stringent disclosure requirements are intended to prevent creditors or advertisers from burying the cost of credit in the price of the goods sold. TILA does not set interest rates, but it does establish a uniform actuarial method for calculating consumer credit charges. TILA also establishes certain requirements for the advertisement of credit terms. The Act applies only to persons who, in the ordinary course of business, lend funds, sell on credit, or arrange for the extension of credit. Thus, loan transactions between two individuals are not regulated by TILA. In addition, TILA protects only *natural persons*, not artificial persons, such as corporations or other legal entities.

TILA's *disclosure* requirements are found in Regulation Z.[51] This regulation applies to any transaction governed by TILA involving an installment sales contract in which payment is to be made in more than four installments and the credit is primarily for personal, family, or household purposes. Generally, installment loans, retail and installment sales, car loans, student loans, home-improvement loans, and certain real estate loans of less than $25,000 are subject to Regulation Z. In particular, Regulation Z requires disclosure of the finance charge (defined as the interest charged over the life of the loan expressed as a dollar amount) and the annual percentage rate (APR), which is interest expressed as a percentage.

Regulation Z also contains provisions regarding the *advertising* of credit. Any advertised specific credit terms must be available, and any credit terms mentioned in the advertisement must be fully explained. The FTC enforces these provisions of Regulation Z; consumers do not have a private cause of action to sue advertisers directly.

TILA sets forth very specific requirements regarding the procedures that must be followed in complying with the Act. If the creditor deviates from any of these procedures, the contract may be rescinded or cancelled.

TILA also has specific provisions regarding credit cards. For example, the liability of a cardholder is limited to $50 per card for unauthorized charges made before the credit company is notified that a card has been lost or stolen. There are also provisions detailing procedures for the consumer and the credit card company to follow in resolving disputes about billing errors or withholding of payment for faulty purchases. In addition, while card issuers may send out unsolicited credit cards, the addressee is not liable for any charges made on an unsolicited card that is lost or stolen prior to receipt and acceptance by the addressee. If the addressee accepts the card, she becomes liable for any authorized charges made with it.

Finally, if advertising promotes consumer credit, the advertiser must comply with Regulation X.[52] This provision applies to all advertisers, not merely to creditors, and so includes parties like manufacturers, real estate brokers, builders, and government agencies. It does not include the media in which the advertisements appear, however. This regulation requires disclosure of certain types of information, such as the APR, depending upon the type of credit being advertised. Advertisements promoting home equity lines of credit are subject to additional disclosure rules as well as Regulation X.

---

[51] 12 C.F.R. § 226.
[52] *See generally* http://www.ftc.gov/bcp/conline/pubs/buspubs/creditad/general.htm

As already noted, TILA has been amended several times since its enactment. Some of these amendments are described below.

The Equal Credit Opportunity Act

The *Equal Credit Opportunity Act*[53] (ECOA) was enacted as an amendment to TILA in 1974. The ECOA prohibits the denial of credit solely on the basis of race, religion, national origin, color, gender, marital status, or age. (While the ECOA prohibits discrimination against older applicants, it does allow them to be afforded more favorable treatment.) The Act also prohibits discrimination on the basis of whether an individual receives certain forms of income, such as public assistance. Creditors may, of course, deny credit for valid reasons relating to creditworthiness, such as inadequate income, excessive debts, or poor credit history. Creditors must provide applicants with the reasons that credit was denied if the applicant so requests.

The ECOA applies to all creditors who extend or arrange credit in the ordinary course of their business, including banks, small loan and finance companies, retail and department stores, credit card companies, and credit unions. Unlike most provisions of TILA, the ECOA protects businesses as well as individuals. States may adopt equal credit opportunity acts that are more protective than the ECOA.

The Consumer Leasing Act

Consumer leases have become very popular in recent years, particularly automobile leases. The *Consumer Leasing Act*,[54] which was a 1988 amendment to TILA, and its accompanying Regulation M, offer protection to consumers who lease goods priced at $25,000 or less for personal, household, or family use, provided the lease term exceeds four months. The Act applies to anyone who advertises consumer leases and imposes specific disclosure requirements upon such parties. It does not apply to the media in which such advertisements appear.[55]

The Fair Credit Reporting Act

Congress enacted the *Fair Credit Reporting Act*[56] (FCRA) as part of TILA in 1970. The FCRA provides that consumer credit reporting agencies may issue credit reports to users only for specific purposes, including the extension of credit, the issuance of insurance policies, employment evaluation, compliance with a court order, and compliance with a consumer's request for a copy of his own credit report. If a consumer is denied credit or insurance on the basis of the credit report or is charged more than others ordinarily would be for such credit or insurance, the consumer must be notified and must be given the name and address of the credit reporting agency that issued the credit report.

In addition, consumers may request the source of any information being given out by a credit agency, as well as the identity of anyone who has received an agency report. Consumers are also entitled to access to the information about themselves contained within a credit reporting agency's files. The agency is obligated, upon the consumer's written request, to investigate and delete any unverifiable or inaccurate information within a reasonable time period. If the agency does not find an error, the consumer is entitled to file a 100-word written statement of her version of the disputed information. Any subsequent credit reports must note the disputed item and must contain the consumer's statement.

[54] 15 U.S.C. § 1691. *See* http://www.ftc.gov/bcp/conline/pubs/credit/ecoa.htm
[54] 15 U.S.C. §§ 1667–1667e.
[55] *See generally* http://www.ftc.gov/bcp/conline/pubs/buspubs/adlease.htm
[56] 15 U.S.C. § 1681 *et seq. See* http://www.ftc.gov/bcp/conline/pubs/credit/fcra.htm

A credit reporting agency that negligently violates the provisions of the FCRA is potentially liable for actual damages, costs, and attorneys fees. An agency that willfully violates the FCRA may be liable for punitive damages as well. A credit reporting agency is not liable under the FCRA for reporting inaccurate information, however, if it followed reasonable procedures to assure maximum possible accuracy.

The Fair Credit and Charge Card Disclosure Act of 1988

The *Fair Credit and Charge Card Disclosure Act of 1988*[57] amended TILA to require disclosure of certain credit terms on credit and charge card solicitations and applications. In particular, the disclosure must reveal (1) the annual percentage rate (APR); (2) the annual membership fee, if any; (3) any minimum or fixed finance charge; (4) any transaction charge for use of the card for purchases; and (5) a statement that charges are due when the periodic statement is received by the cardholder.

The Fair Debt Collections Practices Act

Congress enacted the *Fair Debt Collection Practices Act*[58] (FDCPA) in 1977 in an attempt to prevent collection agencies from engaging in abusive, deceptive, and unfair practices. "Debt" is defined in the FDCPA as "any obligation or alleged obligation of a consumer to pay money arising out of a transaction in which the money, property, insurance, or services which are the subject of the transaction are primarily for personal, family, or household purposes . . . ."[59]

The FDCPA applies only to third-party debt collectors, i.e., to persons who routinely attempt to collect debts on behalf of other creditors (usually in return for a percentage of the amount owed), including specialized debt-collection agencies and attorneys. Creditors who attempt to collect their own debts are not covered by the FDCPA, unless they misrepresent to debtors that they are collection agencies (see Focus Case 8.5).

In particular, the FDCPA prohibits collections agencies from

- contacting the debtor at the debtor's place of employment if the employer objects;
- contacting the debtor during inconvenient or unusual times (the FDCPA provides that convenient hours are generally between 8 A.M. and 9 P.M. unless the debtor's particular circumstances, such as working the night shift, make those times inconvenient);
- contacting the debtor at inconvenient places, such as social events or worship services;
- contacting the debtor at all if the debtor is being represented by an attorney (the collection agency must deal with the attorney instead);
- using harassing or intimidating tactics (such as abusive language or threatening violence) or using false and misleading information (such as pretending to be a police officer); and
- any communication with the debtor after receiving written notice that the debtor is refusing to pay the debt or does not want to be contacted again, except to advise the debtor of further action to be taken by the collection agency (such as the filing of a lawsuit).

The FDCPA also requires collection agencies to provide a "validation notice" when they initially contact a debtor or within five days of that initial contact. The

---

[57] 15 U.S.C. § 1637.
[58] 15 U.S.C. § 1692.
[59] 15 U.S.C. § 1692a(5).

Focus Case 8.5

Facts: Desert Palace, Inc., which does business as Caesars Palace, provides resort hotel and casino amenities. Desert Palace extends lines of gambling credit to patrons who complete a preprinted application form. Once the application is approved, the patron can request "markers," which are used to obtain casino chips for gambling at Desert Palace establishments. Each marker identifies its value in U.S. dollars and states "Pay to the Order of." The markers also include a stipulation that the marker is a negotiable instrument and that the payee is authorized to fill in missing information, such as missing amounts, dates, names, and account numbers.

Matthew Fleeger executed several markers in November 1997 and January 1998. By April 1998, Fleeger owed over $183,000 to Desert Palace in unpaid markers. When Desert Palace deposited some of the markers, they were returned by Fleeger's banks with "NSF" and "Returned Not Paid" notations. After sending a payment demand letter to Fleeger, Desert Palace requested that the County District Attorney collect the debt under Nevada's "bad check" statute. The District Attorney then filed criminal charges, which led to Fleeger's arrest.

Fleeger filed suit, alleging that Desert Palace had violated the Fair Debt Collection Practice Act (FDCPA).

Ordinarily, the FDCPA applies only to entities that collect debts for third parties. However, the Act does provide that "any creditor who, in the process of collecting his own debts, uses any name other than his own which would indicate that a third person is collecting or attempting to collect such debts" may also be deemed a "debt collector" for purposes of the Act. Fleeger alleged that by using the name "Caesars Palace" in attempting to collect the debts, Desert Palace had brought itself within the ambit of the FDCPA.

Decision: The court rejected Fleeger's argument, noting that the markers were made payable to "Caesars Palace" and that the demand letter sent by Desert Palace bore the "Caesars Palace" name, as did the credit application filled out by Fleeger. Because Fleeger incurred the debt with an entity using the "Caesars Palace" name, the use of that name by Desert Palace indicated that the original creditor, not some third party, was collecting or attempting to collect the debt.

The FDCPA thus did not apply to this transaction and Fleeger's allegations that Desert Palace had violated the Act were dismissed. *Fleeger v. Bell*, 95 F. Supp. 2d 1126 (D. Nev., 2000).

---

notice must indicate that the debtor has 30 days in which to dispute the debt and to request (in writing) a written verification of the debt from the collection agency. An agency that fails to comply with the Act is liable for actual damages, plus additional damages not to exceed $1000, plus costs and attorneys fees. The FTC may also seek cease-and-desist orders against debt collectors.

DISCUSSION CASES

8.1 First Amendment Challenge to the TCPA

Destination Ventures, Ltd. v. FCC, 46 F.3d 54 (9th Cir. 1995)

Destination Ventures, Inc., ("Destination") appeals the district court's dismissal of its action for failure to state a claim. It asserts a First Amendment challenge to a provision of the Telephone Consumer Protection Act of 1991 banning unsolicited faxes that contain advertisements. Destination contends that the district court erred in holding that it could not present facts to demonstrate that the ban was not a reasonable means of preventing the shifting of advertising costs to consumers. We affirm.

I

The Telephone Consumer Protection Act of 1991 took effect on December 20, 1992. It states in part:

(b)(1) It shall be unlawful for any person within the United States-

. . . (C) to use any telephone facsimile machine, computer, or other device to send an unsolicited advertisement to a telephone facsimile machine . . . .

The statute defines "unsolicited advertisement" as "any material advertising the commercial availability or quality of any property, goods or services which is transmitted to any person without that person's prior express invitation or permission."

Destination conducts seminars for travel agents and advertised these seminars by fax prior to passage of the ban. It and several other business owners filed suit in district court against the FCC on August 23, 1993, claiming that the ban violated the [First Amendment] . . . . * * *

II

* * * Regulation of commercial speech must directly advance a substantial governmental interest in a manner that forms a "reasonable fit" with the interest. The burden is on the government to demonstrate the reasonable fit. The government's burden "is not satisfied by mere speculation or conjecture; rather, a governmental body seeking to sustain a restriction on commercial speech must demonstrate that the harms it recites are real and that its restriction will in fact alleviate them to a material degree."

Destination does not contest the government's substantial interest in preventing the shifting of advertising costs to consumers. Instead, Destination argues that the FCC failed to sustain its burden of demonstrating a "reasonable fit" between this interest and the ban on fax advertisements. Specifically, it contends that the government has not shown that faxes containing advertising are any more costly to consumers than other unsolicited faxes such as those containing political or "prank" messages. According to Destination, Congress may not single out advertisements for regulation when other types of unsolicited faxes produce the same cost-shifting.

We disagree. Because Congress's goal was to prevent the shifting of advertising costs, limiting its regulation to faxes containing advertising was justified. The ban is even-handed, in that it applies to commercial solicitation by any organization, be it a multinational corporation or the Girl Scouts. * * * The plaintiffs have not disputed that unsolicited commercial fax solicitations are responsible for the bulk of advertising cost-shifting. Thus, banning them is a reasonable means to achieve Congress's goal of reducing cost-shifting. The First Amendment does not require Congress to forgo addressing the problem at all unless it completely eliminates cost-shifting.

Destination also argues that further proceedings are necessary to examine whether the government's solution is excessive in light of what it asserts is minimal cost-shifting caused by unsolicited advertising faxes. It acknowledges that recipients of faxes incur at least some costs. However, it suggests that such costs may be de minimis, and that computer technology is rendering these costs, as well as the problem of tying up fax machines, obsolete.

In a declaration submitted in support of Destination's summary judgment motion, Don McGrath, owner of plaintiff National Faxlist, stated that "the cost of one page of paper used by the typical fax machine in use today is two and one-half cents," and "it takes between 30 and 45 seconds for a fax machine to print an 8-inch by 11-inch page of text." In its Response, the FCC agreed that transmission of a single page by fax takes 35 to 40 seconds, but submitted news articles estimating the cost of fax paper from 3 to 40 cents per sheet.

* * * *

Viewing the facts in the light most favorable to Destination, we conclude that Destination's own figures do not rebut the admitted facts that unsolicited fax advertisements shift significant advertising costs to consumers. The possibility of future technological advances allowing simultaneous transmission and eliminating the need for paper does not alter this conclusion. We look at the problem as it existed when Congress enacted the statute, rather than speculate upon what solutions may turn up in the future. Therefore, we hold that the ban on unsolicited fax advertisements meets the [Supreme Court's] test for restrictions on commercial speech.

* * * *

AFFIRMED.

Questions for Discussion for Case 8.1

1. How would you summarize Destination's argument that the TCPA violated the First Amendment?

2. Why does the court determine that the TCPA is constitutional? What does it state that Congress's purpose was in enacting the TCPA?

3. eFax.com is an Internet service that assigns its members their own telephone numbers for receiving and sending faxes. The members then review the faxes in an electronic format before deciding to print them out. Do you think sending out mass faxes to only eFax numbers would violate the TCPA?

8.2 First Amendment Challenge to the TCPA
Moser v. FCC, 46 F.3d 970 (9th Cir. 1995)

The Federal Communications Commission ("FCC") appeals the district court's ruling on summary judgment that a provision of the Telephone Consumer Protection Act of 1991, banning prerecorded telemarketing calls, violates the First Amendment. The FCC argues . . . that the district court erred in finding that the statute did not constitute a "reasonable fit" with the government's legitimate interest in protecting residential privacy. * * * We reverse . . . .

I

Congress held extensive hearings on telemarketing in 1991. Based upon these hearings, it concluded that telemarketing calls to homes constituted an unwarranted intrusion upon privacy. The volume of such calls increased substantially with the advent of automated devices that dial up to 1,000 phone numbers an hour and play prerecorded sales pitches. By the fall of 1991, more than 180,000 solicitors were using automated machines to telephone 7 million people each day.

In addition to the sheer volume of automated calls, Congress determined that such calls were "more of a nuisance and a greater invasion of privacy than calls placed by 'live' persons" because such calls "cannot interact with the customer except in preprogrammed ways" and "do not allow the caller to feel the frustration of the called party . . . ." Customers who wanted to remove their names from calling lists were forced to wait until the end of taped messages to hear the callers' identifying information. Prerecorded messages cluttered answering machines, and automated devices did not disconnect immediately after a hang up. In a survey conducted for a phone company, 75 percent of respondents favored regulation of automated calls, and half that number favored a ban on all phone solicitation. * * *

The Telephone Consumer Protection Act . . . was passed on December 20, 1991, to take effect a year later. It provides in part:

> It shall be unlawful for any person within the United States
>
> . . . (B) to initiate any telephone call to any residential line using an artificial or prerecorded voice to deliver a message without the prior express consent of the called party, unless the call is initiated for emergency purposes or is exempted by rule or order by the Commission under paragraph (2)(B) . . . .

Under the statute, prerecorded messages may be used only if a live operator introduces the message or if the consumer consents. All live solicitation calls, as well as automated calls to most businesses, are permitted. The statute authorizes the FCC to enact limited exemptions from the ban, including an exemption for calls not made "for a commercial purpose." The FCC adopted regulations on September 17, 1992, that exempted calls by tax-exempt, nonprofit organizations.

II

The nonprofit National Association of Telecomputer Operators ("NATO") . . . suit on November 12, 1992 . . . NATO alleged that the law created a content-based restriction not narrowly tailored to further a substantial government interest, in violation of the First Amendment. * * *

The district court granted a preliminary injunction on December 18, 1992. On May 21, 1993, the court granted summary judgment for the plaintiffs, declaring that the statute violated the First Amendment. * * *

* * * *

IV

* * * *

Because the district court held that the statute itself distinguished between commercial and noncommercial calls, it analyzed the statute's constitutionality under the test for regulation of commercial speech articulated in *Central Hudson Gas & Electric Corp. v. Public Service Comm'n*, 447 U.S. 557, 564 (1980) and *Board of Trustees v. Fox*, 492 U.S. 469, 480 (1989).

Because nothing in the statute requires the Commission to distinguish between commercial and noncommercial speech, we conclude that the statute should be analyzed as a content-neutral time, place, and manner restriction. It regulates all automated telemarketing calls without regard to whether they are commercial or noncommercial. * * *

NATO does not challenge the government's significant interest in residential privacy, and does not dispute that curbs on telemarketing advance that interest. Rather, it asserts that a selective ban on automated, commercial calls is unjustified because there is no evidence that such calls are more intrusive than either "live" or noncommercial calls. The district court reasoned that, because prerecorded calls constitute a fraction of all telemarketing calls, a selective ban on these calls would not advance the governmental interest in protecting privacy. * * *

Because the statute does not require that the FCC distinguish between commercial and noncommercial calls, the appropriate inquiry is whether a ban on automated telemarketing calls is narrowly tailored to the residential privacy interest, and whether ample alternative channels of communication remain open.

There was significant evidence before Congress of consumer concerns about telephone solicitation in general and about automated calls in particular. Congress made extensive findings. The district court did not give sufficient weight to these findings. "When Congress makes findings on essentially factual issues . . . those findings are of course entitled to a great deal of deference, inasmuch as Congress is an institution better equipped to amass and evaluate the vast amounts of data bearing on such an issue." Such deference does not foreclose the court's independent judgment of the facts bearing on an issue of constitutional law.

We conclude that Congress accurately identified automated telemarketing calls as a threat to privacy. Further, Congress could regulate a portion of these calls without banning all of them. The Supreme Court has repeatedly stated that "underinclusiveness" may be the basis of a First Amendment violation only when a regulation represents an "attempt to give one side of a debatable public question an advantage in expressing its views to the people." The ban on automated, prerecorded calls is not an attempt to favor a particular viewpoint.

* * * *

The district court also found that Congress had failed to consider adequately less restrictive alternatives. This conclusion is at odds with the court's finding that Congress considered and rejected less restrictive forms of regulation, including a bill that would have required solicitors to give their names, addresses, and phone numbers in their messages and to use machines with certain disconnect features.

The restrictions in the Act leave open many alternative channels of communication, including the use of taped messages introduced by live speakers or taped messages to which consumers have consented, as well as all live solicitation calls. That some companies prefer the cost and efficiency of automated telemarketing does not prevent Congress from restricting the practice. * * *

CONCLUSION

The provision in the Telephone Consumer Protection Act of 1991 banning automated, prerecorded calls to residences is content-neutral. Congress adequately demonstrated that such calls pose a threat to residential privacy. The ban is narrowly tailored to advance that interest, and leaves open ample alternative channels of communication. Thus, it does not violate the First Amendment.

REVERSED.

Questions for Discussion for Case 8.2

1. Do you think that an automated phone message is any more intrusive than having a live person call?

2. Does it take more or less effort to hang up on a recorded message versus a live operator? If you think that it is easier to end the prerecorded call, how compelling do you think that the government's interest is in regulating prerecorded calls versus live operator calls?

8.3 Home Solicitations

Rossi v. 21st Century Concepts, Inc., **162 Misc. 2d 932, 618 N.Y.S. 2d 182 (City Ct. 1994)**

The plaintiff, soon to be a new bride, attended the Great Bridal Expo. * * * Amongst the many exhibitors was the defendant, 21st Century Concepts, Inc. doing business as Royal Prestige ("Royal Prestige"). Royal Prestige, a direct marketing company, displayed a variety of knives, china, glassware, water filters and cookware. * * *

Royal Prestige sells its products through door-to-door sales. Royal Prestige became aware of the plaintiff and her bridal needs when she filled out a "lead" card at the Bridal Expo. Thereafter, Royal Prestige salesman Larry Kieffer called the plaintiff seeking to arrange a home sales visit. To induce the plaintiff to listen to his sales pitch, Mr. Kieffer

offered plaintiff $100 in cash, a free facial and 100 rolls of free film.

Intrigued, the plaintiff agreed and on September 28, 1993 Mr. Kieffer knocked on the plaintiff's door, gave her $100 in cash, a free facial and one roll of free film. To obtain the remaining 99 rolls of "free" film the plaintiff had to use the first roll and have it processed by Royal Prestige's chosen film processor. After paying for her prints the plaintiff would be given one new roll of free film and so on. In addition, after the sale Mr. Kieffer offered plaintiff a reduced cost Caribbean vacation which plaintiff later rejected because of the poor quality and location of the offered hotels.

Once inside the plaintiff's home, Mr. Kieffer spent 2½ hours extolling the alleged virtues of the entire line of Royal Prestige products. Most of that time (1½ hours) was spent on selling plaintiff a set of pots and pans pretentiously identified as the Royal Prestige Health System (the "Health System"). The Health System consisted of several cooking pots which appeared to be small pressure cookers. These miniature pressure cookers were beautifully photographed and described in elegant terms as sauce pan, skillet, dutch oven and steamer/colander. The Health System was wildly expensive, e.g., the cost (including freight, handling and local sales tax) of the Royal Prestige "22 piece Health System" which consisted of seven pots plus accessories was $1,505.63 or nearly $200 a pot.

Mr. Kieffer pitched the Health System as a technically advanced means of retaining the nutritional value of cooked food. This claim was presented without any supporting documentation such as a Consumer Union Report or the like. * * * In addition, Mr. Kieffer tailored his pitch to the young expectant bride by suggesting a direct relationship between using the Health System pots and preventing heart disease and having healthier babies. The plaintiff relied upon Mr. Kieffer's representations about the benefits of the Health System, agreed to purchase the 22-piece Health System and gave Mr. Kieffer a check for the total cost of $1,505.63.

The front of the sales contract, dated September 28, 1993 contained the following: "You, the Purchaser, may cancel this transaction at any time prior to midnight of the third business day after the date of this transaction. See the attached notice of cancellation form for an explanation of this right." On the reverse side of the sales contract under the title of "Notice of Cancellation" there was extensive language regarding plaintiff's cancellation rights. The Notice of Cancellation contained blanks for the date, the name and address of the seller and the last possible day to cancel the contract. Mr. Kieffer failed to complete any of these blanks.

After receiving her ordered Health System on October 27, 1993, the plaintiff decided to cancel the sales contract and returned the pots with a letter demanding a full refund. Royal Prestige rejected plaintiff's cancellation of the sales contract and sent the purchased pots back to the plaintiff with a letter stating "[t]he quality of our cookware is considered by many experts to be the finest manufactured in the world today."

DISCUSSION

* * * *

The marketing of goods and services through door-to-door sales can be cost effective for manufacturers and distributors. Some manufacturers and distributors favor door-to-door sales for several reasons. *First*, the per unit cost of generating a sale is relatively low. This is because there is no retail store overhead such as rent, salaries, insurance and so forth. Instead a salesman working on a straight commission will use the consumer's living room to sell his wares and take his orders. *Second*, the selling price may be several times greater than that which would be obtainable in a more competitive environment where consumers compare different brands of the same product. * * * *Third*, consumers are less defensive and more comfortable in their own homes and because of this are, especially, susceptible to high pressure sales tactics.

Violation of Door-To-Door Sales Protection Act

Because of all of these factors door-to-door sales often lead to abuses, over-reaching, misrepresentations and fraud. As a consequence several States including New York have enacted remedial statutes which, within the limited context of retail sales made in the home, give consumers contractual rescission rights not otherwise available at common law. These statutes . . . have as their purpose "to afford consumers a 'cooling-off' period to cancel contracts which are entered into as a result of high pressure door-to-door sales tactics."

The contract between Royal Prestige and the plaintiff violated Personal Property Law § 428(1)(b). This section provides that with respect to the required notice of cancellation on the back of the contract, "the seller shall complete both copies by entering the name of the seller, the address of the seller's place of business, the date of the transaction, and the date, not earlier than the third business day following the date of the transaction . . . ." Mr. Kieffer failed to fill in the required information in the Royal Prestige sales contract. A failure to properly inform the plaintiff of her cancellation rights is a violation and allows the plaintiff to cancel her contract until a reasonable time after Royal Prestige has properly informed her of her cancellation rights. Royal Prestige has yet to complete the contract as required. Plaintiff timely cancelled her contract on October 27, 1993, demanded a refund of her contract payment of $1,505.63, returned the Health System to defendant (which she was not required to do [—] consumers may tender goods at residence), which refused to accept the rejected Health System returning it yet again to plaintiff.

The contract also violated Personal Property Law § 428 (4). This section provides that the sales contract "shall disclose conspicuously the seller's refund policy as to all goods . . . subject to the door-to-door sales agreement." The Royal Prestige sales contract blissfully states that the "Seller promises you fair and honorable treatment." This statement is not only not true within the facts of this case, but it is virtually meaningless and does not rise to the level of disclosing "seller's refund policy." Within twenty days after receiving the Health System the plaintiff timely notified Royal Prestige of her intent to cancel and demanded a full refund.

Demand for Rescission

Notwithstanding the statutory right of rescission afforded plaintiff by Personal Property Law § 428, the Royal Prestige sales contract should be rescinded based upon the application of several common-law doctrines. Whether viewed as a want of consideration or failure of consideration, it is clear that the plaintiff was grossly overcharged for the Health System she purchased.

Through high pressure sales tactics the plaintiff was induced to pay nearly $200 a pot for cookware of dubious and undocumented nutritional, medical or technical value. Royal Prestige misrepresented, implicitly or explicitly, that its Health System provided exceptional nutritional value, that it would prevent heart disease, that it would help the plaintiff have healthier babies and that many experts consider the Health System "to be the finest manufactured in the world today."

The Health System was grossly misrepresented, overpriced and the transaction was unconscionable.

Violation of General Business Law § 349

New York General Business Law § 349 prohibits deceptive business practices. General Business Law § 349 is a broad, remedial statute directed towards giving consumers a powerful remedy to right consumer wrongs. The elements of a violation of General Business Law § 349 are (1) proof that the practice was deceptive or misleading in a material respect, and (2) proof that plaintiff was injured. There is no requirement under General Business Law § 349 that plaintiff prove that defendant's practices or acts were intentional, fraudulent or even reckless. Nor is there any requirement under General Business Law § 349 that plaintiff prove that she relied upon defendant's misrepresentations and deceptive practices.

Initially, the failure of Royal Prestige to comply with the disclosure requirements of Personal Property Law § 428 regarding cancellation and refund rights also constitutes an unfair and deceptive business practice under General Business Law § 349.

Secondly, Royal Prestige's unsupported representations regarding the nutritional value of the Health System and its relationship to preventing heart disease and having healthier babies are misleading and deceptive.

Thirdly, the inducements used by Royal Prestige salesman Larry Kieffer to convince the plaintiff to open the door of her home and listen to his sales pitch were themselves misleading and deceptive. Mr. Kieffer promised plaintiff $100 and a free facial and he delivered these two inducements. Mr. Kieffer also promised 100 rolls of "free" film and delivered only one roll while the remaining 99 were available only if plaintiff spent monies on processing exposed film, one roll at a time. This "free" offer was misleading and deceptive. Mr. Kieffer promised a reduced price vacation which plaintiff rejected after discovering the poor quality and location of the hotels offered. This vacation offer was misleading and deceptive and failed to disclose material information regarding the actual value of the vacation package.

DAMAGES

The court awards the following damages to the plaintiff.

First, damages will include the full contract price of $1,505.63 which includes freight, handling and local sales tax; the cost of mailing the Health System back to Royal Prestige of $49.70; and $100 because Royal Prestige refused to refund the contract price.

Second, . . . the Court finds that defendant willfully violated General Business Law § 349. Although the Court would like to treble plaintiff's actual damages of $1,555.33, this amount exceeds the maximum $1,000 permissible.

Third, pursuant to Personal Property Law § 429(3) and General Business Law § 349(h) the Court awards plaintiff attorney's fees and costs of $344.66. Considering plaintiff's counsel's vigorous efforts during trial and an excellent posttrial memorandum of law, the Court would have awarded greater fees and costs but at the time this lawsuit was filed the jurisdictional limit of this court was $2,000.

Questions for Discussion for Case 8.3

1. The court found that the defendant had violated the state cooling-off statute such that the plaintiff was permitted to cancel the contract one month after the sale had occurred. What should the defendant have done differently to have avoided this result?

2. The court also found that the defendant's actions violated the state's statute prohibiting deceptive business practices. Which actions of the defendant were deceptive?

3. What does the plaintiff ultimately recover? The court seems to feel that this amount is inadequate yet states that it is unable to award more to the plaintiff. Why?

8.4 Food, Drug and Cosmetic Act

United States v. Gel Spice Co. **601 F. Supp. 1205 (E.D. N.Y. 1984), aff'd, 773 F.2d 427 (2d Cir. 1985)**

This criminal prosecution under the Federal Food, Drug and Cosmetic Act (the "Act") was initiated with the filing of a ten-count Information on December 3, 1980. The information charges Gel Spice Co., Inc. ("Gel Spice"), its President, Barry Engel, and its Vice-President, Andre S. Engel, with causing various articles of food that had been shipped in interstate commerce to be held for sale in a building accessible to rodents, thereby exposing the food to contamination of rodent filth. This, it is charged, resulted in the food becoming adulterated (a) within the meaning of 21 U.S.C. § 342(a)(4) (1976),[1] in that various lots of food were held under insanitary conditions whereby they may have become contaminated with filth (all Counts); and (b) within the meaning of 21 U.S.C. § 342(a)(3) (1976),[2] in that the food consisted in part of a filthy substance by reason of the presence therein of rodent excreta pellets, rodent gnawings, rodent hair or rodent urine (Counts I, II, III and VIII). Proof of either charge is a violation of 21 U.S.C. § 331(k) (1976),[3] which prohibits the doing of any act that results in food becoming adulterated while being held for sale after shipment in interstate commerce.

* * * *

FINDINGS OF FACT

* * * Since 1969, [Gel Spice] has had an office and warehouse at 593 McDonald Avenue, Brooklyn, New York. Gel Spice imports, processes, and packages spices. The processing involves grinding, blowing, sifting, and repackaging the spices into consumer and industrial size containers.

Barry Engel has been the President of Gel Spice since 1963, and is responsible for the purchasing of spices and their storing, processing and packaging at the McDonald Avenue facility. His brother, Andre Engel, is responsible for sales. Their mother, Margaret Engel, handles the financial opera-

tion of the company. All have equal shares in Gel Spice and may sign checks and documents on behalf of the company.

* * * *

Gel Spice imports spices from abroad, particularly from South America, Europe and the Middle East. The spices are imported by ship and unloaded at piers. When the spices arrive, an official sampler from an outside firm is sent by Gel Spice to take a random sample from the bags.

The sampler follows procedures and standards published by the American Spice Trade Association and the sample is tested for Gel Spice by an independent laboratory using those standards. Gel Spice's decisions regarding the acceptance and use of the merchandise are based on the results of that test. It is notable that no examination is made at the pier of the outside of the bags, and only a random number of bags have samples drawn from within.

If the sampled spices pass the pier inspection, then the entire shipment is brought to the McDonald Avenue warehouse. Everyone in the trade knows that imported spices can arrive at the Gel Spice facility in a contaminated state; accordingly, measures must be taken to avoid bringing rodents into the building. When the spices arrive, a Gel Spice employee looks for evidence of rodent activity. Employees also scan the bags with a "black light" that will expose possible urine stains. At any given time, there may be 10,000 or more bags of spice stored at Gel's premises.

From 1976 through 1979 Gel Spice had an ongoing sanitation and rodent control program. The firm once used DDT before that insecticide was banned. * * * When DDT was banned, the company's exterminator recommended bait stations, traps, and then glue boards. * * *

* * * Between 1974 and 1979 Gel Spice had four different outside exterminators, who would come once each week or every two weeks. During this period, Gel Spice was inspected four times by the FDA. Those inspections form the basis of this Information.

A. *The July 1976 Inspection (Counts I, II)*

In July 1976 FDA Investigators Thomas Gardine and Brian Landesberg inspected the McDonald Avenue warehouse. They examined a lot of chili peppers in the warehouse's cool room. Inspector Gardine saw several dead rodents on bags of a different spice next to the lot of chili peppers. He also observed several dead rodents on the floor, one of which was covered with maggots and which, in Gardine's opinion, had been decomposing for at least one week.

---

[1] Subsection (a)(4) of 21 U.S.C. § 342 (1976) provides: "A food shall be deemed to be adulterated . . . (a)(4) if it has been prepared, packed or held under insanitary conditions whereby it may have become contaminated with filth, or whereby it may have been rendered injurious to health. . . ."

[2] Subsection (a)(3) provides: "A food shall be deemed to be adulterated . . . (a)(3) if it consists in whole or in part of any filthy, putrid or decomposed substance, or if it is otherwise unfit for food. . . ."

[3] Subsection (k) of 21 U.S.C. § 331 provides: The following acts and the causing thereof are hereby prohibited: . . . the doing of any . . . act with respect to, a food . . . if such act is done while such article is held for sale (whether or not the first sale) after shipment in interstate commerce and results in such article being adulterated."

Throughout various areas of the cool room Inspector Gardine observed rodent excreta pellets. Burlap cuttings from the bags of chili pepper tested positively for mammalian urine, as did samples of the peppers themselves.

In the raw material storage room Inspector Gardine examined a lot of sesame seed, which forms the basis of Count II of the Information. He observed a decomposing rodent along the east wall of that room, and what appeared to be a rodent gnaw hole through one of the bags to the sesame seed. Burlap cuttings from various bags tested positively for mammalian urine, as did samples of the sesame seed. Several product samples also tested positively for rodent excreta.

On the other side of the warehouse, in the packaging materials storage room, Gardine observed several decomposing rodents, both in and out of bait boxes. Additionally, he saw numerous access holes for rodents throughout the warehouse.

B. *The March 1977 Inspection (Counts IV, V)*

Counts IV and V of the Information arise out of a March 1977 inspection of lots of marjoram and basil. Investigator Edward Miracco testified that the marjoram was in the main storage room. On the bags of marjoram, Miracco found rodent excreta pellets and numerous dead beetle-like insects. Sifting through the marjoram itself, Miracco found dead insects. Samples of marjoram later tested positively for rodent excreta pellets and red flour beetles.

Miracco also examined a lot of basil, finding rodent excreta pellets on six of the 34 bags he inspected. Burlap cuttings from seven of the bags tested positively for mammalian urine. On the floor of the main storage room was spilled sodium bisulfate; Miracco saw rodent tracks through the chemical. He also saw a hole in a sliding door opening from the area adjacent to the cool room on to McDonald Avenue.

C. *The July 1977 Inspection (Counts III, VI, VII)*

Counts III, VI and VII arise respectively from a July 1977 FDA Inspection of lots of arrowroot flour, sesame seed and whole chili pepper. The arrowroot flour was in the main storage room. Investigator Bodner observed rodent pellets on and around the various bags. Rodent hairs were found around a gnaw hole in one bag, and 28 different cuttings tested positively for mammalian urine.

The sesame seed was stored in the cool room. Rodent pellets were scattered throughout the various bags of seed, and one pellet was lying on sesame seed in a torn bag. Eight samples of burlap bag cuttings tested positively for mammalian urine, and thirteen samples of the sesame seed itself tested positively for rodent pellets. Also stored in the cool room was a lot of whole chili pepper. There were many rodent excreta pellets on and around the bags.

In the course of this inspection, Investigators Bodner and Lesser observed other signs of rodent activity throughout the plant: live rodents; a dead rodent; and rodent excreta pellets. Four bait boxes had no bait in them and the hole in the sliding door to McDonald Avenue, first noticed by Investigator Miracco in the March 1977 inspection, still had not been closed.

D. *The January 1979 Inspection (Counts VIII, IX, X)*

The final FDA Inspection of Gel Spice's warehouse occurred in January 1979. * * *

Investigator Richard Pecora inspected a lot of basil, which was stored in the main storage room. He observed more than 300 rodent pellets on the bags and surrounding floor. He also observed, and photographed, four live rodents nesting inside one of the bags of basil. From that bag he extracted a sample of basil, which was found to contain rodent hair and excreta as well as nesting material.

Also located in the main storage room was the aniseed involved in Count IX. Pecora counted over 200 rodent excreta pellets on and around the bags of aniseed. He found the remnants of a rodent's nest in one of the bags, as well as a roll of toilet paper, which appeared to have been gnawed by a rodent, on the floor next to the bag.

Finally, Pecora inspected a lot of bay leaves, which was stored approximately 30 feet from the aniseed. He discovered rodent excreta pellets on the bags, and a 7.6 ounce sample of bay leaf contained two more rodent pellets. A general inspection of the entire warehouse revealed more rodent pellets, a decomposed rodent in the cool room, and open drums of spices as well as spilled spices.

CONCLUSIONS OF LAW

The information charges ten violations of 21 U.S.C. § 331(k). These charges may be proven by showing the following: (1) the articles involved in the Information were food; (2) they were held for sale by Gel Spice after shipment in interstate commerce; and (3) the articles were adulterated within the meaning of either 21 U.S.C. § 342(a)(3) or § (a)(4). There is no dispute regarding the first two elements of the offense. The case, therefore, turns on whether the government has proven the third element beyond a reasonable doubt. There is also a question as to the applicability of certain defenses.

A. *Corporate Liability*

All ten counts of the Information charge Gel Spice Co. with violating 21 U.S.C. § 342(a)(4), which states that food shall be deemed adulterated "if it has been prepared, packed or held under insanitary conditions whereby it may have become contaminated with filth, or whereby it may have been rendered injurious to health." To prove a violation of this subsection, the government need only prove that the food was held under insanitary conditions, creating a reasonable possibility of contamination; proof of actual contamination is not required. Proof of actual contamination is, however, evidence that the food has been held under insanitary conditions. Moreover, when insanitary conditions are adjacent to food there exists a reasonable possibility that the food may become contaminated.

Filth, as that term is used in §§ 342(a)(3) and § 342(a)(4), is given its common meaning. It is defined as "foul matter; offensive or disgusting." *Random House, Inc., Dictionary of the English Language Unabridged* 53 (1966). Thus, food is adulterated within the meaning of § 342(a)(4) when it is stored in conditions creating a reasonable possibility that it may become contaminated with foul, offensive or disgusting matter.

Applying this standard, the evidence that Gel Spice violated § 342(a)(4) is overwhelming. The testimony of the F.D.A. investigators, corroborated by the results of laboratory analyses and by graphic photographs, proves beyond a reasonable doubt that Gel Spice held food for sale after it had been shipped in interstate commerce, under conditions whereby it may have become adulterated with filth. Accordingly, I find the corporate defendant, Gel Spice Co., guilty of ten counts of violating § 331(k), by violating § 342(a)(4).

B. *Individual Liability*

Defendant Barry Engel, President of Gel Spice Co., is named in all ten counts of the Information. His brother, Andre Engel, is Vice President of Gel Spice Co. and is named in Counts I through VII of the Information. For the reasons developed below, I find Barry Engel guilty and Andre Engel not guilty of all counts charged against them.

Under the Act, individual culpability for criminal acts of a business attaches to any person who exercises responsibility in the conduct of the business, whether or not the individual intended to violate the law or knew of the violative acts. All the government must prove is that the individual was in a position of power or authority to prevent, detect or correct violations of the Act.

The Act "dispenses with the need to prove 'consciousness of wrongdoing.'" As the Supreme Court stated in [*United States v. Park*, 421 U.S. 658, 672–74 (1975)]:

[I]n providing sanctions which reach and touch the individuals who execute the corporate mission . . . the Act imposes not only a positive duty to seek out and remedy violations when they occur but also, and primarily, a duty to implement measures that will insure that violations will not occur.

. . .

[T]he Government establishes a prima facie case when it introduces evidence sufficient to warrant a finding by the trier of the facts that the defendant had, by reason of his position in the corporation, responsibility and authority either to prevent in the first instance, or promptly to correct, the violation complained of, and that he failed to do so. The failure thus to fulfill the duty imposed by the interaction of the corporate agent's authority and the statute furnishes a sufficient causal link. The considerations which prompted the imposition of this duty, and the scope of the duty, provide the measure of culpability.

The government's proof at trial demonstrated beyond a reasonable doubt that Barry Engel was in a position of authority in the corporation to prevent or correct violations of the Act and that he did not do so. He was not "powerless to prevent or correct the violation[s]."

Barry Engel testified that he was principally responsible for plant sanitation. He also admitted this to Investigator Gardine. Although there was testimony that day-to-day plant management is delegated to Mr. Jonas Grunzweig, the evidence is clear that Mr. Grunzweig reported to Barry Engel, that Barry Engel decided what methods of sanitation were to be used, and that Barry Engel controlled the hiring and firing of outside exterminators. Barry Engel was in a position of responsibility and authority to control the insanitary conditions at Gel Spice Co. He is guilty of violating 21 U.S.C. § 331(k), as charged in all ten counts of the Information, because he did not exercise his responsibility and authority to control violations of § 342(a)(4) at the Gel Spice plant.

The government has not proved beyond a reasonable doubt that Andre Engel had the requisite responsibility and authority to warrant a finding of guilt against him. The government makes much of Andre Engel's position as Vice President, and the fact that he was present at the warehouse during the three inspections on which the Counts against him are predicated. Guilt may not be assigned, however, solely by virtue of a defendant's corporate position. Moreover, while Andre Engel was indeed present during three inspections, the FDA investigators were repeatedly told that he was filling in for Barry Engel, that Andre's primary responsibility was sales, and that Barry was the person in charge of plant operation and sanitation. There is more than a reasonable doubt that Andre Engel had responsibility and authority to control sanitary conditions at Gel Spice Co. Accordingly, I find Andre Engel not guilty of the charges contained against him in Counts I through VII.

C. *The Impossibility Defense*

Defendants contend that even if conditions at the warehouse were insanitary within the meaning of the Act, those conditions were impossible to prevent, and thus defendants are not guilty of violating § 342(a)(4). I find that defendants have not established the defense of impossibility.

The impossibility defense derives from the Supreme Court's discussion in *United States v. Park*, 421 U.S. 658 (1975), of the criminal liability of corporate agents for violations of the Act:

> The duty imposed by Congress on responsible corporate agents is, we emphasize, one that requires the highest standard of foresight and vigilance, but the Act, in its criminal aspect, does not require that which is objectively impossible. The theory upon which responsible corporate agents are held criminally accountable for "causing" violations of the Act permits a claim that a defendant was "powerless" to prevent or correct the violation to "be raised defensively at a trial on the merits."

Id. at 673.

* * * [T]he impossibility defense is not available to a corporation. While the defense is available to Barry Engel, I find that he has not offered sufficient evidence to make it a genuine issue in this case . . . .

To establish the impossibility defense the corporate officer must introduce evidence that he exercised extraordinary care, but was nevertheless unable to prevent violations of the Act. * * *

The evidence is clear that, notwithstanding Barry Engel's protestations to the contrary, he did not exercise "extraordinary care" in administering Gel Spice's sanitation program. The shocking amount of rodent filth observed during the four inspections, including live maggots, the remains of dead rodents, and rodent nesting material belies any claim that the exercise of extraordinary care would not have resulted in the removal of much of this filth. Addition-ally, the FDA investigators observed untended bait boxes, and numerous rodent access holes throughout the plant, such as broken windows, cracks in walls, and a hole in the sliding door opening on to McDonald Avenue. Barry Engel, President of Gel Spice and responsible for its sanitation program, was clearly not "powerless to protect against this kind of contamination."

Although defendants did introduce evidence of an ongoing rodent control program, that program did not constitute the extraordinary care required to establish the impossibility defense. Defendants passed an FDA inspection in 1972, and there is no evidence that the spice trade or the conditions surrounding the Gel Spice warehouse changed so much after 1972 that it became impossible for them to control rodent activity inside the warehouse. Indeed, defendants' own pictures of the warehouse, taken shortly before trial and introduced as exhibits, portray the warehouse as far cleaner than when it was inspected by the FDA between 1976 and 1979. * * *

For the foregoing reasons, I find defendants Gel Spice Company and Barry Engel guilty of all ten Counts of the Information, which charged them with violating 21 U.S.C. § 331(k) in that they held food that had been shipped in interstate commerce for sale, in an adulterated condition as defined in 21 U.S.C. § 342(a)(4). I find defendant Andre Engel not guilty of violating 21 U.S.C. § 331(k). Because of my finding that defendants violated § 331(k) by violating § 342(a)(4), I need not discuss violations of § 342(a)(3).

Defendants shall report forthwith to the Probation Department. Sentencing shall take place at 10:00 a.m., February 8, 1985. * * *

SO ORDERED.

[Gel Spice was fined $10,000 and Barry Engel was sentenced to two years' probation on each count and fined a total of $10,000. 773 F.2d 427, 432 (2d Cir.1985).]

Questions for Discussion for Case 8.4

1. What was the court's basis for finding the corporation guilty?

2. Why was Barry Engel found guilty and Andre Engel found not guilty?

3. What is the "impossibility" defense? Why were the corporation and Barry Engel unable to successfully assert this defense?

DISCUSSION QUESTIONS

1. Andrew Ladick brought suit against Gerald J. Van Gemert, an attorney, alleging that Van Gemert had sent him a letter on behalf of a California condominium association demanding payment of a past-due condominium assessment fee. He alleged that the letter violated the Fair Debt Collection Practices Act (FDCPA) because it failed to give a "validation notice" and did not expressly disclose that Van Gemert was attempting to collect a debt and that any information obtained would be used for that purpose. The trial court found that the condominium assessment that Van Gemert sought to collect was not a "debt" under the FDCPA and granted summary judgment to Van Gemert. Ladick appealed. On appeal, Van Gemert argued that a condominium assessment does not involve an extension of credit and is more like a tax than a debt. Should the FDCPA apply to this transaction? *Ladick v. Van Gemert*, 146 F.3d 1205 (10th Cir. 1998).

2. On November 9, 1997, Angel, a Spanish-speaking salesperson working for Credit Express Furniture, made a sales presentation at the home of the Spanish-speaking plaintiffs, Rigoberto and Pilar Filpo. The presentation was in Spanish as the Filpos spoke little or no English. Angel showed Pilar a catalogue, from which she ordered six pieces of furniture for a total of $3,676. The contract signed by Rigoberto was in English. And contained a provision stating that if the buyer cancelled their order or refused delivery, the buyer could pay 20 percent of the contract price as liquidated damage. The contract also stated that the merchandise could only be exchanged up to 30 days after delivery.

Under New York State's Door-to-Door Sales Protection Act, door-to-door sales contracts must contain, in the same language as the presentation and in 10-point type, the following notice:

YOU, THE BUYER MAY CANCEL THIS TRANSACTION AT ANY TIME PRIOR TO MIDNIGHT OF THE THIRD BUSINESS DAY AFTER THE DATE OF THIS TRANSACTION. SEE THE ATTACHED NOTICE OF CANCELLATION FORM FOR AN EXPLANATION OF THIS RIGHT.

The Act also requires door-to-door sales contracts to have attached to them "a completed form in duplicate, captioned 'NOTICE OF CANCELLATION,'" also in the language of the oral presentation, informing consumers of their right to (1) cancel the contract within 3 days, (2) demand a full refund, (3) receive a refund within 3 days, and (4) return the unwanted goods by making them available at the consumer's home.

Rigoberto paid for the furniture in cash when the furniture was delivered the following month. When Pilar arrived home several hours later and inspected the furniture, she found several nonconformities, including loose trim, holes in the fabric, and an incorrect fabric design and color. The next day, Pilar telephoned Credit Express Furniture, reported the damage, canceled the contract, and demanded a full refund. Credit refused to refund the purchase price but offered to exchange the furniture and to give the Filpos $300. Twice, a deliveryperson from Credit Express Furniture showed up at the Filpos' apartment with a replacement set of furniture and a check for $300, but both times the Filpos refused to accept the new furniture or the check, demanding instead that Credit Express Furniture take back the original set and return their $3,676 purchase price.

The Filpos filed suit against Credit Express Furniture. At this point, the Filpos have had the original set of furniture for two and one-half years. Should the court order Credit Express Furniture to accept the return of the furniture and to refund the Filpos' purchase price? *Filpo v. Credit Express Furniture, Inc.*, New York Law Journal, Aug. 26, 1997, at p. 21.

3. In November 1988, Joyce Crystal purchased a waterfront home in Caroline County, Maryland. Soon afterward, she decided that a second-floor skylight should be removed for safety reasons. Her real estate agent brought a contractor named Callahan, from the firm of West & Callahan, Inc., over to the house. While Callahan was evaluating the skylight project, Crystal also asked him about remodeling her screened-in porch. She wanted the porch extended by six to eight feet and enclosed with windows and doors. The parties did not sign an agreement, and Callahan did not provide a notice of the right to cancel the agreement.

Crystal understood that the project would cost $10,000, while Callahan contends that he quoted a figure of approximately $10,000 for time and did not include materials. The final construction bill was $23,769.78, of which Crystal paid $2,000. She refused to pay the balance, arguing poor workmanship and defects, including problems such as incorrect paint color. She had not complained during the construction project, however.

West & Callahan, Inc., sued Crystal for nonpayment, and she counterclaimed, alleging Callahan violated the door-to-door sales act by failing to give her the notice of cancellation required by the Maryland Door-to-Door Sales Act and that she had the right to cancel the agreement at any point until proper notice was given. Thus, she stated in her counterclaim that she was canceling the entire agreement. May Crystal cancel the door-to-door transaction nearly one and one-half years after the work has been completed? *Crystal v. West & Callahan, Inc.*, 614 A.2d 560 (Md. Ct. App. 1992).

4. Prior to September 1, 1994, Richard Whiteside signed a lease with Park Towne Place Apartments in Philadelphia for an apartment to be leased from September 1, 1994, to March 31, 1997. Whiteside failed to pay the rent and voluntarily vacated the apartment in early March 1997. Whiteside owed Park Town Place $4,342 for back rent. Park Town Place then retained National Credit Systems (NCS) to collect the back rent due.

During the first week of May 1999, NCS telephoned Whiteside attempting to collect payment. On May 25, 1999, an NCS representative and Whiteside discussed on the telephone resolving the debt for less than the full amount owing but did not come to an agreement. Whiteside received one additional call from NCS after May 25, 1999. On June 9, 1999, NCS forwarded collection correspondence addressed collectively to Larry Hill (Whiteside's former roommate) and Whiteside to Hill and Whiteside.

Whiteside had also lost his job, had numerous other debts, and was forced to sleep on a friend's couch because of lack of money. He testified at trial that he experienced headaches and that his blood pressure increased because of these multiple problems.

Whiteside filed suit, alleging that NCS's debt collection practices violated the Fair Debt Collection Practices Act. Do they? Explain. *Whiteside v. National Credit Systems, Inc.*, 2000 U.S. Dist. LEXIS 3707 (E.D. Pa. Mar. 27, 2000).

5. James Lee Anthony Jr. brought suit, arguing that the Top Tobacco Company negligently violated the Federal Labeling Act by failing to provide purchasers of its loose-leaf tobacco products with the Surgeon General's warning. The Federal Labeling Act provides that "it is unlawful for any person to manufacture, import, or package for sale or distribution within the United States any cigarettes, the package of which fails to bear the Surgeon General's warning." "Cigarette" is defined under the Federal Labeling Act as: (A) "any roll of tobacco wrapped in paper or in any substance not containing tobacco, and (B) any roll of tobacco wrapped in any substance containing tobacco which, because of its appearance, the type of tobacco used in the filler, or its packaging and labeling, is likely to be offered to, or purchased by, consumers as a cigarette described in subparagraph (A)."

Anthony indicated that he smoked products from Top Tobacco Company because there was no warning on the loose-leaf products. He claims he has numerous physical problems as a result of smoking Top Tobacco products. Should Top Tobacco Company be liable under the Federal Labeling Act for failure to put the Surgeon General's warning on loose-leaf tobacco products? *Anthony v. Top Tobacco Company*, 1999 U.S. Dist. LEXIS 9814 (M.D. Fla. June 14, 1999).

6. John Stevenson began receiving a number of phone calls from bill collectors about arrearages in accounts that were not his. He spoke with TRW, Inc., a credit-reporting firm, to try to correct the problem. In August 1989, he wrote TRW and obtained a copy of his credit report. He discovered many errors, including some accounts that belonged to an individual of the same name living in a different location and some accounts that apparently belonged to his estranged son, John Stevenson, Jr. In total, Stevenson disputed approximately 16 accounts, 7 inquiries, and much of the identifying information.

Stevenson wrote TRW on October 6, 1989, requesting that his credit report be corrected. On November 1, TRW began a reinvestigation by contacting subscribers that had reported the disputed accounts. As a result of this investigation, TRW removed several of the disputed accounts by November 30. TRW retained one account on the record because the subscriber insisted that the information was accurate, and investigations on several other accounts were still pending. TRW also added a warning statement to Stevenson's account in December, indicating that his son had apparently used his social security number without his consent to obtain credit. By February 1990, TRW claimed that all disputed accounts with "negative" credit information had been removed. Inaccurate information continued to appear on Stevenson's report, however, and some of the disputed information was reentered after Stevenson had had it deleted.

Stevenson filed suit, alleging that TRW had violated the Fair Credit Reporting Act. Has TRW done so? Explain. *Stevenson v. TRW, Inc.*, 987 F.2d 288 (5th Cir. 1993).

7. In July 1990, the Bartholomew Circuit Court in Columbus, Indiana, rendered a deficiency judgment against Jeff Henson in the amount of $4,075.54. The Clerk of the Court incorrectly recorded the judgment in the Judgment Docket, stating that a money judgment in that amount had been entered against both Jeff Henson and his brother Greg Henson.

Trans Union Corp. and CSC Credit Services, both credit reporting agencies, listed the information on Greg Henson's credit report. Greg and his wife Mary filed suit against both companies, arguing that the companies had violated the Fair Credit Reporting Act by including this erroneous judgment in his account.

The agencies argued that the information that they had reported was accurate and that a judgment had been entered against Greg. Under Indiana law, the actual judgment entered by the court is the official act that renders the judgment legally binding; the entry of the judgment on the Judgment Docket is merely an administrative task undertaken by the Clerk.

While Greg alleged that he had contacted Trans Union twice in writing regarding the error and that no correction had been made, he did not allege that he had contacted CSC. Trans Union argued that it had no duty to investigate beyond the Judgment Docket to verify the accuracy of the reported information.

How should the court resolve this dispute? *Henson v. CSC Credit Servces*, 29 F.3d 280 (7th Cir. 1994).

8. Sam Nicholson, a Georgia attorney, filed a class action lawsuit on behalf of 1,322 plaintiffs against the Hooters restaurant chain after receiving an unsolicited lunch coupon on his law office fax machine in 1995. Nicholson alleged the unsolicited fax violated the TCPA. The fax was one of several coupons faxed by a company called Value-Fax. Value-Fax had been hired by Hooters and other businesses to distribute advertisements to local fax machines.

The state court certified the class in 1999, allowing the class action case to go forward. Nicholson is seeking $12 million in recovery for repeat faxes of the discount coupon. Nicholson argues that such cases should be brought as class actions because most consumers do not know how to file such suits on their own and the small amount of possible recovery makes it cost-prohibitive to hire a lawyer.

A second lawsuit was filed against a Charleston, South Carolina, Ramada Inn and a fax service. The fax, which promoted a New Year's Eve party, allegedly was sent to as many as 2,700 fax machines. The attorney who filed the case is seeking class certification as

well. The attorney for Ramada Inn has contended, however, that the intent of the TCPA is to allow a hassle-free forum for private citizens to sue, such as small claims court, and that a class action would result in an unintended and unwarranted financial windfall for attorneys. Other suits are also pending against other businesses that sent junk faxes.

The law regarding the availability of class actions in TCPA suits is unclear, and these cases are being closely watched to see how the courts resolve this issue. Should the courts allow class actions to proceed against businesses that send junk faxes? What are the pros and cons of allowing this type of litigation to proceed? Do you think that Congress intended such lawsuits to occur when it passed the TPCA? Does allowing class actions further the purposes of the TCPA or does it simply allow a financial windfall for the attorneys filing such actions? *Hooters of Augusta, Inc. v. Nicholson*, 245 Ga. App. 363 (2000); Emily Heller, *Lawyers Jump on the Junk Fax*, THE NATIONAL LAW JOURNAL, Jan. 17, 2000, at p. A11.

9. On January 24, 1994, Frederick Hantske Jr. was telephoned at home by Paul Kallina, an employee of Brandenburger & Davis, Inc. Kallina told Hantske that he could possibly be an heir to an estate and arranged a meeting with him on the following day.

Kallina met with Hantske at his home in Charlottesville, Virgina, for one and one-half hours. Kallina explained that his firm searched official records for missing heirs. Kallina stated that the firm believed that Hantske was an heir to a certain estate and that the firm would undertake to prove Hantske's claim and would "fight for" Hantske to receive his inheritance. Kallina then presented a contract to Hantske under which Brandenburger & Davis would receive one-fourth of the inheritance received by Hantske in exchange for locating Hantske, notifying him, and proving his interests. If Hantske did not inherit anything, he would owe the firm nothing. Kallina estimated that Hantske's interest in the estate was approximately $30,000 and that the firm would receive a fee of $7,500. Hantske signed the written agreement that same day.

Hantske then went to court seeking to have the contract voided, arguing that under the Virginia Home Solicitation Sales Act of 1970 he had a right to cancel the contract after it was signed. The court found that the agreement between Hantske and Brandenburger & Davis fit the definition of a sale under the Virginia Act. Home solicitation statutes of this type normally provide a three-day "cooling off" time period in which the homeowner has an unwaivable right to cancel the sale. Because the agreement signed by Hantske did not include a right to cancel, the court found that it was unenforceable under the Act.

Should a homeowner such as Hanske be permitted to take advantage of information provided to him by a seller that he would not have easily learned about on his own? Should homeowners be allowed to cancel a signed agreement and retain the financial results? Is it ethical and fair to keep the benefits, cancel the agreement, and not pay for services and information provided? What interests is the Virginia Home Solicitation Sales Act trying to protect? *Hantske v. Brandenburger & Davis, Inc.*, 36 Va. Cir. 423 (1995).

CHAPTER 9

Legal Issues Relating to the Sale of Services and Goods

Contracts and Sales of Goods Law

Although most people do not realize it, they form and execute contracts repeatedly during their daily lives. Every time you purchase gas, buy groceries, go to a movie, or visit a doctor or a dentist, you have formed a contract with the provider of the good or service you are acquiring.

Overview

In most instances, we do not even think about these informal contracts. They are typically oral, not written, transactions; they are formed and executed almost simultaneously; and, unless the goods or services purchased turn out to be defective, the transaction is complete almost immediately, with no lingering legal ramifications to worry about. Nonetheless, the law recognizes these transactions as creating legal relationships known as *contracts*.

Businesses likewise form frequent contractual relationships as they go about their normal, routine activities. Contract law issues arise at several stages in the marketing of goods and services. A manufacturer, for example, enters into purchase contracts with its suppliers and sales contracts with its distributors or retailers. The final sale to the consumer, whether the sale is made by the manufacturer itself, a retailer, or someone else in the chain of distribution, also creates a contractual relationship between the purchaser and the seller.

Businesses tend to pay more attention to their contractual relationships than do individuals. Nonetheless, many routine business transactions occur without the use of a formalized written contract or without the parties explicitly agreeing on the terms of their contract. The law provides default rules that control in the instances in which the parties have not negotiated their own contractual terms. Many of these default rules are discussed in this chapter. You should realize, however, that the law promotes freedom of contract. Explicit agreements of the parties, provided they are not illegal or against public policy, generally override the rules discussed here.

This chapter provides an overview of basic contract law principles, including both common law contracts and the special rules that apply to sales of goods. The law of contracts is considerably more detailed and complex than this necessarily brief description suggests, however, so managers should seek legal advice when confronted with these issues.

Sources of Contract Law

Contract law is a matter of state law. This raises an initial question, however, of *which* state law applies when the parties to the contract are located in two or more states. Many modern commercial transactions involve parties from different states or occur across state lines. If the parties enter into a written contract, they often include a *choice-of-law* provision that indicates which state's law is to govern the contract. Otherwise, the controlling law is the law of the state to which the substance of the contract and the parties are most closely related and the state that has the strongest governmental interest in having its law apply. There are specific *conflict-of-laws* rules that help courts make these determinations.

Two basic sources of law govern the sale of goods and services: the common law and the Uniform Commercial Code (UCC).

THE COMMON LAW OF CONTRACTS

The original source of contract law was the *common law*. As discussed in Chapter 1, common law refers to law that develops in the courts and that is primarily found in judicial decisions. Although state legislatures have passed statutes dealing with certain aspects of specific types of common law contractual relationships, such as employer-employee or landlord-tenant relationships, the common law is still the primary source of contract law. Today, the common law of contracts governs the sale of services (including employment and insurance contracts), intangible personal property (such as trade secrets), and real estate.

The American Law Institute (ALI) has compiled the *Restatement (Second) of Contracts*, which summarizes the generally accepted principles of the common law of contracts.[1] Each state has its own variations on the rules, however, so a marketer needs to be aware of the specific law that controls in the state or states in which it operates.

UNIFORM COMMERCIAL CODE

The *Uniform Commercial Code* (UCC) is a model statute drafted by the National Conference of Commissioners (NCC) on Uniform State Laws[2] and the ALI in the 1940s. It has several parts, called "Articles," which codify the law regarding certain types of commercial transactions.

Originally, commercial law varied from state to state. This imposed a very substantial burden on business, particularly as the economy grew and became national in scope and as businesses began operating across state lines. The UCC was intended to provide the states with a blueprint for commercial law that would standardize the rules across all the states and that would reflect the new legal issues raised by the growth in mass distribution of consumer goods in the early twentieth century.

Article 2 of the UCC, which was drafted in 1951 and which has been adopted in all of the states except Louisiana,[3] governs transactions involving goods.[4] A *sale* is a contract by which title to goods is transferred from one party to another for a price. *Goods* are any tangible personal property. The law pertaining to the sale of goods still is not completely "uniform," as most states altered the UCC somewhat as they adopted it. These alterations tend to be rather minor, however, so businesses can now engage in interstate business activities with a good deal more certainty and ease.

The UCC supplements the common law of contracts with regard to the sale of goods. If the UCC does not contain an explicit provision on a particular point, common law contract rules continue to apply. A marketer of goods thus needs to be aware of both sets of legal rules.

There are some fundamental distinctions between the UCC and the common law. First, the UCC is a lot less formalistic than the common law. This means that its rules are less rigid and that the UCC is more likely to find that an enforceable contract exists than is the common law, even if the parties have failed to agree on seemingly important terms. The UCC has specific "gap-filler" provisions (discussed below) that the courts use to supply certain missing terms.

---

[1] For general information on the ALI, *see* http://www.ali.org

[2] For general information on the NCC, *see* http://www.nccusl.org
  For general information on the UCC, *see* http://www.law.cornell.edu/topics/sales.html

[3] Louisiana follows the civil law tradition of its French heritage rather than the common law system followed in the other 49 states.

[4] Article 2A governs the lease of goods. It was proposed by the drafters of the UCC in the late 1980s in response to uncertainty about how the provisions of Article 2 applied to the burgeoning business of the leasing of goods. Article 2A is substantially similar to Article 2. Some of the major distinctions between the two are that Article 2A contains no battle of the forms provision, the Statute of Frauds provision under Article 2A requires a writing for leases of $1,000 or more, and consumers are provided certain special protections in lease relationships. For general information on Article 2A, *see* http://www.law.cornell.edu/ucc/2A/overview.html

Second, the common law applies equally to all parties. Under the UCC, by contrast, "merchants" are often subject to special rules. The UCC defines a *merchant* as a person who (1) deals in goods of the kind being sold, (2) by his occupation holds himself out as having knowledge or skill peculiar to the practices or goods involved in the transaction, or (3) employs an agent or broker who holds himself out as having such knowledge or skill.[5] For example, the UCC imposes an obligation of good faith upon the parties to a contract.[6] A nonmerchant seller is held to a subjective standard of "honesty in fact."[7] A merchant seller, on the other hand, is held to a higher objective standard that includes not only honesty in fact, but also the "observance of reasonable commercial standards of fair dealing in the trade."[8] Examples of other special merchant rules are provided later in the chapter.

Some contracts involve the sale of both goods and services. For example, if a buyer purchases new carpeting for his home, the sales contract may well include installation of the carpet as well. If a dispute arises, should it be resolved under the UCC (because the sale of goods—carpet—is involved) or the common law (because the sale of a service—carpet installation—is involved)? In *hybrid contracts* involving both goods and services, the courts generally look to see whether the predominant focus of the contract is the sale of the goods or the sale of the service (see Focus Case 9.1 on page 305).

Elements of a Contract

> A contract is a promise or set of promises for breach of which the law gives a remedy, or the performance of which the law in some way recognizes as a duty.[9]

A contract, in short, is a promise or set of promises that the courts will enforce. All contracts involve promises, but not all promises are contracts. For a contract to exist, four elements must be present: (1) mutual assent (i.e., offer and acceptance), (2) consideration, (3) legality, and (4) capacity.

MUTUAL ASSENT

Mutual assent requires a "meeting of the minds" between the two parties and is generally shown by a valid offer and acceptance. An *offer* is a statement by the *offeror* (person making the offer) that indicates a willingness to enter into a bargain. *Acceptance* occurs when the *offeree* (person to whom the offer was made) indicates a willingness to enter into that proposed bargain. Only the intended offeror has the power to accept; third parties may not accept an offer and form a binding contract. Generally, the parties indicate their willingness through words, but conduct can also constitute an offer or acceptance. It is the objective, outward manifestation of the party's words or conduct that counts. The law will not recognize subjective or secret intentions of either party. In addition, offers usually cannot be accepted through *silence* of the offeree.

Offers are effective when received by the offeree. Under the *mailbox rule*, however, acceptances are effective when sent, even if never received by the offeror. This

---

[5] UCC § 2-104(1).
[6] UCC § 1-203.
[7] UCC § 1-201(19).
[8] UCC § 2-103(1)(b).
[9] Restatement (Second) of Contracts § 1 (1979).

Focus Case 9.1

Facts: Ricky Ezell contracted to purchase specially-manufactured interior shutters for his home from The Plantation Shutter Company ("Plantation") for $5,985.75. Plantation was to manufacture and install the shutters. Ezell was not satisfied with 12 of the 37 panels after installation. Plantation agreed to remake the shutters. Ezell continued to complain about several aspects of the shutters, including their exposed hinges. Plantation agreed to specially-manufacture side strips to hide the hinges. Plantation made several attempts to schedule an appointment to install the hinges, but Ezell did not respond to its efforts. Finally, Plantation sent workers to the home to install the hinges, but Ezell refused them access. Plantation sued Ezell for breach of contract to collect the balance owing on the shutters. Ezell argued that the UCC did not apply to this contract because it was a contract for services.

Decision: The court disagreed, stating:

> In considering whether a transaction that provides for both goods and services is a contract for the sale of goods governed by the UCC, courts generally employ the predominant factor test. Under this test, if the predominant factor of the transaction is the rendition of a service with goods incidentally involved, the UCC is not applicable. If, however, the contract's predominant factor is the sale of goods with labor incidentally involved, the UCC applies. In most cases in which the contract calls for a combination of services with the sale of goods, courts have applied the UCC.

* * * *

> Here, the contract does not provide for installation charges. The document is entitled "Terms of Sale." By signing the contract, however, the "customer" authorized the "sales representative" to do the "work" as specified. Although the term "work" sounds more like a service contract term, looking at the contract as a whole, it is predominantly a contract for the sale of goods; therefore, we must apply the UCC.

The court determined that Ezell was liable for breach of contract because he had accepted the shutters by failing to effectively reject them in accordance with UCC requirements. *The Plantation Shutter Co. v. Ezell*, 492 S.E. 2d 404 (S.C. Ct. App. 1997).

---

rule can create risks for the offeror. For example, if a properly addressed acceptance is lost in transmission, it is nonetheless effective and the offeror is bound to the contract even though it may be unaware of the acceptance. To avoid such a result, the offeror should expressly state in its offer that acceptance will be effective only upon receipt of the acceptance by the offeror.

Offers, once made, can be terminated in a number of ways. The offeree may *reject* it or issue a *counteroffer*. The offer may be explicitly *revoked* by the offeror or may expire after a *lapse of time*. The offeror may specify a time limit for acceptance in the offer; otherwise, the offer will automatically expire after a reasonable time period. Finally, the *death* or *incapacity* of either party will terminate the offer.

Bilateral Versus Unilateral Contracts

Contracts can be either *bilateral* or *unilateral*, depending upon whether the offeror requested a promise or an act from the offeree. Most contracts are *bilateral* contracts in which a promise is given in exchange for another promise. If a hospital sends a purchase order for bandages to a medical supply company, for example, and the medical supply company sends back an acknowledgment form, the parties have formed a bilateral contract. The hospital has promised to pay for the bandages ordered, and the medical supply company has promised to provide the bandages in return for payment.

Focus Case 9.2

Facts: In March 1998, McDonald's Corporation began the "1998 McDonald's Monopoly Game" to promote sales of its food items. Customers could win by collecting the entire series of official "Collect to Win" stamps or by obtaining an "Instant Win" stamp. The official rules for the promotion game were posted at all participating McDonald's locations. The official rules stated in part:

> All game materials are subject to verification at a participating McDonald's or the Redemption Center, whichever is applicable. Game materials are null and void and will be rejected if not obtained through authorized, legitimate channels, or if they are mutilated or tampered with in any way (except for the signed initials of the potential winner), or if they contain printing, typographical, mechanical, or other errors. All decisions of McDonald's and the Redemption Center are final, binding and conclusive in all matters.

The official rules also stated: "You are not a winner of any prize until your official game stamp(s) has been verified at the Redemption Center or a participating McDonald's, whichever is applicable."

On April 3, Vernicesa Barnes ordered hash browns at a McDonald's restaurant. The container had a game piece attached that stated: "$200,000 Dream Home Cash—Stamp 818—Need Stamps 818, 819, & 820 to Win—Instant Winner!" Interpreting this to mean that she had an "Instant Win" Stamp, Barnes filled out the forms to begin the redemption process and mailed the stamp and signed forms to the McDonald's Redemption Center.

On May 1, Barnes received a letter from the Redemption Center notifying her that the game stamp was a miscut "Collect to Win" stamp and would not be honored. Barnes filed suit, alleging, among other things, breach of contract.

Decision: The court found that McDonald's promotion constituted the offer of a unilateral contract that could only be accepted by performance of the contract terms. Under the terms of the offer (as spelled out in the official rules), the offeree was required to: (1) possess a valid winning stamp; (2) sign a redemption form indicating that she understood and accepted the official rules; and (3) mail the redemption form and the stamp to the redemption center for a validation procedure.

Barnes did not posses a valid winning ticket and therefore could not comply with the conditions of the offer. The McDonald's Redemption Committee made a decision that the game stamp contained "printing, typographical, mechanical or other errors" and was therefore "null and void" under the terms of the official rules to which Barnes had agreed. Without a valid stamp, Barnes was unable to perform the unilateral contract; thus, no breach had occurred. The court granted McDonald's motion for summary judgment. *Barnes v. McDonald's Corp.,* 72 F. Supp. 2d 1038 (E.D. Ark. 1999), *aff'd,* 230 F.3d 1362 (8th Cir. 2000).

In a *unilateral contract*, a promise is given in exchange for an act (or a refraining from acting) by the other side. Acceptance of the contract occurs when the performance of the act is complete; no promise is requested of or made by the offeree (see Focus Case 9.2).

Generally, businesses prefer to use bilateral contracts. In unilateral contracts, the offeror cannot be certain when or whether the offeree will perform the requested act and form the contract. For example, if the hospital fails to specify its intent regarding acceptance when it places its purchase order for bandages, the medical supply company may accept either by sending back an acknowledgment form promising to ship the bandages or by in fact shipping the requested bandages.[10] In the latter instance, the hospital will not know if the medical supply company has accepted the offer until the bandages actually arrive. For this reason, businesses often prefer to avoid issuing offers that result in unilateral contracts.

[10] UCC § 2-206(1)(b).

Where the language of the offer is ambiguous as to whether a unilateral or bilateral contract is proposed, both the UCC and the Restatement provide that the offeree may accept either by performance or by a promise.

Advertisements as Offers

Marketers often advertise the goods or services they have for sale. Does every such advertisement constitute an offer to every reader of the advertisement to enter into a contract?

Generally, no. Advertisements usually indicate that the marketer has goods or services for sale, describe those goods or services, and indicate prices. They operate as an invitation to the public to make an offer to purchase (which the seller may then accept or reject), but they generally do not rise to the level of an offer to sell. In addition, the courts generally view other sales materials, such as catalogues and price lists, as merely invitations to make an offer as well.

Advertisements that contain definite or specific language that clearly indicates a willingness on the part of the advertiser to be bound to a specific transaction may constitute an offer. For example, a court might interpret as an offer an advertisement to sell "13 SuperLite CoffeeMakers, Model 112B, for $39.95, First come, First served" because the advertiser has specified a definite number and definite type of coffee maker to be sold.

See Discussion Case 9.1.

Option Contracts and Firm Offers

As already stated, offers automatically expire after a reasonable time if they are not accepted. What is reasonable depends upon the circumstances of the offer and practices within the industry. In addition, offers may be revoked by the offeror at any time prior to acceptance. This is true even if the offer states that it will remain open for a certain time period.

However, the offeror can ensure that an offer will remain open if the offeree pays consideration (i.e., provides something of value), thus creating an *option contract*. This is a separate agreement that requires the offeree to provide consideration to the offeror in exchange for the offeror leaving the offer open for a specified time period. Option contracts are commonly used in the sale of real estate or businesses. Consideration is discussed further below.

The UCC provides a special rule for merchants called the *firm offer rule*. Under the UCC's firm offer rule,[11] an offer is not revocable if it is (1) made by a merchant (2) in a signed writing and (3) states that it will remain open for a certain time period. Firm offers do not require the payment of consideration. However, a firm offer cannot be made irrevocable for a period of time longer than three months unless consideration is paid.

Counteroffers and the Battle of the Forms

An offeree, of course, is under no obligation to accept an offer made to it. The offeree may *reject* the offer (which instantly terminates the offer) or may choose simply not to respond (which causes the offer to expire automatically after a reasonable time period).

What if the offeree is interested in the transaction presented to it but is not completely satisfied with the terms of the offer? The offeree may respond with a

[11] UCC § 2-205.

counteroffer. This has the legal effect of rejecting the original offer and putting a new offer on the table instead. Suppose that Amalgamated, Inc., contacts HR Consulting Co. and states that it is interested in having HR prepare new personnel manuals for its operations. Amalgamated has not made an offer at this point but is inviting HR to make an offer to it. HR (the offeror) then sends back a proposal, detailing the work product that it proposes to provide and stating a price of $50,000. Amalgamated (the offeree) believes that the price is too high and responds that it is willing to pay only $45,000 for HR's services.

Because Amalgamated has changed the terms of the offer sent to it, its response is a counteroffer (and Amalgamated is now the offeror). HR is the offeree and may decide whether to accept or reject the counteroffer that Amalgamated has put forth. No contract is formed between the parties unless and until HR agrees to the new terms proposed by Amalgamated.

Suppose HR rejects Amalgamated's counteroffer. May Amalgamated now go back and attempt to accept HR's original offer of $50,000? No. Amalgamated's counteroffer killed the original offer made by HR. At this point, all Amalgamated can do is issue a new offer for $50,000, which HR may choose to accept or reject.

Under the common law, the *mirror image rule* states that no contract is formed unless the offer and acceptance are identical in every respect. Suppose, for example, that Amalgamated, Inc., faxed a letter to Vendors Corp. offering to buy 100 widgets from Vendors, with delivery to occur on Tuesday, May 14. Vendors faxed back an acceptance, but the acceptance indicated that delivery was to occur on Monday, May 13. Under the common law mirror image rule, no contract has been formed and Vendors' purported acceptance is really just a counteroffer.

The common law's rigid mirror image rule does not mesh with the realities of modern day business practice, where companies tend to use preprinted forms with boilerplate language. The buyer, for example, typically sends its purchase order form to the seller. The form contains preprinted provisions (that generally favor the buyer), with blanks where the buyer fills in terms such as price, quantity, and delivery requirements for the goods being ordered. The seller then sends back its preprinted acknowledgment form, which most likely has at least some differing preprinted terms (that generally favor the seller). Neither side typically reads the entire document sent by the other side but, rather, focuses on the terms critical to the immediate transaction, such as price, quantity, and delivery terms. Although the parties may not have reached agreement on all of the remaining terms, they clearly intend that a contract be formed. The mirror image rule frustrates this intention.

The UCC abandons the mirror image rule and focuses instead on the intent (or likely intent) of the parties to the transaction. UCC § 2-207, known as the *"Battle of the Forms"* provision, tells the parties (1) whether a contract has been created when the forms contain differing terms and, if so, (2) what terms control. The rules vary under this section depending upon whether both of the parties are merchants.

Under UCC § 2-207, under most circumstances, a contract is formed even if the offer and acceptance contain differing terms. However, if the second document changes a *fundamental term* (for example, alters the quantity term), there is no acceptance and no contract is formed. In addition, if the second document *expressly states* that no contract will be formed unless the offeror agrees to the new or altered terms, no contract is formed. In both of these instances, the second document operates as a counteroffer.

If there is an acceptance and a contract has been formed, the second question is what terms will control? Different rules apply depending upon whether the second document contains *new* terms or *different* terms.

Whether *new* terms become part of the contract depends upon whether both parties are *merchants*. If *either* the buyer or the seller is *not* a merchant, a contract has been formed under the terms of the first document sent and any new terms in the second document are merely proposals for additions to that contract, which the other side may accept or reject.

If *both* the seller and the buyer *are* merchants, the new terms contained in the second document automatically become part of the contract unless: (1) the new terms materially alter the contract; (2) the other side objects within a reasonable time; or (3) the original offer stated that no new terms would be allowed. Material alterations include things such as disclaimers of warranties or clauses requiring arbitration in the event of a dispute. As a policy matter, the UCC takes the position that material alterations must be negotiated directly with the other side and may not be hidden in boilerplate language.

The UCC's position on *different* terms is much less clear. For example, suppose that the buyer's purchase order provides for one delivery date, but the seller's acknowledgment form states a different date. Some courts treat the different term in the same manner that they would treat a new term. Other courts find that the contract is formed but that the UCC's gap-filler provisions must be used to fill in the term on which the parties disagree. The outcome thus depends upon the state whose law controls the contract.

See Discussion Case 9.2.

CONSIDERATION

The second required element for a contract is *consideration*—that is, a *bargained-for exchange*. Promises made without consideration are considered to be gratuitous or gift promises and are generally not legally enforceable as contracts.

Consideration consists of anything of value exchanged by the parties, such as money, property, services, a promise to do something the person is not otherwise legally required to do, or a promise to refrain from doing something the person is otherwise legally entitled to do. Courts do not inquire into the adequacy of consideration; thus, the exchange of anything of value, no matter how small, suffices, provided that the amount is not nominal or the transaction is not a sham (i.e., the agreement recites the payment of consideration, but no consideration in fact was paid). If a party fails to provide anything of value, however, its promise is *illusory* and no contract is formed (see Focus Case 9.3 on page 310).

Suppose the parties enter into a valid contract for 50 hours of bookkeeping services. One month later, the parties agree that the contract shall now be for 60 hours of such services, not 50. Must this *modification* of the original contract be supported by consideration? Under the common law, the answer is yes—modifications of contracts must be supported by consideration. The UCC, on the other hand, provides that while consideration is necessary for the initial contract, it is not necessary for a modification.[12] Thus, if the contract had been for goods rather than services, consideration would not have been required.

---

[12] UCC § 2-209(1).

Focus Case 9.3

Facts: Carol Poole began working as a travel agent for Incentives Unlimited in April 1992. Four years later, Incentives asked Poole to sign an "Employment Agreement" that contained a covenant not to compete. The covenant prohibited Poole from competing directly with Incentives within a four-county area for one year after ceasing her employment. Poole signed the Agreement.

Poole soon left Incentives and began working at a competing travel agency. Incentives sued to enforce the covenant not to compete. The trial court awarded summary judgment to Poole. Incentives appealed.

Decision: The appellate court affirmed the trial court's decision, finding that the covenant not to compete was not supported by consideration:

Incentives received a benefit when Poole signed the covenant not to compete to her detriment, but it is obvious that Poole received no new benefit. Poole enjoyed no benefit the day after she signed the agreement that she did not have the day before. After Poole signed the covenant not to compete, she remained merely an at-will employee, the same as before. She had no increase in salary, no bonus, and no changed work conditions. The promise of continued employment was illusory because even though Poole signed the covenant, Incentives retained the right to discharge her at any time.

Poole v. Incentives Unlimited, 525 S.E.2d 898 (S.C. App. 1999).

LEGALITY/UNENFORCEABILITY ON PUBLIC POLICY GROUNDS

Although contract law generally favors freedom of bargaining between the parties, the courts do not enforce certain types of bargains or agreements for public policy reasons. Instead, they typically "leave the parties where they find them," which can be very harsh on a party who has fully performed its side of the bargain but has not yet received performance from the other side. There are two rationales behind this rule: (1) to discourage the illegal conduct in the future and (2) to avoid the inappropriate and unseemly sight of having the courts become involved in enforcing a socially undesirable activity.

Some agreements are unenforceable because they are statutory violations. For example, a person engaged in a trade or business required by law to be licensed may not be properly licensed or an individual or firm may be in violation of statutes prohibiting gambling or usury. In such an instance, the statute may well provide that any agreement entered into by such a person or firm is illegal and thus unenforceable. Other types of unenforceable agreements are not statutory violations but are nonetheless found to violate public policy. These would include contracts that attempt to improperly limit one party's liability for its own tortious conduct (*exculpatory clauses* are discussed more below) or contracts that unreasonably restrain trade.

Courts may also decline to enforce contracts they regard as *unconscionable* (i.e., unfair), including *contracts of adhesion*. Contracts of adhesion typically involve standardized documents drafted by a party with grossly disproportionate bargaining power in the relationship, who then presents the document to the other party on a "take it or leave it" basis.

Courts are reluctant to allow businesses to argue that a contract was unconscionable, though they readily use this doctrine to protect consumers.

CAPACITY

To form a contract, both parties must have *contractual capacity*. Most persons have full capacity to enter into a contract, but certain parties have only limited capacity.

Minors (persons under the age of 18), for example, may enter into contracts. However, those contracts are often *voidable* at the option of the minor but not at the option of the other party to the contract. Thus, businesses need to use caution when contracting with minors, particularly as minors increasingly purchase expensive consumer items, such as electronics and automobiles. Businesses often require the minor's parent or another adult to co-sign the contract. Even if the minor is able to void the contract, the adult cosigner will remain bound.

Persons who have been placed under guardianship by a court as a result of incompetency have no capacity to enter into contracts. Persons who are mentally ill or mentally incompetent but who are not under guardianship and intoxicated persons may enter into contracts, but those contracts may be voidable at their option (but not by the other party to the contract).

Corporations make contracts through the acts of their officers, agents, and/or employees. Whether a particular individual has the authority to bind the corporation to a contract is determined by principles of agency or corporate law. The president generally has authority to enter into all contracts relating to business operations. If an individual other than the president is entering into the contract on behalf of the corporation, the other party to the contract would be wise to verify that that individual has the authority to do so.

Promissory Estoppel

There are instances in which a promise does not meet the required elements of a contract but a court nonetheless enforces it under the doctrine of *promissory estoppel*. The *Restatement (Second) of Contracts* defines this doctrine as follows: "A promise which the promisor should reasonably expect to induce action or forbearance on the part of the promisee or a third person and which does induce such action or forbearance is binding if injustice can be avoided only by enforcement of the promise."[13]

Generally, the doctrine of promissory estoppel requires four elements to be present: (1) a clear and unambiguous promise must have been made; (2) the party to whom the promise was made must have relied upon it; (3) that reliance must have been reasonable and foreseeable; and (4) the party relying on the promise must have been injured by that reliance. Under the Restatement (Second), however reasonable reliance is not a required element. Rather, the promisee must show (1) a promise; (2) that the promisor should have reasonably expected to induce action or forbearance; (3) that does induce such action or forbearance; and (4) that injustice can be avoided only through enforcement of the promise. The rationale behind the doctrine of promissory estoppel is to avoid the substantial hardship or injustice that would result if such a promise were not enforced.

See Discussion Case 9.3.

The Statute of Frauds

The law recognizes and enforces oral contracts in most instances. All states have adopted some form of a *Statute of Frauds*, however, that requires that certain types of contracts be in writing in order to be enforceable in court in the event of a

[13] Restatement (Second) of Contracts § 90(a).

dispute. These contracts include (1) contracts that cannot be performed in one year, (2) contracts for the transfer of an interest in real property, and (3) contracts in which one person agrees to assume another's debts.

Under the UCC's Statute of Frauds provision,[14] contracts for $500 or more usually must be in writing in order to be enforceable in court. If a contract is initially for less than $500 (and thus not required to be in writing) but is modified to bring it over $500, the modification must be in writing.

Neither the common law nor the UCC requires that the writing be a formal document—even a handwritten note on a scrap of paper or the back of an envelope will suffice. Under the common law, the document must (1) reasonably identify the subject matter of the contract, (2) indicate that a contract (as opposed to a lease or some other type of transaction) has been made between the parties, (3) state with reasonable certainty the essential terms of the contract, and (4) be signed by the party against whom enforcement is sought.

Returning to our example of Amalgamated, Inc., and HR Consulting, let us suppose that the parties negotiated and agreed on the terms orally. Amalgamated then sent a signed letter to HR, indicating that a contract had been formed and setting forth the terms of the agreement. The letter would be a sufficient writing to allow HR to enforce the contract against Amalgamated. Amalgamated would be unable to enforce the contract against HR, however, if HR failed to perform, because Amalgamated does not have a writing signed by HR.

The lesson for managers, of course, is to never sign a document unless the other side signs as well. Where the document is being exchanged through the mail, and one side necessarily has to sign before the other, the first signatory can be protected by inclusion of a clause to the effect: "This contract shall not be formed or take effect until signed by both parties."

Under the UCC, a writing satisfies the Statute of Frauds if it (1) evidences a contract for the sale of goods, (2) is signed by the party against whom enforcement is sought, and (3) states the quantity.[15] In addition, the UCC has a special Statute of Frauds rule for merchants. Under the *reply doctrine*, if both parties are merchants, a written confirmation that (1) indicates that a contract has been made, (2) has been signed by the sender, and (3) states the quantity is enforceable against the recipient as well as the sender unless the recipient objects in writing within 10 days after receipt.[16]

See Discussion Case 9.1.

Parol Evidence Rule and Contract Interpretation

The *parol evidence rule* provides that evidence of oral agreements and discussion prior to the signing of a writing that is intended to be the final expression of the parties' agreement may not be introduced to contradict that writing. The rule does not bar consideration of oral modifications of a contract made after the signing of the writing, however, unless the writing states that oral modifications are not allowed.

Most modern courts will allow parties to introduce extrinsic evidence to aid in the *interpretation* of an agreement. Thus, the parties can introduce evidence of what

---

[14] UCC § 2-201.
[15] UCC § 2-201(1).
[16] UCC § 2-201(2).

they thought the term in the writing meant. Three sources are particularly important to this interpretation role, particularly in UCC contracts. *Course of performance* refers to the manner in which the parties have conducted themselves with regard to the specific contract at issue.[17] *Course of dealing* refers to the manner in which the parties have acted with respect to past contracts.[18] *Usage of trade* refers to "any practice or method of dealing having such regularity of observance in a place, vocation or trade as to justify an expectation that it will be observed with respect to the transaction in question."[19] Although these sources cannot be used to contradict express terms in a written agreement, they can be used to interpret those terms. Where more than one source applies, the specific controls over the general. That is, an express contractual provision controls over a course of performance, which controls over a course of dealing, which controls over a usage of trade.[20]

Special UCC Rules

The UCC has a number of provisions relating to the sale of goods that differ significantly from the common law of contracts. Some of these special UCC rules are discussed here.

DEFINITENESS AND THE UCC'S "GAP-FILLER" PROVISIONS

Traditionally, the common law required a contract to be very definite in its terms, spelling out all of the material terms of the contract, such as the parties, the subject matter of the contract, the quantity, and the price, in order to be enforceable. Most modern courts have relaxed this requirement and will now supply a missing term where they can find a "reasonable" value for that term.

The UCC has codified this more liberal approach to definiteness of a contract. The UCC does not demand absolute certainty in an agreement in order for a contract to exist. Rather, the UCC requires only three elements to be present: (1) some sort of indication that an agreement exists, (2) the signature of the party against whom enforcement is sought, and (3) a statement of the quantity of goods being sold. The UCC has *gap-filler* rules that will fill in any terms left open or not addressed by the parties, such as price, performance, delivery or payment terms, or remedies.

The UCC will not fill in missing quantity terms—largely because there is no way to tell what the parties intended in terms of quantity if they failed to specify this themselves. The UCC will allow *output* contracts, however, where the buyer agrees to buy all that the seller produces, or *requirements* contracts, where the seller agrees to supply all that the buyer needs. In each case, however, the seller's production or the buyer's requirement is governed by norms of fair dealing and industry custom.

PERFORMANCE OF THE CONTRACT

Under the UCC, the basic obligation of the seller is to tender conforming goods to the buyer. The basic obligation of the buyer is to accept and pay for those goods in accordance with the contract terms.

[17] UCC § 2-208.
[18] UCC § 1-205(1).
[19] UCC § 1-205(2).
[20] UCC § 2-208(2).

Performance by the Seller

Tender of delivery requires the seller to (1) put and hold conforming goods at the buyer's disposition and (2) give the buyer reasonable notification to allow the buyer to take delivery.[21] Tender of conforming goods by the seller entitles the seller to acceptance of them by the buyer and to payment of the contract price.[22]

The *perfect tender rule* requires the seller's tender to conform exactly to the terms of the contract. If the tender deviates in any way—say, the quantity delivered is insufficient, or the widgets are blue instead of green as called for under the contract—the buyer may (1) reject the whole lot, (2) accept the whole lot, or (3) accept any commercial unit or units and reject the rest.[23] The parties can, of course, always contract around the perfect tender rule. For example, they can agree in the contract that the seller has the right to repair or replace any defective goods.

The UCC also creates a number of exceptions to the perfect tender rule. The most important of these is the seller's right to *cure*. The seller can cure—i.e., make a second delivery or substitute a different tender—in two circumstances: (1) when the time for performance under the contract has not yet expired or (2) if the seller reasonably believed that the tender would be acceptable to the buyer with or without a money allowance. If the buyer rejects the goods in this latter instance, the seller has a reasonable time period in which to cure provided the seller notifies the buyer of its intent to do so.[24]

Performance by the Buyer

The buyer's obligation under the UCC is to accept conforming goods and to pay for them. As previously noted, if the tender is nonconforming, the buyer may (1) reject all of the goods, (2) accept all of the goods, or (3) accept any commercial unit or units and reject the rest. The buyer must pay at the contract rate for any units accepted but can recover damages for any nonconformity if the buyer notifies the seller of the breach.

Once the goods have been tendered, the buyer has a number of rights, including:

Inspection: Unless the parties agreed otherwise, the buyer has a right to inspect the goods before payment or acceptance. The buyer loses its right to reject the goods or to revoke its acceptance if it fails to inspect the goods within a reasonable time period. The buyer must pay the expenses of inspection but can recover those expenses from the seller if the goods are rightfully rejected as nonconforming.[25]

Acceptance: Acceptance occurs when the buyer, after a reasonable time to inspect: (1) signifies to the seller that the goods conform, (2) signifies to the seller that the buyer will take or retain the goods despite their nonconformity, or (3) fails to make an effective rejection of the goods.[26] Once the buyer has accepted the goods, the buyer may not reject them.

Revocation of acceptance: The buyer can revoke the acceptance of nonconforming goods if the nonconformity substantially impairs the value of the goods to the buyer, provided that the acceptance (1) was premised on the reasonable assumption that the nonconformity would be cured by the seller, and it was not cured; or (2) was made without discovery of the nonconformity, and the acceptance was

---

[21] UCC § 2-503(1).
[22] UCC § 2-507(1).
[23] UCC § 2-601.
[24] UCC § 2-508.
[25] UCC § 2-513.
[26] UCC § 2-606.

reasonably induced by the difficulty of discovery of the nonconformity before acceptance or by assurances of the seller.[27]

Revocation is not effective until the buyer gives notification of it to the seller. The revocation must be made within a reasonable time after the buyer discovers or should have discovered the grounds for the revocation and before the goods have undergone any substantial change not caused by their defect.[28]

Rejection: Rejection must be made within a reasonable time after the goods are tendered or delivered. It does not take effect unless the buyer seasonably notifies the seller.[29] Rejection can be rightful or wrongful, depending upon whether the goods conform to the contract. The buyer has the right to reject nonconforming goods under the perfect tender rule, of course. The buyer may also reject conforming goods, although the buyer is then in breach of contract and is liable to the seller for damages as described below. Once the buyer has rejected the goods, the buyer cannot exercise any ownership interest in them but must hold the goods for a reasonable time to allow the seller to remove them.

TRANSFER OF TITLE AND RISK OF LOSS

Historically, under the common law, *title* (i.e., legal ownership) governed most aspects of the rights and duties of the buyer and seller arising out of a sales contract, including determining which party bore the risk of loss. Under the UCC, however, transfer of title and passage of risk of loss are considered separate issues. Two key questions thus arise: (1) When does *title* pass from the seller to the buyer? and (2) If the goods are damaged or destroyed before the buyer has accepted them, does the buyer or the seller bear the *risk of loss*?

Transfer of Title

Transfer of title is important for a variety of reasons. In addition to telling us who owns the goods, it tells us which party's creditors can reach the goods and which party is liable in the event that someone is injured by the goods.

Often, the parties specify in their contract at what moment title transfers from the seller to the buyer. For example, the parties may state: "Title and risk of loss in all goods sold hereunder shall pass to the buyer upon seller's delivery to carrier at shipping point." Under the UCC, the agreement of the parties always controls.

If the parties fail to specify in their contract when transfer of title occurs, the UCC provides default rules that will control. These rules fall into two categories: (1) where the goods are to be physically delivered to the buyer and (2) where the goods are not to be moved.

Where the Goods Are to Be Physically Delivered

If the goods are to be physically delivered from the seller to the buyer, the parties may use one of two types of contracts: (1) a shipment contract or (2) a destination contract.

A *shipment contract* requires the seller to turn the goods over to a carrier but does not require the seller to deliver them to a particular destination. Title passes to the buyer when the seller delivers the goods to the carrier for shipment to the buyer. Unless the parties state otherwise, sales contracts involving the transport of goods are presumed to be shipment contracts.

[27] UCC § 2-608(1).
[28] UCC § 2-608(2).
[29] UCC § 2-602.

A *destination contract* requires the seller to deliver the goods to a particular destination (often, the buyer's place of business). Title passes to the buyer when the seller tenders the goods at the specified destination.

Where the Goods Are Not to Be Physically Moved

If the contract provides that the seller is to transfer a *document of title* to the buyer, such as a warehouse receipt, bill of lading, or dock receipt, title transfers when the required document is delivered, even though the goods have not been physically moved.

In some instances, the parties may not intend either the goods or a document of title to be handed over. In such an instance, the title passes at the time of contracting, provided that the goods are identified to the contract; otherwise, title passes at the time of identification. *Identification* occurs when specific goods have been designated as the subject matter of the contract.

Passage of Risk of Loss

Risk of loss determines which party, buyer or seller, will bear the financial impact of the goods being damaged, lost, or destroyed before the buyer has accepted them. (It does not address the issue of whether the party bearing the loss might have a cause of action against a third party, such as a carrier or bailee, who caused the damage to the goods.) The parties to the contract can always agree on how risk of loss should pass. If they fail to do so, the risk of loss passes according to the UCC's default rules. Risk of loss passes differently depending upon whether neither party is in breach of contract or whether one party is in breach (see Focus Case 9.4 on page 317).

In the Absence of a Breach

In the *shipment* and *destination* contracts contexts already discussed, title and risk of loss pass at the same time, provided that neither party is in breach of contract.

In all other cases, title and risk of loss pass separately. Thus, if the seller sells goods to the buyer that are in the possession of a bailee (such as a warehouse), and they are not to be moved, the UCC sets forth three possibilities for transfer of risk of loss:

1. If the buyer receives a negotiable document of title covering the goods, the risk of loss passes at that time.
2. If the bailee acknowledges the buyer's right to take possession of the goods (for example, by sending a notice to the buyer that the goods are available), the buyer assumes the risk of loss upon receipt of the acknowledgment.
3. If the seller gives the buyer a nonnegotiable document of title or a written direction to the bailee to deliver the goods and the buyer has had a reasonable time to present the document or direction, the risk of loss passes to the buyer.[30]

The remaining cases usually involve a buyer who is to take delivery from the seller's premises. In such cases, we would expect that a merchant seller would keep insurance on goods under its control. A buyer, on the other hand, is unlikely to insure goods that are not in its possession. Thus, if the seller *is* a merchant, the risk of loss passes to the buyer only when the buyer receives the goods. If the seller is *not* a merchant, the risk of loss passes to the buyer only when the seller tenders delivery.

---

[30] UCC § 2-509(2).

Focus Case 9.4

Facts: Jordan Systems, Inc., a construction subcontractor, contracted to purchase custom-made windows from Windows, Inc., a fabricator and seller of windows based in South Dakota. The purchase contract provided: "All windows to be shipped properly crated/packaged/boxed suitable for cross country motor freight transit and delivered to New York City."

Windows, Inc. constructed the windows and arranged to have them shipped to Jordan by a common carrier, Consolidated Freightways Corp. During the course of shipment, however, approximately two-thirds of the windows were damaged as a result of "load shift." The damage resulted from the windows being improperly loaded on the truck by Consolidated's employees.

Jordan sued Windows to recover incidental and consequential damages based on Window's alleged breach of contract. The trial court granted summary judgment to Windows and Jordan appealed.

Decision: The appellate court affirmed the decision of the trial court. The court concluded that the contract at issue was a shipment contract, not a destination contract:

Where the terms of an agreement are ambiguous, there is a strong presumption under the UCC favoring shipment contracts. Unless the parties "expressly specify" that the contract requires the seller to deliver to a particular destination, the contract is generally construed as one for shipment.

Here, the language of the contract did not require Windows to deliver the goods to any particular destination, but rather merely to "New York City." The contract was thus a shipment contract and Windows satisfied its contractual obligations when it put the goods, properly packaged, into the possession of the carrier for shipment. Once Windows properly delivered the goods to the carrier, Jordan assumed the risk of loss. Thus, Jordan could not recover damages from Windows for injuries caused by the carrier's negligence.

The court further noted that while Jordan bore the risk of loss as between Jordan and Windows, Jordan was not completely without remedy. Under the Interstate Commerce Act, a buyer or seller can recover from an interstate common carrier for damages goods suffer while in the carrier's care. *Windows, Inc. v. Jordan Panel Sys. Corp.*, 177 F.3d 114 (2d Cir. 1999).

In the Event of a Breach

If the seller tenders or delivers goods that do not conform to the contract, the risk of loss is on the seller until either the seller cures the breach or the buyer agrees to take the goods despite their nonconformity. Similarly, if the buyer wrongfully refuses to take the goods, the risk of loss rests on the buyer for a reasonable time period until the seller can fully insure the goods.[31]

Insurable Interest

Transfer of title and risk of loss are important issues because they help determine which party (or parties) has an *insurable interest* in the goods, i.e., which party (or parties) has the legal right to purchase insurance to protect the goods. The seller has an insurable interest as long as it retains title to or a security interest in the goods. The buyer has an insurable interest when goods are identified to the contract. In addition, any party who has the risk of loss with respect to the goods has an insurable interest in them.[32]

---

[31] UCC § 2-510.
[32] UCC § 2-501.

Breach of Contract and Contract Remedies

ACTUAL AND ANTICIPATORY BREACH

Breach of contract occurs when one party fails to perform its contractual obligations at the time performance is due. *Anticipatory breach*, also known as *anticipatory repudiation*, occurs when one party, through its conduct or words, indicates prior to the time when its performance is due under the contract that it intends to breach.

Under the common law, the nonrepudiating party may treat an anticipatory repudiation as a breach of contract and immediately sue for damages. Alternatively, that party may await the time of performance to see if the repudiating party will withdraw the repudiation and go forward with its performance. Under the UCC, however, the nonrepudiating party may await performance only for a commercially reasonable amount of time and then must undertake mitigation measures.[33] The repudiating party may retract its repudiation unless the nonrepudiating party (1) has cancelled, (2) has materially altered its position, or (3) has otherwise indicated that the repudiation is final.

REMEDIES GENERALLY

Suppose that Buyer and Seller have entered into a contract, and Seller *breaches* (i.e., fails to perform its contractual duties). The law can respond to this in one of two ways: (1) it can permit Seller to breach and simply order Seller to pay Buyer for any damages Buyer may have suffered, or (2) it can treat a breach of contract as being such wrongful behavior that Seller should be punished for its actions.

Generally, contract law wants to promote economic efficiency and wants to put factors of production to their highest and best use. Thus, contract law will permit a breach of contract in most instances if it is more efficient (i.e., cheaper) for the breaching party to breach the contract and pay damages than to go through with performance. As a result, punitive damages are rarely awarded in breach of contract cases (although if the breach of contract also constitutes a tort, such as fraud, punitive damages may be available).

The objective of contract remedies, therefore, is to make the nonbreaching party "whole"—i.e., to put the nonbreaching party in as good a position economically as if the defendant had fully performed. In addition, remedies under contract law are generally *cumulative*, which means that the nonbreaching party can mix and match remedies until it has fully recovered for all of its losses.

Remedies for breach of contract may be *equitable* or *legal*. *Equitable remedies* are generally available only where monetary damages are inadequate to protect the nonbreaching party. Equitable remedies in contract cases usually involve either *specific performance* or issuance of an *injunction*. A decree for specific performance orders the promisor to render the promised performance. An injunction usually orders a party to refrain from a particular act. Specific performance is most commonly given for breach of a contract to convey a piece of land and is never given for personal services contracts. The court cannot order an individual to work for a particular employer, although it may issue an injunction prohibiting the individual from working for a

---

[33] UCC § 2-610.

competitor. Specific performance is also granted when the goods involved in the contract are unique or where it would be difficult to fairly calculate monetary damages.

A court of equity can also order *rescission* (cancellation) of a contract where enforcing the contract would be unfair. When the courts order rescission, they generally order the parties to make *restitution* to each other as well; i.e., they order the parties to return any goods, property, or money that they have exchanged.

Legal remedies typically consists of monetary damages. The common law imposes a *duty to mitigate* upon the plaintiff. This means that if the plaintiff could have avoided a particular item of damage by reasonable effort but fails to do so, he will not be able to collect for that item of damage. The UCC also imposes a duty to mitigate upon plaintiffs who are buyers (but not upon seller-plaintiffs). If the seller fails to deliver or delivers nonconforming goods that the buyer rejects, the buyer must "cover" (i.e., obtain substitute goods in the marketplace) if she can reasonably do so, or she will be unable to recover for those damages that could have been prevented by cover.

Under the common law, if the injured party has fulfilled its duty to mitigate, it is entitled to receive *compensatory damages*, which are intended to put that party in as good a position economically as he would have occupied had the defendant not breached. The injured party generally can recover *consequential damages* as well, which are indirect damages that foreseeably flow from the breach.

Often, the parties to a contract place a *liquidated damages clause* in their written agreement. This is a provision that specifies what will occur and/or what remedies will be available in the event of a breach. Courts generally enforce such provisions provided they are satisfied that the clause is an attempt to estimate actual damages and not to penalize the party for breach of contract. Thus, courts generally require that to be enforceable, the liquidated damages clause (1) be a reasonable estimate of the anticipated or actual loss in the event of breach and (2) address harm that is uncertain or difficult to calculate, even after the fact.

Some contracts also contain an *exculpatory clause*, which is a provision that attempts to excuse one party from liability for its own tortious conduct. Courts generally will not enforce exculpatory clauses that attempt to relieve a party of liability for intentional torts or for willful conduct, fraud, recklessness, or gross negligence but may enforce clauses that address liability for ordinary negligence or contractual breach, provided the clause is conspicuous and clear. Where the party attempting to benefit from the clause has substantially more bargaining power than the other party, the courts may find that the clause is unconscionable and so unenforceable. If the parties have equal bargaining power, however, the courts generally will allow them to allocate risk between themselves via an exculpatory clause.

REMEDIES IN SALES CONTRACTS

The UCC provides special remedies rules that differ from the common law rules. The remedies given will vary depending upon whether the buyer or the seller is the injured party and depending upon whether the goods have been accepted.

Where the Goods Have Not Been Accepted
Buyer's Remedies
If the seller has breached the contract, the buyer has a variety of remedies from which to choose.[34] The more common remedies are discussed here.

---

[34] UCC §§ 2-711 to 2-717.

First, the buyer can *reject* the goods and *cancel* the contract. (This will be the preferred choice of a buyer who has entered into a losing bargain.) Second, the buyer can *cover*, i.e., buy commercially reasonable substitute goods from another seller in good faith and without delay and recover *the difference between the contract price and the cover price, less expenses saved*, from the breaching seller. Third, if the buyer is unable to cover or does not choose to do so, the buyer can recover the *difference between the contract price and the market price at the time the buyer learned of the breach, less expenses saved*.

The buyer may also recover *consequential damages* (e.g., injury to person or property resulting from a breach of warranty) and *incidental damages* (e.g., costs such as inspection, transportation, or storage expenses directly associated with the breach and the buyer's attempt to cover). If the buyer fails to cover, it cannot recover any consequential damages that were preventable by reasonable cover attempts.

Seller's Remedies

Where the buyer has breached, the seller also has a choice of remedies.[35] If the buyer has not accepted the goods, the seller has three options. First, if the seller resells the goods to a third party in good faith and in a "commercially reasonable" manner, the seller may recover the difference between the resale and the contract price, plus incidental damages. Second, the seller may recover the difference between the market price at the time and place for delivery and the unpaid contract price, plus incidental damages. Third, if either of these formulas will not make the seller whole, the seller may instead recover lost profits, plus incidental damages. This remedy is particularly important to a lost volume seller, i.e., a seller who had an adequate supply to have satisfied both the original contract and the resale, who probably would have made both sales in the absence of the breach, and who would have made a profit on both sales (see Focus Case 9.5).

Finally, the seller may sue for the *contract price, plus incidental damages*, in a few specific situations (i.e., where the buyer has accepted the goods, where the risk of loss has passed to the buyer and the goods are lost in transit, or if the seller is unable to resell the goods because they are perishable or custom-made). Note that the seller can always recover incidental damages but cannot recover consequential damages.

Where the Goods Have Been Accepted

Where the buyer has accepted the goods but refuses to pay for them, the seller may sue for the *contract price, plus incidental damages*. If the accepted goods are nonconforming, however, the buyer may sue for *breach of warranty*. Warranties are discussed further in Chapter 10.

Contract Law and E-Commerce

On October 1, 2000, the Electronic Signatures in Global and National Commerce Act (E-SIGN Act)[36] took effect. This federal act provides that any transaction in or affecting interstate or foreign commerce will not be denied legal effect, validity, or enforceability solely because an electronic signature was used. Thus, this Act makes E-signatures as legally binding as handwritten signatures and removes legal barriers to the growth of electronic commerce. The Act does not address other

---

[35] UCC §§ 2-702 to 2-710.
[36] 15 U.S.C. §§ 7001–7006, 7021, and 7031.

Focus Case 9.5

Facts: Blaine McCance purchased a used farming disc from Vanderwerff Implement, Inc. for $2,575. After using the disc for one day, McCance found that the disc was leaving a 6- to 8-inch ridge on one side. Within a day after purchase, McCance telephoned Vanderwerff and informed the company of the problem. McCance stopped payment on his check and returned the disc two weeks later. Vanderwerff checked the disc but found no defect.

The trial court found that Vanderwerff had made an express warranty to McCance that the disc was "field ready," that this warranty had not been breached, and that McCance was in violation of an enforceable contract. The court also found that Vanderwerff was a lost volume seller and awarded damages to Vanderwerff in the amount of $2,575 plus interest.

McCance appealed the trial court's decision.

Decision: The appellate court stated that the normal measure of a seller's damages in the event of a breach is the difference between the market price and the contract price. A "lost volume seller," however, may seek damages for lost profits on the sales contract.

To be a "lost volume seller," one must prove that "even though [it] resold the contract goods, that sale to the third party would have been made regardless of the buyer's breach," using the inventory on hand at the time. Furthermore, "the lost volume seller must establish that had the breaching buyer performed, the seller would have realized profits from two sales." The main inquiry is whether the seller had the ability to sell the product to both the buyer who breached and the resale buyer.

The appellate court agreed with the trial court that Vanderwerff was a lost volume seller. Vanderwerff sold approximately 15 new and 15 used discs each year and typically carried about 10–12 discs in inventory. The "most compelling" evidence that Vanderwerff was a lost volume seller was that Vanderwerff actually resold the disc at issue.

The appellate court found that the trial court had awarded the wrong measure of damages, however. A lost volume seller is entitled to the profit that the seller would have made had the buyer fully performed, plus interest. The trial court, however, awarded Vanderwerff the full contract price, including the profit, plus interest. The appellate court thus remanded the case for a correct determination of damages. *Vanderwerff Implement, Inc. v. McCance,* 561 N.W.2d 24 (S.D. 1997).

---

issues relating to electronic contracting, however, such as how the holder of an electronic document can establish its authenticity.

The E-SIGN Act applies to a wide variety of legal transactions, including those arising under Article 2 of the UCC.[37] Thus, a buyer and seller may contract for a sale of goods over a Web site and be assured that the contract will not fail merely because it was signed electronically rather than formalized in a traditional paper-and-ink contract.

The E-SIGN Act preempts state laws that conflict with its provisions. The E-SIGN Act does not preempt state laws based on the Uniform Electronic Transactions Act (UETA), however. So far, about one-half of the states have adopted UETA.[38] The UETA provides that: (1) a record or signature shall not be denied legal effect or enforceability just because it is in electronic form; (2) a contract shall not be denied legal effect or enforceability just because an electronic record was used in its formation; and (3) an electronic signature satisfies any legal requirement calling for a signature.

---

[37] The E-SIGN Act applies to Article 2A as well.

[38] Information about the UETA, including a listing of the states that have adopted it, can be found on the NCC's Web site at http://www.nccusl.org

Many other countries have also passed electronic signature acts, including Germany in 1997 and Japan[39] and the United Kingdom in 2000. The European Union enacted a Directive regarding the legal effect of electronic signatures in 1999.[40]

Contracts in the International Environment

When the contracting parties are from different countries, a number of special legal issues arise. A U.S. contracting party cannot automatically assume that U.S. law will apply to the transaction, nor can it automatically assume that the contract law of other countries will resemble the U.S. law with which it is familiar. In some countries, for example, title to goods may pass at the time of delivery; in others, it may pass as soon as an agreement is reached, preventing the seller from reclaiming the goods if the buyer fails to pay. Obviously, such distinctions can have profound effects upon the manner in which contractual relationships are formed and handled.

As of February 2001, 58 countries (including the United States) had adopted the *United Nations Convention on the International Sale of Goods* (CISG).[41] The CISG applies to contracts for the sale of goods between parties whose places of business are in different countries but does not apply to sales of personal or consumer goods. Authentic texts of the CISG exist in six languages.[42] The CISG is roughly analogous to the American UCC. It represents, however, a compromise between the common law and civil law traditions of the various member countries.

The CISG automatically applies to relevant contracts between parties whose places of business are in different Contracting States unless the parties select otherwise. Thus, if the parties do not want the CISG to cover their international sales contract, they need to specifically so state and should select an alternative forum. In addition, parties whose contracts are not otherwise subject to the CISG may nonetheless elect to have the CISG apply to their contract.

Articles 1 through 6 of the CISG address its scope of application and general provisions. Articles 7 through 13 address the interpretation of contracts. Article 11 states that a sales contract does not have to be in writing, although several countries that have adopted the CISG have expressly excluded this provision. Articles 14 through 24 address contract formation, including offer and acceptance. Article 25 addresses enforcement issues.

There are some substantial differences between the UCC and the CISG. The UCC, for example, adopts the "mailbox" rule discussed earlier. The CISG, on the other hand, adopts the European principle that an acceptance is not effective until the offeror receives it. The CISG is also not as lenient as the UCC in finding the existence of a contract in battle of the forms situations; rather, most nonconforming acceptances under the CISG operate merely as counteroffers, not acceptances. The UCC supplies a price if necessary, as already discussed. The CISG, on the other hand, does not allow a contract to be formed unless the price term or a provision for determining the price is supplied in the agreement. The UCC requires

[39] The Law Concerning Electronic Signatures and Certification Services can be viewed at http://www.meti.go.jp/english/special/E-Commerce/index.html

[40] The Directive can be viewed at http://europa.eu.int/eur-lex/en/lif/dat/1999/en_399L0093.html

[41] Information on the CISG, including its text, member countries, and cases decided under it may be found at http://www.cisg.law.pace.edu
The United States became a signatory effective January 1, 1988.

[42] Arabic, Chinese, English, French, Russian, and Spanish.

a writing to satisfy the Statute of Frauds for contracts over $500, while the CISG does not require a writing to make a sales contract valid. The CISG also rejects the UCC's perfect tender rule, providing instead that the buyer may reject goods only where the nonconformity amounts to a fundamental breach of contract. This distinction reflects the longer shipping times and greater distances, costs, and complexities of international sales contracts.

Parties entering into international contracts should not rely solely upon the default rules that may apply under the CISG or other applicable laws but, rather, should have an express written agreement that addresses the special issues raised by international contractual relationships. The parties should consider including clauses such as a *forum clause* specifying the location and the court in which disputes are to be litigated; a *governing law clause* specifying which country's or state's law is to apply to the transaction; a *currency of payment clause* specifying the unit of currency that is to be the medium of exchange between the parties; a *force majeure clause* specifying what happens in the event of a war, natural disaster, strike, or extreme shortage; a *language clause* specifying the language in which agreements may be formed, notices sent, or enforcement pursued; and a *notice clause* specifying the manner in which notices are to be sent, taking into account delays caused by long distances, differing holidays, and other factors unique to the international setting. It is also often very important to have a *title passage clause.* The CISG does not address this aspect of international sales. Exporters often prefer to have title transfer outside the United States, so as to avoid adverse U.S. tax consequences.

Parties who enter into commercial contracts often consider including a provision requiring alternative dispute resolution in the event of a problem. Where the contracting parties are from different countries and neither wants to submit to the courts of the other's home country, arbitration clauses are particularly common. To be truly effective, arbitration clauses must be carefully drafted and must provide for a fair and efficient procedure. The clause should identity the arbitrators and the manner in which they are to be selected, the procedural rules that will govern the arbitration, the place of the arbitration, and the language in which it will be conducted.

DISCUSSION CASES

9.1 Advertisements as Offers, Statute of Frauds

Leonard v. PepsiCo., Inc., **88 F. Supp. 2d 116 (S.D. N.Y. 1999),** *aff'd per curiam,* **210 F.3d 88 (2d Cir. 2000)**

Plaintiff brought this action seeking, among other things, specific performance of an alleged offer of a Harrier Jet, featured in a television advertisement for defendant's "Pepsi Stuff" promotion. Defendant has moved for summary judgment . . . [D]efendant's motion is granted.

I. Background

This case arises out of a promotional campaign conducted by defendant, the producer and distributor of the soft drinks Pepsi and Diet Pepsi. The promotion, entitled "Pepsi Stuff," encouraged consumers to collect "Pepsi Points" from specially marked packages of Pepsi or Diet Pepsi and redeem these points for merchandise featuring the Pepsi logo. * * *

A. *The Alleged Offer*

* * * The commercial opens upon an idyllic, suburban morning, where the chirping of birds in sun-dappled trees welcomes a paperboy on his morning route. As the newspaper hits the stoop of a conventional two-story house, the tattoo of a military drum introduces the subtitle, "MONDAY 7:58 AM." The stirring strains of a martial air mark the appearance of a well-coiffed teenager preparing to leave for school, dressed in a shirt emblazoned with the Pepsi logo, a red-white-and-blue ball. While the teenager confidently preens, the military drumroll again sounds as the subtitle "T-SHIRT 75 PEPSI POINTS" scrolls across the screen. Bursting from his room, the teenager strides down the hallway

wearing a leather jacket. The drumroll sounds again, as the subtitle "LEATHER JACKET 1450 PEPSI POINTS" appears. The teenager opens the door of his house and, unfazed by the glare of the early morning sunshine, puts on a pair of sunglasses. The drumroll then accompanies the subtitle "SHADES 175 PEPSI POINTS." A voiceover then intones, "Introducing the new Pepsi Stuff catalog," as the camera focuses on the cover of the catalog.

The scene then shifts to three young boys sitting in front of a high school building. The boy in the middle is intent on his Pepsi Stuff Catalog, while the boys on either side are each drinking Pepsi. The three boys gaze in awe at an object rushing overhead, as the military march builds to a crescendo. The Harrier Jet is not yet visible, but the observer senses the presence of a mighty plane as the extreme winds generated by its flight create a paper mael-strom in a classroom devoted to an otherwise dull physics lesson. Finally, the Harrier Jet swings into view and lands by the side of the school building, next to a bicycle rack. Several students run for cover, and the velocity of the wind strips one hapless faculty member down to his underwear. While the faculty member is being deprived of his dignity, the voiceover announces: "Now the more Pepsi you drink, the more great stuff you're gonna get."

The teenager opens the cockpit of the fighter and can be seen, helmetless, holding a Pepsi. Looking very pleased with himself, the teenager exclaims, "Sure beats the bus," and chortles. The military drumroll sounds a final time, as the following words appear: "HARRIER FIGHTER 7,000,000 PEPSI POINTS." A few seconds later, the fol-lowing appears in more stylized script: "Drink Pepsi—Get Stuff." With that message, the music and the commercial end with a triumphant flourish.

Inspired by this commercial, plaintiff set out to obtain a Harrier Jet. Plaintiff explains that he is "typical of the 'Pepsi Generation' . . . he is young, has an adventurous spirit, and the notion of obtaining a Harrier Jet appealed to him enor-mously." Plaintiff consulted the Pepsi Stuff Catalog. The Catalog features youths dressed in Pepsi Stuff regalia or enjoying Pepsi Stuff accessories, such as "Blue Shades" ("As if you need another reason to look forward to sunny days."), "Pepsi Tees" ("Live in 'em. Laugh in 'em. Get in 'em."), "Bag of Balls" ("Three balls. One bag. No rules."), and "Pepsi Phone Card" ("Call your mom!"). The Catalog spec-ifies the number of Pepsi Points required to obtain promo-tional merchandise. The Catalog includes an Order Form which lists, on one side, fifty-three items of Pepsi Stuff mer-chandise redeemable for Pepsi Points . . . . Conspicuously absent from the Order Form is any entry or description of a Harrier Jet. * * *

The rear foldout pages of the Catalog contain direc-tions for redeeming Pepsi Points for merchandise. These directions note that merchandise may be ordered "only" with the original Order Form. The Catalog notes that in the event that a consumer lacks enough Pepsi Points to obtain a desired item, additional Pepsi Points may be purchased for ten cents each; however, at least fifteen original Pepsi Points must accompany each order.

Although plaintiff initially set out to collect 7,000,000 Pepsi Points by consuming Pepsi products, it soon became clear to him that he "would not be able to buy (let alone drink) enough Pepsi to collect the necessary Pepsi Points fast enough." Reevaluating his strategy, plaintiff "focused for the first time on the packaging materials in the Pepsi Stuff promotion," and realized that buying Pepsi Points would be a more promising option. Through acquaintances, plaintiff ultimately raised about $700,000.

B. *Plaintiff's Efforts to Redeem the Alleged Offer*

On or about March 27, 1996, plaintiff submitted an Order Form, fifteen original Pepsi Points, and a check for $700,008.50. Plaintiff appears to have been represented by counsel at the time he mailed his check; the check is drawn on an account of plaintiff's first set of attorneys. At the bot-tom of the Order Form, plaintiff wrote in "1 Harrier Jet" in the "Item" column and "7,000,000" in the "Total Points" column. In a letter accompanying his submission, plaintiff stated that the check was to purchase additional Pepsi Points "expressly for obtaining a new Harrier jet as advertised in your Pepsi Stuff commercial."

On or about May 7, 1996, defendant's fulfillment house rejected plaintiff's submission and returned the check, explaining that:

> The item that you have requested is not part of the Pepsi Stuff collection. It is not included in the catalogue or on the order form, and only catalogue merchandise can be redeemed under this program.

> The Harrier jet in the Pepsi commercial is fanciful and is sim-ply included to create a humorous and entertaining ad. We apologize for any misunderstanding or confusion that you may have experienced and are enclosing some free product coupons for your use.

Plaintiff's previous counsel responded on or about May 14, 1996, as follows:

> Your letter of May 7, 1996 is totally unacceptable. We have reviewed the video tape of the Pepsi Stuff commercial . . . and it clearly offers the new Harrier jet for 7,000,000 Pepsi Points. Our client followed your rules explicitly. . . .

> This is a formal demand that you honor your commitment and make immediate arrangements to transfer the new Harrier jet to our client. If we do not receive transfer instructions within ten (10) business days of the date of this letter you will leave us no choice but to file an appropriate action against Pepsi. . . .

This letter was apparently sent onward to the advertising company responsible for the actual commercial, BBDO New York ("BBDO"). In a letter dated May 30, 1996, BBDO Vice President Raymond E. McGovern, Jr., explained to plaintiff that:

> I find it hard to believe that you are of the opinion that the Pepsi Stuff commercial ("Commercial") really offers a new Harrier Jet. The use of the Jet was clearly a joke that was meant to make the Commercial more humorous and entertaining. In my opinion, no reasonable person would agree with your analysis of the Commercial.

On or about June 17, 1996, plaintiff mailed a similar demand letter to defendant.

* * * *

II. Discussion

* * * *

B. *Defendant's Advertisement Was Not An Offer*

1. Advertisements as Offers

The general rule is that an advertisement does not constitute an offer. The Restatement (Second) of Contracts explains that:

> Advertisements of goods by display, sign, handbill, newspaper, radio or television are not ordinarily intended or understood as offers to sell. The same is true of catalogues, price lists and circulars, even though the terms of suggested bargains may be stated in some detail. It is of course possible to make an offer by an advertisement directed to the general public, but there must ordinarily be some language of commitment or some invitation to take action without further communication.

Restatement (Second) of Contracts § 26 cmt. b (1979). Similarly, a leading treatise notes that:

> It is quite possible to make a definite and operative offer to buy or sell goods by advertisement, in a newspaper, by a handbill, a catalog or circular or on a placard in a store window. It is not customary to do this, however; and the presumption is the other way . . . . Such advertisements are understood to be mere requests to consider and examine and negotiate; and no one can reasonably regard them as otherwise unless the circumstances are exceptional and the words used are very plain and clear.

1 Arthur Linton Corbin & Joseph M. Perillo, *Corbin on Contracts* § 2.4, at 116–17 (rev. ed. 1993). * * *

An advertisement is not transformed into an enforceable offer merely by a potential offeree's expression of willingness to accept the offer through, among other means, completion of an order form. * * * Under these principles, plaintiff's letter of March 27, 1996, with the Order Form and the appropriate number of Pepsi Points, constituted the offer. There would be no enforceable contract until defendant accepted the Order Form and cashed the check.

The exception to the rule that advertisements do not create any power of acceptance in potential offerees is where the advertisement is "clear, definite, and explicit, and leaves nothing open for negotiation," in that circumstance, "it constitutes an offer, acceptance of which will complete the contract." Lefkowitz v. Great Minneapolis Surplus Store, 86 N.W.2d 689, 691 (Minn. 1957). In *Lefkowitz*, defendant had published a newspaper announcement stating: "Saturday 9 AM Sharp, 3 Brand New Fur Coats, Worth to $100.00, First Come First Served $1 Each." Mr. Morris Lefkowitz arrived at the store, dollar in hand, but was informed that under defendant's "house rules," the offer was open to ladies, but not gentlemen. The court ruled that because plaintiff had fulfilled all of the terms of the advertisement and the advertisement was specific and left nothing open for negotiation, a contract had been formed.

The present case is distinguishable from *Lefkowitz*. First, the commercial cannot be regarded in itself as sufficiently definite, because it specifically reserved the details of the offer to a separate writing, the Catalog. The commercial itself made no mention of the steps a potential offeree would be required to take to accept the alleged offer of a Harrier Jet. The advertisement in *Lefkowitz*, in contrast, "identified the person who could accept." Second, even if the Catalog had included a Harrier Jet among the items that could be obtained by redemption of Pepsi Points, the advertisement of a Harrier Jet by both television commercial and catalog would still not constitute an offer. [T]he absence of any words of limitation such as "first come, first served," renders the alleged offer sufficiently indefinite that no contract could be formed. "A customer would not usually have reason to believe that the shopkeeper intended exposure to the risk of a multitude of acceptances resulting in a number of contracts exceeding the shopkeeper's inventory." There was no such danger in *Lefkowitz*, owing to the limitation "first come, first served."

The Court finds, in sum, that the Harrier Jet commercial was merely an advertisement. * * *

* * * *

C. *An Objective, Reasonable Person Would Not Have Considered the Commercial an Offer*

Plaintiff's understanding of the commercial as an offer must also be rejected because the Court finds that no objective person could reasonably have concluded that the commercial actually offered consumers a Harrier Jet.

1. Objective Reasonable Person Standard

In evaluating the commercial, the Court must not consider defendant's subjective intent in making the commercial, or plaintiff's subjective view of what the commercial offered, but what an objective, reasonable person would have understood the commercial to convey.

If it is clear that an offer was not serious, then no offer has been made:

> What kind of act creates a power of acceptance and is therefore an offer? It must be an expression of will or intention. It must be an act that leads the offeree reasonably to conclude that a power to create a contract is conferred. This applies to the content of the power as well as to the fact of its existence. It is on this ground that we must exclude invitations to deal or acts of mere preliminary negotiation, and acts evidently done in jest or without intent to create legal relations.

Corbin on Contracts, § 1.11 at 30 (emphasis added). An obvious joke, of course, would not give rise to a contract. On the other hand, if there is no indication that the offer is "evidently in jest," and that an objective, reasonable person would find that the offer was serious, then there may be a valid offer.

* * *

3. Whether the Commercial Was "Evidently Done In Jest"

Plaintiff's insistence that the commercial appears to be a serious offer requires the Court to explain why the commercial is funny.* * * The commercial is the embodiment of what defendant appropriately characterizes as "zany humor."

First, the commercial suggests, as commercials often do, that use of the advertised product will transform what, for most youth, can be a fairly routine and ordinary experience. * * * The implication of the commercial is that Pepsi Stuff merchandise will inject drama and moment into hitherto unexceptional lives. The commercial in this case thus makes the exaggerated claims similar to those of many television advertisements: that by consuming the featured clothing, car, beer, or potato chips, one will become attractive, stylish, desirable, and admired by all. A reasonable viewer would understand such advertisements as mere puffery, not as statements of fact, and refrain from interpreting the promises of the commercial as being literally true.

Second, the callow youth featured in the commercial is a highly improbable pilot, one who could barely be trusted with the keys to his parents' car, much less the prize aircraft of the United States Marine Corps. Rather than checking the fuel gauges on his aircraft, the teenager spends his precious preflight minutes preening. The youth's concern for his coiffure appears to extend to his flying without a helmet.

Finally, the teenager's comment that flying a Harrier Jet to school "sure beats the bus" evinces an improbably insouciant attitude toward the relative difficulty and danger of piloting a fighter plane in a residential area, as opposed to taking public transportation.

Third, the notion of traveling to school in a Harrier Jet is an exaggerated adolescent fantasy. * * * This fantasy is, of course, extremely unrealistic. No school would provide landing space for a student's fighter jet, or condone the disruption the jet's use would cause.

Fourth, the primary mission of a Harrier Jet, according to the United States Marine Corps, is to "attack and destroy surface targets under day and night visual conditions." * * * In light of the Harrier Jet's well-documented function in attacking and destroying surface and air targets, armed reconnaissance and air interdiction, and offensive and defensive anti-aircraft warfare, depiction of such a jet as a way to get to school in the morning is clearly not serious even if, as plaintiff contends, the jet is capable of being acquired "in a form that eliminates [its] potential for military use."

Fifth, the number of Pepsi Points the commercial mentions as required to "purchase" the jet is 7,000,000. To amass that number of points, one would have to drink 7,000,000 Pepsis (or roughly 190 Pepsis a day for the next hundred years—an unlikely possibility), or one would have to purchase approximately $700,000 worth of Pepsi Points. The cost of a Harrier Jet is roughly $23 million dollars, a fact of which plaintiff was aware when he set out to gather the amount he believed necessary to accept the alleged offer. Even if an objective, reasonable person were not aware of this fact, he would conclude that purchasing a fighter plane for $700,000 is a deal too good to be true.

Plaintiff argues that a reasonable, objective person would have understood the commercial to make a serious offer of a Harrier Jet because there was "absolutely no distinction in the manner" in which the items in the commercial were presented. Plaintiff also relies upon a press release highlighting the promotional campaign, issued by defendant, in which "no mention is made by [defendant] of humor, or anything of the sort." These arguments suggest merely that the humor of the promotional campaign was tongue in cheek. * * * In light of the obvious absurdity of the commercial, the Court rejects plaintiff's argument that the commercial was not clearly in jest.

* * * *

D. The Alleged Contract Does Not Satisfy the Statute of Frauds

The absence of any writing setting forth the alleged contract in this case provides an entirely separate reason for granting summary judgment. Under the New York Statute of Frauds, a contract for the sale of goods for the price of $500 or more is not enforceable by way of action or defense unless there is some writing sufficient to indicate that a contract for sale has been made between the parties and signed by the party against whom enforcement is sought or by his authorized agent or broker.

N.Y.U.C.C. § 2-201(1). Without such a writing, plaintiff's claim must fail as a matter of law.

There is simply no writing between the parties that evidences any transaction. * * *

* * * Because the alleged contract does not meet the requirements of the Statute of Frauds, plaintiff has no claim for breach of contract or specific performance.

* * * *

III. Conclusion

In sum, there are three reasons why plaintiff's demand cannot prevail as a matter of law. First, the commercial was merely an advertisement, not a unilateral offer. Second, the tongue-in-cheek attitude of the commercial would not cause a reasonable person to conclude that a soft drink company would be giving away fighter planes as part of a promotion. Third, there is no writing between the parties sufficient to satisfy the Statute of Frauds.

For the reasons stated above, the Court grants defendant's motion for summary judgment. * * *

Questions for Discussion for Case 9.1

1. Under what circumstances do advertisements constitute offers? Why did this advertisement not constitute an offer?

2. The court finds that an "objective, reasonable person" would interpret this advertisement merely as humor and not as a legitimate offer. Do you think that the line between jest and offer may be harder to draw in other advertisements? Can you think of any adver-

tisements you have seen where the distinction was less clear than it was in this case?

3. The court also finds that PepsiCo was entitled to summary judgment under the Statute of Frauds. Why? Under what circumstances would a contract arising from an advertisement satisfy the Statute of Frauds?

9.2 UCC Battle of the Forms
Bayway Refining Co. v. Oxygenated Marketing and Trading A.G., 215 F.3d 219 (2d Cir. 2000)

Plaintiff-appellee Bayway Refining Company ("Bayway") paid federal excise tax on a petroleum transaction, as the Internal Revenue Code requires a petroleum dealer to do in a sale to a buyer who has not procured an exemption under the applicable tax provision. In this diversity suit against the buyer, Oxygenated Marketing and Trading A.G. ("OMT"), Bayway seeks to recover the amount of the tax it paid. One question in this "battle of the forms" contract case is whether, under N.Y. U.C.C. § 2-207(2)(b), a contract term allocating liability to the buyer for an excise tax is an additional term presumed to have been accepted (as the seller contends) or (as the buyer contends) a material alteration presumed to have been rejected. The United States District Court . . . granted summary judgment in favor of the seller, Bayway.

* * * [W]e affirm.

BACKGROUND

Bayway and OMT are in the business of buying and selling petroleum products. Bayway contracted to sell to OMT 60,000 barrels of a gasoline blendstock called [MTBE]. On February 12, 1998, OMT faxed Bayway a confirmation letter, which operated as the offer, and which stated in pertinent part:

> We are pleased to confirm the details of our purchase from you of MTBE as agreed between Mr. Ben Basil and Roger Ertle on [February 12, 1998.]
>
> * * * *
>
> This confirmation constitutes the entire contract and represents our understanding of the terms and conditions of our agreement. . . . Any apparent discrepancies or omissions should be brought to our notice within the next two working days.

Bayway faxed its confirmation to OMT the next day. That document, which operated as the acceptance, stated in pertinent part: "We are pleased to confirm the following verbal agreement concluded on February 12, 1998 with your company. This document cancels and supersedes any correspondence in relation to this transaction." Bayway's acceptance then set forth the parties, price, amount and delivery terms, and undertook to incorporate the company's standard terms:

> Notwithstanding any other provision of this agreement, where not in conflict with the foregoing, the terms and conditions as set forth in Bayway Refining Company's General Terms and Conditions dated March 01, 1994 along with Bayway's Marine Provisions are hereby incorporated in full by reference in this contract.

The Bayway General Terms and Conditions were not transmitted with Bayway's fax, but Paragraph 10 of its General Terms and Conditions states:

> Buyer shall pay seller the amount of any federal, state and local excise, gross receipts, import, motor fuel, superfund and spill taxes and all other federal, state and local taxes however designated, other than taxes on income, paid or incurred by seller directly or indirectly with respect to the oil or product sold hereunder and/or on the value thereof.

This term is referenced as the "Tax Clause."

OMT did not object to Bayway's acceptance or to the incorporation of its General Terms and Conditions (which included the Tax Clause). OMT accepted delivery of the MTBE barrels on March 22, 1998.

The Internal Revenue Code imposes an excise tax, payable by the seller, on the sale of gasoline blendstocks such as MTBE "to any person who is not registered . . . for a tax exemption." After delivery, Bayway learned that OMT was not registered with the Internal Revenue Service for the tax exemption. The transaction therefore created a tax liability of $464,035.12, which Bayway paid.

Invoking the Tax Clause, Bayway demanded payment of the $464,035.12 in taxes in addition to the purchase price of the MTBE. OMT denied that it had agreed to assume the tax liability and refused to pay that invoice item. In response, Bayway filed this diversity suit alleging breach of contract by OMT.

* * * The [trial] court . . . granted summary judgment in favor of Bayway.

DISCUSSION

* * * *

A. *Battle of the Forms.*

* * * *

Under New York law, the rules of engagement for the "battle of the forms" are set out in the Uniform Commercial Code ("U.C.C."), § 2-207:

(1) A definite and seasonable expression of acceptance or a written confirmation which is sent within a reasonable time operates as an acceptance even though it states terms additional to or different from those offered or agreed upon, unless acceptance is expressly made conditional on assent to the additional or different terms.

(2) The additional terms are to be construed as proposals for addition to the contract. Between merchants such terms become part of the contract unless:
    (a) the offer expressly limits acceptance to the terms of the offer;
    (b) they materially alter it; or
    (c) notification of objection to them has already been given or is given within a reasonable time after notice of them is received.

N.Y. U.C.C. § 2-207.

[Bayway's] confirmation fax is effective to form a contract as an acceptance—even though it stated or referenced additional terms (including the Tax Clause)—because it was not made expressly conditional on OMT's assent to the additional terms. Therefore, under § 2-207(2), the Tax Clause is a proposal for an addition to the contract. The parties are both merchants within the meaning of the U.C.C. The Tax Clause therefore is presumed to become part of the contract unless one of the three enumerated exceptions applies. In its defense, OMT invokes the "material alteration" exception of § 2-207(2)(b).

* * * *

2. *Materiality.* . . .

A material alteration is one that would "result in surprise or hardship if incorporated without express awareness by the other party."

* * * *

3. *Surprise.*

Surprise, within the meaning of the material alteration exception of § 2-207(2)(b), has both the subjective element of what a party actually knew and the objective element of what a party should have known. A profession of surprise and raised eyebrows are not enough . . . . To carry the burden of showing surprise, a party must establish that, under the circumstances, it cannot be presumed that a reasonable merchant would have consented to the additional term.

OMT has adduced evidence that the Tax Clause came as an amazement to OMT's executives, who described the term's incorporation as "contract by ambush" and a "sleight-of-hand proposal." Thus OMT has sufficiently exhibited its subjective surprise. As to objective surprise, however, OMT has alleged no facts and introduced no evidence to show that a reasonable petroleum merchant would be surprised by the Tax Clause. * * *

* * * *

[Rather], Bayway has adduced compelling proof that shifting tax liability to a buyer is the custom and practice in the petroleum industry. Two industry experts offered unchallenged testimony that it is customary for the buyer to pay all the taxes resulting from a petroleum transaction. One expert stated that "this practice is so universally understood among traders in the industry, that I cannot recall an instance, in all my years of trading and overseeing trades, when the buyer refused to pay the seller for excise or sales taxes."

* * * *

Moreover, common sense supports Bayway's evidence of custom and practice. The federal excise tax is imposed when taxable fuels are sold "to any person who is not registered . . . ." The buyer thereby controls whether any tax liability is incurred in a transaction. A trade practice that reflects a rational allocation of incentives (as trade practices usually do) would place the burden of the tax on the party that is in the position to obviate it—here, on OMT as the buyer.

Viewing Bayway's evidence in the light most favorable to OMT, we conclude that allocating the tax liability to the buyer is the custom and practice in the petroleum industry. OMT could not be objectively surprised by the incorporation of an additional term in the contract that reflects such a practice.

4. Hardship.

* * * *

* * * OMT's only evidence of hardship is (generally) that it is a small business dependent on precarious profit margins, and it would suffer a loss it cannot afford. That does not amount to hardship in the present circumstances.

Typically, courts that have relied on hardship to find that an additional term materially alters a contract have done so when the term is one that creates or allocates an open-ended and prolonged liability.

The Tax Clause places on a buyer a contractual responsibility that bears on a specific sale of goods, that is (at least) not uncommon in the industry, and that the buyer could avoid by registration. The cry of hardship rings hollow, because any loss that the Tax Clause imposed on OMT is limited, routine and self-inflicted.

OMT failed to raise a factual issue as to hardship or surprise. Summary judgment was therefore appropriately granted in favor of Bayway.

Questions for Discussion for Case 9.2

1. What makes an alteration "material" for purposes of § 2-207? Is this a subjective or an objective determination?

2. What role does industry custom and practice play in this decision?

9.3 Promissory Estoppel, Contract Remedies
Tour Costa Rica v. Country Walkers, Inc., 758 A.2d 795 (Vt. 2000)

Defendants Country Walkers, Inc. (CW) and Robert Maynard (Maynard) appeal from the superior court's denial of their . . . motion for judgment as a matter of law, following a jury verdict for plaintiff, Tour Costa Rica (TCR), on its promissory estoppel claim. The jury awarded plaintiff, a company that runs tours in Costa Rica, damages after finding that defendant had breached a promise of a two-year commitment to use TCR to develop, organize and operate Costa Rican walking tours for defendant during that period. We affirm.

* * * *

CW is a Vermont business, owned by Maynard and his wife, that sells guided tours at locations around the world. In 1994, Leigh Monahan, owner of TCR, contacted Maynard

and offered to design, arrange and lead walking tours in Costa Rica for defendant. During negotiations, Monahan explained to Maynard that she had just incorporated the tour company and, because the company had limited resources, she could not afford to develop specialized tours for defendant unless she had a two-year commitment from CW to run its Costa Rican tours through TCR. In the summer of 1994, the parties entered into a verbal agreement under which plaintiff was to design, arrange and lead customized walking tours in Costa Rica for CW from 1995 through 1997. * * *

In March and April 1995, plaintiff conducted two walking tours for CW.

* * * Between the end of April and June of 1995, the parties discussed the details of, and scheduled the dates for,

approximately eighteen walking tours for 1996 and 1997. Due to limited resources, plaintiff could not conduct tours for anyone else while working with defendant and, therefore, stopped advertising and promoting its business, did not pursue other business opportunities and, in fact, turned down other business during this period. In August 1995, a few weeks before the next tour was to occur, defendant informed plaintiff that it would be using another company for all of its future tours in Costa Rica. When challenged by plaintiff with its promised commitment, Maynard responded: "If I did and I certainly may have promised you a two year commitment, I apologize for not honoring it."

Notwithstanding this apology, defendant went on to operate tours in Costa Rica using a rival company. * * * Due to the suddenness of the break with CW, plaintiff was left without tours to run during a prime tourist season, and without sufficient time to market any new tours of its own.

Plaintiff filed suit against defendant, alleging . . . promissory estoppel . . . . * * *

* * * *

* * * The case went to the jury, and the jury found for . . . plaintiff on the promissory estoppel claim, and awarded expectation damages in the amount of $22,520.00. * * * This appeal followed.

* * * *

I.

Defendant first argues that plaintiff failed to make out a prima facie case of promissory estoppel. Under the doctrine of promissory estoppel: "A promise which the promisor should reasonably expect to induce action or forbearance on the part of the promisee or a third person and which does induce such action or forbearance is binding if injustice can be avoided only by enforcement of the promise." The action or inaction taken in reliance on the promise must be "of a definite and substantial character." In other words, the promisee must have detrimentally relied on the promise. Defendant does not seriously dispute that there was a promise or that plaintiff did take action based on the promise. Rather, defendant argues that plaintiff's reliance was not reasonable or detrimental, and that this is not a case where injustice can be avoided only by enforcement of the promise. We first address defendant's argument that plaintiff's reliance was not reasonable.

A.

In determining whether a plaintiff reasonably relied on a defendant's promise, courts examine the totality of the circumstances. Here, plaintiff presented evidence that it relied on defendant's promise of a two-year exclusive commitment by (a) ceasing to advertise and promote the business, failing to pursue other business opportunities, and turning down other business; (b) making hotel and restaurant reservations and arranging for transportation for the tours it was to operate for CW; and (c) making purchases related to the tours it was to operate for CW. Plaintiff suggests that this reliance was reasonable because, in negotiations with Maynard, plaintiff made clear that it required a two-year commitment due to its limited resources, the time it would have to devote to develop specialized tours for CW, and the ongoing communication between the parties as to future dates and requirements for tours.

Defendant argues that plaintiff's reliance was not reasonable based solely on standard industry practice that permits the cancellation of tours upon thirty to sixty days' notice.

While there was no dispute that tours could be canceled with appropriate notice, there was evidence that this industry practice did not apply to the parties' two-year commitment. Monahan testified that she and Maynard specifically agreed to the two-year time frame because she wanted a measure of security for her fledgling company. She further testified that it was her understanding, from negotiations with Maynard, that the two-year commitment was unaffected by the possibility that some scheduled tours might be canceled if, for example, too few people signed.

* * * *

[W]e find that plaintiff presented sufficient evidence to enable the jury to conclude that plaintiff's reliance on defendant's promise was reasonable.

B.

Defendant next argues that plaintiff's reliance on defendant's promise was not detrimental. Defendant suggests that the only evidence of detriment offered by plaintiff was Monahan's testimony concerning expenses for a few minor equipment purchases. Plaintiff disagrees.

Plaintiff maintains that its reliance was detrimental because (1) it lost business due to the fact that (a) it stopped advertising and promoting the business, did not pursue other business opportunities, and turned down other business in reliance on the parties' agreement, and (b) after defendant breached the agreement, plaintiff had no money to advertise or conduct other tours; (2) it spent money in preparation for the tours it was to operate for defendant; and (3) its reputation in the industry suffered because it had to cancel two-years' worth of reservations it had made on behalf of defendant.

Defendant does not dispute that plaintiff stopped advertising and promoting the business, did not pursue other business opportunities and turned down other business, or that plaintiff's reputation was harmed.

Instead, defendant contends that (1) plaintiff would have had to arrange for transportation and make reservations at hotels and restaurants for any tours it arranged for CW, whether or not the tours were part of an exclusive two-year arrangement, and (2) the money plaintiff spent in preparation for the tours is not, in and of itself, sufficient to show detrimental reliance.

Defendant's first argument is flawed because, as noted above, Monahan testified that she told Maynard that plaintiff could not afford to arrange tours for CW without an exclusive two-year agreement. There was no evidence that plaintiff would have prepared tours for CW if the parties did not have an exclusive two-year agreement. Defendant's second argument is flawed because it overlooks the facts that plaintiff stopped advertising and promoting the business, did not pursue other business opportunities, and in fact turned down other business. In reliance on a two-year commitment, plaintiff stopped soliciting business from other sources and declined other bookings, a substantial change in position for a fledgling tour business. Further, plaintiff's reputation in Costa Rica's tourism industry was damaged.

The evidence shows that, as a result of defendant's breach of the parties' agreement, plaintiff suffered significant harm for each of the above-mentioned reasons. Accordingly, the jury could reasonably conclude that plaintiff's reliance on defendant's promise was detrimental.

C.

Whether injustice can be avoided only by enforcement of the promise is a question of law informed by several factors, including:

(a) the availability and adequacy of other remedies, particularly cancellation and restitution;

(b) the definite and substantial character of the action or forbearance in relation to the remedy sought;

(c) the extent to which the action or forbearance corroborates evidence of the making and terms of the promise, or the making and terms are otherwise established by clear and convincing evidence;

(d) the reasonableness of the action or forbearance; [and]

(e) the extent to which the action or forbearance was foreseeable by the promisor.

Restatement (Second) of Contracts § 139(2) (1981).

* * * Damages available in a promissory estoppel action depend upon the circumstances of the case. * * *

Expectation damages, which the jury awarded in this case, provide the plaintiff with an amount equal to the benefit of the parties' bargain.

One potential component of expectation damages is loss of future profits.

The purpose of expectation damages is to "put the non-breaching party in the same position it would have been [in] had the contract been fully performed." Restitution damages seek to compensate the plaintiff for any benefit it conferred upon the defendant as a result of the parties' contract. The purpose of restitution damages is to return the plaintiff to the position it held before the parties' contract. Reliance damages give the plaintiff any reasonably foreseeable costs incurred in reliance on the contract. As with restitution, the purpose of reliance damages is to return the plaintiff to the position it was in prior to the parties' contract. Restitution damages are inapplicable in the instant case because there is no evidence that plaintiff conferred any benefit on defendant as a result of defendant's promise. Further, cancellation is inapplicable, as defendant had already breached its promise, and cancellation would provide no remedy for plaintiff. Reliance damages are also inappropriate because the majority of the harm plaintiff suffered was not expenditures it made in reliance on defendant's promise, but rather, lost profits from the tours it had scheduled with defendant, lost potential profits because it failed to pursue other business opportunities, and harm to its reputation.

Therefore, an award of expectation damages is the only remedy that adequately compensates plaintiff for the harm it suffered.

As to the other factors considered, plaintiff's actions and inactions were of a definite and substantial character. * * * As previously discussed, plaintiff's reliance on defendant's promise was reasonable, and plaintiff's actions and inactions were foreseeable by defendant. Defendant expected plaintiff to take specific actions on defendant's behalf and to design and conduct tours to defendant's specifications. Further, defendant was aware that plaintiff was a new company without a lot of capital, and that it was spending much of that capital preparing tours for defendant.

Taking the above factors into consideration, there was sufficient evidence to allow the jury to conclude that, in this case, injustice could be avoided only by enforcement of the promise through an award of monetary damages.

* * * *

The jury's damage award was not clearly erroneous. Affirmed.

Questions for Discussion for Case 9.3

1. Why is this a promissory estoppel case and not a breach of contract case?

2. What are the elements of promissory estoppel? Which of those elements are at issue in this case?

DISCUSSION QUESTIONS

1. From 1988 to 1992, Dennis McInerney served as a sales representative for Charter Golf, Inc., a company that manufactures and sells golf apparel and supplies. McInerney's sales territory originally covered Illinois but was later expanded to include Indiana and Wisconsin. In 1989, Hickey-Freeman, which manufactures a competing line of golf apparel, offered McInerney a position as an exclusive sales representative that included an 8 percent commission. McInerney contacted Jerry Montiel, Charter Golf's president, to notify him of his intention to accept Hickey-Freeman's offer. Montiel wanted McInerney to continue to work for Charter Golf and offered McInerney a 10 percent commission on sales in Illinois and Wisconsin "for the remainder of his life" in a position where he could be discharged only for dishonesty or disability. McInerney then refused the Hickey-Freeman offer and continued working for Charter Golf. The working relationship between McInerney and Charter Golf deteriorated, and Charter Golf fired McInerney. McInerney sued for breach of contract. In response, Charter Golf argued that: (1) McInerney's promise to forego the Hickey-Freeman job was not sufficient consideration to turn an existing employment-at-will contract into a contract for lifetime employment; and that, (2) if there was a contract, the Statute of Frauds requires that a lifetime employment contract be in writing. How should the court rule on these two claims, and why? *McInerney v. Charter Golf, Inc., 680 N.E.2d 1347 (Ill. 1997).*

2. In August 1995, Carl Merritt contacted RxP Prods., Inc. ("RxP"), about selling "RxP Gas Kicker," a fuel additive, as a private label product. The parties entered into an agreement, which stated, in its entirety:

This agreement is made on this 28th day of September, 1995, between RxP Products, Inc., hereafter referred to as RxP, and Merritt-Campbell, Incorporated, hereinafter referred to as Merritt-Campbell. In consideration of the sum of ten dollars ($10.00), the receipt of which is acknowledged, RxP agrees to sell to Merritt-Campbell the product marketed as "RxP Gas Kicker" under the following terms:

1. RxP guarantees the following price to Merritt-Campbell for a period of five (5) years from the date of first order.
   a. RxP Gas Kicker bottled in 2.5 ounce quantities—$ 1.25 per bottle (excluding labels).
   b. RxP Gas Kicker in 55 gallon drum quantity—$ 1,280,00 (sic) per drum.

Said pricing may be increased only in the case of documented price increases to RxP for raw materials.

2. RxP will bottle RxP Gas Kicker in either green or black bottles, as provided as samples, upon request for Merritt-Campbell.

3. RxP guarantees shipment within fourteen (14) days from receipt of order from Merritt-Campbell.

4. Both RxP and Merritt-Campbell agree unconditionally to maintain confidentiality regarding the relationship between the two companies. This confidentiality includes, but is not limited to, any disclosure of the source product market by RxP and Merritt-Campbell. The scope of this confidentiality includes, but is not limited to, any director, officer, employee, or agent of both RxP and Merritt-Campbell.

5. It is understood by RxP that it is the intention of Merritt-Campbell to market the product heretofore referred to as "RxP Gas Kicker" under a private label.

A dispute arose between the two parties. Merritt-Campbell filed suit against RxP alleging that RxP had breached a requirements contract entered into by the parties. Merritt-Campbell sought specific performance as a remedy. RxP responded that the contract did not satisfy the UCC Statute of Frauds because it failed to state a quantity term. Who is correct? *Merritt-Campbell, Inc. v. RxP Prods., Inc., 164 F.3d 957 (5th Cir. 1999).*

3. Gary Trimble placed a written order for advertising for his business in Ameritech's 1994–95 PAGES-PLUS Directory. Ameritech failed to publish

Trimble's advertisement. The contract that Trimble had signed provided:

> if publisher should be found liable for loss or damage due to a failure on the part of the publisher or its directory, in any respect, regardless of whether customer's claim is based on contract, tort, strict liability, or otherwise, the liability shall be limited to an amount equal to the contract price for the disputed advertisement, or that sum of money actually paid by the customer toward the disputed advertisements, whichever sum shall be less, as liquidated damages and not as a penalty, and this liability shall be exclusive. In no event shall publisher be liable for any loss of customer's business, revenues, profits, the cost to the customer of other advertisements or any other special, incidental, consequential or punitive damages of any nature, or for any claim against the customer by a third party . . . .

Trimble was not charged for the advertisement. He filed suit for damages arising from loss of business. The trial court granted Ameritech's request for summary judgment and Trimble appealed. Is the clause in the parties' contract limiting Ameritech's liability valid and enforceable? *Trimble v. Ameritech Publishing, Inc., 700 N.E.2d 1128 (Ind. 1998).*

4. Kathleen F. Liarikos purchased a 1984 Jaguar XJS from Pine Grove Auto Sales in 1988. She asserted that Pine Grove made various representations about the car's low mileage. In 1990, after the car had had a variety of mechanical problems, Liarikos discovered that the Jaguar's odometer had been turned back. She then sent a letter to Pine Grove that she asserted was a revocation of her acceptance of the Jaguar. Liarikos received no response from Pine Grove. Liarikos continued to use the vehicle as she needed a car in order to conduct her business. Did Liarikos negate her revocation of acceptance by continuing to use the Jaguar? *Liarikos v. Mello, 639 N.E.2d 716 (Mass. 1994).*

5. Bertha Jamison contracted to purchase a set of encyclopedias from Encyclopedia Britannica for $1,652.08. She made a $100 down payment and signed a document entitled "Britannica Revolving Credit Agreement—Retail Installment Contract," in which she agreed to pay $57 per month until the purchase price was fully paid. The contract specified Jamison's street address as the location to which the encyclopedias were to be shipped. Soon thereafter, Encyclope-

dia Britannica assigned the contract to Merchants Acceptance, Inc.

Jamison never received the encyclopedias. A United Parcel Service (UPS) tracking slip revealed the encyclopedias were shipped to Jamison's post office box, not to her street address. Jamison refused to make any of the payments on her account. Merchants sued for payment of the outstanding balance. How should the court rule, and why? *Merchants Acceptance, Inc. v. Jamison, 752 So.2d 422 (Miss. Ct. App. 1999).*

6. Sunset Trails, Inc., provides private recreational facilities, entertainment, and catering for large corporate groups, conventions, and other private parties. On March 25, 1996, Nortex Drug Distributors, Inc., signed a contract reserving Sunset Trails' facilities and catering for a company picnic on July 7, 1996. The contract provided for a minimum of 400 persons at $17.50 per person, for a total of $7,000. The contract contained the following cancellation damages provision:

> Due to the exclusive nature of the CIRCLE R RANCH for group bookings only, the Client will be responsible for payment of the full contract . . . in the event that this function is cancelled.

On July 2, 1996, five days before the scheduled event, Nortex informed Sunset Trails that it was canceling the picnic. Because of the late notice, Sunset Trails was unable to rebook the facilities for July 7. Sunset Trails sent Nortex a bill for $7,000. Nortex refused to pay the bill and contended that the cancellation provision in the contract was an unlawful penalty provision. Sunset Trails argued that the provision was a valid liquidated damages provision. How should the court rule, and why? *Nortex Drug Distributors, Inc. v. Sunset Trails, Inc., 2000 Tex. App. LEXIS 5949 (Aug. 31, 2000).*

7. On August 21, 1992, Miguel A. Diaz Rodriguez ("Diaz") contracted with Learjet, Inc., to purchase a model 60 aircraft. The contract called for a $250,000 deposit to be made upon execution of the contract; $750,000 to be paid on September 18; $1 million to be paid 180 days before the delivery date of July 30, 1993; and the balance to be paid on delivery. Learjet anticipated making a profit of $1.8 million on the sale to Diaz.

Diaz paid the $250,000 deposit on August 21, but made no further payments. At the end of September 1992, Diaz called Learjet, indicated he did not want the aircraft, and requested a return of his deposit.

Learjet indicated that it would not return the deposit but, rather, would retain it as liquidated damages in accordance with the express terms of the contract, which provided for the retention of such payments in the event of breach.

Learjet then contracted with Circus Circus Enterprise, Inc., for sale of the aircraft. Learjet realized a $1,887,464 profit on the sale of the aircraft to Circus Circus, which was larger than the profit it would have made on the sale to Diaz. Diaz filed suit for return of the $250,000 deposit, alleging that the retention of the deposit was an unreasonable and unenforceable penalty. At the time that Diaz breached the contract, Learjet was operating at 60 percent capacity. Learjet would have been able to accelerate its production schedule to produce more model 60 planes during any given year. How should the court rule? *Diaz Rodriguez v. Learjet, Inc., 946 P.2d 1010 (Kan. Ct. App. 1997).*

8. Frigidaire, which manufactures freezers, contacted McGill Manufacturing Co. about purchasing an electrical switch that McGill had advertised as "water resistant." McGill sent Frigidaire some samples of the switches and a price quotation that contained the conditions of sale on its reverse side. Among those conditions was a statement that limited McGill's warranty obligations to either repayment of the purchase price or replacement of the returned parts. The samples were not completely water resistant, so the parties agreed upon a slight redesign of the switches, with a corresponding increase in price.

Frigidaire then sent McGill a blanket purchase order for the redesigned switches. The purchase order set forth Frigidaire's terms and conditions of purchase, which included express warranties of merchantability and fitness for a particular purpose. The purchase order also stated:

This Purchase Order is to be accepted in writing by Seller by signing and returning promptly to Buyer the Acknowledgment Copy, but if for any reason Seller should fail to sign and return to Buyer the Acknowledgment Copy, the commencement of any work or performance of any services hereunder by Seller shall constitute acceptance by Seller of this Purchase Order and all its terms and condi-

tions. Acceptance of this Purchase Order is hereby expressly limited to the terms hereof. Any terms proposed by Seller which add to, vary from, or conflict with the terms herein shall be void and the terms hereof shall govern. If this Purchase Order has been issued by Buyer in response to an offer the terms of which are additional to or different from any of the provisions hereof, then the issuance of this Purchase Order by Buyer shall constitute an acceptance of such offer subject to the express condition that the Seller assent that this Purchase Order constitutes the entire agreement between Buyer and Seller with respect to the subject matter hereof and the subject matter of such offer.

The purchase order stated the original price of the switches, not the increased price that reflected the agreed-upon redesign.

The next day, McGill sent a computer-generated acknowledgment form, which set forth terms similar to the terms on the original price quotation but which included additional limitations and exclusions of warranties. Ten days later, McGill's sales representative changed the incorrect price on the purchase order form, signed it, and returned it to Frigidaire.

Frigidaire produced several thousand freezers containing McGill's switches. The switches began to fail within a matter of months. Frigidaire filed suit, alleging breach of contract and breach of express and implied warranties and seeking in excess of $1.5 million in damages. Frigidaire argues that the terms found in its blanket purchase order should control; McGill argues that the terms found in its acknowledgment form should control. Which party is correct, and why? *White Consolidated Industries, Inc. v. McGill Manufacturing Co., 165 F.3d 1185 (8th Cir. 1999).*

9. On April 14, 1993, Saint Switch, Inc., offered to sell fuel pumps to Norca Corp., stating that its offer was firm until July 31, 1994. On August 18, 1993, Saint Switch forwarded to Norca a new offer stating different price terms for the fuel pumps. On November 4, 1993, Norca attempted to accept the original offer made on April 14, 1993. Is Norca permitted to accept that original offer? Why or why not? *Norca Corp. v. Tokheim Corp., 643 N.Y.S. 2d 139 (1996).*

CHAPTER 10

Legal Issues Relating to the Sale of Goods

Warranties and Products Liability

This chapter addresses (1) warranties and (2) products liability law. The first topic arises under contract law (which is the topic of Chapter 9), the second under tort law. We are concerned here with the civil liability that manufacturers and sellers of goods incur to buyers, users, and bystanders for damages or injury caused by defective goods. This is an area in which proactive management, such as careful planning during the design, manufacturing, and labeling processes, can substantially reduce, though not eliminate, the likelihood of litigation and the potential liability that a company might face. Liability for product defects can extend beyond manufacturers to a number of additional parties in the supply chain (including retailers, wholesalers, and suppliers of raw materials and component parts), so marketers of goods, as well as manufacturers, need to be aware of the law regarding products liability and warranties.

Overview

Originally, the law provided little protection for purchasers when goods turned out to be defective in some manner. In the nineteenth century, product sales were governed by the notion of *caveat emptor* ("let the buyer beware"). Sellers and manufacturers were not held liable for product defects unless they had behaved wrongfully toward or had breached a specific promise made to the buyer with whom the manufacturer had contracted to sell goods. This state of affairs evolved for a number of reasons, including the general notions of laissez-faire and economic individualism that prevailed at that time. Because buyers and sellers typically were of relatively equal size and bargaining ability, courts believed that the parties should be permitted to negotiate the transaction themselves, without interference from the law. The buyer often purchased directly from the manufacturer, and the long lines of distribution that we see today did not exist. Goods were typically uncomplicated, and purchasers could more easily examine them for defects prior to purchase. Finally, the courts wanted to promote the industrialization process by protecting infant industries from lawsuits.

By the twentieth century, however, commerce had changed dramatically. Lines of distribution had become long, and buyers seldom dealt directly with manufacturers. Large corporations evolved, which meant that sellers often had far more bargaining power than buyers. The increased complexity of the goods being sold made it more difficult for consumers to identify defects in products they were about to purchase, and the growth in consumer goods was accompanied by a growth in consumer injuries. Ultimately, as a matter of public policy, the courts determined that sellers and manufacturers could best bear the costs of product defects because they could spread those costs throughout society by increasing prices if necessary. There was a rapid growth in products liability law in the 1960s and the 1970s, and some commentators now argue that the governing rule is *caveat venditor* ("let the seller beware").

Today, the law seeks to protect consumers and purchasers, who are typically the weaker parties in the sales relationship. This goal is accomplished through *warranties*, which are contractual obligations created and enforced under the Uniform Commercial Code (UCC) and through *products liability law*, which imposes tort liability upon manufacturers and sellers of defective products for the injuries caused by their products. Warranties and products liability law protect not only buyers who are individual consumers but also buyers who are businesses. Thus, companies involved in business-to-business sales must be aware of these legal rules as well as those involved in consumer sales.

This chapter first examines the contractual obligations of warranty law, then turns to the tort liabilities created by products liability law.

Warranties

A *warranty* is a contractual promise by a seller or lessor that the goods that he sells or leases conform to certain standards, qualities, or characteristics. Warranties are primarily governed by state law—in particular, by the UCC. Warranties are made to purchasers and users of the product and possibly to third parties injured in their person or property by the goods. The UCC applies only to the sale of goods and does not extend to the sale of services, real estate transactions, or bailments.

Focus Case 10.1

Facts: In March 1998, Plaintiff purchased a Corvette from Defendant for the sum of $8,500 in cash. In April 1998, after consulting with the local police department, he discovered that the car's vehicle identification number had been altered and that the vehicle had been reported stolen in March 1992. The car was seized by the police and Plaintiff brought suit against Defendant for breach of the warranty of title.

Defendant testified that she did not know of the alleged theft at the time she sold the car to Plaintiff. She had purchased the car from Vincent Garofala in July 1997, who in turn had purchased the car from Bright Bay Lincoln Mercury in June 1994. Garofala had a copy of a Retail Certificate of Sale and a copy of a New York title issued to Gail M. DiFede by the New York Department of Motor Vehicles, which was apparently Bright Bay's source of title to the car. Defendant argued she was not liable for breach of warranty of title because she had received good title from Garofala, who had received good title from Bright Bay, who had received good title from DiFede.

Decision: The court rejected Defendant's argument, stating:

> [A] thief cannot pass title to stolen goods and mere delivery of the goods does not relieve the seller of the obligation of warranty of title. By transferring a stolen vehicle to the Plaintiff, irrespective of whether or not she had knowledge of the theft, the Defendant breached the warranty of title codified in section 2-312(1)(a) of the Uniform Commercial Code. One who sells a stolen automobile is liable to the buyer thereof for breach of warranty of title.

The court thus awarded the Plaintiff the purchase price of $8,500 plus $709.68 he had spent on repairs on the car. *Curran v. Ciaramelli*, reported in New York Law Journal, Nov. 10, 1998, p. 25.

Sellers of goods are generally not required to warrant their goods and may disclaim or modify warranties provided they undertake the necessary steps in doing so. Article 2 of the UCC recognizes four types of warranties: (1) warranties of title, (2) express warranties, (3) implied warranties of merchantability, and (4) implied warranties of fitness for a particular purpose. The last three are known as warranties of quality. All of these warranties (or any combination thereof) may arise in a single sale. Under the UCC, all warranties are to be construed as cumulative and consistent to the extent possible.

WARRANTY OF TITLE

Under UCC § 2-312, the seller of goods automatically warrants that (1) the title conveyed is good, (2) the seller has the right to convey the title, and (3) the goods are free from any security interest or other lien upon them of which the buyer was not aware at the time of the sale. This warranty arises automatically in most sales; no special action by the seller or buyer is required to create it (see Focus Case 10.1).

If the seller is a *merchant*,[1] the seller also automatically warrants that the goods are free from any rightful claims of patent, trademark, or similar infringement by

---

[1] Recall from Chapter 9 that a "merchant" is defined under UCC § 2-104 as "a person who deals in goods of the kind or otherwise by his occupation holds himself out as having knowledge or skill peculiar to the practices or goods involved in the transaction or to whom such knowledge or skill may be attributed by his employment of an agent or broker or other intermediary who by his occupation holds himself out as having such knowledge or skill."

any third party. If the buyer provided the specifications to the seller for the goods, however, the buyer must hold the seller harmless for any infringement claims arising out of the seller's compliance with those specifications.

EXPRESS WARRANTIES

If the seller expressly represents that her goods have certain qualities and if the goods do not have those qualities, the buyer may sue for breach of *express warranty*. This is true even if the seller believed that the representation was true and had no way of knowing that it was not true and even if the seller had no intention of creating an express warranty. Express warranties may be written or oral and may be formed by the conduct of the seller as well as by words.

UCC § 2-313 states two requirements for creating an express warranty. First, the seller must (1) make an affirmation of fact or promise regarding the goods, (2) provide a description of the goods, or (3) furnish a sample or model of the goods. Second, that statement or promise, description, or sample or model must be "part of the basis of the bargain" that the buyer made. All statements by a seller are considered to be part of the basis of the bargain unless the seller can demonstrate that the buyer did not rely upon them.

Only statements of fact create an express warranty; statements of opinion do not. Sellers are permitted to "puff their wares." Thus, the statement "this computer is capable of running any software program in the marketplace" creates an express warranty, but the statement "this is an excellent computer" does not. It is often hard to tell whether a particular statement is one of fact or opinion, e.g., "this computer is well designed." In such instances, the courts often consider the relative knowledge of the parties involved. If the buyer is not knowledgeable about the seller's goods, the courts are more likely to treat the statement as one of fact that creates an express warranty. If the buyer knows as much or almost as much about the goods as the seller, the courts are more likely to treat the statement as one of opinion that does not create an express warranty.

See Discussion Case 10.1.

IMPLIED WARRANTIES

Implied warranties do not arise from some statement or act by the seller, as do express warranties, but rather are imposed by law to promote higher commercial standards and to discourage sharp dealing in business. The UCC recognizes two types of implied warranties: (1) the implied warranty of merchantability and (2) the implied warranty of fitness for a particular purpose.

These implied warranties arise automatically in contracts for the sale of goods. If the state has adopted Article 2A (Leases) of the UCC, the same implied warranties will apply to the lease relationship. Some states that have not adopted Article 2A nonetheless find that lessors of personal property are also subject to these implied warranties under common law. In addition, where a transaction involves both the sale of a service and the sale of a good, the courts generally impose warranty liability where the injury is attributable to the product being sold, as opposed to the service being provided. For example, a hairdresser who sells and applies a permanent wave solution may be held liable for breach of warranty if the solution is defective and burns the scalp of the consumer.

See Discussion Case 10.4.

Implied Warranty of Merchantability

Under UCC § 2-314, a seller who is a merchant in the type of goods being sold impliedly warrants that the goods are of merchantable quality, i.e., that they are fit for the ordinary purpose for which they are being sold. The *implied warranty of merchantability* would apply, therefore, to sales of bicycles by a bike shop owner but not to sales of furniture by that same individual at a yard sale. Similarly, an individual selling even a brand-new bike at a yard sale would not create an implied warranty of merchantability because he would not be a merchant of bicycles. The implied warranty of merchantability arises automatically in every sale of goods by a merchant unless expressly disclaimed by the seller as discussed below.

Any merchant seller of goods, including a retailer or wholesaler, impliedly warrants the merchantability of goods, even if the seller did not manufacture the goods. For goods to be "merchantable," they must (1) pass without objection in the trade under the contract description; (2) in the case of fungible goods, be of fair, average quality; (3) be fit for the ordinary purpose for which such goods are sold; (4) be of even kind, quality, and quantity within each unit and among all units; (5) be adequately contained, packaged, and labeled; and (6) conform to any promises or affirmations of fact made on the container or label.

Under UCC § 2-314(1), the implied warranty of merchantibility extends explicitly to "the serving for value of food or drink to be consumed either on the premises or elsewhere." It is not clear whether this warranty extends to used goods, however, even where the seller deals regularly in goods of that kind (e.g., used car dealers or secondhand merchandise stores).

See Discussion Case 10.2.

Implied Warranty of Fitness for a Particular Purpose

Under UCC § 2-315, an implied warranty of fitness for a particular purpose arises when (1) the seller has reason to know of the particular purpose for which the buyer intends to use the goods; (2) the seller has reason to know that the buyer is relying upon the seller's skill or judgment to select or furnish suitable goods; and (3) the buyer actually relies upon the seller's skill or judgment in selecting or furnishing the goods. The seller does *not* have to be a merchant for this implied warranty to arise, although the seller must have some sort of expertise in the goods (see Focus case 10.2 on page 340).

The distinction between the implied warranty of merchantability and the implied warranty of fitness for a particular purpose is an important one. Suppose that a buyer informs an appliance store that she is seeking an oven for use in her commercial bakery. The store sells her a nondefective oven that is designed for residential use but is not capable of handling commercial baking applications. The appliance store has not breached the implied warranty of merchantability because the oven is fit for its ordinary purpose—residential baking. The store has breached the implied warranty of fitness for a particular purpose, however.

PRIVITY

Privity of contract is a requirement that the plaintiff demonstrate that he contracted directly with the defendant in order to bring a cause of action. Historically, the doctrine of privity was applied in warranty actions in such a way as to prevent plaintiffs

Facts: The Ball Works, Inc. operated a driving range. Carl Morrison, its vice-president, approached Lima Lawnmower, Inc. with regard to purchasing a lighter mower that could be used with Ball Works' existing tractor. He testified that he informed Lima Lawnmower's sales associate of the type of tractor that Ball Works owned and that it was a 20-horsepower diesel. He also testified that the sales associate recommended the LasTec 521 mower, and that he relied upon the associate's representation when he purchased the mower that the tractor should have no difficulty in pulling the mower.

The mower never cut the grass satisfactorily. The belt came off the mower repeatedly and the mower tore the grass instead of cutting it. Ball Works contacted other LasTec dealers, who reportedly stated that Ball Works' tractor was not powerful enough to run the LasTec 521 mower. Ball Works filed suit against Lima Lawnmower, alleging, among other things, breach of the implied warranty of fitness for a particular purpose.

Decision: The trial court ruled that Lima Lawnmower had breached the implied warranty of fitness for a particular purpose. On appeal, the appellate court stated:

[T]hree requirements must be met in order for an implied warranty of fitness for a particular purpose to exist: (1) the seller must have reason to know the buyer's particular purpose; (2) the seller must have reason to know that the buyer is relying on the seller's skill or judgment to furnish appropriate goods; and (3) the buyer must, in fact, rely upon the seller's skill or judgment.

First, with regard to the seller knowing the buyer's particular purpose, Carl Morrison testified that he informed Lima Lawnmower's associate that he was looking for a lighter mower to use on a driving range with Ball Works' John Deere 755, 20-horsepower diesel tractor. Lima Lawnmower argues that it was never told what type of tractor Ball Works had or was planning to use with the mower. However, the trial court is in the best position to weigh the credibility of the witnesses and the proffered testimony. There being some competent credible evidence that Lima Lawnmower knew Ball Works' particular purpose, the trial court's finding is not against the manifest weight of the evidence.

Second, there was also some competent, credible evidence that Lima Lawnmower must have had reason to know that Ball Works was relying on Lima Lawnmower's skill or judgment to furnish appropriate goods. Although Lima Lawnmower did not sell tractors, it did sell mowers that had to be propelled by tractors. Additionally, [Lima's general manager] testified that, in the past, when a customer stated what kind of "tractor they were using," sales had been turned down because the tractor the customer was planning on using was underpowered for the mower. Also, although Lima Lawnmower testified that they never recommend what mower a customer should use, Carl Morrison testified that the sales associate recommended the LasTec 521 to him and assured him that it would work with the tractor Ball Works had. Any seller making recommendations and assurances to customers regarding the compatibility of their equipment with the buyer's equipment would have reason to know that the buyer is relying on the seller's skill or judgment.

Third, there is ample testimony that Ball Works relied on Lima Lawnmower's skill or judgment. Both Carl Morrison [and Ball Works' groundskeeper] stated that they relied on the representations and assurances given by Lima Lawnmower that their tractor would operate the LasTec mower. Lima Lawnmower argues that Ball Works' reliance is unjustified. However, this court finds that when a mower can only function in conjunction with a tractor, it is not unreasonable for the buyer to rely on the assurances of a seller that the mower will properly operate with the customer's tractor, regardless of whether the seller sells the tractor in question.

Finally, there is competent, credible evidence that the mower did not operate in the manner required. Witnesses for both parties testified that the PTO [power takeoff] horsepower on the tractor was too low to operate the mower well and that using the tractor to run the mower would result in a poor quality of cut. Further, there was testimony from [three members of Ball Works' firm] that the mower never functioned properly. Hence, this court finds that there was competent, credible evidence to support the trial court's finding that the mower sold to Ball Works by Lima Lawnmower was not fit for the particular purpose intended.

The appellate court thus affirmed the trial court's ruling that Lima Lawnmower had breached the implied warranty of fitness for a particular purpose. *The Ball Works, Inc. v. Lima Lawnmower, Inc.,* 1997 Ohio App. LEXIS 2730 (June 27, 1997).

Focus Case 10.3

Facts: Chrysler Corporation manufactured a car with a defective steering mechanism. Claus Henningson purchased the car from Bloomfield Motors, a Chrysler dealer, and gave the car to his wife, Helen. Helen Henningson was injured when the steering mechanism failed with 468 miles on the odometer. She sued both Bloomfield Motors and Chrysler Corp. for breach of the implied warranty of merchantability.

Decision: Helen Henningson clearly was not in privity with Chrysler Corp. because: (1) the actual purchase was made by her husband, Claus, and (2) he had purchased the car from Bloomfield Motors, a dealer, and not Chrysler Corp. directly. Nonetheless, the New Jersey Supreme Court held that as a matter of public policy, the doctrine of privity ought not to be allowed to act as a bar to Helen Henningson's recovery from Chrysler. The court stated:

> The limitations of privity in contracts for the sale of goods developed their place in the law when marketing conditions were simple, when maker and buyer frequently met face to face on an equal bargaining plane and when many of the products were

relatively uncomplicated and conducive to inspection by a buyer competent to evaluate their quality. With the advent of mass marketing, the manufacturer became remote from the purchaser, sales were accomplished through intermediaries, and the demand for the product was created by advertising media. In such an economy it became obvious that the consumer was the person being cultivated. Manifestly, the connotation of "consumer" was broader than that of "buyer." He signified such a person who, in the reasonable contemplation of the parties to the sale, might be expected to use the product.

The court thus concluded: "[W]here the commodities sold are such that if defectively manufactured they will be dangerous to life or limb, then society's interests can only be protected by eliminating the requirement of privity between the maker and his dealers and the reasonably expected ultimate consumer." Because Helen Henningson was "a person who, in the reasonable contemplation of the parties to the warranty, might be expected to become a user of the automobile," she was protected by the warranty. *Henningsen v. Bloomfield Motors, Inc.*, 161 A.2d 69 (N.J. 1960).

---

from suing manufacturers or other parties within the chain of distribution with whom the plaintiff had not directly contracted. Rather, the "vertical" privity requirement limited the plaintiff to suing his immediate seller. Similarly, only the buyer who had purchased the goods could sue the seller; family members, guests, and bystanders who were injured by the product had no right to recover for breach of warranty because they lacked "horizontal" privity.

The 1960 decision of the New Jersey Supreme Court in *Henningson v. Bloomfield Motors, Inc.*, radically changed the law regarding privity in warranty actions (see Focus case 10.3).

Today, UCC § 2-318 offers states a choice of three positions regarding privity. *Alternative A* provides that if the final purchaser is a beneficiary of a warranty, express or implied, any member of her household and any houseguest are also covered by the warranty "if it is reasonable to expect that such person may use, consume or be affected by the goods" and if such person is personally injured as a result of the breach. Most states have officially adopted this alternative, although in many states the courts have interpreted the language more broadly in their case law.

Alternative B provides that warranty protection extends "to any natural person who may reasonably be expected to use, consume or be affected by the goods and who is injured in person by breach of the warranty." Thus, this alternative gives a cause of action for breach of warranty to parties such as employees or passersby who suffer personal injury as a result of the breach. Even if a state has not officially adopted *Alternative B*, its products liability case law may well provide for the same result that would be reached under this statutory language.

Alternative C extends breach of warranty protection even further by allowing artificial persons (such as corporations) to recover as well as natural persons and by allowing recovery for property damage as well as personal injury.

WARRANTY DISCLAIMERS

Warranty disclaimers are permitted, but not favored, under the UCC. The courts also tend to be hostile to attempts by manufacturers or sellers to disclaim express or implied warranties. Any ambiguities as to whether a disclaimer was made generally are construed against the seller. As a general rule, sellers should make their disclaimers explicit, unequivocal, and conspicuous.

The UCC imposes specific requirements for disclaiming each of the warranties described above. It is easier for the parties to disclaim or limit implied warranties than it is to disclaim or limit express warranties. The UCC specifically notes, for example, that implied warranties can be excluded or modified by course of dealing or course of performance or usage of trade.[2] This means that if the parties actually do or reasonably should understand as a result of their prior dealings with each other or as a result of common knowledge within the trade that no implied warranties are contemplated by the transaction, none arise.

Warranty disclaimers limit only the plaintiff's warranty claim, which arises in contract. Disclaimers do not affect any claims that the plaintiff might have in tort (e.g., negligence or strict products liability claims) for personal injury or property damage that might have occurred as a result of the product defect. These tort actions are discussed below.

Warranty of Title

A warranty of title can only be disclaimed by specific language in the contract or by special circumstances surrounding the transaction that clearly indicate to the buyer that the seller is not claiming title or is only purporting to sell whatever title the seller might have. For example, a statement such as "I convey only such right and title as I have in the goods" would suffice to disclaim the warranty of title. The buyer could not later complain if it turns out that the seller did not have good title to convey. Similarly, goods sold pursuant to a judicial sale carry no warranty of title, as the circumstances of the sale should make it clear to the buyer that the seller has no way of knowing or guaranteeing whether title is good.

Express Warranty

Because it is difficult to disclaim an express warranty, it is best simply not to create an express warranty in the first place. Express warranties can be excluded or modified but only by clear and unambiguous language of the parties. The courts do not like sellers giving a warranty with one hand and then taking it back with the other through a disclaimer, so they tend to view disclaimers of express warranties with a harsh eye.

See Discussion Case 10.1.

[2] UCC § 2-316(3)(c).

Focus Case 10.4

Facts: Plaintiff Catherine Baker purchased a fake fur coat for $127.99 from defendant Burlington Coat Factory Warehouse in Scarsdale, New York. She returned the coat two days later after it began shedding profusely. She demanded a refund of her $127.99 cash payment. Burlington offered either a store credit or a new coat of equal value, but refused to issue a cash refund. Baker filed suit, alleging, among other things, breach of contract and breach of the implied warranty of merchantability.

Burlington noted that it displayed several large signs in its store, which stated: "Warehouse policy: Merchandise, in New Condition, May be Exchanged Within 7 Days of Purchase for Store Credit and Must be Accompanied by a Ticket and Receipt. No Cash Refunds or Charge Credits." In addition, the front of Baker's sales receipt stated: "Holiday Purchases May Be Exchanged Through January 11th, 1998 In House Store Credit Only No Cash Refunds or Charge Card Credits." The back of the receipt stated: "We Will Be Happy to Exchange Merchandise In New Condition Within 7 days When Accompanied By Ticket and Receipt. However, Because Of Our Unusually Low Prices: No Cash Refunds or Charge Card Credits Will Be Issued. In House Store Credit Only." Baker stated that she had not read this language and was not aware of Burlington's "no cash refunds" policy.

Decision: The court found for Baker, stating:

> Under most circumstances retail stores in New York State are permitted to establish a no cash and no credit card charge refund policy and enforce it.
>
> Retail store refund policies are governed, in part, by General Business Law § 218-a, which requires conspicuous signs on the item or at the cash register or on signs visible from the cash register or at each store entrance, setting forth its refund policy including whether it is "in cash, or as credit or store credit only". * * *

> * * * Although plaintiff professed ignorance of defendant's refund policy, the court finds that defendant's signs and the front and back of its sales receipt reasonably inform consumers of its no cash and no credit card charge refund policy.
>
> Notwithstanding its visibility, the defendant's no cash and no credit card charge refund policy as against the plaintiff is unenforceable. Stated, simply, when a product is defective as was the plaintiff's . . . shedding Fake Fur, the defendant cannot refuse to return the consumer's payment whether made in cash or with a credit card.
>
> UCC 2-314(2)(c) mandates that "a warranty that the goods shall be merchantable is implied in a contract for their sale if the seller is a merchant with respect to goods of that kind . . . . (2) Goods to be merchantable must be . . . (c) . . . fit for the ordinary purposes for which such goods are used."
>
> Should there be a breach of the implied warranty of merchantability then consumers may recover all appropriate damages including the purchase price in cash. The court finds that defendant sold plaintiff a defective and unwearable Fake Fur and breached the implied warranty of merchantability. The plaintiff is entitled to the return of her purchase price of $127.99 in cash and all other appropriate damages.

The court specifically noted that the UCC's provisions regarding the implied warranty of merchantability preempt any contrary provisions in General Business Law § 218-a permitting a no-cash-refund policy. If the coat had not been defective and Baker had simply had a change-of-heart about her purchase, § 218-a would have applied and Baker would not have been entitled to a refund. Because the coat was defective, however, the limitations in the exchange policy did not apply. *Baker v. Burlington Coat Factory*, 175 Misc. 2d 951, 673 N.Y.S.2d 281 (1998).

Implied Warranty of Merchantability

Under UCC § 2-316(2), disclaimers of the implied warranty of merchantability must mention the word "merchantability." The disclaimer may be oral, but, if it is made in writing, it must be conspicuous (e.g., capital letters, larger type, contrasting typeface or color) (see Focus Case 10.4).

Implied Warranty of Fitness for a Particular Purpose

The implied warranty of fitness for a particular purpose can only be disclaimed in writing, and the disclaimer must be conspicuous. The disclaimer need not mention the word "fitness." In fact, the UCC notes that the statement that "[t]here are no warranties which extend beyond the description on the face hereof" is sufficient to disclaim all implied warranties of fitness.[3]

"As Is"

Selling goods "as is" or "with all faults" (or with "other language which in common understanding calls the buyer's attention to the exclusion of warranties and makes plain that there is no implied warranty"[4]) disclaims *all* implied warranties, including the implied warranty of merchantability, even if the word "merchantability" is not used. This language does not disclaim any express warranties that the seller might have made, however, nor does it relieve the seller of products liability based in tort. A number of states will not allow consumer products to be sold "as is."

THE BUYER'S OBLIGATIONS IN WARRANTY ACTIONS

As mentioned in Chapter 9, the UCC gives the buyer the right to inspect the goods. If the buyer refuses to examine the goods, or if the buyer actually examines the goods (or a sample or model) as fully as the buyer desires before entering into the contract, there is no implied warranty with respect to defects that a reasonable examination would disclose. Refusal or failure to inspect does not affect any express warranties that might have been made.

In addition, the buyer must give the seller written or oral notice of a breach of warranty within a reasonable time after the breach should have been discovered. If the buyer fails to provide notice of the breach, the buyer will not be permitted to recover from the seller in a warranty action. The requirement of notice protects the seller's right to cure, if cure is appropriate or possible under the circumstances. "Cure" is discussed in Chapter 9.

REMEDIES AND DEFENSES

If the breach of warranty occurs before the buyer has accepted the goods, the buyer's remedies are the same as they would be in any other breach of contract situation: the buyer may reject the goods, demand specific performance, cover, or recover damages in accordance with various UCC formulas. These remedies are discussed in Chapter 9.

If the buyer has accepted the goods, the buyer's damages for breach of warranty are generally calculated as *the difference between the value of the goods as warranted and the value of the goods as accepted, plus consequential and incidental damages.*[5] Recall from Chapter 9 that *incidental damages* include any costs or expenses directly associated with the seller's delay or delivery of defective goods, such as storage or inspection charges, costs of return shipping, or costs of cover. *Consequential damages* include personal or property damage arising from the breach of warranty. The seller is liable for consequential damages for economic losses, such as loss of profits from the anticipated resale of the goods or loss of goodwill or business reputation, only where the seller at the time of the contract had reason to know of such losses. This

---

[3] UCC § 2-316(2).
[4] UCC § 2-316(3)(a).
[5] UCC § 2-714(2) and (3).

foreseeability requirement does not apply to consequential damages claims for noneconomic losses, such as personal injury (including medical expenses and recovery for pain and suffering) and property damage. Punitive damages generally are not available in breach of warranty claims.

The seller may raise a number of defenses to warranty actions, including misuse or abuse of the product by the plaintiff, failure to follow instructions, improper maintenance, or ordinary wear of the product. These defenses often arise in the products liability context as well and are discussed more fully below.

It is very common for sellers to try to limit their liability for the quality of their goods by limiting the remedies that are available to the buyer in the event of a breach. The UCC permits the parties to specify the remedy available in the event of the breach and to make that remedy exclusive.[6] Sellers often use a contractual provision that limits the seller's liability to the repair or replacement of the defective goods. The UCC does not permit the limitation of consequential damages where the plaintiff has suffered personal injury as a result of defective consumer goods. Limitation of "commercial" damages (i.e., economic losses in a business setting) is permitted. State or federal legislation (such as the Magnuson-Moss Federal Warranty Act, discussed below) may also restrict the ability of sellers to limit the remedies available in the event of a breach of warranty. Warranty actions have been on the decline in recent years, as plaintiffs have increasingly turned to the strict liability cause of action discussed below.

THE MAGNUSON-MOSS FEDERAL WARRANTY ACT

The UCC's provisions regarding warranty protection for buyers of consumer goods have been supplemented by both federal and state legislation. The *Magnuson-Moss Federal Warranty Act*[7] applies to *written* warranties on *consumer products*. The Act does not address oral warranties, nor does it apply to products sold for resale or for commercial purposes. Congress's goals in passing the Act were to (1) ensure that consumers could get complete information about warranty terms and conditions, (2) ensure that consumers could compare warranty coverage prior to purchase, (3) promote competition on the basis of warranty coverage, and (4) strengthen incentives for companies to perform their warranty obligations and resolve consumer disputes quickly and without unnecessary expense to consumers.

The Act does not require sellers to make any warranties on consumer products. It does provide, however, that, if a seller makes a written warranty on a consumer product, that warranty must be conspicuously labeled as either a *full warranty* or a *limited warranty* and must contain specific information. The Act also provides that if the seller makes any written warranty, the seller is prohibited from disclaiming the implied warranties of merchantability and fitness for a particular purpose. The warranty information must be provided in a single, easy-to-read document and must be available to consumers prior to purchase.

A *full warranty* entitles the consumer to free repair of the product within a reasonable time period or, after a reasonable number of failed attempts to fix the product, entitles the consumer to choose either a full refund or replacement of a defective product. A full warranty also prevents the warrantor from placing any time limit on the warranty's duration; rather, full warranties last for a reasonable

---

[6] UCC § 2-719(1)(b).

[7] 15 U.S.C. §§ 2301 *et seq.* The Federal Trade Commission's (FTC's) "A Businessperson's Guide to Federal Warranty Law" is available on-line at http://www.ftc.gov/bcp/conline/pubs/buspubs/warranty/ index.htm

time period. (What is reasonable is a question of fact.) Finally, a full warranty prevents the warrantor from excluding or limiting damages for breach of warranty unless such exclusions are conspicuous on the face of the warranty.

A *limited warranty* is anything less than a full warranty. Under a limited warranty, liability for implied warranties cannot be disclaimed altogether but may be limited in duration if the time period stated is reasonable and if the limitation is conspicuously disclosed.

Under rules promulgated by the Federal Trade Commission (FTC) under the Act, all warranties must answer five basic questions: (1) What does the warranty cover or not cover? (2) What is the period of coverage? (3) What will the company do to correct problems? (4) How can the customer obtain warranty service? and (5) How will state law affect consumers' rights under the warranty?[8] Because of the difficulty that national sellers of goods could have in answering the last question, the FTC permits companies to use the following "boilerplate" language:

> This warranty gives you specific legal rights, and you may also have other rights which vary from state to state.

If a limited warranty attempts to limit the duration of implied warranties, the warranty document must contain the following language:

> Some states do not allow limitations on how long an implied warranty lasts, so the above limitation may not apply to you.

If the warranty purports to limit or eliminate the seller's potential liability for consequential or incidental damages, it must state:

> Some states do not allow the exclusion or limitation of incidental or consequential damages, so the above limitation or exclusion may not apply to you.

Consumers who successfully sue for breach of the Magnuson-Moss Act may recover legal and equitable relief and may receive costs and reasonable attorneys fees.

Several states also have consumer protection statutes that provide additional protection to purchasers of consumer goods. This legislation may prohibit or limit the use of disclaimers, specify that warranties last for a reasonable time period, require that the seller provide reasonable service and repair facilities, or expand the remedies available to consumers. Marketers thus need to inform themselves of the specific laws that apply in each state in which they market their goods.

Note that a consumer uses the Magnuson-Moss Act and implied and/or express warranties to obtain satisfaction when the good purchased disappoints the consumer and is not worth the price paid. In such a situation, both the seller and the consumer are bound by whatever limitations or disclaimers exist, provided such limitations or disclaimers are allowed by the law. When a product causes physical injury, however, the injured party turns to products liability law and many of the rules discussed above do not apply.

Products Liability Law

Products liability refers to the liability incurred by a seller of goods when the goods, because of a defect in them, cause personal injury or property damage to the buyer,

---

[8] The FTC has issued a document, "Writing Readable Warranties," which is available on-line at http://www.ftc.gov/bcp/conline/pubs/buspubs/writwarr.htm

a user, or a third party. In recent years, products liability has been stretched to reach beyond tangible goods to include items such as gas, pets, and real estate.

Products liability is based in tort law, while warranties are based in contract law. Although products liability claims can be brought under a number of different tort theories, including misrepresentation and fraud, this chapter focuses on the two most common theories: negligence and strict liability.

Products liability law is state, not federal, law. Although it originally started out as a form of common law, several states have enacted comprehensive products liability statutes that supplement or supplant various aspects of the common law.

NEGLIGENCE

Many products liability claims are based in negligence. The basic notion behind *negligence* is a failure on the part of the defendant to exercise "due care." If the defendant's conduct imposes an unreasonable risk of harm to another person that results in an injury to that person or to his property, the defendant is liable for negligence. Generally, to prove negligence, the plaintiff must show that: (1) the defendant owed a legal duty to the plaintiff; (2) the defendant failed to comply with this legal duty (i.e., failed to exercise due care); (3) the defendant's failure to exercise due care was the "proximate" (legal) cause of plaintiff's harm; and (4) the plaintiff suffered actual damages as a result of the defendant's actions. In judging whether the defendant's behavior posed an unreasonable risk of harm, the courts apply the "reasonable person" standard: Would a reasonable person of ordinary prudence behave as the defendant did under the circumstances?

See Discussion Cases 10.3, 10.4.

Historically, a manufacturer's duty was limited to those who were in privity of contract with the manufacturer; i.e., an injured plaintiff could sue in negligence only if she had contracted directly with the manufacturer for the purchase of the good. In a famous 1916 case, *MacPherson v. Buick Motor Co.*,[9] the New York Court of Appeals rejected the notion of privity in cases where negligently made products caused personal injury. All of the other states have since adopted the holding of *MacPherson*, and it is now the rule that a party who has negligently manufactured a product is liable for personal injuries proximately caused by her negligence, regardless of whether privity is present. A manufacturer's duty now extends to remote purchasers of products, as well as to users and bystanders, provided they are foreseeable plaintiffs. Moreover, a manufacturer can be liable in negligence for property damage as well as for physical injury.

The range of potential defendants is broad. Manufacturers of component parts, assembling manufacturers, wholesalers, retailers, bailors, and other suppliers all potentially may be held liable in negligence for product defects if it can be shown that they acted carelessly toward the plaintiff. The *manufacturer* owes the broadest duty of care of any category of potential defendant. The manufacturer of a product must exercise "due care" in making the product so that it is safe to be used as intended. This means that the manufacturer must exercise due care in (1) designing the product; (2) selecting the materials; (3) using the appropriate production processes; (4) assembling, testing, and inspecting the product; (5) placing adequate warnings on the label informing the user of the dangers of which an ordinary

[9] 111 N.E. 1050 (N.Y. 1916).

person might not be aware; (6) packaging, handling, and shipping the product; and (7) inspecting and testing component parts used in the final product.

Plaintiffs often find it difficult to hold a wholesaler or retailer liable for negligence. The wholesaler or retailer is not held liable for merely selling a negligently designed or manufactured product, as that party might have no duty to inspect or might have no reasonable opportunity to discover the defect even upon inspection. The seller has no duty to inspect goods packaged in sealed containers that are not to be opened before sale to the consumer, for example. The seller may be held liable for negligence, however, if the defect is obvious or if the seller has received other defective goods from the manufacturer in the past and has failed to inspect the current goods. The seller may also be liable for negligence if he knows or should know that the product is dangerous and fails to warn his customers; if the seller fails to use due care in selling the product to a person incapable of using it safely (e.g., selling explosives to a child); or if the seller has done something negligent with the product, such as carelessly assembling it or otherwise preparing it for final sale.

Sellers and manufacturers have a duty to warn buyers and users of *foreseeable* risks of harm associated with their products, but they do not have duty to warn of every risk that might be associated with a product. For example, a Louisiana appellate court held that the manufacturer and the seller of a portable propane tank were not liable for failure to warn when a teenager died after filling a plastic bag with propane and sniffing it with the expectation of getting high. The court found that the teenager's use of the product was neither reasonable nor reasonably anticipated by the manufacturer and seller.[10]

See Discussion Case 10.4.

STRICT PRODUCTS LIABILITY

Since the 1960s, the courts have been fashioning a new kind of relief for plaintiffs in products liability actions—*strict liability*. The objective of strict products liability is to encourage manufacturers and sellers to produce and sell safer products and to spread the costs of injuries caused by defective products among all consumers, rather than forcing random victims to bear the full cost of their injuries.

How does strict liability differ from negligence in products liability cases? First, strict liability focuses on the product itself: Was the product unreasonably dangerous? If so, the seller may be held liable even if the seller was as careful as possible in the preparation and sale of the product. Negligence, on the other hand, focuses on the defendant's behavior: Did the defendant fail to exercise its duty of care? Second, under strict liability, the injured plaintiff has a claim against anyone in the chain of distribution, including the immediate seller, the wholesaler, the manufacturer, and the manufacturer of component parts, regardless of fault. Under negligence, the plaintiff only has a claim against the party or parties whose lack of due care caused the injury.

The Restatements

As discussed in Chapter 1, a Restatement is a compilation of common law principles drafted by the American Law Institute (ALI), which is a group of distinguished scholars and practitioners. Restatements are not legally binding law, although

---

[10] Kelley v. Hanover Insurance Co., 722 So.2d 1133 (La. App. 1998).

courts often adopt the principles contained within the various Restatements as binding rules within their jurisdictions.

Strict products liability law was originally based upon the *Restatement (Second) of Torts*, which was adopted in 1965. In the decades since then, virtually all states have accepted the theory of strict liability for dangerously defective products, and most have incorporated some form of Section 402A as part of their common law. In 1997, the ALI issued the *Restatement (Third) of Torts: Products Liability*. The ALI hopes that the Restatement (Third) will eventually be adopted by the courts as binding precedent, but unless and until that occurs (a process that may take several years), Section 402A of the Restatement (Second) remains the prevailing legal rule on strict products liability.

The Restatement (Second) of Torts

The foundation for modern strict products liability is Section 402A of the Restatement (Second) of Torts, which provides:

> *§ 402A. Special Liability of Seller of Product for Physical Harm to User or Consumer.*
>
> (1) One who sells any product in a defective condition unreasonably dangerous to the user or the consumer or to his property is subject to liability for physical harm thereby caused to the ultimate user or consumer, or to his property, if
>
> > (a) the seller is engaged in the business of selling such a product, and
> >
> > (b) it is expected to and does reach the user or consumer without substantial change in the condition in which it is sold.
>
> (2) The rule stated in Subsection (1) applies although
>
> > (a) the seller has exercised all possible care in the preparation and sale of his product, and
> >
> > (b) the user or consumer has not bought the product from or entered into any contractual relation with the seller.

Section 402A of the Restatement (Second) thus provides that a seller engaged in the business of selling a particular product is liable for physical harm or property damage suffered by the ultimate user or consumer of that product *if* the product was in a defective condition unreasonably dangerous to the user or the consumer or to her property. Section 402A applies to all commercial sellers of products, whether manufacturers, wholesalers, or retailers, but does not apply to casual, one-time sellers (see Focus Case 10.5).

In addition, the strict liability doctrine does *not* make the seller an insurer of the product. Sellers are held liable only for products that are both defective and unreasonably dangerous; they are not held liable for every injury to a user of a product. Under Section 402A, the plaintiff must show that the defect existed at the time that the product left the defendant's hands and that the defect was not the result of a subsequent modification or alteration by another party. It can be hard for a plaintiff to show this against a manufacturer if the product passed through several intermediate suppliers before reaching the plaintiff.

Courts applying Section 402A generally use either the consumer expectations test or the risk-utility test to determine whether a product is defective. *Comment i* of Section 402A states that a product is considered to be "in a defective condition unreasonably dangerous" if it is "dangerous to an extent beyond that which would be contemplated by the ordinary consumer who purchases it, with the ordinary knowledge common to the community as to its characteristics."[11] Under this

---

[11] Restatement (Second) of Torts § 402A, comment i.

Focus Case 10.5

Facts: Scott Gebo's hand was crushed at work in the rollers of a paper embossing machine when a protective guard system failed. Gebo filed a products liability suit against Filtration Sciences, Inc. Filtration Sciences had originally purchased the embosser in 1966 and it had modified the machine by designing and installing the guard system. Three years prior to Gebo's injury, Filtration Science sold its paper mill and all the machinery contained therein, including the embosser, to Knowlton Specialty Papers, Inc.

Decision: The court held that a "casual manufacturer" cannot be held strictly liable for design defects. Imposing strict liability on manufacturers for product defects reflects a public policy decision that manufacturers are in the best position to know when a product is safely made for its intended purpose, and that manufacturers often have the only "practical opportunity, as well as a considerable incentive, to turn out useful, attractive, but safe products." The court found that "Filtration Sciences' single act of design and assembly does not without more make it equivalent to a product manufacturer." *Gebo v. Black Clawson Co.*, 703 N.E.2d 1234 (N.Y. Ct. App. 1998).

consumer expectations test, if a plaintiff, applying the knowledge of an ordinary consumer, sees a danger and can appreciate that danger, the plaintiff cannot recover for any injury she incurs as a result of that danger.

For example, a Texas appellate court found that the trial court had erroneously granted summary judgment to a tequila manufacturer that had been sued by the parents of a college student who had died from acute alcohol poisoning. The appellate court stated: "Although there is no question that drinking alcoholic beverages will cause intoxication and possibly even cause illness is a matter of common knowledge, we are not prepared to hold, as a matter of law, that the general public is aware that the consumption of an excessive amount of alcohol can result in death." Summary judgment was inappropriate because "a trier of fact could properly find that the amount of alcohol consumed by [the student] was potentially lethal and that it was dangerous to an extent beyond that which would be contemplated by the ordinary user of the product with ordinary knowledge common to the community as to the products' characteristics."[12]

Most courts have moved away from the consumer expectations test and have embraced the *risk-utility test* instead. Under this test, a product is "unreasonably dangerous" if a reasonable person would conclude that the danger, whether foreseeable or not, outweighs the utility of the product. However, if a product is *unavoidably unsafe* but its benefits outweigh its dangers, the seller is not held strictly liable for any injuries that occur. The Restatement recognizes, for example, that the rabies vaccine carries a risk of severe side effects. The Restatement also notes, however, that "since the disease itself invariably leads to a dreadful death, both the marketing and the use of the vaccine are fully justified, notwithstanding the unavoidable high degree of risk which they involve. Such a product, properly prepared, and accompanied by proper directions and warning, is not defective, nor is it unreasonably dangerous."[13]

See Discussion Case 10.3.

---

[12] *Brune v. Brown Forman Corp.*, 758 S.W.2d 827 (Tex. App. 1988).
[13] Restatement (Second) of Torts § 402A, comment k.

The Restatement (Third) of Torts: Products Liability

The Restatement (Second) focused primarily on products with manufacturing defects and did not directly address two other major categories of defects: defective warnings and defective design. Many commentators argued that strict liability was inappropriate for these two categories of defects because it was unfair that manufacturers should be held liable for failure to warn of unknowable risks or failure to make their products safer than was technologically feasible.

In May 1997, the ALI adopted the Restatement (Third) of Torts: Products Liability as part of its periodic review and updating process. The Restatement (Third) sets forth 21 black-letter rules for products liability. In particular, Section 2 of the Restatement (Third) provides explicit rules for the three categories of product defects: (1) manufacturing defects, (2) design defects, and (3) inadequate warnings. The Restatement (Third) maintains the strict liability standard for manufacturing defects adopted in the Restatement (Second) but moves toward a fault-based (i.e., negligence) standard for design and warning defects. Section 2 provides:

Section 2   Categories of Product Defect

A product is defective when, at the time of sale or distribution, it contains a manufacturing defect, is defective in design, or is defective because of inadequate instructions or warnings. A product:

(a) contains a manufacturing defect when the product departs from its intended design even though all possible care was exercised in the preparation and marketing of the product;

(b) is defective in design when the foreseeable risks of harm posed by the product could have been reduced or avoided by the adoption of a reasonable alternative design by the seller or other distributor, or by a predecessor in the commercial chain of distribution, and the omission of the alternative design renders the product not reasonably safe;

(c) is defective because of inadequate instructions or warnings when the foreseeable risks of harm posed by the product could have been reduced or avoided by the provision of reasonable instructions or warnings by the seller or other distributor, or a predecessor in the commercial chain of distribution, and the omission of the instructions or warnings renders the product not reasonably safe.[14]

Perhaps the most controversial provision of the Restatement is the requirement that a plaintiff suing a manufacturer over a defectively designed product must show that a reasonable alternative design (RAD) would have prevented the harm, a standard that many commentators believe tilts the law in favor of the manufacturer and away from the consumer. Section 402A of the Restatement (Second) did not require the plaintiff to show the existence of a RAD but, rather, found that a product that is "unreasonably dangerous to the user or consumer or to his property" is defective even if there is no way to eliminate that danger.

Issues Raised by Strict Products Liability

Strict products liability raises a number of unique legal issues.

Subsequent Remedial Design

Plaintiffs often try to show that the defendant redesigned the product after the plaintiff's injury in order to make it safer, arguing that the redesign indicates that the original design was defective and that a safer design was available and should

---

[14] Restatement (Third) of Torts: Products Liability § 2.

have been used. Traditionally, most courts have not allowed this evidence in to prove that the product was defective on the public policy grounds that admitting such evidence would discourage manufacturers from engaging in redesign and from producing safer products.

Latent Defects

Plaintiffs in several mass products liability class actions have attempted to argue that the product has some sort of latent defect such that it might fail under certain circumstances and cause injury, even though no plaintiff has suffered actual injury yet. Most of these claims have involved automotive defects, involving child seats, passive restraints, tires, and transmissions, but cases have also been brought involving cell phones and heart valves.

The heart valve cases illustrate the conflicting policy concerns that such cases can raise. Shiley, Inc., a subsidiary of Pfizer, Inc., had manufactured and sold the Bjork-Shiley Concavo-Convex heart valve from 1979 to 1986. The heart valves had been marketed in several sizes worldwide. The heart valves were withdrawn from the market in 1986 after a number of recipients died from sudden failure of the valves. The valves failed without warning and seemingly at random, making it impossible for doctors to pinpoint which patients would be likely to incur a problem with the valves. Unless the patient received open heart surgery to replace the valve within several hours of the failure, the patient would die.

A study indicated that the overall cumulative failure rate for the size of valve sold in the United States was 4.2 percent over eight years. Over 500 failures had occurred worldwide, killing about two-thirds of the patients involved. Removal and replacement of the valves entails open heart surgery, which itself carries a mortality risk of 5 percent, which is higher than the failure rate associated with the valves.

In a settlement of a class action suit brought against it, Pfizer agreed to pay $75 million to a patient fund; $80 million to $130 million for medical and psychological consultations, depending upon the number of claims; $500,000 to $2 million to each recipient whose heart valve breaks; and $10 million to patients' spouses.[15]

A number of heart valve recipients who had not suffered valve failure attempted to bring suits based upon the latent defects in the valves and their fears that that their valves might fail in the future. The courts uniformly rejected their claims.[16] In *Farsian v. Pfizer*,[17] for example, the plaintiff, who had had a Bjork-Shiley heart valve implant in 1981, sued Pfizer, arguing that the manufacturer had engaged in fraudulent conduct by marketing the valve even though the manufacturer knew of serious manufacturing problems that directly related to the fracture problem in the valve. Although the plaintiff's heart valve was functioning properly at the time of suit, he argued that the higher rate of fracture and risk of death associated with the valve reduced the value of the valve and that he had suffered mental anguish and emotional distress since he learned of the fraud. The Alabama Supreme Court rejected his claim, finding that the plaintiff had no cause of action

---

[15] *See generally* Ben L. Kaufman, *Flat-Rate Fees Denied for Class-Action Lawyers*, THE CINCINNATI ENQUIRER, Jan. 11, 1998, p. B04; Milt Freudenheim, *Pfizer Settles Suit Over Heart Valve*, THE NEW YORK TIMES, Late Edition-Final, Sept. 3, 1993, sec. D, p. 3; *FDA Suggests Removal of Heart Valve*, FACTS ON FILE WORLD NEWS DIGEST, Apr. 2, 1992, p. 233; Gina Kolata, *Heart Valve Called So Risky Its Removal Must be Considered*, THE NEW YORK TIMES, Late Edition-Final, Mar. 13, 1992, Sec. A, p. 1.

[16] *See* Angus v. Shiley, Inc., 989 F.2d 142 (3d Cir. 1993); Walus v. Pfizer, Inc., 812 F. Supp. 41 (D.N.J. 1993); Spuhl v. Shiley, Inc., 795 S.W.2d 573 (Mo. App. 1990); Brinkman v. Shiley, Inc., 732 F. Supp. 33 (M.D. Pa.), *aff'd without op.*, 902 F.2d 1558 (3d Cir. 1989).

[17] 682 So. 2d 405 (Ala.), *dismissed*, 97 F.3d 508 (11th Cir. 1996).

where he had not suffered an injury-producing malfunction of the product. A *fear* of failure of a product, absent a failure itself, is insufficient to support a products liability claim.

Liability for Misrepresentations

Section 9 of the Restatement (Third) also imposes liability upon commercial product sellers and distributors for harm to persons or property caused by misrepresentations of material fact, whether fraudulent, negligent, or innocent. Thus, a seller could be held liable for written or oral statements about a product made by salespersons or advertisements. Moreover, under this section, it does not matter if the product was nondefective, if the seller honestly believed that the representation was accurate, or if the plaintiff did not actually see or rely upon the misrepresentation.

Section 402B of the Restatement (Second) contains a similar provision, though it requires that the plaintiff show that he had "justifiably" relied upon the misrepresentation.

Marketers should be alert to the liability created by these sections and should take care to ensure that salespersons and advertising agencies do not make inaccurate representations about their products.

Market Share Liability

Generally, the plaintiff bears the burden of showing that the defendant caused the plaintiff's injury. Causation can be difficult to show in many instances, however. For example, many women who suffered injury as result of their mothers' taking the drug DES during their pregnancies 20 or more years earlier were unable to demonstrate which of over 300 manufacturers made the precise pills that their mothers took.[18] Each manufacturer used the identical formula in producing the drug.

In such instances, where several manufacturers produced a similar product with a common defect and where the plaintiff is unable to demonstrate which manufacturer in particular was the cause of her injury, many (but not all) courts are willing to impose *market share liability*. Under this approach, liability is apportioned among all of the firms in the industry that might have produced the product that caused the plaintiff's injury. In such an instance, most courts give each defendant the opportunity to prove that it did not produce the product that injured that particular plaintiff. Some courts, however, do not permit defendants to exculpate themselves in this way. For example, the New York Court of Appeals stated in a 1989 case: "[B]ecause liability here is based on the over-all risk produced, and not causation in a single case, there should be no exculpation of a defendant who, although a member of the market producing DES for pregnancy use, appears not to have caused a particular plaintiff's injury."[19]

Successor Liability

A corporation that purchases or acquires the assets of another corporation may well find it has purchased or acquired liability for product defects as well. Traditionally, a corporation purchasing or acquiring the assets of another may be held liable for the obligations and liabilities of the seller if: (1) the purchaser expressly or impliedly agreed to assume such obligations or liabilities; (2) the transaction is in effect a consolidation or merger of the seller and the purchaser; (3) the purchaser

---

[18] *See* Sindell v. Abbott Laboratories, 607 P.2d 924 (Cal. 1980).
[19] *Id.* at 1072.

is merely a continuation of the seller; or (4) the transaction is a fraudulent attempt to escape liability for such obligations or debts.

Some modern courts also impose liability on the acquiring corporation where: (1) the purchaser continues the manufacture of the product line of the seller; or (2) the purchaser continues the enterprise of the seller. The Restatement (Third) rejects these new theories of successor liability and adopts only the four traditional categories.[20]

Remedies

In most states, a plaintiff must suffer an "economic loss" in order to recover in tort. This doctrine requires that the product defect cause personal injury or physical damage to property other than the defective product itself. Remedies available in products liability actions include recovery for personal injury, property damage, and possibly punitive damages. Indirect economic loss (such as lost profits and loss of business goodwill) and basis-of-the-bargain damages are difficult to recover in tort but are available in breach of warranty actions.

Thus, the type of remedy that the plaintiff wishes to recover often guides the plaintiff's decision as to which theory (warranty or tort liability) to sue under. Plaintiffs need not necessarily choose a single cause of action, however. A plaintiff may, and usually does, sue for breach of warranty, negligence, and strict liability all arising out of a single sale and injury, for example.

Manufacturers and sellers often try to limit the remedies available to purchasers of their products, often by excluding recovery for consequential damages or by limiting recovery to repair or replacement of the defective good. The courts are unlikely to uphold such limitations in tort actions involving ordinary consumers but may well do so in actions involving buyers who are businesses or other sophisticated consumers of relatively equal bargaining power.

Similarly, manufacturers or sellers often insert a disclaimer of liability for negligence or strict liability within their sales contracts. The courts are reluctant to allow manufacturers or sellers to disclaim their liability for their own negligence or strict liability in consumer cases, however, and rarely give effect to such disclaimers in that setting. The courts are more likely to allow such disclaimers when the parties are of equal bargaining power, as in a business-to-business transaction.

Defenses to Products Liability Actions

There are several defenses that a defendant may attempt to raise in a products liability action: (1) contributory or comparative negligence, (2) voluntary assumption of risk, (3) misuse or abuse of product, (4) the state-of-the-art defense, (5) compliance with government standards, and (6) the learned intermediaries and sophisticated purchasers rules. Each is discussed below.

Contributory/Comparative Negligence

Contributory negligence was once the majority rule but today applies only in a minority of states. This doctrine provides that if both the plaintiff and the defendant were negligent and the plaintiff's negligence is *a* (though not necessarily the *sole*) proximate cause of her injuries, the plaintiff receives no recovery. Some states apply this doctrine in some types of strict liability cases, such as those involving product misuse or abuse, as well as in negligence cases.

---

[20] Restatement (Third) of Torts: Products Liability § 12.

Comparative negligence (also known as comparative fault) applies in the majority of states. This doctrine provides that if the plaintiff and the defendant were both negligent, plaintiff's recovery will be reduced by his relative degree of fault. Thus, if the plaintiff was 30 percent at fault and the defendant 70 percent at fault, the plaintiff will recover 70 percent of his damages but will not recover for the 30 percent of his damages attributable to his own lack of due care. In a *pure* comparative fault system, the plaintiff will always recover for the portion of the injury attributable to the defendant. In a *mixed* comparative fault system, the plaintiff will recover nothing if the plaintiff is more than 50 percent at fault for his injuries. As you can imagine, it can be very difficult factually to assign relative degrees of fault to the plaintiff and defendant. Typically, much time and effort are devoted to this issue during the trial stage of the litigation.

In jurisdictions that have adopted comparative negligence, the defense always applies in negligence actions, and some courts apply it in strict liability actions as well.

Voluntary Assumption of Risk

Voluntary assumption of risk occurs when the plaintiff knew of the risk of harm presented and voluntarily and unreasonably chose to encounter it. Historically, voluntary assumption of risk operated as a complete bar to the plaintiff's recovery. In recent years, however, the doctrine has fallen into disfavor with many courts. Where it is still followed, this defense applies in both strict liability and negligence cases, as well as in warranty actions.

The defense typically applies only where it is clear beyond question that the plaintiff voluntarily and knowingly proceeded in the face of an obvious and dangerous condition and only where it is clear from the circumstances that the plaintiff willingly accepted the risk. Mere contributory negligence does not show a voluntary assumption of risk.

In addition, many courts reject the doctrine in the employment context, finding "an employee does not voluntarily and unreasonably assume the risk of danger during the course of employment because 'the competitiveness and pragmatism' of the real world workplace compels employees to either perform risky tasks or suffer various adverse employment consequences, ranging from termination to more subtle sanctions."[21] These courts generally continue to apply comparative negligence in such cases, however, so that an employee cannot completely abdicate responsibility for her own safety.

Misuse or Abuse of Product

Misuse or abuse of product differs from voluntary assumption of risk in that misuse or abuse includes actions that the injured party did not know to be dangerous, while assumption of risk does not. This defense is only available to the seller where the misuse or abuse is not reasonably foreseeable. If it is foreseeable, the seller must take reasonable actions to guard against the misuse or abuse. Where the defense is available to the seller, however, it is a complete defense for both negligence and strict liability actions, as well as warranty actions (see Focus Case 10.6 on page 356).

State-of-the-Art Defense and Post-Sale Duties to Warn

Generally, in determining whether a product is "in a defective condition unreasonably dangerous" to the consumer or user or to his property, the courts consider the state of human knowledge at the time that the product was sold, not at the time

---

[21] Staub v. Toy Factory, Inc., 749 A.2d 522, 532 n.11 (Pa. Super. Ct. 2000) (citation omitted).

Focus Case 10.6

Facts: Roy Mercurio drove his Nissan Altima into a tree at a speed of between 30 and 40 miles per hour. At the time his blood alcohol content was at least .18%. When the car struck the tree, the passenger compartment collapsed and Mercurio suffered a severe closed head injury. Mercurio's wife brought a products liability action against Nissan, the car's manufacturer, claiming that the car was not crashworthy.

Decision: The defendant first argued that evidence of Mercurio's blood alcohol content should be admitted into court to show that Mercurio had engaged in unforeseeable misuse of the car. The court rejected the defendant's argument, stating that the "[t]he fact that a collision may have been caused by the driver's intoxication, as opposed to another form of negligence, does not reduce the manufacturer's duty to provide a reasonably safe vehicle."

The court noted that "although the intended purpose of automobiles is not to participate in collisions, it is foreseeable that the collisions do occur, and an automobile manufacturer is under an obligation under Ohio law to use reasonable care in the design of its vehicle to avoid subjecting the user to an unreasonable risk of injury in the event of a collision." The court concluded that "[r]egardless of the cause of Mercurio's accident, the type of accident that is at issue in this case—a frontal collision with a stationary object at thirty to forty miles per hour—is foreseeable." Thus, evidence of Mercurio's blood alcohol content was not admissible to demonstrate unforeseeable misuse of the car.

The defendant next argued that by driving under the influence of alcohol, Mercurio voluntarily assumed the risk of whatever injuries he suffered. Under Ohio law, a plaintiff assumes the risk of a unreasonably dangerous condition when: (1) he knows of the condition; (2) the condition is patently dangerous; and (3) he voluntarily exposes himself to the condition.

Here, the court found, the dangerous condition that Mercurio allegedly assumed was the alleged uncrashworthiness of the car, not the risk of an accident generally. The defendant had not alleged, however, that Mercurio knew that the vehicle's subfloor posed a risk of buckling or that the subfloor was patently dangerous, or that Mercurio voluntarily exposed himself to the dangers of driving in a vehicle that was not crashworthy. Under these facts, the defendant could not raise the defense of assumption of risk.

Thus, the court granted the plaintiff's motion to exclude any reference to Mercurio's consumption of alcohol on the night of his automobile accident. *Mercurio v. Nissan Motor Corp.*, 81 F. Supp. 2d 859 (N.D. Ohio 2000).

---

that the products liability case is heard. The seller should only be held liable for what it reasonably could have known at the time the product was sold. Many states have statutes that specifically provide that a product is not defective if it is designed and sold in a manner consistent with industry customs or the state of the art at the time of sale[22] (see Focus Case 10.7 on page 357).

Some states that apply the state-of-the-art defense require only that the manufacturer conform to industry standards.[23] The problem with such an approach, of course, is that an entire industry may be lax in requiring safety devices or in developing safer technologies. Other states go to the opposite extreme, requiring that the manufacturer conform to cutting-edge technology within its industry.[24] An

---

[22] *See, e.g.*, Ariz. Rev. Stat. Ann. § 12-681 *et seq.*; N.H. Rev. Stat. Ann. § 507:8-g; Tenn. Code Ann. §§ 29-28-104-105.

[23] *See, e.g.*, Beech v. Outboard Marine Corp., 584 So.2d 447 (Ala. 1991); Gosewisch v. American Honda Motor Co., 737 P.2d 365 (Ariz. Ct. App. 1985).

[24] *See* Fibreboard Corp. v. Fenton, 845 P.2d 1168 (Colo. 1993).

Focus Case 10.7

Facts: Carl Anderson filed a suit in strict liability against Owens-Corning Fiberglas Corp. and other manufacturers of products containing asbestos, alleging that he had contracted asbestosis and other lung ailments through exposure to asbestos and asbestos products while working at a naval shipyard from 1946 to 1976. His complaint alleged that the defendants were liable in strict liability for failing to warn the users of the risk of danger associated with asbestos and asbestos-containing products. The defendants responded by raising the state-of-the-art defense; i.e., "that even those at the vanguard of scientific knowledge at the time the products were sold could not have known that asbestos was dangerous to users in the concentrations associated with defendants' products."

Decision: The California Supreme Court ruled that: "Exclusion of state-of-the-art evidence, *when the basis of* *liability is a failure to warn*, would make a manufacturer the virtual insurer of its product's safe use, a result that is not consonant with established principles underlying strict liability." The court stated that public policy grounds supported such an outcome: "[I]f a manufacturer could not count on limiting its liability to risks that were known or knowable at the time of manufacture or distribution, it would be discouraged from developing new and improved products for fear that later significant advances in scientific knowledge would increase its liability."

Thus, the court held that "a defendant in a strict products liability action based upon an alleged failure to warn of a risk of harm may present evidence of the state of the art, i.e., evidence that the particular risk was neither known nor knowable by the application of scientific knowledge available at the time of manufacture and/or distribution." *Anderson v. Owens-Corning Fiberglas Corp.*, 810 P.2d 549 (Cal. 1991).

intermediate, third approach, which was adopted in the Restatement (Third),[25] requires the manufacturer to act reasonably in keeping up with technological advances within its industry and in including safe components and safety devices.[26] In a few states, such as Hawaii and Pennsylvania, the manufacturer is held liable for the harm caused by a defect even if discovery of the defect was scientifically and/or technically impossible at the time the product was marketed.

In some instances, the manufacturer may have no reason to know of a defect at the time of sale but may later discover a defect. The state-of-the-art defense would not have required a warning at the time of sale. The question then becomes whether the manufacturer must issue a warning at the time the defect is discovered.

The common law of many states requires manufacturers to provide a *post-sale warning* in such instances. The Restatement (Third) also imposes such a duty on manufacturers. Section 10 states:

(a) One engaged in the business of selling or otherwise distributing products is subject to liability for harm to persons or property caused by the seller's failure to

---

[25] Restatement (Third) of Torts: Products Liability § 2(b) and (c). These subsections provide that a product:

(b) is defective in design when the foreseeable risks of harm posed by the product could have been reduced or avoided by the adoption of a reasonable alternative design by the seller or other distributor, or a predecessor in the commercial chain of distribution, and the omission of the alternative design renders the product not reasonably safe;

(c) is defective because of inadequate instructions or warnings when the foreseeable risks of harm posed by the product could not have been reduced or avoided by the provision of reasonable instructions or warnings by the seller or other distributor, or a predecessor in the commercial chain of distribution, and the omission of the instructions or warnings renders the product not reasonably safe.

[26] *See* Vassallo v. Baxter Healthcare Corp., 696 N.E.2d 909 (Mass. 1998).

provide a warning after the time of sale or distribution of a product if a reasonable person in the seller's position would provide such a warning.

(b) A reasonable person in a seller's position would provide a warning after the time of sale if:

(1) the seller knows or reasonably should know that the product poses a substantial risk of harm to persons or property; and

(2) those to whom a warning might be provided can be identified and can reasonably assume to be unaware of the risk of harm; and

(3) a warning can be effectively communicated to and acted on by those to whom a warning might be provided; and

(4) the risk of harm is sufficiently great to justify the burden of providing a warning.[27]

Other states reject a post-sale duty to warn if the product met standards of reasonableness when it was sold.[28]

Does a seller have a duty to monitor products post-sale to discover defects? *Comment c* to the Restatement (Third) says no, because such monitoring would be too burdensome for manufacturers. Rather, "[a]s a practical matter, most post-sale duties to warn arise when new information is brought to the attention of the seller, after the time of sale, concerning risks accompanying the product's use or consumption."[29]

In addition, there is no general duty to *recall* defective products. The Restatement (Third) imposes liability for a post-sale failure to recall a product upon commercial product sellers and distributors only if: (1) a government directive has been issued specifically requiring the recall or (2) the seller or distributor voluntarily undertakes such a recall but then does not act reasonably in recalling the product.[30] This limited duty to recall is not as broad as the duty to provide post-sale warnings of defects; i.e., there are situations in which a manufacturer has a duty to issue post-sale warnings but does not have a duty to undertake a recall.

Manufacturers, distributors, and retailers of consumer products who discover information that a product violates applicable consumer product safety rules or contains a defect that would create a substantial hazard have a duty to immediately inform the Consumer Product Safety Commission. This topic is discussed further in Chapter 8.

Compliance with Government Standards

Suppose that the seller's product is regulated and that the state or federal government has set standards for it. If the seller is in compliance with those standards, does the seller have an automatic defense for products liability actions? The answer is no. Government standards generally set *minimum* requirements, and compliance with those standards does not automatically shield the manufacturer or seller from liability, though it may be considered as evidence by the judge or jury that the product is not defective. Several states do have statutes that make regulatory compliance a defense in certain situations. New Jersey, for example, has such a statute for FDA-approved drugs and drug labels.

---

[27] Restatement (Third) of Torts: Products Liability § 10.
[28] *See, e.g.,* Romero v. International Harvester Co., 979 F.2d 1444 (10th Cir. 1992) (applying Colorado law); Carrizales v. Rheem Mfg. Co., 589 N.E.2d 569 (Ill. App. 1991).
[29] Restatement (Third) of Torts: Products Liability § 10 comment c.
[30] Restatement (Third) of Torts: Products Liability § 11 comment c.

The Restatement (Third) creates a rule of absolute liability for *non*compliance with safety statutes or regulations, stating that where the person injured is in the class of persons whom the statute or regulation was intended to protect and the danger is one against which the statute or regulation was intended to protect, the noncompliance renders the product defective.[31]

The Learned Intermediaries and Sophisticated Purchaser Rules

In some instances, a manufacturer or supplier may satisfy its duty to warn by providing warnings to a "learned intermediary," as opposed to the end user of the product. For example, drug manufacturers may provide doctors with adequate information of the risks and hazards associated with drugs; the prescribing or treating physician then intervenes between the manufacturer and the consumer.[32] This rule has also been used to shield a cobalt manufacturer who informed an employer (who was a sophisticated cobalt user) but not the employee of the risks of dust inhalation,[33] and a supplier of naphtha who warned an employer of the chemical's combustability but did not warn the worker who was ultimately injured in an explosion.[34] The theory behind this defense is that the learned intermediary or sophisticated user is better able to make an "informed choice" and to tailor the warnings to meet the end user of the product.

The doctrine has come under fire in recent years, however, as drug manufacturers increasingly advertise their products to consumers. In April 1999, for example, the New Jersey Supreme Court ruled that if a manufacturer markets its products directly to consumers, it has a duty to warn consumers directly of the foreseeable risks associated with the drug.[35]

Statutes of Limitation/Statutes of Repose

Statutes of limitation require that a cause of action be brought within a certain time period (usually measured in a matter of a few years). Thus, if the plaintiff delays too long in filing the suit, she will be prevented by law from doing so. Breach of warranty actions are subject to the statute of limitations for contract claims. Generally, breach of warranty actions must be brought within four years after the cause of action has accrued, which is ordinarily the date at which the seller delivers the goods to the buyer.

In tort actions, the statute of limitations is usually two or three years. It does not begin to run, however, until the time of the injury or until the defect was or should have been discovered by the plaintiff. This may be many years after the purchase of the product. Thus, despite being shorter, the tort statute of limitations can actually be more favorable to the plaintiff than the breach of warranty statute of limitations in many instances.

Statutes of repose are state statutes that limit manufacturer and/or seller liability for defective goods to a specific time period. Most such statutes provide that the seller or manufacturer cannot be held liable for defects that manifest themselves after a certain time period, usually 10 to 12 years after purchase of the goods by the consumer. Thus, these statutes relieve sellers and manufacturers of liability for defects in older goods.

---

[31] Restatement (Third) of Torts: Products Liability § 4.
[32] Restatement (Second) of Torts § 402A .
[33] Tasca v. GTE Prods. Corp., 438 N.W.2d 625 (Mich. App. 1988).
[34] Whitehead v. Dycho Co., 775 S.W.2d 593 (Tenn. 1989).
[35] Perez v. Wyeth Laboratories, Inc., 734 A.2d 1245 (N.J. 1999).

Products Liability Reform

Tort reform in general, and products liability reform in particular, have been hot topics before state and federal legislatures for the past several years. In virtually every legislative session for the past two decades, a products liability reform bill has been introduced in Congress, though none has been successful. These bills would reform existing products liability law by providing for measures such as:

- making it more difficult to obtain punitive damage awards;
- capping the amount of punitive damages awarded in any one case; and
- shielding sellers from liability for manufacturing defects.

Many states have passed their own tort reform measures. These state laws generally limit recoveries (often by capping them at $250,000 or $500,000) for noneconomic losses, such as pain and suffering or mental or emotional distress. About two-thirds of the states restrict or limit the recovery of punitive damages. Some states also have statutes limiting the liability of nonmanufacturers.

International Products Liability Laws

Products liability laws typically develop in nations with economies marked by both mass production and mass consumption. In such settings, older, more traditional negligence standards cease to function well because they impose a difficult burden of proof on injured consumers. In the United States, with its common law tradition, the inequities that resulted from the negligence standard were reformed primarily through judicial decisions and the development of an extensive body of case law of products liability, including strict liability. In civil law nations, the movement from a products liability system based on negligence to one based on strict products liability has developed more commonly through legislation. Two of the more prominent recent legislative actions involved the European Union in 1985 and Japan in 1995.

European Union

On July 25, 1985, the members of the to-be-formed European Union sought to standardize products liability laws among the member states through promulgation of the *Products Liability Directive*.[36] The Directive itself does not have the force of law but, rather, requires the member nations to create legislation implementing the Directive's standards. Many member states, such as the United Kingdom, already had products liability laws and simply needed to conform those existing laws to the Directive. For nations that did not have products liability laws, however, the Directive provided an important model for the drafting of such legislation.

Article 1 of the Directive provides that the producer shall be strictly liable for damages caused by defects in its products. The Directive defines "producer" as the manufacturer of a finished product, producers of any raw materials used in the final product, and producers of components used in the assembly of the final product. A "product" is any physical property and goods, part of another product, or part of a fixture attached to real property.

Under Article 1, consumers do not have to prove that the producer is "at fault," nor do they have to demonstrate the existence of a contractual relationship (i.e., privity) between the consumer and the producer. The standard for determining the defectiveness of a product is the "lack of safety which the general public is entitled

---

[36] The full name of this directive is the *Council Directive on the Approximation of the Laws, Regulations, and Administrative Provisions of the Member States Concerning Liability for Defective Products.*

to expect," considering such factors as the presentation of the product, its reasonable use, and the time when the product was put into circulation. The Directive allows for many of the same defenses available in the United States, such as the state-of-the-art defense and a statute of repose.

Japan

On July 1, 1995, Japan's consumer protection laws moved from a negligence-based system to a strict products liability law through the implementation of the *Products Liability Law*. Formerly, Japan's negligence law required (1) damage, (2) a willful or negligent intention on behalf of the producer, and (3) a causal relationship between the defect in the product and the resulting damage. The Products Liability Law now provides for a strict liability cause of action that requires. (1) damage, (2) a defect in the product, and (3) a causal relationship between the defect and the damage. Japan had been heavily pressured to undertake such reforms by its major trading partners, who felt that the playing field needed to be leveled. The Products Liability Law embraces many of the concepts found in the EU Directive.

The Products Liability Law defines a "product" as a movable property that is manufactured or processed. The Japanese law explicitly excludes agricultural and game products and incorporeal (i.e., nonphysical) products, such as electricity and computer software. Liability extends to manufacturers, processors, importers, and any person or corporation who places its name or mark on the product, but it does not extend to mere "sellers."

"Defect" is defined in the Products Liability Law as "lack of safety that the product ordinarily should provide, taking into account the nature of the product, the ordinarily foreseeable manner and use of the product, the time when the manufacturer, etc. delivered the product, and other circumstances concerning the product." The Products Liability Law allows for a state-of-the-art defense. Producers of raw materials or components are explicitly exempted if they have produced their materials or components in compliance with the specifications given them by the manufacturer or assembler of the final product. In those situations, the final producer is liable under a cause of action similar to that of a design defect.

DISCUSSION CASES

10.1 Express Warranties—Creation and Disclaimer

Hayes v. Bering Sea Reindeer Products, 983 P.2d 1280 (Alaska 1999)

I. Introduction

North Coast Industries (NCI) contracted to purchase an aircraft from Bering Sea Reindeer Products but stopped making payments because the aircraft was defective. Bering Sea successfully sued NCI and its partners, including Michael Hayes, for breach of contract. Michael Hayes appeals on various grounds. * * * [W]e affirm the judgment against him.

II. Facts and Proceedings

NCI contracted to purchase a Beechcraft E-18 aircraft for $73,000 from Bering Sea, a tribal enterprise established by the Native Village of Mekoryuk. NCI intended to use the aircraft for commercial purposes. NCI claimed that after it made the $25,000 down payment and took possession, it discovered that the aircraft would require extensive repairs before it would pass Federal Aviation Administration (FAA) inspection. It made no further payments on the purchase price.

Bering Sea sued brothers Arthur and Michael Hayes individually and in their capacity as partners in NCI. * * *

Michael asserted defenses to Bering Sea's breach of contract claim and counterclaimed for breach of contract and misrepresentation. * * *

After a bench trial . . ., the trial court entered judgment against Michael on all claims. * * *

III. Discussion

* * * *

C. *Counterclaims*

We turn to Michael's counterclaims against Bering Sea for breach of contract. * * *

1. *Express warranties*

Michael contends that Bering Sea made and breached express warranties; Bering Sea counters that it explicitly disclaimed all express and implied warranties. The trial court held that Bering Sea made no warranty concerning the condition of the aircraft at the time of sale because Bering Sea expressly disavowed any warranty in the contract of sale.

Michael argues that Bering Sea made three express warranties during the sale negotiation. He first claims that Bering Sea made an express warranty about the aircraft's airworthiness by presenting its airworthiness certificate to NCI before the sale. Michael next contends that Will Sherman, a representative of Bering Sea, created an express warranty when he assured NCI that the aircraft would meet FAA standards and that it would easily pass inspection. Michael last asserts that Bering Sea made an express warranty that the aircraft would conform to a description Bering Sea faxed to NCI. He claims there were numerous disparities and defects, particularly in the radios, avionics systems, and anti-icing systems.

Denying that it made any express warranties, Bering Sea also argues that it disclaimed any express warranties it arguably made. The contract included the following disclaimer:

> Prior to entering into this agreement, buyer agrees that he has had ample opportunity to inspect aircraft and its logs, and acknowledges that he is purchasing aircraft with no warranty, either express or implied, as to the condition of the aircraft or its components.
>
> Seller states that they have in no way misrepresented the aircraft, its condition, and equipment, and have allowed buyer to make any reasonable "pre-buying" inspections of the aircraft. Seller further states that to the best of their knowledge the aircraft is being delivered in an airworthy condition.

We assume for the sake of discussion that, but for the disclaimer and the thorough pre-sale inspection opportunity, Bering Sea's actions could have created express warranties regarding the aircraft's condition. A description of the item to be sold or promise regarding its condition can create an express warranty under the Uniform Commercial Code as long as it forms part of the basis of the bargain. Such descriptions need not be verbal; technical specifications or documents such as airworthiness certificates can create warranties.

But we are not convinced that these representations formed part of the basis of the parties' bargain, or that the trial court erred in concluding that Bering Sea made no warranty concerning the condition of the aircraft "as of the time of sale." * * * Bering Sea offered NCI ample opportunity to inspect the aircraft, and NCI fully exercised this opportunity before it entered into the contract. A qualified airframe and powerplant mechanic selected by NCI inspected the aircraft on December 16 and 17, 1994. He observed numerous discrepancies between the faxed description and the actual condition of the aircraft and its components. He reported to Arthur Hayes his opinions concerning the condition of the aircraft and whether it could pass an FAA inspection. As a result of problems the mechanic perceived in the propellers during his inspection, NCI negotiated a lower purchase price.

Two days after completion of the inspection, NCI and Bering Sea entered into the contract on December 19. The first paragraph of the disclaimer refers to the inspection. This paragraph permits a conclusion that the inspection, not the prior fax or conversation with Sherman, formed the basis for NCI's understanding of the aircraft's condition. It also supports the trial court's conclusion that Bering Sea, at the time of sale, made no warranty of condition.

* * * *

A seller cannot negate express warranties through generalized disclaimers. But the clear, forceful, specific disclaimer in this contract defeats Michael's claim that Bering Sea made any enforceable express warranty. This is not a fine-print boilerplate disclaimer which NCI could not have negotiated or understood; it is a conspicuous, clearly written provision in a two-page contract between parties with equal bargaining power. Its recitation that the "buyer . . . had ample opportunity to inspect [the] aircraft and its logs" is not a mere formalism, but reflects NCI's actual conduct. We therefore conclude that it was both an enforceable disclaimer and evidence of the basis of the parties' bargain. The numerous discrepancies the mechanic observed and the clear language of the disclaimer could not have left NCI with any illusions that Bering Sea was warrantying the aircraft's condition. We therefore affirm the trial court's conclusion that Bering Sea "made no warranty concerning the condition of the subject aircraft as of the time of sale."

* * * *

IV. Conclusion

We AFFIRM the judgment.

Questions for Discussion for Case 10.1

1. Do you think that Sherman's statements that the aircraft would meet FAA standards and that it would easily pass inspection were statements of opinion or statements of fact? Why does this distinction matter?

2. Do you think that NCI relied primarily on the documents or on the inspection in purchasing this aircraft? Why is reliance important in this context?

3. What must a seller do in order to disclaim an express warranty?

4. If express warranties were important to this buyer, what should the buyer have done to ensure that such warranties existed?

10.2 Implied Warranty of Merchantability, Definition of "Merchant," Damages

Frantz v. Cantrell, 711 N.E.2d 856 (Ind. Ct. App. 1999)

Defendant-appellants Joseph R. Frantz and Frantz Lumber Co., Inc. (collectively "Frantz") appeal from the judgment in favor of plaintiff-appellee Bill Cantrell ("Cantrell") on his breach of implied warranty action. Frantz presents three issues for our review which we restate as follows:

  I.   Whether Frantz's sale of shingles to Cantrell gave rise to an implied warranty of merchantability.
  II. If the sale did give rise to an implied warranty of merchantability, whether the evidence was sufficient to support the trial court's finding that Frantz breached such warranty.
  III. If Frantz did breach such warranty, whether the evidence was sufficient to support the trial court's award of damages to Cantrell.

We affirm.

FACTS AND PROCEDURAL HISTORY

The facts most favorable to the trial court's determination reveal that in the summer of 1994, Cantrell entered into a contractual arrangement with Frantz, whereby Frantz agreed to install a new shingled roof on Cantrell's residence. At that time, Cantrell's only specification was that the shingles be of a good quality asphalt, as opposed to fiberglass shingles. The representative of Frantz obliged by selecting a particular brand of three-tabbed asphalt shingles which the lumber company routinely dealt with and which carried a twenty-year warranty from the manufacturer. The agreed upon price for the shingles and the installation of the new roof was $1,985.15.

Frantz completed the roof later that summer. Cantrell was initially satisfied with the work and with the shingles which had no apparent defects and paid Frantz for the work.

However, in the winter months following the installation, Cantrell noticed that some of the shingles were curling up at the edges and that the tabs of many of the shingles had failed to seal down properly. This caused Cantrell concern not only for the integrity of the roof, but its appearance as well.

Cantrell notified Frantz of the problem and a representative of Frantz came to Cantrell's home to inspect the shingles. Upon examining the roof, the representative noted that while the workmanship was competent, there was a problem with the shingles which he had never encountered before. The representative indicated he would contact the manufacturer of the shingles in an effort to determine an appropriate course of action.

In the months following Cantrell's initial inquiries, Frantz mailed a document to Cantrell which detailed a phenomenon known as "cold curl," a peculiarity to the type of asphalt shingles which had been used on Cantrell's roof. The document advised that this occurrence should correct itself when the roof warms up either by sunlight or an increase in the ambient temperature, but did not address the failure of a number of the shingles' tabs to seal down.

In light of this information, Cantrell waited until the summer of 1995 to see if the warmer weather would in fact remedy the problem. However, when the cold curl and defective sealing did not rectify itself with the increase in temperature, Cantrell again contacted Frantz in an attempt to resolve these issues. When that attempt failed, Cantrell filed his Complaint For Damages against Frantz, claiming breach of implied warranty for the sale of the defective shingles. Following a bench trial, the court entered its order of judgment against Frantz in the amount of $3,904.97, the cost of repair or replacement less the value and use of the installed roof. Frantz now appeals.

DISCUSSION AND DECISION

I. Implied Warranty of Merchantability

Frantz contends that absent evidence of a special relationship between Frantz and the manufacturer of the shingles, there can be no basis for a breach of implied warranty suit against Frantz. We cannot agree.

* * * *

Unless excluded or modified, a warranty that goods shall be merchantable is implied in all sales contracts if the seller is a merchant with respect to goods of that kind. IC 26-1-2-314(1). The warranty of merchantability arises out of the relationship between the buyer and the seller who is a merchant. An implied warranty of merchantability is imposed by operation of law for the protection of the buyer and must be liberally construed in favor of the buyer. To exclude this warranty, one must exercise special care. There is no requirement that any specific relationship between the seller and the manufacturer exist for the warranty to be implied.

Frantz next argues that it is not a "merchant" within the meaning of IC 26-1-2-314. A seller who makes casual or occasional sales of goods of a particular kind is not a merchant in those goods. Because a person making an isolated sale of goods is not a "merchant" within the scope of the Indiana UCC provision, no warranty of merchantability applies.

IC 26-1-2-104(1) defines "merchant" as "a person who deals in goods of the kind or otherwise by his occupation holds himself out as having knowledge or skill peculiar to the practices or goods involved in the transaction . . . ." Applying this definition here, we note that the Frantz family has been affiliated with the lumber company since 1910, and during those eighty-nine years it has sold more than just lumber. Indeed, its business accounting statements bear the phrase "ALL KINDS OF BUILDING MATERIAL" directly beneath the company logo. By Cantrell's own testimony, Frantz was the only establishment he approached to install the new roof on his house, because he had heard of the company's local reputation to do good construction and roofing work. Cantrell also testified that upon specifying he wanted asphalt shingles for his new roof, the representative from Frantz promptly advised that the lumber company did deal with an asphalt shingle which carried a twenty-year warranty. Moreover, the Record as a whole demonstrates Frantz to be extremely knowledgeable about the construction and installation of new roofs, and in turn, the shingles which are used during the course of such work, and supports the trial court's finding that Frantz was a merchant.

Frantz next invokes IC 26-1-2-316(3)(c) for the argument that it is excused from liability under the implied warranty of merchantability because of certain usages of trade prevalent in the roofing business. This statute provides in pertinent part that an implied warranty may be excluded or modified by usage of trade. A usage of trade is "any practice or method of dealing having such regularity of observance in a place, vocation or trade as to justify an expectation that it will be observed with respect to the transaction in question." IC 26-1-1-205(2). In support of its position, Frantz notes that Cantrell's own expert witness testified that a roofer traditionally does not provide any warranties as to the shingles themselves, and as such, argues that the implied warranty of merchantability is inapplicable in the instant case.

In *Martin Rispens & Son v. Hall Farms, Inc.*, 621 N.E.2d 1078 (Ind. 1993), our supreme court held that in order for the exception to be applicable, the usage of trade must be used in the vocation or trade in which both the contracting parties are engaged or be one of which both parties are or should be aware. Here, the parties in the present case are not in the same trade and there is no evidence that Cantrell was or should have been aware of the asserted usage of trade.

II. Breach of Implied Warranty of Merchantability

Because we find that the trial court did not err in its determination that an implied warranty of merchantability arose out of Frantz's sale of the asphalt shingles to Cantrell, the question becomes whether the evidence is sufficient to support the trial court's finding of a breach of that warranty. "Any action based on breach of warranty requires evidence showing not only the existence of the warranty but that the warranty was broken and that the breach of warranty was the proximate cause of the loss sustained." Frantz contends that the Record in this case does not contain any evidence to sustain a judgment against it for breach of implied warranty of merchantability. Again, we cannot agree.

* * * *

Here, the court determined that "the shingles were defective in that they would not seal properly causing curling of the edges. This curling of the edges resulted in a very unsightly roof with a great potential for failure at an early age." In opposition to the court's findings, Frantz contends that the sole purpose of shingles is to roof a house thereby securing the structure from the elements, and that because none of the shingles ever blew off or the roof had never leaked, there was no breach.

* * * [O]ur supreme court stated that a good may be defective as the result of some sort of imperfection or dereliction. The trial court's finding that the shingles in this case were defective is more than adequately supported by the evidence of their imperfections, namely, the curling and failure to seal. Shingles which fail to seal and which curl in an unsightly manner even in warm weather cannot be said to "conform to ordinary standards and . . . be of the same average grade, quality, and value as similar goods sold under similar circumstances." In addition, a roof which is not flat and smooth and whose shingles curl up at the edges and fail to seal cannot be said to "pass without objection in the trade," IC 26-1-2-314(2)(a), even if it does shield the structure from the elements. As such, the trial court's determination that Frantz breached the implied warranty of merchantability in its sale of shingles to Cantrell is supported by the Record and was not clearly erroneous.

III. Damages

Finally, Frantz argues that the evidence is insufficient to support the trial court's award of damages in the amount of $3,904.97. We disagree. IC 26-1-2-714(1) states that a buyer may recover compensatory damages resulting in the ordinary course of events from the seller's breach as determined in any manner which is reasonable. IC 26-1-2-715 further provides for the recovery of incidental and consequential damages which are reasonably foreseeable.

The evidence adduced at trial revealed that the condition of Cantrell's roof as a result of the defective shingles sold by Frantz had detracted from the value of Cantrell's entire property, in that the shingles were unsightly and gave the roof the appearance of being fifteen to twenty years old when in fact it was only four years old at the time of trial. Cantrell's witnesses testified that complete elimination of the curling shingles which had failed to seal was the only remedy available to cure this problem. Moreover, the entire roof required replacement. The roof would have to be stripped of two layers of shingles and completely redone, a reasonably foreseeable consequence of the installation of the faulty shingles in question.

Based on this testimony, Cantrell submitted an estimate for the replacement of the roof at $4,897.55, a usual and customary bid amount for this type of work in his particular locale. There was no evidence offered by Frantz to the contrary. Thereafter, the court determined that Frantz should be credited for the value and use of the installed roof which Cantrell had received up to the time of trial, which was calculated at 50% of the original purchase price of the new roof, or $992.58.

As such, the court's judgment against Frantz for its breach of implied warranty of merchantability in the amount of $3,904.97 was reasonable and comports with UCC guidelines. The evidence in the Record is more than sufficient to support such an award and the trial court's determination was not clearly erroneous.

We affirm.

Questions for Discussion for Case 10.2

1. What two types of implied warranties arise under the UCC? Which is implicated here? Why?

2. Why does the court find that there was a breach of implied warranty?

3. Was the seller a "merchant" for purposes of the UCC? Why, or why not?

10.3 Products Liability—Negligence, Strict Liability
Gaines-Tabb v. ICI Explosives, USA, Inc., 160 F.3d 613 (10th Cir. 1998)

Individuals injured by the April 19, 1995, bombing of the Alfred P. Murrah Federal Building ("Murrah Building") in Oklahoma City, Oklahoma, filed suit against the manufacturers of the ammonium nitrate allegedly used to create the bomb. * * * The district court dismissed the complaint for failure to state a claim upon which relief may be granted, and the plaintiffs appealed. We affirm.

* * * *

BACKGROUND

On April 19, 1995, a massive bomb exploded in Oklahoma City and destroyed the Murrah Building, causing the deaths of 168 people and injuries to hundreds of others. On May 10, 1995, plaintiffs filed this diversity action, on behalf of themselves and all persons who incurred personal injuries during, or may claim loss of consortium or wrongful death resulting from, the bombing, against ICI Explosives ("ICI"), ICI's parent company, Imperial Chemical Industries, PLC, and another of Imperial Chemical's subsidiaries, ICI Canada.

ICI manufactures ammonium nitrate ("AN"). Plaintiffs allege that AN can be either "explosive grade" or "fertilizer grade." According to plaintiffs, "explosive-grade" AN is of low density and high porosity so it will absorb sufficient amounts of fuel or diesel oil to allow detonation of the AN, while "fertilizer-grade" AN is of high density and low porosity and so is unable to absorb sufficient amounts of fuel or diesel oil to allow detonation.

Plaintiffs allege that ICI sold explosive-grade AN mislabeled as fertilizer-grade AN to Farmland Industries, who in turn sold it to Mid-Kansas Cooperative Association in McPherson, Kansas. Plaintiffs submit that a "Mike Havens" purchased a total of eighty 50-pound bags of the mislabeled AN from Mid-Kansas. According to plaintiffs, "Mike Havens" was an alias used either by Timothy McVeigh or Terry Nichols, the two men tried for the bombing. Plaintiffs further allege that the perpetrators of the Oklahoma City bombing used the 4000 pounds of explosive-grade AN purchased from Mid-Kansas, mixed with fuel oil or diesel oil, to demolish the Murrah Building.

* * * *

ANALYSIS

* * * *

I. Negligence

Plaintiffs allege that ICI was negligent in making explosive-grade AN available to the perpetrators of the Murrah Building bombing. Under Oklahoma law, the three essential elements of a claim of negligence are: "(1) a duty owed by the defendant to protect the plaintiff from injury, (2) a failure to properly perform that duty, and (3) the plaintiff's injury being proximately caused by the defendant's breach." The district court held that ICI did not have a duty to protect plaintiffs and that ICI's actions or inactions were not the proximate cause of plaintiffs' injuries. Although causation is generally a question of fact, "the question becomes an issue of law when there is no evidence from which a jury could reasonably find the required proximate, causal nexus between the careless act and the resulting injuries." Because we determine that there is a failure of causation as a matter of law, we need not discuss whether under Oklahoma law defendants owed plaintiffs a duty of care.

* * * Under Oklahoma law, "the causal nexus between an act of negligence and the resulting injury will be deemed broken with the intervention of a new, independent and efficient cause which was neither anticipated nor reasonably foreseeable." Such an intervening cause is known as a "supervening cause." To be considered a supervening cause, an intervening cause must be: (1) independent of the original act; (2) adequate by itself to bring about the injury; and (3) not reasonably foreseeable. "When the intervening act is intentionally tortious or criminal, it is more likely to be considered independent."

"A third person's intentional tort is a supervening cause of the harm that results—even if the actor's negligent conduct created a situation that presented the opportunity for the tort to be committed—unless the actor realizes or should realize the likelihood that the third person might commit the tortious act." If "the intervening act is a reasonably foreseeable consequence of the primary negligence, the original wrongdoer will not be relieved of liability." * * *

Oklahoma has looked to the Restatement (Second) of Torts § 448 for assistance in determining whether the intentional actions of a third party constitute a supervening cause of harm. Section 448 states:

> The act of a third person in committing an intentional tort or crime is a superseding cause of harm to another resulting therefrom, although the actor's negligent conduct created a situation which afforded an opportunity to the third person to commit such a tort or crime, unless the actor at the time of his negligent conduct realized or should have realized the likelihood that such a situation might be created, and that a third person might avail himself of the opportunity to commit such a tort or crime.

Comment b to § 448 provides further guidance in the case before us. * * * [U]nder comment b, the criminal acts of a third party may be foreseeable if (1) the situation provides a temptation to which a "recognizable percentage" of persons would yield, or (2) the temptation is created at a place where "persons of a peculiarly vicious type are likely to be." There is no indication that a peculiarly vicious type of person is likely to frequent the Mid-Kansas Co-op, so we shall turn our attention to the first alternative.

We have found no guidance as to the meaning of the term "recognizable percentage" as used in § 448, comment b. However, we believe that the term does not require a showing that the mainstream population or the majority would yield to a particular temptation; a lesser number will do. Equally, it does not include merely the law-abiding population. In contrast, we also believe that the term is not satisfied by pointing to the existence of a small fringe group or the occasional irrational individual, even though it is foreseeable generally that such groups and individuals will exist.

We note that plaintiffs can point to very few occasions of successful terrorist actions using ammonium nitrate, in fact only two instances in the last twenty-eight years—a 1970 bombing at the University of Wisconsin-Madison and the bombing of the Murrah Building. Due to the apparent complexity of manufacturing an ammonium nitrate bomb, including the difficulty of acquiring the correct ingredients (many of which are not widely available), mixing them properly, and triggering the resulting bomb, only a small number of persons would be able to carry out a crime such as the bombing of the Murrah Building. We simply do not believe that this is a group which rises to the level of a "recognizable percentage" of the population.

As a result, we hold that as a matter of law it was not foreseeable to defendants that the AN that they distributed to the Mid-Kansas Co-op would be put to such a use as to blow up the Murrah Building. Because the conduct of the bomber or bombers was unforeseeable, independent of the acts of defendants, and adequate by itself to bring about plaintiffs' injuries, the criminal activities of the bomber or bombers acted as the supervening cause of plaintiffs' injuries. Because of the lack of proximate cause, plaintiffs have failed to state a claim for negligence.

* * * *

III. Manufacturers' products liability

Plaintiffs assert that ICI is strictly liable for manufacturing a defective product. We read their complaint as alleging both that the AN was defectively designed because, as designed, it was more likely to provide explosive force than an alternative formula, and that ICI failed to issue adequate warnings to Mid-Kansas that the AN was explosive grade rather than fertilizer grade so that Mid-Kansas could take appropriate precautions in selling the AN.

"In Oklahoma, a party proceeding under a strict products liability theory—referred to as manufacturer's products liability—must establish three elements: (1) that the product was the cause of the injury, (2) that the defect existed in the product at the time it left the manufacturer, retailer, or supplier's control, and (3) that the defect made the product unreasonably dangerous." "Unreasonably dangerous" means "dangerous to an extent beyond that which would be contemplated by the ordinary consumer who purchases it, with the ordinary knowledge common to the community as to its characteristics." A product may be unreasonably dangerous

because it is defectively designed or manufactured, or because it is not accompanied by the proper warnings regarding use of the product.

As the basis of their defective design claim plaintiffs contend that ICI could have made the AN safer by using an alternate formulation or incorporating additives to prevent the AN from detonating. Plaintiffs' suggestion that the availability of alternative formulas renders ICI strictly liable for its product contradicts Oklahoma law. "Apparently, the plaintiff would hold the manufacturer responsible if his product is not as safe as some other product on the market. That is not the test in these cases. Only when a defect in the product renders it less safe than expected by the ordinary consumer will the manufacturer be held responsible." The "ordinary consumer" is "one who would be foreseeably expected to purchase the product involved." As plaintiffs acknowledge, the ordinary consumer of AN branded as fertilizer is a farmer. There is no indication that ICI's AN was less safe than would be expected by a farmer.

Similarly, plaintiffs have failed to state a claim regarding ICI's alleged failure to warn Mid-Kansas that the AN was explosive grade rather than fertilizer grade. "Under Oklahoma law, a manufacturer may have a duty to warn consumers of potential hazards which occur from the use of its product." If the manufacturer does not fulfill this duty, the product may be unreasonably dangerous. Interpreting Oklahoma law, this court has held that the duty to warn extends only to "ordinary consumers and users of the products." Under this rationale, defendants had no duty to warn the suppliers of its product of possible criminal misuse.

* * * *

CONCLUSION

We AFFIRM the dismissal of plaintiffs' complaint for failure to state a claim upon which relief may be granted.

Questions for Discussion for Case 10.3

1. Products liability typically arises under state law. Why is this case being heard in federal court? What law does the court apply—federal or state?

2. The court determines that the defendant is not liable in negligence because there is no proximate causation between the plaintiff's injury and the defendant's breach. Explain.

3. The court also determines that the defendant is not strictly liable for the plaintiff's injuries. Why? What

two types of strict liability claims does the plaintiff allege?

4. If the use of AN fertilizer as an explosive device is widely published on the Internet, do you think that such a use would then be reasonably foreseeable? If a manufacturer's product is used by a third party in a way that was unforeseen and someone is injured as a result, do you think that the manufacturer loses the defense that the use was unforeseeable in future lawsuits involving similar conduct by other third parties?

10.4 Products Liability—Strict Liability, Negligence, Warranty

The American Tobacco Co. v. Grinnell, 951 S.W.2d 420 (Tex. 1997)

In this wrongful death case, we confront an issue with profound health and public policy consequences: whether "common knowledge" of the health risks of cigarette smoking relieves tobacco companies of any duty to warn smokers of those risks. [W]e conclude that the defendant has conclusively established the defense of common knowledge with regard to the general health risks of smoking. We also conclude, however, that the defendant has not conclusively established the common knowledge defense with regard to the addictive nature of cigarettes. Accordingly, we conclude that the defendant is entitled to summary judgment on most, but not all of the plaintiffs' claims, and remand the surviving claims to the trial court for further proceedings.

In 1952, nineteen-year-old Wiley Grinnell began smoking Lucky Strikes, cigarettes manufactured by the American Tobacco Company. Almost a year later, Grinnell changed to Pall Malls, also manufactured by American. After smoking for approximately thirty-three years, Grinnell was diagnosed with lung cancer in July 1985. Shortly thereafter, he filed this lawsuit. He died less than a year later. Grinnell's family continued this suit after his death, adding wrongful death and survival claims. The family alleges that American failed to warn of, and actively concealed, facts that it knew or should have known, including the facts that Grinnell could quickly become addicted to cigarettes and that his smoking could result in injury or death from the cancer-causing ingredients if he used the cigarettes as American intended. They also allege that, even though American knew or should have known that its cigarettes were dangerous and could not be used safely, American represented to consumers that cigarettes were not harmful, dangerous, or capable of causing injury.

* * * The gravamen of [the Grinnells'] complaint is that Grinnell began smoking because American did not warn him of the potential dangers of smoking, and once he began smoking he could not stop because he became addicted to cigarettes.

* * * The trial court granted all three motions [for summary judgment filed by American] and dismissed the Grinnells' suit. The court of appeals reversed the trial court's judgment and remanded the entire case. [The case is now on appeal before the Texas Supreme Court.]

* * * *

I. Common-Law Duties

A. *Strict Liability*

The Grinnells allege that cigarettes are both defective and unreasonably dangerous under section 402A of the Restatement (Second) of Torts. Specifically, they assert that American's cigarettes are (1) defectively designed because ingredients found in cigarettes cause cancer, addiction, and disease, (2) defectively marketed, because the cigarette packages contain inadequate warnings, and (3) defectively manufactured because cigarettes contain pesticide residue. In his deposition taken one month before his death, Grinnell testified that had he known of the dangers inherent in cigarettes he would never have started smoking in the first place.

* * * We address each of the Grinnells' claims in turn.

1. *Marketing Defect*

A defendant's failure to warn of a product's potential dangers when warnings are required is a type of marketing defect. * * * Generally, a manufacturer has a duty to warn if it knows or should know of the potential harm to a user because of the nature of its product. Nevertheless, this Court has recognized that there is no duty to warn when the risks associated with a particular product are matters "within the ordinary knowledge common to the community." American argues that it had no duty to warn Grinnell of the risks associated with smoking its cigarettes because the dangers of smoking were common knowledge when Grinnell began smoking in 1952.

* * * *

Common knowledge * * * connotes a general societal understanding of the risks inherent in a specific product or class of products. * * *

[C]ommon knowledge is an extraordinary defense that applies only in limited circumstances. As the court in [*Brune v. Brown Forman Corp.*, 758 S.W.2d 827, 830–31 (Tex. App. 1988)] noted, common knowledge encompasses only those things "so patently obvious and so well known to the community generally, that there can be no question or dispute concerning their existence." * * *

* * * *

The party asserting the common-knowledge defense must establish that the dangers attributable to alcohol, tobacco, or other products were a matter of common knowledge when the consumer began using the product. Based on the summary judgment record, we hold American established that the general ill-effects of smoking were commonly known when Grinnell started smoking in 1952. However, we also hold that American did not establish that the addictive quality of cigarettes was commonly known when Grinnell began smoking in 1952.

Regarding the general health risks associated with smoking, the Tennessee Supreme Court held as early as 1898 that these risks were "generally known." * * * Other early courts also recognized the harmful effects of smoking cigarettes. More recently, courts have similarly acknowledged that the inherent dangers of smoking cigarettes are within the community's common knowledge.

Moreover, by 1962, when the Surgeon General's advisory committee began examining the health risks associated with smoking, there were already more than seven thousand publications of professional and general circulation examining the relationship between smoking and health. Of these publications, articles published in nationally circulated magazines dating back to the early 1900s informed readers about the deleterious effects of smoking.

During this same period, many books examined the health risks associated with smoking and argued against the use of cigarettes. These books and articles published before 1952 indicate that the general dangers of smoking were common knowledge even before Grinnell began smoking.

Not only does historical evidence illustrate the public's pre-1952 awareness of smoking's dangerous effects, but the Grinnells' experts also confirmed that the health hazards of smoking were common knowledge when Grinnell began smoking. * * *

We conclude that the general health dangers attributable to cigarettes were commonly known as a matter of law by the community when Grinnell began smoking. We cannot conclude, however, that the specific danger of nicotine addiction was common knowledge when Grinnell began smoking. Addiction is a danger apart from the direct physical dangers of smoking because the addictive nature of cigarettes multiplies the likelihood of and contributes to the smoker's ultimate injury, in Grinnell's case, lung cancer. This Court has also recognized the seriousness of addiction and the need for manufacturers to warn of this danger in the context of prescription drugs. We acknowledge that some authorities support the proposition that some members of the community associated addiction with smoking cigarettes earlier in this century.

The Surgeon General spoke to the addictive nature of tobacco in the most recent and comprehensive report on the subject in 1988. In that report, the Surgeon General concluded that: (1) cigarettes and other forms of tobacco are addicting, (2) nicotine is the drug in tobacco that causes addiction, and (3) the pharmacologic and behavioral processes that determine tobacco addiction are similar to those that determine addiction to drugs such as heroin and cocaine. More recently, the Food and Drug Administration has concluded that tobacco products are addictive.

But we cannot simply assume that common knowledge of the general health risks of tobacco use naturally includes common knowledge of tobacco's addictive quality. Indeed, as David Kessler, former head of the FDA, has pointed out:

> Before 1980, when FDA last considered its jurisdiction over tobacco products, no major public health organization had determined that nicotine was an addictive drug. Today, however, *all* major public health organizations in the United States and abroad with expertise in tobacco or drug addiction recognize that the nicotine delivered by cigarettes and smokeless tobacco is addictive.

Kessler et al., *The Legal and Scientific Basis for FDA's Assertion of Jurisdiction over Cigarettes and Smokeless Tobacco*, 277 JAMA 405, 406 (1997). * * * Thus, unlike the general dangers associated with smoking, as late as 1988 and certainly in 1952, the danger of addiction from smoking cigarettes was not widely known and recognized in the community in general, or, particularly, by children or adolescents. * * *

* * * *

Because we conclude that American did not conclusively establish that the danger of addiction to nicotine was common knowledge, the Grinnells may maintain their strict liability marketing defect claims to the extent they are based on the addictive qualities of cigarettes, if no other defenses defeat those claims.

* * * *

2. Design Defect

The duty to design a safe product is "an obligation imposed by law." Whether a seller has breached this duty, that is, whether a product is unreasonably dangerous, is a question of fact for the jury. In determining whether a product is defectively designed, the jury must conclude that the product is unreasonably dangerous as designed, taking into consideration the utility of the product and the risk involved in its use.

In [*Turner v. General Motors Corp.*, 584 S.W.2d 844, 848 (Tex. 1979)], we held that evidence of the following factors of risk and utility were admissible in design defect cases: (1) the utility of the product to the user and to the public as a whole weighed against the gravity and likelihood of injury from its use; (2) the availability of a substitute product which would meet the same need and not be unsafe or unreasonably expensive; (3) the manufacturer's ability to eliminate the unsafe character of the product without seriously impairing its usefulness or significantly increasing its costs; (4) the user's anticipated awareness of the dangers inherent in the product and their avoidability because of general public knowledge of the obvious condition of the product, or of the existence of suitable warnings or instructions; and (5) the expectations of the ordinary consumer.

American argues that the common-knowledge defense bars the Grinnells' design defect claims as a matter of law. But, as we stated in *Turner*, "the user's anticipated awareness of the dangers inherent in the product and their avoidability because of general public knowledge of the obvious condition of the product," and "the expectations of the ordinary consumer," are but two factors for the jury to consider when determining whether a product was defectively designed. * * * Accordingly, American's attempt to invoke the common-knowledge defense in the context of an alleged design defect is without merit.

Alternatively, American argues that it is entitled to summary judgment because no safer alternative cigarette design exists. In *Turner*, we held that "the availability of a substitute product which would meet the same need and not be unsafe or unreasonably expensive," was one factor for juries to consider when determining whether a product was defectively designed. We reaffirmed this holding in *Caterpillar, Inc. v. Shears*, [911 S.W.2d 379 (Tex. 1995)], by stating that "if there are no safer alternatives, a product is not unreasonably dangerous as a matter of law." Accordingly, if there is no safer alternative to the cigarette manufactured by American, then its cigarettes are not unreasonably dangerous as a matter of law.

The Grinnells assert that American's cigarettes could have been made reasonably safer by filtration, and by reducing the amount of tobacco, tar, nicotine, and toxins in them. In making its argument that no reasonably safer alternative design exists, American relies on the testimony of the Grinnells' experts, Drs. Greenberg, Stevens, and Ginzel. These experts testified that Grinnell would have developed cancer and died regardless of whether filters, lower tar, or less tobacco had been used. * * *

Ultimately, the Grinnells essentially concede that no reasonably safer alternatives exist, but argue that all cigarettes are defective and unreasonably dangerous nonetheless. Because American conclusively proved that no reasonably safer alternative design exists for its cigarettes, we hold that summary judgment was proper on all of the Grinnells' design defect claims, including those based on the addictive quality of cigarettes.

3. Manufacturing Defect

We turn next to the Grinnells' strict liability claim based on a manufacturing defect. The Grinnells assert that American's products were defectively manufactured because they contained carcinogens and other toxic chemicals, including pesticide residue. During discovery, the Grinnells obtained internal documents showing that American fumigated its Turkish tobacco with Acritet 34, a chemical composed of acrylonitrile and carbon tetrachloride. American uses Turkish tobacco in all of its cigarettes. In 1978, American circulated a memorandum noting new government regulations requiring all materials containing acrylonitrile to be affixed with a "Cancer Hazard" warning label. Likewise, the Grinnells allege that American knew that methyl bromide pesticide residue remained in its tobacco after fumigation. The Grinnells alleged that this potentially cancerous pesticide residue contributed to Grinnell's cancer and resulting death.

Under Texas law, a plaintiff has a manufacturing defect claim when a finished product deviates, in terms of its construction or quality, from the specifications or planned output in a manner that renders it unreasonably dangerous. The common-knowledge defense does not apply to this type of claim because a user does not anticipate a manufacturing defect. This type of defect is a deviation from the planned output.

American, conceding that its cigarettes contain pesticide residue, argues that summary judgment was proper because all cigarette manufacturers fumigate their tobacco with some type of pesticide, and residue inevitably remains after fumigation. Thus, American concludes that the Grinnells' claims based on the presence of pesticide residue are actually design defect claims masquerading as manufacturing defect claims.

According to the undisputed facts, pesticide residue is incidentally, yet normally, found in tobacco after it is fumigated. The presence of pesticide residue is not an anomaly attributable only to the cigarettes Grinnell smoked. Nevertheless, the fact that all cigarettes potentially contain pesticide residue does not transform the Grinnells' manufacturing defect claim into a design defect claim subject to the common-knowledge defense. Simply because certain precautions or improvements in manufacturing technology, which could eliminate pesticide residue from cigarettes, are universally disregarded by an entire industry does not excuse their omission. Although pesticide residue may be found in many if not all cigarettes, it is not an ingredient American intended to incorporate into its cigarettes. Analyzed in this light, the presence of pesticide residue could be a manufacturing defect, not a design defect. Therefore, American did not conclusively negate the existence of a defect in its cigarettes.

* * * *

B. Implied Warranty

Next, we consider the Grinnells' implied warranty claims. We hold that the common-knowledge defense applies and bars these claims to the extent they relate to the general health risks of cigarettes. The Grinnells' implied warranty claims stem from the allegation that American impliedly warranted that its cigarettes were merchantable and fit for their intended purpose. The Grinnells allege that American's cigarettes are neither merchantable nor fit for their intended purpose because they are not safe for human consumption, cause injury to the user, and are addictive. * * * Knowledge common to the community about a certain product is also a factor that must be considered when deciding whether an implied warranty exists.

An implied warranty contrary to the community's common knowledge cannot exist. Because the general health dangers of cigarettes are commonly known by the community, no expectation of safety arises with respect to cigarettes when they are purchased. As American established the common-knowledge defense for the general health risks associated with cigarettes as a matter of law, it also conclusively negated the claims asserting that it impliedly warranted that its cigarettes were safe for consumption. To the extent this claim relates to the general health risks of cigarettes, summary judgment was proper. However, as we explained above, American did not conclusively establish that the danger of nicotine addiction was common knowledge in 1952. The common-knowledge defense does not preclude the Grinnells' implied warranty claims to the extent they relate to the addictive quality of cigarettes.

* * * *

D. *Negligence*

We next consider the Grinnells' claims for negligent design, manufacture, testing, and failure to warn. The Grinnells' negligent design and manufacturing claims are conceptually distinguishable from the strict liability claims. While strict liability focuses on the condition of the product, "negligence looks at the acts of the manufacturer and determines if it exercised ordinary care in design and production." Negligent design and manufacturing claims are predicated on the existence of a safer alternative design for the product. Absent an alternative design, a claim for negligent design or manufacturing fails as a matter of law. As we previously discussed, American conclusively proved that no reasonably safer alternative design exists for its cigarettes. Accordingly, the Grinnells cannot maintain their claims for negligent manufacturing and design as a matter of law.

Questions for Discussion for Case 10.4

1. The court determines that the defendant is entitled to summary judgment on part of the plaintiff's "marketing defect" claims but not on all. What distinction does the court draw, and why?

2. The court refers to the risk/utility test in discussing the plaintiff's design defect claim. What is this test and

Additionally, as we held above, American conclusively established the common-knowledge defense with regard to the general health risks associated with smoking. Therefore, summary judgment was proper on the Grinnells' negligent failure to warn claim to the extent it relates to the general health risks of smoking. The Grinnells' negligent testing claim is predicated on American's duty to test and ascertain the dangers inherent in its products about which it must warn consumers. Because the negligent testing claim is inextricably intertwined with the Grinnells' negligent failure to warn claim, we hold that summary judgment was also proper on this claim to the extent it relates to the general health risks of cigarettes. However, American did not conclusively establish that the specific danger of addiction was knowledge common to the community in 1952. Accordingly, the common-knowledge defense does not preclude the Grinnells' pre-1969* negligent failure to warn and negligent testing claims to the extent these claims relate to the addictive qualities of cigarettes and are not preempted by federal law.

* * * *

III. Conclusion

To summarize, the following of the Grinnells' claims survive summary judgment: pre-1969 strict liability marketing defect, pre-1969 negligent failure to warn, and pre-1969 negligent testing to the extent these claims relate to the addictive quality of cigarettes; the implied warranty claims relating to the addictive quality of cigarettes to the extent they arose within four years before the Grinnells filed suit; and the manufacturing defect claim to the extent that it is based on the alleged addictive nature of cigarettes. Accordingly, we reverse in part and affirm in part the judgment of the court of appeals, and remand the Grinnells' surviving claims to the trial court for further proceedings.

* [The federal Public Health Cigarette Smoking Act, which took effect in 1969, preempts claims arising after 1969 based on failure-to-warn or on misrepresentations designed to neutralize the effect of federally-mandated warnings on cigarette packages.—*Ed.*]

how does it apply in these circumstances? Do you think that the fact that no safer alternative cigarette designs are available means that the product is not defectively designed? What incentive does such a holding give to companies to improve products?

3. The defendant repeatedly raises the "common knowledge" defense. What is this defense? To which claims does the court find it applicable?

4. How does the court distinguish between strict liability and negligence claims?

5. Does this opinion resolve the dispute between these parties? Where does this case go next?

6. In your opinion, if a product is correctly designed for its particular purpose, but the purpose is of little social utility, should courts make a more concentrated effort to focus on the lack of social utility or instead focus on making sure that the public is adequately warned of the product's dangers?

DISCUSSION QUESTIONS

1. Donald Josue Jr. was rendered paraplegic as a result of a single-vehicle accident in which he was ejected from the bed of an Isuzu pickup truck. Josue sued Isuzu, the manufacturer of the truck, asserting, among other things, that Isuzu was liable for (1) negligent failure to warn and (2) strict liability for failure to warn. Both claims were based on the allegation that the pickup truck was defectively designed because it did not contain a warning label informing users of the truck of the dangers associated with riding in the bed of the truck. How does negligent failure to warn differ from strict liability failure to warn? How should the court rule in this case? *Josue v. Isuzu Motors America, Inc.*, 958 P.2d 535 (Haw. 1998).

2. David Weiner was transporting a 54-inch long, 180-pound canister of nitrous oxide (to use in inflating balloons), which he took to rock concerts in his girlfriend's two-door, hatchback Acura. Weiner flipped down the back of the rear seats to make room for the canister. He suffered personal injuries when he hit a guardrail and the unrestrained canister slid into the back of the driver's seat, pinning him between the seat and the shoulder harness. Weiner sued the manufacturers and sellers of the Acura on two strict liability theories: (1) design defect (because the front seats could not withstand the impact of a 180-pound object and because no restraints were provided to secure the cargo) and (2) failure to warn. How should the court rule on these claims? *Weiner v. American Honda Motor Co.*, 718 A.2d 305 (Pa. Super. 1998).

3. Werner Co. manufactures an eight-foot aluminum stepladder, which passed the safety standards of the ANSI and the Underwriter's Laboratory, two independent organizations that evaluate stepladders. Daniel Gawenda was injured when he fell from one of these ladders. He sued Werner, alleging that Werner's failure to build more rigid rear rails into the stepladder constituted negligent design. Gawenda offered no evidence of a stepladder that used more rigid rear rails than Werner's, nor did his expert present evidence describing the feasibility of alternative designs. How should the court rule on Werner's negligence claim? *Gawenda v. Werner Co.*, 127 F.3d 1102 (6th Cir. 1997).

4. Mr. and Mrs. Holowaty, a Canadian couple, stopped at McDonald's for breakfast while traveling through Rochester, Minnesota. Mr. Holowaty purchased a cup of coffee containing the warnings "HOT!" and "CAUTION: CONTENTS HOT" on both the lid and the cup. McDonald's requires its franchises to serve their coffee at between 175 and 185 degrees in containers carrying such warnings. Mrs. Holowaty sat in the passenger seat with the beverage tray on her lap. While exiting the parking lot, the coffee tipped and spilled half its contents on Mrs. Holowaty, causing second-degree burns to her thighs and permanent scars. Mr. and Mrs. Holowaty sued McDonald's as the franchisor, alleging that the coffee was defective because it was excessively hot and because McDonald's failed to provide adequate warnings about the severity of burns that could result. Although the Holowatys admitted that they knew that the coffee would be hot and could cause burns, they argue that reasonable consumers would not anticipate second-degree burns. How should the court rule on their claim? *Holowaty v. McDonald's Corp.*, 10 F. Supp. 2d 1078 (D. Minn. 1998).

5. K2 Corporation, a subsidiary of Anthony Industries, marketed the "Dan Donnelly XTC," a snowboard without predrilled holes for bindings. Without such a pattern, purchasers could install their choice of any bindings by simply screwing them into a fiberglass retention panel in the snowboard's core. Hyjek purchased this model and was injured in March 1991 when his binding came loose from the snowboard, striking him inside his left ankle. In 1993, he sued Anthony Industries, claiming that the design was not reasonably safe and the system of threaded screws was a foreseeably inadequate and unsafe binding retention method. In 1992, K2 had begun to design a new system involving "through-core inserts" molded into the snowboard. Fine threaded screws were then screwed into the inserts to hold the bindings in place. Hyjek sought to enter into evidence K2's subsequent change in design to support his claim for design defect. Should the judge allow the evidence into trial? *Hyjek v. Anthony Industries*, 944 P.2d 1036 (Wash. 1997).

6. Larry Moss purchased a Crosman 760 Pumpmaster BB gun from a local K-Mart store for his seven-year-old son Josh. Larry saw a warning on the box that stated "May cause death or injury" but thought that it might refer just to birds or small animals. The box also contained the following warning, which Larry did not read:

> WARNING: NOT A TOY. ADULT SUPERVISION REQUIRED. MISUSE OR CARELESS USE MAY CAUSE SERIOUS INJURY OR DEATH. MAY BE DANGEROUS UP TO 475 YARDS (435 METERS). THIS AIR GUN IS INTENDED FOR USE BY THOSE 16 YEARS OF AGE OR OLDER. FOR COMPLETE OPERATING INSTRUCTIONS, REVIEW OWNERS MANUAL INSIDE BOX BEFORE USING THIS AIR GUN.

Additional warnings and flyers were contained inside the box, but Larry did not read them before allowing Josh to use the gun. Larry's instructions to Josh on the proper use of the gun indicated that Larry was aware that the gun could be dangerous if misused, however.

Josh and his cousin Tim were playing with the gun in the woods. Josh hid behind a tree about 15 feet in front of Tim and stuck his head out from behind the tree just as Tim fired. The BB pierced Josh's eye, entered his brain, and killed him. Josh's parents brought a suit against Crosman Corp. and K-Mart Corp., alleging that the defendants caused Josh's death by failing to provide adequate warnings detailing the dangers associated with the gun. How should the court rule on this claim? *Moss v. Crosman Corp.*, 136 F.3d 1169 (7th Cir. 1998).

7. Greg Presto's mental illness was being treated with Clozaril, an antipsychotic medication manufactured by Sandoz Pharmaceuticals Corp. Because Clozaril can damage a patient's immune system, pharmacists and nurses at Caremark, Inc., a distributor of the drug, dispensed the medicine, drew Greg's blood each week, monitored the results of those tests, and provided the results to Dr. Warren, the prescribing physician. The Clozaril helped Greg's condition, but it had undesirable side effects. Greg and his mother requested that Greg be taken off the medication, and Dr. Warren allegedly agreed. In August 1991, Greg stopped taking the medication, but he failed to heed the warning included in the drug's packaging to gradually reduce the dosage over a one- or two-week period lest the patient's psychotic symptoms recur. Greg committed suicide. The Prestos sued Sandoz, alleging that the manufacturer failed to warn Greg of the dangers he faced if he discontinued use of the drug suddenly. What defense might Sandoz raise? How should the court rule on this claim? *Presto v. Sandoz Pharmaceuticals Corp.*, 487 S.E.2d 70 (Ga. App. 1997).

8. In early October 1989, Sandra Ruffin purchased "Compelling Everglade" carpet, manufactured by Salem Carpet Mills, Inc. (which later merged with Shaw Industries). The store manager told Ruffin that the carpet "was a higher quality carpet than what she brought in [to the store]" and that she was getting "a very good grade of material." Ruffin alleges that shortly after she purchased the carpet and had it installed, she and her minor daughter began experiencing physical symptoms such as nosebleeds, rashes, extreme sweating, chills, sleeplessness, and racing of the heart. After repeated complaints, the store removed the carpet from her home less than a month after its installation. Ruffin alleges that she and her daughter have suffered severe toxic injuries as a result of the chemicals in the carpet installed in her house and asserts a claim for breach of express warranty. Has an express warranty been created? *Ruffin v. Shaw Industries, Inc.*, 149 F.3d 294 (4th Cir. 1998).

9. Skip Wright, a firefighter with 13 years' experience, was operating a Stang deck gun attached to a fire engine while extinguishing a fire. During the course of the fire, the water reaching the water cannon had to be routed from the hydrant through the truck's water pump. The extreme pressure created an unusual force, called a "water hammer," where the force of the water is four to six times greater than normal, detaching the water cannon from the truck and throwing Wright into the air. He landed on the ground with the water cannon falling on top of him. Wright brought suit under a failure-to-warn theory. Stang argued that anyone familiar with fire apparatus would recognize the risk of a water hammer. Stang did not produce evidence to the court that it had provided any warnings regarding the potential hazards of a water hammer. How should the court resolve this dispute? *Wright v. Stang Manufacturing Co.*, 54 Cal. App. 4th 1218.

10. The Black Talon bullet, designed and manufactured by Olin Corp., is a hollowpoint bullet designed to bend upon impact into six, ninety-degree-angle, razor-sharp petals or "talons" that increase the wounding power of the bullet by stretching, cutting, and tearing tissue and bone. On December 7, 1993, Colin Ferguson opened fire on the passengers of a commuter train departing from New York City. Ferguson, using the Black Talons in a 9mm semiautomatic handgun, killed six people, including Dennis McCarthy, and injured nineteen, including Kevin McCarthy. Their injuries were enhanced because the bullets performed as designed. Kevin McCarthy and the estate of Dennis McCarthy sued Olin Corp. under design-defect theories based in negligence and strict liability. How should the court resolve this dispute? *McCarthy v. Olin Corp.*, 119 F.3d 148 (2d Cir. 1997).

11. Ronald Anderson Jr. is a self-employed construction contractor from New York. While working on a project in Connecticut, Anderson purchased lumber from a Home Depot in Danbury, Connecticut. Wishing to protect the lumber from the rain, Anderson also purchased a tarp and bungee stretch cords to cover the lumber that sat in the bed of his pickup. The bungee cords came in an assortment pack of various lengths. Anderson purchased the cords after examining the package, noticing two statements: "Made in the U.S.A. We Make Our Products Where We Make Our Home[s]—America" and "Premium Quality." He failed, however, to read the warnings on the package regarding proper use, including the importance of wearing protective eye wear while using the cords, the maximum stretching capacity of the cords, and admonitions against stretching the cords toward or away from one's body.

After Anderson strapped the tarp over the bed of his truck, one of the hooks on the cords became dislodged, hitting him in the left eye. Anderson alleges that the manufacturer, Bungee Int'l Mfg. Corp., breached an express warranty created by the "Made in the U.S.A." and "Premium Quality" statements as well as the drawings showing proper usage. Anderson alleged that the "Made in the U.S.A." and the "Premium Quality" labeling on the packaging, along with the five drawings showing recommended uses, caused

him to believe that the cord was "a good, strong, top notch American-made product suitable for numerous uses." The hooks on the cord were made in Taiwan, but the product was assembled in the United States and under federal regulations could be advertised as "Made in the U.S.A." Has there been a breach of express warranty? *Anderson v. Bungee Int'l Mfg. Corp.*, 44 F. Supp. 2d 534 (S.D. N.Y. 1999).

12. In 1994, Daniel Scoggin hired Broward Marine for $5,000 to perform a "bottom job" on his 77-foot sailboat, the "Jubilem." A "bottom job" is a final paint job involving sandblasting the hull to the bare metal and applying a protective coat that prevents barnacles from attaching to the hull of the ship. New Nautical Coatings, Inc., manufactured the paint used on the Jubilem. New Nautical's products contained an express warranty that, if used properly, the paint would protect the hull for one year, and a booklet contained detailed instructions as to use.

Three months after the paint job, the coating began to peel. New Nautical determined that this was because Broward had not properly sandblasted the boat, as prescribed by the detailed instructions, and supplied replacement paint at no cost. Once again, the boat was not sandblasted because Scoggin did not want to pay the extra cost. Broward applied a test patch to the boat, and a representative of Nautical approved the new paint job, saying "yeah, go ahead and apply it and [Nautical] would warranty it." The coating did not last. Scoggin sued for breach of an express warranty. Has there been a breach of express warranty? *New Nautical Coatings, Inc. v. Scoggin*, 731 So.2d 145 (Fla. Dist. Ct. App. 1999).

13. In an attempt to save on utility costs, Metro National Corp. decided to construct a thermal-energy-storage system to replace its central-air-conditioning system at Memorial City Medical Center. Metro contacted Morris & Associates about purchasing three of its ice harvesters (which are essentially industrial icemakers). Dunham-Bush manufactured a specially engineered compressor, the 1216SE, for use in the Morris harvesters. Hoping to enter this burgeoning market, Dunham-Bush assured Morris that the compressors were specially designed, reliable, and suitable for use under the predicted field conditions. In addition, Dunham-Bush extended its usual one-year warranty to a five-year one on the 1216SE. On several occasions, Morris assured Metro that the compressors were extremely reliable, and Dunham-Bush quickly replaced a compressor that immediately failed. Metro ordered two more units later that year. The compressors experienced a 70 percent failure rate. Metro gave up on the Morris systems and purchased instead a new 200-ton central-air-conditioning system. If Metro were to sue Dunham-Bush for breach of warranty, what warranties should they allege were breached? Should the court find that the warranties had been breached? *Metro Nat'l Corp. v. Dunham-Bush, Inc.*, 984 F. Supp. 538 (S.D. Tex. 1997).

14. Reliance Granite Company, run by James R. Noggle, manufactures gravestone monuments for monument dealers. Willis Mining, Inc., quarries granite, cuts it into blocks, and sells it to such manufacturers. Noggle purchased blocks from Willis, created monuments, and sold them. Within 18 months, the monuments sold by Noggle became discolored, forcing Noggle to replace them. When Noggle sought reimbursement from Willis, Willis refused to pay. Noggle brought this suit against Willis alleging, among other claims, breach of an implied warranty of merchantability. Willis claims that no breach occurred because Noggle inspected the blocks and selected them with monument manufacturing in mind. How should the court resolve this dispute? *Willis Mining, Inc. v. Noggle*, 509 S.E.2d 731 (Ga. Ct. App. 1998).

The United States Constitution

We the People of the United States, in Order to form a more perfect Union, establish Justice, insure domestic Tranquility, provide for the common defence, promote the general Welfare, and secure the Blessings of Liberty to ourselves and our Posterity, do ordain and establish this Constitution for the United States of America.

ARTICLE I

Section 1

All legislative Powers herein granted shall be vested in a Congress of the United States, which shall consist of a Senate and House of Representatives.

Section 2

The House of Representatives shall be composed of Members chosen every second Year by the People of the several States, and the Electors in each State shall have the Qualifications requisite for Electors of the most numerous Branch of the State Legislature.

No Person shall be a Representative who shall not have attained to the Age of twenty five Years, and been seven Years a Citizen of the United States, and who shall not, when elected, be an Inhabitant of that State in which he shall be chosen.

Representatives and direct Taxes shall be apportioned among the several States which may be included within this Union, according to their respective Numbers, which shall be determined by adding to the whole Number of free Persons, including those bound to Service for a Term of Years, and excluding Indians not taxed, three fifths of all other Persons. The actual Enumeration shall be made within three Years after the first Meeting of the Congress of the United States, and within every subsequent Term of ten Years, in which Manner as they shall by Law direct. The Number of Representatives shall not exceed one for every thirty Thousand, but each State shall have at Least one Representative; and until such enumeration shall be made, the State of New Hampshire shall be entitled to choose three, Massachusetts eight, Rhode Island and Providence Plantations one, Connecticut five, New York six, New Jersey four, Pennsylvania eight, Delaware one, Maryland six, Virginia ten, North Carolina five, South Carolina five, and Georgia three.

When vacancies happen in the Representation from any State, the Executive Authority thereof shall issue Writs of Election to fill such Vacancies.

The House of Representatives shall choose their Speaker and other Officers; and shall have the sole Power of Impeachment.

Section 3

The Senate of the United States shall be composed of two Senators from each State, chosen by the Legislature thereof, for six Years; and each Senator shall have one Vote.

Immediately after they shall be assembled in Consequence of the first Election, they shall be divided as equally as may be into three Classes. The Seats of the Senators of the first Class shall be vacated at the Expiration of the second Year, of the second Class at the Expiration of the fourth Year, and of the third Class at the Expiration of the sixth Year, so that one third may be chosen every second Year; and if Vacancies happen by Resignation, or otherwise, during the Recess of the Legislature of any State, the Executive thereof may make temporary Appointments until the next Meeting of the Legislature, which shall then fill such Vacancies.

No Person shall be a Senator who shall not have attained to the Age of thirty Years, and been nine Years a Citizen of the United States, and who shall not, when elected, be an Inhabitant of that State for which he shall be chosen.

The Vice President of the United States shall be President of the Senate, but shall have no Vote, unless they be equally divided.

The Senate shall chuse their other Officers, and also a President pro tempore, in the Absence of the Vice President, or when he shall exercise the Office of President of the United States.

The Senate shall have the sole Power to try all Impeachments. When sitting for that Purpose, they shall be on Oath or Affirmation. When the President of the United States is tried the Chief Justice shall preside: And no Person shall be convicted without the Concurrence of two thirds of the Members present.

Judgment in Cases of Impeachment shall not extend further than to removal from Office, and disqualification to hold and enjoy any Office of honor, Trust or Profit under the United States: but the Party convicted shall nevertheless be liable and subject to Indictment, Trial, Judgment and Punishment, according to Law.

Section 4

The Times, Places and Manner of holding Elections for Senators and Representatives, shall be prescribed in each State by the Legislature thereof; but the Congress may at any time by Law make or alter such Regulations, except as to the Places of chusing Senators.

The Congress shall assemble at Least once in every Year, and such Meeting shall be on the first Monday in December, unless they shall by Law appoint a different Day.

Section 5

Each House shall be the Judge of the Elections, Returns and Qualifications of its own Members, and a Majority of each shall constitute a Quorum to do Business; but a smaller Number may adjourn from day to day, and may be authorized to compel the Attendance of absent Members, in such Manner, and under such Penalties as each House may provide.

Each House may determine the Rules in its Proceedings, punish its Members for disorderly Behaviour, and, with the Concurrence of two thirds, expel a Member.

Each House shall keep a Journal of its Proceedings, and from time to time publish the same, excepting such Parts as may in their Judgment require Secrecy; and the Yeas and Nays of the Members of either House on any question shall, at the Desire of one fifth of those Present, be entered on the Journal.

Neither House, during the Session of Congress, shall, without the Consent of the other, adjourn for more than three days, nor to any other Place than that in which the two Houses shall be sitting.

Section 6

The Senators and Representatives shall receive a Compensation for their Services, to be ascertained by Law, and paid out of the Treasury of the United States. They shall in all Cases, except Treason, Felony and Breach of the Peace, be privileged from Arrest during their Attendance at the Session of their respective Houses, and in going to and returning from the same; and for any Speech or Debate in either House, they shall not be questioned in any other Place.

No Senator or Representative shall, during the Time for which he was elected, be appointed to any civil Office under the Authority of the United States, which shall have been created, or the Emoluments whereof shall have been encreased during such time; and no Person holding any Office under the United States, shall be a Member of either House during his Continuance in Office.

Section 7

All Bills for raising Revenue shall originate in the House of Representatives; but the Senate may propose or concur with amendments as on other Bills.

Every Bill which shall have passed the House of Representatives and the Senate, shall, before it become a Law, be presented to the President of the United States; If he approve he shall sign it, but if not he shall return it, with his Objections to that House in which it shall have originated, who shall enter the Objections at large on their Journal, and proceed to reconsider it. If after such Reconsideration two thirds of that House shall agree to pass the Bill, it shall be sent, together with the Objections, to the other House, by which it shall likewise be reconsidered, and if approved by two thirds of that House, it shall become a Law. But in all such Cases the Votes of both Houses shall be determined by Yeas and Nays, and the names of the Persons voting for and against the Bill shall be entered on the Journal of each House respectively. If any Bill shall not be returned by the President within ten Days (Sundays excepted) after it shall have been presented to him, the Same shall be a Law, in like Manner as if he had signed it, unless the Congress by their Adjournment prevent its Return, in which Case it shall not be a Law.

Every Order, Resolution, or Vote to which the Concurrence of the Senate and House of Representatives may be necessary (except on a question of Adjournment) shall be presented to the President of the United States; and before the Same shall take Effect, shall be approved by him, or being disapproved by him, shall be repassed by two thirds of the Senate and House of Representatives, according to the Rules and Limitations prescribed in the Case of a Bill.

Section 8

The Congress shall have Power To lay and collect Taxes, Duties, Imposts and Excises, to pay the Debts and provide for the common Defense and general Welfare of the United States; but all Duties, Imposts and Excises shall be uniform throughout the United States;

To borrow Money on the credit of the United States;

To regulate Commerce with foreign Nations, and among the several States, and with the Indian Tribes;

To establish an uniform Rule of Naturalization, and uniform Laws on the subject of Bankruptcies throughout the United States;

To coin Money, regulate the Value thereof, and of foreign Coin, and fix the Standard of Weights and Measures;

To provide for the Punishment of counterfeiting the Securities and current Coin of the United States;

To establish Post Offices and post Roads;

To promote the Progress of Science and useful Arts, by securing for limited Times to Authors and Inventors the exclusive Right to their respective Writings and Discoveries;

To constitute Tribunals inferior to the supreme Court;

To define and punish Piracies and Felonies committed on the high Seas, and Offenses against the Law of Nations;

To declare War, grant Letters of Marque and Reprisal, and make Rules concerning Captures on Land and Water;

To raise and support Armies, but no Appropriation of Money to that Use shall be for a longer Term than two Years;

To provide and maintain a Navy;

To make Rules for the Government and Regulation of the land and naval Forces;

To provide for calling forth the Militia to execute the Laws of the Union, suppress Insurrections and repel Invasions;

To provide for organizing, arming, and disciplining, the Militia, and for governing such Part of them as may be employed in the Service of the United States, reserving to the States respectively, the Appointment of the Officers, and the Authority of training the Militia according to the discipline prescribed by Congress;

To exercise exclusive Legislation in all Cases whatsoever, over such District (not exceeding ten Miles square) as may, by Cession of particular States, and the Acceptance of Congress, become the Seat of the Government of the United States, and to exercise like Authority over all Places purchased by the Consent of the Legislature of the State in which the Same shall be, for the Erection of Forts, Magazines, Arsenals, dock-Yards, and other needful Buildings;—And

To make all Laws which shall be necessary and proper for carrying into Execution the foregoing Powers, and all other Powers vested by this Constitution in the Government of the United States, or in any Department or Officer thereof.

Section 9

The Migration or Importation of such Persons as any of the States now existing shall think proper to admit, shall not be prohibited by the Congress prior to the Year one thousand eight hundred and eight, but a Tax or duty may be imposed on such Importation, not exceeding ten dollars for each Person.

The Privilege of the Writ of Habeas Corpus shall not be suspended, unless when in Cases of Rebellion or Invasion the public Safety may require it.

No Bill of Attainder or ex post facto Law shall be passed.

No Capitation, or other direct, Tax shall be laid, unless in Proportion to the Census or Enumeration herein before directed to be taken.

No Tax or Duty shall be laid on Articles exported from any State.

No Preference shall be given to any Regulation of Commerce or Revenue to the Ports of one State over those of another; nor shall Vessels bound to, or from, one State, be obliged to enter, clear or pay Duties in another.

No Money shall be drawn from the Treasury, but in Consequence of Appropriations made by Law; and a regular Statement and Account of the Receipts and Expenditures of all public Money shall be published from time to time.

No Title of Nobility shall be granted by the United States: And no Person holding any Office of Profit or Trust under them, shall, without the Consent of the Congress, accept of any present, Emolument, Office, or Title, of any kind whatever, from any King, Prince or foreign State.

Section 10

No State shall enter into any Treaty, Alliance, or Confederation; grant Letters of Marque and Reprisal; coin Money; emit Bills of Credit; make any Thing but gold and silver Coin a Tender in Payment of Debts; pass any Bill of Attainder, ex post facto Law or law impairing the Obligation of Contracts, or grant any Title of Nobility.

No State shall, without the Consent of the Congress, lay any Imposts or Duties on Imports or Exports, except what may be absolutely necessary for executing its inspection Laws: and the net Produce of all Duties and Imposts, laid by any State on Imports or Exports, shall be for the Use of the Treasury of the United States; and all such Laws shall be subject to the Revision and Control of the Congress.

No State shall, without the Consent of Congress, lay any Duty on Tonnage, keep Troops, or Ships of War in time of Peace, enter into any Agreement or Compact with another State, or with a foreign Power, or engage in War, unless actually invaded, or in such imminent Danger as will not admit of delay.

ARTICLE II

Section I

The executive Power shall be vested in a President of the United States of America. He shall hold his Office during the Term of four Years, and, together with the Vice President, chosen for the same Term, be elected, as follows:

Each State shall appoint, in such Manner as the Legislature thereof may direct, a Number of Electors, equal to the whole Number of Senators and Representatives to which the State may be entitled in the Congress: but no Senator or Representative, or Person holding an Office of Trust or Profit under the United States, shall be appointed an Elector.

The Electors shall meet in their respective States, and vote by Ballot for two Persons, of whom one at least shall not be an Inhabitant of the same State with themselves. And they shall make a List of all the Persons voted for, and of the Number of Votes for each; which List they shall sign and certify, and transmit sealed to the Seat of the Government of the United States, directed to the President of the Senate. The President of the Senate shall, in the Presence of the Senate and House of Representatives, open all the Certificates, and the Votes shall then be counted. The Person having the greatest Number of Votes shall be the President, if such Number be a Majority of the whole Number of Electors appointed; and if there be more than one who have such Majority, and have an equal Number of Votes, then the House of Representatives shall immediately chuse by Ballot one of them for President; and if no Person have a Majority, then from the five highest on the List the said House shall in like Manner chuse the President. But in chusing the President, the Votes shall be taken by States, the Representation from each State having one Vote; a quorum for this Purpose shall consist of a Member or Members from two thirds of the States, and a Majority of all the States shall be necessary to a Choice. In every Case, after the Choice of the President, the Person having the greatest Number of Votes of the Electors shall be the Vice President. But if there should remain two or more who have equal Votes, the Senate shall chuse from them by Ballot the Vice President.

The Congress may determine the Time of chusing the Electors, and the Day on which they shall give their Votes; which Day shall be the same throughout the United States.

No Person except a natural born Citizen, or a Citizen of the United States, at the time of the Adoption of this Constitution, shall be eligible to the Office of President; neither shall any Person be eligible to that Office who shall not have attained to the Age of thirty five Years, and been fourteen years a Resident within the United States.

In Case of the Removal of the President from Office, or of his Death, Resignation, or Inability to discharge the Powers and Duties of the said Office, the Same shall devolve on the Vice President, and the Congress may by Law provide for the Case of Removal, Death, Resignation, or Inability, both of the President and Vice President, declaring what Officer shall then act as President, and such Officer shall act accordingly, until the Disability be removed, or a President shall be elected.

The President shall, at stated Times, receive for his Services, a Compensation, which shall neither be encreased nor diminished during the Period for which he shall have been elected, and he shall not receive within that Period any other Emolument from the United States, or any of them.

Before he enter on the Execution of his Office, he shall take the following Oath or Affirmation:—"I do solemnly swear (or affirm) that I will faithfully execute the Office of

President of the United States, and will to the best of my Ability, preserve, protect, and defend the Constitution of the United States."

Section 2

The President shall be Commander in Chief of the Army and Navy of the United States, and of the Militia of the several States, when called into the actual Service of the United States; he may require the Opinion, in writing, of the principal Officer in each of the executive Departments, upon any Subject relating to the Duties of their respective Offices, and he shall have Power to grant Reprieves and Pardons for Offenses against the United States, except in Cases of Impeachment.

He shall have Power, by and with the Advice and Consent of the Senate, to make Treaties, provided two thirds of the Senators present concur; and he shall nominate, and by and with the Advice and Consent of the Senate, shall appoint Ambassadors, other public Ministers and Consuls, Judges of the supreme Court, and all other Officers of the United States, whose Appointments are not herein otherwise provided for, and which shall be established by Law: but the Congress may by Law vest the Appointment of such inferior Officers, as they think proper, in the President alone, in the Courts of Law, or in the Heads of Departments.

The President shall have Power to fill up all Vacancies that may happen during the Recess of the Senate, by granting Commissions which shall expire at the End of their next Session.

Section 3

He shall from time to time give to the Congress Information of the State of the Union, and recommend to their Consideration such Measures as he shall judge necessary and expedient; he may, on extraordinary Occasions, convene both Houses, or either of them, and in Case of Disagreement between them, with Respect to the Time of Adjournment, he may adjourn them to such Time as he shall think proper; he shall receive Ambassadors and other public Ministers; he shall take Care that the Laws be faithfully executed, and shall Commission all the Officers of the United States.

Section 4

The President, Vice President and all Civil Officers of the United States, shall be removed from Office on Impeachment for, and Conviction of, Treason, Bribery, or other high Crimes and Misdemeanors.

ARTICLE III

Section 1

The judicial Power of the United States, shall be vested in one supreme Court, and in such inferior Courts as the Congress may from time to time ordain and establish. The Judges, both of the supreme and inferior Courts, shall hold their Offices during good Behaviour, and shall, at stated Times, receive for their Services, a Compensation, which shall not be diminished during their Continuance in Office.

Section 2

The judicial Power shall extend to all Cases, in Law and Equity, arising under this Constitution, the Laws of the United States, and Treaties made, or which shall be made, under their Authority;—to all Cases affecting Ambassadors, other public Ministers and Consuls;—to all Cases of admiralty and maritime Jurisdiction;—to Controversies to which the United

States shall be a Party;—to Controversies between two or more States;—between a State and Citizens of another State;—between Citizens of different States,—between Citizens of the same State claiming Lands under Grants of different States, and between a State, or the Citizens thereof, and foreign States, Citizens or Subjects.

In all Cases affecting Ambassadors, other public Ministers and Consuls, and those in which a State shall be Party, the Supreme Court shall have original Jurisdiction. In all the other Cases before mentioned, the supreme Court shall have appellate Jurisdiction, both as to Law and Fact, with such Exceptions, and under such Regulations as the Congress shall make.

The Trial of all Crimes, except in Cases of Impeachment, shall be by Jury; and such Trial shall be held in the State where the said Crimes shall have been committed; but when not committed within any State, the Trial shall be at such Place or Places as the Congress may by Law have directed.

Section 3

Treason against the United States, shall consist only in levying War against them, or in adhering to their Enemies, giving them Aid and Comfort. No Person shall be convicted of Treason unless on the Testimony of two Witnesses to the same overt Act, or on Confession in open Court.

The Congress shall have Power to declare the Punishment of Treason, but no Attainder of Treason shall work Corruption of Blood, or Forfeiture except during the Life of the Person attainted.

ARTICLE IV

Section 1

Full Faith and Credit shall be given in each State to the public Arts, Records, and judicial Proceedings of every other State. And the Congress may by general Laws prescribe the Manner in which such Acts, Records and Proceedings shall be proved, and the Effect thereof.

Section 2

The Citizens of each State shall be entitled to all Privileges and Immunities of Citizens in the several States.

A Person charged in any State with Treason, Felony, or other Crime, who shall flee from Justice, and be found in another State, shall on Demand of the executive Authority of the State from which he fled, be delivered up, to be removed to the State having Jurisdiction of the Crime.

No Person held to Service or Labour in one State, under the Laws thereof, escaping into another, shall, in Consequence of any Law or Regulation therein, be discharged from such Service or Labour, but shall be delivered up on Claim of the Party to whom such Service or Labour may be due.

Section 3

New States may be admitted by the Congress into this Union; but no new State shall be formed or erected within the Jurisdiction of any other State; nor any State be formed by the Junction of two or more States, or Parts of States, without the Consent of the Legislatures of the States concerned as well as of the Congress.

The Congress shall have Power to dispose of and make all needful Rules and Regulations respecting the Territory or other Property belonging to the United States; and nothing in this Constitution shall be so construed as to Prejudice any Claims of the United States, or of any particular State.

Section 4

The United States shall guarantee to every State in this Union a Republican Form of Government, and shall protect each of them against Invasion; and on Application of the Legislature, or of the Executive (when the Legislature cannot be convened) against domestic Violence.

ARTICLE V

The Congress, whenever two thirds of both Houses shall deem it necessary, shall propose Amendments to this Constitution, or, on the Application of the Legislatures of two thirds of the several States, shall call a Convention for proposing Amendments, which, in either Case, shall be valid to all Intents and Purposes, as Part of this Constitution, when ratified by the Legislatures of three fourths of the several States, or by Conventions in three fourths thereof, as the one or the other Mode of Ratification may be proposed by the Congress; Provided that no Amendment which may be made prior to the Year One thousand eight hundred and eight shall in any Manner affect the first and fourth Clauses in the Ninth Section of the first Article; and that no State, without its Consent, shall be deprived of its equal Suffrage in the Senate.

ARTICLE VI

All Debts contracted and Engagements entered into, before the Adoption of this Constitution, shall be as valid against the United States under this Constitution, as under the Confederation.

This Constitution, and the Laws of the United States which shall be made in Pursuance thereof; and all Treaties made, or which shall be made, under the Authority of the United States, shall be the supreme Law of the Land; and the judges in every State shall be bound thereby, any Thing in the Constitution or Laws of any State to the Contrary notwithstanding.

The Senators and Representatives before mentioned, and the Members of the several State Legislatures, and all executive and judicial Officers, both of the United States and of the several States, shall be bound by Oath or Affirmation, to support this Constitution; but no religious Test shall ever be required as a Qualification to any Office or public Trust under the United States.

ARTICLE VII

The Ratification of the Conventions of nine States, shall be sufficient for the Establishment of this Constitution between the States so ratifying the Same.

AMENDMENT I (1791)

Congress shall make no law respecting an establishment of religion, or prohibiting the free exercise thereof; or abridging the freedom of speech, or of the press; or the right of the people peaceably to assemble, and to petition the Government for a redress of grievances.

AMENDMENT II (1791)

A well regulated Militia, being necessary to the security of a free State, the right of the people to keep and bear Arms, shall not be infringed.

AMENDMENT III (1791)

No Soldier shall, in time of peace be quartered in any house, without the consent of the Owner, nor in time of war, but in a manner to be prescribed by law.

AMENDMENT IV (1791)

The right of the people to be secure in their persons, houses, papers, and effects, against unreasonable searches and seizures, shall not be violated, and no Warrants shall issue, but upon probable cause, supported by Oath or affirmation, and particularly describing the place to be searched, and the persons or things to be seized.

AMENDMENT V (1791)

No person shall be held to answer for a capital or otherwise infamous crime, unless on a presentment or indictment of a Grand Jury, except in cases arising in the land or naval forces, or in the Militia, when in actual service in time of War or public danger; nor shall any person be subject for the same offense to be twice put in jeopardy of life or limb; nor shall be compelled in any criminal case to be a witness against himself, nor be deprived of life, liberty, or property, without due process of law; nor shall private property be taken for public use, with out just compensation.

AMENDMENT VI (1791)

In all criminal prosecutions, the accused shall enjoy the right to a speedy and public trial, by an impartial jury of the State and district wherein the crime shall have been committed, which district shall have been previously ascertained by law, and to be informed of the nature and cause of the accusation; to be confronted with the witnesses against him; to have compulsory process for obtaining Witnesses in his favor, and to have the Assistance of Counsel for his defense.

AMENDMENT VII (1791)

In Suits at common law, where the value in controversy shall exceed twenty dollars, the right of trial by jury shall be preserved, and no fact tried by a jury, shall be otherwise reexamined in any Court of the United States, than according to the rules of the common law.

AMENDMENT VIII (1791)

Excessive bail shall not be required nor excessive fines imposed, nor cruel and unusual punishments inflicted.

AMENDMENT IX (1791)

The enumeration in the Constitution, of certain rights, shall not be construed to deny or disparage others retained by the people.

AMENDMENT X (1791)

The powers not delegated to the United States by the Constitution, nor prohibited by it to the States, are reserved to the States respectively, or to the people.

AMENDMENT XI (1798)

The Judicial power of the United States shall not be construed to extend to any suit in law or equity, commenced or prosecuted against one of the United States by Citizens of another State, or by Citizens or Subjects of any Foreign State.

AMENDMENT XII (1804)

The Electors shall meet in their respective states and vote by ballot for President and Vice President, one of whom, at least, shall not be an inhabitant of the same state with themselves; they shall name in their ballots the person voted for as President, and in distinct ballots the person voted for as Vice-President, and they shall make distinct lists of all persons voted for as President, and of all persons voted for as Vice-President, and of the number of votes for each, which lists they shall sign and certify, and transmit sealed to the seat of the government of the United States, directed to the President of the Senate;—The President of the Senate shall, in the presence of the Senate and House of Representatives, open all the certificates and the votes shall then be counted;—The person having the greatest number of votes for President, shall be the President, if such number be a majority of the whole number of Electors appointed; and if no person have such majority, then from the persons having the highest numbers not exceeding three on the list of those voted for as President, the House of Representatives shall choose immediately, by ballot, the President. But in choosing the President, the votes shall be taken by states, the representation from each state having one vote; a quorum for this purpose shall consist of a member or members from two-thirds of the states, and a majority of all the states shall be necessary to a choice. And if the House of Representatives shall not choose a President whenever the right of choice shall devolve upon them, before the fourth day of March next following, then the Vice-President shall act as President, as in the case of the death or other constitutional disability of the President—The person having the greatest number of votes as Vice-President, shall be the Vice-President, if such number be a majority of the whole number of Electors appointed, and if no person have a majority, then from the two highest numbers on the list, the Senate shall choose the Vice-President; a quorum for the purpose shall consist of two-thirds of the whole numbers of Senators, and a majority of the whole number shall be necessary to a choice. But no person constitutionally ineligible to the office of President shall be eligible to that of Vice President of the United States.

AMENDMENT XIII (1865)

Section 1
Neither slavery nor involuntary servitude, except as a punishment for crime whereof the party shall have been duly convicted, shall exist within the United States, or any place subject to their jurisdiction.

Section 2
Congress shall have power to enforce this article by appropriate legislation.

AMENDMENT XIV (1868)

Section 1

All persons born or naturalized in the United States and subject to the jurisdiction thereof, are citizens of the United States and of the State wherein they reside. No State shall make or enforce any law which shall abridge the privileges or immunities of citizens of the United States; nor shall any State deprive any person of life, liberty, or property, without due process of law; nor deny to any person within its jurisdiction the equal protection of the laws.

Section 2

Representatives shall be apportioned among the several States according to their respective numbers, counting the whole number of persons in each State, excluding Indians not taxed. But when the right to vote at any election for the choice of electors for President and Vice President of the United States, Representatives in Congress, the Executive and Judicial officers of a State, or the members of the Legislature thereof, is denied to any of the male inhabitants of such State, being twenty-one years of age, and citizens of the United States, or in any way abridged, except for participation in rebellion, or other crime, the basis of representation therein shall be reduced in the proportion which the number of such male citizens shall bear to the whole number of male citizens twenty-one years of age in such State.

Section 3

No person shall be a Senator or Representative in Congress, or elector of President and Vice President, or hold any office, civil or military, under the United States, or under any State, who, having previously taken an oath, as a member of Congress, or as an officer of the United States, or as a member of any State legislature, or as an executive or judicial officer of any State, to support the Constitution of the United States, shall have engaged in insurrection or rebellion against the same, or given aid or comfort to the enemies thereof. But Congress may by a vote of two-thirds of each House, remove such disability.

Section 4

The validity of the public debt of the United States, authorized by law, including debts incurred for payment of pensions and bounties for services in suppressing insurrection or rebellion, shall not be questioned. But neither the United States nor any State shall assume or pay any debt or obligation incurred in aid of insurrection or rebellion against the United States, or any claim for the loss or emancipation of any slave; but all such debts, obligations and claims shall be held illegal and void.

Section 5

The Congress shall have power to enforce, by appropriate legislation, the provisions of this article.

AMENDMENT XV (1870)

Section 1

The right of citizens of the United States to vote shall not be denied or abridged by the United States or by any State on account of race, color, or previous condition of servitude.

Section 2

The Congress shall have power to enforce this article by appropriate legislation.

AMENDMENT XVI (1913)

The Congress shall have power to lay and collect taxes on incomes, from whatever source derived, without apportionment among the several States, and without regard to any census or enumeration.

AMENDMENT XVII (1913)

The Senate of the United States shall be composed of two Senators from each State, elected by the people thereof, for six years; and each Senator shall have one vote. The electors in each State shall have the qualifications requisite for electors of the most numerous branch of the State legislatures.

When vacancies happen in the representation of any State in the Senate, the executive authority of such State shall issue writs of election to fill such vacancies: Provided, That the legislature of any State may empower the executive thereof to make temporary appointments until the people fill the vacancies by election as the legislature may direct.

This amendment shall not be so construed as to affect the election or term of any Senator chosen before it becomes valid as part of the Constitution.

AMENDMENT XVIII (1919)

Section 1
After one year from the ratification of this article the manufacture, sale, or transportation of intoxicating liquors within, the importation thereof into, or the exportation thereof from the United States and all territory subject to the jurisdiction thereof for beverage purposes is hereby prohibited.

Section 2
The Congress and the several States shall have concurrent power to enforce this article by appropriate legislation.

Section 3
This article shall be inoperative unless it shall have been ratified as an amendment to the Constitution by the legislatures of the several States, as provided in the Constitution, within seven years from the date of the submission hereof to the States by the Congress.

AMENDMENT XIX (1920)

Section 1
The right of citizens of the United States to vote shall not be denied or abridged by the United States or by any State on account of sex.

Section 2
Congress shall have power to enforce this article by appropriate legislation.

AMENDMENT XX (1933)

Section 1
The terms of the President and Vice President shall end at noon on the 20th day of January, and the terms of Senators and Representatives at noon on the 3d day of January, of the years

in which such terms would have ended if this article had not been ratified; and the terms of their successors shall then begin.

Section 2
The Congress shall assemble at least once in every year, and such meeting shall begin at noon on the 3d day of January, unless they shall by law appoint a different day.

Section 3
If, at the time fixed for the beginning of the term of the President, the President elect shall have died, the Vice President elect shall be come President. If a President shall not have been chosen before the time fixed for the beginning of his term, or if the President elect shall have failed to qualify, then the Vice President elect shall act as President until a President shall have qualified; and the Congress may by law provide for the case wherein neither a President elect nor a Vice President elect shall have qualified, declaring who shall then act as President, or the manner in which one who is to act shall be selected, and such person shall act accordingly until a President or Vice President shall have qualified.

Section 4
The Congress may by law provide for the case of the death of any of the persons from whom the House of Representatives may choose a President whenever the right of choice shall have devolved upon them, and for the case of the death of any of the persons from whom the Senate may choose a Vice President whenever the right of choice shall have devolved upon them.

Section 5
Sections 1 and 2 shall take effect on the 15th day of October following the ratification of this article.

Section 6
This article shall be inoperative unless it shall have been ratified as an amendment to the Constitution by the legislatures of three fourths of the several States within seven years from the date of its submission.

AMENDMENT XXI (1933)

Section 1
The eighteenth article of amendment to the Constitution of the United States is hereby repealed.

Section 2
The transportation or importation into any State, Territory, or possession of the United States for delivery or use therein of intoxicating liquors, in violation of the laws thereof, is hereby prohibited.

Section 3
This article shall be inoperative unless it shall have been ratified as an amendment to the Constitution by conventions in the several States, as provided in the Constitution, within seven years from the date of the submission hereof to the States by the Congress.

AMENDMENT XXII (1951)

Section 1
No person shall be elected to the office of the President more than twice, and no person, who has held the office of President, or acted as President, for more than two years of a term to which some other person was elected President shall be elected to the Office of the President more than once. But this Article shall not apply to any person holding the office of President when this Article was proposed by the Congress, and shall not prevent any person who may be holding the office of President, or acting as President, during the term within which this Article becomes operative from holding the Office of President or acting as President during the remainder of such term.

Section 2
This article shall be inoperative unless it shall have been ratified as an amendment to the Constitution by the legislatures of three fourths of the several States within seven years from the date of its submission to the States by the Congress.

AMENDMENT XXIII (1961)

Section 1
The District constituting the seat of Government of the United States shall appoint in such manner as the Congress may direct:

A number of electors of President and Vice President equal to the whole number of Senators and Representatives in Congress to which the District would be entitled if it were a State, but in no event more than the least populous State; they shall be in addition to those appointed by the States, but they shall be considered, for the purposes of the election of President and Vice President, to be electors appointed by a State; and they shall meet in the District and perform such duties as provided by the twelfth article of amendment.

Section 2
The Congress shall have power to enforce this article by appropriate legislation.

AMENDMENT XXIV (1964)

Section 1
The right of citizens of the United States to vote in any primary or other election for President or Vice President, for electors for President or Vice President, or for Senator or Representative in Congress, shall not be denied or abridged by the United States or any State by reason of failure to pay any poll tax or other tax.

Section 2
The Congress shall have power to enforce this article by appropriate legislation.

AMENDMENT XXV (1967)

Section 1
In case of the removal of the President from office or of his death or resignation, the Vice President shall become President.

Section 2

Whenever there is a vacancy in the office of the Vice President, the President shall nominate a Vice President who shall take office upon confirmation by a majority vote of both Houses of Congress.

Section 3

Whenever the President transmits to the President pro tempore of the Senate and the Speaker of the House of Representatives his written declaration that he is unable to discharge the powers and duties of his office, and until he transmits to them a written declaration to the contrary, such powers and duties shall be discharged by the Vice President as Acting President.

Section 4

Whenever the Vice President and a majority of either the principal officers of the executive departments or of such other body as Congress may by law provide, transmit to the President pro tempore of the Senate and the Speaker of the House of Representatives their written declaration that the President is unable to discharge the powers and duties of his office, the Vice President shall immediately assume the powers and duties of the office as Acting President.

Thereafter, when the President transmits to the President pro tempore of the Senate and the Speaker of the House of Representatives his written declaration that no inability exists, he shall resume the powers and duties of his Office unless the Vice President and a majority of either the principal officers of the executive department or of such other body as Congress may by law provide, transmit within four days to the President pro tempore of the Senate and the Speaker of the House of Representatives their written declaration that the President is unable to discharge the powers and duties of his office. Thereupon Congress shall decide the issue, assembling within forty-eight hours for that purpose if not in session. If the Congress, within twenty-one days after receipt of the latter written declaration, or, if Congress is not in session, within twenty-one days after Congress is required to assemble, determines by two-thirds vote of both Houses that the President is unable to discharge the powers and duties of his office, the Vice President shall continue to discharge the same as Acting President; otherwise, the President shall resume the powers and duties of his office.

AMENDMENT XXVI (1971)

Section 1

The right of citizens of the United States, who are eighteen years of age or older, to vote shall not be denied or abridged by the United States or by any State on account of age.

Section 2

The Congress shall have power to enforce this article by appropriate legislation.

AMENDMENT XXVII (1992)

No law varying the compensation for services of the Senators and Representatives shall take effect until an election of representatives shall have intervened.

Selected UCC Provisions

ARTICLE 1-GENERAL PROVISIONS

PART 2

§ 1-201. General Definitions.
(19) "Good faith" means honesty in fact in the conduct or transaction concerned.

§ 1-203. Obligation of Good Faith.
Every contract or duty within this Act imposes an obligation of good faith in its performance or enforcement.

§ 1-204. Time; Reasonable Time; "Seasonably".
(1) Whenever this Act requires any action to be taken within a reasonable time, any time which is not manifestly unreasonable may be fixed by agreement.

(2) What is a reasonable time for taking any action depends on the nature, purpose and circumstances of such action.

(3) An action is taken "seasonably" when it is taken at or within the time agreed or if no time is agreed at or within a reasonable time.

§ 1-205. Course of Dealing and Usage of Trade.
(1) A course of dealing is a sequence of previous conduct between the parties to a particular transaction which is fairly to be regarded as establishing a common basis of understanding for interpreting their expressions and other conduct.

(2) A usage of trade is any practice or method of dealing having such regularity of observance in a place, vocation or trade as to justify an expectation that it will be observed with respect to the transaction in question. The existence and scope of such a usage are to be proved as facts. If it is established that such a usage is embodied in a written trade code or similar writing the interpretation of the writing is for the court.

(3) A course of dealing between parties and any usage of trade in the vocation or trade in which they are engaged or of which they are or should be aware give particular meaning to and supplement or qualify terms of an agreement.

(4) The express terms of an agreement and an applicable course of dealing or usage of trade shall be construed wherever reasonable as consistent with each other; but when such construction is unreasonable express terms control both course of dealing and usage of trade and course of dealing controls usage of trade.

(5) An applicable usage of trade in the place where any part of performance is to occur shall be used in interpreting the agreement as to that part of the performance.

(6) Evidence of a relevant usage of trade offered by one party is not admissible unless and until he has given the other party such notice as the court finds sufficient to prevent unfair surprise to the latter.

ARTICLE 2-SALES

PART 1
SHORT TITLE, GENERAL CONSTRUCTION AND SUBJECT MATTER

§ 2-103. Definitions and Index of Definitions.

(1) In this Article unless the context otherwise requires

(a) "Buyer" means a person who buys or otherwise contracts to buy goods.
(b) "Good faith" in the case of a merchant means honesty in fact and the observance of reasonable commercial standards of fair dealing in the trade.
(c) "Receipt" of goods means taking physical possession of them.
(d) "Seller" means a person who sells or contracts to sell goods.

§ 2-104. Definitions:"Merchant"; "Between Merchants"; "Financing Agency".

(1) "Merchant" means a person who deals in goods of the kind or otherwise by his occupation holds himself out as having knowledge or skill peculiar to the practices or goods involved in the transaction or to whom such knowledge or skill may be attributed by his employment of an agent or broker or other intermediary who by his occupation holds himself out as having such knowledge or skill.

(3) "Between Merchants" means in any transaction with respect to which both parties are chargeable with the knowledge or skill of merchants.

§ 2-105. Definitions: Transferability; "Goods"; "Future" Goods; "Lot"; "Commercial Unit".

(1) "Goods" means all things (including specially manufactured goods) which are movable at the time of identification to the contract for sale other than the money in which the price is to be paid, investment securities (Article 8) and things in action. "Goods" also includes the unborn young of animals and growing crops and other identified things attached to realty as described in the section on goods to be severed from realty (Section 2-107).

(2) Goods must be both existing and identified before any interest in them can pass. Goods which are not both existing and identified are "future" goods. A purported present sale of future goods or of any interest therein operates as a contract to sell.

(3) There may be a sale of a part interest in existing identified goods.

(4) An undivided share in an identified bulk of fungible goods is sufficiently identified to be sold although the quantity of the bulk is not determined. Any agreed proportion of such a bulk or any quantity thereof agreed upon by number, weight or other measure may to the extent of the seller's interest in the bulk be sold to the buyer who then becomes an owner in common.

(5) "Lot" means a parcel or a single article which is the subject matter of a separate sale or delivery, whether or not it is sufficient to perform the contract.

(6) "Commercial unit" means such a unit of goods as by commercial usage is a single whole for purposes of sale and division of which materially impairs its character or value on the market or in use. A commercial unit may be a single article (as a machine) or a set of articles (as a suite of furniture or an assortment of sizes) or a quantity (as a bale, gross, or carload) or any other unit treated in use or in the relevant market as a single whole.

§ 2-106. Definitions: "Contract"; "Agreement"; "Contract for sale"; "Sale"; "Present Sale"; "Conforming" to Contract; "Termination"; "Cancellation".

(1) In this Article unless the context otherwise requires "contract" and "agreement" are limited to those relating to the present or future sale of goods. "Contract for sale" includes both a present sale of goods and a contract to sell goods at a future time. A "sale" consists in the passing of title from the seller to the buyer for a price (Section 2-401). A "present sale" means a sale which is accomplished by the making of the contract.

(2) Goods or conduct including any part of a performance are "conforming" or conform to the contract when they are in accordance with the obligations under the contract.

(3) "Termination" occurs when either party pursuant to a power created by agreement or law puts an end to the contract otherwise than for its breach. On "termination" all obligations which are still executory on both sides are discharged but any right based on prior breach or performance survives.

(4) "Cancellation" occurs when either party puts an end to the contract for breach by the other and its effect is the same as that of "termination" except that the cancelling party also retains any remedy for breach of the whole contract or any unperformed balance.

PART 2
FORM, FORMATION AND READJUSTMENT OF CONTRACT

§ 2-201. Formal Requirements; Statute of Frauds.

(1) Except as otherwise provided in this section a contract for the sale of goods for the price of $500 or more is not enforceable by way of action or defense unless there is some writing sufficient to indicate that a contract for sale has been made between the parties and signed by the party against whom enforcement is sought or by his authorized agent or broker. A writing is not insufficient because it omits or incorrectly states a term agreed upon but the contract is not enforceable under this paragraph beyond the quantity of goods shown in such writing.

(2) Between merchants if within a reasonable time a writing in confirmation of the contract and sufficient against the sender is received and the party receiving it has reason to know its contents, it satisfies the requirements of subsection (1) against such party unless written notice of objection to its contents is given within 10 days after it is received.

§ 2-204. Formation in General.

(1) A contract for sale of goods may be made in any manner sufficient to show agreement, including conduct by both parties which recognizes the existence of such a contract.

(2) An agreement sufficient to constitute a contract for sale may be found even though the moment of its making is undetermined.

(3) Even though one or more terms are left open a contract for sale does not fail for indefiniteness if the parties have intended to make a contract and there is a reasonably certain basis for giving an appropriate remedy.

§ 2-205. Firm Offers.

An offer by a merchant to buy or sell goods in a signed writing which by its terms gives assurance that it will be held open is not revocable, for lack of consideration, during the time stated or if no time is stated for a reasonable time, but in no event may such period of irrevocability exceed three months; but any such term of assurance on a form supplied by the offeree must be separately signed by the offeror.

§ 2-206. Offer and Acceptance in Formation of Contract.

(1) Unless otherwise unambiguously indicated by the language or circumstances

(a) An offer to make a contract shall be construed as inviting acceptance in any manner and by any medium reasonable in the circumstances.

(b) an order or other offer to buy goods for prompt or current shipment shall be construed as inviting acceptance either by a prompt promise to ship or by the prompt or current shipment of conforming or non-conforming goods, but such a shipment of non-conforming goods does not constitute an acceptance if the seller seasonably notifies the buyer that the shipment is offered only as an accommodation to the buyer.

§ 2-207. Additional Terms in Acceptance or Confirmation.

(1) A definite and seasonable expression of acceptance or a written confirmation which is sent within a reasonable time operates as an acceptance even though it states terms additional to or different from those offered or agreed upon, unless acceptance is expressly made conditional on assent to the additional or different terms.

(2) The additional terms are to be construed as proposals for addition to the contract. Between merchants such terms become part of the contract unless:

(a) the offer expressly limits acceptance to the terms of the offer;

(b) they materially alter it; or

(c) notification of objection to them has already been given or is given within a reasonable time after notice of them is received.

(3) Conduct by both parties which recognizes the existence of a contract is sufficient to establish a contract for sale although the writings of the parties do not otherwise establish a contract. In such case the terms of the particular contract consist of those terms on which the writings of the parties agree, together with any supplementary terms incorporated under any other provisions of this Act.

§ 2-208. Course of Performance or Practical Construction.

(1) Where the contract for sale involves repeated occasions for performance by either party with knowledge of the nature of the performance and opportunity for objection to it by the other, any course of performance accepted or acquiesced in without objection shall be relevant to determine the meaning of the agreement.

(2) The express terms of the agreement and any such course of performance, as well as any course of dealing and usage of trade, shall be construed whenever reasonable as consistent with each other; but when such construction is unreasonable, express terms shall control course of performance and course of performance shall control both course of dealing and usage of trade (Section 1-205).

(3) Subject to the provisions of the next section on modification and waiver, such course of performance shall be relevant to show a waiver or modification of any term inconsistent with such course of performance.

§ 2-209. Modification, Rescission and Waiver.

(1) An agreement modifying a contract within this Article needs no consideration to be binding.

PART 3
GENERAL OBLIGATION AND CONSTRUCTION OF CONTRACT

§ 2-301. General Obligations of Parties.

The obligation of the seller is to transfer and deliver and that of the buyer is to accept and pay in accordance with the contract.

§ 2-305. Open Price Term.

(1) The parties if they so intend can conclude a contract for sale even though the price is not settled. In such a case the price is a reasonable price at the time for delivery if

(a) nothing is said as to price; or

(b) the price is left to be agreed by the parties and they fail to agree; or

(c) the price is to be fixed in terms of some agreed market or other standard as set or recorded by a third person or agency and it is not so set or recorded.

(2) A price to be fixed by the seller or by the buyer means a price for him to fix in good faith.

(3) When a price left to be fixed otherwise than by agreement of the parties fails to be fixed through fault of one party the other may at his option treat the contract as cancelled or himself fix a reasonable price.

(4) Where, however, the parties intend not to be bound unless the price be fixed or agreed and it is not fixed or agreed there is no contract. In such a case the buyer must return any goods already received or if unable so to do must pay their reasonable value at the time of delivery and the seller must return any portion of the price paid on account.

§ 2-306. Output, Requirements and Exclusive Dealings.

(1) A term which measures the quantity by the output of the seller or the requirements of the buyer means such actual output or requirements as may occur in good faith, except that no quantity unreasonably disproportionate to any stated estimate or in the absence of a stated estimate to any normal or otherwise comparable prior output or requirements may be tendered or demanded.

(2) A lawful agreement by either the seller or the buyer for exclusive dealing in the kind of goods concerned imposes unless otherwise agreed an obligation by the seller to use best efforts to supply the goods and by the buyer to use best efforts to promote their sale.

§ 2-307. Delivery in Single Lot or Several Lots.

Unless otherwise agreed all goods called for by a contract for sale must be tendered in a single delivery and payment is due only on such tender but where the circumstances give either party the right to make or demand delivery in lots the price if it can be apportioned may be demanded for each lot.

§ 2-308. Absence of Specified Place for Delivery.

Unless otherwise agreed

(a) the place for delivery of goods is the seller's place of business or if he has none his residence; but

(b) in a contract for sale of identified goods which to the knowledge of the parties at the time of contracting are in some other place, that place is the place for their delivery; and

(c) documents of title may be delivered through customary banking channels.

§ 2-309. Absence of Specific Time Provisions; Notice of Termination.

(1) The time for shipment or delivery or any other action under a contract if not provided in this Article or agreed upon shall be a reasonable time.

(2) Where the contract provides for successive performances but is indefinite in duration it is valid for a reasonable time but unless otherwise agreed may be terminated at any time by either party.

(3) Termination of a contract by one party except on the happening of an agreed event requires that reasonable notification be received by the other party and an agreement dispensing with notification is invalid if its operation would be unconscionable.

§ 2-310. Open Time for Payment or Running of Credit; Authority to Ship Under Reservation.

Unless otherwise agreed

(a) payment is due at the time and place at which the buyer is to receive the goods even though the place of shipment is the place of delivery; and

(b) if the seller is authorized to send the goods he may ship them under reservation, and may tender the documents of title, but the buyer may inspect the goods after their arrival before payment is due unless such inspection is inconsistent with the terms of the contract (Section 2-513); and

(c) if delivery is authorized and made by way of documents of title otherwise than by subsection (b) then payment is due at the time and place at which the buyer is to receive the documents regardless of where the goods are to be received; and

(d) where the seller is required or authorized to ship the goods on credit the credit period runs from the time of shipment but post-dating the invoice or delaying its dispatch will correspondingly delay the starting of the credit period.

§ 2-312. Warranty of Title and Against Infringement; Buyer's Obligation Against Infringement.

(1) Subject to subsection (2) there is in a contract for sale a warranty by the seller that

(a) the title conveyed shall be good, and its transfer rightful; and

(b) the goods shall be delivered free from any security interest or other lien or encumbrance of which the buyer at the time of contracting has no knowledge.

(2) A warranty under subsection (1) will be excluded or modified only by specific language or by circumstances which give the buyer reason to know that the person selling does not claim title in himself or that he is purporting to sell only such right or title as he or a third person may have.

(3) Unless otherwise agreed a seller who is a merchant regularly dealing in goods of the kind warrants that the goods shall be delivered free of the rightful claim of any third person by way of infringement or the like but a buyer who furnishes specifications to the seller must

hold the seller harmless against any such claim which arises out of compliance with the specifications.

§ 2-313. Express Warranties by Affirmation, Promise, Description, Sample.

(1) Express warranties by the seller are created as follows:

(a) Any affirmation of fact or promise made by the seller to the buyer which relates to the goods and becomes part of the basis of the bargain creates an express warranty that the goods shall conform to the affirmation or promise.

(b) Any description of the goods which is made part of the basis of the bargain creates an express warranty that the goods shall conform to the description.

(c) Any sample or model which is made part of the basis of the bargain creates an express warranty that the whole of the goods shall conform to the sample or model.

(2) It is not necessary to the creation of an express warranty that the seller use formal words such as "warrant" or "guarantee" or that he have a specific intention to make a warranty, but an affirmation merely of the value of the goods or a statement purporting to be merely the seller's opinion or commendation of the goods does not create a warranty.

§ 2-314. Implied Warranty: Merchantability; Usage of Trade.

(1) Unless excluded or modified (Section 2-316), a warranty that the goods shall be merchantable is implied in a contract for their sale if the seller is a merchant with respect to goods of that kind. Under this section the serving for value of food or drink to be consumed either on the premises or elsewhere is a sale.

(2) Goods to be merchantable must be at least such as

(a) pass without objection in the trade under the contract description; and

(b) in the case of fungible goods, are of fair average quality within the description; and

(c) are fit for the ordinary purposes for which such goods are used; and

(d) run within the variations permitted by the agreement, of even kind, quality and quantity within each unit and among all units involved; and

(e) are adequately contained, packaged, and labeled as the agreement may require; and

(f) conform to the promise or affirmations of fact made on the container or label if any.

(3) Unless excluded or modified (Section 2-316) other implied warranties may arise from course of dealing or usage of trade.

§ 2-315. Implied Warranty: Fitness for Particular Purpose.

Where the seller at the time of contracting has reason to know any particular purpose for which the goods are required and that the buyer is relying on the seller's skill or judgment to select or furnish suitable goods, there is unless excluded or modified under the next section an implied warranty that the goods shall be fit for such purpose.

§ 2-316. Exclusion or Modification of Warranties.

(1) Words or conduct relevant to the creation of an express warranty and words or conduct tending to negate or limit warranty shall be construed wherever reasonable as consistent with each other; but subject to the provisions of this Article on parol or extrinsic evidence

(Section 2-202) negation or limitation is inoperatiave to the extent that such construction is unreasonable.

(2) Subject to subsection (3), to exclude or modify the implied warranty of merchantability or any part of it the language must mention merchantability and in case of a writing must be conspicuous, and to exclude or modify any implied warranty of fitness the exclusion must be by a writing and conspicuous. Language to exclude all implied warranties of fitness is sufficient if it states, for example, that "There are no warranties which extend beyond the description on the face hereof."

(3) Notwithstanding subsection (2)

(a) unless the circumstances indicate otherwise, all implied warranties are excluded by expressions like "as is", "with all faults" or other language which in common understanding calls the buyer's attention to the exclusion of warranties and makes plain that there is no implied warranty; and

(b) When the buyer before entering into the contract has examined the goods or the sample or model as fully as he desired or has refused to examine the goods there is no implied warranty with regard to defects which an examinatiaon ought in the circumstances to have revealed to him; and

(c) an implied warranty can also be excluded or modified by course of dealing or course of performance or usage of trade.

(4) Remedies for breach of warranty can be limited in accordance with the provisions of this Article on liquidation or limitation of damages and on contractual modification of remedy (Sections 2-718 and 2-719).

§ 2-317. Cumulation and Conflict of Warranties Express or Implied.

Warranties whether express or implied shall be construed as consistent with each other and as cumulative, but if such construction is unreasonable the intention of the parties shall determine which warranty is dominant. In ascertaining that intention the following rules apply:

(a) Exact or technical specifications displace an inconsistent sample or model or general language of description.

(b) A sample from an existing bulk displaces inconsistent general language of description.

(c) Express warranties displace inconsistent implied warranties other than an implied warranty of fitness for a particular purpose.

§ 2-318. Third Party Beneficiaries of Warranties Express or Implied.

[**Note:** *If this Act is introduced in the Congress of the United States this section should be omitted. (States to select one alternative.)*]

Alternative A

A seller's warranty whether express or implied extends to any natural person who is in the family or household of his buyer or who is a guest in his home if it is reasonable to expect that such person may use, consume or be affected by the goods and who is injured in person by breach of the warranty. A seller may not exclude or limit the operation of this section.

Alternative B

A seller's warranty whether express or implied extends to any natural person who may reasonably be expected to use, consume or be affected by the goods and who is injured in person by breach of the warranty. A seller may not exclude or limit the operation of this section.

Alternative C

A seller's warranty whether express or implied extends to any person who may reasonably be expected to use, consume or be affected by the goods and who is injured by breach of the warranty. A seller may not exclude or limit the operation of this section with respect to injury to the person of an individual to whom the warranty extends.

[**Note:** *As amended in 1966.*]

PART 5
PERFORMANCE

§ 2-501. Insurable Interest in Goods; Manner of Identification of Goods.

(1) The buyer obtains a special property and an insurable interest in goods by identification of existing goods as goods to which the contract refers even though the goods so identified are non-conforming and he has an option to return or reject them. Such identification can be made at any time and in any manner explicitly agreed to by the parties. In the absence of explicit agreement identification occurs

(a) when the contract is made if it is for the sale of goods already existing and identified;

(b) if the contract is for the sale of future goods other than those described in paragraph (c) when goods are shipped, marked or otherwise designated by the seller as goods to which the contract refers;

(c) when the crops are planted or otherwise become growing crops or the young are conceived if the contract is for the sale of unborn young to be born within twelve months after contracting or for the sale of crops to be harvested within twelve months or the next normal harvest reason after contracting whichever is longer.

(2) The seller retains an insurable interest in goods so long as title to or any security interest in the goods remains in him and where the identification is by the seller alone he may until default or insolvency or notification to the buyer that the identification is final substitute other goods for those identified.

(3) Nothing in this section impairs any insurable interest recognized under any other statute or rule of law.

§ 2-503. Manner of Seller's Tender of Delivery.

(1) Tender of delivery requires that the seller put and hold conforming goods at the buyer's disposition and give the buyer any notification reasonably necessary to enable him to take delivery. The manner, time and place for tender are determined by the agreement and this Article, and in particular

(a) tender must be at a reasonable hour, and if it is of goods they must be kept available for the period reasonably necessary to enable the buyer to take possession; but

(b) unless otherwise agreed the buyer must furnish facilities reasonably suited to the receipt of the goods.

§ 2-504. Shipment by Seller.

Where the seller is required or authorized to send the goods to the buyer and the contract does not require him to deliver them at a particular destination, then unless otherwise agreed he must

(a) put the goods in the possession of such a carrier and make such a contract for their transportation as may be reasonable having regard to the nature of the goods and other circumstances of the case; and

(b) obtain and promptly deliver or tender in due form any document necessary to enable the buyer to obtain possession of the goods or otherwise required by the agreement or by usage of trade; and

(c) promptly notify the buyer of the shipment.

Failure to notify the buyer under paragraph (c) or to make a proper contract under paragraph (a) is a ground for rejection only if material delay or loss ensues.

§ 2-507. Effect of Seller's Tender; Delivery on Condition.

(1) Tender of delivery is a condition to the buyer's duty to accept the goods and, unless otherwise agreed, to his duty to pay for them. Tender entitles the seller to acceptance of the goods and to payment according to the contract.

§ 2-508. Cure by Seller of Improper Tender or Delivery; Replacement.

(1) Where any tender or delivery by the seller is rejected because non-conforming and the time for performance has not yet expired, the seller may seasonably notify the buyer of his intention to cure and may then within the contract time make a conforming delivery.

(2) Where the buyer rejects a non-conforming tender which the seller had reasonable grounds to believe would be acceptable with or without money allowance the seller may if he seasonably notifies the buyer have a further reasonable time to substitute a conforming tender.

§ 2-509. Risk of Loss in the Absence of Breach.

(1) Where the contract requires or authorizes the seller to ship the goods by carrier

(a) if it does not require him to deliver them at a particular destination, the risk of loss passes to the buyer when the goods are duly delivered to the carrier even though the shipment is under reservation (Section 2-505); but

(b) if it does require him to deliver them at a particular destination and the goods are there duly tendered while in the possession of the carrier, the risk of loss passes to the buyer when the goods are there duly so tnedered as to enable the buyer to take delivery.

(2) Where the goods are held by a bailee to be delivered without being moved, the risk of loss passes to the buyer

(a) on his receipt of a negotiable document of title covering the goods; or

(b) on acknowledgment by the bailee of the buyer's right to possession of the goods; or

(c) after his receipt of a non-negotiable document of title or other written direction to deliver, as provided in subsection (4)(b) of Section 2-503.

(3) In any case not within subsection (1) or (2), the risk of loss passes to the buyer on his receipt of the goods if the seller is a merchant; otherwise the risk passes to the buyer on tender of delivery.

(4) The provisions of this section are subject to contrary agreement of the parties and to the provisions of this Article on sale on approval (Section 2-327) and on effect of breach on risk of loss (Section 2-510).

§ 2-510. Effect of Breach on Risk of Loss.

(1) Where a tender or delivery of goods so fails to conform to the contract as to give a right of rejection the risk of their loss remains on the seller until cure or acceptance.

(2) Where the buyer rightfully revokes acceptance he may to the extent of any deficiency in his effective insurance coverage treat the risk of loss as having rested on the seller from the beginning.

(3) Where the buyer as to conforming goods already identified to the contract for sale repudiates or is otherwise in breach before risk of their loss has passed to him, the seller may to the extent of any deficiency in his effective insurance coverage treat the risk of loss as resting on the buyer for a commercially reasonable time.

§ 2-511. Tender of Payment by Buyer; Payment by Check.

(1) Unless otherwise agreed tender of payment is a condition to the seller's duty to tender and complete any delivery.

(2) Tender of payment is sufficient when made by any means or in any manner current in the ordinary course of business unless the seller demands payment in legal tender and gives any extension of time reasonably necessary to procure it.

(3) Subject to the provisions of this Act on the effect of an instrument on an obligation (Section 3-310), payment by check is conditional and is defeated as between the parties by dishonor of the check on due presentment.

§ 2-513. Buyer's Right to Inspection of Goods.

(1) Unless otherwise agreed and subject to subsection (3), where goods are tendered or delivered or identified to the contract for sale, the buyer has a right before payment or acceptance to inspect them at any reasonable place and time and in any reasonable manner. When the seller is required or authorized to send the goods to the buyer, the inspection may be after their arrival.

(2) Expenses of inspection must be borne by the buyer but may be recovered from the seller if the goods do not conform and are rejected.

(3) Unless otherwise agreed and subject to the provisions of this Article on C.I.F. contracts (subsection (3) of Section 2-321), the buyer is not entitled to inspect the goods before payment of the price when the contract provides

(a) for delivery "C.O.D." or on other like terms; or

(b) for payment against documents of title, except where such payment is due only after the goods are to become available for inspection.

(4) A place or method of inspection fixed by the parties is presumed to be exclusive but unless otherwise expressly agreed it does not postpone identification or shift the place for delivery or for passing the risk of loss. If compliance becomes impossible, inspection shall be as provided in this section unless the place or method fixed was clearly intended as an indispensable condition failure of which avoids the contract.

PART 6
BREACH, REPUDIATION AND EXCUSE

§ 2-601. Buyer's Rights on Improper Delivery.

Subject to the provisions of this Article on breach in installment contracts (Section 2-612) and unless otherwise agreed under the sections on contractual limitations of remedy (Sections 2-718 and 2-719), if the goods or the tender of delivery fail in any respect to conform to the contract, the buyer may

(a) reject the whole; or

(b) accept the whole; or

(c) accept any commercial unit or units and reject the rest.

§ 2-602. Manner and Effect of Rightful Rejection.

(1) Rejection of goods must be within a reasonable time after their delivery or tender. It is ineffective unless the buyer seasonably notifies the seller.

(2) Subject to the provisions of the two following sections on rejected goods (Sections 2-603 and 2-604),

(a) after rejection any exercise of ownership by the buyer with respect to any commercial unit is wrongful as against the seller; and

(b) if the buyer has before rejection taken physical possession of goods in which he does not have a security interest under the provisions of this Article (subsection (3) of Section 2-711), he is under a duty after rejection to hold them with reasonable care at the seller's disposition for a time sufficient to permit the seller to remove them; but

(c) the buyer has no further obligations with regard to goods rightfully rejected.

(3) The seller's rights with respect to goods wrongfully rejected are governed by the provisions of this Article on seller's remedies in general (Section 2-703).

§ 2-603. Merchant Buyer's Duties as to Rightfully Rejected Goods.

(1) Subject to any security interest in the buyer (subsection (3) of Section 2-711), when the seller has no agent or place of business at the market of rejection a merchant buyer is under a duty after rejection of goods in his possession or control to follow any reasonable instructions received from the seller with respect to the goods and in the absence of such instructions to make reasonable efforts to sell them for the seller's account if they are perishable or threaten to decline in value speedily. Instructions are not reasonable if on demand indemnity for expenses is not forthcoming.

(2) When the buyer sells goods under subsection (1), he is entitled to reimbursement from the seller or out of the proceeds for reasonable expenses of caring for and selling them, and if the expenses include no selling commission then to such commission as is usual in the trade or if there is none to a reasonable sum not exceeding ten per cent on the gross proceeds.

(3) In complying with this section the buyer is held only to good faith and good faith conduct hereunder is neither acceptance nor conversion nor the basis of an action for damages.

§ 2-606. What Constitutes Acceptance of Goods.

(1) Acceptance of goods occurs when the buyer

(a) after a reasonable opportunity to inspect the goods signifies to the seller that the goods are conforming or that he will take or retain them in spite of their non-conformity; or

(b) fails to make an effective rejection (subsection (1) of Section 2-602), but such acceptance does not occur until the buyer has had a reasonable opportunity to inspect them; or

(c) does any act inconsistent with the seller's ownership; but if such act is wrongful as against the seller it is an acceptance only if ratified by him.

(2) Acceptance of a part of any commercial unit is acceptance of that entire unit.

§ 2-607. Effect of Acceptance; Notice of Breach; Burden of Establishing Breach After Acceptance; Notice of Claim or Litigation to Person Answerable Over.

(1) The buyer must pay at the contract rate for any goods accepted.

(2) Acceptance of goods by the buyer precludes rejection of the goods accepted and if made with knowledge of a non-conformity cannot be revoked because of it unless the acceptance was on the reasonable assumption that the non-conformity would be seasonably cured but acceptance does not of itself impair any other remedy provided by this Article for non-conformity.

(3) Where a tender has been accepted

(a) the buyer must within a reasonable time after he discovers or should have discovered any breach notify the seller of breach or be barred from any remedy; and

(b) if the claim is one for infringement or the like (subsection (3) of Section 2-312) and the buyer is sued as a result of such a breach he must so notify the seller within a reasonable time after he receives notice of the litigation or be barred from any remedy over for liability established by the litigation.

(4) The burden is on the buyer to establish any breach with respect to the goods accepted.

(5) Where the buyer is sued for breach of a warranty or other obligation for which his seller is answerable over

(a) he may give his seller written notice of the litigation. If the notice states that the seller may come in and defend and that if the seller does not do so he will be bound in any action against him by his buyer by any determination of fact common to the two litigations, then unless the seller after seasonable receipt of the notice does come in and defend he is so bound.

(b) if the claim is one for infringement or the like (subsection (3) of Section 2-312) the original seller may demand in writing that his buyer turn over to him control of the litigation including settlement or else be barred from any remedy over and if he also agrees to bear all expense and to satisfy any adverse judgment, then unless the buyer after seasonable receipt of the demand does turn over control the buyer is so barred.

(6) The provisions of subsections (3), (4) and (5) apply to any obligation of a buyer to hold the seller harmless against infringement or the like (subsection (3) of Section 2-312).

§ 2-608. Revocation of Acceptance in Whole or in Part.

(1) The buyer may revoke his acceptance of a lot or commercial unit whose non-conformity substantially impairs its value to him if he has accepted it

(a) on the reasonable assumption that its non-conformity would be cured and it has not been seasonably cured; or

(b) without discovery of such non-conformity if his acceptance was reasonably induced either by the difficulty of discovery before acceptance or by the seller's assurances.

(2) Revocation of acceptance must occur within a reasonable time after the buyer discovers or should have discovered the ground for it and before any substantial change in condition of the goods which is not caused by their own defects. It is not effective until the buyer notifies the seller of it.

(3) A buyer who so revokes has the same rights and duties with regard to the goods involved as if he had rejected them.

§ 2-609. Right to Adequate Assurance of Performance.

(1) A contract for sale imposes an obligation on each party that the other's expectation of receiving due performance will not be impaired. When reasonable grounds for insecurity arise with respect to the performance of either party the other may in writing demand adequate assurance of due performance and until he receives such assurance may if commercially reasonable suspend any performance for which he has not already received the agreed return.

(2) Between merchants the reasonableness of grounds for insecurity and the adequacy of any assurance offered shall be determined according to commercial standards.

(3) Acceptance of any improper delivery or payment does not prejudice the aggrieved party's right to demand adequate assurance of future performance.

(4) After receipt of a justified demand failure to provide within a reasonable time not exceeding thirty days such assurance of due performance as is adequate under the circumstances of the particular case is a repudiation of the contract.

§ 2-610. Anticipatory Repudiation.

When either party repudiates the contract with respect to a performance not yet due the loss of which will substantially impair the value of the contract to the other, the aggrieved party may

(a) for a commercially reasonable time await performance by the repudiating party; or

(b) resort to any remedy for breach (Section 2-703 or Section 2-711), even though he has notified the repudiating party that he would await the latter's performance and has urged retraction; and

(c) in either case suspend his own performance or proceed in accordance with the provisions of this Article on the seller's right to identify goods to the contract notwithstanding breach or to salvage unfinished goods (Section 2-704).

§ 2-611. Retraction of Anticipatory Repudiation.

(1) Until the repudiating party's next performance is due he can retract his repudiation unless the aggrieved party has since the repudiation cancelled or materially changed his position or otherwise indicated that he considers the repudiation final.

(2) Retraction may be by any method which clearly indicates to the aggrieved party that the repudiating party intends to perform, but must include any assurance justifiably demanded under the provisions of this Article (Section 2-609).

(3) Retraction reinstates the repudiating party's rights under the contract with due excuse and allowance to the aggrieved party for any delay occasioned by the repudiation.

PART 7
REMEDIES

§ 2-702. Seller's Remedies on Discovery of Buyer's Insolvency.

(1) Where the seller discovers the buyer to be insolvent he may refuse delivery except for cash including payment for all goods theretofore delivered under the contract, and stop delivery under this Article (Section 2-705).

(2) Where the seller discovers that the buyer has received goods on credit while insolvent he may reclaim the goods upon demand made within ten days after the receipt, but if misrepresentation of solvency has been made to the particular seller in writing within three months before delivery the ten day limitation does not apply. Except as provided in this subsection the seller may not base a right to reclaim goods on the buyer's fraudulent or innocent misrepresentation of solvency or of intent to pay.

(3) The seller's right to reclaim under subsection (2) is subject to the rights of a buyer in ordinary course or other good faith purchaser under this Article (Section 2-403). Successful reclamation of goods excludes all other remedies with respect to them.

[**Note:** *As amended in 1966.*]

§ 2-703. Seller's Remedies in General.

Where the buyer wrongfully rejects or revokes acceptance of goods or fails to make a payment due on or before delivery or repudiates with respect to a part or the whole, then with respect to any goods directly affected and, if the breach is of the whole contract (Section 2-612), then also with respect to the whole undelivered balance, the aggrieved seller may

    (a) withhold delivery of such goods;

    (b) stop delivery by any bailee as hereafter provided (Section 2-705);

    (c) proceed under the next section respecting goods still unidentified to the contract;

    (d) resell and recover damages as hereafter provided (Section 2-706);

    (e) recover damages for non-acceptance (Section 2-708) or in a proper case the price (Section 2-709);

    (f) cancel.

§ 2-704. Seller's Right to Identify Goods to the Contract Notwithstanding Breach or to Salvage Unfinished Goods.

(1) An aggrieved seller under the preceding section may

    (a) identify to the contract conforming goods not already identified if at the time he learned of the breach they are in his possession or control;

(b) treat as the subject of resale goods which have demonstrably been intended for the particular contract even though those goods are unfinished.

(2) Where the goods are unfinished an aggrieved seller may in the exercise of reasonable commercial judgment for the purposes of avoiding loss and of effective realization either complete the manufacture and wholly identify the goods to the contract or cease manufacture and resell for scrap or salvage value or proceed in any other reasonable manner.

§ 2-705. Seller's Stoppage of Delivery in Transit or Otherwise.

(1) The seller may stop delivery of goods in the possession of a carrier or other bailee when he discovers the buyer to be insolvent (Section 2-702) and may stop delivery of carload, truckload, planeload or larger shipments of express or freight when the buyer repudiates or fails to make a payment due before delivery or if for any other reason the seller has a right to withhold or reclaim the goods.

(2) As against such buyer the seller may stop delivery until

(a) receipt of the goods by the buyer ; or

(b) acknowledgment to the buyer by any bailee of the goods except a carrier that the bailee holds the goods for the buyer; or

(c) such acknowledgment to the buyer by a carrier by reshipment or as warehouseman; or

(d) negotiation to the buyer of any negotiable document of title covering the goods.

(3) (a) To stop delivery the seller must so notify as to enable the bailee by reasonable diligence to prevent delivery of the goods.

(b) After such notification the bailee must hold and deliver the goods according to the directions of the seller but the seller is liable to the bailee for any ensuing charges or damages.

(c) If a negotiable document of title has been issued for goods the bailee is not obliged to obey a notification to stop until surrender of the document.

(d) A carrier who has issued a non-negotiable bill of lading is not obliged to obey a notification to stop received from a person other than the consignor.

§ 2-706. Seller's Resale Including Contract for Resale.

(1) Under the conditions stated in Section 2-703 on seller's remedies, the seller may resell the goods concerned or the undelivered balance thereof. Where the resale is made in good faith and in a commercially reasonable manner the seller may recover the difference between the resale price and the contract price together with any incidental damages allowed under the provisions of this Article (Section 2-710), but less expenses saved in consequence of the buyer's breach.

(2) Except as otherwise provided in subsection (3) or unless otherwise agreed resale may be at public or private sale including sale by way of one or more contracts to sell or of identification to an existing contract of the seller. Sale may be as a unit or in parcels and at any time and place and on any terms but every aspect of the sale including the method, manner, time, place and terms must be commercially reasonable. The resale must be reasonably identified as referring to the broken contract, but it is not necessary that the goods be in existence or that any or all of them have been identified to the contract before the breach.

(3) Where the resale is at private sale the seller must give the buyer reasonable notification of his intention to resell.

(4) Where the resale is at public sale

(a) only identified goods can be sold except where there is a recognized market for a public sale of futures in goods of the kind; and

(b) it must be made at a usual place or market for public sale if one is reasonably available and except in the case of goods which are perishable or threaten to decline in value speedily the seller must give the buyer reasonable notice of the time and place of the resale; and

(c) if the goods are not to be within the view of those attending the sale the notification of sale must state the place where the goods are located and provide for their reasonable inspection by prospective bidders; and

(d) the seller may buy.

(5) A purchaser who buys in good faith at a resale takes the goods free of any rights of the original buyer even though the seller fails to comply with one or more of the requirements of this section.

(6) The seller is not accountable to the buyer for any profit made on any resale. A person in the position of a seller (Section 2-707) or a buyer who has rightfully rejected or justifiably revoked acceptance must account for any excess over the amount of his security interest, as hereinafter defined (subsection (3) of Section 2-711).

§ 2-707. "Person in the Position of a Seller".

(1) A "person in the position of a seller" includes as against a principal an agent who has paid or become responsible for the price of goods on behalf of his principal or anyone who otherwise holds a security interest or other right in goods similar to that of a seller.

(2) A person in the position of a seller may as provided in this Article withhold or stop delivery (Section 2-705) and resell (Section 2-706) and recover incidental damages (Section 2-710).

§ 2-708. Seller's Damages for Non-acceptance or Repudiation.

(1) Subject to subsection (2) and to the provisions of this Article with respect to proof of market price (Section 2-723), the measure of damages for non-acceptance or repudiation by the buyer is the difference between the market price at the time and place for tender and the unpaid contract price together with any incidental damages provided in this Article (Section 2-710), but less expenses saved in consequence of the buyer's breach.

(2) If the measure of damages provided in subsection (1) is inadequate to put the seller in as good a position as performance would have done then the measure of damages is the profit (including reasonable overhead) which the seller would have made from full performance by the buyer, together with any incidental damages provided in this Article (Section 2-710), due allowance for costs reasonably incurred and due credit for payments or proceeds of resale.

§ 2-709. Action for the Price.

(1) When the buyer fails to pay the price as it becomes due the seller may recover, together with any incidental damages under the next section, the price

(a) of goods accepted or of conforming goods lost or damaged within a commercially reasonable time after risk of their loss has passed to the buyer; and

(b) of goods identified to the contract if the seller is unable after reasonable effort to resell them at a reasonable price or the circumstances reasonably indicate that such effort will be unavailing.

(2) Where the seller sues for the price he must hold for the buyer any goods which have been identified to the contract and are still in his control except that if resale becomes possible he may resell them at any time prior to the collection of the judgment. The net proceeds of any such resale must be credited to the buyer and payment of the judgment entitles him to any goods not resold.

(3) After the buyer has wrongfully rejected or revoked acceptance of the goods or has failed to make a payment due or has repudiated (Section 2-610), a seller who is held not entitled to the price under this section shall nevertheless be awarded damages for non-acceptance under the preceding section.

§ 2-710. Seller's Incidental Damages.
Incidental damages to an aggrieved seller include any commercially reasonable charges, expenses or commissions incurred in stopping delivery, in the transportation, care and custody of goods after the buyer's breach, in connection with return or resale of the goods or otherwise resulting from the breach.

§ 2-711. Buyer's Remedies in General; Buyer's Security Interest in Rejected Goods.
(1) Where the seller fails to make delivery or repudiates or the buyer rightfully rejects or justifiably revokes acceptance then with respect to any goods involved, and with respect to the whole if the breach goes to the whole contract (Section 2-612), the buyer may cancel and whether or not he has done so may in addition to recovering so much of the price as has been paid

(a) "cover" and have damages under the next section as to all the goods affected whether or not they have been identified to the contract; or

(b) recover damages for non-delivery as provided in this Article (Section 2-713).

(2) Where the seller fails to deliver or repudiates the buyer may also

(a) if the goods have been identified recover them as provided in this Article (Section 2-502); or

(b) in a proper case obtain specific performance or replevy the goods as provided in this Article (Section 2-716).

(3) On rightful rejection or justifiable revocation of acceptance a buyer has a security interest in goods in his possession or control for any payments made on their price and any expenses reasonably incurred in their inspection, receipt, transportation, care and custody and may hold such goods and resell them in like manner as an aggrieved seller (Section 2-706).

§ 2-712. "Cover"; Buyer's Procurement of Substitute Goods.
(1) After a breach within the preceding section the buyer may "cover" by making in good faith and without unreasonable delay any reasonable purchase of or contract to purchase goods in substitution for those due from the seller.

(2) The buyer may recover from the seller as damages the difference between the cost of cover and the contract price together with any incidental or consequential damages as hereinafter defined (Section 2-715), but less expenses saved in consequence of the seller's breach.

(3) Failure of the buyer to effect cover within this section does not bar him from any other remedy.

§ 2-713. Buyer's Damages for Non-delivery or Repudiation.

(1) Subject to the provisions of this Article with respect to proof of market price (Section 2-723), the measure of damages for non-delivery or repudiation by the seller is the difference between the market price at the time when the buyer learned of the breach and the contract price together with any incidental and consequential damages provided in this Article (Section 2-715), but less expenses saved in consequence of the seller's breach.

(2) Market price is to be determined as of the place for tender or, in cases of rejection after arrival or revocation of acceptance, as of the place of arrival.

§ 2-714. Buyer's Damages for Breach in Regard to Accepted Goods.

(1) Where the buyer has accepted goods and given notification (subsection (3) of Section 2-607) he may recover as damages for any non-conformity of tender the loss resulting in the ordinary course of events from the seller's breach as determined in any manner which is reasonable.

(2) The measure of damages for breach of warranty is the difference at the time and place of acceptance between the value of the goods accepted and the value they would have had if they had been as warranted, unless special circumstances show proximate damages of a different amount.

(3) In a proper case any incidental and consequential damages under the next section may also be recovered.

§ 2-715. Buyer's Incidental and Consequential Damages.

(1) Incidental damages resulting from the seller's breach include expenses reasonably incurred in inspection, receipt, transportation and care and custody of goods rightfully rejected, any commercially reasonable charges, expenses or commissions in connection with effecting cover and any other reasonable expense incident to the delay or other breach.

(2) Consequential damages resulting from the seller's breach include

(a) any loss resulting from general or particular requirements and needs of which the seller at the time of contracting had reason to know and which could not reasonably be prevented by cover or otherwise; and

(b) injury to person or property proximately resulting from any breach of warranty.

§ 2-716. Buyer's Right to Specific Performance or Replevin.

(1) Specific performance may be decreed where the goods are unique or in other proper circumstances.

(2) The decree for specific performance may include such terms and conditions as to payment of the price, damages, or other relief as the court may deem just.

(3) The buyer has a right of replevin for goods identified to the contract if after reasonable effort he is unable to effect cover for such goods or the circumstances reasonably indicate that such effort will be unavailing or if the goods have been shipped under reservation and satisfaction of the security interest in them has been made or tendered.

§ 2-717. Deduction of Damages From the Price.

The buyer on notifying the seller of his intention to do so may deduct all or any part of the damages resulting from any breach of the contract from any part of the price still due under the same contract.

§ 2-718. Liquidation or Limitation of Damages; Deposits.

(1) Damages for breach by either party may be liquidated in the agreement but only at an amount which is reasonable in the light of the anticipated or actual harm caused by the breach, the difficulties of proof of loss, and the inconvenience or nonfeasibility of otherwise obtaining an adequate remedy. A term fixing unreasonably large liquidated damages is void as a penalty.

(2) Where the seller justifiably withholds delivery of goods because of the buyer's breach, the buyer is entitled to restitution of any amount by which the sum of his payments exceeds

(a) the amount to which the seller is entitled by virtue of terms liquidating the seller's damages in accordance with subsection (1), or

(b) in the absence of such terms, twenty per cent of the value of the total performance for which the buyer is obligated under the contract or $500, whichever is smaller.

(3) The buyer's right to restitution under subsection (2) is subject to offset to the extent that the seller establishes

(a) a right to recover damages under the provisions of this Article other than subsection (1), and

(b) the amount or value of any benefits received by the buyer directly or indirectly by reason of the contract.

(4) Where a seller has received payment in goods their reasonable value or the proceeds of their resale shall be treated as payments for the purposes of subsection (2); but if the seller has notice of the buyer's breach before reselling goods received in part performance, his resale is subject to the conditions laid down in this Article on resale by an aggrieved seller (Section 2-706).

2-719. Contractual Modification or Limitation of Remedy.

(1) Subject to the provisions of subsections (2) and (3) of this section and of the preceding section on liquidation and limitation of damages,

(a) the agreement may provide for remedies in addtion to or in substitution for those provided in this Article and may limit or alter the measure of damages recoverable under this Article, as by limiting the buyer's remedies to return of the goods and repayment of the price or to repair and replacement of non-conforming goods or parts; and

(b) resort to a remedy as provided is optional unless the remedy is expressly agreed to be exclusive, in which case it is the sole remedy.

APPENDIX C

Selected Statutes

Sec. 1051. Registration of Trademarks

(a) Application for use of trademark

(1) The owner of a trademark used in commerce may request registration of its trademark on the principal register hereby established by paying the prescribed fee and filing in the Patent and Trademark Office an application and a verified statement, in such form as may be prescribed by the Director,and such number of specimens or facsimiles of the mark as used as may be required by the Director.

(2) The application shall include specification of the applicant's domicile and citizenship, the date of the applicant's first use of the mark, the date of the applicant's first use of the mark in commerce, the goods in connection with which the mark is used, and a drawing of the mark.

(3) The statement shall be verified by the applicant and specify that—

(A) the person making the verification believes that he or she, or the juristic person in whose behalf he or she makes the verification, to be the owner of the mark sought to be registered;

(B) to the best of the verifier's knowledge and belief, the facts recited in the application are accurate;

(C the mark is in use in commerce; and

(D) to the best of the verifier's knowledge and belief, no other person has the right to use such mark in commerce either in the identical form thereof or in such near resemblance thereto as to be likely, when used on or in connection with the goods of such other person, to cause confusion, or to cause mistake, or to deceive, except that, in the case of every application claiming concurrent use, the applicant shall—

(i) state exceptions to the claim of exclusive use; and

(ii) shall specify, to the extent of the verifier's knowledge—

(I) any concurrent use by others;

(II) the goods on or in connection with which and the areas in which each concurrent use exists;

(III) the periods of each use; and

(IV) the goods and area for which the applicant desires registration.

(4) The applicant shall comply with such rules or regulations as may be prescribed by the Director. The Director shall promulgate rules prescribing the requirements for the application and for obtaining a filing date herein.

(b) Application for bona fide intention to use trademark

(1) A person who has a bona fide intention, under circumstances showing the good faith of such person, to use a trademark in commerce may request registration of its trademark on the principal register hereby established by paying the prescribed fee and filing in the Patent and Trademark Office an application and a verified statement, in such form as may be prescribed by the Director.

(2) The application shall include specification of the applicant's domicile and citizenship, the goods in connection with which the applicant has a bonafide intention to use the mark, and a drawing of the mark.

(3) The statement shall be verified by the applicant and specify—

(A) that the person making the verification believes that he or she, or the juristic person in whose behalf he or she makes the verification, to be entitled to use the mark in commerce;

(B) the applicant's bona fide intention to use the mark in commerce;

(C) that, to the best of the verifier's knowledge and belief, the facts recited in the application are accurate; and

(D) that, to the best of the verifier's knowledge and belief, no other person has the right to use such mark in commerce either in the identical form thereof or in such near resemblance thereto as to be likely, when used on or in connection with the goods of such other person, to cause confusion, or to cause mistake, or to deceive.

Except for applications filed pursuant to [15 U.S.C. § 1126], no mark shall be registered until the applicant has met the requirements of subsections (c) and (d) of this section.

(4) The applicant shall comply with such rules or regulations as may be prescribed by the Director. The Director shall promulgate rules prescribing the requirements for the application and for obtaining a filing date herein.

Sec. 1052. Trademarks registrable on principal register; concurrent registration

No trademark by which the goods of the applicant may be distinguished from the goods of others shall be refused registration on the principal register on account of its nature unless it—

(a) Consists of or comprises immoral, deceptive, or scandalous matter; or matter which may disparage or falsely suggest a connection with persons, living or dead, institutions, beliefs, or national symbols, or bring them into contempt, or disrepute; or a geographical indication which, when used on or in connection with wines or spirits, identifies a place other than the origin of the goods and is first used on or in connection with wines or spirits by the applicant on or after one year after the date on which the WTO Agreement (as defined in [19 U.S.C. § 3501 (9)]) enters into force with respect to the United States.

(b) Consists of or comprises the flag or coat of arms or other insignia of the United States, or of any State or municipality, or of any foreign nation, or any simulation thereof.

(c) Consists of or comprises a name, portrait, or signature identifying a particular living individual except by his written consent, or the name, signature, or portrait of a deceased President of the United States during the life of his widow, if any, except by the written consent of the widow.

(d) Consists of or comprises a mark which so resembles a mark registered in the Patent and Trademark Office, or a mark or trade name previously used in the United States by another and not abandoned, as to be likely, when used on or in connection with the goods of the applicant, to cause confusion, or to cause mistake, or to deceive: Provided, That if the Director determines that confusion, mistake, or deception is not likely to result from the continued use by more than one person of the same or similar marks under conditions and limitations as to the mode or place of use of the marks or the goods on or in connection with which such marks are used, concurrent registrations may be issued to such persons when they have become entitled to use such marks as a result of their concurrent lawful use in commerce prior to (1) the earliest of the filing dates of the applications pending or of any registration issued under this chapter; (2) July 5, 1947, in the case of registrations previously issued under the Act of March 3, 1881, or February 20, 1905, and continuing in full force and effect on that date; or (3) July 5, 1947, in the case of applications filed under the Act of February 20, 1905, and registered after July 5, 1947. Use prior to the filing date of any pending application or a registration shall not be required when the owner of such application or registration consents to the grant of a concurrent registration to the applicant. Concurrent registrations may also be issued by the Director when a court of competent jurisdiction has finally determined that more than one person is entitled to use the same or similar marks in commerce. In issuing concurrent registrations, the Director shall prescribe conditions and limitations as to the mode or place of use of the mark or the goods on or in connection with which such mark is registered to the respective persons.

(e) Consists of a mark which (1) when used on or in connection with the goods of the applicant is merely descriptive or deceptively misdescriptive of them, (2) when used on or in connection with the goods of the applicant is primarily geographically descriptive of them, except as indications of regional origin may be registrable under section 1054 of this title, (3) when used on or in connection with the goods of the applicant is primarily geographically deceptively misdescriptive of them, (4) is primarily merely a surname, or (5) comprises any matter that, as a whole, is functional.

(f) Except as expressly excluded in subsections (a), (b), (c), (d), (e) (3), and (e) (5) of this section, nothing herein shall prevent the registration of a mark used by the applicant which has become distinctive of the applicant's goods in commerce. The Director may accept as prima facie evidence that the mark has become distinctive, as used on or in connection with the applicant's goods in commerce, proof of substantially exclusive and continuous use thereof as a mark by the applicant in commerce for the five years before the date on which the claim of distinctiveness is made. Nothing in this section shall prevent the registration of a mark which, when used on or in connection with the goods of the applicant, is primarily geographically deceptively misdescriptive of them, and which became distinctive of the applicant's goods in commerce before December 8, 1993. A mark which when used would cause dilution under section 1125(c) of this title may be refused registration only pursuant to a proceeding brought under section 1063 of this title. A registration for a mark which when used would cause dilution under section 1125(c) of this title may be canceled pursuant to a proceeding brought under either section 1064 of this title or section 1092 of this title.

Sec. 1058. Duration

(a) Each registration shall remain in force for 10 years, except that the registration of any mark shall be canceled by the Director for failure to comply with the provisions of subsection (b) of this section, upon the expiration of the following time periods, as applicable:

(1) For registrations issued pursuant to the provisions of this chapter, at the end of 6 years following the date of registration.

(2) For registrations published under the provisions of section 1062(c) of this title, at the end of 6 years following the date of publication under such section.

(3) For all registrations, at the end of each successive 10-year period following the date of registration.

Sec. 1059. Renewal of registration

(a) Subject to the provisions of section 1058 of this title, each registration may be renewed for periods of 10 years at the end of each successive 10-year period following the date of registration upon payment of the prescribed fee and the filing of a written application, in such form as may be prescribed by the Director. Such application may be made at any time within 1 year before the end of each successive 10-year period for which the registration was issued or renewed, or it may be made within a grace period of 6 months after the end of each successive 10-year period, upon payment of a fee and surcharge prescribed therefor. If any application filed under this section is deficient, the deficiency may be corrected within the time prescribed after notification of the deficiency, upon payment of a surcharge prescribed therefor.

Sec. 1064. Cancellation of registration

A petition to cancel a registration of a mark, stating the grounds relied upon, may, upon payment of the prescribed fee, be filed as follows by any person who believes that he is or will be damaged, including as a result of dilution under section 1125(c) of this title, by the registration of a mark on the principal register established by this chapter, or under the Act of March 3, 1881, or the Act of February 20, 1905:

(1) Within five years from the date of the registration of the mark under this chapter.

(2) Within five years from the date of publication under section 1062(c) of this title of a mark registered under the Act of March 3, 1881, or the Act of February 20, 1905.

(3) At any time if the registered mark becomes the generic name for the goods or services, or a portion thereof, for which it is registered, or is functional, or has been abandoned, or its registration was obtained fraudulently or contrary to the provisions of section 1054 of this title or of subsection (a), under this chapter, or contrary to similar prohibitory provisions of such prior Acts for a registration under such Acts, or if the registered mark is being used by, or with the permission of, the registrant so as to misrepresent the source of the goods or services on or in connection with which the mark is used. If the registered mark becomes the generic name for less than all of the goods or services for which it is registered, a petition to cancel the registration for only those goods or services may be filed. A registered mark shall not be deemed to be the generic name of goods or services solely because such mark is also used as a name of or to identify a unique product or service. The primary significance of the registered mark to the relevant public rather than purchaser motivation shall be the test for determining whether the registered mark has become the generic name of goods or services on or in connection with which it has been used.

(4) At any time if the mark is registered under the Act of March 3, 1881, or the Act of February 20, 1905, and has not been published under the provisions of subsection (c) of section 1062 of this title.

(5) At any time in the case of a certification mark on the ground that the registrant (A) does not control, or is not able legitimately to exercise control over, the use of such mark, or (B) engages in the production or marketing of any goods or services to which the certification mark is applied, or (C) permits the use of the certification mark for purposes other than to certify, or (D) discriminately refuses to certify or to continue to certify the goods or services of any person who maintains the standards or conditions which such mark certifies: Provided, That the Federal Trade Commission may apply to cancel on the grounds specified in paragraphs (3) and (5) of this section any mark registered on the principal register established by this chapter, and the prescribed fee shall not be required. Nothing in paragraph (5) shall be deemed to prohibit the registrant from using its certification mark in advertising or promoting recognition of the certification program or of the goods or services meeting the certification standards of the registrant. Such uses of the certification mark shall not be grounds for cancellation under paragraph (5), so

long as the registrant does not itself produce, manufacture, or sell any of the certified goods or services to which its identical certification mark is applied.

Sec. 1111. Notice of registration; display with mark; recovery of profits and damages in infringement suit

Notwithstanding the provisions of section 1072 of this title, a registrant of a mark registered in the Patent and Trademark Office, may give notice that his mark is registered by displaying with the mark the words "Registered in U.S. Patent and Trademark Office" or "Reg. U.S. Pat. & Tm. Off." or the letter R enclosed within a circle, thus (inch(s)); and in any suit for infringement under this chapter by such a registrant failing to give such notice of registration, no profits and no damages shall be recovered under the provisions of this chapter unless the defendant had actual notice of the registration.

Sec. 1114. Remedies; infringement; innocent infringement by printers and publishers

(1) Any person who shall, without the consent of the registrant—

(a) use in commerce any reproduction, counterfeit, copy, or colorable imitation of a registered mark in connection with the sale, offering for sale, distribution, or advertising of any goods or services on or in connection with which such use is likely to cause confusion, or to cause mistake, or to deceive; or

(b) reproduce, counterfeit, copy, or colorably imitate a registered mark and apply such reproduction, counterfeit, copy, or colorable imitation to labels, signs, prints, packages, wrappers, receptacles or advertisements intended to be used in commerce upon or in connection with the sale, offering for sale, distribution, or advertising of goods or services on or in connection with which such use is likely to cause confusion, or to cause mistake, or to deceive, shall be liable in a civil action by the registrant for the remedies hereinafter provided. Under subsection (b) hereof, the registrant shall not be entitled to recover profits or damages unless the acts have been committed with knowledge that such imitation is intended to be used to cause confusion, or to cause mistake, or to deceive.

As used in this paragraph, the term "any person" includes the United States, all agencies and instrumentalities thereof, and all individuals, firms, corporations, or other persons acting for the United States and with the authorization and consent of the United States, and any State, any instrumentality of a State, and any officer or employee of a State or instrumentality of a State acting in his or her official capacity. The United States, all agencies and instrumentalities thereof, and all individuals, firms, corporations, other persons acting for the United States and with the authorization and consent of the United States, and any State, and any such instrumentality, officer, or employee, shall be subject to the provisions of this chapter in the same manner and to the same extent as any nongovernmental entity.

(2) Notwithstanding any other provision of this chapter, the remedies given to the owner of a right infringed under this chapter or to a person bringing an action under section 1125(a) or (d) of this title shall be limited as follows:

(A) Where an infringer or violator is engaged solely in the business of printing the mark or violating matter for others and establishes that he or she was an innocent infringer or innocent violator, the owner of the right infringed or person bringing the action under section 1125(a) of this title shall be entitled as against such infringer or violator only to an injunction against future printing.

(B) Where the infringement or violation complained of is contained in or is part of paid advertising matter in a newspaper, magazine, or other similar periodical or in an electronic communication as defined in section 2510(12) of title 18, the remedies of the owner of the right infringed or person bringing the action under section 1125(a) of this title as against the publisher or distributor of such newspaper,magazine, or other similar periodical or electronic communication shall be limited to an injunction against the presentation of such advertising matter in future issues of such newspapers, magazines, or other similar periodicals or in future transmissions of such electronic communications. The limitations of this subparagraph shall apply only to innocent infringers and innocent violators.

(C) Injunctive relief shall not be available to the owner of the right infringed or person bringing the action under section 1125(a) of this title with respect to an issue of a newspaper, magazine, or other similar periodical or an electronic communication containing infringing matter or violating matter where restraining the dissemination of such infringing matter or violating matter in any particular issue of such periodical or in an electronic communication would delay the delivery of such issue or transmission of such electronic communication after the regular time for such delivery or transmission, and such delay would be due to the method by which publication and distribution of such periodical or transmission of such electronic communication is customarily conducted in accordance with sound business practice, and not due to any method or device adopted to evade this section or to prevent or delay the issuance of an injunction or restraining order with respect to such infringing matter or violating matter.

(D) (i) (I) A domain name registrar, a domain name registry, or other domain name registration authority that takes any action described under clause (ii) affecting a domain name shall not be liable for monetary relief or, except as provided in subclause (II) per injunctive relief, to any person for such action, regardless of whether the domain name is finally determined to infringe or dilute the mark.

(II) A domain name registrar, domain name registry, or other domain name registration authority described in subclause (I) may be subject to injunctive relief only if such registrar, registry, or other registration authority has—

(aa) not expeditiously deposited with a court, in which an action has been filed regarding the disposition of the domain name, documents sufficient for the court to establish the court's control and authority regarding the disposition of the registration and use of the domain name;

(bb) transferred, suspended, or otherwise modified the domain name during the pendency of the action, except upon order of the court; or

(cc) willfully failed to comply with any such court order.

(ii) An action referred to under clause (i)(I) is any action of refusing to register, removing from registration, transferring, temporarily disabling, or permanently canceling a domain name—

(I) in compliance with a court order under section 1125(d) of this title; or

(II) in the implementation of a reasonable policy by such registrar, registry, or authority prohibiting the registration of a domain name that is identical to, confusingly similar to, or dilutive of another's mark.

(iii) A domain name registrar, a domain name registry, or other domain name registration authority shall not be liable for damages under this section for the registration or maintenance of a domain name for another absent a showing of bad faith intent to profit from such registration or maintenance of the domain name.

(iv) If a registrar, registry, or other registration authority takes an action described under clause (ii) based on a knowing and material misrepresentation by any other person that a domain name is identical to, confusingly similar to, or dilutive of a mark, the person making the knowing and material misrepresentation shall be liable for any damages, including costs and attorney's fees, incurred by the domain name registrant as a result of such action. The court may also grant injunctive relief to the domain name registrant, including the reactivation of the domain name or the transfer of the domain name to the domain name registrant.

(v) A domain name registrant whose domain name has been suspended, disabled, or transferred under a policy described under clause (ii)(II) may, upon notice to the mark owner, file a civil action to establish that the registration or use of the domain name by such registrant is not unlawful under this chapter. The court may grant injunctive relief to the domain name registrant, including the reactivation of the domain name or transfer of the domain name to the domain name registrant.

(E) As used in this paragraph—

(i) the term "violator" means a person who violates section 1125(a) of this title; and

(ii) the term "violating matter" means matter that is the subject of a violation under section 1125(a) of this title.

Sec. 1117. Recovery for violation of rights; Profits; damages and costs; attorney fees; treble damages

(a) When a violation of any right of the registrant of a mark registered in the Patent and Trademark Office, a violation under section 1125(a), (c), or (d) of this title, or a willful violation under section 1125(c) of this title, shall have been established in any civil action arising under this chapter, the plaintiff shall be entitled, subject to the provisions of sections 1111 and 1114 of this title, and subject to the principles of equity, to recover (1) defendant's profits, (2) any damages sustained by the plaintiff, and (3) the costs of the action. The court shall assess such profits and damages or cause the same to be assessed under its direction. In assessing profits the plaintiff shall be required to prove defendant's sales only; defendant must prove all elements of cost or deduction claimed. In assessing damages the court may enter judgment, according to the circumstances of the case, for any sum above the amount found as actual damages, not exceeding three times such amount. If the court shall find that the amount of the recovery based on profits is either inadequate or excessive the court may in its discretion enter judgment for such sum as the court shall find to be just, according to the circumstances of the case. Such sum in either of the above circumstances shall constitute compensation and not a penalty. The court in exceptional cases may award reasonable attorney fees to the prevailing party.

(b) Treble damages for use of counterfeit mark

In assessing damages under subsection (a) of this section, the court shall, unless the court finds extenuating circumstances, enter judgment for three times such profits or damages, whichever is greater, together with a reasonable attorney's fee, in the case of any violation of section 1114(1)(a) of this title or section 220506 of title 36 that consists of intentionally using a mark or designation, knowing such mark or designation is a counterfeit mark (as defined in section 1116(d) of this title), in connection with the sale, offering for sale, or distribution of goods or services. In such cases, the court may in its discretion award prejudgment interest on such amount at an annual interest rate established under section 6621 of title 26, commencing on the date of the service of the claimant's pleadings setting forth the claim for such entry and ending on the date such entry is made, or for such shorter time as the court deems appropriate.

(c) Statutory damages for use of counterfeit marks In a case involving the use of a counterfeit mark (as defined in section 1116(d) of this title) in connection with the sale, offering for sale, or distribution of goods or services, the plaintiff may elect, at any time before final judgment is rendered by the trial court, to recover, instead of actual damages and profits under subsection (a) of this section, an award of statutory damages for any such use in connection with the sale, offering for sale, or distribution of goods or services in the amount of—

(1) not less than $500 or more than $100,000 per counterfeit mark per type of goods or services sold, offered for sale, or distributed, as the court considers just; or

(2) if the court finds that the use of the counterfeit mark was willful, not more than $1,000,000 per counterfeit mark per type of goods or services sold, offered for sale, or distributed, as the court considers just.

(d) In a case involving a violation of section 1125(d)(1) of this title, the plaintiff may elect, at any time before final judgment is rendered by the trial court, to recover, instead of actual damages and profits, an award of statutory damages in the amount of not less than $1,000 and not more than $100,000 per domain name, as the court considers just.

Sec. 1125. False designations of origin, and false descriptions forbidden

(a) Civil action

(1) Any person who, on or in connection with any goods or services, or any container for goods, uses in commerce any word, term, name, symbol, or device, or any combination thereof, or any false designation of origin, false or misleading description of fact, or false or misleading representation of fact, which—

(A) is likely to cause confusion, or to cause mistake, or to deceive as to the affiliation, connection, or association of such person with another person, or as to the origin, sponsorship, or approval of his or her goods, services, or commercial activities by another person, or

(B) in commercial advertising or promotion, misrepresents the nature, characteristics, qualities, or geographic origin of his or her or another person's goods, services, or commercial activities, shall be liable in a civil action by any person who believes that he or she is or is likely to be damaged by such act.

(2) As used in this subsection, the term "any person" includes any State, instrumentality of a State or employee of a State or instrumentality of a State acting in his or her official capacity. Any State, and any such instrumentality, officer, or employee, shall be subject to the provisions of this chapter in the same manner and to the same extent as any nongovernmental entity.

(3) In a civil action for trade dress infringement under this chapter for trade dress not registered on the principal register, the person who asserts trade dress protection has the burden of proving that the matter sought to be protected is not functional.

(b) Importation

Any goods marked or labeled in contravention of the provisions of this section shall not be imported into the United States or admitted to entry at any customhouse of the United States. The owner, importer, or consignee of goods refused entry at any customhouse under this section may have any recourse by protest or appeal that is given under the customs revenue laws or may have the remedy given by this chapter in cases involving goods refused entry or seized.

(c) Remedies for dilution of famous marks

(1) The owner of a famous mark shall be entitled, subject to the principles of equity and upon such terms as the court deems reasonable, to an injunction against another person's commercial use in commerce of a mark or trade name, if such use begins after the mark has become famous and causes dilution of the distinctive quality of the mark, and to obtain such other relief as is provided in this subsection. In determining whether a mark is distinctive and famous, a court may consider factors such as, but not limited to—

(A) the degree of inherent or acquired distinctiveness of the mark;

(B) the duration and extent of use of the mark in connection with the goods or services with which the mark is used;

(C) the duration and extent of advertising and publicity of the mark;

(D) the geographical extent of the trading area in which the mark is used;

(E) the channels of trade for the goods or services with which the mark is used;

(F) the degree of recognition of the mark in the trading areas and channels of trade used by the marks' owner and the person against whom the injunction is sought;

(G) the nature and extent of use of the same or similar marks by third parties; and

(H) whether the mark was registered under the Act of March 3, 1881, or the Act of February 20, 1905, or on the principal register.

(2) In an action brought under this subsection, the owner of the famous mark shall be entitled only to injunctive relief as set forth in section 1116 of this title unless the person against whom the injunction is sought willfully intended to trade on the owner's reputation or to cause dilution of the famous mark. If such willful intent is proven, the owner of the famous mark shall also be entitled to the remedies set forth in sections 1117(a) and 1118 of this title, subject to the discretion of the court and the principles of equity.

(3) The ownership by a person of a valid registration under the Act of March 3, 1881, or the Act of February 20, 1905, or on the principal register shall be a complete bar to an action against that person, with respect to that mark, that is brought by another person under the common law or a statute of a State and that seeks to prevent dilution of the distinctiveness of a mark, label, or form of advertisement.

(4) The following shall not be actionable under this section:

(A) Fair use of a famous mark by another person in comparative commercial advertising or promotion to identify the competing goods or services of the owner of the famous mark.

(B) Noncommercial use of a mark.

(C) All forms of news reporting and news commentary.

(d) Cyberpiracy prevention

(1) (A) A person shall be liable in a civil action by the owner of a mark, including a personal name which is protected as a mark under this section, if, without regard to the goods or services of the parties, that person—

(i) has a bad faith intent to profit from that mark, including a personal name which is protected as a mark under this section; and

(ii) registers, traffics in, or uses a domain name that—

(I) in the case of a mark that is distinctive at the time of registration of the domain name, is identical or confusingly similar to that mark;

(II) in the case of a famous mark that is famous at the time of registration of the domain name, is identical or confusingly similar to or dilutive of that mark; or

(III) is a trademark, word, or name protected by reason of section 706 of title 18 or section 220506 of title 36.

(B) (i) In determining whether a person has a bad faith intent described under subparagraph (A), a court may consider factors such as, but not limited to—

(I) the trademark or other intellectual property rights of the person, if any, in the domain name;

(II) the extent to which the domain name consists of the legal name of the person or a name that is otherwise commonly used to identify that person;

(III) the person's prior use, if any, of the domain name in connection with the bona fide offering of any goods or services;

(IV) the person's bona fide noncommercial or fair use of the mark in a site accessible under the domain name;

(V) the person's intent to divert consumers from the mark owner's online location to a site accessible under the domain name that could harm the goodwill represented by the mark, either for commercial gain or with the intent to tarnish or disparage the mark, by creating a likelihood of confusion as to the source, sponsorship, affiliation, or endorsement of the site;

(VI) the person's offer to transfer, sell, or otherwise assign the domain name to the mark owner or any third party for financial gain without having used, or having an intent to use, the domain name in the bona fide offering of any goods or services, or the person's prior conduct indicating a pattern of such conduct;

(VII) the person's provision of material and misleading false contact information when applying for the registration of the domain name, the person's intentional failure to maintain accurate contact information, or the person's prior conduct indicating a pattern of such conduct;

(VIII) the person's registration or acquisition of multiple domain names which the person knows are identical or confusingly similar to marks of others that are distinctive at the time of registration of such domain names, or dilutive of famous marks of others that are famous at the time of registration of such domain names, without regard to the goods or services of the parties; and

(IX) the extent to which the mark incorporated in the person's domain name registration is or is not distinctive and famous within the meaning of subsection (c)(1) of this section.

(ii) Bad faith intent described under subparagraph (A) shall not be found in any case in which the court determines that the person believed and had reasonable grounds to believe that the use of the domain name was a fair use or otherwise lawful.

(C) In any civil action involving the registration, trafficking, or use of a domain name under this paragraph, a court may order the forfeiture or cancellation of the domain name or the transfer of the domain name to the owner of the mark.

(D) A person shall be liable for using a domain name under subparagraph (A) only if that person is the domain name registrant or that registrant's authorized licensee.

(E) As used in this paragraph, the term "traffics in" refers to transactions that include, but are not limited to, sales, purchases, loans, pledges, licenses, exchanges of currency, and any other transfer for consideration or receipt in exchange for consideration.

(2) (A) The owner of a mark may file an in rem civil action against a domain name in the judicial district in which the domain name registrar, domain name registry, or other domain name authority that registered or assigned the domain name is located if—

    (i) the domain name violates any right of the owner of a mark registered in the Patent and Trademark Office, or protected under subsection (a) or (c) of this section; and

    (ii) the court finds that the owner—

        (I) is not able to obtain in personam jurisdiction over a person who would have been a defendant in a civil action under paragraph (1); or

        (II) through due diligence was not able to find a person who would have been a defendant in a civil action under paragraph (1) by—

            (aa) sending a notice of the alleged violation and intent to proceed under this paragraph to the registrant of the domain name at the postal and e-mail address provided by the registrant to the registrar; and

            (bb) publishing notice of the action as the court may direct promptly after filing the action.

(B) The actions under subparagraph (A)(ii) shall constitute service of process.

(C) In an in rem action under this paragraph, a domain name shall be deemed to have its situs in the judicial district in which—

    (i) the domain name registrar, registry, or other domain name authority that registered or assigned the domain name is located; or

    (ii) documents sufficient to establish control and authority regarding the disposition of the registration and use of the domain name are deposited with the court.

(D) (i) The remedies in an in rem action under this paragraph shall be limited to a court order for the forfeiture or cancellation of the domain name or the transfer of the domain name to the owner of the mark. Upon receipt of written notification of a filed, stamped copy of a complaint filed by the owner of a mark in a United States district court under this paragraph, the domain name registrar, domain name registry, or other domain name authority shall—

    (I) expeditiously deposit with the court documents sufficient to establish the court's control and authority regarding the disposition of the registration and use of the domain name to the court; and

    (II) not transfer, suspend, or otherwise modify the domain name during the pendency of the action, except upon order of the court.

(ii) The domain name registrar or registry or other domain name authority shall not be liable for injunctive or monetary relief under this paragraph except in the case of bad faith or reckless disregard, which includes a willful failure to comply with any such court order.

(3) The civil action established under paragraph (1) and the in rem action established under paragraph (2), and any remedy available under either such action, shall be in addition to any other civil action or remedy otherwise applicable.

(4) The in rem jurisdiction established under paragraph (2) shall be in addition to any other jurisdiction that otherwise exists, whether in rem or in personam.

SELECTED PROVISIONS OF THE COPYRIGHT ACT
17 U.S.C.

Sec. 101. Definitions

Except as otherwise provided in this title, as used in this title, the following terms and their variant forms mean the following:

An "anonymous work" is a work on the copies or phonorecords of which no natural person is identified as author.

An "architectural work" is the design of a building as embodied in any tangible medium of expression, including a building, architectural plans, or drawings. The work includes the overall form as well as the arrangement and composition of spaces and elements in the design, but does not include individual standard features.

"Audiovisual works" are works that consist of a series of related images which are intrinsically intended to be shown by the use of machines, or devices such as projectors, viewers, or electronic equipment, together with accompanying sounds, if any, regardless of the nature of the material objects, such as films or tapes, in which the works are embodied.

The "Berne Convention" is the Convention for the Protection of Literary and Artistic Works, signed at Berne, Switzerland, on September 9, 1886, and all acts, protocols, and revisions thereto.

The "best edition" of a work is the edition, published in the United States at any time before the date of deposit, that the Library of Congress determines to be most suitable for its purposes.

A person's "children" are that person's immediate offspring, whether legitimate or not, and any children legally adopted by that person.

A "collective work" is a work, such as a periodical issue, anthology, or encyclopedia, in which a number of contributions, constituting separate and independent works in themselves, are assembled into a collective whole.

A "compilation" is a work formed by the collection and assembling of preexisting materials or of data that are selected, coordinated, or arranged in such a way that the resulting work as a whole constitutes an original work of authorship. The term "compilation" includes collective works.

"Copies" are material objects, other than phonorecords, in which a work is fixed by any method now known or later developed, and from which the work can be perceived, reproduced, or otherwise communicated, either directly or with the aid of a machine or device. The term "copies" includes the material object, other than a phonorecord, in which the work is first fixed.

"Copyright owner", with respect to any one of the exclusive rights comprised in a copyright, refers to the owner of that particular right.

A work is "created" when it is fixed in a copy or phonorecord for the first time; where a work is prepared over a period of time, the portion of it that has been fixed at any particular time constitutes the work as of that time, and where the work has been prepared in different versions, each version constitutes a separate work.

A "derivative work" is a work based upon one or more preexisting works, such as a translation, musical arrangement, dramatization, fictionalization, motion picture version, sound recording, art reproduction, abridgment, condensation, or any other form in which a work may be recast, transformed, or adapted. A work consisting of editorial revisions, annotations, elaborations, or other modifications which, as a whole, represent an original work of authorship, is a "derivative work".

A "device", "machine", or "process" is one now known or later developed.

A "digital transmission" is a transmission in whole or in part in a digital or other non-analog format.

To "display" a work means to show a copy of it, either directly or by means of a film, slide, television image, or any other device or process or, in the case of a motion picture or other audiovisual work, to show individual images nonsequentially.

An "establishment" is a store, shop, or any similar place of business open to the general public for the primary purpose of selling goods or services in which the majority of the gross square feet of space that is nonresidential is used for that purpose, and in which nondramatic musical works are performed publicly.

A "food service or drinking establishment" is a restaurant, inn, bar, tavern, or any other similar place of business in which the public or patrons assemble for the primary purpose of being served food or drink, in which the majority of the gross square feet of space that is nonresidential is used for that purpose, and in which nondramatic musical works are performed publicly.

The term "financial gain" includes receipt, or expectation of receipt, of anything of value, including the receipt of other copyrighted works.

A work is "fixed" in a tangible medium of expression when its embodiment in a copy or phonorecord, by or under the authority of the author, is sufficiently permanent or stable to permit it to be perceived, reproduced, or otherwise communicated for a period of more than transitory duration. A work consisting of sounds, images, or both, that are being transmitted, is "fixed" for purposes of this title if a fixation of the work is being made simultaneously with its transmission.

The "Geneva Phonograms Convention" is the Convention for the Protection of Producers of Phonograms Against Unauthorized Duplication of Their Phonograms, concluded at Geneva, Switzerland, on October 29, 1971.

The "gross square feet of space" of an establishment means the entire interior space of that establishment, and any adjoining outdoor space used to serve patrons, whether on a seasonal basis or otherwise.

The terms "including" and "such as" are illustrative and not limitative.

An "international agreement" is—

(1) the Universal Copyright Convention;

(2) the Geneva Phonograms Convention;

(3) the Berne Convention;

(4) the WTO Agreement;

(5) the WIPO Copyright Treaty;

(6) the WIPO Performances and Phonograms Treaty; and

(7) any other copyright treaty to which the United States is a party.

A "joint work" is a work prepared by two or more authors with the intention that their contributions be merged into inseparable or interdependent parts of a unitary whole.

"Literary works" are works, other than audiovisual works, expressed in words, numbers, or other verbal or numerical symbols or indicia, regardless of the nature of the material objects, such as books, periodicals, manuscripts, phonorecords, film, tapes, disks, or cards, in which they are embodied.

"Motion pictures" are audiovisual works consisting of a series of related images which, when shown in succession, impart an impression of motion, together with accompanying sounds, if any.

To "perform" a work means to recite, render, play, dance, or act it, either directly or by means of any device or process or, in the case of a motion picture or other audiovisual work, to show its images in any sequence or to make the sounds accompanying it audible.

A "performing rights society" is an association, corporation, or other entity that licenses the public performance of nondramatic musical works on behalf of copyright owners of such works, such as the American Society of Composers, Authors and Publishers (ASCAP), Broadcast Music, Inc. (BMI), and SESAC, Inc. "Phono records" are material objects in which sounds, other than those accompanying a motion picture or other audiovisual work, are fixed by any method now known or later developed, and from which the sounds can be perceived, reproduced, or otherwise communicated, either directly or with the aid of device. The term "phonorecords" includes the material object in which the sounds are first fixed.

"Pictorial, graphic, and sculptural works" include two-dimensional and three-dimensional works of fine, graphic, and applied art, photographs, prints and art reproductions, maps, globes, charts, diagrams, models, and technical drawings, including architectural plans. Such works shall include works of artistic craftsmanship insofar as their form but not their mechanical or utilitarian aspects are concerned; the design of a useful article, as defined in this section, shall be considered a pictorial, graphic, or sculptural work only if, and only to the extent that, such design incorporates pictorial, graphic, or sculptural features that can be identified separately from, and are capable of existing independently of, the utilitarian aspects of the article.

For purposes of section 513, a "proprietor" is an individual, corporation, partnership, or other entity, as the case may be, that owns an establishment or a food service or drinking establishment, except that no owner or operator of a radio or television station licensed by the Federal Communications Commission, cable system or satellite carrier, cable or satellite carrier service or programmer, provider of online services or network access or the operator of facilities therefor, telecommunications company, or any other such audio or audiovisual service or programmer now known or as may be developed in the future, commercial subscription music service, or owner or operator of any other transmission service, shall under any circumstances be deemed to be a proprietor.

A "pseudonymous work" is a work on the copies or phonorecords of which the author is identified under a fictitious name.

"Publication" is the distribution of copies or phonorecords of a work to the public by sale or other transfer of ownership, or by rental, lease, or lending. The offering to distribute copies or phonorecords to a group of persons for purposes of further distribution, public performance, or public display, constitutes publication. A public performance or display of a work does not of itself constitute publication.

"Registration", for purposes of sections 205 (c)(2), 405, 406, 410(d), 411, 412, and 506(e), means a registration of a claim in the original or the renewed and extended term of copyright.

To perform or display a work "publicly" means—

(1) to perform or display it at a place open to the public or at any place where a substantial number of persons outside of a normal circle of a family and its social acquaintances is gathered; or

(2) to transmit or otherwise communicate a performance or display of the work to a place specified by clause (1) or to the public, by means of any device or process, whether the members of the public capable of receiving the performance or display receive it in the same place or in separate places and at the same time or at different times.

"Sound recordings" are works that result from the fixation of a series of musical, spoken, or other sounds, but not including the sounds accompanying a motion picture or other audiovisual work, regardless of the nature of the material objects, such as disks, tapes, or other phonorecords, in which they are embodied.

"State" includes the District of Columbia and the Commonwealth of Puerto Rico, and any territories to which this title is made applicable by an Act of Congress.

A "transfer of copyright ownership" is an assignment, mortgage, exclusive license, or any other conveyance, alienation, or hypothecation of a copyright or of any of the exclusive rights comprised in a copyright, whether or not it is limited in time or place of effect, but not including a nonexclusive license.

A "transmission program" is a body of material that, as an aggregate, has been produced for the sole purpose of transmission to the public in sequence and as a unit.

To "transmit" a performance or display is to communicate it by any device or process whereby images or sounds are received beyond the place from which they are sent.

A "treaty party" is a country or intergovernmental organization other than the United States that is a party to an international agreement.

The "United States", when used in a geographical sense, comprises the several States, the District of Columbia and the Commonwealth of Puerto Rico, and the organized territories under the jurisdiction of the United States Government.

For purposes of section 411, a work is a "United States work" only if—

(1) in the case of a published work, the work is first published—

(A) in the United States;

(B) simultaneously in the United States and another treaty party or parties, whose law grants a term of copyright protection that is the same as or longer than the term provided in the United States;

(C) simultaneously in the United States and a foreign nation that is not a treaty party; or

(D) in a foreign nation that is not a treaty party, and all of the authors of the work are nationals, domiciliaries, or habitual residents of, or in the case of an audiovisual work legal entities with headquarters in, the United States;

(2) in the case of an unpublished work, all the authors of the work are nationals, domiciliaries, or habitual residents of the United States, or, in the case of an unpublished audiovisual work, all the authors are legal entities with headquarters in the United States; or

(3) in the case of a pictorial, graphic, or sculptural work incorporated in a building or structure, the building or structure is located in the United States.

A "useful article" is an article having an intrinsic utilitarian function that is not merely to portray the appearance of the article or to convey information. An article that is normally a part of a useful article is considered a "useful article".

The author's "widow" or "widower" is the author's surviving spouse under the law of the author's domicile at the time of his or her death, whether or not the spouse has later remarried.

A "work of visual art" is—

(1) a painting, drawing, print, or sculpture, existing in a single copy, in a limited edition of 200 copies or fewer that are signed and consecutively numbered by the author, or, in the case of a sculpture, in multiple cast, carved, or fabricated sculptures of 200 or fewer that are consecutively numbered by the author and bear the signature or other identifying mark of the author; or

(2) a still photographic image produced for exhibition purposes only, existing in a single copy that is signed by the author, or in a limited edition of 200 copies or fewer that are signed and consecutively numbered by the author. A work of visual art does not include—

(A) (i) any poster, map, globe, chart, technical drawing, diagram, model, applied art, motion picture or other audiovisual work, book, magazine, newspaper, periodical, data base, electronic information service, electronic publication, or similar publication;

(ii) any merchandising item or advertising, promotional, descriptive, covering, or packaging material or container;

(iii) any portion or part of any item described in clause (i) or (ii);

(B) any work made for hire; or

(C) any work not subject to copyright protection under this title.

A "work of the United States Government" is a work prepared by an officer or employee of the United States Government as part of that person's official duties.

A "work made for hire" is—

(1) a work prepared by an employee within the scope of his or her employment; or

(2) a work specially ordered or commissioned for use as a contribution to a collective work, as a part of a motion picture or other audiovisual work, as a sound recording, as a translation, as a supplementary work, as a compilation, as an instructional text, as a test, as answer material for a test, or as an atlas, if the parties expressly agree in a written instrument signed by them that the work shall be considered a work made for hire. For the purpose of the foregoing sentence, a "supplementary work" is a work prepared for publication as a secondary adjunct to a work by another author for the purpose of introducing, concluding, illustrating, explaining, revising, commenting upon, or assisting in the use of the other work, such as forewords, afterwords, pictorial illustrations, maps, charts, tables, editorial notes, musical arrangements, answer material for tests, bibliographies, appendixes, and indexes, and an "instructional text" is a literary, pictorial, or graphic work prepared for publication and with the purpose of use in systematic instructional activities.

The terms "WTO Agreement" and "WTO member country" have the meanings given those terms in paragraphs (9) and (10), respectively, of section 2 of the Uruguay Round Agreements Act. A "computer program" is a set of statements or instructions to be used directly or indirectly in a computer in order to bring about a certain result.

Sec. 102. Subject matter of copyright: In general

(a) Copyright protection subsists, in accordance with this title, in original works of authorship fixed in any tangible medium of expression, now known or later developed, from which they can be perceived, reproduced, or otherwise communicated, either directly or with the aid of a machine or device. Works of authorship include the following categories:

(1) literary works;

(2) musical works, including any accompanying words;

(3) dramatic works, including any accompanying music;

(4) pantomimes and choreographic works;

(5) pictorial, graphic, and sculptural works;

(6) motion pictures and other audiovisual works;

(7) sound recordings; and

(8) architectural works.

(b) In no case does copyright protection for an original work of authorship extend to any idea, procedure, process, system, method of operation, concept, principle, or discovery, regardless of the form in which it is described, explained, illustrated, or embodied in such work.

Sec. 106. Exclusive rights in copyrighted works

Subject to sections 107 through 121, the owner of copyright under this title has the exclusive rights to do and to authorize any of the following:

(1) to reproduce the copyrighted work in copies or phonorecords;

(2) to prepare derivative works based upon the copyrighted work;

(3) to distribute copies or phonorecords of the copyrighted work to the public by sale or other transfer of ownership, or by rental, lease, or lending;

(4) in the case of literary, musical, dramatic, and choreographic works, pantomimes, and motion pictures and other audiovisual works, to perform the copyrighted work publicly;

(5) in the case of literary, musical, dramatic, and choreographic works, pantomimes, and pictorial, graphic, or sculptural works, including the individual images of a motion picture or other audiovisual work, to display the copyrighted work publicly; and

(6) in the case of sound recordings, to perform the copyrighted work publicly by means of a digital audio transmission.

Sec. 106A. Rights of certain authors to attribution and integrity

(a) Rights of Attribution and Integrity. Subject to section 107 and independent of the exclusive rights provided in section 106, the author of a work of visual art—

(1) shall have the right—

(A) to claim authorship of that work, and

(B) to prevent the use of his or her name as the author of any work of visual art which he or she did not create;

(2) shall have the right to prevent the use of his or her name as the author of the work of visual art in the event of a distortion, mutilation, or other modification of the work which would be prejudicial to his or her honor or reputation; and

(3) subject to the limitations set forth in section 113(d), shall have the right—

(A) to prevent any intentional distortion, mutilation, or other modification of that work which would be prejudicial to his or her honor or reputation, and any intentional distortion, mutilation, or modification of that work is a violation of that right, and

(B) to prevent any destruction of a work of recognized stature, and any intentional or grossly negligent destruction of that work is a violation of that right.

(b) Scope and Exercise of Rights.—Only the author of a work of visual art has the rights conferred by subsection (a) in that work, whether or not the author is the copyright owner. The authors of a joint work of visual art are coowners of the rights conferred by subsection (a) in that work.

(c) Exceptions.

(1) The modification of a work of visual art which is a result of the passage of time or the inherent nature of the materials is not a distortion, mutilation, or other modification described in subsection (a)(3)(A).

(2) The modification of a work of visual art which is the result of conservation, or of the public presentation, including lighting and placement, of the work is not a destruction, distortion, mutilation, or other modification described in subsection (a)(3) unless the modification is caused by gross negligence.

(3) The rights described in paragraphs (1) and (2) of subsection (a) shall not apply to any reproduction, depiction, portrayal, or other use of a work in, upon, or in any connection with any item described in subparagraph (A) or (B) of the definition of "work of visual art" in section 101, and any such reproduction, depiction, portrayal, or other use of a work is not a destruction, distortion, mutilation, or other modification described in paragraph (3) of subsection (a).

(d) Duration of Rights.

(1) With respect to works of visual art created on or after the effective date set forth in section 610(a) of the Visual Artists Rights Act of 1990, the rights conferred by subsection (a) shall endure for a term consisting of the life of the author.

(2) With respect to works of visual art created before the effective date set forth in section 610(a) of the Visual Artists Rights Act of 1990, but title to which has not, as of such effective date, been transferred from the author, the rights conferred by subsection (a) shall be coextensive with, and shall expire at the same time as, the rights conferred by section 106.

(3) In the case of a joint work prepared by two or more authors, the rights conferred by subsection (a) shall endure for a term consisting of the life of the last surviving author.

(4) All terms of the rights conferred by subsection (a) run to the end of the calendar year in which they would otherwise expire.

Sec. 107. Limitations on exclusive rights: Fair use

Notwithstanding the provisions of sections 106 and 106A, the fair use of a copyrighted work, including such use by reproduction in copies or phonorecords or by any other means specified by that section, for purposes such as criticism, comment, news reporting, teaching (including multiple copies for classroom use), scholarship, or research, is not an infringement of copyright. In determining whether the use made of a work in any particular case is a fair use the factors to be considered shall include—

(1) the purpose and character of the use, including whether such use is of a commercial nature or is for nonprofit educational purposes;

(2) the nature of the copyrighted work;

(3) the amount and substantiality of the portion used in relation to the copyrighted work as a whole; and

(4) the effect of the use upon the potential market for or value of the copyrighted work.

The fact that a work is unpublished shall not itself bar a finding of fair use if such finding is made upon consideration of all the above factors.

Sec. 201. Ownership of copyright

(a) Initial ownership. Copyright in a work protected under this title vests initially in the author or authors of the work. The authors of a joint work are coowners of copyright in the work.

(b) Works made for hire. In the case of a work made for hire, the employer or other person for whom the work was prepared is considered the author for purposes of this title, and, unless the parties have expressly agreed otherwise in a written instrument signed by them, owns all of the rights comprised in the copyright.

Sec. 302. Duration of copyright: Works created on or after January 1, 1978

(a) In general. Copyright in a work created on or after January 1, 1978, subsists from its creation and, except as provided by the following subsections, endures for a term consisting of the life of the author and 70 years after the author's death.

(b) Joint works. In the case of a joint work prepared by two or more authors who did not work for hire, the copyright endures for a term consisting of the life of the last surviving author and 70 years after such last surviving author's death.

(c) Anonymous works, pseudonymous works, and works made for hire. In the case of an anonymous work, a pseudonymous work, or a work made for hire, the copyright endures for a term of 95 years from the year of its first publication, or a term of 120 years from the year of its creation, whichever expires first. If, before the end of such term, the identity of one or more of the authors of an anonymous or pseudonymous work is revealed in the records of a registration made for that work under subsections (a) or (d) of section 408, or in the records provided by this subsection, the copyright in the work endures for the term specified by subsection (a) or (b), based on the life of the author or authors whose identity has been revealed. Any person having an interest in the copyright in an anonymous or pseudonymous work may at any time record, in records to be maintained by the Copyright Office for that purpose, a statement identifying one or more authors of the work; the statement shall also identify the person filing it, the nature of that person's interest, the source of the information recorded, and the particular work affected, and shall comply in form and content with requirements that the Register of Copyrights shall prescribe by regulation.

(d) Records relating to death of authors. Any person having an interest in a copyright may at any time record in the Copyright Office a statement of the date of death of the author of the copyrighted work, or a statement that the author is still living on a particular date. The statement shall identify the person filing it, the nature of that person's interest, and the source of the information recorded, and shall comply in form and content with requirements that the Register of Copyrights shall prescribe by regulation. The Register shall maintain current records of information relating to the death of authors of copyrighted works, based on such recorded statements and, to the extent the Register considers practicable, on data contained in any of the records of the Copyright Office or in other reference sources.

(e) Presumption as to author's death. After a period of 95 years from the year of first publication of a work, or a period of 120 years from the year of its creation, whichever expires first, any person who obtains from the Copyright Office a certified report that the records provided by subsection (d) disclose nothing to indicate that the author of the work is living, or died less than 70 years before, is entitled to the benefits of a presumption that the author has been dead for at least 70 years. Reliance in good faith upon this presumption shall be a complete defense to any action for infringement under this title.

Sec. 401. Notice of copyright: Visually perceptible copies

(a) General provisions. Whenever a work protected under this title is published in the United States or elsewhere by authority of the copyright owner, a notice of copyright as provided by this section may be placed on publicly distributed copies from which the work can be visually perceived, either directly or with the aid of a machine or device.

(b) Form of notice. If a notice appears on the copies, it shall consist of the following three elements:

(1) the symbol (©) (the letter C in a circle), or the word "Copyright", or the abbreviation "Copr."; and

(2) the year of first publication of the work; in the case of compilations, or derivative works incorporating previously published material, the year date of first publication of the compilation or derivative work is sufficient. The year date may be omitted where a pictorial, graphic, or sculptural work, with accompanying text matter, if any, is reproduced in or on greeting cards, postcards, stationery, jewelry, dolls, toys, or any useful articles; and

(3) the name of the owner of copyright in the work, or an abbreviation by which the name can be recognized, or a generally known alternative designation of the owner.

(c) Position of notice. The notice shall be affixed to the copies in such manner and location as to give reasonable notice of the claim of copyright. The Register of Copyrights shall prescribe by regulation, as examples, specific methods of affixation and positions of the notice on various types of works that will satisfy this requirement, but these specifications shall not be considered exhaustive.

(d) Evidentiary weight of notice. If a notice of copyright in the form and position specified by this section appears on the published copy or copies to which a defendant in a copyright infringement suit had access, then no weight shall be given to such a defendant's interposition of a defense based on innocent infringement in mitigation of actual or statutory damages, except as provided in the last sentence of section 504(c)(2).

Sec. 407. Deposit of copies or phonorecords for Library of Congress

(a) Except as provided by subsection (c), and subject to the provisions of subsection (e), the owner of copyright or of the exclusive right of publication in a work published in the United States shall deposit, within three months after the date of such publication—

(1) two complete copies of the best edition; or

(2) if the work is a sound recording, two complete phonorecords of the best edition, together with any printed or other visually perceptible material published with such phonorecords. Neither the deposit requirements of this subsection nor the acquisition provisions of subsection (e) are conditions of copyright protection.

Sec. 408. Copyright registration in general

(a) Registration permissive. At any time during the subsistence of the first term of copyright in any published or unpublished work in which the copyright was secured before January 1, 1978, and during the subsistence of any copyright secured on or after that date, the owner of copyright or of any exclusive right in the work may obtain registration of the copyright claim by delivering to the Copyright Office the deposit specified by this section, together with the application and fee specified by sections 409 and 708. Such registration is not a condition of copyright protection.

(b) Deposit for copyright registration. Except as provided by subsection (c), the material deposited for registration shall include—

(1) in the case of an unpublished work, one complete copy or phonorecord;

(2) in the case of a published work, two complete copies or phonorecords of the best edition;

(3) in the case of a work first published outside the United States, one complete copy or phonorecord as so published;

(4) in the case of a contribution to a collective work, one complete copy or phonorecord of the best edition of the collective work.

Copies or phonorecords deposited for the Library of Congress under section 407 may be used to satisfy the deposit provisions of this section, if they are accompanied by the prescribed application and fee, and by any additional identifying material that the Register may, by regulation, require. The Register shall also prescribe regulations establishing requirements under which copies or phonorecords acquired for the Library of Congress under subsection (e) of section 407, otherwise than by deposit, may be used to satisfy the deposit provisions of this section.

Sec. 412. Registration as prerequisite to certain remedies for infringement

In any action under this title, other than an action brought for a violation of the rights of the author under section 106A(a) or an action instituted under section 411(b), no award of statutory damages or of attorney's fees, as provided by sections 504 and 505, shall be made for—

(1) any infringement of copyright in an unpublished work commenced before the effective date of its registration; or

(2) any infringement of copyright commenced after first publication of the work and before the effective date of its registration, unless such registration is made within three months after the first publication of the work.

Sec. 502. Remedies for infringement: Injunctions

(a) Any court having jurisdiction of a civil action arising under this title may, subject to the provisions of section 1498 of title 28, grant temporary and final injunctions on such terms as it may deem reasonable to prevent or restrain infringement of a copyright.

(b) Any such injunction may be served anywhere in the United States on the person enjoined; it shall be operative throughout the United States and shall be enforceable, by proceedings in contempt or otherwise, by any United States court having jurisdiction of that person. The clerk of the court granting the injunction shall, when requested by any other court in which enforcement of the injunction is sought, transmit promptly to the other court a certified copy of all the papers in the case on file in such clerk's office.

Sec. 503. Remedies for infringement: Impounding and disposition of infringing articles

(a) At any time while an action under this title is pending, the court may order the impounding, on such terms as it may deem reasonable, of all copies or phonorecords claimed to have been made or used in violation of the copyright owner's exclusive rights, and of all plates, molds, matrices, masters, tapes, film negatives, or other articles by means of which such copies or phonorecords may be reproduced.

(b) As part of a final judgment or decree, the court may order the destruction or other reasonable disposition of all copies or phonorecords found to have been made or used in violation of the copyright owner's exclusive rights, and of all plates, molds, matrices, masters, tapes, film negatives, or other articles by means of which such copies or phonorecords may be reproduced.

Sec. 504. Remedies for infringement: Damages and profits

(a) In general. Except as otherwise provided by this title, an infringer of copyright is liable for either—

(1) the copyright owner's actual damages and any additional profits of the infringer, as provided by subsection (b); or

(2) statutory damages, as provided by subsection (c).

(b) Actual damages and profits. The copyright owner is entitled to recover the actual damages suffered by him or her as a result of the infringement, and any profits of the infringer that are attributable to the infringement and are not taken into account in computing the actual damages. In establishing the infringer's profits, the copyright owner is required to present proof only of the infringer's gross revenue, and the infringer is required to prove his or her deductible expenses and the elements of profit attributable to factors other than the copyrighted work.

(c) Statutory damages.

(1) Except as provided by clause (2) of this subsection, the copyright owner may elect, at any time before final judgment is rendered, to recover, instead of actual damages and profits, an award of statutory damages for all infringements involved in the action, with respect to any one work, for which any one infringer is liable individually, or for which any two or more infringers are liable jointly and severally, in a sum of not less than $750 or more than $30,000 as the court considers just. For the purposes of this subsection, all the parts of a compilation or derivative work constitute one work.

(2) In a case where the copyright owner sustains the burden of proving, and the court finds, that infringement was committed willfully, the court in its discretion may increase the award of statutory damages to a sum of not more than $150,000. In a case where the infringer sustains the burden of proving, and the court finds, that such infringer was not aware and had no reason to believe that his or her acts constituted an infringement of copyright, the court in its discretion may reduce

the award of statutory damages to a sum of not less than $200. The court shall remit statutory damages in any case where an infringer believed and had reasonable grounds for believing that his or her use of the copyrighted work was a fair use under section 107, if the infringer was: (i) an employee or agent of a nonprofit educational institution, library, or archives acting within the scope of his or her employment who, or such institution, library, or archives itself, which infringed by reproducing the work in copies or phonorecords; or (ii) a public broadcasting entity which or a person who, as a regular part of the nonprofit activities of a public broadcasting entity (as defined in subsection (g) of section 118) infringed by performing a published nondramatic literary work or by reproducing a transmission program embodying a performance of such a work.

Sec. 505. Remedies for infringement: Costs and attorney's fees

In any civil action under this title, the court in its discretion may allow the recovery of full costs by or against any party other than the United States or an officer thereof. Except as otherwise provided by this title, the court may also award a reasonable attorney's fee to the prevailing party as part of the costs.

Sec. 506. Criminal offenses

(a) Criminal infringement. Any person who infringes a copyright willfully either—

 (1) for purposes of commercial advantage or private financial gain, or

 (2) by the reproduction or distribution, including by electronic means, during any 180-day period, of 1 or more copies or phonorecords of 1 or more copyrighted works, which have a total retail value of more than $1,000, shall be punished as provided under section 2319 of title 18, United States Code. For purposes of this subsection, evidence of reproduction or distribution of a copyrighted work, by itself, shall not be sufficient to establish willful infringement.

(b) Forfeiture and destruction. When any person is convicted of any violation of subsection (a), the court in its judgment of conviction shall, in addition to the penalty therein prescribed, order the forfeiture and destruction or other disposition of all infringing copies or phonorecords and all implements, devices, or equipment used in the manufacture of such infringing copies or phonorecords.

(c) Fraudulent copyright notice. Any person who, with fraudulent intent, places on any article a notice of copyright or words of the same purport that such person knows to be false, or who, with fraudulent intent, publicly distributes or imports for public distribution any article bearing such notice or words that such person knows to be false, shall be fined not more than $2,500.

(d) Fraudulent removal of copyright notice. Any person who, with fraudulent intent, removes or alters any notice of copyright appearing on a copy of a copyrighted work shall be fined not more than $2,500.

(e) False Representation.—Any person who knowingly makes a false representation of a material fact in the application for copyright registration provided for by section 409, or in any written statement filed in connection with the application, shall be fined not more than $2,500.

(f) Rights of attribution and integrity. Nothing in this section applies to infringement of the rights conferred by section 106A(a).

SELECTED PROVISIONS OF THE FEDERAL ECONOMIC ESPIONAGE ACT 18 U.S.C.

Sec. 1831. Economic espionage

(a) In general. Whoever, intending or knowing that the offense will benefit any foreign government, foreign instrumentality, or foreign agent, knowingly—

(1) steals, or without authorization appropriates, takes, carries away, or conceals, or by fraud, artifice, or deception obtains a trade secret;

(2) without authorization copies, duplicates, sketches, draws, photographs, downloads, uploads, alters, destroys, photocopies, replicates, transmits, delivers, sends, mails, communicates, or conveys a trade secret;

(3) receives, buys, or possesses a trade secret, knowing the same to have been stolen or appropriated, obtained, or converted without authorization;

(4) attempts to commit any offense described in any of paragraphs (1) through (3); or

(5) conspires with one or more other persons to commit any offense described in any of paragraphs (1) through (3), and one or more of such persons do any act to effect the object of the conspiracy, shall, except as provided in subsection (b), be fined not more than $500,000 or imprisoned not more than 15 years, or both.

(b) Organizations.—Any organization that commits any offense described in subsection (a) shall be fined not more than $10,000,000.

Sec. 1832. Theft of trade secrets

(a) Whoever, with intent to convert a trade secret, that is related to or included in a product that is produced for or placed in interstate or foreign commerce, to the economic benefit of anyone other than the owner thereof, and intending or knowing that the offense will, injure any owner of that trade secret, knowingly—

(1) steals, or without authorization appropriates, takes, carries away, or conceals, or by fraud, artifice, or deception obtains such information;

(2) without authorization copies, duplicates, sketches, draws, photographs, downloads, uploads, alters, destroys, photocopies, replicates, transmits, delivers, sends, mails, communicates, or conveys such information;

(3) receives, buys, or possesses such information, knowing the same to have been stolen or appropriated, obtained, or converted without authorization;

(4) attempts to commit any offense described in paragraphs (1) through (3); or

(5) conspires with one or more other persons to commit any offense described in paragraphs (1) through (3), and one or more of such persons do any act to effect the object of the conspiracy, shall, except as provided in subsection (b), be fined under this title or imprisoned not more than 10 years, or both.

(b) Any organization that commits any offense described in subsection (a) shall be fined not more than $5,000,000.

Sec. 1833. Exceptions to prohibitions

This chapter does not prohibit—

(1) any otherwise lawful activity conducted by a governmental entity of the United States, a State, or a political subdivision of a State; or

(2) the reporting of a suspected violation of law to any governmental entity of the United States, a State, or a political subdivision of a State, if such entity has lawful authority with respect to that violation.

Sec. 1834. Criminal forfeiture

(a) The court, in imposing sentence on a person for a violation of this chapter, shall order, in addition to any other sentence imposed, that the person forfeit to the United States—

(1) any property constituting, or derived from, any proceeds the person obtained, directly or indirectly, as the result of such violation; and

(2) any of the person's property used, or intended to be used, in any manner or part, to commit or facilitate the commission of such violation, if the court in its discretion so determines, taking into consideration the nature, scope, and proportionality of the use of the property in the offense.

(b) Property subject to forfeiture under this section, any seizure and disposition thereof, and any administrative or judicial proceeding in relation thereto, shall be governed by section 413 of the Comprehensive Drug Abuse Prevention and Control Act of 1970 (21 U.S.C. 853), except for subsections (d) and (j) of such section, which shall not apply to forfeitures under this section.

Sec. 1836. Civil proceedings to enjoin violations

(a) The Attorney General may, in a civil action, obtain appropriate injunctive relief against any violation of this section.

(b) The district courts of the United States shall have exclusive original jurisdiction of civil actions under this subsection.

Sec. 1837. Applicability to conduct outside the United States

This chapter also applies to conduct occurring outside the United States if—

(1) the offender is a natural person who is a citizen or permanent resident alien of the United States, or an organization organized under the laws of the United States or a State or political subdivision thereof; or

(2) an act in furtherance of the offense was committed in the United States.

Sec. 1839. Definitions

As used in this chapter—

(1) the term "foreign instrumentality" means any agency, bureau, ministry, component, institution, association, or any legal, commercial, or business organization, corporation, firm, or entity that is substantially owned, controlled, sponsored, commanded, managed, or dominated by a foreign government;

(2) the term "foreign agent" means any officer, employee, proxy, servant, delegate, or representative of a foreign government;

(3) the term "trade secret" means all forms and types of financial, business, scientific, technical, economic, or engineering information, including patterns, plans, compilations, program devices, formulas, designs, prototypes, methods, techniques, processes, procedures, programs, or codes, whether tangible or intangible, and whether or how stored, compiled, or memorialized physically, electronically, graphically, photographically, or in writing if—

(A) the owner thereof has taken reasonable measures to keep such information secret; and

(B) the information derives independent economic value, actual or potential, from not being generally known to, and not being readily ascertainable through proper means by, the public; and

(4) the term "owner", with respect to a trade secret, means the person or entity in whom or in which rightful legal or equitable title to, or license in, the trade secret is reposed.

SELECTED PROVISIONS OF THE PATENT ACT
35 U.S.C.

Sec. 100. Definitions
When used in this title unless the context otherwise indicates—

(a) The term "invention" means invention or discovery.

(b) The term "process" means process, art or method, and includes a new use of a known process, machine, manufacture, composition of matter, or material.

(c) The terms "United States" and "this country" mean the United States of America, its territories and possessions.

(d) The word "patentee" includes not only the patentee to whom the patent was issued but also the successors in title to the patentee.

Sec. 101. Inventions patentable
Whoever invents or discovers any new and useful process, machine, manufacture, or composition of matter, or any new and useful improvement thereof, may obtain a patent therefor, subject to the conditions and requirements of this title.

Sec. 102. Conditions for patentability; novelty and loss of right to patent
A person shall be entitled to a patent unless—

(a) the invention was known or used by others in this country, or patented or described in a printed publication in this or a foreign country, before the invention thereof by the applicant for patent, or

(b) the invention was patented or described in a printed publication in this or a foreign country or in public use or on sale in this country, more than one year prior to the date of the application for patent in the United States, or

(c) he has abandoned the invention, or

(d) the invention was first patented or caused to be patented, or was the subject of an inventor's certificate, by the applicant or his legal representatives or assigns in a foreign country prior to the date of the application for patent in this country on an application for patent or inventor's certificate filed more than twelve months before the filing of the application in the United States, or

(e) The invention was described in—

(1) an application for patent, published under section 122(b), by another filed in the United States before the invention by the applicant for patent, except that an international application filed under the treaty defined in section 351(a) shall have the effect under this subsection of a national application published under section 12(b) only if the international application designating the United States was published under Article 21(2)(a) of such treaty in the English language; or

(2) a patent granted on an application for patent by another filed in the United States before the invention by the applicant for patent, except that a patent shall not be deemed filed in the United States for the purposes of this subsection based on the filing of an international application filed under the treaty defined in section 351(a); or

(f) he did not himself invent the subject matter sought to be patented, or

(g) (1) during the course of an interference conducted under section 135 or section 291, another inventor involved therein establishes, to the extent permitted in section 104, that before such person's invention thereof the invention was made by such other inventor and not abandoned, suppressed, or concealed, or (2) before such person's invention thereof, the invention was made in this country by another inventor who had not abandoned, suppressed, or concealed it. In determining priority of invention under this subsection, there shall be considered not only the respective dates of conception and reduction to practice of the invention, but also the reasonable diligence of one who was first to conceive and last to reduce to practice, from a time prior to conception by the other.

Sec. 103. Conditions for patentability; non-obvious subject matter

(a) A patent may not be obtained though the invention is not identically disclosed or described as set forth in section 102 of this title, if the differences between the subject matter sought to be patented and the prior art are such that the subject matter as a whole would have been obvious at the time the invention was made to a person having ordinary skill in the art to which said subject matter pertains. Patentability shall not be negatived by the manner in which the invention was made.

Sec. 111. Application

(a) In general.

(1) Written application. An application for patent shall be made, or authorized to be made, by the inventor, except as otherwise provided in this title, in writing to the Commissioner.

(2) Contents. Such application shall include—

(A) a specification as prescribed by section 112 of this title;

(B) a drawing as prescribed by section 113 of this title; and

(C) an oath by the applicant as prescribed by section 115 of this title.

(3) Fee and oath. The application must be accompanied by the fee required by law. The fee and oath may be submitted after the specification and any required drawing are submitted, within such period and under such conditions, including the payment of a surcharge, as may be prescribed by the Commissioner.

(4) Failure to submit. Upon failure to submit the fee and oath within such prescribed period, the application shall be regarded as abandoned, unless it is shown to the satisfaction of the Commissioner that the delay in submitting the fee and oath was unavoidable or unintentional. The filing date of an application shall be the date on which the specification and any required drawing are received in the Patent and Trademark Office.

Sec. 116. Inventors

When an invention is made by two or more persons jointly, they shall apply for patent jointly and each make the required oath, except as otherwise provided in this title. Inventors may apply for a patent jointly even though (1) they did not physically work together or at the same time, (2) each did not make the same type or amount of contribution, or (3) each did not make a contribution to the subject matter of every claim of the patent.

If a joint inventor refuses to join in an application for patent or cannot be found or reached after diligent effort, the application may be made by the other inventor on behalf of himself and the omitted inventor. The Commissioner, on proof of the pertinent facts and after such notice to the omitted inventor as he prescribes, may grant a patent to the inventor making the application, subject to the same rights which the omitted inventor would have had if he had been joined. The omitted inventor may subsequently join in the application.

Whenever through error a person is named in an application for patent as the inventor, or through error an inventor is not named in an application, and such error arose without any deceptive intention on his part, the Commissioner may permit the application to be amended accordingly, under such terms as he prescribes.

Sec. 122. Confidential status of applications; publication of patent applications

(a) Confidentiality. Except as provided in subsection (b), applications for patents shall be kept in confidence by the Patent and Trademark Office and no information concerning the same given without authority of the applicant or owner unless necessary to carry out the provisions of an Act of Congress or in such special circumstances as may be determined by the Director.

(b) Publication.

(1) In general.

(A) Subject to paragraph (2), each application for a patent shall be published, in accordance with procedures determined by the Director, promptly after the expiration of a period of 18 months from the earliest filing date for which a benefit is sought under this title. At the request of the applicant, an application may be published earlier than the end of such 18-month period.

(B) No information concerning published patent applications shall be made available to the public except as the Director determines.

(C) Notwithstanding any other provision of law, a determination by the Director to release or not to release information concerning a published patent application shall be final and nonreviewable.

(2) Exceptions.

(A) An application shall not be published if that application is

(i) no longer pending;

(ii) subject to a secrecy order under section 181 of this title;

(iii) a provisional application filed under section 11(b) of this title; or

(iv) an application for a design patent filed under chapter 16 of this title [35 USCS §§ 171 et seq.].

(B) (i) If an applicant makes a request upon filing, certifying that the invention disclosed in the application has not and will not be the subject of an application filed in another country, or under a multilateral international agreement, that requires publication of applications 18 months after filing, the application shall not be published as provided in paragraph (1).

(ii) An applicant may rescind a request made under clause (i) at any time.

(iii) An applicant who has made a request under clause (i) but who subsequently files, in a foreign country or under a multilateral international agreement specified in clause (i), an application directed to the invention disclosed in the application filed in the Patent and Trademark Office, shall notify the Director of such filing not later than 45 days after the date of the filing of such foreign or international application. A failure of the applicant to provide such notice within the prescribed period shall result in the application being regarded as abandoned, unless it is shown to the satisfaction of the Director that the delay in submitting the notice was unintentional.

(iv) If an applicant rescinds a request made under clause (i) or notifies the Director that an application was filed in a foreign country or under a multilateral international agreement specified in clause (i), the application shall be published in accordance with the provisions of paragraph (1) on or as soon as is practical after the date that is specified in clause (1) on or as soon as is practical after the date that is specified in clause (i).

(v) If an applicant has filed applications in one or more foreign countries, directly or through a multilateral international agreement, and such foreign filed applications corresponding to an application filed in the Patent and Trademark Office or the description of the invention in such foreign filed applications is less extensive than the application or description of the invention in the application filed in the Patent and Trademark Office, the applicant may submit a redacted copy of the application filed in the Patent and Trademark Office eliminating any part or description of the invention in such application that is not also contained in any of the corresponding applications filed in a foreign country. The Director may only publish the redacted copy of the application unless the redacted copy of the application is not received within 16 months after the earliest effective filing date for which a benefit is sought under this title. The provisions of section 154(d) shall not apply to a claim if the description of the invention published in the redacted application filed under this clause with respect to the claim does not enable a person skilled in the art to make and use the subject matter of the claim.

(C) Protest and pre-issuance opposition. The Director shall establish appropriate procedures to ensure that no protest or other form of pre-issuance opposition to the grant of a patent on an application may be initiated after publication of the application without the express written consent of the applicant.

(D) National security. No application for patent shall be published under subsection (b) (1) if the publication or disclosure of such invention would be detrimental to the national security. The Director shall establish appropriate procedures to ensure that such applications are promptly identified and the secrecy of such inventions is maintained in accordance with chapter 17 of this title [35 USCS §§ 181 et seq.].

HISTORY: (July 19, 1952, ch 950, § 1, 66 State. 801; Jan. 2, 1975, P.L. 93-596, § 1, 88 Stat. 1949; Nov. 29, 1999, P.L. 106-113, Div B, § 1000(a) (9), 113 Stat. 1536.)

History; Ancillary Laws and Directives

Prior law and revision:

This section enacts the Patent Office rule of secrecy of applications.

Explanatory notes:

The amendment made by § 1000(a)(9) of Act Nov. 29, 1999, P.L. 106-113, is based on § 4502 of Subtitle E of Title IV of S. 1948 (113 Stat. 1501A-561), as introduced on Nov. 17,1999, which was enacted into law by such § 1000(a)(9).

Amendments:

1975. Act Jan. 2, 1975 (effective 1/2/75, as provided by § 4 of such Act, which appears as #4 15 USCS § 1111 note), substituted "Patent and Trademark Office" for "Patent Office."

1999. Act Nov. 29, 1999 (effective one year after enactment, as provided by § 4508 of S. 1948, as enacted into law by such Act, which appears as #5 35 USCS § 11 note), substituted this section for one which read:

"§ 122. Confidential status of applications

"Application for patents shall be kept in confidence by the Patent and Trademark Office."

Sec. 154. Contents and term of patent; provisional rights

(a) In general.

(1) Contents. Every patent shall contain a short title of the invention and a grant to the patentee, his heirs or assigns, of the right to exclude others from making, using, offering for sale, or selling the invention throughout the United States or importing the invention into the United States, and, if the invention is a process,

of the right to exclude others from using, offering for sale or selling throughout the United States, or importing into the United States, products made by that process, referring to the specification for the particulars thereof.

(2) Term. Subject to the payment of fees under this title, such grant shall be for a term beginning on the date on which the patent issues and ending 20 years from the date on which the application for the patent was filed in the United States or, if the application contains a specific reference to an earlier filed application or applications under section 120, 121, or 365(c) of this title, from the date on which the earliest such application was filed.

(3) Priority. Priority under section 119, 365(a), or 365(b) of this title shall not be taken into account in determining the term of a patent.

(4) Specification and drawing. A copy of the specification and drawing shall be annexed to the patent and be a part of such patent.

Sec. 171. Patents for designs

Whoever invents any new, original and ornamental design for an article of manufacture may obtain a patent therefor, subject to the conditions and requirements of this title.

The provisions of this title relating to patents for inventions shall apply to patents for designs, except as otherwise provided.

Sec. 173. Term of design patent

Patents for designs shall be granted for the term of fourteen years from the date of grant.

Sec. 271. Infringement of patent

(a) Except as otherwise provided in this title, whoever without authority makes, uses, offers to sell, or sells any patented invention, within the United States or imports into the United States any patented invention during the term of the patent therefor, infringes the patent.

(b) Whoever actively induces infringement of a patent shall be liable as an infringer.

(c) Whoever offers to sell or sells within the United States or imports into the United States a component of a patented machine, manufacture, combination or composition, or a material or apparatus for use in practicing a patented process, constituting a material part of the invention, knowing the same to be especially made or especially adapted for use in an infringement of such patent, and not a staple article or commodity of commerce suitable for substantial noninfringing use, shall be liable as a contributory infringer.

(d) No patent owner otherwise entitled to relief for infringement or contributory infringement of a patent shall be denied relief or deemed guilty of misuse or illegal extension of the patent right by reason of his having done one or more of the following: (1) derived revenue from acts which if performed by another without his consent would constitute contributory infringement of the patent; (2) licensed or authorized another to perform acts which if performed without his consent would constitute contributory infringement of the patent; (3) sought to enforce his patent rights against infringement or contributory infringement; (4) refused to license or use any rights to the patent; or (5) conditioned the license of any rights to the patent or the sale of the patented product on the acquisition of a license to rights in another patent or purchase of a separate product, unless, in view of the circumstances, the patent owner has market power in the relevant market for the patent or patented product on which the license or sale is conditioned.

(e) (1) It shall not be an act of infringement to make, use, offer to sell, or sell within the United States or import into the United States a patented invention (other than a new animal drug or veterinary biological product (as those terms are used in the Federal Food, Drug, and Cosmetic Act and the Act of March 4, 1913) which is primarily manufactured using recombinant DNA, recombinant RNA, hybridoma technology, or other processes involving site specific genetic manipulation techniques) solely for uses reasonably related to the development and submission of information under a Federal law which regulates the manufacture, use, or sale of drugs or veterinary biological products.

(2) It shall be an act of infringement to submit—

(A) an application under section 505(j) of the Federal Food, Drug, and Cosmetic Act or described in section 505(b)(2) of such Act for a drug claimed in a patent or the use of which is claimed in a patent, or

(B) an application under section 512 of such Act or under the Act of March 4, 1913 (21 U.S.C. 151-158) for a drug or veterinary biological product which is not primarily manufactured using recombinant DNA, recombinant RNA, hybridoma technology, or other processes involving site specific genetic manipulation techniques and which is claimed in a patent or the use of which is claimed in a patent, if the purpose of such submission is to obtain approval under such Act to engage in the commercial manufacture, use, or sale of a drug or veterinary biological product claimed in a patent or the use of which is claimed in a patent before the expiration of such patent.

(3) In any action for patent infringement brought under this section, no injunctive or other relief may be granted which would prohibit the making, using, offering to sell, or selling within the United States or importing into the United States of a patented invention under paragraph (1).

(4) For an act of infringement described in paragraph (2)—

(A) the court shall order the effective date of any approval of the drug or veterinary biological product involved in the infringement to be a date which is not earlier than the date of the expiration of the patent which has been infringed,

(B) injunctive relief may be granted against an infringer to prevent the commercial manufacture, use, offer to sell, or sale within the United States or importation into the United States of an approved drug or veterinary biological product, and

(C) damages or other monetary relief may be awarded against an infringer only if there has been commercial manufacture, use, offer to sell, or sale within the United States or importation into the United States of an approved drug or veterinary biological product.

The remedies prescribed by subparagraphs (A), (B), and (C) are the only remedies which may be granted by a court for an act of infringement described in paragraph (2), except that a court may award attorney fees under section 285.

(f) (1) Whoever without authority supplies or causes to be supplied in or from the United States all or a substantial portion of the components of a patented invention, where such components are uncombined in whole or in part, in such manner as to actively induce the combination of such components outside of the United States in a manner that would infringe the patent if such combination occurred within the United States, shall be liable as an infringer.

(2) Whoever without authority supplies or causes to be supplied in or from the United States any component of a patented invention that is especially made or especially adapted for use in the invention and not a staple article or commodity of commerce suitable for substantial noninfringing use, where such component is

uncombined in whole or in part, knowing that such component is so made or adapted and intending that such component will be combined outside of the United States in a manner that would infringe the patent if such combination occurred within the United States, shall be liable as an infringer.

(g) Whoever without authority imports into the United States or offers to sell, sells, or uses within the United States a product which is made by a process patented in the United States shall be liable as an infringer, if the importation, offer to sell, sale, or use of the product occurs during the term of such process patent. In an action for infringement of a process patent, no remedy may be granted for infringement on account of the noncommercial use or retail sale of a product unless there is no adequate remedy under this title for infringement on account of the importation or other use, offer to sell, or sale of that product. A product which is made by a patented process will, for purposes of this title, not be considered to be so made after—

(1) it is materially changed by subsequent processes; or

(2) it becomes a trivial and nonessential component of another product.

(h) As used in this section, the term "whoever" includes any State, any instrumentality of a State, and any officer or employee of a State or instrumentality of a State acting in his official capacity. Any State, and any such instrumentality, officer, or employee, shall be subject to the provisions of this title in the same manner and to the same extent as any nongovernmental entity.

(i) As used in this section, an "offer for sale" or an "offer to sell" by a person other than the patentee, or any designee of the patentee, is that in which the sale will occur before the expiration of the term of the patent.

Sec. 283. Injunction

The several courts having jurisdiction of cases under this title may grant injunctions in accordance with the principles of equity to prevent the violation of any right secured by patent, on such terms as the court deems reasonable.

Sec. 284. Damages

Upon finding for the claimant the court shall award the claimant damages adequate to compensate for the infringement, but in no event less than a reasonable royalty for the use made of the invention by the infringer, together with interest and costs as fixed by the court.

When the damages are not found by a jury, the court shall assess them. In either event the court may increase the damages up to three times the amount found or assessed.

The court may receive expert testimony as an aid to the determination of damages or of what royalty would be reasonable under the circumstances.

Sec. 285. Attorney fees

The court in exceptional cases may award reasonable attorney fees to the prevailing party.

Sec. 287. Limitation on damages and other remedies; marking and notice

(a) Patentees, and persons making, offering for sale, or selling within the United States any patented article for or under them, or importing any patented article into the United States, may give notice to the public that the same is patented, either by fixing thereon the word "patent" or the abbreviation "pat.", together with the number of the patent, or when, from the character of the article, this can not be done, by fixing to it, or to the package wherein one or more of them is contained, a label containing a like notice. In the event of failure so to mark, no damages shall be recovered by the patentee in any action for infringement, except on proof that the infringer was notified of the infringement and continued to infringe thereafter, in which event damages may be recovered only for infringement occurring after such notice. Filing of an action for infringement shall constitute such notice.

UNIFORM TRADE SECRETS ACT
WITH 1985 AMENDMENTS

SECTION 1. DEFINITIONS. AS USED IN THIS [ACT], UNLESS THE CONTEXT REQUIRES OTHERWISE:

(1) "Improper means" includes theft, bribery, misrepresentation, breach or inducement of a breach of a duty to maintain secrecy, or espionage through electronic or other means;

(2) "Misappropriation" means:

(i) acquisition of a trade secret of another by a person who knows or has reason to know that the trade secret was acquired by improper means; or

(ii) disclosure or use of a trade secret of another without express or implied consent by a person who

(A) used improper means to acquire knowledge of the trade secret; or

(B) at the time of disclosure or use, knew or had reason to know that his knowledge of the trade secret was

(I) derived from or through a person who had utilized improper means to acquire it;

(II) acquired under circumstances giving rise to a duty to maintain its secrecy or limit its use; or

(III) derived from or through a person who owed a duty to the person seeking relief to maintain its secrecy or limit its use; or

(C) before a material change of his [or her] position, knew or had reason to know that it was a trade secret and that knowledge of it had been acquired by accident or mistake.

(3) "Person" means a natural person, corporation, business trust, estate, trust, partnership, association, joint venture, government, governmental subdivision or agency, or any other legal or commercial entity.

(4) "Trade secret" means information, including a formula, pattern, compilation, program, device, method, technique, or process, that:

(i) derives independent economic value, actual or potential, from not being generally known to, and not being readily ascertainable by proper means by, other persons who can obtain economic value from its disclosure or use, and

(ii) is the subject of efforts that are reasonable under the circumstances to maintain its secrecy.

Section 2. Injunctive Relief.

(a) Actual or threatened misappropriation may be enjoined. Upon application to the court, an injunction shall be terminated when the trade secret has ceased to exist, but the injunction may be continued for an additional reasonable period of time in order to eliminate commercial advantage that otherwise would be derived from the misappropriation.

(b) If the court determines that it would be unreasonable to prohibit future use In exceptional circumstances, an injunction may condition future use upon payment of a reasonable royalty for no longer than the period of time the for which use could have been prohibited. Exceptional circumstances include, but are not limited to, a material and prejudicial change of position prior to acquiring knowledge or reason to know of misappropriation that renders a prohibitive injunction inequitable.

(c) In appropriate circumstances, affirmative acts to protect a trade secret may be compelled by court order.

Section 3. Damages.

(a) In addition to or in lieu of injunctive relief Except to the extent that a material and prejudicial change of position prior to acquiring knowledge or reason to know of misappropriation renders a monetary recovery inequitable, a complainant is entitled to recover damages for the actual loss caused by misappropriation. A complainant also may recover for Damages can include both the actual loss caused by misappropriation and the unjust enrichment caused by misappropriation that is not taken into account in computing damages for actual loss. In lieu of damages measured by any other methods, the damages caused by misappropriation may be measured by imposition of liability for a reasonable royalty for a misappropriator's unauthorized disclosure or use of a trade secret.

(b) If willful and malicious misappropriation exists, the court may award exemplary damages in an amount not exceeding twice any award made under subsection (a).

Section 4. Attorney's Fees.

If (i) a claim of misappropriation is made in bad faith, (ii) a motion to terminate an injunction is made or resisted in bad faith, or (iii) willful and malicious misappropriation exists, the court may award reasonable attorney's fees to the prevailing party.

Section 5. Preservation of Secrecy.

In an action under this [Act], a court shall preserve the secrecy of an alleged trade secret by reasonable means, which may include granting protective orders in connection with discovery proceedings, holding in-camera hearings, sealing the records of the action, and ordering any person involved in the litigation not to disclose an alleged trade secret without prior court approval.

Section 6. Statute of Limitations.

An action for misappropriation must be brought within 3 years after the misappropriation is discovered or by the exercise of reasonable diligence should have been discovered. For the purposes of this section, a continuing misappropriation constitutes a single claim.

Section 7. Effect on Other Law.

(a) This Except as provided in subsection (b), this [Act] displaces conflicting tort, restitutionary, and other law of this State pertaining to providing civil liability remedies for misappropriation of a trade secret.

(b) This [Act] does not affect:

    (1) contractual or other civil liability or relief that is remedies, whether or not based upon misappropriation of a trade secret; or

    (2) criminal liability for other civil remedies that are not based upon misappropriation of a trade secret. ; or

    (3) criminal remedies, whether or not based upon misappropriation of a trade secret.

Glossary

Ab initio from the beginning.

Abrogate recall or repeal; make void or inoperative.

Absolute liability liability for an act that causes harm even though the actor was not at fault.

Acceptance unqualified assent to the act or proposal of another; as the acceptance of a draft (bill of exchange), of an offer to make a contract, of goods delivered by the seller, or of a gift or deed.

Accident an event that occurs even though a reasonable person would not have foreseen its occurrence, because of which the law holds no one responsible for the harm caused.

Accord agreement to a different performance other than what was originally specified in the contract.

Accord and satisfaction an agreement to substitute a different performance for that called for in the contract and the performance of this substitute agreement.

Acknowledgment an admission or confirmation, generally of an instrument and usually made before a person authorized to administer oaths, such as a notary public; the purpose being to declare that the instrument was executed by the person making the instrument, or that it was a voluntary act or that that person desires that it be recorded.

Action a proceeding to enforce any right.

Action in personam an action brought to impose liability upon a person, such as a money judgment.

Action in rem an action brought to declare the status of a thing, such as an action to declare the title to property to be forfeited because of its illegal use.

Action of assumpsit a common law action brought to recover damages for breach of a contract.

Act of God a natural phenomenon that is not reasonably foreseeable.

Act-of-state doctrine the doctrine whereby every sovereign state is bound to respect the independence of every other sovereign state, and the courts of one country will not sit in judgment of another government's acts done within its own territory.

Actual the physical delivery of an agreement.

Administrative agency a governmental commission or board given authority to regulate particular matters.

Administrative law the law governing administrative agencies.

Administrative Procedure Act (APA) a federal law governing the operations and process of federal administraaive agencies.

Administrative regulations rules made by state and federal administrative agencies.

Advisory opinion an opinion that may be rendered in a few states when there is no actual controversy before the court and the matter is submitted by private persons, or in some instances by the governor of the state, to obtain the court's opinion.

Affidavit a statement of facts set forth in written form and supported by the oath or affirmation of the person making the statement setting forth that such facts are true on the basis of actual knowledge or on information and belief. The affidavit is executed before a notary public or other person authorized to administer oaths.

Affirmative covenant an express undertaking or promise in a contract or deed to do an act.

Agency the relationship that exists between a person identified as a principal and another by virtue of which the latter may make contracts with third persons on behalf of the principal. (Parties—**principal, agent, third person**)

Agent one who is authorized by the principal or by operation of law to make contracts with third persons on behalf of the principal.

Airbill a document of title issued to a shipper whose goods are being sent via air.

Aktiengesellschaft German version of the société anonyme, very similar to the U.S. corporate form of business organization.

Alteration any material change of the terms of a writing fraudulently made by a party thereto.

Ambiguous having more than one reasonable interpretation.

Amicus curiae literally, a friend of the court; one who is approved by the court to take part in litigation and to assist the court by furnishing an opinion in the matter.

Answer what a defendant must file to admit or deny facts asserted by the plaintiff.

Anticipatory breach the repudiation by a promisor of the contract prior to the time that performance is required when such repudiation is accepted by the promisee as a breach of the contract.

Anticipatory repudiation the repudiation made in advance of the time for performance of the contract obligations.

Antitrust acts statutes prohibiting combinations and contracts in restraint of trade—notably, the federal Sherman Antitrust Act of 1890.

Apparent authority appearance of authority created by the principal's words or conduct.

Appeal taking a case to a reviewing court to determine whether the judgment of the lower court or administrative agency was correct. (Parties—**appellant, appellee**)

Appellate jurisdiction the power of a court to hear and decide a given class of cases on appeal from another court or administrative agency.

Arbitration the settlement of disputed questions, whether of law or fact, by one or more arbitrators by whose decision the parties agree to be bound.

Article 2 section of Uniform Commercial Code that governs contracts for the sale of goods.

Article 2A the portion of the UCC that governs the lease of goods.

Assignee a third party to whom contract benefits are transferred.

Assignment transfer of a right. Generally used in connection with personal property rights, as rights under a contract, commercial paper, an insurance policy, a mortgage, or a lease. (Parties—**assignor, assignee**)

Assumption of risk the common law rule that an employee could not sue the employer for injuries caused by the ordinary risks of employment on the theory that the employee assumed such risks by undertaking the work. The rule has been abolished in those areas governed by workers' compensation laws and most employers' liability statutes.

Attorney in fact a private attorney authorized to act for another under a power of attorney.

Attorneys counselors at law who are officers of the court.

Authenticate make or establish as genuine, official, or final, such as by signing, countersigning, sealing, or performing any other act indicating approval.

Bailee person who accepts possession of a property.

Bailment the relationship that exists when personal property is delivered into the possession of another under an agreement, express or implied, that the identical property will be returned or will be delivered in accordance with the agreement. (Parties—**bailor, bailee**)

Bailment for hire a contract in which the bailor agrees to pay the bailee.

Bailor the person who turns over the possession of a property.

Battle of the forms merchants' exchanges of invoices and purchase orders with differing boiler plate terms.

Bilateral contract an agreement under which one promise is given in exchange for another.

Bill of lading a document issued by a carrier reciting the receipt of goods and the terms of the contract of transportation. Regulated by the federal Bills of Lading Act or the UCC.

Bill of sale a writing signed by the seller reciting that the personal property therein described has been sold to the buyer.

Bona fide in good faith; without any fraud or deceit.

Boycott a combination of two or more persons to cause harm to another by refraining from patronizing or dealing with such other person in any way or inducing others to so refrain.

Breach the failure to act or perform in the manner called for in a contract.

Cancellation a crossing out of a part of an instrument or a destruction of all legal effect of the instrument, whether by act of party, upon breach by the other party, or pursuant to agreement or decree of court.

Carrier an individual or organization undertaking the transportation of goods.

Case law law that includes principles that are expressed for the first time in court decisions.

Cause of action the right to damages or other judicial relief when a legally protected right of the plaintiff is violated by an unlawful act of the defendant.

Caveat emptor Let the buyer beware. This maxim has been nearly abolished by warranty and strict tort liability concepts and consumer protection laws.

Cease and desist order an order issued by a court or administrative agency to stop a practice that it decides is improper.

Certiorari a review by a higher court of the regularity of proceedings before a lower court. Originally granted within the discretion of the reviewing court. The name is derived from the language of the writ, which was in Latin and directed the lower court to certify its record and transfer it to the higher court. In modern practice, the scope of review has often been expanded to include a review of the merits of the case and, also, to review the action of administrative agencies.

CF cost and freight.

Choice-of-law clause a clause in an agreement that specifies which law will govern should a dispute arise.

C.I.F. cost, insurance, and freight.

Circumstantial evidence relates to circumstances surrounding the facts in dispute from which the trier of fact may deduce what has happened.

C.I.S.G. uniform international contract code contracts for international sale of goods.

Civil action in many states a simplified form of action combining all or many of the former common law actions.

Civil court a court with jurisdiction to hear and determine controversies relating to private rights and duties.

Clayton Act a federal law that prohibits price discrimination.

COD cash on delivery.

Comity a principle of international and national law that the laws of all nations and states deserve the respect legitimately demanded by equal participants.

Commerce clause that section of the U.S. Constitution allocating business regulation.

Commercial impracticability when costs of performance rise suddenly and performance of a contract will result in a substantial loss.

Commercial unit the standard of the trade for shipment or packaging of a good.

Common carrier a carrier that holds out its facilities to serve the general public for compensation without discrimination.

Common law the body of unwritten principles originally based upon the usages and customs of the community that were recognized and enforced by the courts.

Comparative negligence a defense to negligence that allows plaintiff to recover reduced damages based on his level of fault.

Compensatory damages a sum of money that will compensate an injured plaintiff for actual loss.

Complaint the initial pleading filed by the plaintiff in many actions, which in many states may be served as original process to acquire jurisdiction over the defendant.

Condition an event that affects the existence of a contract or the obligation of a party to a contract.

Condition precedent event that if unsatisfied would mean that no rights would arise under a contract.

Condition subsequent an event whose occurrence or lack thereof terminates a contract.

Conflict of interest conduct that compromises an employee's allegiance to that company.

Conflict of laws the body of law that determines the law of which state is to apply when two or more states are involved in the facts of a given case.

Consent decrees informal settlements of enforcement actions brought by agencies.

Consequential damages damages the buyer experiences as a result of the seller's breach with respect to a third party.

Consequential loss a loss that does not result directly from a party's act but from the consequences of that act.

Consideration the promise or performance that the promisor demands as the price of the promise.

Consignee person to whom goods are shipped.

Consignment a bailment made for the purpose of sale by the bailee. (Parties—**consignor, consignee**)

Consignor person who delivers goods to the carrier for shipment.

Conspiracy an agreement between two or more persons to commit an unlawful act.

Constitution a body of principles that establishes the structure of a government and the relationship of the government to the people who are governed.

Constitutional law the branch of law that is based on the constitutions in force in a particular area or territory.

Consumer credit credit for personal, family, and household use.

Consumer credit transaction a transaction referred to by the FTC rule limiting the rights of a holder in due course in this type of transaction to protect consumers of goods or services for personal, family, or household use.

Consumer goods goods used or bought primarily for personal, family, or household use.

Consumer lease lease of goods by a natural person for personal, family, or household use.

Contract a binding agreement based upon the genuine assent of the parties, made for a lawful object, between competent parties, in the form required by law, and generally supported by consideration.

Contract of adhesion a contract offered by a dominant party to a party with inferior bargaining power on a take-it-or-leave-it basis.

Contractual capacity the ability to understand that a contract is being made and to understand its general meaning.

Contributory negligence negligence of the plaintiff.

Cooperative a group of two or more persons or enterprises that acts through a common agent with respect to a common objective, such as buying or selling.

Copyright a grant to an author or artist of an exclusive right to publish and sell the copyrighted work for the life of the author or artist and fifty years thereafter. For a "work made for hire," a grant of an exclusive right to publish and sell the copyrighted work for 100 years from its creation or 75 years from its publication, whichever is shorter.

Costs the expenses of suing or being sued, recoverable in some actions by the successful party and, in others, subject to allocation by the court. Ordinarily, costs do not include attorney's fees or compensation for loss of time.

Counterclaim a claim that the defendant in an action may make against the plaintiff.

Counterfeiting manufacturing, with fraudulent intent, of a document or coin that appears genuine.

Counteroffer a proposal by an offeree to the offeror that changes the terms of, and thus rejects, the original offer.

Course of dealing pattern of performance between two parties to a contract.

Court a tribunal established by government to hear and decide matters properly brought to it.

Covenants obligations of parties in a lease.

Creditor person (seller or lender) who is owed money; also may be a secured party.

Crime a violation of the law that is punished as an offense against the state or government.

Cross complaint a claim that the defendant may make against the plaintiff.

Cross-examination the examination made of a witness by the attorney for the adverse party.

Customary authority authority of an agent to do any act that, according to the custom of the community, usually accompanies the transaction for which the agent is authorized to act.

Cybersquatters the term for those who register and set up domain names on the Internet for resale to the famous users of the names in question.

Damages a sum of money recovered to redress or make amends for the legal wrong or injury done.

Debtor a buyer on credit, i.e., a borrower.

Declaratory judgment a procedure for obtaining the decision of a court on a question before any action has been taken or loss sustained. It differs from an advisory opinion in that there must be an actual, imminent controversy.

De facto existing in fact as distinguished from as of right, as in the case of an officer or a corporation purporting to act as such without being elected to the office or having been properly incorporated.

Defamation libel, the attacking of someone's reputation.

Defendant party charged with a violation of civil or criminal law in a proceeding.

Delegated powers powers expressly granted the national government by the Constitution.

Delegation the transfer to another of the right and power to do an act.

Demurrer a pleading that may be filed to attack the sufficiency of the adverse party's pleading as not stating a cause of action or a defense.

Deposition the testimony of a witness taken out of court before a person authorized to administer oaths.

Design patents patents that protect new and nonobvious ornamental features that appear in connection with an article of manufacture.

Detrimental reliance see **reliance** and **promissory estoppel**.

Dicta see obiter dictum.

Direct damages losses that are caused by breach of a contract.

Directed verdict a direction by the trial judge to the jury to return a verdict in favor of a specified party to the action.

Direct examination the asking of witnesses about details pertinent to a case.

Directors the persons vested with control of the corporation, subject to the elective power of the shareholders.

Discharge of contract termination of a contract by performance, agreement, impossibility, acceptance of breach, or operation of law.

Discovery procedures for ascertaining facts prior to the time of trial in order to eliminate the element of surprise in litigation.

Dismiss a procedure to terminate an action by moving to dismiss on the ground that the plaintiff has not pleaded a cause of action entitling the plaintiff to relief.

Disparagement of goods the making of malicious, false statements as to the quality of the goods of another.

Dispute Settlement Body a means, provided by the World Trade Organization, for member countries to resolve trade disputes rather than engage in unilateral trade sanctions or a trade war.

Distributor the entity that takes title to goods and bears the financial and commercial risks for the subsequent sale of the goods.

Domicile the home of a person or the state of incorporation, to be distinguished from a place where a person lives but does not regard as home, or a state in which a corporation does business but in which it was not incorporated.

Donee recipient of a gift

Donor person making a gift.

Draft see **bill of exchange**.

Due care the degree of care that a reasonable person would exercise to prevent the realization of harm, which under all the circumstances was reasonably foreseeable in the event that such care was not taken.

Due process the constitutional right to be heard, question witnesses, and present evidence.

Due Process Clause the process of checking the environmental history and nature of land prior to purchase.

Dumping selling goods in another country at less than their fair value.

Duress conduct that deprives the victim of free will and that generally gives the victim the right to set aside any transaction entered into under such circumstances.

Duty an obligation of law imposed on a person to perform or refrain from performing a certain act.

Economic duress threat of financial loss.

Effects doctrine the doctrine that states U.S. courts will assume jurisdiction and will apply antitrust laws to conduct outside of the United States where the activity of business firms has direct and substantial effect on U.S. commerce.

Electronic funds transfer (EFTA) any transfer of funds (other than a transaction originated by a check, draft, or similar paper instrument) that is initiated through an electronic terminal, telephone, computer, or magnetic tape so as to authorize a financial institution to debit or credit an account.

Employment-at-will doctrine doctrine in which the employer has historically been allowed to terminate the employment contract at any time for any reason or for no reason.

En banc the term used when the full panel of judges on the appellate court hears a case.

Equity the body of principles that originally developed because of the inadequacy of the rules then applied by the common law courts of England.

Estoppel the principle by which a person is barred from pursuing a certain course of action or of disputing the truth of certain matters.

Ethica a branch of philosophy dealing with values that relate to the nature of human conduct and values associated with that conduct.

European Union (EU) name used to describe the union of the fifteen member countries of Europe who seek to unify their economic, monetary, and political policies.

Evidence that which is presented to the trier of fact as the basis upon which the trier is to determine what happened.

Exculpatory clause a provision in a contract stating that one of the parties shall not be liable for damages in case of breach; also called limitation-of-liability clause.

Execute to carry out a judgment.

Executed contract an agreement that has been completely performed.

Executive branch the branch of government (e.g., the president) formed to execute the laws.

Executory contract an agreement by which something remains to be done by one or both parties.

Exemplary damages damages, in excess of the amount needed to compensate for the plaintiff's injury, that are awarded in order to punish the defendant for malicious or wanton conduct; also called "punitive damages."

Exhaustion of administrative remedies the requirement that an agency make its final decision before the parties can go to court.

Existing goods goods that physically exist and are owned by the seller at the time of a transaction.

Expert witness one who has acquired special knowledge in a particular field as through practical experience or study, or both, whose opinion is admissible as an aid to the trier of fact.

Export sale a direct sale to customers in a foreign country.

Express authority authority of an agent to perform a certain act.

Express contract an agreement of the parties manifested by their words, whether spoken or written.

Express warranty a statement by the defendant relating to the goods, which statement is part of the basis of the bargain.

Ex-ship the obligation of a seller to deliver or unload goods from a ship that has reached its port of destination.

Fair use a principle that allows the limited use of copyrighted material for teaching, research, and news reporting.

FAS free alongside the named vessel.

FCPA Foreign Corrupt Practices Act; prohibits bribery by U.S.-based companies in their international operations.

Federal district court a general trial court of the federal system.

Federal Register a government publication issued five days a week that lists all administrative regulations, all presidential proclamations and executive orders, and other documents and classes of documents that the president or Congress direct to be published.

Federal sentencing guidelines federal standards used by judges to determine mandatory sentencing terms for convicted criminals.

Federal supremacy declared by constitution for use when direct conflict between state and federal statutes exist.

Federal system the system of government in which a central government is given power to administer to national concerns while individual states retain the power to administer to local concerns.

Federal Trade Commission Act a statute prohibiting unfair methods of competition in interstate commerce.

Fifth Amendment constitutional protection against self incrimination which also guarantees due process.

Firm offer an offer stated to be held open for a specified time, which must be so held in some states even in the absence of an option contract, or under the UCC, with respect to merchants.

FOB free on board, indicating a seller is providing for the shipping of goods to the buyer.

FOB place of destination general commercial language for delivery to the buyer.

FOB place of shipment a 'ship to' contract.

Food, Drug, and Cosmetic Act a federal statute prohibiting the interstate shipment of misbranded or adulterated foods, drugs, cosmetics, and therapeutic devices.

Forbearance refraining from doing an act.

Foreign corporation a corporation incorporated under the laws of another state.

Forgery the fraudulent making or altering of an instrument that apparently creates or alters a legal liability of another.

Formal contracts written contracts or agreements whose formality signifies the parties' intention to abide by the terms.

Forum a court in which any lawsuit should be brought.

Franchise a privilege or authorization, generally exclusive, to engage in a particular activity within a particular geographic area, such as a government franchise to operate a taxi company within a specified city, or a private franchise as the grant by a manufacturer of a right to sell products within a particular territory or for a particular number of years.

Franchise agreement sets forth rights of franchisee to use trademarks, etc., of franchisor.

Franchisee person to whom franchise is granted.

Franchising the granting of permission to use a trademark, trade name, or copyright under specified conditions.

Franchisor party granting the franchise.

Fraud the making of a false statement of a past or existing fact, with knowledge of its falsity or with reckless indifference as to its truth, with the intent to cause another to rely thereon, and such person does rely thereon and is harmed thereby.

Fraud in the inducement is fraud in the obtaining of a promise to an instrument, not fraud as to the nature of the instrument itself.

Freedom of Information Act federal law permitting citizens to request documents and records from administrative agencies.

Freight insurance insures that shipowner will receive payment for transportation charges.

Full warranty the obligation of a seller to fix or replace a defective product within a reasonable time without cost to the buyer.

Funds transfer communication of instructions or requests to pay a specific sum of money to the credit of a specified account or person without an actual physical passing of money.

Fungible goods goods of a homogeneous nature of which any unit is the equivalent of any other unit or is treated as such by mercantile usage.

Future goods goods that exist physically but are not owned by the seller as well as goods that have not yet been produced.

Gambling making a bet with a chance for profit and similar to a lottery in that there are the three elements of payment, prize, and chance.

General agent an agent authorized by the principal to transact all affairs in connection with a particular kind of business or trade or to transact all business at a certain place.

General damages damages that in the ordinary course of events follow naturally and probably from the injury caused by the defendant.

General jurisdiction the power to hear and decide all controversies involving legal rights and duties.

Gift the title to an owner's personal property voluntarily transferred by a party not receiving anything in exchange.

Good faith the absence of knowledge of any defects in or problems.

Goods anything movable at the time it is identified as the subject of a transaction.

Gray market goods foreign-made goods with U.S. trademarks brought into the United States without the consent of the trademark owners to compete with these owners.

Guarantor one who undertakes the obligation of guaranty.

Guaranty an undertaking to pay the debt of another if the creditor first sues the debtor and is unable to recover the debt from the debtor or principal. (In some instances the liability is primary, in which case it is the same as suretyship.)

Horizontal price fixing a violation of antitrust law whereby competitive businesses—manufacturers, for example—agree on the price they will charge for a good or service.

Identification point in the transaction when the buyer acquires an interest in the goods subject to the contract.

Identified term applied to particular goods selected by either the buyer or the seller as the goods called for by the sales contract.

Illusory promise a promise that in fact does not impose any obligation on the promisor.

Immunity not being subject to liability ordinarily imposed by law.

Implied contract a contract expressed by conduct or implied or deduced from the facts. Also used to refer to a quasi contract.

Implied warranty a warranty that was not made but is implied by law.

Imputed vicariously attributed to or charged to another; for instance, the knowledge of an agent obtained while acting in the scope of authority is imputed to the principal.

Incidental authority authority of an agent that is reasonably necessary to execute express authority.

Incidental damages incurred by the nonbreaching party as part of the process of trying to cover or sell; includes storage fees, commissions and the like.

Incorporation by reference a contract consisting of both the original or skeleton document and the detailed statement that is incorporated in it.

Indemnity the right of a person secondarily liable to require that a person primarily liable pay for loss sustained when the secondary party discharges the obligation that the primary party should have discharged; the right of an agent to be paid the amount of any loss or damage sustained without fault because of obedience to the principal's instructions; an undertaking by one person for a consideration to pay another person a sum of money to indemnify that person when a specified loss is incurred.

Indemnity contract an undertaking by one person, for a consideration, to pay another person a sum of money in the event that the other person sustains a specified loss.

Independent contractor a contractor who undertakes to perform a specified task according to the terms of a contract but over whom the other contracting party has no control except as provided for by the contract.

Informal contract a simple oral or written contract.

Infringement the violation of trademarks, patents, or copyrights by copying or using material without permission.

Injunction an order of a court of equity to refrain from doing (negative injunction) or to do (affirmative or mandatory injunction) a specified act. Its use in labor disputes has been greatly restricted by statute.

In pari delicto equally guilty; used in reference to a transaction as to which relief will not be granted to either party because both are equally guilty of wrongdoing.

Instructions summary of the law given to jurors by the judge before deliberation begins.

Insurable interest an interest in the nonoccurrence of the risk insured against, generally because such occurrence would cause financial loss, although sometimes merely because of the close relationship between the insured and the beneficiary.

Insurance a plan of security against risks by charging the loss against a fund created by the payments made by policyholders.

Insured person to whom the promise in an insurance contract is made.

Insurer promisor in an insurance contract.

Integrity the adherence to one's values and principles despite the costs and consequences.

Intellectual property rights Trademark, copyright, and patent rights protected by law.

Intentional tort a civil wrong that results from intentional conduct.

Interlineation a writing between the lines or adding to the provisions of a document, the effect thereof depending upon the nature of the document.

Interpleader a form of action or proceeding by which a person against whom conflicting claims are made may bring the claimants into court to litigate their claims between themselves, as in the case of a bailee when two persons each claim to be the owner of the bailed property, or an insurer when two persons each claim to be the beneficiary.

Interrogatories written questions used as a discovery tool that must be answered under oath.

Invasion of privacy tort of intentional intrusion in to the private affairs of another.

Inventory goods held primarily for sale or lease to others; raw materials, work in progress, materials consumed in a business.

Investigative consumer report a report on a person based on personal investigation and interviews.

Ipso facto by the very act or fact in itself without any further action by anyone.

Irrebuttable presumption a presumption that cannot be rebutted by proving that the facts are to the contrary; not a true presumption but merely a rule of law described in terms of a presumption.

Joint and several contract a contract in which two or more persons are jointly and separately obligated or under which they are jointly and separately entitled to recover.

Joint contract a contract in which two or more persons are jointly liable or jointly entitled to performance under the contract.

Judge primary officer of the court.

Judgment the final sentence, order, or decision entered into at the conclusion of the action.

Judgment n.o.v. a judgment that may be entered after verdict upon the motion of the losing party on the ground that the verdict is so wrong that a judgment should be entered the opposite of the verdict, or *non obstante veredicto* (notwithstanding the verdict).

Judgment on the pleadings a judgment that may be entered after all the pleadings are filed when it is clear from the pleadings that a particular party is entitled to win the action without proceeding any further.

Judicial branch the branch of government (courts) formed to interpret the laws.

Jurisdiction the power of a court to hear and determine a given class of cases; the power to act over a particular defendant.

Jury a body of citizens sworn by a court to determine by verdict the issues of fact submitted to them.

Laches the rule that the enforcement of equitable rights will be denied when the party has delayed so long that rights of third persons have intervened or the death or disappearance of witnesses would prejudice any party through the loss of evidence.

Last clear chance the rule that a defendant who had the last clear chance to have avoided injuring the plaintiff is liable even though the plaintiff had also been contributorily negligent. In some states also called the humanitarian doctrine.

Law the order or pattern of rules that society establishes to govern the conduct of individuals and the relationships among them.

Law of the case matters decided in the course of litigation that are binding on the parties in the subsequent phases of litigation.

Law of the forum the law of state in which the court is located.

Legislative branch the branch of government (e.g., Congress) formed to make the laws.

Letter of credit a written agreement by which the issuer of the letter, usually a bank, agrees with the other contracting party, its customer, that the issuer will honor drafts drawn upon it by the person named in the letter as the beneficiary. Domestic letters are regulated by the UCC, Article 5; international letters, by the Customs and Practices for Commercial Documentary Credits. Commercial or payment letter: the customer is the buyer of goods sold by the beneficiary and the letter covers the purchase price of the goods. Standby letter: a letter obtained instead of a suretyship or guaranty contract requiring the issuer to honor drafts drawn by the beneficiary upon the issuer when the customer of the issuer fails to perform a contract between the customer and the beneficiary. Documentary letter: a letter of credit that does not obligate the issuer to honor drafts unless they are accompanied by the documents specified in the letter.

Libel written or visual defamation without legal justification.

Licensing the transfer of technology rights to a product.

Limitation-of-liability clause a provision in a contract stating that one of the parties shall not be liable for damages in case of breach; also called "exculpatory clause."

Limited jurisdiction a court's power to hear and determine cases within certain restricted categories.

Limited warranty any warranty that does not provide the complete protection of a full warranty.

Liquidated damages a provision stipulating the amount of damages to be paid in the event of default or breach of contract.

Liquidation of damages clause the specification of exact compensation in case of a breach of contract.

Lis pendens the doctrine that certain kinds of pending action are notice to everyone so that if any right is acquired from a party to such action, the transferee takes that right subject to the outcome of the pending action.

Lottery any plan by which a consideration is given for a chance to win a prize; it consists of three elements: (1) there must be a payment of money or something of value for an opportunity to win, (2) a prize must be available, and (3) the prize must be offered by lot or chance.

Mailbox rule timing for acceptance tied to proper acceptance.

Majority of age, as contrasted with being a minor; more than half of any group, as a majority of stockholders.

Mark any word, name, symbol, or device used to identify a product or service.

Market power the ability to control price and exclude competitors

Mask work the specific form of expression embodied in a chip design, including the stencils used in manufacturing "semiconductor chip products."

Mediation the settlement of a dispute through the use of a messenger who carries to each side of the dispute the issues and offers in the case.

Merchant a seller who deals in specific goods classified by the UCC.

Minor at common law anyone under 21 years of age, but now any person under 18 in most states, and 19 in a few.

Misdemeanor a criminal offense that is neither treason nor a felony.

Misrepresentation a false statement of fact although made innocently without any intent to deceive.

Money a medium of exchange.

Most-favored-nation clause a clause in treaties between countries whereby any privilege subsequently granted to a third country in relation to a given treaty subject is extended to the other party to the treaty.

Motion for summary judgment request that the court decide case on basis of law only because there are no material issues disputed by the parties.

Motion to dismiss a pleading that may be filed to attack the sufficiency of the adverse party's pleading as not stating a cause of action or a defense.

Natural law a system of principles to guide human conduct independent of, and sometimes contrary to, enacted law and discovered by man's rational intelligence.

Necessaries things indispensable or absolutely necessary for the sustenance of human life.

Negligence the failure to exercise due care under the circumstances in consequence of which harm is proximately caused to one to whom the defendant owed a duty to exercise due care.

Negligence per se an action that is regarded as so improper that it is declared by law to be negligent in itself without regard to whether due care was otherwise exercised.

Negotiable warehouse receipt a receipt that states the covered goods will be delivered 'to the bearer' or 'to the order of.'

Nominal damages a nominal sum awarded the plaintiff in order to establish that legal rights have been violated although the plaintiff in fact has not sustained any actual loss or damages.

Nonnegotiable bill of lading see 'straight bill of lading.'

Nonnegotiable warehouse receipt a receipt that states the covered goods received will be delivered to a specific person.

Obiter dictum that which is said in the opinion of a court in passing or by the way, but which is not necessary to the determination of the case and is therefore not regarded as authoritative as though it were actually involved in the decision.

Objective intent the intent of parties to an agreement that is manifested outwardly and will be enforced.

Offer the expression of an offeror's willingness to enter into a contractual agreement.

Offeree person to whom an offer is made.

Offeror person who makes an offer.

Operation of law the attaching of certain consequences to certain facts because of legal principles that operate automatically, as contrasted with consequences that arise because of the voluntary action of a party designed to create those consequences.

Option contract a contract to hold an offer to make a contract open for a fixed period of time.

Order designates payment to a particular person or entity for their further direction.

Ordinary contract defenses any defense that a party to an ordinary contract may raise, such as a lack of capacity of parties, absence of consideration, fraud, concealment, or mistake.

Original jurisdiction the authority to hear a controversy when it is first brought to court.

Output contract the contract of a producer to sell its entire production or output to a given buyer.

Parol evidence rule the rule that prohibits the introduction in evidence of oral or written statements made prior to or contemporaneously with the execution of a complete written contract, deed, or instrument, in the absence of clear proof of fraud, accident, or mistake causing the omission of the statement in question.

Past consideration something that has been performed in the past and which, therefore, cannot be consideration for a promise made in the present.

Patent the grant to an inventor of an exclusive right to make and sell an invention for a nonrenewable period of 20 years.

Patentable a term used to describe an invention that is new and not obvious to a person of ordinary skill and knowledge in the art or technology to which the invention is related.

Per se in, through, or by itself.

Person a term that includes both natural persons, or living persons, and artificial persons, such as corporations which are created by act of government.

Personal property property that is movable or intangible, or rights in such things.

Physical duress threat of physical harm to person or property.

Plant patents patents that protect the developers of a sexual reproduction of new plants.

Pleadings the papers filed by the parties in an action in order to set forth the facts and frame the issues to be tried, although, under some systems, the pleadings merely give notice or a general indication of the nature of the issues.

Postdate to insert or place on an instrument a later date than the actual date on which it was executed.

Power of appointment a power given to another, commonly a beneficiary of a trust, to designate or appoint who shall be beneficiary or receive the fund after the death of the grantor.

Power of attorney a written authorization to an agent by the principal.

Precedent a decision of a court that stands as the law for a particular problem in the future.

Preempt to take precedence over.

Preemption the federal government's superior regulatory position over state laws on the same subject area.

Presumption a rule of proof that permits the existence of a fact to be assumed from the proof that another fact exists when there is a logical relationship between the two or when the means of disproving the assumed fact are more readily within the control or knowledge of the adverse party against whom the presumption operates.

Price the consideration for sale of goods.

Prima facie evidence that, if believed, is sufficient by itself to lead to a particular conclusion.

Principal Register a federal register maintained for recording trademarks and service marks.

Private carrier a carrier owned by the shipper, such as a company's own fleet of trucks.

Privity a succession or chain of relationship to the same thing or right, such as privity of contract, privity of estate, privity of possession.

Privity of contract the relationship between a promisor and the promisee.

Procedural law the law that must be followed in enforcing rights and liabilities.

Product disparagement false statements made about a product or business.

Product liability liability imposed upon the manufacturer or seller of goods for harm caused by a defect in the goods, comprising liability for (a) negligence, (b) fraud, (c) breach of warranty, and (d) strict tort.

Promisee a person to whom a promise is made.

Promisor a person who makes a promise.

Promissory estoppel the doctrine that a promise will be enforced although it is not supported by consideration when the promisor should have reasonably expected that the promise would induce action or forbearance of a definite and substantial character on the part of the promised and injustice can be avoided only by enforcement of the promise.

Proximate cause the act that is the natural and reasonably foreseeable cause of the harm or event that occurs and injures the plaintiff.

Proximate damages damages that in the ordinary course of events are the natural and reasonably foreseeable result of the defendant's violation of the plaintiff's rights.

Punitive damages damages, in excess of those required to compensate the plaintiff for the wrong done, that are imposed in order to punish the defendant because of the particularly wanton or willful character of wrongdoing; also called "exemplary damages."

Pur curiam opinion an opinion written by the court rather than by a named judge when all the judges of the court are in such agreement on the matter that it is not deemed to merit any discussion and may be simply disposed of.

Quantum meruit an action brought for the value of the services rendered the defendant when there was no express contract as to the purchase price.

Quasi as if, as though it were, having the characteristics of; a modifier employed to indicate that the subject is to be treated as though it were in fact the noun that follows the word quasi, as in quasi contract, quasi corporation, quasi-public corporation.

Quasi contract a court-imposed obligation to prevent unjust enrichment in the absence of a contract.

Quasi-judicial proceedings forms of hearings in which the rules of evidence and procedure are more relaxed but each side still has a chance to be heard.

Quid pro quo literally 'what for what.' An early form of the concept of consideration by which an action for debt could not be brought unless the defendant had obtained something in return for the obligation sued upon.

Reasonable care the degree of care that a reasonable person would take under all the circumstances then known.

Rebuttable presumption a presumption that may be overcome or rebutted by proof that the actual facts were different from those presumed.

Reformation a remedy by which a written instrument is corrected when it fails to express the actual intent of both parties because of fraud, accident, or mistake.

Remand decision of appellate court to send a case back to trial court for additional hearings or a new trial.

Remedy the action or procedure that is followed in order to enforce a right or to obtain damages for injury to a right.

Repudiation the result of a buyer or seller refusing to perform the contract as stated.

Requirements contract a contract to buy all requirements of the buyer from the seller.

Rescission by agreement the setting aside of a contract by the action of the parties as though the contract had never been made.

Rescission upon breach the action of one party to a contract to set the contract aside when the other party is guilty of a breach of the contract.

Res ipsa loquitur the permissible inference that the defendant was negligent in that the thing speaks for itself when the circumstances are such that ordinarily the plaintiff could not have been injured had the defendant not been at fault.

Respondeat superior the doctrine that the principal or employer is vicariously liable for the unauthorized torts committed by an agent or employee while acting within the scope of the agency or the course of the employment, respectively.

Reverse the term used when the appellate court sets aside the verdict or judgment of a lower court.

Right legal capacity to require another person to perform or refrain from an action.

Right of privacy the right to be free from unreasonable intrusion by others.

Right to cure the second chance for a seller to make a proper tender of conforming goods.

Risk the peril or contingency against which the insured is protected by the contract of insurance.

Risk of loss in contract performance is the cost of damage or injury to the goods contracted for.

Robinson-Patman Act a federal statute designed to eliminate price discrimination in interstate commerce.

Sale of goods a present transfer of title to movable property for a price.

Sale on approval term indicating that no sale takes place until the buyer approves or accepts the goods.

Seasonable timely.

Service mark any word, name, symbol, or device that identifies a service.

Several contracts separate or independent contracts made by differerent persons undertaking to perform the same obligation.

Sherman Antitrust Act a federal statute prohibiting combinations and contracts in restraint of interstate trade, now generally inapplicable to labor union activity.

Shop right the right of an employer to use in business without charge an invention discovered by an employee during working hours and with the employer's material and equipment.

Slander defamation of character by spoken words or gestures.

Sovereign immunity doctrine the doctrine that states that a foreign sovereign generally cannot be sued unless an exception to the Foreign Sovereign Immunities act of 1976 applies.

Special agent an agent authorized to transact a specific transaction or to do a specific act.

Special damages damages that do not necessarily result from the injury to the plaintiff but at the same time are not so remote that the defendant should not be held liable therefor provided that the claim for special damages is properly made in the action.

Special jurisdiction a court with power to hear and determine cases within certain restricted categories.

Specific performance an action brought to compel the adverse party to perform a contract on the theory that merely suing for damages for its breach will not be an adequate remedy.

Statute of frauds a statute that, in order to prevent fraud through the use of perjured testimony, requires that certain kinds of transactions be evidenced in writing in order to be binding or enforceable.

Statute of limitations a statute that restricts the period of time within which an action may be brought.

Statutory law legislative acts declaring, commanding, or prohibiting something.

Stop delivery the right of an unpaid seller under certain conditions to prevent a carrier or a bailee from delivering goods to the buyer.

Straight (or nonnegotiable) bill of lading a document of title that consigns transported goods to a named person.

Strict liability a civil wrong for which there is absolute liability because of the inherent danger in the underlying activity, for example, the use of explosives.

Strict tort liability a product liability theory that imposes liability upon the manufacturer, seller, or distributor of goods for harm caused by defective goods.

Subjective intent a secret intent of a person.

Subject matter jurisdiction judicial authority to hear a particular type of case.

Substantial impairment material defect in a good.

Substantial performance the equitable doctrine that a contractor substantially performing a contract in good faith is entitled to recover the contract price less damages for noncompletion or defective work.

Substantive law the law that defines rights and liabilities.

Substitution discharge of a contract by substituting another in its place.

Sui generis in a class by itself, or its own kind.

Sui juris legally competent, possessing capacity.

Summary judgment a judgment entered by the court when no substantial dispute of fact is present, the court acting on the basis of affidavits or depositions that show that the claim or defense of a party is a sham.

Summons a writ by which an action was commenced under the common law.

Tariff domestically a government-approved schedule of charges that may be made by a regulated business, such as a common carrier or warehouser. Internationally a tax imposed by a country on goods crossing its borders, without regard to whether the purpose is to raise revenue or to discourage the traffic in the taxed goods.

Tender an offer of money as part of a contract.

Tender of goods to present goods for acceptance.

Tender of payment an unconditional offer to pay the exact amount of money due at the time and place specified by the contract.

Tender of performance an unconditional offer to perform at the time and in the manner specified by the contract.

Testimony the answers of witnesses under oath to questions given at the time of the trial in the presence of the trier of fact.

Theory of the case the rule that, when a case is tried on the basis of one theory, the appellant in taking an appeal cannot argue a different theory to the appellate court.

Third party beneficiary a third person whom the parties to a contract intend to benefit by the making of the contract and to confer upon such person the right to sue for breach of contract.

Tie-in sale the requirement imposed by the seller that the buyer of particular goods or equipment also purchase certain other goods from the seller in order to obtain the original property desired.

Toll the statute stop the running of the period of the Statute of Limitations by the doing of some act by the debtor.

Tort a civil wrong that interferes with one's property or person.

Tortious interference *see* "contract interference."

Trade dress a product's total image including its overall packaging look.

Trade libel written defamation about a product or service.

Trademark a name, device, or symbol used by a manufacturer or seller to distinguish goods from those of other persons.

Trade name a name under which a business is carried on and, if fictitious, it must be registered.

Trade-secrets secrets of any character peculiar and important to the business of the employer that have been communicated to the employee in the course of confidential employment.

Transferee buyer or vendee.

Transferor seller or vendor.

Treble damages three times the damages actually sustained.

Trespass an unauthorized action with respect to person or property (Party—**trespasser**).

Trial de novo a trial required to preserve the constitutional right to a jury trial by allowing an appeal to proceed as though there never had been any prior hearing or decision.

Trier of fact in most cases a jury, although it may be the judge alone in certain classes of cases (as in equity) or in any case when jury trial is waived, or when an administrative agency or commission is involved.

Trust a transfer of property by one person to another with the understanding or declaration that such property be held for the benefit of another; the holding of property by the owner in trust for another, upon a declaration of trust, without a transfer to another person. (Parties—**settlor, trustee, beneficiary**)

Trust agreement instrument creating a trust.

Unconscionable unreasonable, not guided or restrained by conscience and often referring to a contract grossly unfair to one party because of the superior bargaining powers of the other party.

Undisclosed principal a principal on whose behalf an agent acts without disclosing to the third person the fact of agency or the identity of the principal.

Undue influence the influence that is asserted upon another person by one who dominates that person.

Unfair competition the wrong of employing competitive methods that have been declared unfair by statute or an administrative agency.

Unilateral contract a contract under which only one party is obligated to perform.

Universal agent an agent authorized by the principal to do all acts that can lawfully be delegated to a representative.

Usage of trade language and customs of an industry.

Usury the lending of money at greater than the maximum rate of interest allowed by law.

Utility patents the patents that grant inventors of any new and useful process, machine, manufacture, or composition of matter or any new useful improvement of such devices the right to obtain a patent.

Vacating of judgment the setting aside of a judgment.

Valid legal.

Valid contract an agreement that is binding and enforceable.

Value consideration or antecedent debt or security given in exchange for the transfer of a negotiable instrument.

Verdict the decision of the trial or petty jury.

Vertical price fixing an agreement by a retailer with a producer, for example, not to resell below a stated price, which is a violation of antitrust law.

Vicarious liability imposing liability for the fault of another.

Void of no legal effect and not binding on anyone.

Voidable a transaction that may be set aside by one party thereto because of fraud or similar reason but which is binding on the other party until the injured party elects to avoid.

Voidable contract an agreement that is otherwise binding and enforceable but may be rejected at the option of one of the parties as the result of specific circumstances.

Voidable title title of goods that carries with it the contingency of an underlying problem.

Void agreement an agreement that cannot be enforced.

Voir dire examination the preliminary examination of a juror or a witness to ascertain fitness to act as such.

Volenti non fit injuria the maxim that the defendant's act cannot constitute a tort if the plaintiff has consented thereto.

Waiver the release or relinquishment of a known right or objection.

Warehouser a person engaged in the business of storing the goods of others for compensation.

Warehouse receipt a receipt issued by the warehouser for stored goods. Regulated by the UCC, which clothes the receipt with some degree of negotiability.

Warranties of seller of goods warranties consisting of express warranties that relate to matters forming part of the basis of the bargain; warranties as to title and right to sell; and the implied warranties that the law adds to a sale depending upon the nature of the transaction.

Warranty a promise either express or implied about the nature, quality, or performance of the goods.

Warranty of title implied warranty that title to the goods is good and transfer is proper.

Willful intentional, as distinguished from accidental or involuntary. In penal statutes, with evil intent or legal malice, or without reasonable ground for believing one's act to be lawful.

World Trade Organization (WTO) agency responsible for administering the objectives of the General Agreement on Tariffs and Trade (GATT).

Writ of certiorari ordered by the U.S. Supreme Court granting a right of review by the court of a lower court decision.

Index